Handbook of Pseudonyms and Personal Nicknames

compiled by
HAROLD S. SHARP

Volume II: K-Z

The Scarecrow Press, Inc.
Metuchen, N.J.   1972

Copyright 1972 by Harold S. Sharp

K - Z

K

K. A. Bediako. See:
    KONADU, SAMUEL
        ASARE
K. Allen Saddler. See:
    RICHARDS, RONALD
        CHARLES WILLIAM
K. C., The Docker's. See:
    BEVIN, ERNEST
K. Caj Doog. See:
    GOOD, IRVING JOHN
K. F. Hill. See:
    BAER, MRS.
K. F. Hill, Mrs. See:
    BAER, MRS.
K. F. Pasternak. See:
    KRASZEWSKI, JÓZEF
        IGNACY
K. G. Ballard. See:
    ROTH, HOLLY
K. H. Thomas. See:
    KIRK, THOMAS
        HOBSON
K. Harrington. See:
    BEAN, KEITH FENWICK
K. K. McGinnis. See:
    PAGE, GROVER, JR.
K. S. Karol. See:
    KEWES, KAROL
K. T. Stevens. See:
    WOOD, GLORIA
K. Werner. See:
    CASEWIT, CURTIS
KAC, ISSER (1896-1958)
    [Polish motion picture
    actor]
    Kurt Katch
Kadra Maysi. See:
    SIMONS, KATHERINE
        DRAYTON MAYRANT
Kaffir King, The. See:
    BARNATO, BARNETT
        ISAACS
KAGEY, RUDOLF (1905-46)

[American author of
detective stories]
    Kurt Steel
Kah-Ge-Ga-Gah-Bowh. See:
    COPWAY, GEORGE
KAHAKALAU, ROBERT (1922-)
    [American jazz musician
    (bass)]
    Bob Carter
KAHN, ALBERT (1869-1942)
    [German-American architect]
    The World's No. 1 Industrial
    Architect
KAHN, NORMAN (1924-53)
    [American jazz musician
    (arranger, drums)]
    Tiny Kahn
KAHN, STEPHEN (1940-)
    [American editor and
    author]
    Steve Kahn
Kai-Shek, Chiang. See:
    CHIANG CHUNG-CHENG
Kaine, George S. See:
    MORRIS, CHARLES SMITH
KAISER, ARNOLD (1889-1956)
    [American motion picture
    actor]
    Norman Kerry
KAISER, HENRY J. (1882-1967)
    [American industrialist]
    Hurry Up Henry
Kaiser, The. See:
    WILLIAM II
KALB, JOHANN (1721-80)
    [German-born general in
    the American Revolution]
    Baron de Kalb
KALBFUS, EDWARD CLIFFORD
    (1877-) [American ad-
    miral]
    The Old Man
    Durable Ned
KALED. See:
    KHALID (KALED)

558

KALER, JAMES OTIS (1848-1912)
[American writer of
juvenile literature]
James Otis
Kalita, Ivan (The Moneybag).
See: IVAN I
DANILOVICH
Kalmus, Ain. See:
MAND, EWALD
Kalojoannes. See:
JOHN II
Kamba Thorpe. See:
BELLAMY, ELIZABETH
WHITEFIELD
CROOM
Kambu, Joseph. See:
AMAMOO, JOSEPH
GODSON
Kambujiya. See:
CAMBYSES II
KAMEHAMEHA I (1737?-1819)
[King of Hawaii]
The Great (Nui)
The Napoleon of the Pacific
Kamerman, Sylvia E. See:
BURACK, SYLVIA
KAMINKER, SIMONE-
HENRIETTE-CHARLOTTE
(1921-) [French
actress]
Simone Signoret
KAMINSKY, DAVID DANIEL
(1913-) [American
singer and entertainer]
Danny Kaye
KAMPF, ABRAHAM (1920-)
[American educator and
author]
Avram Kampf
Kandahar, Pretoria and
Waterford, Roberts of.
See: ROBERTS,
FREDERICK SLEIGH
KANE [Kane]. See also:
CAIN
Cain
CAINE
Caine
Kayne
Kane, Bernie. See:
AQUINO, FRANK J.
Kane, Dr. Elisha Kent. See:
FOX, MARGARET

KANE, FRANK (1912-68)
[American columnist,
editor and author]
Frank Boyd
Kane Richmond. See:
BOWDITCH, FREDERICK
W.
Kane, Saul. See:
SASSOON, SIEGFRIED
LORAINE
Kang Teh. See:
HSUAN T'UNG
Kansas. See:
FIELDS, CARL DONNELL
Kansas Coolidge, The. See:
LANDON, ALFRED
MOSSMAN
Kansas Dry, The. See:
GUYER, ULYSSES SAMUEL
Kansas Hero, The. See:
MONTGOMERY, JAMES
KANT, IMMANUEL (1724-1804)
[German philosopher]
The Founder of the Critical
Philosophy
Kant, The Spiritual Father of.
See: HUME, DAVID
KANTO, PETER (1932-)
[American journalist and
author]
John Dexter
Ginny Gorman
Derel Pilgrim
E.R. Rangely
Olivia Rangely
KANTOROWICZ, HERMANN
(1877-) [German educator
and author]
Snaeus Flavius
Kanuni (The Lawgiver). See:
SULAIMAN I or II
KAPLAN, ANNE BERNAYS
(1930-) [American editor
and author]
Anne Bernays
KAPLAN, BOCHE (1926-)
[American textile
designer, educator and
author]
A.K. Roche
Kapnio. See:
REUCHLIN, JOHANN
Kapp, Paul. See:

HARDT, RICHARD
Karadjordje (Black George).
    See: CZERNY, GEORGE
Karageorgevich. See:
    PETER I
KARAMZIN, NICHOLAS
    MIKHAELOVITCH (1765-
    1826) [Russian poet,
    historian and novelist]
    The Russian Livy
Karen. See also:
    Karin
Karen Morley. See:
    LINTON, MILDRED
Karen Verne. See:
    KLINCKERFUSS, INGABOR
    KATRINE
KARIG, WALTER (1898-1956)
    [American novelist and
    naval officer]
    Julia K. Duncan
    James Cody Ferris
    Carolyn Keene
    Keats Patrick
KARIM AL HUSSAINI SHAH
    (1936-   ) [Moslem
    religious leader]
    Aga Kahn IV
Karin. See also:
    Karen
Karin Krog. See:
    BERGH, KARIN KROG
Karin Michaëlis. See:
    STANGELAND, KATHARINE
    MARIE BECH-BRÖNDUM
KARK, NINA MARY MABEY
    (1925-   ) [British author]
    Nina Bawden
Karl. See also:
    Carl
    Carle
Karl Albrecht. See:
    CHARLES VII
Karl Carl. See:
    VON BERNBRUNN, KARL
    ANDREAS
Karl Hohenthal. See:
    MAY, KARL FRIEDRICH
Karl Johan (Charles John). See:
    BERNADOTTE, JEAN
    BAPTISTE JULES
Karl Knuttson. See:
    CHARLES VIII

Karl Malden. See:
    SEKULOVICH, MLADEN
Karl Maras. See:
    BULMER, HENRY KENNETH
Karl Prentiss. See:
    PURDY, KEN WILLIAM
Karl Van Kampen. See:
    CAMPBELL, JOHN WOOD
Karloff, Boris. See:
    PRATT, WILLIAM HENRY
Karol. See also:
    Carol
    Carole
    Carrel
    CARROLL
    Carroll
Karol, K. S. See:
    KEWES, KAROL
Karpis, Alvin. See:
    KARPOVIECZ, FRANCIS
    ALBIN
KARPOVIECZ, FRANCIS ALBIN
    (1907-   ) [Canadian kid-
    napper and outlaw]
    Old Creepy
    Alvin Karpis
Karta, Nat. See:
    NORWOOD, VICTOR GEORGE
    CHARLES
Kartikeya Skylar Mushafir. See:
    TIKEKAR, SHRIPAD
    RAMCHANDRA
KIRWAN, MOLLY (fl. mid-20th
    cent.) [English author]
    Charlotte Morrow
Karweem, Musheed. See:
    POWELL, EVERARD
    STEPHEN
KASATKIN, IVAN (1835-1912)
    [Russian Orthodox missionary
    to Japan]
    Nicolai
Kasimir Edschmid. See:
    SCHMIDT, EDUARD
Kassai, Dejaz. See:
    JOHN IV
Katch, Kurt. See:
    KAC, ISSER
Kate. See:
    SMITH, KATHRYN
    ELIZABETH
Kate F. Hill. See:
    BAER, MRS.

Kate Garnett Wells. See:
WELLS, CATHERINE
BOOTH GARNETT
Kate Norway. See:
NORTON, OLIVE MARION
Kate Thorn. See:
TRASK, CLARA AUGUSTA
JONES
Kate Vaughan. See:
CANDELON, CATHERINE
Katharine. See also:
CATHERINE
Catherine
Cathrine
Katherine
Kathryn
Katrin
Katrina
Katharine Gibson. See:
WICKS, KATHARINE
GIBSON
Katharine Susannah Prichard.
See: THROSSELL,
KATHARINE SUSANNAH
PRICHARD
Katharine Tynan. See:
HINKSON, MRS.
KATHARINE TYNAN
Katharine Whitehorn. See:
LYALL, KATHARINE
ELIZABETH
Katherine. See also:
CATHERINE
Catherine
Cathrine
Katharine
Kathryn
Katrin
Katrina
Katherine Blake. See:
WALTER, DOROTHY
BLAKE
Katherine C. LaMancusa. See:
KOOP, KATHERINE C.
Katherine Lee. See:
JENNER, KATHERINE LEE
Katherine Mansfield. See:
MURRY, KATHLEEN
BEAUCHAMP
Katherine Pierce. See:
ST. JOHN, WYLLY FOLK
Katherine Ross. See:
WALTER, DOROTHY BLAKE

Kathey. See also:
Cathie
Cathy
Kathey Wilde. See:
KING, PATRICIA
Kathleen. See:
ROBINSON, CHAILLE PAYNE
Kathleen Fidler. See:
GOLDIE, KATHLEEN ANNIE
Kathleen Gough. See:
ABERLE, KATHLEEN
GOUGH
Kathleen Harris. See:
HUMPHRIES, ADELAIDE M.
Kathleen Kellow. See:
HIBBERT, ELEANOR
BURFORD
Kathleen Partridge. See:
WOODERIDGE, KATHLEEN
Kathleen Treves. See:
WALKER, EMILY
KATHLEEN
Kathryn. See also:
CATHERINE
Catherine
Cathrine
Katharine
Katherine
Katrin
Katrina
Kathryn Culver. See:
DRESSER, DAVIS
Kathryn Forbes. See:
McLEAN, KATHRYN
ANDERSON
Kathryn Grant. See:
GRANDSTAFF, KATHERINE
Kathryn Grayson. See:
HEDRICK, ZELMA
Kathryn Kenny. See:
STACK, NICOLETE
Kathryn Porter. See:
SWINFORD, BETTY JUNE
WELLS
Katie. See:
LOUCHEIM, KATHLEEN
SCOFIELD
Katie from the Kostur Hotel.
See: CUMPANAS, ANA
Katina Paxinou. See:
CONSTANTOPOULOS,
KATINA
Katrin. See also:

CATHERINE
Catherine
Cathrine
Katharine
Katherine
Kathryn
Katrina
Katrin Holland. See:
    FREYBE, HEIDI
        HUBERTA
Katrina. See:
    CATHERINE
    Catherine
    Cathrine
    Katharine
    Katherine
    Kathryn
    Katrin
    TRASK, KATE NICHOLS
KATT. See also:
    Cat
KATT, WILLIAM (1926-)
    [American motion picture
    actor]
    Bill Williams
Katy Jurado. See:
    GARCÍA, MARÍA JURADO
KATZ. See also:
    CATS
    Cats
    Catz
KATZ, MENKE (1906-)
    Lithuanian-American
    educator, editor and poet]
    Elchik Hiat
KAUFMAN, MARTIN ELLIS
    (1899-) [American
    composer and conductor]
    Whitey Kaufman
Kaufman, Sue. See:
    BARONDESS, SUE
        KAUFMAN
KAULITZ-NIEDECK, ROSA
    (1881-) [German
    author]
    Rosa Anderson
KAUMEYER, DOROTHY (1914-)
    [American singer and
    motion picture actress]
    Dorothy Lamour
    The Mary Pickford of This
        War
    The Paratrooper Pet

The Sarong Girl
The Sweetheart of the Foxholes
Uncle Sam's Favorite Niece
Kavan, Anna. See:
    EDMONDS, HELEN WOODS
Kay. See:
    HILL, KATHLEEN
        LOUISE
    KYSER, JAMES KING KERN
    MILLET, KADISH
Kay, Barbara. See:
    KELLER, ETHEL MAY
Kay Blake. See:
    WALTER, DOROTHY BLAKE
Kay Davis. See:
    WIMP, KATHRYN
        ELIZABETH
KAY, ERNEST (1915-) [British
    journalist, editor and
    author]
    George Ludlow
    Alan Random
Kay Fenwick. See:
    BEAN, KEITH FENWICK
Kay Francis. See:
    GIBBS, KATHARINE
Kay, George. See:
    LAMBERT, ERIC
Kay Hamilton. See:
    DE LEEUW, CATEAU
        WILHELMINA
Kay Hammond. See:
    STANDING, DOROTHY
Kay, Helen. See:
    GOLDFRANK, HELEN CO-
        LODNY
Kay Starr. See:
    STARKS, KATHRYN
Kay Talbot. See:
    ROWLAND, DONALD
        SYDNEY
KAY, TERENCE (1918-)
    [Anglo-American author]
    Terry Kay
Kaye Ballard. See:
    BALOTTA, CATHERINE
        GLORIA
Kaye, Barbara. See:
    MUIR, BARBARA KEN-
        RICK GOWING
Kaye, Danny. See:
    KAMINSKY, DAVID DANIEL
Kaye, Nora. See:

562

KOREFF, NORA
Kayne. See also:
CAIN
Cain
CAINE
Caine
KANE
Kane
Kayne, Humphrey St. See:
CRAWFURD, OSWALD
Kazan, Elia. See:
KAZANJOGLOUS, ELIA
KAZANJIAN, ARLINE
FRANCIS (1908-)
[American actress and
television personality]
Arlene Francis
KAZANJOGLOUS, ELIA
(1909-) [Greek actor
and motion picture and
theater director]
Elia Kazan
Keal Setis. See:
STILES, EZRA CLARKE
KEAN. See also:
KEANE
KEEN
Keene
KEAN, EDMUND (1787-1833)
[English actor]
Edmund Carey
KEANE. See also:
KEAN
KEEN
Keene
KEANE, CONSTANCE
(1919-) [American
motion picture actress]
Veronica Lake
KEANE, ELLSWORTH
McGRANAHAN (1927-)
[American jazz musician
(trumpet, flugel horn)]
Shake
KEARNEY, DENIS (1847-1907)
[Irish-American labor
agitator in San
Francisco]
The Sand Lot Agitator
KEARNY, PHILIP (1815-62)
[American general officer
in Mexican War]
Dashing Phil Kearny

The One-armed Devil
One-armed Phil
KEATING, JOHN HENRY
(1870-1963) [American
composer]
Lyn Udall
KEATING, LAWRENCE A.
(1903-) [American author]
John Keith Bassett
H. C. Thomas
KEATON, JOSEPH FRANCIS
(1896-1966) [American
motion picture comedian]
Buster Keaton
KEATS, JOHN (1795-1821)
[English poet]
The Immortal Keats
Keats of Kentucky, The. See:
CAWEIN, MADISON JULIUS
Keats Patrick. See:
KARIG, WALTER
KEEFER, ROSE (1906-)
[American motion picture
actress]
Rose Hobart
KEEGAN, MARY HEATHCOTT
(1914-) [British
journalist and author]
Mary Heathcott
Mary Raymond
KEEL, HAROLD (1919-)
[American singer, stage
and motion picture actor]
Howard Keel
Keel, Laura. See:
BERGE, CAROL
Keelboatmen, The King of the.
See: FINK, MIKE
KEELER, WILLIAM HENRY
(1872-1923) [American
professional baseball
player]
Wee Willie Keeler
Keely. See:
SMITH, DOROTHY
JACQUELINE KEELY
KEEN. See also:
KEAN
KEANE
Keene
KEEN, FREDERICK (1858-c.1933)
[British stage and
motion picture actor]

Frederick Kerr
Keene. See also:
   KEAN
   KEANE
   KEEN
Keene, Bob. See:
   KUHN, ROBERT
Keene, Carolyn. See:
   ADAMS, HARRIET
     STRATEMEYER
   KARIG, WALTER
   STRATEMEYER,
     EDWARD L.
Keene, Faraday. See:
   JARRETT, CORA HARDY
Keene, James. See:
   COOK, WILLIAM
     EVERETT
Keene, Laura. See:
   UNKNOWN
Keene, Lieut. See:
   RATHBONE, ST. GEORGE
     HENRY
KEENEY, CHARLES JAMES
   (1912-) [American edu-
   cator and author]
Chuck Keeney
KEESHAN, ROBERT JAMES
   (1927-) [American
   television actor and
   producer]
Bob Keeshan
KEEVIL, HENRY JOHN (1914-)
   [British civil servant
   and author]
Clay Allison
Bill Bonney
Wes Hardin
Frank McLowery
Johnny Ringo
Keg. See:
   JOHNSON, FREDERIC H.
   PURNELL, WILLIAM
KEHL, MARY ANNE (1815-95)
   [English actress]
Fanny Stirling
Keighley. See:
   SNOWDEN, JAMES
Keir. See:
   HARDIE, JAMES KEIR
Keir, Christine. See:
   POPESCU, CHRISTINE
     PULLEIN-THOMPSON

KEISCHNER, SIDNEY (1906-)
   [American playwright]
Sidney Kingsley
Keiser, Robert. See:
   KING, ROBERT
Keith, Carlton. See:
   ROBERTSON, KEITH
Keith Christie. See:
   HAYNES, ALFRED HENRY
Keith, Donald. See:
   MONROE, KEITH
Keith Grantland. See:
   BEAUMONT, CHARLES
Keith, Ian. See:
   ROSS, KEITH
Keith, Marion. See:
   MACGREGOR, MARY
     ESTHER MILLER
KEITH, ROBERT, JR. (1921-)
   [American motion picture
   actor]
Brian Keith
Keith Woodcott. See:
   BRUNNER, JOHN KILIAN
     HOUSTON
Kel Holland. See:
   WHITTINGTON, HARRY
Kell, Joseph. See:
   BURGESS, ANTHONY
KELLAND, CLARENCE
   BUDINGTON (1881-1964)
   [American novelist and
   short story writer]
Bud Kelland
KELLAR, HARRY (1849-1922)
   [American illusionist and
   magician]
The Dean of American
   Magicians
KELLER, ETHEL MAY (1878-)
   [American author]
Barbara Kay
Lucia Whitney
KELLER, KENT ELLSWORTH
   (1867-) [American
   politician; Congressman from
   Illinois]
The Big Man from Little
   Egypt
KELLEY. See also:
   KELLY
   Kelly
KELLEY, DAVID CAMPBELL

(1833-1909) [American
Methodist Episcopal clergy-
man and Civil War officer]
The Fighting Parson
KELLEY, MARTHA MOTT.
See: Patrick, Q.
KELLEY, WILLIAM DARRAGH
(1848-90) [American
politician Congressman
from Pennsylvania]
The Father of the House
Pig Iron Kelley
KELLNER, ESTHER (fl. 1956-
64) [American editor
and author]
Esther Cooper
KELLOGG, JEAN (1916-)
[American editor and
author]
Sally Jackson
KELLOGG, VERNON LYMAN
(1867-1937) [American
educator, zoologist and
author]
Max Vernon
Kellow, Kathleen. See:
HIBBERT, ELEANOR
BURFORD
KELLY [Kelly]. See also:
KELLEY
KELLY, ALVIN (1885? 1893?-
1952) [American
flagpole sitter]
The Luckiest Fool Alive
Sailor Kelly
Shipwreck Kelly
KELLY, CLINTON WAYNE
(1844-1923) [American
physician]
Big Medicine
KELLY, EDWARD AUSTIN
(1892-) [American
politician; Congressman
from Illinois]
Baseball Eddy
KELLY, EUGENE JOSEPH
(1912-) [American
dancer, choreographer
and actor]
Gene Kelly
KELLY, GEORGE (190?-54)
[American bank robber
and kidnapper]

Machine Gun Kelly
KELLY, GEORGE C. (1849-95)
[Irish journalist and author]
Harold Payne
Kelly, Glenn. See:
McNEILLY, MILDRED
MASTERSON
KELLY, JAMES EDWARD
(1855-1933) [American
sculptor]
The Sculptor of American
History
KELLY, JOHN (1821-86) [Amer-
ican politician and grafter;
member of Tammany Hall]
Boss Kelly
Honest John Kelly
The Sachem of Tammany Hall
KELLY, JOHN (1862-95)
[Irish professional boxer;
world's middleweight
champion]
Jack Dempsey
The Nonpareil
KELLY, JONATHAN FALCON-
BRIDGE (1817-c. 55)
[American editor and
humorist]
Cerro Gordo
Falconbridge
Jack Humphries
O. K.
KELLY, JOSEPH WILLIAM
(1901-) [American
radio commentator and
script writer]
Joe Kelly
KELLY, LUTHER SAGE (1849-
1928) [American army scout]
Yellowstone Kelly
KELLY, MICHAEL J. (1857-94)
[American professional
baseball player]
King Kelly
The Ten Thousand Dollar
Beauty
Kelly, Ralph. See:
GEIS, DARLENE STERN
KELLY, THOMAS RAYMOND
(1927-) [American jazz
musician (bass)]
Red Kelly
KELLY, WALTER C. (1873-1939)

[American actor]
The Virginia Judge
KELLY, WALTER CRAWFORD
(1913-) [American
cartoonist]
Walt Kelly
KELSEY, JOAN MARSHALL
(1907-) [British
author]
Joan Grant
Kelvin McKay. See:
STRONG, CHARLES
STANLEY
Kemal Bey. See:
NAMIK, MEHMED
KEMAL, MUSTAFA (MUSTAPHA)
[1881-1938] [Turkish
soldier; first president
of the Turkish Republic]
Kemal Atatürk
Kemal Pasha
KEMBLE, FRANCES ANNE
(1809-93) [British actress,
poet and dramatist]
Fanny Kemble
KEMBLE, JOHN PHILIP
(1757-1823) [English
tragedian]
Black Jack
KEMP, HIBBARD (1883-1960)
[American poet]
Harry Kemp
The Tramp Poet
Kemp, Jeremy. See:
WALKER, EDMUND
KEMPEN, THOMAS HAMERKEN
VAN (1380-1471) [German
Catholic ecclesiastic and
writer]
Thomas à Kempis
Thomas Hämmerlein
Kemper Campbell, Mrs. See:
CAMPBELL, LITTA
BELLE
Kempis, Thomas à. See:
KEMPEN, THOMAS
HAMERKEN VAN
KEMPLING, WILLIAM BAILEY
(1869-) [British author
and journalist]
W. B. K.
KEMPNER, LYDIA
RABINOWITSCH (1871-)

[Russian bacteriologist and
author]
Lydia Rabinowitsch
Ken. See:
BOYER, KENTON LLOYD
CROSSEN, KENDELL
FOSTER
DARBY, KENNETH LORIN
HARRELSON, KENNETH
SMITH
ROSEWALL, KENNETH R.
VENTURI, KENNETH
Ken Bourbon. See:
BAUER, ERWIN A.
Ken Ranger. See:
CREASEY, JOHN
Ken Wanstall. See:
GREEN-WANSTALL,
KENNETH
Kenbrovin, Jaan. See:
VINCENT, NATHANIEL
HAWTHORNE
Kendal, Madge. See:
GRIMSON, MARGARET
BRUNTON
Kendal, William Hunter. See:
GRIMSTON, WILLIAM
HUNTER
KENDALL, JOHN KAYE (1869-
1952) [British author]
Dum-Dum
Kendall, Lace. See:
STOUTENBURG, ADRIEN
PEARL
KENDALL, W. S. (-1876) [Amer-
ican Poet]
The Mad Poet of California
KENDALL, WILLMOORE (1909-)
[American correspondent,
educator and author]
Alan Monk
Kendrake, Carleton. See:
GARDNER, ERLE STANLEY
KENDRICK, BAYNARD HARD-
WICK (1894-) [American
author]
Richard Hayward
KENDRICK, FRANCES (fl. late
17th cent.) [English noble-
woman]
The Berkshire Lady
Kendricks, James. See:
FOX, GARDNER FRANCIS

KENNEALLY, GEORGE V.
(1902-) [American
professional football
player and coach]
The Old Man of the Grid-
iron
Kennedy, Captain, J. L. See:
HARBAUGH, THOMAS
CHALMERS
KENNEDY, CRAMMOND (1842-
1918) [American juvenile
preacher]
The Boy Preacher
KENNEDY, EDWARD MOORE
(1932-) [American
politician; senator from
Massachusetts]
Ted Kennedy
Teddy Kennedy
KENNEDY, GERALD HAMILTON
(1907-) [American
Methodist clergyman,
educator and author]
G. Hobab Kish
KENNEDY, JACQUELINE
BOUVIER (MRS.
ARISTOTLE SOCRATES
ONASSIS) (1929-)
[Widow of JOHN FITZ-
GERALD KENNEDY,
thirty-fifth President of
the United States]
Jackie
KENNEDY, JOHN FITZGERALD
(1917-63) [Thirty-fifth
President of the United
States]
J. F. K.
Jack
KENNEDY, JOHN PENDLETON
(1795-1870) [American
cabinet officer, edu-
cator, editor and author]
Mark Littleton
Solomon Secondthoughts
KENNEDY, JOSEPH (1929-)
[American educator and
author]
X. J. Kennedy
KENNEDY, REV. GEOFFREY
ANKETELL STUDDERT
(18??-1929) [English
author, churchman and

World War I army chaplain]
Woodbine Willie
KENNEDY, ROBERT FRANCIS
(1925-68) [American
politician]
Bobbie
R. F. K.
Kennedy, Rose. See:
VICTOR, MRS. METTA
VICTORIA FULLER
MORSE
Kenneth. See:
Johns, Kenneth
KENNETH I (fl. 9th cent.)
[King of the Dalriad Scots]
Macalpine
Kenneth Conrad. See:
LOTTICH, KENNETH VERNE
Kenneth Eric. See:
HENLEY, ARTHUR
Kenneth MacFarlane. See:
WALKER, KENNETH
MACFARLANE
Kenneth, Mr. See:
MARLOWE, KENNETH
KENNEY. See also:
KENNY
Kenny
KENNEY, EDWARD A. (1884-)
[American real estate
dealer and politician;
representative from New
Jersey]
Lottery Kenney
Kenninghall, Henry Howard of.
See: HOWARD, HENRY
Kenny. See:
CLARKE, KENNETH
SPEARMAN
DORHAM, McKINLEY
HOWARD
Kenney
Kenny, Charles J. See:
GARDNER, ERLE STANLEY
KENNY, ELIZABETH (1886-1952)
[Australian nurse active in
the treatment of infantile
paralysis]
Sister Kenny
Kenny, George. See:
WHITCOMB, KENNETH G.
Kenny, Kathryn. See:
STACK, NICOLETE

Kent, Alexander. See:
    METHOLD, KENNETH
    WALTER
KENT, JAMES (1763-1847)
    [American jurist and
    writer on legal subjects]
    The American Blackstone
Kent, Jean. See:
    SUMMERFIELD, JOAN
KENT, LOUISE ANDREWS
    (1886-) [American
    author]
    Theresa Tempest
Kent, Philip. See:
    BULMER, HENRY
    KENNETH
KENT, ROCKWELL (1882-)
    [American artist, illus-
    trator, muralist and
    author]
    Hogarth, Jr.
Kent Sanders. See:
    WILKES-HUNTER,
    RICHARD
Kent Taylor. See:
    WEISS, LOUIS
Kent, The Captain of. See:
    CADE, JOHN
Kent, The Fair Maid of. See:
    JOAN
Kent, The Maid of. See:
    BARTON, ELIZABETH
Kent, The Nun of. See:
    BARTON, ELIZABETH
Kent, Warren F. See:
    MANNING, WILLIAM
    HENRY
KENTIGERN (518-603)
    [Celtic missionary]
    St. Mungo
Kenton, Maxwell, joint pseud.
    of MASON HOFFENBERG
    (-) and TERRY
    SOUTHERN (1926-)
    [American authors]
KENTON, STANLEY NEWCOMB
    (1912-) [American
    jazz musician (piano,
    leader, composer)]
    Stan Kenton
Kentucky Duel Fighter, The.
    See: CLAY, CASSIUS
    MARCELLUS, SR.

Kentucky, The Daniel Boone of
    Southern. See:
    LYNN, BENJAMIN
Kentucky, The Keats of. See:
    CAWEIN, MADISON
    JULIUS
Kenyon Gambier. See:
    LATHROP, LORIN
    ANDREWS
Kenyon West. See:
    HOWLAND, FRANCES
    LOUISE MORSE
KEOGH, LILIAN GILMORE
    (1927-) [Irish educator
    and author]
    Lilian Patrick
Kepha (Petros) (Rock). See:
    PETER
Kerala Putra. See:
    PANIKKAR, KAVALAM
    MADHAVA
KEREKES, TIBOR (1893-)
    [Hungarian educator,
    lecturer and author]
    Rotarius
KERLIN, LOUISE (1882-1965)
    [American vaudevillian and
    motion picture actress]
    Louise Dresser
Kern, E.R. See:
    KERNER, FRED
KERN, JEROME DAVID
    (1885-1945) [American
    composer]
    The Dean of America's Show
    Music Composers
    Jerry Kern
KERNAHAN, JEAN GWYNNE
    (1856-) [British novelist]
    Mrs. Coulson Kernahan
KERNER, FRED (1921-)
    [Canadian journalist and
    author]
    Frohm Fredricks
    E.R. Kern
    Frederick Kerr
KEROUAC, JEAN-LOUIS
    LEBRID DE (1922-)
    [American author]
    Jack Kerouac
    Jean-Louis
    Jean-Louis Inconiteau
    John Kerouac

KERR, ANDREW (1878-)
[American football
coach]
Andy Kerr
Kerr, Ben. See:
ARD, WILLIAM THOMAS
Kerr, Frederick. See:
KEEN, FREDERICK
KERNER, FRED
Kerr, Norman D. See:
SIEBER, SAM DIXON
Kerr, Orpheus C. See:
NEWELL, ROBERT
HENRY
KERR-TRIMMER, DEBORAH
JANE (1921-)
[British actress]
Deborah Kerr
Kerry. See:
MILLS, FREDERICK
ALLEN
Kerry, Lois. See:
CARDOZO, LOIS
STEINMETZ
Kerry Mitchell. See:
WILKES-HUNTER,
RICHARD
Kerry, Norman. See:
KAISER, ARNOLD
Kerry Scott. See:
SWANSON, HAROLD
NORLING
KERTESZ, MIHALY (1888-1962)
[Hungarian-American
motion picture director]
Michael Curtiz
KESSEL, LIPMANN (1914-)
[English orthopedic
surgeon and author]
Daniel Paul
KESSLER, JASCHA FREDERICK
(1929-) [American
educator and author]
Frederick Ely
KETCH, JOHN (died 1686)
[English executioner]
Jack Ketch
KETCHAM, HENRY KING
(1920-) [American
cartoonist]
Hank Ketcham
Ketchel, Stanley. See:
KIECHAL, STANISLAUS

KETTELL, SAMUEL (fl. early
19th cent.) [American
author]
Peter Parley
Kettenfeier, Petri. See:
ROSEGGER, PETER
KETTERING, CHARLES
FRANKLIN (1876-1958)
[American engineer, in-
ventor and business execu-
tive]
Boss Kettering
Ketti. See:
FRINGS, KETTI
Ketty
Kitty
Ketty. See also:
Ketti
Kitty
Ketty Lester. See:
FRIERSON, REVOYDA
Keverne, Richard. See:
HOSKEN, CLIFFORD
Kevin Matthews. See:
FOX, GARDNER FRANCIS
Kevin O'Hara. See:
CUMBERLAND, MARTEN
Kevin O'Malley. See:
HOSSENT, HARRY
KEWES, KAROL (1924-)
[Polish correspondent and
author]
K. S. Karol
KEY, THEODORE (1912-)
[American cartoonist and
writer]
Ted Key
Keyber, Mr. Conny. See:
FIELDING, HENRY
Keys, The Old Tomcat of the.
See: ZURKE, ROBERT
Khaireddin. See:
BARBAROSSA, KHIZR
KHALID (KALED) (died 642)
[Saracen general officer]
The Sword of God
Khan, Aga, III. See:
AGA SULTAN SIR
MOHAMED SHAH
Khan, Carlo. See:
FOX, CHARLES JAMES
Khan, Chinghiz (Precious
Warrior). See:

TEMUJIN
Khan, Genghis (Precious
Warrior). See:
TEMUJIN
Khan, Genghis (Very Mighty
Ruler). See:
TEMUJIN
KHAN, ABDULLAH JAFFA
ANVER BEY (1930-)
[Afghanistan-American
ballet dancer and
choreographer]
Robbert Joffrey
Khan, Jenghiz (Precious
Warrior). See:
TEMUJIN
KHAN, TAIDJE (1917-)
[Mongolian-Swiss
actor]
Yul Brynner
Khan, The Great. See:
KUBLAI KHAN
(KHUBILAI KHAN)
(KUBLA KHAN)
KHARE, NARAYAN BHASKAR
(1882-) [Indian
surgeon and author]
Bapu
KHAURY, HERBERT
BUCKINGHAM (193?-)
[American singer and
entertainer]
Darry Dover
Tiny Tim
Khazar, The. See:
LEO IV
KHOSRAU I (died 579 A.D.)
[King of Persia]
Anushirvan (Having an
Immortal Soul)
KHOSRAU II (died 628 A.D.)
[King of Persia]
Parvez (The Victorious)
KHUBILAI KHAN. See:
KUBLAI KHAN
(KHUBILAI KHAN)
(KUBLA KHAN)
Khudavendighiar. See:
MURAD (AMURATH) I
Khufu. See:
CHEOPS
KHUSRAU (CHOSROES) I
(fl. 6th cent. A.D.) [King

of Persia]
The Generous
The Great
The Just
Kid. See:
GLEASON, WILLIAM
HOWARD, AVERY
KIDD
Kidd
ORY, EDWARD
RENA, HENRY
Kid, Billie the. See:
Billy the Kid
RUSSELL, WILLIAM EUSTIS
Kid, Billy the. See:
Billie the Kid
BONNEY, WILLIAM H.
SOUTHWORTH,
WILLIAM H.
Kid-gloves. See:
HARRISON, BENJAMIN
Kid McCoy. See:
SELBY, NORMAN
Kid Sheriff of Nebraska, The.
See: WEDGWOOD,
EDGAR A.
Kid Shots. See:
MADISON, LOUIS
Kid, The. See:
WILLIAMS, THEODORE
SAMUEL
Kid, The Candy. See:
BROCK, WILLIAM
EMERSON
Kid, The Cherokee. See:
ROGERS, WILLIAM PENN
ADAIR
Kid, The Missouri. See:
RUDOLPH, WILLIAM
Kid, The Panavision. See:
BOWERING, GEORGE
Kid, The Pianner. See:
LOPEZ, VINCENT
Kid, The Sailor. See:
LONDON, JOHN GRIFFITH
Kid, The Sweatshirt. See:
FISCHER, ROBERT JAMES
Kid Thomas. See:
VALENTINE, THOMAS
Kidd, Russ. See:
DONSON, CYRIL
KIDD, WALTER E. (1917-)
[American educator, poet

and author]
Conrad Pendleton
KIDD, WILLIAM (1645?-1701)
[British pirate and
privateer]
Captain Kidd
Kiddo. See:
DAVIS, GEORGE WILLIS
Kids. See:
Dead End Kids, The
Kids, The East Side. See:
Dead End Kids, The
KIECHAL, STANISLAUS
(1887-1910) [American
professional boxer;
world's middleweight
champion]
Stanley Ketchel
KIENZLE, RAYMOND
NICHOLAS (1911-)
[American motion
picture director]
Nicholas Ray
Kieron Moore. See:
O'HANRAHAN, KIERON
KIES, MARGARET (1910-)
[American stage and
motion picture actress]
Margaret Lindsay
Kiki. See:
CUYLER, HAZEN S.
KILBRACKEN, JOHN RAYMOND
GODLEY (1920-)
[British journalist,
columnist and author]
John Godley
Kildare, John. See:
KING, JOHN BOSWELL
Kill Crazy. See:
DILLINGER, JOHN
HERBERT
Kill Devil, Old. See:
FREEMAN, AUSTIN
KILLEFER, WILLIAM
(1888-) [American
baseball manager]
Reindeer
Killer, Jack the Giant. See:
DEMPSEY, WILLIAM
HARRISON
JACKSON, ROBERT
HOUGHWOUT
RANDOLPH, JOHN

Killer, Owney the. See:
MADDEN, OWEN
Killer, The Buffalo. See:
MATTHEWSON, WILLIAM
Killer, The Corduroy. See:
FISCHER, ROBERT JAMES
KILLIGREW, THOMAS (1612-83)
[English dramatist]
Killigrew the Elder
KILLIGREW, THOMAS
(1657-1719) [English
dramatist]
Killigrew the Younger
KILMER, ALFRED JOYCE
(1886-1918) [American
poet]
Joyce Kilmer
Kilpatrick, Sarah. See:
UNDERWOOD, MARVIS
EILEEN
Kim. See:
GANNON, JAMES
KIMBALL
NOVAK, MARILYN PAULINE
SIMENON, GEORGES
Kim Hunter. See:
COLE, JANET
Kim Stanley. See:
REID, PATRICIA
KIMSEY, CLYDE (1906-)
[American professional
baseball player]
Chad
KIMURA, HENRY SEIMATSU
(1875-1958) [Japanese
Congregational minister]
The Billy Sunday of Japan
Kin. See:
HUBBARD, FRANK
McKINNEY
Kincaid, Alan. See:
RIKHOFF, JAMES C.
KINCHELOE, CHARLES
(1934-) [American jazz
musician (piano, com-
poser)]
Kirk Stuart
Kindergarten, The Mother of
the. See:
BLOW, SUSAN ELIZABETH
Kinderhook Fox, The. See:
VAN BUREN, MARTIN
Kinderhook, The Red Fox of.

See: VAN BUREN,
MARTIN
Kinderhook, The Sage of. See:
VAN BUREN, MARTIN
Kinderhook, The Wizard of.
See: VAN BUREN,
MARTIN
KINDI, AL (ABU YŪSUF YA
IQUB IBN-ISHAQ AL
KINDI) (died c. 873) [Arabian
philosopher]
The Philosopher of the Arabs
KINES, THOMAS ALVIN
(1922-) [Canadian
singer, broadcaster and
author]
Tom Kines
King. See:
BOLDEN, CHARLES
CANUTE (CNUT) (KNUT) II
CARTER, ROBERT
HANCOCK, JOHN
HOOPER, ROBERT
KELLY, MICHAEL J.
OLIVER, JOSEPH
PYM, JOHN
SEARS, ISAAC
King, Alan. See:
KNIBERG, IRWIN ALAN
King and Queen of Hospitality,
The, joint nickname of
ANDREW JACKSON
(1767-1845) [American
general officer and 7th
President of the United
States] and his wife
RACHEL DONELSON
JACKSON (1767-1828)
King and Queen of Hospitality,
The. See also:
JACKSON, ANDREW
JACKSON, RACHEL
DONELSON
King, Andrea. See:
BARRY, GEORGETTA
King Andrew the First. See:
JACKSON, ANDREW
King Andy. See:
JOHNSON, ANDREW
King Andy the First. See:
JOHNSON, ANDREW
KING ARTHUR (fl. 6th cent.)
[semi-legendary

British king]
The Flower of Kings
King, Arthur. See:
CAIN, ARTHUR HOMER
King, Australia's Martin
Luther. See:
PERKINS, CHARLES
NELSON
King Bomba. See:
FERDINAND II
King, Botanist to the. See:
BARTRAM, JOHN
King Caucus. See:
STILWELL, SILAS MOORE
King Cole, Nat. See:
COLES, NATHANIEL
ADAMS
King Coody. See:
TANEY, ROGER BROOKE
KING, CYRUS MURDOCK
(1860-1922) [American
advocate of highway im-
provement in Minnesota]
Good Roads King
King, Dennis. See:
PRATT, DENNIS
King, Farmer (Rei Lavrador).
See: DINIZ (DENIS)
KING, FRANCIS HENRY (1923-
) [British lecturer and
author]
Frank Cauldwell
King Franconi. See:
MURAT, JOACHIM
King, Godfre Ray. See:
BALLARD, GUY WARREN
King Hal, Bluff. See:
HENRY VIII
KING-HALL, WILLIAM STEPHEN
RICHARD (1893-) [British
journalist, politician and
author]
Etienne
King Harry. See:
HENRY VIII
King Hill. See:
ROBERTSON, FRANK
CHESTER
King, Jo. See:
BELLAW, AMERICUS
WELLINGTON
King, John. See:
McKEAG, ERNEST LIONEL

KING, JOHN BOSWELL (fl. mid-
20th cent) [English
author]
John Boswell
John Kildare
King Josiah the First. See:
QUINCY, JOSIAH
King Kong. See:
KLINE, ROBERT GEORGE
King-maker, The. See:
GUFFEY, JOSEPH F.
NEVIL (NEVILLE),
RICHARD
King Martin the First. See:
VAN BUREN, MARTIN
KING, MARY LOUISE (1911-)
[American editor and
author]
Mary Louise Johnson
King, Minnesota's Potato. See:
SCHROEDER, HENRY
KING, MOIRA SHEARER
(1926-) [English bal-
lerina and actress]
The First Lady of
Hollywood
Moira Shearer
King, Most Faithful. See:
JOHN V
King, Norman A. See:
TRALINS, S. ROBERT
King of America, The Wire.
See: GATES, JOHN
WARNE
King of American Clowns, The.
See: RICE, DANIEL
King of Bark, The. See:
CHRISTOPHER III
King of Bath, The. See:
NASH, RICHARD
King of Brave Men, The. See:
HENRY IV
King of Chefs, The. See:
ESCOFFIER, AUGUSTE
King of Comedy, The. See:
SENNETT, MACK
King of Corsica, Theodore.
See: VAN NEUHOFF,
BARON
King of Cotswold, The. See:
BRYDGES, GREY
King of Dullness, The. See:
CIBBER, COLLEY

King of Dunces, The. See:
CIBBER, COLLEY
King of England's Viceroy, The.
See: LOUIS XVIII
King of Escape Artists, The.
See: GARDNER, ROY
King of Escapologists, The.
See: WEISS, EHRICH
(ERIK WEISZ)
King of "Feuilletons," The. See:
JANIN, JULES GABRIEL
King of Florida, The. See:
PLANT, HENRY BRADLEY
King of Handcuffs, The. See:
WEISS, EHRICH (ERIK
WEISZ)
King of Handcuffs, Undisputed.
See: WEISS, EHRICH
(ERIK WEISZ)
King of Hi De Ho, The. See:
CALLOWAY, CABELL,
3RD
King of Iceland. See:
JÖRGENSSEN, JÖRGEN
King of Ireland, The Uncrowned.
See: PARNELL, CHARLES
STEWART
King of Jazz. See:
WHITEMAN, PAUL
King of Kings. See:
MAILS, WALTER
King of Moonshiners, The. See:
GOOCH, WAYNE B.
King of Musical Corn, The.
See: WELK, LAWRENCE
King of Painters, The. See:
PARRHASIUS
King of Preachers, The. See:
BOURDALONE, LOUIS
King of Roads (Rhodes), The.
See: MACADAM, JOHN
LOUDON
King of Rome. See:
BONAPARTE, NAPOLEON
FRANÇOIS CHARLES
JOSEPH
King of Rum Runners, The. See:
McCOY, CAPTAIN WILLIAM
King of Scotland, The Un-
crowned. See:
DUNDAS, HENRY
King of Sweden (Charles XIV).
See: BERNADOTTE,

JEAN BAPTISTE
JULES
King of Swing, The. See:
  GOODMAN, BENJAMIN
  DAVID
King of the Barricades, The.
  See: LOUIS PHILIPPE
King of the Beggars, The.
  See: CAREW, BAMP-
  FYLDE MOORE
King of the Bohemians, The.
  See:
  CLAPP, HENRY, JR.
  COLLINS, MORTIMER
King of the Bootleggers, The.
  See: DWYER, WILLIAM
  VINCENT
King of the Border, The. See:
  SCOTT, ADAM, OF
  TUSHIELAW
King of the Commons, The.
  See: JAMES V
King of the Drums. See:
  KRUPA, EUGENE
  BERTRAM
King of the Electric Guitar,
  The. See:
  McBURNEY, ALBERT
King of the Feds, The. See:
  HAMILTON, ALEXANDER
King of the Flower Painters,
  The. See:
  DE LONGPRÉ, PAUL
King of the Jukes, The. See:
  COMO, PIERINO
King of the Keelboatmen, The.
  See: FINK, MIKE
King of the Lobby, The. See:
  WARD, SAMUEL
King of the Links, The. See:
  JONES, ROBERT TYRE,
  JR.
King of the Marine Insurance
  Business, The. See:
  TOWNSEND, HAWORTH
  NOTTINGHAM
King of the Markets, The.
  See: BEAUFORT, DUC
  DE
King of the Mellers, The.
  See: TAYLOR,
  CHARLES A.
King of the Missouri, The.

See: MACKENZIE,
  KENNETH
King of the Never-Made-Good
  Crack Downs, The. See:
  JOHNSON, HUGH SAMUEL
King of the New Dealers, The.
  See: MINTON, SHERMAN
King of the Pulps. See:
  FAUST, FREDERICK
  SCHILLER
King of the Quakers, The. See:
  PEMBERTON, ISRAEL
King of the Ragtime Composers,
  The. See:
  JOPLIN, SCOTT
King of the Reptiles, The. See:
  VILLE, BERNARD
  GERMAIN ÉTIENNE DE
  LA
King of the Smugglers. See:
  HANCOCK, JOHN
King of the Squatters, The.
  See: ROBINSON, SOLON
King of the Texas Wildcatters,
  The. See:
  CULLEN, HUGH TROY
King of the Wildcatters, The.
  See: BENEDUM,
  MICHAEL
King of Thieves, The. See:
  SCOTT, ADAM, OF
  TUSHIELAW
KING OF WILLIAM, JAMES
  (18??-56) [California
  pioneer and newspaper
  editor]
  James King of William
KING, PATRICIA (1930-)
  [American educator and
  author]
  Kathey Wilde
King, Paul. See:
  DRACKETT, PAUL
King Pepin, Little. See:
  CHANNING, WILLIAM
  ELLERY
King Philip. See:
  METACOM (METACOMET)
King, Philip the. See:
  MARSTON, PHILIP
  BOURKE
King Pleasure. See:
  BEEKS, CLARENCE

KING, RILEY B. (1925-)
[American jazz musician
(guitar, singer)]
B.B.
B.B. King
Blues Boy King
KING, ROBERT (1862-1932)
[American composer]
Mary Earl
Robert Keiser
Mrs. Ravenhall
R.A. Wilson
King Solomon. See:
HOLCOMBE, SOLOMON
King, T.W. See:
INGRAHAM, COLONEL
PRENTISS
King, The Advertising. See:
BARTON, BRUCE
King, The Ammonia. See:
MALLINKRODT, EDWARD
King, The Apple. See:
WELLHOUSE, FREDERICK
King, The Barley. See:
BUERGER, JOHN
King, The Borax. See:
SMITH, FRANCIS
MARION
King, The Cattle. See:
KLEBERG, RICHARD
MIFFIN
King, The Circus. See:
RINGLING, JOHN
King, The Citizen. See:
CHAMBORD, HENRI
CHARLES DIEUPONNÉ,
COMTE DE
LOUIS PHILIPPE
King, The Dandy. See:
MURAT, JOACHIM
King, The Distillery. See:
DIRKSEN, EVERETT
McKINLEY
King, The Do-nothing. See:
CLOVIS II
King, The Factory. See:
OASTLER, RICHARD
King, The Farmer. See:
GEORGE III
King, The Flivver. See:
FORD, HENRY
King, The Handcuff. See:
WEISS, EHRICH (ERIK

WEISZ)
King, The Hawaiian Pineapple.
See: DOLE, JAMES
DRUMMOND
King, The Honest. See:
VICTOR EMMANUEL II
King, The Ice. See:
MORSE, CHARLES
WYMAN
TUDOR, FREDERIC
King, The Kaffir. See:
BARNATO, BARNETT
ISAACS
King, The Lap. See:
OLAF
King, The Locksmith. See:
LOUIS XVI
King, The March. See:
SOUSA, JOHN PHILIP
King, The Martyr. See:
HENRI VI
LOUIS XVI
King, The Match. See:
KREUGER, IVAR
King, The Orange. See:
HARRIS, JAMES
ARMSTRONG
King, The Paper. See:
LAW, JOHN
King, The Patriot. See:
ST. JOHN, HENRY
King, The Peanut. See:
GWALTNEY, PEMBROKE
DECATUR
OBICI, AMEDEO
King, The Pittsburgh Candy.
See: CLARK, DAVID
LYTLE
King, The Policy. See:
ADAMS, ALBERT J.
King, The Railroad. See:
GOULD, JASON
King, The Railway. See:
CORNING, ERASTUS
HUDSON, GEORGE
King, The Red. See:
WILLIAM II
King, The Rubber. See:
HARTER, DOW WATTERS
King, The Sailor. See:
WILLIAM IV
King, The Seven Days'. See:
MASANIELLO (TOMMASO

ANIELLO) (ANELLO)
King, The Snow. See:
FREDERICK V
GUSTAVUS II
King, The Standard Oil. See:
ROCKEFELLER, JOHN
DAVISON
King, The Storm. See:
ESPEY, JAMES POLLARD
King, The Sugar. See:
SPRECKLES, CLAUS
King, The Sulphur. See:
FRASCH, HERMAN
King, The Sun (Le Roi Soleil).
See: LOUIS XIV
King, The Theatrical. See:
MURAT, JOACHIM
King, the Waltz. See:
KING, WAYNE HAROLD
King, The White. See:
CHARLES I
King, The Winter. See:
FREDERICK V
King, The Yankee. See:
SICKLES, DANIEL EDGAR
KING TUTANKAHAMEN
(died 1346 B.C.) [Egyptian
ruler]
King Tut
King, Uncrowned. See:
BLAINE, JAMES
GILLESPIE
King Wampum. See:
PEMBERTON, ISRAEL
KING, WAYNE HAROLD (1901-)
[American jazz musician
(clarinet, alto saxophone,
leader, composer)]
The Waltz King
King Wenceslaus, Good. See:
WENCESLAUS
KING, WILLIAM BASIL (1859-
1928) [American clergy-
man and author]
Basil King
KING, WILLIAM HENRY
(1864-) [American
politician; Senator from
Utah]
King of the District
King of Investigators
The Mormon Bishop
Kingdom, Protector and

Defender of the. See:
JOHN OF LANCASTER
Kingfish (George Stevens). See:
GOSDEN, FREEMAN F.
Kingfish of the Italian Motion
Picture Industry, The. See:
LAURENTIS, DINO DE
Kingfish, The. See:
LONG, HUEY PIERCE
King's Daughter, The Sea. See:
ALEXANDRA, CAROLINE
MARIE CHARLOTTE
LOUISA JULIA
Kings, King of. See:
MAILS, WALTER
King's Mountain, The Hero of.
See:
CLEVELAND, BENJAMIN
Kings, The Flower of. See:
KING ARTHUR
Kingsbury, Vernon L. See:
LUKENS, HENRY CLAY
KINGSLEY, HENRY (1830-76)
[English novelist]
Granby Dixon
KINGSLEY, OMAR (1840-79)
[American circus
equestrian and female
impersonator]
Ella Zoyara
KINGSLEY, REV. CHARLES
(1819-75) [English
clergyman and author]
The Chartist Clergyman
The Chartist Preacher
Parson Lot
Kingsley, Robert. See:
CLARKE, JOHN CAMP-
BELL
Kingsley, Sidney. See:
KEISCHNER, SIDNEY
Kingston, Gertrude. See:
KONSTAM, GERTRUDE
Kinkaid, Matt. See:
ADAMS, CLIFTON
KINLEYSIDE, DOUGLAS
(1905-45) [American
motion picture actor]
Donald Douglas
Kinmont Willy. See:
ARMSTRONG, WILLIAM
KINROSS, PATRICK, LORD
(1904-) [Scottish

576

journalist, broadcaster and
author]
Patrick Balfour
Kinsayder, W. See:
MARSTON, JOHN
Kinver, Richard. See:
VOGEL, HARRY BEN-
JAMIN
KINZIE, JOHN (1763-1828)
[Canadian fur trader]
Shaw-nee-aw-kee (The
Silver Man]
KIPLING, JOSEPH RUDYARD
(1865-1936) [English
novelist, short story writer
and poet]
Rudyard Kipling
Kipling, The American. See:
LONDON, JOHN GRIFFITH
Kirby. See:
THORNE, BLISS KIRBY
Kirby Grant. See:
HORN, KIRBY GRANT
Kirby, Jean. See:
McDONNELL, VIRGINIA
BLEECKER
ROBINSON, CHAILLE
PAYNE
Kirby Mack. See:
McEVOY, HARRY KIRBY
KIRCHOFF, THEODORE (1828-
99) [German-American
poet; resident of San
Francisco]
The Poet of the Golden Gate
Kirk Deming. See:
DRAGO, HENRY SINCLAIR
Kirk Douglas. See:
DEMSKY, ISSUR
DANIELOVITCH
Kirk, Eleanor. See:
AMES, ELEANOR MARIA
EASTERBROOK
KIRK, ELLEN WARNER
OLNEY (1842-1928) [Amer-
ican novelist]
Henry Hayes
KIRK, IRENE (1926-)
[American journalist and
educator]
Irina Kirk
KIRK, JAMES PRIOR (1850-
1922) [English novelist]

James Prior
KIRK, JOHN ROBERT
(18? ?-1937) [American
educator]
The Grand Old Man of
Missouri
Kirk, Phyllis. See:
KIRKEGAARD, PHYLLIS
KIRK, RICHARD EDMUND
(1931-) [American
editor, correspondent
and author]
Jeffrey Church
KIRK, RONALD T. (1936-)
[American jazz musician
(flute, tenor saxophone,
others, composer)]
Roland Kirk
Kirk Stuart. See:
KINCHELOE, CHARLES
KIRK, THOMAS HOBSON
(1899-) [English
physician and author]
K.H. Thomas
Kirk Wood. See:
STAHL, LEROY
Kirke, Edmund. See:
GILMORE, JAMES
ROBERTS
KIRKEBY, WALLACE T.
(1891-) [American
musician]
Ed Kirkeby
KIRKEGAARD, PHYLLIS
(1930-) [American
dancer, model and motion
picture actress]
Phyllis Kirk
KIRKLAND, CAROLINE MATILDA
STANSBURY (1801-64)
[American social
historian]
Mrs. Mary Clavers
KIRKLAND, RICHARD R.
(1841-63) [American
Civil War sergeant]
The Hero of Fredericksburg
KIRKPATRICK, JOHN MILTON
(1825-18? ?) [American
attorney]
The Silver-tongued Orator
Kirkpatrick West. See:
HARRIS, FRANK BRAYTON

KIRKUP, JAMES (1927-)
[British poet]
James Falconer
Andrew James
Ivy B. Summerforest
Kirkus, Virginia. See:
  GLICK, VIRGINIA
  KIRKUS
KIRKWOOD, JAMES (1930-)
[American actor and
author]
Jim Kirkwood
KIRSCHNER, ALOISIA (1854-)
[Australian author]
Ossip Schubin
Kirtland, G.B. See:
  HINE, SESYLE JOSLIN
Kirwan. See:
  MURRAY, NICHOLAS
KIRWAN, MOLLY MORROW
(1906-) [British author]
Charlotte Morrow
Kish, G. Hobab. See:
  KENNEDY, GERALD
  HAMILTON
KISKADDEN, MAUDE
(1872-1953) [American
actress]
Maude Adams
Kiss-of-death. See:
  OLIVER, ELI L.
Kissing-bug. See:
  HOBSON, RICHMOND
  PEARSON
Kisskiss Bangbang, Mr.
  See: CONNERY, THOMAS
Kit. See:
  CARSON, CHRISTOPHER
  CARSON, WALTER LLOYD
  CORNELL, KATHARINE
  MARLOWE, CHRIS-
    TOPHER
  REED, LILLIAN CRAIG
Kit Clyde. See:
  SENARENS, LUIS PHILIP
Kit, Father. See:
  CARSON, CHRISTOPHER
Kitchell, Iva. See:
  BAUGH, EMMA
KITCHENER, HORATIO HER-
BERT, 1ST EARL
KITCHENER (1850-1916)
[British general officer]

Lord Kitchener
KITCHIN, FREDERICK HAR-
COURT (1867-) [English
author]
Bennett Copplestone
Kite, Larry. See:
  SCHNECK, STEPHEN
KITMAN, MARVIN. See:
  Hirsch, William Randolph
Kitty. See:
  CHEATHAM, KATHERINE
  SMILEY
  Ketti
  Ketty
Kitty, Aunt. See:
  McINTOSH, MARIA JANE
Kitty Clive. See:
  RAFTOR, CATHERINE
Kivi, Aleksis. See:
  STENVALL, ALEKSIS
KLAGES, THEODORE (1911-)
[American musician]
Ted Klages
Klainikite, Anne. See:
  GEHMAN, BETSY
  HOLLAND
KLASS, EUGENE (1921-)
[American motion picture
and television actor]
Gene Barry
KLAUE, LOLA SHELTON
(1903-) [American
teacher and author]
Lola Shelton
Klaus, Bruder. See:
  LÖWENBRUGGER,
  NIKOLAS
Klaus, Santa. See:
  NICOLAUS, ST.
KLEBE, CHARLES EUGENE
(1907-) [American
artist and author]
Gene Klebe
KLEBERG, RICHARD MIFFIN
(1887-) [American
ranchman and politician;
Congressman from Texas]
The Cattle King
KLEIN-LUCKOW, MAX (1905-)
[German professional
boxer; world's heavyweight
champion]
Der Max

Max Schmeling
Klenovsky, Paul. See:
WOOD, SIR HENRY
JOSEPH
Klikspaan. See:
KNEPPELHOUT,
JOHANNES
KLINCKERFUSS, INGABOR
KATRINE (c.1918-)
[Norwegian motion
picture actress]
Karen Verne
KLINE, FRANK (1925-)
[American stage and
motion picture actor]
Frank Latimore
KLINE, ROBERT GEORGE
(1910-) [American
professional baseball
player]
King Kong
Klook. See:
CLARKE, KENNETH
SPEARMAN
KLOPSTOCK, FRIEDRICH
GOTTLIEB (1724-1803)
[German poet]
The German Milton
The Milton of Germany
KNAPP, SAMUEL LORENZO
(1783-1838) [American
lawyer and editor]
Ignatius Loyola Robertson
Shahcoolen
Marshall Soult
Knaresborough, Blind Jack of.
See: METCALF, JACK
KNAUTH, ROBERT
(1814-85) [German
musician and composer]
Robert Franz
KNEF, HILDEGARDE
(1925-) [German artist,
film cartoonist and
actress]
Hildegarde Neff
KNEPPELHOUT, JOHANNES
(1814-85) [Dutch
essayist and man of
letters]
Klikspaan
KNIBERG, IRWIN ALAN
(1927-) [American

comedian, author, actor
and producer]
An Aggressive Jack Benny
Alan King
Knickerbocker, Cholly. See:
PAUL, MAURY HENRY
BIDDLE
Knickerbocker, Diedrich. See:
IRVING, WASHINGTON
KNICKERBOCKER, HERMAN
(1782-1855) [American
resident of Schaghticoke,
N.Y.]
The Prince of Knickerbocker
The Prince of Schaghticoke
Knife, Long. See:
LEWIS, MERIWETHER
Knife, The Sharp. See:
JACKSON, ANDREW
Knife, The Two-edged. See:
BILBO, THEODORE
GILMORE
Knifesmith. See:
CUTLER, IVOR
Knight, Adam. See:
LARIAR, LAWRENCE
KNIGHT-ADKIN, JAMES H.
(1879-) [British educator
and author]
Knight Adkin
Knight, David. See:
PRATHER, RICHARD
SCOTT
KNIGHT, GOODWIN JESS
(1896-1970) [American
lawyer and politician;
Governor of California]
Goody Knight
KNIGHT, HENRY COGSWELL
(1789-1835) [American
author]
Arthur Singleton
Arthur Singleton, Esq.
KNIGHT, J. FORREST (1901-)
[American night club
entertainer and motion
picture actor]
Fuzzy Knight
Knight, James. See:
SCHNECK, STEPHEN
Knight of Germany, The Red.
See: VON RICHTHOFEN,
BARON MANFRED

Knight of Liddesdale, The. See:
DOUGLAS, SIR WILLIAM
Knight of Our Round Table,
The. See:
AEGIDIUS OF ASSISI
Knight of the Border, The
Black. See:
MALONE, PERCY LAY
Knight of the Confederacy, The
Plumed. See:
STUART, JAMES EWELL
BROWN
Knight of the Golden Spurs,
The. See:
STUART, JAMES EWELL
BROWN
Knight of the Most Honorable
Order of Starvation. See:
LIVINGSTON, WILLIAM
Knight of the Red Rose, The.
See: TAYLOR, ALFRED
ALEXANDER
Knight of the South, The Black.
See: McCLUNG,
ALEXANDER
Knight of the White Rose, The.
See: TAYLOR, ROBERT
LOVE
Knight-Patterson, W. M. See:
KULSKI, WLADYSLAW
WSZEBOR
Knight, Plumed. See:
BLAINE, JAMES
GILLESPIE
KNIGHT, SARAH KEMBLE
(1666-1727) [American
teacher and journalist]
Madame Knight
Knight, Tattooed. See:
BLAINE, JAMES
GILLESPIE
Knight, The Red Cross. See:
GEORGE, ST.
Knight, The Serving. See:
McCONNELL, JOHN
PRESTON
Knight Without Fear and
Without Reproach, The.
See: BAYARD,
PIERRE DU TERRAIL,
CHEVALIER DE
Knight Without Reproach, The.
See: BARNAZAN,

ARNAULD GUILHELM
DE
Knights, The Last of the. See:
MAXIMILIAN I
KNIPE, EMILIE BENSON
(1870-1958) [American
artist and author]
Therese Benson
Knish, Anne
Emanuel Morgan, joint
pseuds. of WITTER
BYNNER (1881-1968) and
ARTHUR DAVISON
FICKE (1883-1945)
[American authors and
poets]
Knitting Hattie. See:
CARAWAY, HATTIE
WYATT
Knobby. See:
TOTAH, NABIL MARSHALL
KNOBLAUGH, GLEN GRAY
(1906-63) [American jazz
musician (saxophones,
leader of the Casa Loma
orchestra)]
Glen Gray
Spike
KNOPF, ALFRED A. (1892-)
[American publisher]
The Perfect Publisher
KNOTHE, WILFRED EDGAR
(1905-   ) [American
professional baseball
player]
Fritz
Knott, Herman. See:
SMITH, WALTER
CHALMERS
KNOTT, WILLIAM CECIL, JR.
(1927-) [American
teacher and author]
Bill Knott
Bill J. Carol
KNOTTS, DON (1924-)
[American comedian]
Windy Wales
Knowall, George. See:
O'NUALLAIN, BRIAN
Knowledge, The Cyclopedia of.
See: BROWN, JOHN
JACKSON
KNOWLES, MABEL WINIFRED

(1875-) [British church
worker and author]
May Wynne
Knox, Calvin M. See:
SILVERBERG, ROBERT
KNOX, EDMUND GEORGE VALPY
(1881-) [English humorous
writer and parodist]
Evoe
Knox, Jackson. See:
HARBAUGH, THOMAS
CHALMERS
KNOX, JOHN (1505-72) [Scottish
religious reformer and
writer]
The Apostle of the Scots
The Apostle of the Scottish
Reformation
KNOX, PHILANDER CHASE
(1853-1921) [American
politician; Attorney
General in cabinet of
WILLIAM McKINLEY
Sleepy Phil
KNOX, WILLIAM (1928-)
[Scottish newspaperman
and author]
Bill Knox
Robert MacLeod
KNOX, WILLIAM FRANKLIN
(1874-1944) [American
newspaper publisher and
politician]
Frank Knox
KNUDSEN, WILLIAM S.
(1879-1948) [Danish-
American industrialist]
Bill Knudsen
KNUT. See:
CANUTE (CNUT) (KNUT) II
Knut Hamsun. See:
PEDERSEN, KNUT
KNUTSON, CORNELIA GJESDAL
(1912-) [American
politician; U.S. representa-
tive from Minnesota]
Coya Knutson
The Farm Woman's Congress-
woman
KNUTSON, HAROLD (1880-)
[American journalist and
politician; congressman
from Minnesota]
Anti-war Knutson

Knuttson, Karl. See:
CHARLES VIII
KOBAYASHI, MASAKO
MATSUNO (1935-)
[Japanese author]
Masako Matsuno
KOCH, ILSE (-1967) [Sadistic
German wife of commander
of Buchenwald Nazi con-
centration camp]
The Bitch of Buchenwald
KOCH, JODOCUS (1493-1555)
[German reformer]
Justus Jonas
Koch, Judith. See:
ECKER, JUDITH K.
KOENIG, MARIE ADRIENNE
(1889-1965) [American
dancer and silent motion
picture actress]
Mae Murray
KOERBER, LEILA (1871-1934)
[Canadian-American
comedienne and actress]
Marie Dressler
The Grand Old Lady of the
Movies
The Old Trouper
Queen Marie of Hollywood
KOFFLER, CAMILLA (died 1955)
[Austrian photographer of
animals]
Ylla
KOFORD, HELEN (1932-)
[American motion picture
actress]
Terry Moore
KOHN-BEHRENS, CHARLOTTE
(fl. mid-20th cent.)
[German author]
Viktoria Rehn
Koizumi, Yakumo. See:
HEARN, PATRICIO
LAFCADIO TESSIMA
CARLOS
KOLB, REUBEN FRANCIS
(1839-1918) [American
politician; unsuccessful
candidate for governorship
of Alabama]
Genial Reuben
Our Patrick Henry
Run Forever Kolb

Kole. See also:
COLE
Cole
COLL
Kole, Robert. See:
KOLODIN, ROBERT
KOLLONTAY, ALEXANDRA
(fl. early 20th cent.)
[Russian diplomat and
author]
Schura
KOLODIN, ROBERT (1932-)
[American composer]
Robert Kole
Kolta, Bautier De. See:
BAUTIER, JOSEPH
Komed. See:
LANGER, ALFONS
KOMISARJEVSKY, FEDOR
(1882-1954) [Russian
producer of plays and
operas]
Theodore Komisarjevsky
KOMISS, VIRGINIA (1913-)
[American radio and
television personality]
Virginia Graham
KONADU, SAMUEL ASARE
(1932-) [African
journalist and author]
K. A. Bediako
Asare Konadu
Kong, King. See:
KLINE, ROBERT
GEORGE
KONSTAM, GERTRUDE (1866-
1937) [English actress
and theater manager]
Gertrude Kingston
KONSTANTY, CASIMER JAMES
(1917-) [American
professional baseball
player]
Jim Konstanty
Kookie. See:
BYRNES, EDD
KOOP, KATHERINE C. (1923-)
[American educator and
author]
Katherine C. LaMancusa
KOOWESKOOWE. See:
COOWESCOOWE
(KOOWESKOOWE)

KOREFF, NORA (1920-)
[American ballerina]
The Duse of the Dance
Nora Kaye
KORNBLUTH, C. M. See:
Judd, Cyril
KORNGOLD, ERICH WOLFGANG
(1897-) [Moravian-
American composer]
The Modern Mozart
KORSOMO, EMIL (1863-)
[Norwegian biologist,
educator and author]
E. K.
KORZENIOWSKI, TEODOR
JÓZEF KONRAD (1857-
1924) [English author
of Polish
extraction]
Joseph Conrad
KOSINSKI, JERZY NIKODEM
(1933-) [Polish-American
author]
Joseph Novak
Kosleck, Martin. See:
YOSHKIN, NICOLAI
Koster, Henry. See:
KOSTERLITZ, HERMANN
KOSTERLITZ, HERMANN
(1905-) [German motion
picture director]
Henry Koster
KOSTRABA, DANIEL (1924-)
[American jazz musician
(leader, trumpet,
arranger)]
Dan Terry
KOSTROWITZKY, APOLLINARIS
(1880-1918) [French poet]
Guillaume Apollinaire
Kostur Hotel, Katie from the.
See: CUMPANAS, ANA
KOUFAX, SANFORD (1935-)
[American professional
baseball player]
The Man With the Golden Arm
Sandy Koufax
KOUTS, HERTHA PRETORIUS
(1922-) [American author]
Hertha Pretorius
KOUYOUMDJIAN, DIKRAN
(1895-1956) [English
novelist born at Ruschuk,

Bulgaria]
Michael Arlen
KOVACS, EDITH ENKE
(1927-) [American
singer, actress and
comedienne]
Edie Adams
KRAENZEL, MARGARET
POWELL (1899-)
[American librarian and
author]
Wallace Blue
KRAMER. See also:
CRAMER
KREMER
KRAMER, JOHN ALBERT
(1921-) [American tennis
player]
Big Jake Kramer
Jack Kramer
Jake Kramer
KRAMER, STANLEY E.
(1913-) [American
motion picture producer]
Genius on a Low Budget
Wonder Boy
KRAMISH, ARNOLD (1923-)
[American scientist and
author]
J. Lincoln Paine
KRAMPKE, HUGH (1925-)
[American television and
motion picture actor]
Hugh O'Brian
KRANZ, JACOB (1899-)
[Viennese-American
motion picture actor]
Ricardo Cortez
KRANZ, STANISLAUS (1908-)
[Viennese-American
cinematographer]
Stanley Cortez
Krapp, R. M. See:
ADAMS, ROBERT
MARTIN
Kraselchik, R. See:
DYER, CHARLES
KRASNEY, SAMUEL A.
(1922-) [American
editor, columnist and
author]
Sam Curzon
Krasny, Ivan (The Red). See:

IVAN II
KRASZEWSKI, JÓZEF IGNACY
(1812-87) [Polish writer]
R. Bołeslawita
K.F. Pasternak
KRAUSÉ, LYDA FARRINGTON
(1864-) [Danish author]
Barbara Yechton
KRAUSS, ROBERT G. (1924-)
[American reporter,
columnist and author]
Bob Krauss
KRAUTH, VIOLET (1913-)
[American motion
picture actress]
Marion Marsh
KRAUTTER, ELISA BIALK
(fl. 1930-60) [American
author]
Elisa Bialk
KRAVCHINSKY, SERGIUS
MIKHAILOVICH (1852-95)
[Russian revolutionary]
Stepnyak (Son of the Steppe)
KREBS, MARY TOMLINSON
(1890-) [American motion
picture actress]
Marjorie Main
KREBS, RICHARD JULIUS
HERMAN (1905-51) [Com-
munist saboteur and author]
Jan Valtin
KRECH, WARREN (c.1895-1948)
[American stage and motion
picture actor]
Warren William
KREIG, MARGARET B. (1922-)
[American author]
Peggy Craig
KREMER. See also:
CRAMER
KRAMER
KREMER, GERHARD (1512-94)
[Flemish mathematician,
geographer and cartographer]
The Father of Modern
Geography
Gerhardus Mercator
KRENTEL, MILDRED WHITE
(1921-) [American
broadcast programmer,
editor and author]
Mrs. Miggy

KRETZER, MARY (1854-1941)
[German novelist]
The German Zola
KREUGER. See also:
KRUGER
KREUGER, IVAR (1800-1932)
[Swedish industrialist and
financier]
The Match King
Kris. See also:
Chris
Cris
Kris Giles. See:
NIELSEN, HELEN
BERNIECE
Kristian. See also:
CHRISTIAN
Christian
Kristian Pagan. See:
SEBELIEN, JOHN
ROBERT FRANCIS
KROEGER, HENRY (1819-18??)
[Prussian-American
ice manufacturer]
Ice-bear Kroeger
Krog, Karin. See:
BERGH, KARIN KROG
KROHN, JOHN ALBERT (fl.
1908-10) [American
transcontinental walker]
Colonel Jack
Kroll, Burt. See:
ROWLAND, DONALD
SYDNEY
KROLL, JOHN JACOB
(1885-) [American
trade union leader]
Jack Kroll
KROUT, CAROLINE VIRGINIA
(1853-1931) [American
author]
Caroline Brown
KRUGER. See also:
KREUGER
KRUGER, STEPHANUS
JOHANNES PAULUS
(1825-1904) [South
African statesman]
Oom Paul
Krull, Felix. See:
WHITE, JAMES DILLON
KRUMBEIN, MAURICE (1908-)
[American composer,

conductor and pianist]
Ray Carter
KRUPA, EUGENE BERTRAM
(1909-) [American jazz
musician (drums, leader)]
That Ace Drummer Man
Gene Krupa
King of the Drums
KRUPP, MAJOR D. DUDLEY
(1894-) [American soldier,
composer, radiologist and
physician]
Dudley Manners
Krutzsch, Gus. See:
ELIOT, THOMAS STEARNS
KUBELIK, JAN (1880-1940)
[Czech violin virtuoso and
composer]
Polgar
KUBELSKY, BENNY (1894-)
[American comedian,
violinist and actor]
Ben Benny
Jack Benny
KUBLAI KHAN (KHUBILAI KHAN)
(KUBLA KHAN) (1216-94)
[Mongol military leader;
founder and first emperor
of the Mongol Yuan
Dynasty]
The Great Khan
KUEHN, DOROTHY DALTON
(1915-) [American poet]
Dorothy Dalton
KUEHNELT-LEDDIHN, ERIK
RITTER VON (1909-)
[Austrian educator and
author]
Francis Stuart Campbell
Chester F. O'Leary
Tomislav Vitezovic
KUHHORN, MARTIN (1491-1551)
[German Protestant
theologian]
Martin Buccer (Butzer)
Aretius Felinus
KUHN, ROBERT (1922-)
[American jazz musician
(clarinet, leader)]
Bob Keene
KUJNIR-HERESCU, NADIA
(1923-) [Russian-Rumanian
motion picture actress]

Nadia Gray
KULSKI, WLADYSLAW
WSZEBOR (1903-)
[Polish-American educator
and author]
W. W. Coole
W. M. Knight-Patterson
Politicus
KUMMER, FREDERIC ARNOLD
(1873-1943) [American
novelist and playwright]
Arnold Fredericks
KUNCEWICZ, MARIA
SZCZEPANSKA (1899-)
(Polish educator, broad-
caster and author]
Maria Kuncewiczowa
KUNITZ, RICHARD E. (1919-)
[American banker and
composer]
Richard Evans
KUNITZ, STANLEY JASSPON
(1905-) [American poet
and author of reference
books]
Dilly Tante
KUPFERBERG, NAPHTALI (1923-)
[American editor, librar-
ian, folk singer and
author]
Tuli Kupferberg
Kurowski, Eugeniusz. See:
DOBRACZYNSKI, JAN
KURSH, CHARLOTTE OLMSTED
(1912-) [American anthro-
pologist and writer]
Charlotte Olmsted
Kurshu. See:
CYRUS
Kurt Katch. See:
KAC, ISSER
Kurt Steel. See:
KAGEY, RUDOLF
KURTZ, MANNY (1911-)
[American composer and
author]
Mann Curtis
Kurz, Artur R. See:
SCORTIA, THOMAS
NICHOLAS
Kyd. See also:
Kid
Kyd, Thomas. See:

HARBAGE, ALFRED
BENNETT
Kyle, Alexander. See:
MARLOWE, ALAN
STEPHEN
Kyle, Elizabeth. See:
DUNLOP, AGNES MARY
ROBERTSON
Kyle Hunt. See:
CREASEY, JOHN
Kylie Tennant. See:
RODD, KYLIE TENNANT
KYNER, SYLVESTER (1932-)
[American jazz musician
(alto saxophone)]
Sonny Red
Kyrle, Harold. See:
BELLEW, HAROLD KYRLE
KYRLE, JOHN (1637-1724)
[English humanist]
The Man of Ross
Kyrre, Olaf (The Quiet). See:
OLAF III
KYSER, JAMES KING KERN
(1906-) [American jazz
musician (leader)]
Kay Kyser
The Old Professor

L

L. See:
LANDON, LETITIA ELIZA-
BETH
L.A. G. See:
STRONG, LEONARD AL-
FRED GEORGE
L. B. J. See:
JOHNSON, LYNDON
BAINES
L David Barnett. See:
LASCHEVER, BARNETT D.
L. Dunton Green. See:
GREIN, JACOB THOMAS
L.E. L. See:
LANDON, LETITIA
ELIZABETH
L. Fairfax. See:
CONNELLY, LELIA LOGAN
L. Frank Baum. See:
BAUM, LYMAN FRANK
L.J. Arnold. See:

CAMERON, LOU
L. L. Case. See:
LEWIN, LEONARD CASE
L. M. See:
LIM, BOON KENG
L. M. Montgomery. See:
MACDONALD, LUCY
MAUDE MONTGOMERY
L. W. See:
UNKNOWN
Laage, Barbara. See:
COLOMBAT, CLAIRE
LAAR, PIETER VAN (c. 1592-
1642) [Dutch genre painter]
Il Bamboccio (The Deformed)
LABÉ, LOUISE (1526-66)
[French poet]
La Belle Cordière (The
Beautiful Rope Maker)
La Bolina, Jack. See:
VECCHI, AUGUSTUS
VICTOR
Labor Loves, The Loquacious
Linguist Whom. See:
PERKINS, FRANCES
Labor Mayor, The. See:
DORE, JOHN FRANCIS
Labor Movement, The Dean of
the American. See:
FURUSETH, ANDREW
Labor, The Father of Ohio. See:
CROSSER, ROBERT
Labor, The Grand Old Man of.
See: GOMPERS, SAMUEL
Labrador, Grenfell of. See:
GRENFELL, SIR
WILFRED THOMASON
LABRUNIE, GERARD (1808-55)
[French writer]
Gerard de Nerval
Lace Kendall. See:
STOUTENBURG, ADRIEN
PEARL
LACHOFF, SOL (1911-) [Amer-
ican composer]
Sol Lake
LACK, PEARL (1922-)
[American dancer and
choreographer]
Pearl Lang
Lackland. See:
JOHN I
LA COCK, JOANNE (1923-)

[American motion picture
actress]
Joanne Dru
Lacon. See:
WATSON, EDMUND
HENRY LACON
LACKRITZ, STEVEN (1934-)
[American jazz musician
(soprano saxophone)]
Steve Lacy
LACROIX, PAUL (1806-64)
[French scholar]
Pierre Dufour
P. L. Jacob, Bibliophile
Lacroix, Ramón. See:
McKEAG, ERNEST
LIONEL
Lacrymal, The Poète. See:
BOUILLY, JEAN
NICOLAS
Lacy, John. See:
DARLEY, GEORGE
Lacy, Steve. See:
LACKRITZ, STEVEN
Lad, The. See:
ALMAGRO, DIEGO DE
LADD, WILLIAM (1778-1841)
[American peace advocate]
The Apostle of Peace
Laddie, The Highland. See:
STUART, CHARLES
EDWARD LOUIS PHILIP
CASIMIR
Ladolas, Magnus (Barn Lock).
See: MAGNUS I
Lady. See:
GODIVA (GODGIFU)
HAMILTON, EMMA LYON
PACKER, JOY PETERSEN
WU, LADY
Lady, A. See:
AUSTEN, JANE
BOTSFORD, MARGARET
COOPER, SUSAN
FENIMORE
FIELDING, SUSAN
HOWE, JULIA WARD
SMITH, SARAH POGSON
WINCHILSEA, ANNE
FINCH, COUNTESS OF
Lady Augusta Gregory. See:
PERSSE, ISABELLA
AUGUSTA

Lady, Berkshire. See:
  KENDRICK, FRANCES
Lady Bird, See:
  JOHNSON, CLAUDIA ALTA
    TAYLOR
Lady Caroline Lascelles. See:
  BRADDON, MARY
    ELIZABETH
Lady, Chicago's Grand Old. See:
  HUDLUN, ANNA
    ELIZABETH
Lady Day. See:
  McKAY, ELEANOR
    GOUGH
Lady de Frece. See:
  POWLES, MATILDA
    ALICE
Lady Esther Hope. See:
  ST. JOHN, PERCY
    BOLLINGBROKE
Lady Geralda. See:
  BRONTË, ANNE
Lady of Christ's, The. See:
  MILTON, JOHN
Lady of England, A (A. L. O. E.)
  See: TUCKER,
    CHARLOTTE MARIA
Lady of England, The. See:
  MATILDA
Lady of Hollywood, The First.
  See: DUNNE, IRENE
    GARSON, GREER
    KING, MOIRA SHEARER
Lady of Literacy, The First.
  See: FISHER, WELTHY
    BLAKESLEY
    HONSINGER
Lady of Maine, A. See:
  BARRELL, SARAH
    SAYWARD
Lady of Massachusetts, A. See:
  BARRELL, SARAH SAY-
    WARD
Lady of Opera, The Grand Old.
  See: SCHUMANN-
    HEINK, MME.
    ERNESTINE
Lady of Philadelphia, A. See:
  BOTSFORD, MARGARET
Lady of Quality, A. See:
  BAGNOLD, ENID
Lady of Song, The First. See:
  FITZGERALD, ELLA

Lady of Supper Clubs, The
  First. See:
    SELL, HILDEGARDE
      LORETTA
Lady of Television, The First.
  See: BALL, LUCILLE
Lady of the American Dance,
  The First. See:
    DENNIS, RUTH
Lady of the American Theater,
  The First. See:
    BROWN, HELEN HAYES
Lady of the Iron Watchdog, The.
  See: INGALLS,
    MARILLA BAKER
Lady of the Land, The First.
  See: WILSON, EDITH
    BOLLING GALT
Lady of the Mercians, The. See:
  AETHELFLAED
Lady of the Movies, The Grand
  Old. See:
    KOERBER, LEILA
Lady of the Screen, The First.
  See: GUICHE, LILLIAN
    DE
Lady of the Stars, The. See:
  PROCTOR, MARY
Lady of the Sun, The. See:
  PETERS (PERRERS)
    (PIERCE) (PERREN),
    ALICE
Lady of the Vale. See:
  BUTLER, LADY ELEANOR
    PONSONBY, MISS
    SARAH
Lady of the World, The First.
  See: WILSON, EDITH
    BOLLING GALT
Lady Peel. See:
  LILLIE, BEATRICE
    GLADYS
Lady, The Poppy. See:
  MICHAEL, MOINA
Lady, The Singing Story. See:
  WICKER, IREENE
    SEATON
Lady, The Story. See:
  FAULKNER, GEORGENE
Lady, The Texas Doll. See:
  WEAVER, GUSTINE
    NANCY COURSON
Lady, The Ukulele. See:

BREEN, MAY SINGHI
Lady With the Hatchet, The.
   See: NATION, CARRY
      AMELIA MOORE
Lady With the Lamp, The. See:
   NIGHTINGALE, FLORENCE
Lael Tucker. See:
   WERTENBAKER, LAEL
      TUCKER
Laelius. See:
   DISRAELI, BENJAMIN,
      1ST EARL OF BEACONS-
      FIELD
LAENGSDORFF, JULIA VIRGINIA
   (1878-) [German author]
   Julia Virginia
Lafayette, Marquis de. See:
   MOTIER, MARIE JEAN
      PAUL ROCH YVES
      GILBERT
Lafayette of the Greek Revolu-
   tion, The. See:
   HOWE, SAMUEL GRIDLEY
Lafayette Smith. See:
   HIGDON, HAL
Lafcadio. See:
   HEARN, PATRICIO LAF-
      CADIO TESSIMA
      CARLOS
Lafitte, Colonel Leon. See:
   INGRAHAM, COLONEL
      PRENTISS
LAFITTE, JEAN (c. 1780-c. 1826)
   [French privateer and
   smuggler on Gulf of
   Mexico]
   The Boss
   The Gentleman Smuggler
   The Pirate of the Gulf
   The Terror of the Gulf
LA FLESCHE, SUZETTE
   (1854-1903) [American
   Indian educator, lecturer
   and author]
   Inshtatheanba (Bright Eyes)
LA FOLLETTE, ROBERT
   MARION, SR. (1855-
   1925) [American
   politician; Congressman
   from Wisconsin]
   Battling Bob
Lagartijo. See:
   MOLINA, RAFAEL

LAGERY. See:
   ODA OF LAGERY
Laggan, Mrs. Grant of. See:
   GRANT, ANNE MACVICAR
Lagoböter (Reformer of the Laws).
   See: MAGNUS VI
LA GUARDIA, FIORELLO
   HENRY (1882-1947) [Amer-
   ican politician; Mayor of
   New York City]
   Butch
   The Little Flower
Lahovary, His Highness Prince.
   See: MANOLESCO, GEORGE
Lahr, Bert. See:
   LARHEIM, IRVING
LAHRHEIM, IRVING (1895-1967)
   [American comedian]
   Bert Lahr
Laidlaw, A.K. See:
   GRIEVE, CHRISTOPHER
      MURRAY
LAINE [Laine]. See also:
   LANE
   Lane
   Lanne
Laine Fisher. See:
   HOWARD, JAMES ARCH
Laine, Frankie. See:
   LOVECCHIO, FRANK PAUL
LAINE, GEORGE VITELLE
   (1873-) [American jazz
   musician (leader, drums)]
   Jack Laine
   Papa Laine
Laing, Hugh. See:
   SKINNER, HUGH
Laird, Dorothy. See:
   CARR, DOROTHY
      STEVENSON LAIRD
Laird of Skibo Castle, The. See:
   CARNEGIE, ANDREW
Laird of Skibo, The. See:
   CARNEGIE, ANDREW
Laird of Woodchuck Lodge, The.
   See: BURROUGHS, JOHN
LAISNÉ, JEANNE (fl. 15th cent.)
   [French heroine]
   Fourquet
   Jeanne Hachette
LAJOIE, NAPOLEON (1875-1959)
   [American professional
   baseball player]

Larry Lajoie
Nap Lajoie
Lake Erie, The Hero of.
    See: PERRY, OLIVER
    HAZARD
LAKE, HARRIETTE (1909-)
    [American stage and motion
    picture actress]
Ann Sothern
Lake, Sol. See:
    LACHOFF, SOL
Lake, Turk Van. See:
    HOUSEPIAN, VANIG
Lake, Veronica. See:
    KEANE, CONSTANCE
Laklan, Carli, joint pseud. of
    VIRGINIA CARLI LAUGH-
    LIN (1907-) and
    FREDERICK THOMAS (-)
    [American authors]
Laklan, Carli. See also:
    LAUGHLIN, VIRGINIA CARLI
Lalo. See:
    SCHIFRIN, BORIS
LA LOCA, JOANNA (1479-1555)
    [Daughter of FERDINAND
    King of Castile, and
    ISABELLA, Queen of
    Spain]
Crazy Jane
LaMancusa, Katherine C. See:
    KOOP, KATHERINE C.
Lamar, Ashton. See:
    SAYLER, HARRY
    LINCOLN
LAMARE, HILTON (1910-)
    [American jazz musician
    (guitar, banjo, singer)]
Nappy Lamare
La Marr, Barbara. See:
    WATSON, REATHA
Lamarr, Hedy. See:
    LEISLER, HEDWIG
LAMB, CHARLES (1775-1834)
    [British author, critic
    and essayist]
Elia
LAMB, MARY ANN (1764-1847)
    [English author]
Bridget Elia
LAMB, WILLIAM (1835-1909)
    [American Civil War
    Confederate officer]

The Hero of Fort Fisher
Lambert, Christine. See:
    FREYBE, HEIDI HUBERTA
LAMBERT, EDWARD (1809-94)
    [English actor and play-
    wright]
Edward Stirling
LAMBERT, ERIC (1918-)
    [British biologist, cricket
    player and author]
Frank Brennand
George Kay
LAMBERT, JONATHAN (fl. late
    17th cent.) [American
    pirate]
Brother Jonathan
Lambert, Louis. See:
    GILMORE, PATRICK
    SARSFIELD
LAMBERTINI, PROSPERO
    (1675-1758) [Supreme
    Pontiff of Roman Catholic
    Church]
Pope Benedict XIV
LAMBURN, JOHN BATTERSBY
    CROMPTON (1893-)
    [British author]
John Crompton
LAMBURN, RICHMAL CROMP-
    TON (1890-) [British
    author]
Richmal Crompton
Lame, The. See:
    CHARLES I
    HENRY II
    HERMANN
Lame, Timur the. See:
    TIMUR LENK
LA MENTHE, FERDINAND
    JOSEPH (1885-1941)
    [American jazz musician
    (piano, composer, leader,
    singer)]
Jelly Roll Morton
Lamia. See:
    AUSTIN, ALFRED
Lamoille, The Silver-tongued
    Orator of. See:
    SHAW, HOWARD ELWIN
Lamont, Victor See:
    MAIORANA, VICTOR E.
Lamour, Dorothy. See:
    KAUMEYER, DOROTHY

L'AMOUR, LOUIS DEARBORN
(1908-) [American author
and lecturer]
Tex Burns
Lamp, The Lady With the. See:
NIGHTINGALE,
FLORENCE
LAMPMAN, EVELYN SIBLEY
(1907-) [American
broadcasting executive
and author]
Lynn Bronson
Lana. See:
TURNER, JULIA JEAN
MILDRED FRANCES
Lancashire Burns, The. See:
WAUGH, EDWIN
Lancashire Poet, The. See:
WAUGH, EDWIN
LANCASTER. See:
JOHN OF LANCASTER
LANCASTER, BURTON
STEPHEN (1913-)
[American motion picture
actor and producer]
Burt Lancaster
Lang
Lancaster, Henry of. See:
HENRY IV
Lancaster, William. See:
WARREN, JOHN BYRNE
LEICESTER
Lance. See:
SIEVEKING, LANCELOT
DE GIBERNE
Lance Falconer. See:
HAWKER, MARY
ELIZABETH
Lancelot. See also:
Launcelot
Lancelot Wagstaff. See:
THACKERAY, WILLIAM
MAKEPEACE
Lancewood, Lawrence. See:
WISE, DANIEL
Lanchester, Elsa. See:
LAUGHTON, ELIZABETH
SULLIVAN
Land Admiral, The. See:
REESIDE, JAMES
Land, Fallow (Novalis). See:
HARDENBERG,
FRIEDRICH LEOPOLD,
BARON VON

Land, First Gentleman of the.
See:
ARTHUR, CHESTER ALAN
Land Hero of 1812, The. See:
JACKSON, ANDREW
Land, Rosina. See:
HASTINGS, PHYLLIS DORA
HODGE
Land, The First Lady of the.
See: WILSON, EDITH
BOLLING GALT
LANDAU-ALDANOV, MARK
(1888-) [Russian
novelist and essayist]
M.A. Aldanov
Landers, Ann. See:
FRIEDMAN, ESTHER
PAULINE
Landers, Lew. See:
FRIEDLANDER, LEWIS
LANDESBERG, PHYLLIS G.
(1927-) [American
composer]
Phyllis Fairbanks
LANDESMAN, FRANCES
(1927-) [American
composer]
Fran Landesman
LANDESMANN, HEINRICH
(1821-1902) [German
deaf and blind poet and
prose writer]
Hieronymus Lorm
Landi, Elissa. See:
ZANARDI-LANDI,
ELIZABETH MARIE
Landis, Carole. See:
RIDSTE, FRANCES
LANDIS, KENESAW MOUNTAIN
(1866-1944) [Amerian
attorney and baseball
commissioner]
The Czar of American
Baseball
The Czar of Baseball
The Czar of the National
Pastime
Judge Landis
LANDON [Landon]. See also:
LENDON
LONDON
London
LANDON, ALFRED MOSSMAN
(1887-) [American

590

politician; Governor of
Kansas, Presidential
nominee]
Alf Landon
The Coolidge of the West
The Kansas Coolidge
LANDON, LETITIA ELIZABETH
(1802-38/39) [English
poet and novelist]
The English Sappho
L.
L.E.L.
Landon, Louise. See:
HAUCK, LOUISE PLATT
LANDON, MELVILLE DE
LANCEY (1839-1910)
[American humorist and
lecturer]
Eli Perkins
Landon, Michael. See:
OROWITZ, MICHAEL
LANDREAUX, ELIZABETH
MARY (1895-1963) [Amer-
ican jazz singer]
Lizzie Miles
Landscape Gardening, The Cre-
ator of French. See:
LENÔTRE, ANDRÉ
Landscape Gardening, The
Father of. See:
LENÔTRE, ANDRÉ
Landseer, The Liverpool. See:
HUGGINS, WILLIAM
Landsfield, The Countess of.
See: GILBERT,
MARIE DOLORES
ELIZA ROSANNA
LANDUS (died 914) [Supreme
Pontiff of Roman
Catholic Church]
Pope Landus
LANE [Lane]. See also:
LAINE
Laine
Lanne
Lane, Allan. See:
ALBERSHART, HARRY
Lane Archer. See:
HAUCK, LOUISE PLATT
Lane, Burton. See:
LEVY, BURTON
LANE-JACKSON, NICHOLAS
(1849-) [English

journalist and author]
Creston
LANE, JAMES HENRY (1814-66)
[American abolitionist and
general officer]
Fighting Jim
The Grim Chieftain
LANE, JOSEPH (1801-81)
[American general officer]
The Marion of the Mexican
Army
LANE, RALPH NORMAN
ANGELL (1872-1967)
[English economist and
author]
Norman Angell
Sir Norman Angell
Lane, Rocky. See:
ALBERSHART, HARRY
LANE, YOTI (fl. 1930-50)
[Irish author]
Mark Mayo
Lang. See:
LANCASTER, BURTON
STEPHEN
LANG, ANDREW (1844-1912)
[Scottish author]
Hugo Langway
Lang, Eddie. See:
MASSARO, SALVATORE
Lang, Frances. See:
MANTLE, WINIFRED
LANGFORD
Lang, Gregor. See:
BIRREN, FABER
Lang, June. See:
VLASEK, JUNE
Lang, Martin. See:
BIRREN, FABER
Lang, Pearl. See:
LACK, PEARL
Langdon, Mary. See:
PIKE, MARY HAYDEN
GREEN
LANGE, CARL GUSTAV
ALBERT (1885-) [German
author]
Penklub
LANGE, ERNST PHILIPP KARL
(1819-99) [German
novelist]
Philipp Galen
LANGER, ALFONS (1859-)

[German chemist and
author]
Komed
Paul Schultze
Langford, Jane. See:
MANTLE, WINIFRED
LANGFORD
LANGFORD, SAM (1880-1956)
[American Negro profes-
sional boxer]
The Boston Tar Baby
LANGHANKE, LUCILE V.
(1906-) [American
actress and author]
Mary Astor
Langley, Helen. See:
ROWLAND, DONALD
SYDNEY
Langley, John Prentice. See:
RATHBONE, ST. GEORGE
HENRY
LANGNER, ARMINA MARSHALL
See: Child, Alan
LANGNER, LAWRENCE. See:
Child, Alan
Langstaff, Launcelot joint
pseud. of WASHINGTON
IRVING (1783-1859); his
brother WILLIAM IRVING
(1766-1821); and JAMES
KIRKE PAULDING (1779-
1860) [American authors]
Langstaff, Launcelot. See also:
IRVING, WASHINGTON
PAULDING, JAMES KIRKE
Langstaff, Tristram. See:
LORD, WILLIAM WILBER-
FORCE
Langston. See:
HUGHES, JAMES
LANGSTON
LANGSTROTH, LORENZO
LORRAINE (1810-95)
[American apiarist,
educator and clergyman]
The Father of American
Apiculture]
Langtry, Lily. See:
BRETON, EMILY CHAR-
LOTTE LE
Languaged Daniel, The Well.
See: DANIEL,
SAMUEL

Langway, Hugo. See:
LANG, ANDREW
LANIER, SIDNEY (1842-81)
[American poet]
The Sunrise Poet
LANMAN, CHARLES (1819-95)
[American author and
painter]
The Picturesque Explorer of
the United States
Lanne. See also:
LAINE
Laine
LANE
Lane
Lanne, William F. See:
LEOPOLD, NATHAN F.
Lanny. See:
ROSS, LANCELOT PATRICK
Lansing, Henry.
See: ROWLAND, DONALD
SYDNEY
Lant, Harvey. See:
ROWLAND, DONALD SYD-
NEY
Lanza, Mario. See:
COCOZZA, ALFRED
LAON. See:
ALSELM OF LAON
Lap King, The. See:
OLAF
LAPAUZE, JEANNE LOISEAU
(1860-1921) [French writer]
Daniel Lesueur
LAPIDE, PINCHAS E. (1922-)
[Canadian diplomat and
author]
Phinn E. Lapide
LAPIZE, ALICE (1889-)
[French actress and singer]
Alice Delysia
Laporte. See:
LE FEBVRE, MATHIEU
LARA, MANUEL (1867-1912)
[Spanish bullfighter]
Jerezano
LARAIA, CAROL MARIA (1932-)
[American dancer, singer
and actress]
Carol Lawrence
Laraine Day. See:
JOHNSON, LARAINE
LARDNER. See also:

LARNER
LARDNER, RING, JR. See:
Hollywood Ten, The
LARDNER, RINGGOLD WIL-
MER (1885-1933)
[American short story
writer and humorist]
Ring Lardner
Laredo, Johnny. See:
CAESAR, EUGENE LEE
Largesse, He of the (El de
las Mercedes). See:
HENRY II
Largest Congregation in the
United States, A Lay
Preacher to the. See:
BOK, EDWARD WILLIAM
LARIAR, LAWRENCE (1908-)
[American commercial
artist, cartoonist and
author]
Adam Knight
Michael Lawrence
Michael Stark
Larking, C. B. See:
SHAW, GEORGE BERNARD
LARNER. See also:
LARDNER
LARNER, JEREMY (1937-)
[American author]
Orson Gouge
LA ROCCA, DOMINICK JAMES
(1889-1961) [American
jazz musician (cornet,
composer, leader)]
Nick La Rocca
La Rocca, Pete. See:
SIMS, PETER
Laroche, René. See:
McKEAG, ERNEST LIONEL
La Rocque, Rod. See:
LA ROUR, RODERICK LA
ROCQUE DE
LA ROUR, RODERICK LA
ROCQUE DE (1896-)
[American motion picture
actor]
Rod La Rocque
LA ROZE, CLAUDE (c. 1640-86)
[French actor]
Rosimond
LARRALDE, ROMULO (1902-)
[Mexican motion picture

actor]
Romney Brent
Larrimore, Lida. See:
TURNER, LIDA LAR-
RIMORE
Larruper, The Livermore. See:
BAER, MAXIMILIAN
ADELBERT
Larruping Lou. See:
GEHRIG, HENRY LOUIS
Larry. See:
ABBOTT, LAWRENCE
GILBERT
ADLER, LAWRENCE
CECIL
ALLEN, LAURENCE
EIGNER, LAURENCE J.
FREEMAN, GRAYDON
LA VERNE
LAJOIE, NAPOLEON
McPHAIL, LELAND
STANFORD
NIVEN, LAURENCE VAN
COTT
Larry Baxter. See:
SETARO, PETER D.
Larry Craig. See:
COUGHRAN, LARRY C.
Larry Dey. See:
DEYBROOK, L. M.
Larry Kite. See:
SCHNECK, STEPHEN
Larry, Loud. See:
McPHAIL, LELAND
STANFORD
Larry M. Harris. See:
JANIFER, LAURENCE
MARK
Larry McPhail, A Midwestern.
See: VEECK, WILLIAM
LOUIS, JR.
Larry Maddock. See:
JARDINE, JACK
Larry Rivers. See:
GROSSBERG, YITZROCH
LOIZA
Larry Young. See:
YASIN, KHALID
LARSEN, ERLING (1909-)
[American educator and
author]
Peter Brand
LARSEN, SUZAN (1924-)

[American operatic singer
and motion picture
actress]
Susanna Foster
Larson, Eve. See:
    ST. JOHN, WYLLY
    FOLK
LARSSON, SIGNE (1915-)
[Swedish stage and
motion picture actress]
Signe Hasso
La Rue, Jack. See:
    BIONDOLILLO,
    GASPARE
LaSalle, Charles E. See:
    ELLIS, EDWARD
    SYLVESTER
Lascaris. See:
    JOHN IV
LAS CASAS, BARTOLOMÉ DE
(1474-1566) [Spanish
priest]
The Apostle of the Indians
The Protector of the Indians
Lascelles, Alison. See:
    PARRIS, JOHN
Lascelles, Lady Caroline. See:
    BRADDON, MARY
    ELIZABETH
LASCELLES, WALTER (1898-)
[Irish author]
Patrick Downe
LASCHEVER, BARNETT D.
(1924-) [American
editor and author]
L. David Barnett
LASHA, WILLIAM B. (1929-)
[American jazz musician
(flute, composer)]
Prince Lasha
LASLEY, JOHN WAYNE III
(1925-) [American
attorney and author]
Jack Lasley
LASSERAN-MASSENCOME,
    SEIGNEUR DE MONT-
    LUC (1501-77)
[French marshal]
Le Royaliste Boucher
Last Astrologer, The. See:
    LILLY, WILLIAM
Last Cocked Hat, The. See:
    MONROE, JAMES
Last Literary Cavalier, The.

See: HAYNE, PAUL
    HAMILTON
Last Man, The. See:
    CHARLES I
Last Man, The Son of the. See:
    CHARLES II
Last Minstrel of the English
    Stage, The. See:
    SHIRLEY, JAMES
Last of the Barons, The. See:
    NEVIL (NEVILLE),
    RICHARD
Last of the Boatmen, The. See:
    FINK, MIKE
Last of the Cocked Hats, The.
    See: MEASE, JOHN
Last of the Dandies, The. See:
    D'ORSAY, ALFRED
    GUILLAUME GABRIEL,
    COUNT
Last of the Elizabethans, The.
    See: FORD, JOHN
Last of the Fathers, The. See:
    BERNARD OF CLAIRVAUX
Last of the Goths, The. See
    RODERICK
Last of the Great Scouts, The.
    See: CODY, WILLIAM
    FREDERICK
Last of the Greeks, The. See:
    PHILOPOEMEN
Last of the Incas, The. See:
    ATAHUALPA
Last of the Knights, The. See:
    MAXIMILIAN I
Last of the Makars, The. See:
    LINDSAY (LYNDSAY), SIR
    DAVID
Last of the Puritans, The. See:
    ADAMS, SAMUEL
Last of the Red-hot Mammas, The.
    See: ABUZA, SOPHIE
Last of the Romans, The. See:
    RIENZI, COLA DI
Last of the Saxons, The. See:
    HAROLD II
Last of the Schoolmen, The.
    See: BIEL (BYLL), GABRIEL
    MAJOR (MAIR), JOHN
    SUAREZ, FRANCISCO
Last of the Scottish Chaucerians,
    The. See:
    LINDSAY (LYNDSAY), SIR
    DAVID

Last of the Tribunes, The. See:
RIENZI, COLA DI
Last of the Troubadours, The.
See: BOÉ, JACQUES
Last of the Unholy Trio, The.
See: SHEIL, LILY
LATAS, MICHAEL (1806-71)
[Ottoman general officer]
Omar Pasha
Late Ben Smith, The. See:
MATHEWS, CORNELIUS
Late Henry Allen, Esq., The.
See: HOPE, JAMES
BARRON
LATEUR. See also:
LA TOUR
LATEUR, FRANK (1871-)
[Flemish writer]
Stijn Streuvels
Latham C. Carleton, Captain
See: ELLIS, EDWARD
SYLVESTER
Latham, O'Neill. See:
O'NEILL, ROSE CECIL
LATHROP, LORIN ANDREWS
(1858-) [American
novelist]
Kenyon Gambier
Lathyrus. See:
PTOLEMY VIII
Latimore, Frank. See:
KLINE, FRANK
Latouche, John. See:
CRAWFURD, OSWALD
LA TOUR. See also:
LATEUR
LA TOUR D'AUVERGNE,
THÉOPHILE MALO COR-
RET DE (1743-1800)
[French soldier]
The First Grenadier of
France
Latreaumont. See:
MAY, KARL
FRIEDRICH
LAUDENBACH, PIERRE-JULES
(1897-) [French actor
and director]
Pierre Fresnay
Lauder, Sir Harry. See:
MacLENNAN, HUGH
LAUDERDALE, DUKE OF (JOHN
MAITLAND). See:

Cabal, The
LAUDET, FERNAND CHARLES
(1860-) [French author]
Film
Laughing-gas Man, The. See:
SHORT, DEWEY
Laughing Philosopher, The. See:
DEMOCRITUS
LAUGHLIN, VIRGINIA CARLI
(1907-) [American author]
John Clarke
LAUGHLIN, VIRGINIA CARLI.
See also: Laklan, Carli
LAUGHTON, ELIZABETH
SULLIVAN (1902-)
[British stage and motion
picture actress]
Elsa Lanchester
Laugier, R. See:
CUMBERLAND, MARTEN
Lauingen, Albert of. See:
ALBERTUS MAGNUS,
SAINT, COUNT OF
BOLLSTÄDT
Launce Poyntz. See:
WHITTAKER, FREDERICK
Launcelot. See also:
Lancelot
Launcelot Langstaff. See:
Langstaff, Launcelot
PAULDING, JAMES KIRKE
Laura Keel. See:
BERGE, CAROL
Laura Keene. See:
UNKNOWN
Laura Lee Hope. See:
STRATEMEYER,
EDWARD L.
Laura Riding. See:
JACKSON, LAURA RIDING
Laura Riding Gottschalk. See:
JACKSON, LAURA RIDING
Laurati da Siena. See:
LORENZETTI, PIETRO
Laurati, Pietro. See:
LORENZETTI, PIETRO
Laureate of California, The
Poet. See:
COOLBRITH, IDA DONNA
McGROARTY, JOHN STEVEN
Laureate of New England, The
Poet. See: WHITTIER,
JOHN GREENLEAF

Laureate of Song, The. See:
  LONGFELLOW, HENRY
    WADSWORTH
Laureate of the Army, The
  Poet. See:
    PATTEN, GEORGE
      WASHINGTON
Laureate of the Bluestockings.
  See: MORE, HANNAH
Laureate of the Confederacy,
  The Poet. See:
    TIMROD, HENRY
Laureate of the Gentle Craft,
  The. See:
    SACHS, HANS
Laureate of the Nursery, The.
  See: MILLER, WILLIAM
    RANDS, WILLIAM BRIGHTY
Laureate of the South, The
  Poet. See:
    HAYNE, PAUL HAMILTON
Laureate, Our Battle. See:
  BROWNELL, HENRY
    HOWARD
Laureate, The Canadian. See:
  FRÉCHETTE, LOUIS
    HONORÉ
Laureate, The Georgian. See:
  ABERCROMBIE,
    LASCELLES
Laureate, The People's. See:
  RILEY, JAMES
    WHITCOMB
Laureate to the Congress,
  Camillo Querno, Poet.
  See: ODELL,
    JONATHAN
Laurel, Stan. See:
  JEFFERSON, ARTHUR
    STANLEY
Laurel, Stanley. See:
  JEFFERSON, ARTHUR
    STANLEY
Lauren Bacall. See:
  BOGART, BETTY JOAN
    PEPSKE BACALL
Laurence. See:
  Hazard, Laurence
  Lawrance
  LAWRENCE
  Lawrence
Laurence Harvey. See:
  SKIKNE, LARUSHKA

MISCHA
Laurence Hope. See:
  NICHOLSON, ADELA
    FLORENCE
Laurence Naismith. See:
  JOHNSON, LAWRENCE
Laurence Templeton. See:
  SCOTT, SIR WALTER
Laurence, Will. See: SMITH,
  WILLARD LAURENCE
LAURENS, JOHN (1754-82)
  [American soldier]
  The Bayard of the Revolution
LAURENTIS, DINO DE (1919-)
  [Italian motion picture
  producer]
  The Dynamo of the Italian
    Motion Picture Industry
  The Garibaldi of the Italian
    Motion Picture Industry
  The Kingfish of the Italian
    Motion Picture Industry
Laurette, La Belle. See:
  COONEY, HELEN LAURETTE
    MAGDALENE
Laurette Taylor. See:
  COONEY, HELEN LAURETTE
    MAGDALENE
Laurie, Harry C. See:
  CAHN, ZVI
Laurie, Piper. See:
  JACOBS, ROSETTA
Laurie Todd. See:
  THORBURN, GRANT
Lauscher, Hermann. See:
  HESSE, HERMANN
LAUSEN, JOHN R. (1911-)
  [American jazz musician
  (trumpet)]
  Yank Lawson
Lauter. See:
  CHAMSON, ANDRÉ JULES
    LOUIS
Lautréamont, Le Comte de. See:
  DUCASSE, ISIDORE
    LUCIEN
Lautrec, Toulouse. See:
  MONFA, HENRI MARIE
    RAYMOND DE
      TOULOUSE-LAUTREC
LAVATER, JOHANN CASPAR
  (1741-1801) [Swiss poet,
  theologian and founder of

physiognomy]
The Fénelon of Germany
Lavengro (Word Master). See:
BORROW, GEORGE HENRY
LAVER, JAMES (1899-)
[British museum director
and author]
Jacques Reval
LAVER, RODNEY GEORGE
(1938-) [Australian
tennis player]
Rod Laver
Lavin, Mary. See:
WALSH, MARY
Lavinia. See:
PONTI, DIANA DA
Lavinia Warren. See:
BUMP, MERCY LAVINIA
WARREN
Lavrador, Rei (Farmer King).
See: DINIZ (DENIS)
LAW, GEORGE (1806-81)
[American shipbuilder]
Live Oak George
LAW, JOHN (1671-1729)
[Scottish financier and
speculator]
The Paper King
LAW, SALLIE CHAPMAN
GORDON (1805-94)
[American Confederate
sympathizer]
The Mother of the Con-
federacy
Law, The Father of International.
See: GROTIUS, HUGO
Law, The Father of the Homestead.
See: GROW, GALUSHA
AARON
Law, The Father of the Maine.
See: DOW, NEAL
Law West of the Pecos, The.
See: BEAN, ROY
LAWEMAN. See:
LAYAMON (LAWEMAN)
Lawgiver of Parnassus, The.
See: BOILEAU-
DESPRÉAUX, NICHOLAS
Lawgiver, The (Kanuni). See:
SULAIMAN I or II
Lawless, Anthony. See:
MACDONALD, PHILIP
LAWLOR, PATRICK ANTHONY

(1893-) [New Zealand
journalist and author]
Shibli Bagarag
Pat Lawler
Christopher Penn
Lawrance. See also:
Laurence
LAWRENCE
Lawrence
Lawrance, Jody. See:
GODDARD, JOSEPHINE
LAWRENCE
LAWRENCE [Lawrence]. See also:
Laurence
Lawrance
Lawrence, Brother. See:
HERMAN, NICHOLAS
Lawrence, Carol. See:
LARAIA, CAROL MARIA
LAWRENCE, CORNELIUS C.
(1902-) [American com-
poser, publisher and actor]
Neil Lawrence
LAWRENCE, DAVID HERBERT
(1885-1930) [English author,
poet and essayist]
Lawrence H. Dawson
D. H. Lawrence
Lawrence, Elliot. See:
BROZA, ELLIOT LAWRENCE
Lawrence Ferling. See:
FERLINGHETTI,
LAWRENCE MONSANTO
Lawrence Gardner. See:
BRANNON, WILLIAM T.
Lawrence Ives. See:
WOODS, FREDERICK
Lawrence, Jack. See:
FITZGERALD, LAWRENCE
PENNYBAKER
Lawrence, Jimmie. See:
DILLINGER, JOHN HERBERT
LAWRENCE, JOYCE (1898-)
[British stage and motion
picture actress]
Joyce Carey
LAWRENCE-KLASEN, ALEXANDRE
DAGMAR (1898-1952)
[British musical comedy and
motion picture actress]
Gertrude Lawrence
Lawrence Lancewood. See:
WISE, DANIEL

Lawrence Leslie, Col. See:
  RATHBONE, ST. GEORGE
    HENRY
Lawrence, Michael. See:
  LARIAR, LAWRENCE
Lawrence of Arabia. See:
  LAWRENCE, THOMAS
    EDWARD
Lawrence Peters. See:
  DAVIES, LESLIE
    PURNELL
Lawrence, Richard A. See:
  LEOPOLD, NATHAN F.
Lawrence, Steve. See:
  LEIBOWITZ, SIDNEY
LAWRENCE, THOMAS EDWARD
  (1888-1935) [British
  traveler, archaeologist
  and soldier]
  Aircraftsman Ross
  Lawrence of Arabia
  Private T. E. Shaw
LAWRENCE, WILLIAM JOHN
  (1862-) [Irish
  theatrical historian and
  writer]
  Scaramuccio
Laws, Reformer of the
  (Lagoböter). See:
  MAGNUS VI
LAWSON, HORACE LOWE
  (1900-) [American
  journalist, editor, publisher
  and author]
  H. Lowe Lawson
  M. C. Lawson
  John A. Summers
LAWSON, JOHN DANIEL
  (1816-96) [American
  politician; Congressman
  from New York]
  Sitting Bull
LAWSON, JOHN HOWARD. See:
  Hollywood Ten, The
Lawson, Ted. See:
  LEHRMAN, THEODORE H.
Lawson, W. B. See:
  COOK, WILLIAM WALLACE
  INGRAHAM, COLONEL
    PRENTISS
  JENKS, GEORGE CHARLES
  RATHBONE, ST. GEORGE
    HENRY

Lawson, Wilfrid. See:
  WORSNOP, WILFRID
Lawson, Yank. See:
  LAUSEN, JOHN R.
LAWTON, SHERMAN PAXTON
  (1908-) [American edu-
  cator and author]
  Jack Paxton
  Dr. John Paxton
Lawyer. See:
  SORRELL, VICTOR
    GARLAND
Lawyer, The Honest. See:
  OGDEN, ROBERT
Lawyer, The People's. See:
  BRANDEIS, LOUIS
    DEMBITZ
Lawyer, The Ragged. See:
  GROVER, MARTIN
Laxness, Halldór Kiljan. See:
  GUDJONSSEN, HALLDÓR
Lay Preacher. See:
  DENNIE, JOSEPH
Lay Preacher to the largest
  Congregation in the United
  States, A. See:
  BOK, EDWARD WILLIAM
LAYAMON (LAWEMAN) (fl.
  c. 1200) [English priest and
  author]
  The English Ennius
Lazzari, Bramante. See:
  D'AGNOLO, DONATO
LAZZERI, ANTHONY MICHAEL
  (1903-46) [American pro-
  fessional baseball player]
  Tony Lazzeri
  Push-'em-up Lazzeri
LEA, LUKE (1879-) [American
  politician, Senator from
  Tennessee]
  Young Thunderbolt
LEABO, BETTY (1918-)
  [American model and
  motion picture actress]
  Brenda Joyce
LEACH, ALEXANDER ARCHIBALD
  (1904-) [Anglo-American
  motion picture actor]
  Cary Grant
Leadbelly. See:
  LEDBETTER, HUDDIE
Leader, Great (Quaid-i-azam).

See: JINNAH, MOHAM-
MED ALI
Leader, The. See:
SINATRA, FRANCIS
ALBERT
Leader, The Peerless. See:
CHANCE, FRANK LeROY
LEAF, MUNRO (1905-)
[American artist and
author]
Mun
Leah. See:
MAIZEL, CLARICE
MATTHEWS
Leah Jacobs. See:
GELLIS, ROBERTA L.
JACOBS
Leah Morton. See:
STERN, ELIZABETH
GERTRUDE
Leal Patrick. See:
STONE, PATTI
Lean Jimmy. See:
JONES, JAMES C.
Leaper, Ludwig the. See:
LUDWIG
LEAR, EDWARD (1812-88)
[English water color
painter and humorist]
Limerick Lear
LEARMOUNT, THOMAS, OF
ERCILDOUNE (c. 1220-
c. 1300) [Scottish seer
and poet]
Thomas Rhymour of Ercildoune
Thomas the Rhymer
True Thomas
Learned Blacksmith, The. See:
BURRITT, ELIHU
Learned Fool in Christendom.
The Most. See:
JAMES I
Learned of the Romans, The
Most. See:
VARRO, MARCUS
TERENTIUS
Learned Painter, The. See:
LEBRUN, CHARLES
Learned Printer, The. See:
BOWYER, WILLIAM
Learned Shoemaker, The. See:
SHERMAN, ROGER
Learned Tailor, The. See:

WILD, HENRY
Learned, The. See:
ALFONSO X
Learned, The (El Sabio). See:
FERDINAND VI
Learning in America, The
Father of Biblical. See:
STUART, MOSES
Learning, The Prodigy of. See:
HAHNEMANN, CHRISTIAN
SAMUEL FREDERICK
Learsi, Rufus. See:
GOLDBERG, ISRAEL
Least of the Dukes, The (Duca
Minimo). See:
RAMPAGNETTO, GAETANO
Leather-Dresser, The Literary.
See: DOWSE, THOMAS
Leather, George. See:
SWALLOW, NORMAN
Leatrice Joy. See:
ZEIDLER, LEATRICE
JOY
LEAVITT, DUDLEY (1772-1851)
[American school teacher
and almanac maker]
Old Master Leavitt
LEBENSOHN, ABRAHAM DOB
(1794?-1878) [Hebrew
poet and grammarian]
Adam
LEBLANC, DUDLEY J. (1894-)
[American politician and
patent medicine manufac-
turing executive]
Couzin Dud
LEBRUN, CHARLES (1619-90)
[French historical
painter and author]
The Learned Painter
LEBRUN, PONCE-DENIS
ÉCOUCHARD (1729-1807)
[French lyric poet]
Lebrun-Pindare
le Carré, John. See:
CORNWELL, DAVID JOHN
MOORE
Le Chanois, Jean-Paul. See:
DREYFUS, JEAN-PAUL
LECKIE, ROBERT HUGH
(1920-) [American
journalist and author]
Roger Barlow

Mark Porter
LÉCLUSE, CHARLES DE
(1525-1609) [French
botanist]
Clusius
Le Coq, Monsieur. See:
SIMENON, GEORGES
Leda Burke. See:
GARNETT, DAVID
LEDBETTER, HUDDIE (1885-
1949) [American jazz
musician (singer, guitar)]
Leadbelly
Lee. See:
LEIGH
Leigh
PEARL, LEO J.
RESNICK, LEON
THAYER, EMMA
REDINGTON LEE
THUNA, LEONORA
Lee Abrams. See:
ABRAMSON, LEON
Lee, Alice G. See:
HAVEN, EMILY BRADLEY
NEAL
Lee, Andrew. See:
AUCHINCLOSS, LOUIS
STANTON
Lee Ang Shoy. See:
SHERIDAN, LIONEL
ASTOR
Lee, Anna. See:
WINNIFRITH, JOANNA
Lee, Anne S. See:
MURPHY, MABEL
ANSLEY
LEE, ARTHUR (1740-92)
[American diplomat and
author]
Junius Americanus
LEE, AUSTIN (1904-)
[British Church of England
ordained priest and
author]
John Austwick
Julian Callender
Lee Borden. See:
DEAL, BORDEN
Lee, Canada. See:
CANEGATA, LEONARD
LIONEL CORNELIUS
Lee, Carol. See:

FLETCHER, HELEN JILL
Lee, Carolina. See:
DERN, PEGGY GADDIS
Lee, Catherine. See:
JENNER, KATHERINE LEE
LEE, CHARLES (1731-82)
[Anglo-American soldier
and patriot]
Boiling Water
The Hero of Charleston
Lee Craig. See:
SANDS, LEO GEORGE
Lee Creighton. See:
OVERHOLSER, WAYNE D.
LEE, EDWARD D. (1844-1927)
[American giver of
children's picnics]
The Ain't Gonna Rain No
Mo' Man
LEE, FITZHUGH (1835-1905)
[American general officer]
Flea
Lee, George B. See:
HARBAUGH, THOMAS
CHALMERS
Lee Gibb. See:
Froy, Herald
Lee, Guy Carlton. See:
AYER, JOHN
Lee, Gypsy Rose. See:
HOVICK, ROSE LOUISE
LEE, HAL BURNHAM
(1907-) [American
professional baseball
player]
Sheriff
Lee, Harper. See:
GILLETE, HARPER LEE
LEE, HENRY (1756-1818)
[American general officer]
Light Horse Harry
The Sage of Ashland
Lee J. Cobb. See:
JACOBY, LEE
LEE, JESSE (1758-1816)
[American Methodist
clergyman]
The Apostle of Methodism
LEE, JOSHUA BRYAN (1892-)
[American politician;
Senator and Congressman
from Oklahoma]
The Boy Orator

The Boy Wonder
One Speech Lee
The Second William
Jennings Bryan
Silver-tongued Josh
LEE (LEES), ANN (1736-84)
[Anglo-American
religious leader; founder
of the Shakers in America]
Ann of the Word
Mother Ann
Mother Lee
Lee Leighton. See:
OVERHOLSER, WAYNE D.
LEE, LINCOLN (1922-)
[British aviator and
author]
Neil Collen
LEE, MANFRED BENNINGTON.
See: Queen, Ellery
LEE, MARY EMILY
FRANCES (fl. mid-20th
cent.) [English author]
Cecile Lee
Lee, Mildred. See:
SCUDDER, MILDRED
LEE
Lee Moreton. See:
BOUCICAULT,
DIONYSIUS LARDNER
LEE, NATHANIEL (c.1653-92)
[English playwright]
The Mad Poet
Lee Neville. See:
RICHARDS, LELA HORN
Lee, Norah. See:
BARSTOW, NORAH LEE
HAMMOND
LEE, PALMER (1927-)
[American disc jockey
and motion picture
actor]
Gregg Palmer
Lee, Patty. See:
CAREY, ALICE
Lee, Peggy. See:
ENGSTROM, NORMA
DOLORES (JEAN)
LEE, REV. ALBERT (1858-)
[British archivist and
author]
Adrian Mason
Linton Romaine

LEE, RICHARD HENRY
(1732-94) [American
statesman]
The American Cicero
The Federal Farmer
LEE-RICHARDSON, JAMES
(1913-) [English
author]
Desmond Dunne
LEE, ROBERT EDWARD
(1807-70) [American Civil
War general officer;
commander of Confederate
forces]
Old Ace of Spades
Old Spades Lee
Uncle Robert
Lee Roberts. See:
MARTIN, ROBERT LEE
Lee Rogers. See:
WILSON, ROGER C.
Lee, Ronny. See:
LEVENTHAL, RONALD
Lee, Rowena. See:
BARTLETT, MARIE
SWAN
Lee Roy. See:
ANTHONY, LEO
LE ROI
LE ROY
Le Roy
Lee Sebastian. See:
SILVERBERG, ROBERT
Lee Street. See:
HAMPTON, KATHLEEN
Lee Thomas. See:
FLOREN, LEE
Lee, Vernon. See:
PAGET, VIOLET
Lee, William. See:
BURROUGHS, WILLIAM
SEWARD
LEE, WILLIAM HENRY
FITZHUGH (1837-91)
[American Confederate
soldier]
Rooney
LEE, WILLIAM STORRS
(1906-) [American
editor, educator and
author]
W. Storrs Lee
Leeds, Andrea. See:

LEES, ANTOINETTE
Leeds, Homer Stansbury. See:
    BERNARD, PIERRE A.
LEEMANS, ALPHONSE
    (1913-   ) [American
    professional football
    player]
    Tuffy Leemans
LEES. See:
    LEE (LEES), ANN
LEES, ANTOINETTE (1914-)
    [American motion picture
    actress]
    Andrea Leeds
Lees, Hannah. See:
    FETTER, ELIZABETH
    HEAD
Lee's Old War Horse. See:
    LONGSTREET, JAMES
LEFEBVRE, GERMAINE
    (c. 1935-   ) [French
    model and motion picture
    actress]
    Capucine
LE FEBVRE, MATHIEU
    (c. 1584-c. 1621) [French
    actor-manager]
    Laporte
le Fevre, Félicité. See:
    SMITH-MASTERS,
    MARGARET
LEFEVRE, LAURA ZENOBIA
    (fl. 1928-46) [American
    author]
    Zenobia Bird
Left-Handed Press Agent, The
    Great. See:
    MAILS, WALTER
Lefthander, The Old. See:
    SANDERS, JOSEPH L.
Lefty. See:
    GROVE, ROBERT MOSES
    O'DOUL, FRANK JOSEPH
    SHAUTE, JOSEPH
    BENJAMIN
Leg, Old Silver. See:
    STUYVESANT, PETER
Leg Shackles, The Monarch
    of. See:
    WEISS, EHRICH (ERIK
    WEISZ)
Leg, Wooden. See:
    STUYVESANT, PETER

Legal Interpreter of the Con-
    stitution, The. See:
    MARSHALL, JOHN
Legal Successor of Houdini,
    The. See:
    WEISS, THEO
LE GALLIENNE, RICHARD
    (1866-1947) [Anglo-
    American poet and critic]
    Logroller
LEGENDRE, LOUIS (1756-97)
    [Member of the French
    National Assembly]
    The Peasant of the Danube
LEGER, MARIE-RENÉ
    ALEXIS SAINT-LEGER
    (1887-   ) [French
    diplomat and author]
    Saintleger Leger
    Saint-John Perse
Legion, The Mother of the
    American. See:
    SCHUMANN-HEINK, MME.
    ERNESTINE
Legislature, The Dean of the
    Alabama. See:
    TUNSTALL, ALFRED
    MOORE
LEGMAN, GERSHON (1917-)
    [American author]
    Roger-Maxe de la Glannege
LeGrand. See:
    HENDERSON, LeGRAND
LEGRAND, HENRI (c. 1587-
    1637) [French comic
    actor]
    Turlupin
Legrand, Louis, M.D. See:
    VICTOR, ORVILLE J.
Le Grand, Pierre. See:
    FRANÇOIS PIERRE
LEHMAN, GEORGE (fl. 1856-58)
    [American resort pro-
    prietor]
    George the Baker
    Round House George
LEHMANN,/ELIZABETH NINA
    MARY FREDERIKA (1862-
    1918) [English soprano
    and composer]
    Liza Lehmann
LEHMANN, THEODORE H.
    (1929-   ) [American

composer and teacher]
Ted Lawson
Lei Chen Yuan. See:
    JAEGHER, RAYMOND-
    JOSEPH DE
LEIBOWITZ, SIDNEY
    (1935-) [American
    singer and actor]
    Steve Lawrence
Leif Erickson. See:
    ANDERSON, WILLIAM
Leif the Lucky. See:
    ERICSON, LEIF
Leigh. See:
    HUNT, JAMES HENRY
    LEIGH
    LEE
    Lee
Leigh Carder. See:
    CUNNINGHAM, EUGENE
Leigh, Ione. See:
    MASSADA, IONE
Leigh, Janet. See:
    MORRISON, JEANETTE
Leigh, Johanna. See:
    SAYERS, DOROTHY
    LEIGH
Leigh North. See:
    PHELPS, ELIZABETH
    STEWART
LEIGH, PERCIVAL (1813-89)
    [British humorist]
    Paul Prendergast
Leigh Rives. See:
    SEWARD, WILLIAM
    WARD, JR.
Leigh, Vivien. See:
    HARTLEY, VIVIAN
    MARY
Leigh, W. Rye. See:
    RILEY, WILLIE
Leigh Winfield. See:
    YOUNGBERG, NORMA
    IONE RHOADS
LEIGHTON, JAMES ALBERT
    (1877-1964) [American
    composer and singer]
    Bert Leighton
Leighton, Lee. See:
    OVERHOLSER, WAYNE D.
LEINER, BENJAMIN (1896-
    1947) [American pro-
    fessional boxer; world's

lightweight champion]
    Benny Leonard
Leinster, Murray. See:
    JENKINS, WILLIAM
    FITZGERALD
LEISK, DAVID JOHNSON
    (1906-) [American art
    editor, cartoonist, book
    illustrator and writer]
    Crockett Johnson
LEISY, JAMES FRANKLIN
    (1927-) [American
    editor and author]
    Frank Lynn
Lekain, Henri-Louis. See:
    CAIN, HENRI-LOUIS
LELAND, CHARLES GODFREY
    (1824-1903 [American edi-
    tor, humorist and essayist]
    Hans Breitmann
LELONG, LUCIEN (1889-)
    [French fashion designer]
    The First Gentleman of
    Fashion
Lely, Sir Peter. See:
    VAN DER FAES, PIETER
LEMAÎTRE, ANTOINE-LOUIS-
    PROSPER (1800-76)
    [French actor]
    Frédérick
LEMKE, WILLIAM (1878-)
    [American politician;
    Congressman from North
    Dakota]
    Moratorium Bill
LEMMON. See also:
    LEMON
    Lemons
LEMMON, JOHN UHLER III
    (1925-) [American actor]
    Jack Lemmon
Lemoine, Ernest. See:
    ROY, EWELL PAUL
LEMON. See also:
    LEMMON
    Lemons
LEMON, MEADOW GEORGE
    (1933-) [American
    professional basketball
    player and clown]
    The Clown Prince of Basket-
    ball
    Meadowlark

Lemonade Lucy. See:
    HAYES, LUCY WARE
        WEBB
Lemons. See:
    LEMMON
    LEMON
    SOLTERS, JULIUS JOSEPH
Lemuel Gulliver. See:
    SWIFT, JONATHAN
Lemuel Q. Stoopnagle. See:
    TAYLOR, FREDERICK
        CHASE
Len. See:
    LEWY, LEONARD
Len Turner. See:
    FLOREN, LEE
Lena. See:
    BLACKBURNE, RUSSELL
Lenanton, C. See:
    OMAN, CAROLA MARY
        ANIMA
Lenau, Nikolaus. See:
    VON STREHLENAU,
        NIKOLAUS NIEMBSCH
LENCLOS, ANNE (1616-1706)
    [French courtesan]
    Ninon de Lenclos
LENDON. See also:
    LANDON
    Landon
    LONDON
    London
LENDON, ALFRED AUSTIN
    (1856-) [British
    physician and author]
    Austin Harding
LENDON, KENNETH HARRY
    (1928-) [Canadian
    educator and author]
    Leo Vaughan
LENGEL, WILLIAM CHARLES
    (1888-) [American
    editor and author]
    Charles Grant
    Warren Spencer
L'Engle, Madeleine. See:
    FRANKLIN, MADELEINE
LENGYEL, CORNEL ADAM
    (1915-) [American
    educator, editor and
    author]
    Cornel Adam
LENGYEL, GEZA (1904-)

[Hungarian-American
    violinist and composer]
    George Adams
LENHART, JASON GREGORY
    (c.1905-) [American
    impresario and motion
    picture producer]
    Paul Gregory
Lenin, Nikolai. See:
    ULYANOV, VLADIMIR
        ILYICH
Lenin, Vladimir Ilyich. See:
    ULYANOV, VLADIMIR
        ILYICH
Lennard. See also:
    LEONARD
    Leonard
Lennard Gandalae. See:
    BERNE, ERIC LENNARD
Lennie. See:
    HAYTON, LEONARD
        GEORGE
Lennie Martin. See:
    MARINO, RINALDO R.
LENNON, FLORENCE BECKER
    TANNENBAUM (1895-)
    [American teacher, poet
    and author]
    Florence Becker
LENNON, JOHN. See:
    Beatles, The
    Nurk Twins, The
LENNOX, CHARLOTTE
    RAMSAY (1720-1804)
    [American novelist]
    Harriet Stuart
Lennox Wylder. See:
    TURNER, DR. WILLIAM
        MASON
Leno, Dan. See:
    GALVIN, GEORGE
LENORMAND, MARIE ANNE
    ADÉLAÏDE (1772-1843)
    [French necromancer]
    The Great Lenormand
    La Sibylle du Faubourg
        Saint-Germain
LENÔTRE, ANDRÉ (1613-1700)
    [French horticulturist]
    The Creator of French
        Landscape Gardening
    The Father of Landscape
        Gardening

Lens. See:
  LENZ
  SALEEBY, CALEB
    WILLIAMS
LENT, BLAIR (1930-   )
  [American lawyer,
    educator and author]
Ernest Small
LENT, DORA GENEVA
  (1904-   ) [Canadian
    painter, historian and
    author]
Gene Dorant
LENTHALL, WILLIAM. See:
  Five Members, The
Lenya, Lotte. See:
  BLAMAUER, KAROLINE
LENZ. See also:
  Lens
LENZ, GEORGE MONTGOMERY
  (1916-   ) [American
    motion picture actor]
George Montgomery
LENZ, HEINRICH OSKAR
  (1848-1925) [German
    explorer and geographer]
Oskar Lenz
Leo. See:
  TOLSTOI, COUNT LEV
    NIKOLAEVICH
LEO (died 461) [Supreme
  Pontiff of Roman Catholic
    Church]
  The Great
  Pope Leo I
  St. Leo
LEO (died 683) [Supreme
  Pontiff of Roman
    Catholic Church]
  Pope Leo II
  St. Leo
LEO (died 816) [Supreme
  Pontiff of Roman
    Catholic Church]
  Pope Leo III
  St. Leo
LEO (died 855) [Supreme
  Pontiff of Roman
    Catholic Church]
  Pope Leo IV
  St. Leo
LEO (died 903) [Supreme
  Pontiff of Roman

  Catholic Church]
  Pope Leo V
LEO (died 928/9) [Supreme
  Pontiff of Roman
    Catholic Church]
  Pope Leo VI
LEO (died 939) [Supreme
  Pontiff of Roman
    Catholic Church]
  Pope Leo VII
LEO (died 965) [Supreme
  Pontiff of Roman
    Catholic Church]
  Pope Leo VIII
LEO I (c. 400-74) [Byzantine
  emperor]
  The Butcher (Makeles)
  The Great
  The Thracian
LEO III (c. 680-740) [Byzantine
  emperor]
  The Isaurian
LEO IV (c. 750-80) [Byzantine
  emperor]
  The Khazar
LEO V (died 820) [Byzantine
  emperor]
  The Armenian
LEO VI (866-912) [Byzantine
  emperor]
  The Philosopher
  The Wise
Leo IX, Pope. See:
  BRUNO, COUNT OF
    EGISHEIM-DAGSBURG
Leo X, Pope. See:
  MEDICI, GIOVANNI DE'
Leo XI, Pope. See:
  MEDICI, ALESSANDRO
    OTTAVIANO
Leo XII, Pope. See:
  GENGA, ANNIBALE
    SERMATTEI DELLA
Leo XIII, Pope. See:
  PECCI, GIOACCHINO
    VINCENZO
Leo Africanus. See:
  ALWAZZAN (ALWEZAZ),
    ALHASSAN IBN
    MOHAMMED
Leo Berne. See:
  DAVIES, LESLIE
    PURNELL

Leo, Johannes. See:
ALWAZZAN (ALWEZAZ),
ALHASSAN IBN
MOHAMMED
Leo Leonardo. See:
DE LEO, LIONARDO
ORONZO SALVATORE
Leo, St. See:
BRUNO, COUNT OF
EGISHEIM-DAGSBURG
LEO
Leo Vaughan. See
LENDON, KENNETH
HARRY
LEOFRIC, EARL OF MERCIA.
See: GODIVA (GODGIFU)
Leon. See:
LEONARDI, LEONID
LEWIS, JULIUS WARREN
Leon Ames. See:
WYCOFF, LEON
LEON, JUAN (1788-1854)
[Spanish bullfighter]
Leoncillo
Leon Lafitte, Colonel. See:
INGRAHAM, COLONEL
PRENTISS
Leon Sash. See:
SHASH, LEON ROBERT
Leon Trotsky. See:
BRONSTEIN, LEV
DAVIDOVICH
LEONARD [Leonard]. See also:
Lennard
Leonard, Baird. See:
ZOGBAUM, BAIRD
LEONARD
Leonard, Benny. See:
LEINER, BENJAMIN
LEONARD, DANIEL (1740-1829)
[American Tory lawyer
and writer]
Massachusettensis
Leonard, Eddie. See:
TONEY, LEMUEL
GORDON
LEONARD, FREDERICK
(1881-1954) [English
playwright]
Frederick Lonsdale
LEONARD, HELEN LOUISE
(1861-1922) [American
light opera soprano]
Lillian Russell

LEONARD, JACK E. (1911-)
[American comedian]
The Mean Mr. Clean
Mr. Insult
Leonard Merrick. See:
MILLER, LEONARD
Leonard Q. Ross. See:
ROSTEN, LEO CALVIN
Leonard, Sheldon. See:
BERSHAD, SHELDON
Leonard Spaulding. See:
BRADBURY, RAY
DOUGLAS
LEONARD, WILLIAM AUGUSTUS
(1916-) [American tele-
vision news correspondent
and producer]
Bill Leonard
LEONARDI, LEONID (1901-)
[Russian composer, pianist
and conductor]
Leon Leonardi
Leonardo, Leo. See:
DE LEO, LIONARDO
ORONZO SALVATORE
Leoncillo. See:
LEÓN, JUAN
Leone, Giovanni. See:
ALWAZZAN (ALWEZAZ),
ALHASSAN IBN
MOHAMMED
Leonid Vladimirov. See:
FINKELSTEIN, LEONID
VLADIMIROVITCH
Leonidas. See:
WEDELL, H.C.
Leonidas of America, The. See:
STARK, JOHN
Leonidas of Modern Greece,
The. See:
BOZZARIS (BOTZARIS),
MARKOS
Leonide Moguy. See:
MAGUILEVSKY,
LEONIDE
Leonie. See:
SACHS, NELLY
LEOPOLD (1676-1747) [Prussian
field marshal]
Der Alte Dessauer (The
Old Dessauer)
LEOPOLD I (1790-1865) [King
of the Belgians]
The Nestor of Europe

Uncle Leopold
LEOPOLD, ISAIAH EDWIN
    (1887-1966) [American
    vaudeville, radio, tele-
    vision and motion picture
    comedian]
  The Fire Chief
  The Perfect Fool
  Ed Wynn
LEOPOLD, NATHAN F. (1904-71)
    [American ornithologist,
    social worker and
    author]
  William F. Lanne
  Richard A. Lawrence
Leopold Stokowski. See:
    ANTONI, BOLESLAWO-
      WICZ STANISLAW
Leper, The. See:
    BALDWIN IV
LEPPERT, ALICE (1912-)
    [American singer and
    motion picture actress]
  Alice Faye
le Reunêt, Henri. See:
    POE, EDGAR ALLAN
LERNER, SAMUEL M. (1903-)
    [Rumanian singer and
    composer]
  Sammy Lerner
LE ROI. See also:
    Lee Roy
    LE ROY
    Le Roy
LE ROI, DAVID DE ROCHE
    (1905-) [English
    editor and author]
  John Roche
LE ROY [Le Roy]. See also:
    Lee Roy
    LE ROI
Le Roy, Baby. See:
    WINNEBRENNER,
      LE ROY
LE ROY, WILLIAM EDGAR
    (1818-88) [American
    admiral]
  The Chesterfield of the
    Navy
Les. See also:
    TAYLOR, LIONEL
Les Paul. See:
    POLFUS, LESTER

LeSeig, Theo. See:
    GEISEL, THEODOR
    SEUSS
Leser, Tina. See:
    SHILLARD-SMITH,
      CHRISTINE WETHERILL
LeSHAN, LAWRENCE LEE
    (1920-) [American
    educator and author]
  Edward Grendon
LESHAY, JEROME (1926-)
    [American composer and
    director]
  Jerry Leshay
Lesley Bourne. See:
    MARSHALL, EVELYN
Lesley Conger. See:
    SUTTLES, SHIRLEY
      SMITH
Lesley Egan. See:
    LININGTON,
      ELIZABETH
LESLEY, PETER (1819-1903)
    [American geologist and
    author]
  John W. Allen, Jr.
  J.P. Lesley
Leslie. See:
    PETERS, DONALD L.
Leslie, Amy. See:
    WEST, LILLIE
LESLIE, CECILIE (1914-)
    [British editor and
    author]
  Eve MacAdam
Leslie Charteris. See:
    LIN, LESLIE CHARLES
      BOWYER
Leslie, Col. Lawrence. See:
    RATHBONE, ST. GEORGE
      HENRY
Leslie, Doris. See:
    FERGUSSON HANNAY,
      LADY
LESLIE, ELIZA (1787-1858)
    [American author]
  Miss Leslie
Leslie Ford. See:
    BROWN, ZENITH JONES
Leslie, Frank. See:
    CARTER, HENRY
Leslie Grosofsky. See:
    GROSS, LESLIE

Leslie, Henrietta. See:
SCHUTZE, GLADYS
HENRIETTA
Leslie, Joan. See:
BRODELL, JOAN
Leslie, Marion. See:
TOOLEY, SARAH ANNE
LESLIE, MIRIAM FLORENCE
FOLLINE (1836?-1914)
[American editor and
author]
Frank Leslie
Miriam F. Squire
Leslie, Mrs. Madeline. See:
BAKER, HARRIETTE
NEWALL WOODS
Leslie, O.H. See:
SLESAR, HENRY
Leslie, Sharon. See:
LUSTER, SHIRLEY
Leslie Stuart. See:
MARLOWE, KENNETH
Leslie Vardre. See:
DAVIES, LESLIE
PURNELL
Leslie, Walter. See:
LIVINSKY, WALTER
Leslie, Ward S. See:
WARD, ELIZABETH
HONOR SHEDDEN
LESS. See:
JAMES THE LESS
Lesser, Milton. See:
MARLOWE, STEPHEN
Lessing, Bruno. See:
BLOCK, RUDOLPH
EDGAR
LESSING, GOTTHOLD
EPHRAIM (1729-81)
[German critic and
dramatist]
The Aesop of Germany
The Father of German
Criticism
The Father of German
Literature
Lester. See:
YOUNG, WILLIS LESTER
Lester, Bruce. See:
LISTER, BRUCE
Lester Chadwick. See:
STRATEMEYER,
EDWARD L.

Lester, Frank. See:
USHER, FRANK
Lester, Ketty. See:
FRIERSON, REVOYDA
Lester-Rands, A. See:
JUDD, FREDERICK
CHARLES
L'Estrange, Corrine. See:
HARTSHORNE, HENRY
Lesueur, Daniel. See:
LAPAUZE, JEANNE
LOISEAU
LE SUEUR, EUSTACHE
(1616-55) [French
painter]
The French Raphael
LE SUEUR, LUCILLE (or
BILLIE CASSIN) (1904-)
[American motion picture
actress]
Joan Crawford
LETHINGTON. See:
MAITLAND OF
LETHINGTON, WILLIAM
Lethington, Secretary. See:
MAITLAND OF
LETHINGTON, WILLIAM
Letitia Booth, Mrs. See:
RUSSELL, WILLIAM
CLARK
Letter Carrier's Friend, The.
See: COX, SAMUEL
SULLIVAN
Letters, The Dean of
American. See:
HOWELLS, WILLIAM DEAN
Letters, The Dictator of. See:
AROUET, FRANÇOIS
MARIE
Letters, The Father of. See:
FRANCIS I
Letters, The Prince of
American. See:
IRVING, WASHINGTON
Letts, W.M. See:
VERSCHOYLE, WINIFRED
MABEL LETTS
LE VAYER, FRANÇOIS DE LA
MOTHE (1583-1672)
[French philosopher and
writer]
The Plutarch of France
LEVENSON, SAMUEL (1911-)

[American television
performer and lecturer]
Sam Levenson
LEVENTHAL, RONALD
(1927-) [American
guitarist and composer]
Ronny Lee
LEVER, CHARLES JAMES
(1806-72) [Irish
novelist]
C. O'Malley
Paul Gosslet
Cornelius O'Dowd
LE VERT, OCTAVIA WALTON
(1810-77) [American
actress]
The Belle of the Union
Leviathan of Literature, The.
See: JOHNSON, DR.
SAMUEL
LEVIELLE, GABRIEL (1883-
1925) [French silent
motion picture comedian]
Max Linder
LEVIN, MARCIA OBRASKY
(1918-) [American
author]
Marcia Martin
LEVIN, MARCIA OBRASKY.
See also:
Martin, Jeremy
LEVIN, MARTIN P. See:
Martin, Jeremy
LEVINE, PHILIP (1928-)
[American educator,
poet and editor]
Edgar Poe
Levinson, Bob. See:
WELLS, ROBERT
LEVINSON, NORMAN (1900-)
[American fashion
designer]
Norman Norell
LEVITCH, JOSEPH (1926-)
[American singer and
entertainer]
Jerry Lewis
LEVY, BURTON (1912-)
[American composer]
Burton Lane
LEVY, FREDERICK (1882-
1938) [American motion
picture actor]

Conway Tearle
LEVY, NEWMAN (1888-)
[American author, poet
and humorist]
Flaccus
LEVY, PAUL (1889-1932)
[American motion picture
executive]
Paul Bern
Lew. See:
ALCINDOR, FERDINAND
LEWIS, JR.
BREAU, LOUIS
HOAD, LEWIS A.
Lou
WORSHAM, LEWIS
ELMER, JR.
Lew Ayres. See:
AYER, LEWIS
Lew Bedell. See:
BIDEU, LOU
Lew Cody. See:
COTÉ, LOUIS JOSEPH
Lew Dockstader. See:
CLAPP, GEORGE ALFRED
Lew Fields. See:
SCHANFIELD, LEWIS
MAURICE
Lew Gordon. See:
BALDWIN, GORDON C.
Lew Landers. See:
FRIEDLANDER, LEWIS
Lew Smith. See:
FLOREN, LEE
Lew Wallace. See:
WALLACE, LEWIS
Lew Wallace, General. See:
WALLACE, LEWIS
Lewin, C.L. See:
BRISTER, RICHARD
LEWIN, LEONARD CASE
(1916-) [American
editor and author]
L.L. Case
LEWIN, WILLIAM CHARLES
JAMES (1847-97) [English
actor]
Breezy Bill
No. 1, Adelphi Terriss
William Terriss
Lewis. See:
LOUIS
Louis

PETERS, ROBERT LOUIS
LEWIS, ALFRED HENRY
    (c. 1858-1914) [American
    editor and author]
Dan Quin
LEWIS, ALONZO (1794-1861)
    [American poet]
The Lynn Bard
Lewis Baboon. See:
    LOUIS XIV
LEWIS, BARBARA GEDDES
    (1922-) [American stage
    and motion picture
    actress]
Barbara Bel Geddes
Lewis Brant. See:
    ROWLAND, DONALD
    SYDNEY
Lewis Carroll. See:
    DODGSON, CHARLES
    LUTWIDGE
LEWIS, CHARLES BERTRAND
    (1842-1924) [Anglo-
    American humorist, play-
    wright, dime novelist
    and journalist]
M. Quad
LEWIS, CLIFFORD. See:
    Berrisford, Judith M.
LEWIS, CLIVE STAPLES
    (1898-1963) [English
    author]
Clive Hamilton
C.S. Lewis
Lewis, D.B. See:
    BIXBY, JEROME LEWIS
LEWIS, DAVID JOHN
    (1869-) [American
    coal miner and politician;
    Congressman from
    Maryland]
Little Davey
The Little Giant
LEWIS, DOMINIC BEVAN
    WYNDHAM (1894-)
    [English journalist and
    biographer]
At the Sign of the Blue
    Moon
Beachcomber
Timothy Shy
LEWIS, ESTELLE ANNA
    BLANCHE ROBINSON

(1824-50) [American
    poet]
S. Anna Lewis
Sarah Anna Lewis
The Female Petrarch
The Rival of Sappho
Stella
LEWIS, GEORGE EDWARD
    (1888-) [American
    professional baseball
    player]
Duffy Lewis
Lewis Graham Underwood. See:
    WAGNER, CHARLES
    PETER
Lewis Grassic Gibbon. See:
    MITCHELL, JAMES
    LESLIE
LEWIS, HARRY SINCLAIR
    (1885-1951) [American
    novelist]
Tom Graham
Sinclair Lewis
Red
LEWIS, HENRY CLAY
    (1825-50) [American
    physician and author]
Madison Tensas, M.D.
Lewis, Ian. See:
    BENSMAN, JOSEPH
Lewis J. Swift. See:
    GARDNER, LEWIS J.
LEWIS, JAMES HAMILTON
    (1866-1939) [American
    politician; senator from
    Illinois]
The Beau Brummel of the
    Senate
The Fashion Plate
Pink Whiskers
Lewis, Janet. See:
    WINTERS, JANET LEWIS
Lewis, Jerry. See:
    LEVITCH, JOSEPH
LEWIS, JOHN WOODRUFF
    (1835-1919) [American
    poet and novelist]
Juan Lewis
LEWIS, JULIUS WARREN
    (1833-1920) [American
    poet and novelist]
Leon Lewis
LEWIS, MARY. See:

Berrisford, Judith M.
Lewis, Mary F.W. See:
    BOND, MARY FANNING
    WICKHAM
LEWIS, MATTHEW GREGORY
    (1775-1818) [English
    novelist, playwright
    and poet]
Monk Lewis
LEWIS, MEADE (1905-64)
    [American jazz musician
    (composer, pianist)]
Meade Lux Lewis
Lewis, Mel. See:
    SOKOLOFF, MELVIN
Lewis Melville. See:
    BENJAMIN, LEWIS
    SAUL
LEWIS, MERIWETHER (1774-
    1809) [American
    explorer]
Long Knife
The Sublime Dandy
LEWIS, MILDRED D.
    (1912-) [American
    bookstore owner and
    writer]
James DeWitt
LEWIS, MRS. SINCLAIR
    (1894-) [American
    newspaper columnist
    and commentator]
The Cassandra of the
    Columnists
The Contemporary
    Cassandra
Dorothy Thompson
Lewis Myrtle. See:
    HILL, GEORGE
    CANNING
LEWIS, PERCY WYNDHAM
    (1884-1957) [English
    artist, essayist and
    novelist]
Wyndham Lewis
Lewis, Roger. See:
    ZARCHY, HARRY
LEWIS, SARAH ANN
    ROBINSON (1824-80)
    [American poet]
Estelle Lewis
Lewis, Ted. See:
    FRIEDMAN, THEODORE

LEOPOLD
Lewis W. Carson, Major. See:
    AIKEN, ALBERT W.
LEWIS, WILLIAM THOMAS
    (c.1748-1811) [English
    comedian]
The Mercutio of Actors
LEWIS, WILLIAM WALLER
    (1860-1915) [English
    actor-manager]
Lewis Waller
LEWITON, MINA (1904-)
    [American teacher and
    author]
Mina Lewiton Simon
LEWY, LEONARD (1921-)
    [American composer,
    conductor and teacher]
Len Lewy
Lex Pender. See:
    PENDOWER, JACQUES
Lexy, Edward. See:
    LITTLE, EDWARD
    GERALD
LEY, WILLY (1906-)
    [German-American writer
    and lecturer on space
    research]
Robert Willey
Leyden, Lucas Van. See:
    HUGENSZ, LUCAS
LI HUNG CHANG (1823-1901)
    [Chinese statesman]
The Bismarck of Asia
Lia. See:
    FÉLIX, ADÉLAÏDE
Liam O'Connor. See:
    LIDDY, JAMES
    DANIEL REEVES
Liam Roy. See:
    SCARRY, PATRICIA
    MURPHY
Liancourt, Raoul de. See:
    WINGENBACH, CHARLES
    EDWARD
Liaqat Ali Salaam. See:
    CLARKE, KENNETH
    SPEARMAN
Liars, The Prince of. See:
    PINTO, FERNÃO MENDES
Libby MacCall. See:
    MACHOL, LIBBY
Liberace of the Accordion, The.

See:
WELK, LAWRENCE
LIBERACE, GEORGE J.
(1911-) [American
jazz musician (violin,
leader)]
Brother George
LIBERACE, WLADZIU
VALENTINO
(1920-) [American
pianist, entertainer and
television actor]
Liberace
Liberal Politician, The. See:
PERKINS, FRANCES
Liberal, The Great, See:
WHEELER, BURTON
KENDALL
Liberals, The Dean of the.
See: NORRIS, GEORGE
WILLIAM
Liberator and Father of His
Country. See:
DORIA, ANDREA
Liberator, Europe's. See:
WELLINGTON,
ARTHUR WELLESLEY,
1ST DUKE OF
Liberator of Africa, The.
See: PHILIP, JOHN
Liberator of Genoa, The.
See: DORIA, ANDREA
Liberator of the New World, The.
See: FRANKLIN,
BENJAMIN
Liberator of the Territory.
See: THIERS, LOUIS
ADOLPHE
Liberator, The. See:
MacGAHAN, JANUARIUS
ALOYSIUS
O'CONNELL, DANIEL
Liberator, The (El Libertador).
See: BOLÍVAR, SIMÓN
LIBERIUS (died 366) [Supreme
Pontiff of Roman Catholic
Church]
Pope Liberius
Libertador, El (The Liberator).
See: BOLÍVAR, SIMÓN
Liberty, Radio's Own Statue
of. See:
SMITH, KATHRYN
ELIZABETH

Liberty, The Apostle of. See:
CLAY, HENRY
JEFFERSON, THOMAS
Librarian, The. See:
PEARSON, EDMUND
LESTER
Librarianship, Philosopher of.
See: RANGANATHAN,
SHIYALI RAMAMRITA
Library, The Stalking. See:
MITCHELL, STEPHEN MIX
Library, The Walking. See:
CAMERON, JOHN
HALES, JOHN
Lichfield, The Swan of. See:
SEWARD, ANNA
LICHTENBERG, ELISABETH
JACOBA (1913-) [Dutch
broadcaster and author]
Liesje van Someren
Lida Larrimore. See: TURNER,
LIDA LARRIMORE
Liddesdale, The Knight of. See:
DOUGLAS, SIR WILLIAM
LIDDY, JAMES DANIEL REEVES
(1934-) [Irish lawyer and
author]
Brian Lynch
Liam O'Connor
LIEB, JOHN WILLIAM
(1860-1929) [American
electrician and inventor]
Apostle of Light and Power
The Father of the Electric
Light in Europe
Lieb, Yehudah. See:
GORDON, JUDAH LOEB
LIEB, ZISKIND (1930-)
[American composer,
trombonist and arranger]
Dick Lieb
Lieber (Liebler). See:
ERASTUS, THOMAS
LIEBHARD, JOACHIM
(1500-74) [German scholar]
Joachim Camerarius
Liebler (Lieber).
ERASTUS. THOMAS
LIEBOWICZ, JANKIEW
(1726-91) [Polish
theologian and mystic]
Jacob Frank
Liégeoise, La Belle. See:
TERWAGNE, ANNE

JOSEPH
Lies, The Father of. See:
HERODOTUS
Liesje van Someren. See:
LICHTENBERG, ELISA-
BETH JACOBA
LIESLER, HEDWIG (1914-)
[Austrian motion picture
actress]
Hedy Lamarr
Lieut. A.K. Sims. See:
WHITSON, JOHN HARVEY
Lieut. Alfred B. Thorne. See:
AIKEN, ALBERT W.
Lieut. Frederick Garrison.
See: SINCLAIR,
UPTON BEALL
Lieut. J.H. Randolph. See:
ELLIS, EDWARD
SYLVESTER
Lieut. Keene. See:
RATHBONE, ST. GEORGE
HENRY
Lieut. Murray. See:
BALLOU, MATURIN MUR-
RAY
Lieut. Ned Hunter. See:
ELLIS, EDWARD
SYLVESTER
Lieut. Preston Graham. See:
INGRAHAM, COLONEL
PRENTISS
Lieut. R.H. Jayne. See:
ELLIS, EDWARD
SYLVESTER
LIEVEN, DOROTHEA,
PRINCESS DE (1784-1857)
[Russian politician and
intriguer]
The Egeria of Guizot
Life, The Fountain of. See:
ALEXANDER OF HALES
LIGHT [Light]. See also:
Lite
Lyte
Light and Power, Apostle of.
See: LIEB, JOHN
WILLIAM
LIGHT, BEN (1894-1965)
[American jazz musician
(piano, leader)]
Lightning Fingers
Light Elder, The Blue. See:

JACKSON, THOMAS
JONATHAN
Light Horse Harry. See:
LEE, HENRY
WATTERSON, HENRY
Light in Europe, The Father of
Electric. See:
LIND, JOHN WILLIAM
LIGHT, MAUDE ELLEN
(1879-1934) [American
actress]
Margaret Illington
Light of the West, The. See:
MAIMONIDES
Light of the Western Churches,
The. See:
HOOKER, THOMAS
Light of the World, The. See:
SIGISMUND
LIGHTFOOT, HANNAH (fl. 1759)
[Supposed wife of GEORGE
III of England, then
Prince of Wales]
The Fair Quakeress
Lightner, A.M. See: HOPF,
ALICE LIGHTNER
Lightner, Winnie. See:
HANSON, WINIFRED
Lightnin'. See:
GOSDEN, FREEMAN F.
HOPKINS, SAM
Lightning. See:
ELLSWORTH, GEORGE A.
HAMILCAR BARCA
Lightning Fingers. See:
LIGHT, BEN
Lightning (Ilderm). See:
BAJAZET I
Lightning Pilot, The. See:
BIXBY, HORACE EZRA
Lightning, Tamer of the. See:
FRANKLIN, BENJAMIN
Lightning Williams, Thunder and.
See: WILLIAMS, DAVID
ROGERSON
LIGOURI, ALPHONSUS
(1696-1787) [Italian Catholic
churchman and theologian]
St. Alphonsus
Ligurian Sage, The. See:
AULIS PERSIUS FLACCUS
Lil Dagover. See:
LILETTS, MARTA MARIA

Lil, Diamond. See:
WEST, MAE
LILBURNE, JOHN (c. 1613-57)
[English republican]
Free-born John
LILETTS, MARTA MARIA
(1897-) [German motion
picture actress]
Lil Dagover
Lili. See also:
Lilli
LILLIE
LILLY
Lily
Lili Damita. See:
CARRÉ, LILLIAN
Lilian. See also:
Lillian
Lillian
Lilian Adelaide Neilson. See:
BROWN, ELIZABETH
ANN
Lilian Patrick. See:
KEOGH, LILIAN
GILMORE
Lilian Woodward. See:
MARSH, JOHN
Lilli. See also:
Lili
LILLIE
LILLY
Lily
Lilli Palmer. See:
HARRISON, MARIA LILLI
PEISER
Lillian. See also:
Lilian
Lillien
Lillian Beckwith. See:
COMBER, LILLIAN
Lillian de la Torre. See:
McCUE, LILLIAN BUENO
Lillian de la Torre-Bueno. See:
McCUE, LILLIAN BUENO
Lillian Gish. See:
GUICHE, LILLIAN DE
Lillian R. Drayton. See:
CORYELL, JOHN RUSSELL
Lillian Russell. See:
LEONARD, HELEN
LOUISE
LILLIE. See also:
Lili

Lilli
LILLY
Lily
LILLIE, BEATRICE GLADYS
(1898-) [Canadian actress
and comedienne]
Bea Lillie
The Mistress of Sophisticated
Slapstick
Lady Peel
LILLIE, MAJOR GORDON W.
(1860-1942) [American
frontier scout and showman]
Pawnee Bill
The White Chief of the
Pawnees
Lillien. See also:
Lilian
Lillian
Lillien Blanche Fearing. See:
FEARING, LILIAN BLANCHE
LILLY. See also:
Lili
Lilli
LILLIE
Lily
LILLY, WILLIAM (1602-81)
[English astrologer and
prophet]
The Last Astrologer
Zadkiel
Lily. See:
CHAUCHOIN, CLAUDETTE
Lili
Lilli
LILLIE
LILLY
PONS, ALICE JOSÉPHINE
Lily Langtry. See:
BRETON, EMILY CHAR-
LOTTE LE
Lily, The Jersey. See:
BRETON, EMILY CHAR-
LOTTE LE
Lily, Tiger. See:
BLAKE, LILLIE DEVEREUX
LIM, BOON KENG (1869-)
[Chinese physician and
author]
L.M.
Wen Ching
Limerick. See:
LEAR, EDWARD

LIN [Lin]. See also:
  Lyn
  LYNN
  Lynn
LIN, ADET JUSU (1923-)
  [Chinese correspondent
  and author]
  Tan Yun
LIN, LESLIE CHARLES
  BOWYER (1907-)
  [Anglo-American author
  of detective stories]
  Leslie Charteris
Lin Shao-Yang. See:
  JOHNSTON, SIR
  REGINALD FLEMING
Lina. See:
  FACK, CAROLINE
Lincoln. See:
  STEFFENS, JOSEPH
  LINCOLN
LINCOLN, ABRAHAM (1809-65)
  [Sixteenth President of the
  United States]
  The Ancient
  The Buffoon
  Caesar
  The Emancipation President
  Father Abraham
  The Flatboat Man
  The Grand Wrestler
  The Great Emancipator
  The Great Wrestler
  Honest Abe
  The Illinois Baboon
  The Jester
  The Long 'un
  The Man of the People
  The Martyr President
  Massa Linkum
  Old Abe
  The Rail Splitter
  The Sage of Springfield
  The Sectional President
  The Tycoon
  The Tyrant
  Uncle Abe
Lincoln, Arthur. See:
  HAYDON, ARTHUR
  LINCOLN
Lincoln, Elmo. See:
  LINKENHELT, OTTO ELMO
Lincoln, Howard. See:
  HARBAUGH, THOMAS

CHALMERS
LINCOLN, MARY TODD (1818-82)
  [Wife of President
  ABRAHAM LINCOLN]
  The She-Wolf
Lincoln of the Sea, The Abraham.
  See: FURUSETH,
  ANDREW
L'Inconnue. See:
  FRENCH, LUCY VIRGINIA
  SMITH
LIND, JOHANNA MARIA
  (1820-87) [Swedish soprano,
  introduced in America by
  P. T. BARNUM]
  Madame Otto Goldschmidt
  Jenny Lind
  The Swedish Nightingale
LIND, JOSEPH CONRAD
  (1915-) [American actor
  and comedian]
  Peter Lind Hayes
LIND, RAGNAR (1909-)
  [American motion picture
  actor]
  Jeffrey Lynn
Linda. See:
  DARNELL, MANETTA ELOISA
Linda Boscawen. See:
  SMITHELLS, ANABEL
  DOREEN
Linda Christian. See:
  WELTER, BLANCA
  ROSA
Linda Haynes. See:
  SWINFORD, BETTY JUNE
  WELLS
Linda Tremaine. See:
  MORGAN, DIANA
LINDBERGH, CHARLES
  AUGUSTUS (1902-)
  [American aviator]
  The Ambassador of the Air
  Lindy
  The Lone Eagle
  Lucky Lindy
Lindeman, Edith. See:
  CALISCH, EDITH
Linden, Sara. See:
  BARTLETT, MARIE SWAN
Linden Travers. See
  LINDON-TRAVERS,
  FLORENCE
LINDENBERG, HEDDA (1916-)

[Romanian artist]
Hedda Sterne
Lindenwald, The Sage of. See:
    VAN BUREN, MARTIN
Linder, Max. See:
    LEVIELLE, GABRIEL
LINDLEY, LOUIS BERT (1919-)
    [American motion picture
    actor]
Slim Pickens
LINDON-TRAVERS, FLORENCE
    (1913-) [British stage and
    motion picture actress]
Linden Travers
LINDSAY, BARBARA. See:
    James, Josephine
Lindsay, David. See:
    WALLS, IAN GASCOIGNE
LINDSAY, HAROLD ARTHUR
    BILL (1900-) [Australian
    lecturer and writer]
Bogaduck
A. B. Carrick
Ex-R. S. M.
LINDSAY, JACK (1900-)
    [Australian journalist
    and author]
Peter Meadows
Richard Preston
LINDSAY, JOHN MAURICE
    (1918-) [Scottish critic,
    broadcaster and author]
Gavin Brock
LINDSAY (LYNDSAY,) SIR
    DAVID (1490?-1555)
    [Scottish poet]
The Last of the Makars
The Last of the Scottish
    Chaucerians
Lindsay of the Mount
Lindsay McRae. See:
    SOWERBY, ARTHUR
        LINDSAY McRAE
Lindsay, Margaret. See:
    KIES, MARGARET
LINDSAY, NICHOLAS
    VACHEL (1879-1931)
    [American poet]
Vachel Lindsay
Lindsay, Perry. See:
    DERN, PEGGY GADDIS
LINDSEY, BENJAMIN BARR
    (1869-1943) [American

juvenile court judge]
The Father of the Juvenile
    Court
Ben Lindsey
Judge Lindsey
Lindsey, John. See:
    MURIEL, JOHN
Lindy. See:
    LINDBERGH, CHARLES
        AUGUSTUS
Lindy, Lucky. See:
    LINDBERGH, CHARLES
        AUGUSTUS
Line, Hold That. See:
    BLANTON, THOMAS
        LINDSAY
Line, The Father of the White.
    See: HINES, EDWARD
        NORRIS
Line Whig, Old. See:
    WILLIAMS, JAMES
LINEBARGER, PAUL MYRON
    ANTHONY (1913-) [Amer-
    ican educator and author]
Felix C. Forest
Carmichael Smith
LINEBARGER, PAUL MYRON
    WENTWORTH (1871-1939)
    [American author]
Paul Myron
LINGEMAN, RICHARD ROBERTS
    (1931-   ) [American
    editor, publisher and
    author]
Niles Chignon
LINGEMAN, RICHARD ROBERTS.
    See also: Hirsch,
        William Randolph
Linguist Whom Labor Loves,
    The Loquacious. See:
    PERKINS, FRANCES
LININGTON, ELIZABETH
    (1921-) [American author]
Anne Blaisdell
Lesley Egan
Egan O'Neill
Dell Shannon
LINKENHELT, OTTO ELMO
    (1889-1952) [American
    silent motion picture actor]
Elmo Lincoln
LINKLETTER, ARTHUR GORDON
    (1912-) [Canadian radio

616

and television personality,
actor and writer]
Art Linkletter
Links, The King of the. See:
  JONES, ROBERT
    TYRE, JR.
Linkum, Massa. See:
  LINCOLN, ABRAHAM
LINLEY, ELIZA ANN (1754-92)
  [English soprano; wife of
  RICHARD BRINSLEY
  SHERIDAN]
  The Maid of Bath
Linnaeus, Carolus. See:
  VON LINNÉ, CARL
LINSKILL, MARY (1840-91)
  [English novelist]
  Stephen Yorke
LINTON [Linton]. See also:
  Lynton
LINTON, MILDRED (1905-)
  [American motion picture
  actress]
  Karen Morley
Linton Romaine. See:
  LEE, REV. ALBERT
LINUS (died c. 76) [Supreme
  Pontiff of Roman Catholic
  Church]
  Pope Linus
  St. Linus
Lion. See also:
  LYON
  Lyon
Lion Hearted, The (Coeur de
  Lion). See:
  LOUIS VIII
  RICHARD I
Lion Hearted Thomas. See:
  THOMAS, HENRY
    GEORGE
Lion Hunter, The. See:
  CUMMING, ROUALEYN
    GEORGE GORDON
  TINKHAM, GEORGE
    HOLDEN
Lion, Le. See:
  LOUIS VIII
Lion of Athens, The Grim Old.
  See: GROSVENOR,
    CHARLES HENRY
Lion of God, The. See:
  ALI, CALIPH

Lion of Janina, The. See:
  ALI
Lion of Judah, The. See:
  HAILE SELASSIE, RAS
    TAFFARI (TAFARI)
Lion of Sweden, The. See:
  BANÉR, JOHAN
Lion of the North, The. See:
  GUSTAVUS II
Lion of the Punjab, The. See:
  RANJIT SINGH
Lion of the Senate, The. See:
  BORAH, WILLIAM EDGAR
Lion of the South, The. See:
  HINDMAN, THOMAS
    CARMICHAEL
Lion, Sea. See:
  BENNETT, GEOFFREY
    MARTIN
Lion, The. See:
  ALI PASHA
  HENRY
  WILLIAM
Lion, The Carthaginian. See:
  HANNIBAL
Lion, The Idaho. See:
  BORAH, WILLIAM EDGAR
Lion, The Little. See:
  HAMILTON, ALEXANDER
Lion, The Lone. See:
  BORAH, WILLIAM EDGAR
Lion, The Old. See:
  ROOSEVELT, THEODORE
Lion, The Russian. See:
  HACKENSCHMIDT, GEORGE
Lion, Willie the. See:
  SMITH, WILLIAM HENRY
    JOSEPH BERTHOL
    BONAPARTE BERTHOLOFF
Lion, Yehudah. See:
  GORDON, JUDAH LOEB
Lionel Barrymore. See:
  BLYTHE, LIONEL
Lionel Black. See:
  BARKER, DUDLEY
Lip, The. See:
  DUROCHER, LEO ERNEST
Lip, The Big. See:
  MAILS, WALTER
Lip, The Louisville. See:
  CLAY, CASSIUS
    MARCELLUS, JR.
LIPPARD, GEORGE (1822-54)

[American novelist;
founder of the "Brotherhood
of the Union"]
Our Talisman
LIPPI, FRA FILIPPO (c. 1406-69)
[Italian religious
painter]
Lippo Lippi
LIPPINCOTT, MARTHA
SHEPARD (188?-1949)
[American poet]
The Quaker Poetess
LIPPINCOTT, SARA JANE
CLARKE (1823-1904)
[American poet and
journalist]
Grace Greenwood
LIPPMAN, SIDNEY (1914-)
[American composer]
Sid Lippman
Lippo. See:
LIPPI, FRA FILIPPO
Lippy. See:
DUROCHER, LEO ERNEST
Lips, Hot. See:
BURNETT, CAROL
PAGE, ORAN
LIPSCOMB, ANDREW ADGATE
(1816-90) [American
Methodist minister at the
age of eighteen]
The Boy Preacher
Liquor Czar, The. See:
MORGAN, WILLIAM
FORBES
Liquor Industry, The Czar of
the. See:
MORGAN, WILLIAM
FORBES
Lisa Grenelle. See:
MUNROE, ELIZABETH
LEE
LISBONA, EDWARD (1915-)
[Anglo-American
composer and pianist]
Eddie "Piano" Miller
Lisi, Virna. See:
PIERALISI, VIRNA
Lisl. See:
BEER, ELOISE C. S.
Lisl Drake. See:
BEER, ELOISE C. S.
Lisle, Seward D. See:

ELLIS, EDWARD
SYLVESTER
LISTER, BRUCE (1912-)
[South African motion
picture actor]
Bruce Lester
LISTER, JOSEPH (1827-1912)
[English nobleman and
surgeon]
The Father of Antiseptic
Surgery
LISTON, CHARLES (1930/33-70)
[American Negro pro-
fessional boxer; world's
heavyweight champion]
Sonny Liston
Liston, Jack. See:
MALONEY, RALPH LISTON
Litchfield, The Swan of. See:
SEWARD, ANNA
Lite. See also:
LIGHT
Light
Lyte
Lite, Jams. See:
SCHNECK, STEPHEN
Literacy, The First Lady of.
See: FISHER, WELTHY
BLAKESLEY HONSINGER
Literary Cavalier, The Last.
See: HAYNE, PAUL
HAMILTON
Literary Colossus, The. See:
JOHNSON, DR. SAMUEL
Literary Leather-Dresser, The.
See: DOWSE, THOMAS
Literary Tailor, The. See:
BROWN, THEOPHILUS
Literature, The Alnaschar of
Modern. See:
COLERIDGE, SAMUEL
TAYLOR
Literature, The Black Hussar of.
See:
SCOTT, SIR WALTER
Literature, The Father of
American. See:
IRVING, WASHINGTON
Literature, The Father of
Belgian. See:
DE COSTER, CHARLES
THEODORE HENRI
Literature, The Father of

German. See:
LESSING, GOTTHOLD
EPHRAIM
Literature, The Father of Roman.
See: ENNIUS, QUINTUS
Literature, The Founder of
Danish. See:
HOLBERG, LUDVIG
Literature, The Giant of.
See: JOHNSON,
DR. SAMUEL
Literature, The Great Cham
of. See:
JOHNSON, DR. SAMUEL
Literature, The Leviathan of. See:
JOHNSON, DR. SAMUEL
Literature, The Polyphemus of.
See: JOHNSON, DR.
SAMUEL
Literature, The Voltaire of
Grecian. See:
LUCIAN OF SAMOSATA
Litri. See:
BÁEZ, MANUEL
BAEZ, MIGUEL
Little Alby. See:
BARKLEY, ALBEN
WILLIAM
Little Aleck. See:
STEPHENS, ALEXANDER
HAMILTON
Little Bat. See:
GARNIER, BAPTISTE
Little Ben. See:
HARRISON, BENJAMIN
Little Benny. See:
HARRIS, BENJAMIN
Little Bill. See:
JOHNSTON, WILLIAM M.
Little Billy. See:
SMITH, WILLIAM
RUSSELL
Little Billy Cody the
Messenger. See:
CODY, WILLIAM
FREDERICK
Little Bird. See:
HEATH, JAMES
EDWARD
Little Black Dan. See:
WEBSTER, DANIEL
Little Breeches. See:
HAY, JOHN MILTON

Little Chief. See:
THATCHER, MOSES
Little Colonel, The. See:
SHARP, HAROLD SPENCER
Little Corporal of Unsought
Fields. See:
McCLELLAN, GEORGE
BRINTON
Little Corporal, The. See:
NELSON, KNUTE
Little Corporal, The (Le
Petit Caporal). See:
BONAPARTE, NAPOLEON
Little Coward, The Dirty. See:
FORD, ROBERT
Little Davey. See:
LEWIS, DAVID JOHN
Little David. See:
RANDOLPH, JOHN
Little Doctor, The. See:
HOUGHTON, DOUGLASS
LITTLE, DUDLEY (1930-)
[American jazz musician
(piano, singer, leader)]
Big Tiny Little
Little Duke, The. See:
SCOTT, JAMES
LITTLE, EDWARD GERALD
(1897-) [British motion
picture actor]
Edward Lexy
Little Egypt, The Big Man from.
See: KELLER, KENT
ELLSWORTH
Little Feller, The. See:
SULLIVAN, TIMOTHY P.
Little Flower of Jesus. See:
TERESA OF LISIEUX, ST.
Little Flower, The. See:
LA GUARDIA, FIORELLO
HENRY
Little, Frances. See:
MACAULAY, FANNIE
CALDWELL
Little Giant of Alexandria, The.
See: NELSON, KNUTE
Little Giant, The. See:
DOUGLAS, STEPHEN
ARNOLD
LEWIS, DAVID JOHN
Little Grandmother of the Russian
Revolution, The. See:
BRESHKOVSKY, CATHERINE

Little Hartley. See:
    COLERIDGE, DAVID
    HARTLEY
Little Hero, The. See:
    WHEELER, JOSEPH
Little Hoarse One (Ronquillo).
    See: PELAYO, LUIS
Little Indian Fighter, The. See:
    STANDISH, MILES (MYLES)
Little Jack Little. See:
    LITTLE, JOHN
Little Jazz. See:
    ELDRIDGE, DAVID ROY
Little Joe. See:
    WHEELER, JOSEPH
LITTLE, JOHN (1900-56)
    [Anglo-American enter-
    tainer, singer, pianist
    and composer]
    Little Jack Little
Little King Pepin. See:
    CHANNING, WILLIAM
    ELLERY
Little Lion, The. See:
    HAMILTON, ALEXANDER
LITTLE, LOUIS LAWRENCE
    (1893-) [American
    football coach]
    The Caesar of Football
    Lou Little
Little Mac. See:
    McCLELLAN, GEORGE
    BRINTON
Little Mac the Young Napoleon.
    See: McCLELLAN,
    GEORGE BRINTON
Little Magician, The. See:
    VAN BUREN, MARTIN
LITTLE, MALCOLM (1925-65)
    [American Negro Black
    Power advocate]
    Big Red
    Malcolm X
    Malik El-Shabazz
Little Marlborough, The. See:
    SCHWERIN, COUNT KURT
    CHRISTOPH
Little, Master. See:
    MOORE, THOMAS
Little Masters, joint nickname
    of HANS SEBALD
    BEHAM (1500-50) and his
    brother, BARTHEL BEHAM

(1502-40) [German painters]
Little Minnie Maddern. See:
    DAVEY, MARIE AUGUSTA
Little Miss Poker Face. See:
    WILLS, HELEN NEWING-
    TON
Little Miss Roosevelt. See:
    LONGWORTH, ALICE LEE
    ROOSEVELT
Little Missy. See:
    MOZZEE, PHOEBE ANNE
    OAKLEY
Little Mother of All the Russians,
    The. See:
    ANHALT-ZERBST,
    SOPHIA AUGUSTA
    FREDERICA OF
Little Napoleon. See:
    BRUMBAUGH, CARL
Little Napoleon, The. See:
    BEAUREGARD, PIERRE
    GUSTAVE TOUTANT
Little Norwegian, The. See:
    NELSON, KNUTE
Little Owen the Epigram-maker.
    See: OWEN, JOHN
LITTLE, PAUL H. (1915-)
    [American advertising
    executive and author]
    Paula Little
    Paula Minton
    Hugo Paul
Little Pete. See:
    FUNG JING TOY
Little Phil. See:
    SHERIDAN, PHILIP HENRY
    THOMPSON, PHILIP
    BURTON, JR.
Little Poison. See:
    WANER, LLOYD JAMES
Little Portuguese, My. See:
    BROWNING, ELIZABETH
    BARRETT
Little Queen, The. See:
    ISABELLA OF VALOIS
Little Red. See:
    BARTON, DAVID
Little Rich Girl, The Poor. See:
    VANDERBILT GLORIA
Little Round Man, The. See:
    BUTTS, JAMES
    WALLACE, JR.
Little Round Top, The Hero of.

See:
CHAMBERLAIN, JOSHUA
LAWRENCE
Little Spaniard, The (Lo
Spagnoletto). See:
RIBERA, JUSEPE DE
Little Sure Shot. See: MOZZEE,
PHOEBE ANNE OAKLEY
Little, The. See:
JAMES THE LESS
Little, The (Parvus). See:
JOHN OF SALISBURY
Little, Thomas. See:
MOORE, THOMAS
Little Tich. See:
RELPH, HARRY
Little Tim. See:
SULLIVAN, TIMOTHY P.
Little Tramp, The. See:
CHAPLIN, CHARLES
SPENCER
Little Van. See:
VAN BUREN, MARTIN
Little, Van Dyck in. See:
COOPER, SAMUEL
Little Whig, The. See: ANNE
Little Wonder, The. See:
GRAVELET, JEAN
FRANÇOIS
Littlepage, Cornelius. See:
COOPER, JAMES
FENIMORE
LITTLER, EUGENE (1930-)
[American professional
golfer]
Gene Littler
Littleton, Mark. See:
KENNEDY, JOHN
PENDLETON
Litvinov, Maksim Maksimovich.
See: FINKELSTEIN,
MEYER
LIU, JAMES TZU CHIEN
(1919-) [Chinese edu-
cator and author]
Tsu-chien Liu
LIU, WU-CHI (1907-)
[Chinese educator, editor
and author]
Hsiao Hsia
Live Oak George. See:
LAW, GEORGE
Lively. See:

POPE, JANE
LIVERMORE, GEORGE (1809-65)
[American antiquarian]
The Antiquary
Livermore Larruper, The. See:
BAER, MAXIMILIAN
ADELBERT
Liverpool Landseer, The. See:
HUGGINS, WILLIAM
LIVERTON, JOAN (1913-)
[English author]
Joan Medhurst
LIVI, YVES (YVO) (IVO)
(1921-) [French singer
and actor]
Yves Montand
Living Anatomy, The (l'Anatomie
Vivante). See:
AROUET, FRANÇOIS MARIE
Living Pentecost, The. See:
MEZZOFANTI, CARDINAL
GIUSEPPE
LIVINGSTON, JOHN HENRY
(1746-1825) [American
clergyman; founder of
Rutgers College]
The Father of the Dutch
Reformed Church in America
LIVINGSTON, JOSEPH A.
(1906-57) [American jazz
musician (composer, saxo-
phones, arranger)]
Fud Livingston
LIVINGSTON, ROBERT R.
(1746-1813) [American
lawyer, politician and
orator]
The Cicero of America
LIVINGSTON, WILLIAM
(1723-90) [American
politician; Governor of
New Jersey]
Despot-in-Chief in and over
the Rising State of New
Jersey
Don Quixote of the Jerseys
Extraordinary Chancellor of
the Rising State of New
Jersey
Knight of the Most Honorable
Order of Starvation
Spurious Governor
LIVINSKY, WALTER (1929-)

[American composer,
saxophonist and arranger]
Walter Leslie
Livy. See:
TITUS LIVIUS
Livy of Portugal, The. See:
BARROS, JOÃO DE
Livy of Spain, The. See:
MARIANA, JUAN DE
Livy, The Portuguese. See:
BARROS, JOÃO DE
Livy, The Protestant. See:
PHILIPPI, JOHANNES
Livy, The Russian. See:
KARAMZIN, NICHOLAS
MIKHAELOVITCH
Liz Toby. See:
MINSKY, BETTY JANE
TOEBE
Liza. See:
LEHMANN, ELIZABETH
NINA MARY
FREDERIKA
Lizabeth Scott. See:
MATSO, EMMA
Lizzie Bland. See:
BROWN, ELIZABETH
ANN
Lizzie Miles. See:
LANDREAUX, ELIZA-
BETH MARY
Lizzie W. Champney. See:
CHAMPNEY, ELIZABETH
WILLIAMS
Llancarvan, Caradog of. See:
CARADOG
Llangollen, Maid of. See:
BUTLER, LADY ELEANOR
PONSONBY, MISS
SARAH
LLANO, ISIDRO SANTIAGO
(1811-51) [Spanish bull-
fighter]
Barragán
Llaverito. See:
GUERRA, RAFAEL
Llewellyn. See also:
LLYWELYN
Llewellyn, Richard. See:
LLOYD, RICHARD DOYLE
VIVIAN LLEWELLYN
Lloyd. See:
OSBORNE, SAMUEL

LLOYD
LLOYD, HAROLD CLAYTON
(1893-1971) [American
motion picture comedian]
Lonesome Luke
Lloyd, Hugh. See:
FITZHUGH, PERCY KEESE
LLOYD, JOHN IVESTER (1905-)
[English author]
Babbler
Peter Farmer
The Lodger
LLOYD, MARY (1890-)
[British stage and motion
picture actress]
Mary Merrall
LLOYD, RICHARD DOYLE
VIVIAN LLEWELLYN
(1907-) [Welsh author]
Richard Llewellyn
Lloyd, Stephanie. See:
GOLDING, MORTON JAY
Lloyd, The Australian Marie.
See: FLANAGAN,
FLORENCE
LLYWELYN (died 1240) [Welsh
prince]
The Great
LLYWELYN. See also:
Llewellyn
Lo Zingaro. See:
SOLARIO, ANTONIO
LOADER, WILLIAM REGINALD
(1916-) [British lecturer
and author]
Daniel Nash
Loafers, The Taystee. See:
Happiness Boys, The
Lobby, The King of the. See:
WARD, SAMUEL
Lobrano d'Arlington. See:
DEUBLER, MARY
LOCA. See:
LA LOCA, JOANNA
Loco
LOCHER, CHARLES (1913-)
[American stage and
motion picture actor]
Jon Hall
LOCHER, JACOB (1471-1528)
[German humanist]
Philomusus
Lochiel, Gentle. See:

622

CAMERON, DONALD, OF
LOCHIEL
Lochlons, Colin   See:
JACKSON, CAARY PAUL
Lock, Barn (Magnus Ladolas).
See: MAGNUS I
Locke, Clinton W.   See:
STRATEMEYER,
EDWARD L.
LOCKE, DAVID ROSS (1833-88)
[American humorist]
Petroleum V. Nasby
Reverend Petroleum Vesuvius
Nasby
LOCKE, JOHN (1632-1704)
[English philosopher and
political theorist]
The Father of the Enlighten-
ment in England
Locke, Martin.   See:
DUNCAN, WILLIAM
MURDOCH
Locke, Peter.   See:
McCUTCHAN, JOHN
WILSON
LOCKHART, ARTHUR JOHN
(1850-1926) [American
Methodist clergyman]
Pastor Felix
LOCKHART, EUGENE (1891-)
[Canadian actor]
Gene Lockhart
LOCKHART, JOHN GIBSON
(1794-1854) [Scottish
writer]
Peter Morris
Lockjaw.   See:
DAVIS, EDDIE
LOCKRIDGE, FRANCES
LOUISE.   See:
Richards, Francis
LOCKRIDGE, RICHARD.   See:
Richards, Francis
Locksmith King, The.   See:
LOUIS XVI
LOCKWOOD, INGERSOLL
(1841-1918) [American
lawyer, editor and author]
Irwin Longman
Lockwood, Margaret.   See:
DAY, MARGARET
LOCKWOOD, RALPH
INGERSOLL (1798-1858)

[American novelist and
lawyer]
Mr. Smith
LOCKYER, ROGER (1927-)
[British educator and
author]
Philip Francis
Loco.   See also:
LOCA
Loco, Joe.   See:
ESTEVES, JOSEPH
Locomotive, The Father of the.
See: TREVETHICK,
RICHARD
Lode, Rex.   See:
GOLDSTEIN, WILLIAM
ISAAC
Loder, John.   See:
LOWE, JOHN
Lodge, The Laird of Woodchuck.
See: BURROUGHS, JOHN
LODGE, THOMAS (c.1556-1625)
[English novelist, poet,
dramatist and miscellaneous
writer]
The Young Juvenal
Lodger, The.   See:
LLOYD, JOHN IVESTER
LOEHR, DELORES (1926-72)
[American pianist and
former child motion picture
actress]
Diana Lynn
LOESSER, FRANK HENRY
(1910-) [American song
writer]
The Army's One-man Hit
Parade
The G.I.'s Own Songwriter
LOFLAND, JOHN (1798-1849)
[American poet]
The Milford Bard
LOFTING, HUGH (1886-1947)
[Anglo-American author and
illustrator]
Dr. Dolittle
LOFTON, LAWRENCE (1930-)
[American jazz musician
(trombone)]
Tricky Lofton
LOFTS, NORAH ROBINSON
(1904-) [British educator
and author]

Peter Curtis
LOFTUS, MARIE CECILIA
(1876-1943) [English
actress]
Cissie Loftus
Log Cabin Candidate, The. See:
HARRISON, WILLIAM
HENRY
Log-Cabin Harrison. See:
HARRISON, WILLIAM
HENRY
Log Hall. See:
PHILIPS, MARDIN WILSON
Log Hall, The Sage of. See:
PHILIPS, MARDIN
WILSON
Logan. See:
TAH-GAH-JUTE
Logan, Ford. See:
NEWTON, DWIGHT
BENNETT
LOGAN, JOHN ALEXANDER
(1826-86) [American
general officer]
The Black Eagle of
Illinois
Black Jack
The Jack of Spades
The Murat of the Union Army
Logarithms, The Father of.
See: NAPIER, JOHN
Logic-chopping Machine, The.
See: MILL, JOHN STUART
Logroller. See:
LE GALLIENNE, RICHARD
Lois Barth. See:
FREIHOFER, LOIS DIANE
Lois Duncan. See:
CARDOZO, LOIS
STEINMETZ
Lois Hayden Meek. See:
STOLZ, LOIS MEEK
Lois Kerry. See:
CARDOZO, LOIS
STEINMETZ
Lois Maxwell. See:
HOOKER, LOIS
Lois Montez. See:
GILBERT, MARIE DOLORES
ELIZA ROSANNA
Lola Shelton. See:
KLAUE, LOLA SHELTON
Lolly. See:

PARSONS, LOUELLA
Lom, Herbert. See:
SCHLUDERPACHERU,
HERBERT CHARLES
ANGELO KUCHACEVICH
ZE
Lomas, Steve. See:
BRENNAN, JOSEPH LOMAS
Lomax, Bliss. See:
DRAGO, HENRY SINCLAIR
Lombard, Carole. See:
PETERS, JANE
Lombard, Nap, joint pseud. of
PAMELA HANSFORD
JOHNSON (1912-) and NEIL
STEWART (-) [English
authors]
LOMBARD, PETER (c.1100-64)
[Italian theologian]
Magister Sententiarum
(Master of Sentences)
LOMBARDI, ERNEST NATALI
(1908-) [American pro-
fessional baseball player]
Snozz
LOMBARDI, VINCENT THOMAS
(1913-70) [American
professional football coach]
Vince Lombardi
LOMBARDO, GUY ALBERT
(1902-) [Canadian musician;
leader of Royal Canadian
orchestra]
Mr. New Year's Eve
LOMI, ARTEMISIA (1590-1642?)
[Italian painter]
Artemisia Gentileschi
LOMI, ORAZIO (1563-1647)
[Italian painter]
Orazio Gentileschi
Lon. See:
CHANEY, CREIGHTON
Lon Dunlap. See:
McCORMICK, WILFRED
LONDON [London]. See also:
LANDON
Landon
LENDON
London Bach, The. See:
BACH, JOHANN CHRISTIAN
London, George. See:
BURNSON, GEORGE
London, Jane. See:

GEIS, DARLENE STERN
LONDON, JOHN GRIFFITH (1876-
1916) [American author]
The American Kipling
The Boy Socialist
Jack London
The Sailor Kid
London, St. Thomas of. See:
BECKET, THOMAS À
London, Stewart. See:
WILSON, ROGER C.
Lone Eagle, The. See:
LINDBERGH, CHARLES
AUGUSTUS
Lone Lion, The. See:
BORAH, WILLIAM EDGAR
Lone Star, The. See:
STARR, FREDERICK
Lone Wolf of the Underworld,
The. See:
MILLMAN, HARRY
Loneliness, The Painter of. See:
HOPPER, EDWARD
Lonesome Charley. See:
REYNOLDS, CHARLES
ALEXANDER
Lonesome George. See:
GOBEL, GEORGE LESLIE
Lonesome Luke. See:
LLOYD, HAROLD CLAYTON
Lonesome Singer of the Air,
The. See:
MARVIN, JOHN
LONG ANDY IONA (1902-)
[Hawaiian composer and
musician]
Andy Iona
Long, Ann Marie. See:
JENSEN, PAULINE MARIE
LONG
Long Ben. See:
AVERY, CAPTAIN JOHN
Long Gone. See:
MILES, LUKE
Long, Helen Beecher. See:
STRATEMEYER,
EDWARD L.
LONG, HUEY PIERCE (1893-
1935) [American politician;
political dictator of and
senator from
Louisiana]
The Dictator of Louisiana

The Kingfish
Hooey Long
Louisiana's Loud Speaker
Long John. See:
WENTWORTH, JOHN
LONG, JOHN FREDERICK
LAWRENCE (1917-) [British
educator, editor and
author]
John Longsword
Long Knife. See:
LEWIS, MERIWETHER
LONG, MRS. GABRIELLE
MARGARET VERE CAMP-
BELL (1886-1952) [English
historical novelist and
short story writer]
Marjorie Bowen
Robert Paye
George Preedy
Joseph Shearing
John Winch
Long Peter. See:
AARTSEN, PETER
Long Scribe. See:
DOWLING, VINCENT
Long Sword. See:
WILLIAM
Long Tom. See:
JEFFERSON, THOMAS
PERKINS, THOMAS
HANDASYD
Long 'un, The. See:
LINCOLN, ABRAHAM
LONG, WILLIAM JOSEPH
(1866-1952) [American
author, naturalist and
clergyman]
Peter Rabbit
LONGFELLOW, HENRY WADS-
WORTH (1807-82) [American
poet, educator and man of
letters]
The Children's Poet
Joshua Coffin
The Laureate of Song
The Poet of the Commonplace
Longhanded (Longimanus). See:
See: ARTAXERXES I
Longhi. See:
FALCA, PIETRO
Longimanus (Longhanded). See:
ARTAXERXES I

Longlegs, Daddy. See:
    McADOO, WILLIAM
        GIBBS
Longlegs (Haalegg). See:
    HAAKON V MAGNUSSON
Longman, Irwin. See:
    LOCKWOOD, INGERSOLL
LONGRIGG, JANE CHICHESTER
    (1929-) [British television
    script writer and author]
Jane Chichester
LONGRIGG, ROGER ERSKINE
    (1929-) [Scottish
    author]
Rosalind Erskine
Longshanks. See:
    EDWARD I
LONGSTREET, AUGUSTUS
    BALDWIN (1790-1870)
    [American humorist,
    jurist and educator]
Timothy Crabshaw
LONGSTREET, JAMES
    (1821-1904) [American
    Confederate general
    officer]
The Bulldog
Lee's Old War Horse
Old Pete
Pete
The War Horse of the Con-
    federacy
LONGSTREET, STEPHEN
    (1907-) [American
    cartoonist, artist, critic
    and writer]
Thomas Buxton
Paul Haggard
David Ormsbee
Henri Wiener
Longsword, John. See:
    LONG, JOHN FREDERICK
        LAWRENCE
LONGUEVILLE, ANNE,
    DUCHESSE DE (1619-79)
    [French noblewoman and
    politician]
The Soul of the Fronde
Longueville, Count of Dunois
    and. See:
    DUNOIS, JEAN
LONGWORTH, ALICE LEE
    ROOSEVELT (1884-)
    [Eldest daughter of

President THEODORE
    ROOSEVELT]
Little Miss Roosevelt
Princess Alice
Queen Alice
LONGWORTH, NICHOLAS
    (1782-1863) [American
    horticulturist]
The Father of American
    Grape Culture
Lonnie. See:
    STAGG, AMOS ALONZO
Lonsdale, Frederick. See:
    LEONARD, FREDERICK
LOOMIS, NOEL MILLER (1905-)
    [American newspaperman
    and author]
Sam Allison
Benjamin Miller
Frank Miller
Silas Water
Lope de Vega. See:
    CARPIO, LOPE FÉLIX
        DE VEGA
LOPES, JOSÉ LAURENTINO
    (1922-47) [Spanish
    bullfighter]
Joselillo
LÓPEZ, ALFONSO RAMÓN
    (1908-) [American pro-
    fessional baseball
    manager]
Al Lopez
LOPEZ DE AYALA, PEDRO
    (1332-1407) [Spanish
    chronicler, poet and
    translator]
The Chancellor Ayala
López de Recalde, Íñigo. See:
    LOYOLA, IGNATIUS OF,
        ST. (ÍÑIGO DE OÑEZ
        Y LOYOLA)
LÓPEZ, ENCARNACIÓN
    (1905-45) [Argentine-born
    Spanish dancer]
Argentinita
LÓPEZ, TRINIDAD (1937-   )
    [Mexican-American
    singer]
Trini
LOPEZ, VINCENT (1895-)
    [American jazz musician
    (piano, leader)]
The Pianner Kid

626

Loquacious Linguist Whom
Labor Loves, The. See:
PERKINS, FRANCES
Loquacious Scribble, Esq. See:
HAMILTON, DR.
ALEXANDER
Lord, unauthorized designation
used by JOHN SANGER
(1816-89) and his brother
(GEORGE SANGER (1825-
1911) [English showmen and
circus proprietors]
Lord. See also:
BERNERS, GERALD
HUGH TYRWHITT-
WILSON, 14TH BARON
BYRON, GEORGE GORDON
NOEL
DUNSANY, EDWARD JOHN
MORETON DRAX PLUNK-
ETT, 18TH BARON
KITCHENER, HORATIO
HERBERT, 1ST EARL
KITCHENER
NELSON, HORATIO,
VISCOUNT NELSON
NORTH, FREDERICK, 2D
EARL OF GUILFORD
OGLETHORPE, JAMES
EDWARD
TEDDER, ARTHUR
WILLIAM
TENNYSON, ALFRED,
1ST BARON TENNYSON
LORD ALTHORP (1782-1845)
[English nobleman]
Honest Jack
Honest John
Lord Burgess. See:
BURGIE, IRVING
Lord Caradon. See:
FOOT, HUGH
MACINTOSH
Lord Charles Wellesley. See:
BRONTË, CHARLOTTE
Lord Cobham, The Good. See:
OLDCASTLE, SIR JOHN
LORD, DOREEN MILDRED
DOUGLAS (1904-)
[English author]
Doreen Ireland
Lord Fanny. See:
LORD HERVEY
Lord Gawkey See:

GRENVILLE, RICHARD
TEMPLE
Lord Greenock. See:
CATHCART, CHARLES
MURRAY, 2D EARL
Lord Haw Haw. See:
JOYCE, WILLIAM
LORD HERVEY (1694-1743)
[Baron Hervey of Ickworth,
English nobleman]
Lord Fanny
Sporus
Lord, Jeremy. See:
REDMAN, BEN RAY
Lord Lyttelton, The Good. See:
LYTTELTON, GEORGE,
1ST LORD LYTTELTON
Lord Lyttelton, The Wicked.
See: LYTTELTON,
THOMAS, 2ND LORD
LYTTELTON
Lord Moran. See:
WILSON, CHARLES
McMORAN
Lord O.W.L. (Oh Wonderful
Love), Servant of the.
See: GRAHAM, JAMES
Lord of Galloway. See:
DOUGLAS, ARCHIBALD,
3D LORD OF
Lord of San Simeon, The.
See: HEARST, WILLIAM
RANDOLPH
Lord of the Age, The. See:
SULAIMAN I or II
Lord of the Marshes, First.
See: HATFIELD,
BAZIL MUSE
LORD, PHILLIPS HAYNES
(1902-) [American
author and radio drama-
tist]
Seth Parker
Lord Protector of England. See:
CROMWELL, OLIVER
CROMWELL, RICHARD
Lord Randolph Churchill. See:
CHURCHILL, RANDOLPH
HENRY SPENCER
LORD STANLEY (1799-1869)
[English statesman]
The Hotspur of Debate
The Rupert of Debate
Scorpion Stanley

Lord Stirling. See:
  ALEXANDER, WILLIAM
Lord Strutt. See:
  CHARLES II
Lord, The. See: CRISLER
  HERBERT ORIN
Lord, The Brother of the. See:
  JAMES THE LESS
Lord, The Roundsman of the.
  See: COMSTOCK, ANTHONY
Lord, The Shepherd. See:
  CLIFFORD, HENRY DE
Lord Timothy Dexter. See:
  DEXTER, TIMOTHY
LORD, WILLIAM WILBER-
  FORCE (1819-1907) [Ameri-
  can poet, Civil War chaplain
  and Episcopal clergyman]
  The American Milton
  Tristram Langstaff
Lord's Chore Boy, The. See:
  MAY, SAMUEL JOSEPH
Loren, Sophia. See:
  VILLANI (SCICOLONE),
  SOPHIA
LORENZETTI, AMBROGIO
  (1300?-48) [Italian painter
  of the Sienese school]
  Ambrogio di Lorenzo
LORENZETTI, PIETRO (1280?-
  1348?) [Italian painter of
  the Sienese school]
  Laurati da Siena
  Pietro Laurati
LORENZINI, CARLO
  (1826-90) [Italian
  author]
  Carlo Collodi
Lorenzino. See:
  MEDICI, LORENZO DE'
LORENZO (c.1370-c.1425)
  [Italian painter]
  Il Monaco
Lorenzo, Ambrogio di. See:
  LORENZETTI,
  AMBROGIO
Lorenzo Da Ponte. See:
  CONEGLIANO,
  EMANUELE
Lorenzo, Piero di. See:
  COSIMO, PIERO DI
Lorenzo Stecchetti. See:
  GUERRINI, OLINDO

Lorenzo the Magnificent. See:
  MEDICI, LORENZO DE'
Lorenzo the Younger. See:
  MEDICI, LORENZO DE'
Loretta. See:
  YOUNG, GRETCHEN
Lorez Alexandria. See:
  NELSON, DELOREZ
  ALEXANDRIA
Loring. See:
  Lorring
  MacKaye, Loring
Loring Brent. See:
  WORTS, GEORGE FRANK
LORING, EMILIE BAKER
  (1863/4-1951) [American
  novelist and playwright]
  Josephine Story
Loring, Jules. See:
  MacKaye, Loring
Loring, Peter. See:
  SHELLABARGER,
  SAMUEL
LORING, WILLIAM WING
  (1818-86) [American Con-
  federate general officer]
  Old Blizzards
Loris. See: VON HOFMANNS-
  THAL, HUGO
Lorm, Hieronymus. See:
  LANDESMANN, HEINRICH
Lorna Deane. See:
  WILKINSON, LORNA
  HILDA KATHLEEN
Lorna Page. See:
  ROWLAND, DONALD
  SYDNEY
Lorning, Ray. See:
  BRALY, MALCOLM
Lorrain, Jean. See:
  DUVAL, MARTIN PAUL
  ALEXANDER
LORRAINE. See:
  FRANÇOIS DE LORRAINE
  FREDERICK OF LORRAINE
Lorraine, Anne. See:
  CHISHOLM, LILIAN MARY
Lorraine, Claude. See:
  GELÉE, CLAUDE
Lorraine, Duke of Lower. See:
  GODFREY OF BOUILLON
Lorraine, Mary of. See:
  GUISE, MARY

Lorring. See also:
    Loring
Lorring, Joan. See:
    ELLIS, MAGDALEN
Los Angeles, The Boy
    Preacher of. See:
    IRONSIDE, HENRY
        ALLAN
Los Angeles, Victoria de Los.
    See: CIMA, VICTORIA
        GAMEZ
LOSCH, OTTILIE ETHEL
    (1907-) [Viennese
    dancer and artist]
    Tilly Losch
Loser (The Tyneman). See:
    DOUGLAS, ARCHIBALD
Lost Dauphin, The. See:
    WILLIAMS, ELEAZAR
Lot, Parson. See:
    KINGSLEY, REV.
        CHARLES
LOTHAIR. See:
    SEGNI, LOTHAIR OF
LOTHAIR I (795?-855) [Holy
    Roman Emperor]
    The Pious
LOTHAIR II (died 1137)
    [Emperor of the Holy
    Roman Empire]
    The Saxon
Lothrop, Amy. See:
    WARNER, ANNA
        BARTLETT
LOTHROP, HARRIET MULFORD
    STONE (1844-1924) [Amer-
    ican author]
    Margaret Sidney
Loti, Pierre. See:
    VIAUD, LOUIS MARIE
        JULIEN
Lotta. See:
    CRABTREE, CHARLOTTE
Lotte Lenya. See:
    BLAMAUER, KAROLINE
Lottery. See:
    KENNEY, EDWARD A.
LOTTICH, KENNETH VERNE
    (1904-) [American
    educator and author]
    Kenneth Conrad
Lou. See:
    GEHRIG, HENRY LOUIS

GOTTLIEB, LOUIS E.
    Lew
LITTLE, LOUIS LAW-
    RENCE
MUNSON, MARY LOU
    EASLEY
Lou Bennett. See:
    BENOIT, LOUIS
Lou Capsadell. See:
    HAMMOND, HENRIETTA
        HARDY
Lou Costello. See:
    CRISTELLO, LOUIS
Lou, Larruping. See:
    GEHRIG, HENRY LOUIS
LOUCHEIM, KATHLEEN
    SCOFIELD (1903-)
    [American writer and
    political party official]
    Katie Loucheim
Loud Larry. See:
    McPHAIL, LELAND
        STANFORD
Loud Speaker, Louisiana's. See:
    LONG, HUEY PIERCE
Loudon, Isabelle. See:
    Child, Alan
Louie. See:
    ARMSTRONG, DANIEL
        LOUIS
    JORDAN, LOUIS THOMAS
LOUIS (1682-1712) [Duc de
    Bourgoyne]
    The Second Dauphin
Louis. See:
    EVANS, REDD
        LEWIS
    Lewis
LOUIS I (778-840) [King of
    the Franks and Holy
    Roman Emperor]
    Le Débonnaire (The
    Debonaire)
    Le Pieux (The Pious)
LOUIS I (1326-82) [King of
    Hungary and of Poland]
    The Great
LOUIS II (804?-76) [King of
    Germany]
    The German
LOUIS II (846-79) [King of
    France and Aquitaine]
    The Stammerer

LOUIS III (880?-928) [Holy
Roman emperor]
The Blind
The Blind Emperor
LOUIS III (893-911) [King of
Germany]
The Child
LOUIS IV (921?-54) [King
of France]
D'Outremer (From Over-
seas)
LOUIS IV (1287?-1347)
[Holy Roman Emperor]
The Bavarian
LOUIS V (966?-87) [King of
France]
Le Fainéant (The Sluggard)
LOUIS VI (1081-1137)
[King of France]
The Fat
LOUIS VII (1121?-80) [King of
France]
Le Jeune (The Young)
The Pious
LOUIS VIII (1187-1226)
[King of France]
Coeur de Lion (The Lion
Hearted)
Le Lion
LOUIS IX (1215-70) [King of
France]
St. Louis
The Solomon of France
LOUIS X (1289-1316) [King
of France and of Navarre]
The Quarreler
LOUIS XI (1423-83) [King of
France]
The Universal Spider
LOUIS XII (1462-1515) [King
of France]
Père du Peuple (Father of
the People)
LOUIS XIII (1601-43) [King
of France]
The Just
LOUIS XIV (1638-1715) [King
of France]
God-given
Le Grand Monarque
The Grand Monarch
The Great
Le Roi Soleil (The Sun King)

Lewis Baboon
Old Bona Fide
LOUIS XV (1710-74) [King of
France]
Le Bien-Aimé (The Well-
Beloved)
LOUIS XVI (1754-93) [King of
France]
The Baker
The Locksmith King
The Martyr King
LOUIS XVII (1785-95) [Titular
King of France]
Louis Charles de France
LOUIS XVIII (1755-1824)
[King of France]
The King of England's
Viceroy
Louis Le Désiré
Louis Aldrich. See:
LYON, LOUIS
Louis Alexandre César Bombet.
See: BEYLE, MARIE-
HENRI
Louis Bellson. See:
BALASSONI, LOUIS
Louis Calhern. See:
VOGT, CARL
Louis Charles. See:
STRATEMEYER,
EDWARD L.
Louis Charles de France. See:
LOUIS XVII
Louis, Father M. See:
MERTON, THOMAS JAMES
Louis-Ferdinand Céline. See:
DESTOUCHES, LOUIS
FUCH
Louis Hayward. See:
GRANT, SEAFIELD
Louis Incogniteau, Jean. See:
KEROUAC, JEAN-LOUIS
LEBRID DE
Louis, Jean. See:
KEROUAC, JEAN-LOUIS
LEBRID DE
Louis, Joe. See:
BARROW, JOSEPH LOUIS
Louis Jourdan. See:
GENDRE, LOUIS
Louis Lambert. See:
GILMORE, PATRICK
SARSFIELD

Louis Legrand, M.D. See:
VICTOR, ORVILLE J.
Louis McIntosh. See:
JOHNSON, CHRISTOPHER
LOUIS, MARILYN (1923-)
[American motion picture
actress]
Rhonda Fleming
Louis Moresby. See:
BECK, MRS. LILY
MORESBY ADAMS
Louis, Murray. See:
FUCHS, MURRAY
LOUIS
Louis Napoleon. See:
BONAPARTE, CHARLES
LOUIS NAPOLEON
LOUIS PHILIPPE (1773-1850)
[King of the French]
The Citizen King
Égalité
The King of the Barricades
Mr. Smith
The Napoleon of Peace
Louis Philippe, The American.
See: FILLMORE,
MILLARD
Louis Wilkinson. See:
MARLOW, LOUIS
Louis Zara. See:
ROSENFIELD, LOUIS
ZARA
Louisa. See:
WALLACE, LEWIS
Louisa May Woollcott. See:
WOOLLCOTT, ALEXANDER
HUMPHREYS
Louise. See also:
MICHEL, CLÉMENCE
LOUISE
Louise, Anita. See:
FREMAULT, ANITA
LOUISE
Louise Bellocq See:
BOUDAT, MARIE-
LOUISE
Louise Christopher. See:
HALE, ARLENE
Louise Dresser. See:
KERLIN, LOUISE
Louise Florence Pétronille de
la Live. See:
D'ESCLAVELLES,

LOUISE TARDIEU
Louise Homer. See:
BEATTY, LOUISE
DILWORTH
Louise Landon. See:
HAUCK, LOUISE PLATT
Louisiana Jurisprudence, The
Father of. See:
MARTIN, FRANÇOIS
XAVIER
Louisiana Ram, The. See:
MOUTON, ROBERT L.
Louisiana, The Dictator of.
See: LONG, HUEY
PIERCE
Louisiana's Loud Speaker. See:
LONG, HUEY PIERCE
Louisville Lip, The. See:
CLAY, CASSIUS MAR-
CELLUS, JR.
Lourie, Helen. See:
STORR, CATHERINE COLE
Lovat Marshall. See:
DUNCAN, WILLIAM
MURDOCH
Love and Humanity, The Sweet-
spirited Advocate of
Justice. See:
MOTT, LUCRETIA
Love, Bessie. See:
HORTON, JUANITA
Love, The Great Master of. See:
DANIEL, ARNAUD
(ARNAUT)
Lovebird. See:
ALLEN, WILLIAM
FRANKLIN
LOVECCHIO, FRANK PAUL
(1913-) [American
popular singer]
Frankie Laine
Lovegood, John. See:
GRANT-WATSON, ELLIOT
LOVEGOOD
Lovehill, C.B. See:
BEAUMONT, CHARLES
LOVEJOY, ELIJAH PARRISH
(1802-37) [American
abolitionist and reformer]
The Martyr Abolitionist
LOVELL, JOHN (1710-78)
[American educator]
The Busby of New England

Lover of Candour, A. See:
HOPKINSON, FRANCIS
Lover, The Screen's Greatest.
See: D'ANTONGUOLLA,
RODOLPHO ALFONZO
RAFAELO PIERRE
FILIBERT GUGLIELMO
DI VALENTIN
Lover, The Vagabond. See:
VALLEE, HUBERT PRIOR
Loves, The Loquacious Linguist
Whom Labor. See:
PERKINS, FRANCES
Lovie Austin. See:
CALHOUN, CORA
Loving his Father (New
Philopator). See:
PTOLEMY VII
Loving his Father (Philopator).
See: PTOLEMY IV
Lovingood, Sut. See:
HARRIS, GEORGE
WASHINGTON
LOVRIEN, RUTH ELLEN
(fl. 1951-62) [American
home economist, editor
and writer]
Mary Meade
Low Budget, Genius on a.
See: KRAMER,
STANLEY E.
Low, Gardner. See:
RODDA, CHARLES
Low Hampton, The Poet of.
See: MILLER,
WILLIAM
LOW, LOIS DOROTHEA
(1916-) [English
author]
Dorothy Mackie Low
LOWDEN, FRANK ORREN
(1861-) [American
politician; Congressman
from Illinois]
The Sage of Sinnissippi
LOWE, JOHN (1898-) [British
motion picture actor]
John Loder
Lowell Adams. See:
JOSEPH, JAMES
HERZ
Lowell Blake. See:
SCHOENFELD, WILLIAM C.

Lowell E. Willis. See:
DAVIS, HORACE
BANCROFT
LOWELL, JAMES RUSSELL
(1819-91) [American
author, educator and
diplomat]
The Best Read Man of the
Century
Hosea Biglow
LOWELL, JOHN, JR. (1743-
1840) [American
political writer]
Columella of the New
England States
Lowell Ryerson. See:
VAN ATTA, WINIFRED
LOWELL
LÖWENBRUGGER, NIKOLAUS
(1417-87) [Swiss holy
hermit]
Bruder Klaus
Nikolaus of Flue
Lower Case. See:
CUMMINGS, EDWARD
ESTLIN
Lower Lorraine, Duke of.
See: GODFREY OF
BOUILLON
Lowery, Robert. See:
HANKE, ROBERT
LOWERY
LOWRY, JOAN CATLOW
(1911-) [English
novelist]
Joanna Catlow
Loy, Myrna. See:
WILLIAMS, MYRNA
LOYOLA, IGNATIUS OF, ST.
(IÑIGO DE OÑEZ Y
LOYOLA) (1491-1556)
[Spanish soldier and
ecclesiastic]
Iñigo López de Recalde
LOYSON, CHARLES (1827-
1912) [French Carmelite
preacher]
Hyacinthe
Père Hyacinthe
Lu-ch'iao. See:
WU, NELSON IKON
Lu, L'uan-yi. See:
LUK, CHARLES

L'uan-yu Lu. See:
LUK, CHARLES
Luber, Jet. See:
MEULENBELT-LUBER,
HENRIETTA C.A.
Luc. See also:
LUK
Luk
Luc Dorsan. See:
SIMENON, GEORGES
LUCANESE, NICK (1897-)
[American tenor,
guitarist and
composer]
The Crooning Troubadour
Nick Lucas
LUCAS, CHRISTOPHER
NORMAN (1912-)
[English composer and
conductor]
Norman Davis
LUCAS, DANIEL BEDINGER
(1836-1909) [American
poet]
The Poet of the Shenan-
doah Valley
LUCAS, EMILY BEATRIX
COURSOLLES (1893-)
[British novelist]
E.B.C. Jones
Lucas Malet. See:
HARRISON, MARY ST.
LEGER KINGSLEY
Lucas, Nick. See:
LUCANESE, NICK
Lucas Van Leyden. See:
HUGENSZ, LUCAS
Lucas, Victoria. See:
PLATH, SYLVIA
LUCCIOLA, JOHN (1926-)
[American composer and
saxophonist]
Johnnie Luce
Luce, Johnnie. See:
LUCCIOLA, JOHN
LUCE, ROBERT (1862-1946)
[American politician;
Congressman from
Massachusetts]
The Parliamentarian
Lucerna, Juris, The. See:
IRNERIUS
LUCEY. See also:

LUCY
Lucy
LUCEY, THOMAS ELMORE
(1874-) [American lyceum
entertainer, actor, author]
The Poet Entertainer of the
Ozarks
LUCHESE, GAETANO (1899-)
[Sicilian-American
racketeer]
Three-Finger Brown
Tommy Brown
Thomas Luchese
Lucia Whitney. See:
KELLER, BARBARA MAY
LUCIAN OF SAMOSATA (c. 120-
200) [Greek rhetorician,
satirist and writer]
The Voltaire of Grecian
Literature
LUCIANA, SALVATORE
(1896-1962) [Sicilian-
American racketeer]
Charles Luciano
Lucky Luciano
Luciano, Charles. See:
LUCIANA, SALVATORE
Luciano, Lucky. See:
LUCIANA, SALVATORE
Lucien Bluphocks. See:
SELDES, GILBERT VIVIAN
Lucile. See also:
Lucille
Lucile Blair. See:
YEAKLEY, MARJORY HALL
LUCILIUS, CAIUS (c. 180 B.C. -
103 B.C.) [Latin satirical
poet]
The Father of Roman Satire
Lucilla Andrews. See:
CRICHTON, LUCILLA
MATHEW
Lucille. See also:
Lucile
Lucille Fletcher. See: WALLOP,
LUCILLE FLETCHER
Lucille Jackson. See:
STRAUSS, MARY LUCILLE
JACKSON
LUCIUS (died 254) [Supreme
Pontiff of Roman Catholic
Church]
Pope Lucius I

St. Lucius
LUCIUS. See also:
    SENECA, MARCUS (or
      LUCIUS)
Lucius II, Pope. See:
    CACCIANEMICI, GHERARDO
Lucius III, Pope. See:
    ALLUCINGOLI,
      UBALDO
LUCK. See:
    Luc
    LUK
    Luk
Luckey. See:
    Lucky
    ROBERTS, G. LUCKEYTH
Luckiest Fool Alive, The. See:
    KELLY, ALVIN
LUCKMAN, SIDNEY (1916-)
    [American football
    player]
    Sid Luckman
Lucky. See:
    BALDWIN, ELIAS
      JACKSON
    DEMPSEY, MILES
      CHRISTOPHER
    Luckey
    MILLINDER, LUCIUS
    THOMPSON, ELI
Lucky, Leif the. See:
    ERICSON, LEIF
Lucky Lindy. See:
    LINDBERGH, CHARLES
      AUGUSTUS
Lucky Luciano. See:
    LUCIANA, SALVATORE
Lucy. See:
    BALL, LUCILLE
    LUCEY
Lucy A. Hovell. See:
    HOVELL, LUCILLE A.
      PETERSON
Lucy, Lemonade. See:
    HAYES, LUCY WARE
      WEBB
Lucy May Russell. See:
    CORYELL, JOHN
      RUSSELL
LUCY, SIR HENRY WILLIAM
    (1845-1924) [English
    journalist]
    Toby, M.P.
Lucy Stone. See:

BLACKWELL, MRS.
    HENRY BROWN
Ludlow, George. See:
    KAY, ERNEST
LUDLOW, LOUIS LEON
    (1873-) [American
    journalist, politician and
    Congressman from Indiana]
    Peace Ludlow
Ludlow, Park. See:
    BROWN, THERON
LUDLOW, ROGER (1590-165?)
    [Anglo-American lawyer]
    The Father of Connecticut
    Jurisprudence
Ludlum, Mabel Cleland. See:
    WIDDEMER, MABEL
      CLELAND
LUDOVICI, ANTHONY MARIO
    (1882-) [British lecturer
    and author]
    Cobbett
    Huntley Paterson
    David Valentine
Ludovicus. See:
    VIVES, JUAN LUIS
LUDOVISI, ALESSANDRO
    (1554-1623) [Supreme
    Pontiff of Roman Catholic
    Church]
    Pope Gregory XV
LUDWIG (born 1042) [Margrave
    of Thuringia]
    Ludwig the Leaper
Ludwig. See:
    GRISWOLD, RUFUS
      WILMOT
Ludwig, Emil. See:
    COHN, EMIL
LUFF, STANLEY GEORGE
    ANTHONY (1921-)
    [British educator and
    author]
    Hugh Farnash
Lugosi, Bela. See:
    BLASKO, BELA LUGOSI
LUJACK, JOHN (1925-)
    [American professional
    football player]
    Johnny Lujack
LUK [Luk]. See also:
    Luc
LUK, CHARLES (1898-)
    [Chinese businessman and

translator of Chinese texts]
L'uan-yu Lu
Luk-oie, Ole. See:
SWINTON, SIR ERNEST
DUNLOP
LUKACS, PAL (1895-)
[Hungarian stage and
motion picture actor]
Paul Lukas
Lukas, Paul. See:
LUKACS, PAL
Luke. See:
SEWELL, JAMES LUTHER
Luke Allan. See:
AMY, WILLIAM LACEY
Luke Forward. See:
PATRICK, JOHNSTONE
GILLESPIE
LUKE, FRANK, JR. (1897-
1918) [American World
War I aviator]
The Balloon Buster
Luke Garland. See:
WHITSON, JOHN HARVEY
Luke, Lonesome. See:
LLOYD, HAROLD
CLAYTON
LUKE, ST. (died 74 A.D.)
[Early Christian evangelist]
The Beloved Physician
Luke Sharp. See:
BARR, ROBERT
Luke Short. See:
GLIDDEN, PATRICK
DUDLEY
Luke Thrice. See:
RUSSELL, JOHN
LUKENS, HENRY CLAY
(1838-1900?) [American
journalist and parodist]
Erratic Enrique
Vernon L. Kingsbury
LULLY, RAYMOND (c. 1235-
1315) [Spanish scholar
and alchemist]
Doctor Illuminatus
Lum, Peter. See:
CROWE, BETTINA LUM
Lumpy Willie. See:
CHAPELSKI, ALEX
SAMUEL
LUNCEFORD, JAMES MELVIN
(1902-47) [American

jazz musician (saxophones,
leader)]
Jimmie Lunceford
LUND, A. MORTEN (1926-)
[American editor, film
producer and author]
Ted Borch
LUNDY, BENJAMIN (1789-1839)
[American abolitionist]
Peter the Hermit of the
Abolitionist Movement
LUNGSTRUM, FRANK ALLAN
(1919-) [American
singer and disc jockey]
Frank Allan
Lupe Velez. See:
VILLABOS. GUADALOUPE
VELEZ DE
LUPOFF, RICHARD ALLEN
(1935-) [American
writer and director of
technical films]
Dick Lupoff
Luqueer, Helen. See:
BUSHNELL, MRS.
WILLIAM H.
LURASKA, DIANNE (1928-)
[Canadian motion picture
actress]
Dianne Foster
LURIA, ISAAC BEN SOLOMON
(1534-72) [founder of
modern Cabalism]
Ari
Ha-ari
Luska, Sidney. See:
HARLAND, HENRY
LUSTER, SHIRLEY (1925-)
[American jazz musician
(singer)]
June Christy
Sharon Leslie
Luther, Frank. See:
CROW, FRANCIS
LUTHER
Luther of Sweden, The. See:
PETRI, OLAUS (OLAF)
Luther of the Early Temperance
Reformation, The. See:
HEWIT, NATHANIEL
Luther, The Danish. See:
TAUSEN, HANS
Lux Lewis, Meade. See:

LEWIS, MEADE
Luxemburg, Henry of. See:
    HENRY VII
Luzon, The Napoleon of. See:
    MacARTHUR, DOUGLAS
Lyall, Edna. See:
    BAYLY, ADA ELLEN
LYALL, KATHARINE
    ELIZABETH (1928-)
    [British editor, author
    and columnist]
Katharine Whitehorn
Lydia Rabinowitsch. See:
    KEMPNER, LYDIA
    RABINOWITSCH
Lydia Steptoe. See:
    BARNES, DJUNA
Lyel, Viola. See:
    WATSON, VIOLET
Lying Dick Talbot. See:
    TALBOT, RICHARD
Lyle Monroe. See:
    HEINLEIN, ROBERT
    ANSON
Lyle Talbot. See:
    HENDERSON, LISLE
Lyman, Abe. See:
    SIMON, ABRAHAM
LYMAN, ALBERT
    ROBISON (1880-)
    [American educator,
    Mormon missionary and
    editor]
    The Old Settler
Lyman Hopkins. See:
    FOLSOM, FRANKLIN
    BREWSTER
Lyman R. Lyon. See:
    DE CAMP, LYON SPRAGUE
Lyn. See:
    HARDING, DAVID
    LLEWELLYN
    LIN
    Lin
    LYNN
    Lynn
Lyn Udall. See:
    KEATING, JOHN HENRY
Lynch, B. Suarez. See:
    Domecq, Honorio Bustos
Lynch, Brian. See:
    LIDDY, JAMES DANIEL

REEVES
LYNCH, MARGARET (191?-)
    [American radio and
    television writer and
    actress]
    Peg Lynch
LYND, ROBERT (1879-1949)
    [Irish essayist and
    literary critic]
    Y.Y.
Lynde Palmer. See:
    PEEBLES, MARY LOUISE
LYNDSAY. See:
    LINDSAY (LYNDSAY), SIR
    DAVID
LYNN [Lynn]. See also:
    LIN
    Lin
    Lyn
Lynn Avery. See:
    COLE, LOIS DWIGHT
Lynn Bard, The. See:
    LEWIS, ALONZO
Lynn Bari. See:
    BITZER, MARJORIE
LYNN, BENJAMIN (fl. 1782)
    [American pioneer hunter,
    frontiersman and preacher]
    The Daniel Boone of
    Southern Kentucky
    The Hunter-Preacher
Lynn Brock. See:
    McALLISTER, ALISTER
Lynn Bronson. See:
    LAMPMAN, EVELYN
    SIBLEY
Lynn, Diana. See:
    LOEHR, DELORES
Lynn, Ethel. See:
    BEERS, ETHELINDA
    ELIOT
Lynn, Frank. See:
    LEISY, JAMES FRANKLIN
Lynn, Irene. See:
    ROWLAND, DONALD
    SYDNEY
LYNN, JANE THURSTON
    (1915-) [American com-
    poser]
    Gene Willadsen
Lynn, Jeffrey. See:
    LIND, RAGNAR

Lynn, Patricia. See:
    WATTS, MABEL
    PIZZEY
Lynn Westland. See:
    JOSCELYN, ARCHIE L.
Lynne, Becky. See:
    ZAWADSKY, PATIENCE
Lynton. See also:
    LINTON
    Linton
Lynton, Ann. See:
    RAYNER, CLAIRE
LYNX. See:
    ANGERMAYER, FRED
    ANTOINE
Lynx. See:
    FAIRFIELD, CECILY
    ISABEL
LYON [Lyon]. See also:
    Lion
LYON, BESS (fl. early
    18th cent.) [Associate
    of JOHN SHEPPARD,
    English criminal]
  Edgeworth Bess
Lyon, Elinor. See:
    WRIGHT, ELINOR
    BRUCE
Lyon, Jessica. See:
    DE LEEUW, CATEAU
    WILHELMINA
LYON, LOUIS (1843-1901)
    [American actor]
  Louis Aldrich
  The Ohio Roscius
Lyon, Lyman R. See:
    DE CAMP, LYON
    SPRAGUE
Lyon, The. See:
    WILLIAM
LYONS, A. NEIL (1880-)
    [South African writer
    and dramatist]
  Albert Michael
Lyre, Pinchbeck. See:
    SASSOON, SIEGFRIED
    LORAINE
Lyre, The Michelangelo of the.
    See: PALESTRINA, GIO-
    VANNI PIERLUIGI DA
Lyre, The Theban. See:
    PINDAR

Lyss. See:
    GRANT, HIRAM ULYSSES
Lyte. See also:
    LIGHT
    Light
    Lite
Lyte, Richard. See:
    WHELPTON, GEORGE
    ERIC
LYTELL, BERT (1888-1954)
    [American actor]
  Jimmy Valentine
LYTTELTON, GEORGE, 1ST
    LORD LYTTELTON (1709-
    73) [British nobleman
    and poet]
  The Good Lord Lyttelton
LYTTELTON, THOMAS, 2ND
    LORD LYTTELTON
    (1744-79) [British
    nobleman and poet]
  The Bad
  The Wicked Lord Lyttelton
Lytton. See:
    STRACHEY, GILES
    LYTTON
Lytton, Edward. See:
    MORRIS, CHARLES
    SMITH
    WHEELER, EDWARD
    LYTTON
LYTTON, LORD (EDWARD
    ROBERT BULWER,
    1ST EARL OF LYTTON)
    (1831-91) [British states-
    man and poet]
  Owen Meredith

M

M. See:
    Monsieur
M.A. See:
    BASIT, ABDUL
M.A. Aldanov. See:
    LANDAU-ALDANOV,
    MARK
M.A.C. See:
    MACFAYDEN, DUGALD
M.A.D. See:
    DENISON, MARY

ANDREWS

M.A. Dormie. See:
    SHARROCK, MARIAN
        EDNA DORMITZER
M.A. Titmarsh. See:
    THACKERAY, WILLIAM
        MAKEPEACE
M.B. See:
    FAUST, FREDERICK
        SCHILLER
M.B. Drapier. See:
    SWIFT, JONATHAN
M. Borden. See:
    SAXON, GLADYS RELYEA
M.C. See:
    LAWSON, HORACE LOWE
M. Claire Cross. See:
    CROSS, CLAIRE
M.D.C., 1817, Somebody.
    See: NEAL, JOHN
M.E. Atkinson. See:
    FRANKAU, MARY
        EVELYN ATKINSON
M.E. Chaber. See:
    CROSSEN, KENDELL
        FOSTER
M.E. McCaull. See:
    BOHLMAN, EDNA
        McCAULL
M.E.W.S. See:
    SHERWOOD, MARY
        ELIZABETH WILSON
M.H. Applezweig. See:
    APPLEY, MORTIMER
        HERBERT
M.H.S. See:
    SPIELMANN, MARION
        HARRY
M. Ilin. See:
    MARSHAK, I.A.
M. Immerito. See:
    SPENSER, EDMUND
M.L. Emslie. See:
    SIMPSON, MYRTLE
        LILLIAS
M.M. Michaeles. See:
    GOLDING, MORTON JAY
M. Nott Erasmus. See:
    STUBER, STANLEY IRVING
M.O. Rolfe, The Detective
    Novelist. See:
    ROLFE, MARO O.

M. O'Rolfe, The Irish
    Novelist. See:
    ROLFE, MARO O.
M. Quad. See:
    LEWIS, CHARLES
        BERTRAND
M. St. Vivant. See:
    BIXBY, JEROME LEWIS
M.Y. Ben Gorion. See:
    BERDICHEVSKY,
        MIKHAH YOSEF
Ma. See:
    BARKER, KATE CLARK
    FERGUSON, MIRIAM A.
Ma Rainey. See:
    PRIDGETT, GERTRUDE
        MALISSA NIX
Maartens, Maarten. See:
    SCHWARTZ, JOOST
        WILLEM VAN DER
        POORTEN
MAAS, MELVIN JOSEPH
    (1898-) [American
    aviator, politician and
    Congressman from
    Minnesota]
    The Marine Aviator
Mabel C. Hawley. See:
    STRATEMEYER,
        EDWARD L.
Mabel Cleland. See:
    WIDDEMER, MABEL
        CLELAND
Mabel Cleland Ludlum. See:
    WIDDEMER, MABEL
        CLELAND
Mabel Normand. See:
    FORTESCUE, MABEL
Mabel Yeates. See
    PEREIRA, HAROLD
        BERTRAM
Mabuse, Jan. See:
    GOSSART, JAN
Mac. See:
    MACMANUS, SEUMAS
    PHILLIPS, MAURICE
        JACK
Mac, Little. See:
    McCLELLAN, GEORGE
        BRINTON
Mac the Unready. See:
    McCLELLAN, GEORGE

638

BRINTON
Mac the Young Napoleon,
Little. See:
McCLELLAN, GEORGE
BRINTON
MacAdam, Eve. See:
LESLIE, CECILIE
MACADAM, JOHN LOUDON
(1756-1836) [Scottish
engineer; inventor of
system for paving
roads]
The King of Roads (Rhodes)
McADOO, WILLIAM GIBBS
(1863-1941) [American
politician; Senator from
California]
Bill the Builder
The Crown Prince
Daddy Longlegs
The Dancing Fool
The World War Croesus
MacAedhagan, Eamon. See:
EGAN, EDWARD
WELSTEAD
McAlister, Frank A., joint
pseud. of FRANK DAVIS
HALSEY (1890-1941) and
COLEMAN McALISTER
(-) [American
playwrights]
McALLISTER, ALISTER (1877-)
[English author and
playwright]
Lynn Brock
Anthony Wharton
Macalpine. See:
KENNETH I
MACALPINE, MARGARET
HESKETH MURRAY
(1907-) [Scottish
educator and author]
Ann Carmichael
MacAoidh. See:
MACKIE, ALBERT
DAVID
McArone. See:
ARNOLD, GEORGE
MacARTHUR, DOUGLAS
(1880-1964) [American
general officer]
The Beau Brummel of the Army

The Buck Private's Gary
Cooper
The D'Artagnan of the A.E.F.
The Disraeli of the Chiefs
of Staff
Dugout Doug
The Magnificent
The Napoleon of Luzon
McArthur, John. See:
WISE, ARTHUR
MACAULAY, FANNIE
CALDWELL (1863-1941)
[American author]
Frances Little
McBain, Ed. See:
HUNTER, EVAN
McBRIDE, JOHN JOSEPH
(1898-) [English author]
Jack McBride
McBRIDE, PETER (1854-)
[British physician and
author]
E.C.M.
McBRIDE, ROBERT MEDILL
(1879-) [American
author]
Robert Medill
McBROOM, MARDEN (1914-)
[American motion picture
actor]
David Bruce
McBROOM, R. CURTIS
(1910-) [American
attorney and author]
Nathaniel Dring
McBURNEY, ALBERT
(1909-) [American jazz
musician (leader, guitar)]
The King of the Electric
Guitar
Alvino Rey
MACCABAEUS, JUDAS (died
160 B.C.) [Second of
the five sons of MATTHIAS
THE HASMONEAN]
The Hammer
Maccabaeus, The Swedish. See:
GUSTAVUS II
McCabe, Cameron. See:
BORNEMAN, ERNEST
McCABE, CHARLES CARDWELL
(1836-1906) [American

639

Methodist Episcopalian
minister and chaplain]
The Singing Bishop
The Singing Chaplain
The Singing Secretary
McCABE, JAMES DABNEY
(1842-83) [American author]
Edwin Winslow Martin
MacCall [McCall]. See also:
McCaull
MacCAll, Libby. See:
MACHOL, LIBBY
McCall, Sidney. See:
FENELLOSA, MARY
McNEIL
McCALL, VIRGINIA NIELSEN
(1909-) [American
author]
Virginia Nielsen
McCALLUM, COLIN WHITTON
[1852-1945) [Cockney
stage comedian]
Charles Coburn
McCann, Arthur. See:
CAMPBELL, JOHN
WOOD
McCann, Coolidge. See:
FAWCETT, FRANK
DUBREZ
McCARL, JOHN RAYMOND
(1879-1940) [American
politician; Comptroller
General of the United
States]
The Watchdog of the
Treasury
McCARTHY, JOSEPH VINCENT
(1887-) [American
baseball manager]
Joe McCarthy
Marse Joe
McCARTHY, SHAUN (1928-)
[British journalist,
teacher and author]
Theo Callas
Desmond Cory
McCARTNEY, PAUL. See:
Beatles, The
Nurk Twins, The
McCARTY, DANIEL THOMAS,
JR. (1912-) [American
politician, citrus grower,

cattleman and Governor
of Florida]
Dan McCarty
Macauley of the South, The.
See: JONES, CHARLES
COLCOCK
McCAULEY, ELFRIEDA BAB-
NICK (1915-) [American
editor and author]
Anne W. House
McCAULEY, MARY LUDWIG
HAYS (1744-1823)
[American Revolutionary
War heroine]
Captain Molly
Molly Pitcher
McCaull. See also:
McCALL
McCall
McCaull, M.E. See:
BOHLMAN, EDNA
McCAULL
McCLARY, JANE
STEVENSON (1919-)
[American journalist and
author]
Jane McIlvaine
McCLELLAN, GEORGE
BRINTON (1826-85)
[American Civil War Union
general officer]
The general of the Mackerel
Brigade
Little Corporal of Unsought
Fields
Little Mac
Little Mac the Young
Napoleon
Mac the Unready
Tardy George
McClelland, William. See:
STRONG, CHARLES
STANLEY
McCLINTIC, JAMES V.
(1878-) [American
politician; Congressman
from Texas]
Rivet McClintic
McCLINTOCK, MARSHALL
(1906-) [American book-
man and author]
Gregory Duncan

Mike McClintock
Douglas Marshall
William Starret
McCLOSKEY, ROBERT (1914-)
    [American artist,
    illustrator and author]
Balfour Dangerfield
McCLUNG, ALEXANDER
    (1855-) [American
    editor and orator]
The Black Knight of the
    South
McClure, Greg. See:
    EASTON, DALE
MACLURE, WILLIAM (1763-
    18??) [Scottish-American
    geologist]
The Father of American
    Geology
McCONNELL, JAMES
    DOUGLAS RUTHERFORD
    (1915-) [Irish educator
    and author]
Douglas Rutherford
McCONNELL, JOHN PRESTON
    (18??-1941) [American
    educator and philosopher]
Eci
The Serving Knight
McCord, Whip. See:
    NORWOOD, VICTOR
        GEORGE CHARLES
McCormick, Brooks. See:
    ADAMS, WILLIAM
        TAYLOR
McCormick, F.J. See:
    JUDGE, PETER
McCORMICK, WILFRED
    (1903-) [American
    author]
Rand Allison
Lon Dunlap
McCOWEN, ALEXANDER
    DUNCAN (1925-) [British
    actor]
Alec McCowen
McCOY,CAPTAIN WILLIAM
    (- 1948) [American
    bootlegger and rum runner]
The Founder of Rum Row
The King of Rum Runners
The Real McCoy

McCOY, IOLA FULLER
    (fl. 1964) [American
    librarian, educator and
    author]
Iola Fuller
McCoy, Kid. See:
    SELBY, NORMAN
McCoy, The Real. See:
    McCOY, CAPTAIN
        WILLIAM
    SELBY, NORMAN
McCRARY, EUGENIA LINCOLN
    FALKENBURG (1919-)
    [American radio and
    television commentator
    and producer]
Jinx Falkenburg
McCready, Jack. See:
    POWELL, TALMAGE
McCREADY, WARREN
    THOMAS (1915-)
    [American educator and
    author]
Machiavelli
McCRINDLE, MRS. RONALD
    (c.1894-) [Anglo-
    American novelist]
Susan Ertz
McCUE, LILLIAN BUENO
    (1902-) [American edu-
    cator and author]
Lillian de la Torre
Lillian de la Torre-Bueno
McCUE, WILLIAM (1874-1913)
    [American civic leader
    in New Orleans]
Captain Billy
McCULLERS, LULA CARSON
    (1917-67) [American
    author]
Carson McCullers
McCULLEY, JOHNSTON
    (1883-) [American
    author]
Raley Brien
George Drayne
Frederic Phelps
Rowiena Raley
Harrington Strong
McCUTCHAN, JOHN WILSON
    (1909-) [American
    educator and author]

641

Peter Locke
McCUTCHEON, BEN
FREDERICK (1875-
1934) [American
author]
Benjamin Brace
McCUTCHEON GEORGE
BARR (1866-1928)
[American novelist]
Richard Greaves
McDANIEL, DAVID EDWARD
(1939-) [American
disc jockey, television
actor, photographer
and author]
Ted Johnstone
McDANIEL, IRA C. (1877-
1954) [American farmer
and stock breeder]
Red Rat
MacDermott the Great. See:
FARRELL, GILBERT
HASTINGS
MacDiarmid, Hugh. See:
GRIEVE, CHRISTOPHER
MURRAY
MacDonald, Aeneas. See:
THOMSON, GEORGE
MALCOLM
MacDonald, Anson. See:
HEINLEIN, ROBERT
ANSON
MacDonald, Betty. See:
HESKETT, ANNE
ELIZABETH
CAMPBELL BARD
McDONALD, ERWIN
LAWRENCE (1907-)
[American Baptist
minister, editor and
author]
Clabe Hankins
MacDonald, Golden. See:
BROWN, MARGARET
WISE
MacDonald Harris. See:
HEINEY, DONALD
WILLIAM
Macdonald, John. See:
MILLAR, KENNETH
Macdonald, John Ross. See:
MILLAR, KENNETH

McDONALD, JOSEPH
EWING (1819-91)
[Indiana lawyer and
politician]
Old Saddlebags
MACDONALD, LUCY MAUDE
MONTGOMERY (1874-
1942) [Canadian author]
L.M. Montgomery
MacDonald, Marcia. See:
HILL, GRACE
LIVINGSTON
McDonald, Marie. See:
FRYE, MARIE
MACDONALD, PHILIP (189?-)
[English novelist and
writer of detective
stories]
Oliver Fleming
Anthony Lawless
Martin Porlock
Macdonald, Ross. See:
MILLAR, KENNETH
MACDONALD, SIR JOHN
ALEXANDER (1815-91)
[First Premier of the
Dominion of Canada]
Old Tomorrow
MACDONELL, ARCHIBALD
GORDON (1895-1941)
[Scottish novelist]
John Cameron
Neil Gordon
MACDONNELL, ALASTAIR
RUADH (c.1725-61)
[Scottish chieftain and
spy]
Pickle the Spy
MACDONNELL, JAMES ED-
MOND (1917-)
[Australian journalist and
author]
James MacNell
MACDONNELL, JAMES
FRANCIS CARLIN
(1881-) [American poet]
Francis Carlin
McDONNELL, VIRGINIA
BLEECKER (1917-)
[American journalist,
columnist and author]
Jean Kirby

Jinny McDonnell
McDOUGAL, DAVID STOCKTON (1809-82) [American naval officer]
The American Devil
MacDougall, Robertson. See: MAIR, GEORGE BROWN
McDow, Gerald. See: SCORTIA, THOMAS NICHOLAS
McDOWALL, RODERICK ANDREW (1928-) [British actor]
Roddy McDowall
McDOWELL, JOSEPH (1758-99) [American army officer and politician; Congressman from North Carolina]
Pleasant Gardens Joe
Quaker Meadows Joe
MACDOWELL, KATHERINE SHERWOOD BONNER (1849-83) [American novelist and short story writer]
Sherwood Bonner
McDuff, Brother Jack. See: McDUFFY, EUGENE
McDuffie, The Sage of. See: WATSON, THOMAS EDWARD
McDUFFY, EUGENE (1926-) [American jazz musician (organ, composer, bass, piano)]
Brother Jack McDuff
Macedon, Philip of. See: PHILIP II
Macedonia, The Madman of. See: ALEXANDER III
Macedonian, Basil the. See: BASIL I
Macedonian, The. See: BASIL I
McELFRESH, ELIZABETH ADELINE (1918-) [American journalist and writer]
John Cleveland
Jane Scott
Elizabeth Wesley
McELHENEY, JANE (1836-74)

[American actress and author]
Ada Clare
The Queen of Bohemia
McENERY, DAVID (1914-) [American country music singer]
Red River Dave
McEVOY, ARTHUR (1901-57) [British music-hall comedian]
Frank Randle
McEVOY, HARRY KIRBY (1910-) [American author]
Kirby Mack
McEVOY, MARJORIE HARTE (fl. 1963) [British author]
Marjorie Harte
MACFALL, CHAMBERS HALDANE COOKE (1860-1928) [British novelist and writer of books on art]
Hal Dane
McFALL, FRANCES ELIZABETH CLARK (1862-1943) [English-Irish novelist]
Sarah Grand
McFARLAND, DANIEL (1825-1900) [American politician, active in Ohio]
Black Dan
MacFarlane, Kenneth. See: WALKER, KENNETH MACFARLANE
McFARLANE, WILLIAM DODDRIDGE (1894-) [American politician; Congressman from Texas]
Anti-McFarlane
MACFAYDEN, DUGALD (1867-) [British preacher and author]
M.A.C.
MacFee, Maxwell. See: RENNIE, JAMES ALAN
"M'Fingal," The Celebrated Author of. See: TRUMBULL, JOHN
MacGAHAN, JANUARIUS

ALOYSIUS (1844-78)
[American war correspondent]
The Liberator
McGAW, NAOMI BLANCHE
THOBURN (1920-)
[British businesswoman and author]
Jane Hervey
McGee, Fibber. See:
JORDAN, JAMES
EDWARD
McGee, Molly. See:
JORDAN, MARIAN
DRISCOLL
McGHEE, WALTER
(1915-) [American jazz
musician (singer, guitar)]
Brownie McGhee
McGILLICUDDY, CORNELIUS
(1862-1956) [American
professional baseball
manager]
Connie Mack
MACGILLIVRAY, JAMES
PITTENDRIGH (1856-1938)
[Scottish sculptor and
author]
P.M.
Peter Maitland
McGINNIS, JAMES
ANTHONY (1847-1906)
[American circus
impresario]
James A. Bailey
McGinnis, K.K. See:
PAGE, GROVER, JR.
McGINNITY, JOSEPH JEROME
(1871-1929) [American
professional baseball
player]
Iron Man
McGIVERN, MAUREEN DALY
(1921-) [Irish-
American journalist,
editor and writer]
Maureen Daly
McGLINCHY, F.D. (1904-)
[British stage and
motion picture actress]
Fabia Drake
McGlinn, Dwight. See:
BRANNON, WILLIAM T.

McGLOIN, JOSEPH
THADDEUS (1917-)
[American Catholic
churchman and author]
Thaddeus O'Finn
McGONEGAL, AL (1900-)
[American motion
picture actor]
Allen Jenkins
McGOWEN, THOMAS (1927-)
[American advertising
manager and author]
Tom McGowen
McGrant, Terence. See:
PECK, GEORGE
WILBUR
McGregor. See:
HURLEY, DORAN
MACGREGOR, IRVINE T.
(1915-) [Scottish
composer, singer and
guitarist]
Scotty MacGregor
MACGREGOR, JAMES
MURDOCH (1925-)
[Scottish author]
J.T. McIntosh
MACGREGOR, JOHN (1848-)
[Scottish military officer
and author]
Ralph
MACGREGOR, JOHN CHALMERS
(1903-) [American jazz
musician (piano)]
Chummy MacGregor
MACGREGOR, MARY ESTHER
MILLER (1876-)
[Canadian author]
Marion Keith
MACGREGOR, ROBERT
(1671-1734) [Scottish
freebooter]
Campbell
Red Robert (Rob Roy)
McGROARTY, JOHN STEVEN
(1862-1944) [American
poet]
The Poet Laureate of
California
The Sage of the Verduga Hills
MacGrom, John. See:
McMASTER, GUY
HUMPHRIES

McGuire, Mickey. See:
YULE, JOE, JR.
Machaquito. See:
GÓNZALEZ, RAFAEL
McHARGUE, JAMES EUGENE
(1907-) [American jazz
musician (clarinet)]
Rosy McHargue
McHenry, Colonel Oram R.
See: ROLFE, MARO O.
McHENRY, JAMES (1775-1845)
[Irish-American poet
and novelist]
Solomon Secondsight
McHenry, The Hero of Fort.
See: ARMISTEAD,
GEORGE
Machiavelli. See:
McCREADY, WARREN
THOMAS
Machiavellian Belshazzar, The.
See: VAN BUREN,
MARTIN
MACHIN-GOODALL, DAPHNE
(fl. 1955) [English author
and horse and dog fancier]
Daphne Machin Goodall
Machine Gun. See:
KELLY, GEORGE
Machine, The Father of the
Sewing. See:
HOWE, ELIAS
Machine, The Logic-chopping.
See: MILL, JOHN
STUART
Machito. See:
GRILLO, FRANK
MACHLIN, MILTON ROBERT
(1924-) [American
author]
William Jason
McLean Roberts
MACHOL, LIBBY (1916-)
[American educator and
author]
Libby MacCall
McHugh, Hugh. See:
HOBART, GEORGE
VERE
McHUGH, JAMES FRANCIS
(1895-) [American
composer]

Jimmy McHugh
McHugh, Stuart. See:
ROWLAND, DONALD
SYDNEY
Macie, James Lewis (Louis).
See: SMITHSON, JAMES
McIlvaine, Jane. See:
McCLARY, JANE
STEVENSON
McINERNY, RALPH (1929-)
[American educator and
author]
Harry Austin
Ernan Mackey
McIntosh, J.T. See:
MACGREGOR, JAMES
MURDOCH
McIntosh, Louis. See:
JOHNSON, CHRISTOPHER
McINTOSH, MARIA JANE
(1803-78) [American
author]
Aunt Kitty
MACINTYRE, DR. JOHN
(1869-1947)
[Scottish playwright]
John Brandane
McINTYRE, OSCAR ODD
(1884-1938) [American
newspaper columnist
and author]
The First Citizen of New
York
O.O. McIntyre
Odd McIntyre
MacIre, Esor B. See:
AMBROSE, ERIC
Mack, Cecil. See:
McPHERSON, RICHARD C.
MACK, CHARLES. See:
Two Black Crows
Mack, Connie. See:
McGILLICUDDY,
CORNELIUS
Mack, Evalina. See:
McNAMARA, LENA
BROOKE
Mack Fite. See:
SCHNECK, STEPHEN
Mack, Kirby. See:
McEVOY, HARRY KIRBY
Mack, Marjorie. See:

DIXON, MARJORIE MACK
Mack, Moran and. See:
Two Black Crows
Mack, Noreen. See:
O'FLYNN, HONORIA
Mack, Ted. See:
MAGUINESS, WILLIAM
EDWARD
McKAHAN, RUFUS ALAN
(1892-1950) [American
motion picture actor]
Alan Hale
McKAY, ELEANOR GOUGH
(1915-59) [American
Negro blues singer]
Lady Day
Billie Holiday
McKay, Kelvin. See:
STRONG, CHARLES
STANLEY
MACKAY, LEWIS HUGH
(fl. mid-20th cent.)
[English army officer
and author]
Hugh Matheson
MACKAY, MARY (1855-1924)
[English novelist]
Marie Corelli
Minnie Mackay
MACKAY, ROBERT (1714-78)
[Irish poet]
Rob Donn
MACKAYE, JAMES MORRISON
STEELE (1842-94)
[American dramatist]
Steele MacKaye
Mackaye, Loring
Julian David
Jules Loring, joint
pseuds. of DAVID
LORING MACKAYE
(1890-) and his wife
JULIA JOSEPHINE
GUNTHER MACKAYE
(1892-) [American
librarians and authors]
McKEAG, ERNEST LIONEL
(1896-) [British
journalist and author]
Jacque Braza
Griff
Mark Grimshaw

Pat Haynes
John King
Ramón Lacroix
René Laroche
Jack Maxwell
Eileen McKeay
Roland Vane
McKeay, Eileen. See:
McKEAG, ERNEST
LIONEL
McKECHNIE, FLORENCE
(1901-) [American
stage and motion
picture actress]
Florence Eldridge
McKeen, Captain. See:
ST. JOHN, PERCY
BOLLINGBROKE
McKee's Grandfather, Baby.
See: HARRISON,
BENJAMIN
McKEEVER, EDWARD CLARK
(1910-) [American
football coach]
Ed McKeever
McKELWAY, ST. CLAIR
(1905-) [American
journalist, correspondent
and author]
J. De P. Hall
McKenna, Evelyn. See:
JOSCELYN, ARCHIE L.
MACKENZIE, CHARLES
(1805-77) [English actor]
Henry Compton
Mackenzie, Dr. Willard. See:
STRATEMEYER,
EDWARD L.
MACKENZIE, HENRY
(1745-1831) [Scottish
novelist]
The Addison of the North
The Northern Addison
MACKENZIE, KENNETH
(1779-1861) [Scottish-
American fur trader]
Emperor Mackenzie
The Emperor of the West
The King of the Missouri
McKENZIE, NAN (1913-)
[British author]
Nan Fairbrother

MACKENZIE, SIR GEORGE
(1636-91) [Scottish lawyer
and miscellaneous writer]
Bloody Mackenzie
McKENZIE, WILLIAM (1899-
1948) [American jazz
musician (leader,
singer, kazoo)]
Red McKenzie
Mackerel Brigade, The General
of the. See:
McCLELLAN, GEORGE
BRINTON
Mackey, Ernan. See:
McINERNY, RALPH
MACKIE, ALBERT DAVID
(1904-) [Scottish
journalist and author]
MacAoidh
MacNib
The Walrus
McKILLOP, NORMAN (1892-)
[Scottish engineer,
editor and author]
Toran Beg
McKIM, ANN (1912-)
[American motion picture
actress]
Ann Dvorak
MACKINLAY, LEILA
ANTOINETTE STERLING
(1910-) [British critic
and author]
Brenda Grey
McKINLEY, CARLYLE (1847-
1904) [American poet,
editor and essayist]
Carl McKinley
McKINLEY, CHARLES ROBERT
(1941-) [American
tennis player]
Chuck McKinley
McKINLEY, WILLIAM
(1843-1901) [Twenty-fifth
President of the United
States]
The Idol of Ohio
The Napoleon of Protection
Prosperity's Advance Agent
The Stocking-foot Orator
McKINNIES, HENRY H. (1932-)
[American radio and motion

picture actor]
Jeffrey Hunter
MACKINNON, CHARLES ROY
(1924-) [Scottish book-
man and author]
F. Brown
Vivian Donald
Hilary Rose
Charles Stuart
Iain Torr
MACKINTOSH, ELIZABETH (-
1952) [English novelist and
playwright]
Gordon Daviot
Josephine Tey
Maclagan, Bridget. See:
BORDEN, MARY
McLAIN, DENNIS DALE
(1944-) [American
professional baseball
player]
Denny McLain
MacLaine, Shirley. See:
BEATY, SHIRLEY
MACLEAN
McLandress, Herschel. See:
GALBRAITH, JOHN
KENNETH
MACLANE, MARY (1881-1929)
[Canadian author]
The Butte Bashkirtseff
McLAREN, DANIEL (1823-1900)
[American circus per-
former and entrepreneur]
Dan Rice
MacLaren, Gordon   See:
PATTEN, WILLIAM
GILBERT
Maclaren, Ian. See:
WATSON, JOHN
MacLaren, James. See:
GRIEVE, CHRISTOPHER
MURRAY
McLAUGHLIN, JAMES FAIRFAX
(1839-1903) [American
lawyer and author]
Pasquino
MacLAVERTY, EDMUND
(1882-c.1951) [British
stage and motion picture
actor]
Edmund Breon

McLEAN, KATHRYN
ANDERSON (1909-66)
[American author]
Kathryn Forbes
McLean Roberts. See:
MACHLIN, MILTON
ROBERT
McLean, Sally Pratt. See:
GREENE, SARAH
PRATT McLEAN
MACLEHOSE, AGNES
CRAIG (1759-1841)
[Friend and correspondent
of Robert Burns]
Clarinda
McLELLAN, CHARLES MORTON
STEWART (1865-1916)
[American playwright]
Hugh Morton
McLELLAN, ISAAC (1806-99)
[American poet]
The Poet Sportsman
MacLENNAN, HUGH (1870-1950)
[Scotch entertainer, singer
and composer]
Sir Harry Lauder
MACLEOD, CHARLOTTE
MATILDA HUGHES
(1922-) [Canadian
journalist, author and
painter]
Matilda Hughes
Macleod, Fiona. See:
SHARP, WILLIAM
MACLEOD, JEAN SUTHERLAND
(1908-) [Scottish
author]
Catherine Airlie
McLeod, Margaret Vail. See:
HOLLOWAY, TERESA
BRAGUNIER
MacLeod, Robert. See:
KNOX, WILLIAM
McLowery, Frank. See:
KEEVIL, HENRY JOHN
MACMAHON, PAUL (1924-)
[American dancer and
motion picture actor]
Paul Gilbert
McMANUS, GEORGE (1884-
1954) [American car-
toonist]

Jiggs McManus
MACMANUS, SEUMAS (1869-
[Irish writer and poet]
Mac
McMASTER, GUY HUMPHRIES
(1829-87) [American jurist,
poet and historian]
John MacGrom
McMATH, SIDNEY SANDERS
(1912-) [American
lawyer and politician;
Governor of Arkansas]
Sid McMath
McMATH, VIRGINIA
KATHERINE (1911-)
[American actress and
dancer]
Ginger Rogers
McMEEKAN, DAVID (1914-)
[American actor]
David Wayne
McMeekin, Clark, joint pseud.
of DOROTHY PARK CLARK
(1899-) and ISABEL
McLENNAN McMEEKIN
(1895-) [American
authors]
McMILLIN, BENTON (1845-1933)
[American politician;
Governor of Tennessee]
The Democratic War Horse
The Democratic War Horse
of Tennessee
The Grandest Roman of Them
All
The Noblest Roman of Them
All
McMINN, URSULA (1906-)
[British stage and motion
picture actress]
Ursula Jeans
MACMULLEN, CHARLES KIRK-
PATRICK (1889-) [Irish
playwright and author]
C.K. Munro
McNab, Frances. See:
FRASER, AGNES MAUDE
McNAIR, DONALD ERIE (1910-)
[American professional
baseball player]
Rabbit
McNALLY, HORACE (c. 1916-)

[American motion picture actor]
Stephen McNally
McNAMARA, LENA BROOKE (1891-) [American painter, illustrator and author]
Evalina Mack
McNARY, CHARLES LINZA (1874-1944) [American attorney and politician; Congressman from Oregon]
Wise Charley
McNaughton, Gus. See: HOWARD, AUGUSTUS
MacNeil, Neil. See: BALLARD, WILLIS TODHUNTER
McNEILE, HERMAN CYRIL (1888-1937) [English author]
Sapper
McNEILL, DONALD THOMAS (1907-) [American radio broadcaster]
Don McNeill
McNEILLY, MILDRED MASTERSON (1910-) [American author]
James Dewey
Glenn Kelly
MacNell, James. See: MACDONNELL, JAMES EDMOND
McNellis, Maggi. See: ROCHE, MARGARET ELEANOR
MacNib. See: MACKIE, ALBERT DAVID
McNISH, GEORGE (c.1660-1722) [Anglo-American Presbyterian clergyman]
The Father of Presbyterianism in the State of New York
McNULTY, DOROTHY (1912-) [American vaudevillian and motion picture actress]
Penny Singleton
McNUTT, GEORGE WASHINGTON MORRISON (1843-)

[Midget exhibited by PHINEAS TAYLOR BARNUM]
Commodore Nutt
McNUTT, PAUL VORIES (1891-1955) [American lawyer and politician; governor of Indiana]
Boob McNutt
MACON, NATHANIEL (1758-1837) [American politician; Senator from North Carolina]
The Father of the House
McPhail, A Midwestern Larry. See: VEECK, WILLIAM LOUIS, JR.
McPHAIL, LELAND STANFORD (1890-) [American businessman, army officer and baseball club president]
Larry McPhail
Loud Larry McPhail
McPHERSON, AIMEE SEMPLE (1890-1944) [Canadian evangelist; founder of Four Square Gospel]
Sister Aimee
The World's Most Pulchritudinous Evangelist
McPHERSON, RICHARD C. (1883-1944) [American composer]
Cecil Mack
MACPHERSON, THOMAS GEORGE (1915-) [Anglo-American editor and author]
Tom Parsons
McQUADE, ANN AIKMAN (1928-) [American journalist and author]
Ann Aikman
McQUEEN, MILDRED HARK (1908-) [American editor and author]
Mildred Hark
McQUEEN, TERENCE STEPHEN (1930?-) [American actor]
Steve McQueen

McQuill, Thursty. See:
BRUCE, WALLACE
MACRAE, DONALD G. (1921-)
[Scottish sociologist and
author]
Clive Campbell
McRae, Lindsay. See:
SOWERBY, ARTHUR
LINDSAY McRAE
MacRae, Travis. See:
FEAGLES, ANITA MACRAE
McSHANN, JAY (1909-)
[American jazz musician
(leader, piano)]
Hootie McShann
McSPADDEN, JOSEPH WALKER
(1874-) [American
author]
Joseph Walker
Macumber, Mari. See:
SANDOZ, MARI SUZETTE
McVeigh, Sue. See:
NEARING, ELIZABETH
CUSTER
MacVICAR, MARTHA (1925-)
[American motion picture
actress]
Martha Vickers
McWILLIAMS, JULIA
(1912-) [American author,
food expert and television
personality]
Julia Child
Mad. See:
SHELLEY, PERCY
BYSSHE
SWINBURNE, ALGERNON
CHARLES
Mad Anne. See:
BAILEY, ANNE HENNIS
TROTTER
Mad Anthony. See:
WAYNE, ANTHONY
Mad Cavalier, The. See:
PRINCE RUPERT
Mad Dog of Gangland, The. See:
COLL, VINCENT
Mad, Howlin'. See:
SMITH, HOLLAND
McTYEIRE
Mad Jack. See:
BYRON, CAPTAIN JOHN

PERCIVAL, JOHN
Mad Poet of Broadway, The.
See: CLARKE,
McDONALD
Mad Poet of California, The.
See: KENDALL, W.S.
Mad Poet of New York, The.
See: CLARKE,
McDONALD
Mad Poet, The. See:
CLARKE, MacDONALD
LEE, NATHANIEL
Mad Priest, The. See:
BALL, JOHN
Mad Rudi. See:
HESS, RUDOLF
Mad Tom. See:
SHERMAN, WILLIAM
TECUMSEH
Madaline. See also:
Madeleine
Madeline
Madaline Bridges. See:
DE VERE, MARY AINGE
Madame. See:
ALEXANDER, BEATRICE
CURIE, MARIE
SKLODOWSKA
DuBARRY, MARIE JEANNE
GOMARD DE VAUBER-
NIER, COMTESSE
KNIGHT, SARAH KEMBLE
POMPADOUR, MARQUISE
DE, JEANNE
ANTOINETTE POISSON,
MME. LENORMAND
D'ÉTOILES
RÉCAMIER, JEANNE
FRANÇOISE JULIE
ADÉLAÏDE BERNARD
RUBINSTEIN, HELENA
TUSSAUD, MARIE
GROSHOLTZ
Madame D'Arblay. See:
BURNEY, FRANCES
Madame de Souza. See:
FILLEUL, ADÉLAÏDE
MARIE ÉMILE
Madame de Staël. See:
STAËL-HOLSTEIN, ANNE
LOUISE GERMAINE,
BARONNE DE

Madame E. Farra. See:
FAWCETT, FRANK
DUBREZ
Madame Guyon. See:
MOTTE-GUYON, JEANNE
MARIE BOUVIER DE
LA
Madame Otto Goldschmidt. See:
LIND, JOHANNA MARIA
Madame Roland. See:
ROLAND DE LA
PLATIÈRE, JEANNE
MANON PHILIPON
Madame Vestris. See:
BARTOLOZZI, LUCIA
ELIZABETH
Madcap Maggie. See:
WHITING, MARGARET
ELEANORE
Madcap Maxie. See:
BAER, MAXIMILIAN
ADELBERT
MADDEN, OWEN (1892-1965)
[American gangster]
Owney Madden
Owney the Killer
Madden, Warren. See:
CAMERON, KENNETH
NEILL
Maddern, Little Minnie. See:
DAVEY, MARIE
AUGUSTA
Maddock, Larry. See:
JARDINE, JACK
Madeleine. See also:
Madaline
Madeline
Madeleine L'Engle. See:
FRANKLIN, MADELEINE
Madeleine Paltenghi. See:
ANDERSON, MADELEINE
PALTENGHI
Madeleine Robinson. See:
SVOBODA, MADELEINE
Madeline. See also:
Madaline
Madeleine
Madeline Leslie, Mrs. See:
BAKER, HARRIETTE
NEWALL WOODS
Mademoiselle Desoeillets.
See: FAVIOT, ALIX

Mademoiselle George. See:
WEIMAR, MARGUÉRITE
JOSÉPHINE
Mademoiselle, La Grande. See:
MONTPENSIER, ANNE
MARIE LOUISE
D'ORLÉANS, DUCHESSE
DE
Madge Kendal. See:
GRIMSON, MARGARET
BRUNTON
Madi. See:
CHRISTIANS, MARGUERITA
MARIA
MADISON, DOROTHY PAYNE
TODD (1772-1849) [Wife
of President JAMES
MADISON]
Dolly Madison
The Dowager
The Nation's Hostess
Quaker Dolly
Queen Dolly
The Queen Dowager
Madison, Frank. See:
HUTCHINS, FRANCIS
GILMAN
Madison, Guy. See:
MOSELEY, ROBERT
Madison, Hank. See:
ROWLAND, DONALD
SYDNEY
MADISON, JAMES (1751-1836)
[Fourth President of the
United States]
The Father of the Constitution
The Sage of Montpelier
MADISON, JAMES. See also:
Publius
Madison, Jane. See:
HORNE, HUGH ROBERT
MADISON, LOUIS (1899-1948)
[American jazz musician
(cornet)]
Kid Shots
Madison, Nat. See:
MADISON, NATHANIEL
JOSEPH
MOSCOVITCH, NOEL
MADISON, NATHANIEL
JOSEPH (1896-)
[American composer]

Nat Madison
Madison, Noel. See:
    MOSCOVITCH, NOEL
Madison Tensas, M.D. See:
    LEWIS, HENRY CLAY
MADLEE, DOROTHY HAYNES
    (1917-) [American
    journalist and author]
    Anna Haynes
    Wade Rogers
Madman of Macedonia, The.
    See: ALEXANDER III
Madman of the North, The.
    See: CHARLES XII
Madman, The. See:
    SEBASTIAN
Madman, The Brilliant. See:
    CHARLES XII
Madman, The Divine. See:
    BUONARROTI,
    MICHELANGELO
Madonna of Hall-Moody, The.
    See: HALL, MUSA L.
Madonna Painter, The Modern.
    See: CARRIÈRE, EUGÈNE
Mady. See:
    CHRISTIANS, MARGUERITA
    MARIA
Mae. See:
    MARSH, MARY WARNE
    MAY
    May
Mae Murray. See:
    KOENIG, MARIE
    ADRIENNE
Maend, Evald. See:
    MAND, EWALD
Maeonian Swan, The. See:
    HOMER
Maera. See:
    GARCÍA, MANUEL
Maestro, Il. See:
    NUVOLARI, TAZIO
Maestro, The Old. See:
    ANZELEVITZ,
    BERNARD
Maffy. See:
    FALAY, AHMED
    MUVAFFAX
Magazine Editors, The Dean
    of American. See:
    ALDEN, HENRY MILLS

Magee, Speed. See:
    JOHNSON, HAROLD
MAGEE, WILLIAM KIRK-
    PATRICK (1868-) [Irish
    essayist and poet]
    John Eglinton
Maggi McNellis. See:
    ROCHE, MARGARET
    ELEANOR
Maggie. See:
    MITCHELL, MARGARET
    JULIA
    SMITH, MARGARET
Maggie, Madcap. See:
    WHITING, MARGARET
    ELEANORE
Maggie Teyte. See:
    TATE, MARGARET
Magic Fingers of Radio, The.
    See: DUCHIN, EDWIN
    FRANK
Magic, The Father of Modern.
    See: ROBERT-HOUDIN,
    JEAN EUGÈNE
Magician of the North, The.
    See: HAMANN, JOHANN
    GEORG
    SCOTT, SIR WALTER
Magician of the North, The Great.
    See: SCOTT, SIR
    WALTER
Magician, Simon the. See:
    SIMON MAGUS
Magician, The. See:
    SCOTT, SIR WALTER
Magician, The Child Wonder.
    See: DUNNINGER,
    JOSEPH
Magician, The Great. See:
    SCOTT, SIR WALTER
Magician, The Little. See:
    VAN BUREN, MARTIN
Magicians, The Dean of
    American. See:
    KELLAR, HARRY
MAGIDSON, HERBERT (1906-)
    [American composer]
    Herb Magidson
Magill, Marcus, joint pseud.
    of JOANNA ELDER GILES
    (-) and BRIAN HILL
    (1896-) [English authors of

detective stories]
MAGINN, WILLIAM (1793-
1842) [Irish author]
The Modern Rabelais
Magister Islebius. See:
SNEIDER (SCHNITTER),
JOHANNES
Magister Militum, Patricius
and. See:
THEODORIC
Magister Sententiarum
(Master of Sentences).
See: LOMBARD, PETER
MAGLIE, SALVATORE ANTHONY
(1917-) [American pro-
fessional baseball
player]
Sal Maglie
MAGNANI, ANNA (1908-)
[Italian actress]
Nannerella
Magnanimous, The. See:
ALFONSO V
JOHN FREDERICK I
PHILIP OF HESSE
Magnesia Phillips, Milk of.
See: PHILLIPS, ALFRED
NOROTON, JR.
Magnetic Man. See:
BLAINE, JAMES
GILLESPIE
Magnetic Statesman. See:
BLAINE, JAMES
GILLESPIE
Magnificent, Lorenzo the. See:
MEDICI, LORENZO DE'
Magnificent, The. See:
EDMUND (EADMUND) I
MacARTHUR, DOUGLAS
SULAIMAN I or II
Magno, El (The Great). See:
FERDINAND I
MAGNUS. See:
ALBERTUS MAGNUS,
SAINT, COUNT OF
BOLLSTÄDT
MAGNUS I (died 1047) [King of
Norway and Denmark]
The Good
MAGNUS I (1240-90) [King of
Sweden]
Barn Lock (Magnus Ladolas]

MAGNUS II (1035-69) [King of
Norway]
Haraldsson
MAGNUS II (1316-74) [King of
Sweden (as MAGNUS II)
and of Norway (as MAGNUS
VII)
Eriksson
Smek
MAGNUS III (1073-1103)
[King of Norway]
The Barefoot
MAGNUS IV (1115?-39)
[King of Norway]
The Blind
MAGNUS V (1156-84) [King of
Norway]
Erlingsson
MAGNUS VI (1238-80) [King of
Norway]
Reformer of the Laws
(Lagobøter)
MAGNUS-ALLCROFT, SIR
PHILIP (1906-) [British
government official and
author]
Philip Magnus
Magnus, Carolus. See:
CHARLEMAGNE
Magnus, Gerardus. See:
GROOTE (GROOT) (GROETE),
GERHARD
Magnus Ladolas (Barn Lock).
See: MAGNUS I
Magnus Merriweather. See:
TALBOT, CHARLES
REMINGTON
Magnus of the North, The. See:
HAMANN, JOHANN GEORG
MAGNÚSSON, GUDMUNDUR
(1873-1918) [Icelandic
novelist, playwright and
short story writer]
Jón Trausti
Magnusson, Olaf. See:
OLAF IV
MAGOUN, FREDERICK ALEXANDER
(1896-) [American educator
and author]
Amos Wright
MAGUILEVSKY, LEONIDE
(1899-) [Russian newsreel

653

producer; afterwards
motion picture director]
Leonide Moguy
MAGUINESS, WILLIAM EDWARD
(1904-) [American radio
and television producer and
master of ceremonies]
Ted Mack
MAGUIRE, ROBERT AUGUSTINE
JOSEPH (1898-) [Irish
author]
Michael Taaffe
MAGUS. See:
SIMON MAGUS
Mahatma. See:
GANDHI, MOHANDAS
KARAMCHAND
Mahatma Kane Jeeves. See:
DUKINFIELD, WILLIAM
CLAUDE
MANIDOL, ANANTA (1925-46)
[King of Thailand (Siam)]
Rama VIII
Mahlon A. Brown. See:
PECK, WILLIAM HENRY
MAHMUD OF GHAZNI (c. 971-
1030) [Sultan of Ghazni]
The Great
MAHON, CHARLES JAMES
PATRICK (1800-91)
[Irish politician and
adventurer]
The O'Gorman Mahon
MAHONE, WILLIAM (1826-
95) [American soldier-
hero]
The Hero of the Crater
MAHONEY, BESSIE (1847-96)
[English music-hall per-
former]
Bessie Bellwood
MAHONEY, ELIZABETH
(1911-) [American
author]
Thalia Mara
Mahoney, Jock. See:
O'MAHONEY, JACQUES
MAHONEY, JOHN THOMAS
(1905-) [American
journalist, editor and
author]
Tom Mahoney

MAHONY, FRANCIS SYLVESTER
(1804-66) [Irish humorist]
Father Prout
MAHR, HERMAN CARL
(1901-64) [American
composer]
Curley Mahr
Maia Rodman. See:
WOJCIECHOWSKA,
MAIA
Maid of Anjou, The Fair. See:
PLANTAGENET, LADY
EDITH
Maid of Bath, The. See:
LINLEY, ELIZA ANN
Maid of Galloway, The Fair.
See: MARGARET
Maid of Kent, The. See:
BARTON, ELIZABETH
Maid of Kent, The Fair. See:
JOAN
Maid of Llangollen. See:
BUTLER, LADY ELEANOR
PONSONBY, MISS SARAH
Maid of Norway, The Fair.
See: MARGARET
Maid of Orleans, The (La
Pucelle d'Orléans). See:
JOAN OF ARC, ST.
(JEANNE D'ARC)
Maid of Perth, The Fair. See:
GLOVER, CATHERINE
Maid, The. See:
JOAN OF ARC, ST.
(JEANNE D'ARC)
Maid, The Wondrous. See:
JOAN OF ARC, ST.
(JEANNE D'ARC)
Maiden, Malcolm The. See:
MALCOLM IV
Maiden, The. See:
MALCOLM IV
Maids. See:
Biddenden Maids, The
Mail Contractors, The Prince
of. See:
REESIDE, JAMES
Mail Order Catalog, The Father
of the. See:
FRANKLIN, BENJAMIN
Mailings, Malachi. See:
GALT, JOHN

MAILS, WALTER (1896-)
    [American professional
    baseball player and press
    agent]
  The Big Lip
  Duster
  The Cock o' the Walk of
    Baseball
  The Great Left-Handed
    Press Agent
  The Great Mails
  King of Kings Mails
Maimee. See also:
  Mamie
Maimee Thornton. See:
  JEFFREY-SMITH, MAY
    THORNTON
Maimon, Moses Ben. See:
  MAIMONIDES
MAIMONIDES (1135-1204) [Jewish
    scholar, philosopher
    and writer]
  The Great Eagle
  The Light of the West
  Moses Ben Maimon
  RaMBam (Second Moses)
Main, John. See:
  PARSONS, MRS. ELSIE
    WORTHINGTON CLEWS
Main, Marjorie. See:
  KREBS, MARY TOMLIN-
    SON
Main, The Moralist of the.
  See: CLEMENS, SAMUEL
    LANGHORNE
Mainbocher. See:
  BOCHER, MAIN
Maine, A Lady of. See:
  BARRELL, SARAH
    SAYWARD
Maine Law, The Father of the.
  See: DOW, NEAL
Maine, Man from. See:
  BLAINE, JAMES
    GILLESPIE
MAINPRIZE, DON (1930-)
    [American clergyman and
    author]
  Richard Rock
MAINTENON, MADAME DE
    (1635-1710) [French
    noblewoman]

La Belle Indienne
MAIORANA, VICTOR E.
    (1897-1964) [Italian com-
    poser, pianist and
    organist]
  Victor Lamont
MAIR. See:
  MAJOR (MAIR), JOHN
MAIR, GEORGE BROWN
    (1914-) [Scottish educator,
    surgeon and author]
  Robertson MacDougall
Mair, Margaret. See:
  CROMPTON, MARGARET
    NORAH MAIR
Maire O'Neill. See:
  ALLGOOD, MARIE
Maire Price. See:
  NIC SHIUBHLAIGH,
    MAIRE
Mairi. See also:
  Mari
  MARY
  Mary
Mairi O'Nair. See:
  EVANS, CONSTANCE MAY
Maisie Sharman. See:
  BOLTON, MAISIE
    SHARMAN
MAISON, MARGARET MARY
    BOWLES (1920-)
    [British author, journalist
    and educator]
  Margaret Clare
Mait Metsanurk. See:
  HUBEL, EDUARD
Maitland, James A. See:
  SMITH, FRANCIS SHUBAEL
MAITLAND, JOHN, DUKE OF
    LAUDERDALE. See:
  Cabal, The
MAITLAND OF LETHINGTON,
    WILLIAM (1528?-73)
    [Scottish statesman]
  Secretary Lethington
Maitland, Peter. See:
  MACGILLIVRAY, JAMES
    PITTENDRIGH
MAIZEL, CLARICE MATTHEWS
    (1919-) [British magistrate
    and author]
  C.L. Maizel

Leah Maizel
Majesty, Consort of Her Most
    Gracious. See:
    ALBERT
Major. See:
    BOWES, EDWARD
    HOUK, RALPH GEORGE
    NOAH, MORDECAI
    MANUEL
Major A. F. Grant. See:
    HARBAUGH, THOMAS
    CHALMERS
Major Andy Burton. See:
    RATHBONE, ST. GEORGE
    HENRY
MAJOR, CHARLES (1856-1913)
    [American novelist and
    lawyer]
    Edwin Caskoden
Major E. L. St. Vrain. See:
    MANNING, WILLIAM
    HENRY
Major C. W. Alcalaw. See:
    HARBAUGH, THOMAS
    CHALMERS
Major Goliah Gahagan. See:
    THACKERAY, WILLIAM
    MAKEPEACE
Major Henri Le Caron. See:
    BEACH, THOMAS
Major Henry B. Stoddard. See:
    INGRAHAM, COLONEL
    PRENTISS
Major J. Divine, Reverend.
    See: BAKER, GEORGE
Major J. Downing. See:
    DAVIS, CHARLES
    AUGUSTUS
Major Jack Downing. See:
    SMITH, SEBA
Major Jack Downing of Downing-
    ville. See: SMITH, SEBA
Major Jones. See:
    THOMPSON, WILLIAM
    TAPPAN
Major Lewis W. Carson. See:
    AIKEN, ALBERT W.
MAJOR (MAIR), JOHN (1470?-
    1550) [English educator
    and historian]
    The Last of the Schoolmen
Major Penniman. See:

DENISON, CHARLES
    WHEELER
Major S. S. Scott. See:
    HARBAUGH, THOMAS
    CHALMERS
Major, The Boy. See:
    PELHAM, JOHN
Major, Ursa. See:
    JOHNSON, DR. SAMUEL
Major Walt Wilmot. See:
    HARBAUGH, THOMAS
    CHALMERS
Major Walter Brisbane. See:
    HARBAUGH, THOMAS
    CHALMERS
Makars, The Last of the. See:
    LINDSAY (LYNDSAY), SIR
    DAVID
MAKEBA, ZENSI MIRIAM
    (1932-   ) [Afro-American
    singer]
    Miriam Makeba
Makeles (The Butcher). See:
    LEO I
MAKEMIE, FRANCIS (1658-1708)
    [Irish-American Presby-
    terian clergyman]
    The Apostle of Accomac
    The Saint Francis of
    Presbyterianism
Makepeace, Joan. See:
    JOAN
Maker, Mr. Music. See:
    WELK, LAWRENCE
Maker of Stars, The. See:
    BONESTEELE, LAURA
    JUSTINE
Maker, The Basket. See:
    MILLER, THOMAS
Maker, The Beautiful Rope (La
    Belle Cordière). See:
    LABÉ, LOUISE
Maker, The King. See:
    GUFFEY, JOSEPH F.
    NEVIL (NEVILLE),
    RICHARD
Maker, The President. See:
    CLAY, HENRY
Maker, The Red-headed Music.
    See: HALL, WENDELL
    WOODS
Making, The Father of American

Map. See:
GANNETT, HENRY
Maksim. See also:
MAXIM
Maxim
Maksim Maksimovich
Litvinov. See:
FINKELSTEIN, MEYER
Malachi Mailings. See:
GALT, JOHN
Malachi Malagrowth. See:
SCOTT, SIR WALTER
Malack, Muley. See:
NOAH, MORDECAI MANUEL
Malagrowth, Malachi. See:
SCOTT, SIR WALTER
Malaya, The Tiger of. See:
YAMASHITA, TOMOYUKI
MALCHUS (c. 232-303) [Greek
scholar and philosopher]
Porphyry
MALCOLM III (died 1093)
[King of Scotland]
Canmore (Great Head)
MALCOLM IV (1141-65) [King
of Scotland]
Malcolm the Maiden
The Maiden
Malcolm J. Errym. See:
RYMER, JAMES
MALCOLM
Malcolm J. Merry. See:
RYMER, JAMES
MALCOLM
Malcolm X. See:
LITTLE, MALCOLM
Malden, Karl. See:
SEKULOVICH, MLADEN
Maler. See:
MÜLLER (MUELLER),
FRIEDRICH
Malet, Lucas. See:
HARRISON, MARY ST.
LEGER KINGSLEY
Malik El-Shabazz. See:
LITTLE, MALCOLM
Malin, Peter. See:
CONNOR, PATRICK
REARDON
Malla. See:
GARCÍA, AUGUSTÍN
MALLINCKRODT, EDWARD

(1845-1928) [American
manufacturer of chemicals]
The Ammonia King
Malloch, Peter. See:
DUNCAN, WILLIAM
MURDOCH
MALLON, MARY (1870-1938)
[Irish-American cook;
carrier of typhoid germs]
Typhoid Mary
Malmesbury, The Philosopher of.
See: HOBBES, THOMAS
Malmsbury, William of. See:
SOMERSET, WILLIAM
Malo, Gina. See:
FLYNN, JANET
Malone, Dorothy. See:
MALONEY, DOROTHY
Malone, Mr. See:
GUION, RAYMOND
MALONE, PERCY LAY (1903-)
[American soldier and pro-
fessional baseball
player]
The Black Knight of the Border
Pat Malone
MALONEY, DOROTHY (1925-)
[American motion picture
actress]
Dorothy Malone
Maloney, Pat. See:
MARKUN, PATRICIA
MALONEY
MALONEY, RALPH LISTON
(1927-) [American author]
Jack Liston
MALRAUX, GEORGES-ANDRÉ
(1901-) [French
archaeologist, editor and
author]
Colonel Berger
Maltster, Sam the. See:
ADAMS, SAMUEL
MALTZ, ALBERT. See:
Hollywood Ten, The
Mama Stringbean, Sweet. See:
WATERS, ETHEL
Mamie. See also:
Maimee
Mamie Van Doren. See:
OLANDER, JOAN LUCILLE
Mammas, The Last of the Red-

657

hot. See:
ABUZA, SOPHIE
Man. See also:
MANN
Mann
MANNE
Man Eloquent, Blind. See:
WEST, WILLIAM
HENRY
Man Eloquent of the Senate,
The Old. See:
HOAR, GEORGE
FRISBIE
Man Eloquent, Old. See:
ADAMS, JOHN QUINCY
COLERIDGE, SAMUEL
TAYLOR
CUSTIS, GEORGE
WASHINGTON PARKE
ISOCRATES
Man from Cordoba, The (El
Córdobes). See:
BENITEZ, MANUEL
Man from Little Egypt, The Big.
See: KELLER, KENT
ELLSWORTH
Man from Maine. See:
BLAINE, JAMES
GILLESPIE
Man from Maryland, The Grand
Old. See:
WHYTE, WILLIAM
PINKNEY
Man from Missouri, The. See:
TRUMAN, HARRY S
Man from the North, The. See:
HOBMAN, JOSEPH BURTON
Man, Hollywood's Grand Old.
See: BLYTHE, LIONEL
Man in Canada, The Ugliest. See:
CHAPELSKI, ALEX
SAMUEL
Man in the Commons, The First.
See: BURKE, EDMUND
Man in the Iron Mask, The. See:
MOODY, WILLIAM
VAUGHAN
UNKNOWN
Man in the Straw Hat, The. See:
CHEVALIER, MAURICE
AUGUSTE
Man in the White House, That.

See: ROOSEVELT,
FRANKLIN DELANO
Man in the World, The Biggest
Hotel. See:
HILTON, CONRAD
NICHOLSON
Man, Iron. See:
Ironman
McGINNITY, JOSEPH
JEROME
Man, Magnetic. See:
BLAINE, JAMES
GILLESPIE
Man Milliner, The. See:
HENRY III
Man of a Thousand Faces, The.
See: CHANEY, LON
Man of Adria, The Blind. See:
GROTO, LUIGI
Man of Alexandria, The Grand
Old. See:
DUNN, EMMETT CLARKE
Man of Baseball, The Iron. See:
GEHRIG, HENRY LOUIS
Man of Bath, The. See:
ALLEN, RALPH
Man of Blood and Iron, The. See:
VON BISMARCK, PRINCE
OTTO EDUARD LEOPOLD
Man of Blood, The. See:
CHARLES I
SIMMONS, THOMAS
Man of Chios, The. See:
HOMER
Man of December, The (l'Homme
de Décembre). See:
BONAPARTE, CHARLES
LOUIS NAPOLEON
Man of Destiny, The. See:
BONAPARTE, NAPOLEON
CLEVELAND, STEPHEN
GROVER
Man of Destiny, The Green-eyed.
See: WALKER, WILLIAM
Man of Destiny, The Grey-eyed.
See: WALKER, WILLIAM
Man of Europe, The Mystery.
See: ZACHARIAS,
BASILEIOS
Man of Faith, Shelby's. See:
ANTHONY, JOHN ALSTON
Man of Football, The Grand Old.

See: STAGG, AMOS
ALONZO
Man of Great Heart, The. See:
HOOVER, HERBERT CLARK
Man of Happy Unhappy Answers,
The. See:
TARLTON, RICHARD
Man of Independence, The. See:
TRUMAN, HARRY S
Man of Labor, The Grand Old.
See: GOMPERS, SAMUEL
Man of Many Faces, The. See:
WEISENFREUND, MUNI
Man of Missouri, The Grand Old.
See: KIRK, JOHN
ROBERT
Man of Ross, The. See:
KYRLE, JOHN
Man of Scio's Rocky Isle, The
Blind Old. See:
HOMER
Man of Sedan, The. See:
BONAPARTE, CHARLES
LOUIS NAPOLEON
Man of Silence, The. See:
BONAPARTE, CHARLES
LOUIS NAPOLEON
Man of Sin, The. See:
CROMWELL, OLIVER
Man of Steel, The (Adaman-
tius). See:
ORIGEN (ORIGENES)
Man of the Century, The
Best Read. See:
LOWELL, JAMES
RUSSELL
Man of the Four Nations, The
Beloved. See:
HAWKINS, BENJAMIN
Man of the Gridiron, The
Golden. See:
WILKINSON, CHARLES
BURNHAM
Man of the Gridiron, The Old.
See: KENNEALLY,
GEORGE V.
Man of the Mountain, The Old.
See: HASAN-IBN-AL-
SABBAH
Man of the People, The. See:
FOX, CHARLES JAMES
HENRY, PATRICK
JEFFERSON, THOMAS

LINCOLN, ABRAHAM
Man of the Screen, The Grand
Old. See:
ROBERTS, THEODORE
Man of the Town Meeting. See:
ADAMS, SAMUEL
Man on Horseback, The. See:
BOULANGER, GEORGES
ERNEST JEAN MARIE
ROOSEVELT, THEODORE
Man River, " Football's "Old.
See: STAGG, AMOS
ALONZO
Man, Scat. See:
CROTHERS, SHERMAN
Man Sent from God, The. See:
FRANSON, FREDRIK
Man, Silent. See:
GRANT, HIRAM ULYSSES
Man, Stan the. See:
MUSIAL, STANLEY FRANK
Man, Tattooed. See:
BLAINE, JAMES GILLESPIE
Man, That Ace Drummer. See:
KRUPA, EUGENE BERTRAM
Man, The. See:
SINATRA, FRANCIS ALBERT
Man, The Ain't Gonna Rain No
Mo'. See:
LEE, EDWARD D.
Man, The Bad Old. See:
EARLY, JUBAL ANDERSON
Man, The Belfast. See:
DAVIS, FRANCIS
Man, The Bible-Class. See:
STUART, JAMES EWELL
BROWN
Man, The Burlington Hawkeye.
See: BURDETTE, ROBERT
JONES
Man, The Cinderella. See:
BRADDOCK, JAMES J.
BROWNING, EDWARD
Man, The Danbury News. See:
BAILEY, JAMES MONT-
GOMERY
Man, The Egyptian Miracle. See:
BEY, RAHMAN
Man, The Flatboat. See:
LINCOLN, ABRAHAM
Man, The Forgotten. See:
BRADDOCK, JAMES J.
Man, The Friend of. See:

RIQUETI, VICTOR
Man, The Grand Old. See:
FRANKLIN, BENJAMIN
GLADSTONE, WILLIAM
EWART
PITT, WILLIAM
SAVAGE, GEORGE
MARTIN
Man, The Green. See:
DE SALVO, ALBERT H.
Man, The Hi De Ho. See:
CALLOWAY, CABELL,
3RD
Man, The Last. See:
CHARLES I
Man, The Laughing-gas. See:
SHORT, DEWEY
Man, The Little Round. See:
BUTTS, JAMES WALLACE,
JR.
Man, The Measuring. See:
DE SALVO, ALBERT H.
Man, The Mighty Medicine. See:
See: POWELL, DAVID
FRANK
Man, The Musical Small-coal.
See: BRITTON, THOMAS
Man, The Old. See:
ALEXANDER, WILLIAM
ANDERSON
KALBFUS, EDWARD
CLIFFORD
Man, The Old (Der Alte).
See: ADENAUER,
KONRAD
Man, The Orchid. See:
CARPENTIER, GEORGES
Man, The Peanut. See:
CARVER, DR. GEORGE
WASHINGTON
Man, The Silver (Shaw-nee-aw-
kee). See:
KINZIE, JOHN
Man, The Slogan. See:
SMYTHE JOHN HENRY,
JR.
Man, The Solid. See:
MULDOON, WILLIAM
Man, The Son of the. See:
BONAPARTE, NAPOLEON
FRANÇOIS CHARLES
JOSEPH

Man, The Son of the Last. See:
CHARLES II
Man, The Sweet-potato. See:
CARVER, DR. GEORGE
WASHINGTON
Man, The Union's Grand Old. See:
SAVAGE, GEORGE MARTIN
Man, The Universal (Homo
Universale). See:
VINCI, LEONARDO DA
Man, The World's Wildest Tenor.
See: COBB, ARNETT
CLEOPHUS
Man Who Can Say Anything and
Make Everybody Like it, The.
See: ROGERS, WILLIAM
PENN ADAIR
Man Who Is Always Somebody
Else, The. See:
WEISENFREUND, MUNI
Man Who Won a Fight, The Dead.
See: DOUGLAS, JAMES
Man With the Golden Arm, The.
See: KOUFAX, SANFORD
Man With the Miracle Mind, The.
See: DUNNINGER, JOSEPH
Man with the Sling, The. See:
RANDOLPH, JOHN
Man Without a Skin, The. See:
CUMBERLAND, RICHARD
Manager, Archie the. See:
GARDNER, EDWARD
FRANCIS
Manager Henry Abbott. See:
STRATEMEYER,
EDWARD L.
Manager of the War, The
General. See:
SMITH, WALTER BEDELL
MANAOIS, JOSEPH
(1903-) [Philippine com-
poser and conductor]
Don José
Manassa Mauler, The. See:
DEMPSEY, WILLIAM
HARRISON
MANCE, JULIAN C., JR.
(1928-) [American jazz
musician (piano)]
Junior Mance
Manchester Poet, The. See:
SWAIN, CHARLES

Manchester Poor, Santa Claus
of the. See:
CHENEY, SOPHIE H.
MANCUSO, AUGUST RODNEY
(1905-) [American
professional baseball
player]
Blackie
MANCUSO, RONALD BERNARD
(1933-) [American jazz
musician (baritone horn,
bass)]
Gus Mancuso
MAND, EWALD (1906-)
[Esthonian-American
Baptist clergyman and
author]
Ain Kalmus
Evald Maend
MANDEL, JOHN ALFRED
(1925-) [American
composer, leader and
arranger]
Johnny Mandel
MANDEL, JOSEPH (1880-1954)
[German motion picture
director]
Joe May
MANDELKORN, EUGENIA
MILLER (1916-)
[American author]
Eugenia Miller
MANDER, LIONEL
(1888-1946) [British
stage and motion picture
actor]
Miles Mander
MANDERS, JACK (1909-)
[American professional
football player]
Automatic
Mandeville, Jehan de (Sir
John), pseud. of JEHAN
DE BOURGOGNE (other-
wise JEHAN À LA
BARBE) (died 1372) or
JEAN D'OUTREMEUSE
(fl. 14th cent.) [French
author or translator of
famous book of travels
published c. 1366]
MANFRED, FREDERICK

FEIKEMA (1912-) [Amer-
ican author]
Feike Feikema
Manfred, Robert. See:
MARX, ERICA ELIZABETH
MANGIONE, CHARLES FRANK
(1940-) [American jazz
musician (trumpet, com-
poser)]
Chuck
MANGIONE, GASPARE CHARLES
(1938-) [American jazz
musician (piano, composer)]
Gap
MANGUM, LEO ALLAN
(1900-) [American pro-
fessional baseball player]
Blacky
Manhattan. See:
SCOVILLE, JOSEPH
ALFRED
Manila, The Hero of. See:
DEWEY, GEORGE
MANION, CLYDE JENNINGS
(1896-) [American pro-
fessional baseball player]
Pete
Mankind, Delight of. See:
MAXIMILIAN II
VESPASIANUS, TITUS
FLAVIUS SALINUS
MANKOWSKA, JOYCE KELLS
BATTEN (1919-)
[Scottish interpreter and
author]
Joyce Mortimer Batten
Manly, Marline. See:
RATHBONE, ST. GEORGE
HENRY
MANN [Mann]. See also:
Man
MANNE
Mann, Avery. See:
BREETVELD, JIM
PATRICK
Mann Curtis. See:
KURTZ, MANNY
Mann, D.J. See:
FREEMAN, JAMES DILLET
Mann, Herbie. See:
SOLOMON, HERBERT JAY
MANN, JOHN R. (1928-)

[American jazz musician
(leader, composer, piano)]
Johnny Mann
Mann of the South, The Horace.
See: RUFFNER,
WILLIAM HENRY
MANN, THOMAS (1875-1955)
[German author and man
of letters]
Paul Thomas
Mann Vom Rinn, Der. See:
SPECKBACHER, JOSEPH
MANNA, CHARLES J. (1925-)
[American comedian]
Charlie Manna
Barry DeForest
MANNE. See also:
Man
MANN
Mann
MANNE, SHELDON (1920-)
[American jazz musician
(drums, leader, composer)]
Shelly Manne
Mannering, Julia. See:
BINGHAM, MADELEINE
Manners, David. See:
ACKLON, RAUFF DE
RYTHER DUAN
Manners, Dudley. See:
KRUPP, MAJOR D.
DUDLEY
Manners, Julia. See:
JUDSON, EDWARD ZANE
CARROLL
Manners, Motley. See:
DUGANNE, AUGUSTINE
JOSEPH HICKEY
Manners, Zeke. See:
MANNES, LEO
MANNES, LEO (1911-)
[American composer and
conductor]
Zeke Manners
Mannigan, Peter. See:
MONGER, IFOR DAVID
Manning. See:
Coles, Manning
MANNYNG
MANNING, ADELAIDE FRANCES
OKE. See:
Coles, Manning

Manning, David. See:
FAUST, FREDERICK
SCHILLER
Manning, Irene. See:
HARVET, INEZ
MANNING, REGINALD WEST
(1905-) [American
cartoonist]
Reg Manning
Manning, Rosemary. See:
COLE, MARGARET ALICE
MANNING, ROSEMARY JOY
(1911-) [English author]
Mary Voyle
MANNING, WILLIAM HENRY
(1852-1929) [American
author of dime novels]
Barry DeForest
Warren Edwards
Ben Halliday
W. M. Hoyt
Warren F. Kent
Jo Pierce
Major E. L. St. Vrain
Warren Walters
Marcus H. Waring
Hugh Warren
J. T. Warren
Ned Warren
V. S. Warren
Captain Mark Wilton
Mannon, Warwick. See:
HOPKINS, KENNETH
MANNYNG. See also:
MANNING
Manning
MANNYNG, ROBERT (c. 1260-
1340) [English poet and
chronicler]
Robert de Brunne
Manoel. See also:
MANUEL
Manuel
Manoel, Dom. See:
MANUEL II
Manoello Guideo. See:
IMMANUEL BEN SOLOMON
MANOLESCO, GEORGE
(1871-1911) [Rumanian thief
and card sharp]
His Highness Prince
Lahovary

The Duke of Otranto
The Prince of Thieves
Manolete. See:
    RODRÍGUEZ, MANUEL
    SÁNCHEZ, MANUEL
    RODRÍGUEZ Y
MANONE, JOSEPH
    MATHEWS (1904-)
    [American jazz musician
    (trumpet, singer, leader)]
Wingy Manone
Manor, Jason. See:
    HALL, OAKLEY
    MAXWELL
Manoso, El Neily (The
    Skillful Neily). See:
    NEILY, HARRY
Man's Counsellor, The Poor.
    See: CLARK, ABRAHAM
Man's Friend, The Poor. See:
    COUZENS, JAMES
Man's Priest, The Poor. See:
    DOLLING, FATHER
    RICHARD RADCLYFFE
Mansell Black. See:
    TREVOR, ELLESTON
MANSFIELD, EDWARD
    DEERING (1801-80)
    [American editor,
    biographer and social
    historian]
    E. D. M.
    Veteran Observer
Mansfield, Jayne. See:
    PALMER, JAYNE
Mansfield, Katherine. See:
    MURRY, KATHLEEN
    BEAUCHAMP
MANSFIELD, MILBURG
    FRANCISCO (1871-)
    [American traveler
    and author]
    Francis Miltoun
Mansfield, Norman. See:
    GLADDEN, EDGAR
    NORMAN
Mansfield of the Screen, The.
    See: WALTHALL, HENRY
    B.
MANSON, GEORGE (1844-
    1922) [Scottish doctor,
    pioneer in malaria

research]
Mosquito Manson
MANSUR, ABDUL QASIM (HASAN)
    [c.940-1020 A. D.) [Persian
    epic poet]
    Firdausi (Firdusi) (Firdousi)
    The Homer of Persia
MANTLE, MICKEY CHARLES
    (1931-) [American profes-
    sional baseball player]
    The Infant Prodigy
MANTLE, ROBERT BURNS
    (1873-1948) [American
    dramatic critic]
    The Dean of the Dramatic
    Critics
    Burns Mantle
MANTLE, WINIFRED LANGFORD
    (fl. 1938-61) [British
    educator and author]
    Anne Fellowes
    Frances Lang
    Jane Langford
Manton, Jo. See:
    GITTINGS, JO GREN-
    VILLE MANTON
Manton, Peter. See:
    CREASEY, JOHN
Mantua, Peter of. See:
    GUARNIERI, PIETRO
    GIOVANNI
Mantua, The Swan of. See:
    MARO, PUBLIUS
    VERGILIUS
Mantuan Bard, The. See:
    MARO, PUBLIUS
    VERGILIUS
Mantuan Swan, The. See:
    MARO, PUBLIUS
    VERGILIUS
Mantuan, The Flying. See:
    NUVOLARI, TAZIO
MANUEL. See:
    EMANUEL (MANUEL) I
    Manoel
MANUEL I (1120?-80)
    [Byzantine Emperor]
    Comnenus
MANUEL II (1350-1425)
    [Byzantine emperor]
    Palaeologus
MANUEL II (1889-1932) [King of

663

Portugal]
Dom Manoel
Manuel de Falla. See:
   FALLA Y MATHEU,
      MANUEL MARIA DE
Manufacture, The Father of
   American. See:
      SLATER, SAMUEL
MANUSH, HENRY A. (1902-71)
   [American professional
   baseball player]
   Heinie Manush
Many Faces, The Man of. See:
   WEISENFREUND, MUNI
Many-sided, The. See:
   FRANKLIN, BENJAMIN
Manzanillo, The Dewey of.
   See: TODD, CHAPMAN
      C.
Mao-Tun. See:
   SHEN YEN-PING
Maoris, Apostle to the. See:
   MARSDEN, SAMUEL
Map Making, The Father of
   American. See:
      GANNETT, HENRY
MAPES, VICTOR (1870-)
   [American playwright and
   dramatic critic]
   Maverick Post
   Sidney Sharp
Mar, Esmeralda de. See:
   MELLEN, IDA MAY
MAR, JOHN ERSKINE,
      6TH or 11TH EARL OF
   (1675-1732) [Scottish
   Jacobite]
   Bobbing Joan
Mara, Adele. See:
   DELGADO, ADELAIDA
Mara, Thalia. See:
   MAHONEY, ELIZABETH
Marais, Joan. See:
   VILLAIN-MARAIS, JEAN
Maralee G. Davis. See:
   THIBAULT, MARALEE G.
MARANVILLE, WALTER
      JAMES VINCENT
   (1891-1954) [American
   professional baseball
   player]
   Rabbit Maranville

Maras, Karl. See:
   BULMER, HENRY
      KENNETH
MARAT, JEAN PAUL (1744-93)
   [French revolutionist]
   l'Ami du Peuple (The Friend
   of the People)
MARAVICH, PETER (1949-)
   [American professional
   basketball player]
   Pistol Pete
MARBERRY, FRED (1899-)
   [American professional
   baseball player]
   Firpo
MARBLE, DANFORTH
   (1810-49) [American
   actor]
   The Gamecock of the
   Wilderness
   Dan Marble
Marbourg, Dolores. See:
   BACON, MARY SCHELL
Marc. See:
   CONNELLY, MARCUS
      COOK
Marc Antony Henderson. See:
   STRONG, REV. GEORGE A.
Marc Brandel. See:
   BERESFORD, MARCUS
Marc Brody. See:
   WILKES-HUNTER,
      RICHARD
Marcantonio. See:
   RAIMONDI, MARCANTONIO
MARCANTONIO, VITO (1902-54)
   [American politician;
   Congressman from New
   York]
   The Firebrand
Marceau, Felicien. See:
   CARETTE, LOUIS-ALBERT
MARCEAU, MARCEL (1923-)
   [French pantomimist]
   Bip
Marcelino. See:
   AGNEW, EDITH JOSEPHINE
MARCELLINUS (died 304)
   [Supreme Pontiff of Roman
   Catholic Church]
   Pope Marcellinus
   St. Marcellinus

MARCELLUS (died 309)
[Supreme Pontiff of
Roman Catholic Church]
Pope Marcellus I
St. Marcellus
Marcellus II, Pope. See:
SPANNOCHI, MARCELLO
CERVINI DEGLI
MARCELLUS (MARCUS
CLAUDIUS) (before 268-
208 B.C.) [Roman states-
man and general officer]
The Sword of Rome
March. See also:
MARSH
Marsh
March, Anne. See:
WOOLSON, CONSTANCE
FENIMORE
March, Fredric. See:
BICKEL, FREDERICK
McINTYRE
March King, The. See:
SOUSA, JOHN PHILIP
March, Stella. See:
MARSHALL, MARJORIE
BELL
March, William. See:
CAMPBELL, WILLIAM
EDWARD
Marchant, Catherine. See:
COOKSON, CATHERINE
McMULLEN
Marchbanks, Samuel. See:
DAVIES, ROBERTSON
MARCHEGIANO, ROCCO
FRANCIS (1924-1969)
[American professional box-
er; world's heavyweight
champion]
Rocky Marciano
Marcher, The Great. See:
SHERMAN, WILLIAM
TECUMSEH
MARCHESE, MALACRIDA
(1890-) [Italian
author]
Piermarini
Marchiali. See:
UNKNOWN
Marcia. See:
WARREN, MERCY OTIS

Marcia Ford. See:
RADFORD, RUBY
LORRAINE
Marcia MacDonald. See:
HILL, GRACE LIVINGSTON
Marcia Martin. See:
LEVIN, MARCIA OBRASKY
Marciano, Rocky. See:
MARCHEGIANO, ROCCO
FRANCIS
MARCO, JAIME (1920-)
[Spanish bullfighter]
El Choni
MARCOUREAU, GUILLAUME
(1638-85) [French actor
and playwright]
Brécourt
Marcus. See:
Magill, Marcus
MARCUS (died 336) [Supreme
Pontiff of Roman Catholic
Church]
Pope Marcus
St. Marcus
Marcus Aurelius. See:
VERUS, MARCUS ANNIUS
MARCUS AURELIUS
ANTONINUS (188-217 A.D.)
[Roman emperor]
Caracalla
MARCUS AURELIUS CLAUDIUS.
See: CLAUDIUS
(MARCUS AURELIUS
CLAUDIUS)
MARCUS CLAUDIUS. See:
MARCELLUS (MARCUS
CLAUDIUS)
Marcus H. Waring. See:
MANNING, WILLIAM
HENRY
MARCY, OLIVER (1820-99)
[American scientist and
advocate of Methodism]
The Methodist Agassiz
Mare, Per. See:
BOOTHBY, FREDERICK
LEWIS MAITLAND
MAREK, KURT WILLI (1915-)
[German-American editor
and author]
C.W. Ceram
Margaret. See:

FULLER, SARAH
MARGARET, MAR-
CHIONESS OSSOLI
Margret
MARGUERITE
Marguerite
MARGARET (fl. 14th cent.)
[Daughter of ERIC II
of Norway]
The Fair Maid of Norway
MARGARET (fl. 15th cent.)
[wife of WILLIAM
DOUGLAS, 8th Earl of
Douglas]
The Fair Maid of Galloway
Margaret Ann Hubbard. See:
PRILEY, MARGARET
HUBBARD
Margaret Beebe Sutton. See:
SUTTON, RACHEL
IRENE BEEBE
Margaret Clare. See:
MAISON, MARGARET
MARY BOWLES
Margaret Dean Stevens. See:
ALDRICH, BESS
STREETER
Margaret Grant. See:
CORYELL, JOHN RUSSELL
FRANKEN, ROSE D.
(MRS. WILLIAM BROWN
MELONEY)
Margaret Holt. See:
PARISH, MARGARET
HOLT
Margaret Illington. See:
LIGHT, MAUDE
ELLEN
Margaret J. Miller. See:
DALE, MARGARET
JESSY
Margaret L. Wiley. See:
MARSHALL, MARGARET
WILEY
Margaret Lindsay. See:
KIES, MARGARET
Margaret Lockwood. See:
DAY, MARGARET
Margaret Mair. See:
CROMPTON, MARGARET
NORAH MAIR
Margaret Mayo. See:

CLATTEN, LILIAN
Margaret Neuman. See:
POTTER, MARGARET
NEWMAN
MARGARET OF NAVARRE
(1492-1549) [Queen of
Navarre]
Marguérité d'Angoulême
MARGARET OF VALOIS (1553-
1615) [Wife of HENRY IV,
King of France]
Margaret of France
Queen Margot
Margaret Penrose. See:
STRATEMEYER,
EDWARD L.
Margaret Phipps. See:
TATHAM, LAURA
ESTHER
Margaret Powers. See:
HEAL, EDITH
Margaret Sidney. See:
LOTHROP, HARRIET
MULFORD STONE
Margaret, Sister Teresa. See:
ROWN, MARGARET KEVIN
Margaret Taylor. See:
BURROUGHS, MARGARET
TAYLOR
Margaret Vail McLeod. See:
HOLLOWAY, TERESA
BRAGUNIER
Margaret Vandegrift. See:
JANVIER, MARGARET
THOMPSON
Margaret Warde. See:
DUNTON, EDITH KELLOGG
Margaret Yorke. See:
NICHOLSON, MARGARET
BEDA LARMINIE
Marge. See:
CHAMPION, MARJORIE
CELESTE BELCHER
SHARP, MARJORIE
BARNHILL ZEHR
Margerson, David. See:
DAVIES, DAVID
MARGERISON
Margery. See also:
Marjorie
Marjory
Margery Sharp. See:

666

CASTLE, MRS. GEOFFREY
L.
Margery the Boston Medium.
See: CRANDON, MINA
Margo. See:
CASTILLA, MARIA
MARGUERITA GUADE-
LUPE BOLDAO Y
Margot Fonteyn. See:
HOOKHAM, MARGARET
Margot Fonteyn de Arias, Dame.
See: HOOKHAM,
MARGARET
Margot, Queen. See:
MARGARET OF VALOIS
Margret. See also:
MARGARET
Margaret
MARGUERITE
Marguerite
Margret, Ann. See:
OLSON, ANN-MARGRET
MARGUERITE [Marguerite].
See also: Margaret
Margret
Marguérite d'Angoulême. See:
MARGARET OF NAVARRE
Marguerite Montansier. See:
BRUNET, MARGUERITE
Marguerite Nelson. See:
FLOREN, LEE
MARGUERITE OF FRANCE
(1523-74) [Daughter of
FRANCIS I, King of
France]
The Mother of Peoples
MARGULOIS, DAVID (1912-)
[American theatrical
producer]
The Barnum of Broadway
Producers
David Merrick
Mari. See also:
Mairi
MARY
Mary
Mari Macumber. See:
SANDOZ, MARI SUSETTE
MARIA CHRISTINA (1806-78)
[Queen of Spain]
Christina of Spain
Maria del Occidente. See:

BROOKS, MARIA GOWEN
Maria Jeritza. See:
JEDLITZKA, MARIE
Maria Kuncewiczowa. See:
KUNCEWICZ, MARIA
SZCZEPANSKA
María Montez. See:
SILAS, MARÍA DE SANTO
María Salomé. See:
RODRÍGUEZ, AUGUSTÍN
Maria Zaturenska. See:
GREGORY, MRS. HORACE
MARYA
Mariacourt, Peter de. See:
PEREGRINUS, PETRUS
Marian. See also:
MARION
Marion
Marian Allison. See:
REID, FRANCES PUGH
Marian Douglas. See:
ROBINSON, ANNIE DOUGLAS
GREEN
Marian Gilmore. See:
DEY, FREDERICK VAN
RENSSELAER
Marian Montgomery. See:
HALLOWAY, MARIAN M.
RUNNELS
MARIANA, JUAN DE (1537-1624)
[Spanish Jesuit historian]
The Livy of Spain
Marianne O'Brien. See:
JUDD, MARY ANN
Marice Rutledge. See:
HALE, MARIE LOUISE
GIBSON
MARIE ANTOINETTE (1755-93)
[Queen of France; wife of
LOUIS XVI]
The Baker's Wife
Marie Ault. See:
CRAGG, MARIE
Marie Boas. See:
HALL, MARIE BOAS
Marie Carmichael. See:
STOPES, MRS; MARIE CHAR-
LOTTE CARMICHAEL
MARIE CHARLOTTE (1724-1800)
[Comtesse du
Boufflers-Rouveret]
The Idol of the Temple

Marie Cher. See:
    SCHERR, MARIE
Marie Corelli. See:
    MACKAY, MARY
Marie Dressler. See:
    KOERBER, LEILA
Marie Gaston. See:
    DAUDET, ALPHONSE
Marie Lloyd, The Australian.
    See: FLANAGAN,
    FLORENCE
Marie McDonald. See:
    FRYE, MARIE
Marie of Hollywood, Queen.
    See: KOERBER, LEILA
MARIE OF RUMANIA (1875-
    1938) [Dowager Queen of
    Rumania]
    Queen Marie
Marie Prevost. See:
    DUNN, MARIE BICKFORD
Maria, Queen. See:
    MARIE OF RUMANIA
Marie Stanley. See:
    WEST, LILLIE
Marie Swan. See:
    BARTLETT, MARIE SWAN
Marie Tempest. See:
    ETHERINGTON, MARY
    SUSAN
Marie Wilson. See:
    WHITE, KATHLEEN
    ELIZABETH
Marie Windsor. See:
    BERTELSON, EMILY
    MARIE
Marilyn. See:
    MAXWELL, MARVEL
Marilyn Harris. See:
    SPRINGER, MARILYN
    HARRIS
Marilyn Monroe. See:
    BAKER (MORTENSEN),
    NORMA JEAN
Marilyn Pender. See:
    PENDOWER, JACQUES
Marina Vlady. See:
    POLIAKOPF-BAIDAROV,
    MARINA DE
Marine Aviator, The. See:
    MAAS, MELVIN JOSEPH
Marine Bob. See:

MOUTON, ROBERT L.
Marine Insurance Business, The
    King of the. See:
    TOWNSEND, HAWORTH
    NOTTINGHAM
Marine, The Fighting. See:
    TUNNEY, JAMES JOSEPH
MARINO, RINALDO R. (1916-63)
    [American composer and
    arranger]
    Lennie Martin
MARINUS (died 884) [Supreme
    Pontiff of Roman Catholic
    Church]
    Pope Marinus I
    Pope Martin II
MARINUS (died 946) [Supreme
    Pontiff of Roman Catholic
    Church]
    Pope Marinus II
    Pope Martin III
Mario, Giuseppe. See:
    CANDIA, DON GIOVANNI DE
Mario Lanza. See:
    COCOZZA, ALFRED
MARION [Marion]. See also:
    Marian
Marion Davies. See:
    DOURAS, MARION
Marion E. George. See:
    BENJAMIN, CLAUDE MAX
    EDWARD POHLMAN
Marion Fox. See: WARD,
    MARION INEZ DOUGLAS
MARION, FRANCIS (1732-95)
    [American general officer in
    Revolutionary War]
    The Bayard of the South
    The Old Swamp Fox
    The Swamp Fox
    The Swamp Fox of South
    Carolina
Marion Harland. See: TERHUNE,
    MARY VIRGINIA HAWES
Marion Hutton. See:
    THORNBURG, MARION
Marion Keith. See:
    MACGREGOR, MARY
    ESTHER MILLER
Marion Leslie. See:
    TOOLEY, SARAH ANNE
Marion Marsh. See:

KRAUTH, VIOLET
Marion of the Mexican Army,
The. See:
LANE, JOSEPH
Marion S. Doane. See:
WOODWARD, GRACE
STEELE
Marion Seyton. See:
SAXON, GLADYS
RELYEA
Marion Sunshine. See:
IJAMES, MARY TUNSTALL
Marion Thorne. See:
THURSTON, IDA
TREADWELL
Marionette Emperor, The.
See: MAXIMILIAN,
FERDINAND JOSEPH
Marisa. See: NUCERA,
MARISA LONETTE
Marisa Pavan. See:
PIERANGELI, ANNA
MARIA
Maristan. See:
Chapman, Maristan
MARIUS. See:
CAIUS MARIUS
Marjoram, J. See:
MOTTRAM, RALPH HALE
Marjorie. See also:
Margery
Marjory
Marjorie Bowen. See:
LONG, MRS. GABRIELLE
MARGARET VERE
CAMPBELL
Marjorie Curtis. See:
PREBBLE, MARJORIE
MARY CURTIS
Marjorie Harte. See:
McEVOY, MARJORIE
HARTE
Marjorie Mack. See:
DIXON, MARJORIE
MACK
Marjorie Main. See:
KREBS, MARY TOMLINSON
Marjorie, Pet. See:
FLEMING, MARGARET
Marjorie Reynolds. See:
GOODSPEED, MARJORIE
Marjorie Torrey. See:

CHANSLOR, MARJORIE
TORREY HOOD
Marjory. See also:
Margery
Marjorie
Marjory Hall. See:
YEAKLEY, MARJORY HALL
Mark. See:
Caine, Mark
HANNA, MARCUS ALONZO
Phillips, Mark
Mark Carrel. See:
PAINE, LAUREN
Mark Dane. See:
AVALLONE, MICHAEL
ANGELO, JR.
Mark Epernay. See:
GALBRAITH, JOHN
KENNETH
Mark Finney. See:
MUIR, KENNETH ARTHUR
Mark Forest. See:
DEGNI, LOU
Mark Gault. See:
COURNOS, JOHN
Mark Goodwin. See:
MATTHEWS, STANLEY
GOODWIN
Mark Grimshaw. See:
McKEAG, ERNEST LIONEL
Mark Hampton. See:
NORWOOD, VICTOR
GEORGE CHARLES
Mark Howard. See:
RIGSBY, HOWARD
Mark Littleton. See:
KENNEDY, JOHN PENDLE-
TON
Mark, Matthew. See:
BABCOCK, FREDERIC
Mark Mayo. See:
LANE, YOTI
Mark Merrick. See:
RATHBONE, ST. GEORGE
HENRY
Mark Oliver. See:
TYLER-WHITTLE, MICHAEL
SIDNEY
MARK, PAULINE DAHLIN (1913-)
[American Protestant
missionary and author]
Polly Mark

669

Mark Peabody, Mrs. See:
VICTOR, MRS. METTA
VICTORIA FULLER
MORSE
Mark Philippi. See:
BENDER, ARNOLD
Mark Porter. See:
LECKIE, ROBERT
HUGH
Mark Rothko. See:
ROTHKOVICH,
MARCUS
Mark Rutherford. See:
WHITE, WILLIAM
HALE
Mark Sawyer. See:
GREENHOOD, CLARENCE
DAVID
Mark Twain. See:
CLEMENS, SAMUEL
LANGHORNE
SELLERS, ISAIAH
Mark Twain of Cartoonists, The.
See: WEBSTER, HAROLD
TUCKER
Mark West. See:
RUNYON, CHARLES W.
Mark Wilton, Captain. See:
MANNING, WILLIAM
HENRY
Market Gardener, The. See:
BLACKMORE, RICHARD
DODDRIDGE
Markets, The King of the.
See: BEAUFORT, DUC
DE
MARKEWICH, MAURICE
(1936-) [American
jazz musician (piano,
flute)]
Reese Markewich
Markham, Mrs. See:
PENROSE, ELIZABETH
Markham, Robert. See:
AMIS, KINGSLEY
Markham, Violet Rosa. See:
CARRUTHERS, MRS.
JAMES
MARKLE. See also:
MERKLE
MARKLE, GEORGE BUSHER
(1827-88) [American

inventor]
The Father of the Breaker
Markova, Alicia. See:
MARKS, LILIAN ALICIA
MARKOWITZ, RICHARD
(1926-) [American com-
poser]
Richard Allen
MARKS, JOHN D. (1909-)
[American composer and
publisher]
Johnny Marks
MARKS, LILIAN ALICIA (1910-)
[British prima ballerina]
Alicia Markova
MARKUN, PATRICIA MALONEY
(1924-) [American radio
announcer, editor and
author]
Sybil Forrest
Pat Maloney
Patricio Marroquin
MARLAND, ERNEST WHITWORTH
(1874-) [American poli-
tician; Congressman from
Oklahoma]
Hot Oil Marland
Marlborough, The Little. See:
SCHWERIN, COUNT KURT
CHRISTOPH
Marlene. See also:
Marline
Marlene Dietrich. See:
VON LOSCH, MARIA
MAGDALENE
Marley, Florence. See:
SMEKALOVA, HANA
Marline. See also:
Marlene
Marline Manly. See:
RATHBONE, ST. GEORGE
HENRY
MARLOW, LOUIS (1881-)
[British novelist]
Louis Wilkinson
MARLOW, MRS. LOUIS (1899-)
[British author]
Ann Alexander Reid
MARLOWE, ALAN STEPHEN
(1937-) [American actor
and author]
Kyle Alexander

Marlowe, Amy Bell. See:
STRATEMEYER,
EDWARD L.
Marlowe, Charles. See:
JAY, HARRIET
MARLOWE, CHRISTOPHER
(1564-93) [British
dramatist and poet]
Kit Marlowe
The Second Shakespeare
Marlowe, Hugh. See:
HIPPLE, HUGH
PATTERSON, HENRY
Marlowe, Jerry. See:
MAUTNER, JEROME
Marlowe, Julia. See:
FROST, SARAH FRANCES
MARLOWE, KENNETH (1926-)
[American author]
Mr. Kenneth
Leslie Stuart
MARLOWE, STEPHEN
(1928-) [American
author]
Andrew Frazer
Milton Lesser
Jason Ridgway
C. H. Thames
Marmaduke. See:
DEY, FREDERICK
VAN RENSSELAER
MARMAROSA, MICHAEL
(1925-) [American
jazz musician (piano)]
Dodo Marmarosa
MARO, PUBLIUS VERGILIUS
(70 B.C.-19 B.C.)
[Roman poet]
The Mantuan Bard
The Mantuan Swan
The Swan of Mantua
Vergil
Virgil
MAROT, CLÉMENT (1497-1544)
[French poet]
The Chaucer of France
Marprelate, Martin. See:
HARVEY, GABRIEL
Marpriest, Martin. See:
OVERTON, RICHARD
MARQUAND, JOHN PHILLIPS
(1893-1960) [American

author]
John Phillips
MARQUARD, LEOPOLD (1897-)
[British educator, UNESCO
official and author]
John Burger
MARQUARDT, RICHARD W.
(1889-) [American pro-
fessional baseball player]
Rube Marquardt
MARQUETTE, JACQUES
(1637-75) [French mis-
sionary and explorer in
North America]
Pere Marquette
MARQUEZ, LEONARDO (c. 1820-
) [Mexican general
officer]
The Tiger of Tacubaya
Marquis au Court Nez (Marquis
Short-nose). See:
GUILLAUME D'ORANGE
Marquis de Lafayette. See:
MOTIER, MARIE JEAN
PAUL ROCH YVES
GILBERT
Marquis de Mirabeau. See:
RIQUETI, VICTOR
Marquis de Sade. See:
SADE, COMTE DONATIEN
ALPHONSE FRANÇOIS
DE
MARQUIS, DONALD ROBERT
PERRY (1878-1937) [Amer-
ican journalist, playwright,
humorist and author]
Don Marquis
Marquis of Douro, The. See:
BRONTË, CHARLOTTE
Marquis of Queensberry, The.
DOUGLAS, JOHN SHOLTO
Marquis Short-nose (Marquis au
Court Nez). See:
GUILLAUME D'ORANGE
Marquis, The Great. See:
POMBAL, MARQUÊS DE,
SEBASTIÃO JOSÉ DE
CARVALHO E MELLO
MARR-JOHNSON, DIANA
MAUGHAM (1908-)
[British author]
Diana Maugham

MARRACK, J. F. See:
    Potiphar
MARRERO, JOSÉ (1870-1909)
    [Cuban bullfighter]
    Cheche
Marric, J.J. See:
    CREASEY, JOHN
MARRINER, EDYTHE
    (1918-) [American
    model and motion picture
    actress]
    Susan Hayward
Marriott, Moore. See:
    MOORE-MARRIOTT,
    GEORGE THOMAS
Marroquin, Patricio. See:
    MARKUN, PATRICIA
    MALONEY
MARRYAT, FREDERICK
    (1792-1848) [British
    naval officer and novelist]
    Captain Marryat
Marrying Justice of Worcester
    County, The. See:
    DAVIS, WALTER
    ALONZO
Mars, The Portuguese. See:
    ALBUQUERQUE,
    AFFONSO D'
MARSCHALK, ANDREW
    (fl. late 18th cent.)
    [American journalist]
    The Father of Journalism
    in Mississippi
MARSDEN, SAMUEL (1764-1838)
    [English missionary]
    Apostle to the Maoris
Marse Henry. See:
    WATTERSON, HENRY
Marse Joe. See:
    McCARTHY, JOSEPH
    VINCENT
MARSH [Marsh]. See also:
    March
Marsh, Carol. See:
    SIMPSON, NORMA
Marsh, Garry. See:
    GERAGHTY, LESLIE
    MARCH
Marsh, J.E. See:
    MARSHALL, EVELYN
Marsh, Jean. See:
    MARSHALL, EVELYN

MARSH, JOHN (1907-)
    [British author]
    John Elton
    John Harley
    Harrington Hastings
    Grace Richmond
    Lilian Woodward
Marsh, Marion. See:
    KRAUTH, VIOLET
MARSH, MARY WARNE
    (1895-) [American motion
    picture actress]
    Mae Marsh
Marsh, Paul. See:
    HOPKINS, KENNETH
Marsh, Rebecca. See:
    NEUBAUER, WILLIAM
    ARTHUR
MARSH, SYLVESTER (1803-84)
    [American railroad builder]
    Crazy Marsh
Marsha. See:
    HUNT, MARCIA
MARSHAK, I.A. (1895-)
    [Russian author of
    scientific books for
    juveniles]
    M. Ilin
Marshal. See:
    NEY, MICHEL
Marshal de Saxe. See:
    SAXE, MAURICE, COMTE
    DE
Marshal Forwards. See:
    BLÜCHER, GEBHARD
    LEBERECHT VON, PRINCE
    OF WAHLSTADT
Marshal, The Young. See:
    CHANG HSUEH-LIANG
Marshal Tito. See:
    BROZ, JOSIP
Marshal, William, Gent. See:
    WALPOLE, HORATIO
Marshall, Brenda. See:
    ANKERSON, ARDIS
Marshall, Douglas. See:
    McCLINTOCK, MARSHALL
MARSHALL, EDISON (1894-)
    [American author]
    Hall Hunter
Marshall, Edmund. See:
    HOPKINS, KENNETH
Marshall, Emily. See:

672

HALL, BENNIE CAROLINE
HUMBLE
MARSHALL, EVELYN (1897-)
[British author]
Leslie Bourne
Jean Marsh
J. E. Marsh
Marshall, James. See:
RISTER, CARL COKE
MARSHALL, JAMES VANCE
(fl. 1917- 65) [Australian
author]
Jice Doon
Marshall, James Vance. See:
PAYNE, DONALD GORDON
MARSHALL, JOHN (1755-
1835) [American jurist
and statesman; Chief Jus-
tice of the United States
Supreme Court]
The Greatest American
Jurist
The Legal Interpreter of
the Constitution
Silver Heels
Marshall, Lovat. See:
DUNCAN, WILLIAM
MURDOCH
MARSHALL, MARGARET
WILEY (1908-) [Ameri-
can educator and author]
Margaret L. Wiley
MARSHALL, MARJORIE BELL
(1916-) [English author]
Stella March
Marshall, Percy. See:
YOUNG, PERCY
MARSHALL
Marshall Soult. See:
KNAPP, SAMUEL
LORENZO
MARSHALL, STEPHEN
(1600-66) [English
churchman and
pamphleteer]
The Geneva Bull
MARSHALL, STEPHEN
See also:
Smectymnuus
Marshall, Tully. See:
PHILLIPS, TULLY
MARSHALL

Marshes, First Lord of the.
See: HATFIELD, BAZIL
MUSE
Marsten, Richard. See:
HUNTER, EVAN
MARSTON, JEFFERY EARDLY
(1887-) [British military
officer and author]
Jeffery E. Jeffery
MARSTON, JOHN (c. 1575-1634)
[English satiric poet and
dramatist]
W. Kinsayder
MARSTON, PHILIP BOURKE
(1850-87) [British poet]
Philip the King
Mart. See:
CASEY, MICHAEL T.
MARTEL, CHARLES. See:
CHARLES MARTEL
MARTEL, COMTESSE DE
MIRABEAU DE
(1849-1932) [French
novelist]
Gyp
MARTENS, FERNAND (1904-)
[French motion picture
actor]
Fernand Gravet
Martens, Paul. See:
SOUTHWOLD, STEPHEN
Martha Albrand. See:
FREYBE, HEIDI HUBERTA
Martha Earley. See:
WESTWATER, SISTER
AGNES MARTHA
Martha Edith von Almedingen,
See: ALMEDINGEN, EDITH
MARTHA
Martha Farquharson. See:
FINLEY, MARTHA
FARQUHARSON
Martha James. See:
DOYLE, MARTHA CLAIRE
MACGOWAN
Martha Miller. See:
IVAN, MARTHA MILLER
PFAFF
Martha Raye. See:
O'REED, MAGGIE TERESA
Martha Schlamme. See:
HAFTEL, MARTHA

Martha Trent. See:
SMITH, DOROTHY
WHITEHILL
Martha Vickers. See:
MacVICAR, MARTHA
Martha Wright. See:
WIEDERRECHT, MARTHA
MARTI, ISIDRO (1884-1921)
[Spanish bullfighter]
Flores
Martial. See:
MARTIALIS, MARCUS
VALERIUS
Martial, The British. See:
OWEN, JOHN
MARTIALIS, MARCUS
VALERIUS (c. 40-c. 104)
[Roman epigrammatist]
Martial
MARTIN [Martin]. See also:
Martyn
MARTIN (died 655) [Supreme
Pontiff of Roman
Catholic Church]
Pope Martin I
St. Martin
Martin II, Pope. See:
MARINUS
Martin III, Pope. See:
MARINUS
Martin IV, Pope. See:
BRION, SIMON DE
Martin V, Pope. See:
COLONNA, ODDONE
Martin, Abe. See:
HUBBARD, FRANK
McKINNEY
Martin Agricola. See:
SOHR (SORE), MARTIN
Martin, Allan Langdon, joint
pseud. of JANE COWL (1890-
1950)[American actress and
writer] and JANE MURFIN
(-) [American motion pic-
ture scenario writer]
MARTIN, BASIL KINGSLEY
(1897-) [British editor
and author]
Critic
Martin Buccer (Butzer).
See: KUHHORN, MARTIN
MARTIN, CECILIA (1903-)
[American photographer

and journalist]
Jackie Martin
Martin Colt. See:
EPSTEIN, SAMUEL
Martin Cornwall. See:
CAVENDISH, RICHARD
Martin, Dean. See:
CROCETTI, DINO
Martin Dexter. See: FAUST,
FREDERICK SCHILLER
Martin, Edwin Winslow. See:
McCABE, JAMES DABNEY
Martin, Eugene. See: STRATE-
MEYER, EDWARD L.
Martin Fallon. See:
PATTERSON, HENRY
MARTIN, FRANÇOIS
XAVIER (1762-1846)
[French-American publisher
of legal materials]
The Father of Louisiana
Jurisprudence
Martin, Frederic. See:
CHRISTOPHER, MATTHEW F.
Martin Hare. See:
ZAJDLER, ZOË GIRLING
Martin Hasler. See:
SHURLY, ERNEST WILLIAM
Martin, Hipsch. See:
SCHONGAUER, MARTIN
Martin, Hubsch. See:
SCHONGAUER, MARTIN
MARTIN, JAMES GREEN
(1819-78) [American
Confederate soldier]
Old One Wing
Martin, Jay. See:
GOLDING, MORTON JAY
Martin, Jeremy, joint pseud. of
MARCIA OBRASKY LEVIN
(1918-) and her husband,
MARTIN P. LEVIN (-)
[American authors]
Martin, Jeremy. See also:
LEVIN, MARCIA OBRASKY
Martin, John. See:
SHEPARD, MORGAN VAN
ROERBACH
TATHAM, LAURA ESTHER
MARTIN, JOHNNY LEONARD
(1904-) [American pro-
fessional baseball player]
Pepper Martin

Martin Kosleck. See:
    YOSHKIN, NICOLAI
Martin Lang. See:
    BIRREN, FABER
Martin Leach Warborough See:
    ALLEN, CHARLES GRANT
        BLAIRFINDIE
Martin, Lennie. See:
    MARINO, RINALDO R.
MARTIN, LLOYD (1916-)
    [American jazz
    musician (saxophone,
    arranger)]
    Skip Martin
Martin Locke. See:
    DUNCAN, WILLIAM
        MURDOCH
MARTIN, LUTHER (1748-1826)
    [American Federalist
    lawyer]
    The Federal Bull-dog
Martin Luther King,
    Australia's. See:
    PERKINS, CHARLES
        NELSON
Martin, Marcia. See:
    LEVIN, MARCIA
        OBRASKY
MARTÍN, MARIANO (1937-)
    [Spanish bullfighter]
    Carriles
Martin Marprelate. See:
    HARVEY, GABRIEL
Martin Marpriest. See:
    OVERTON, RICHARD
Martin Mewburn. See:
    HITCHIN, MARTIN
        MEWBURN
Martin Miller. See:
    MÜLLER, RUDOLPH
Martin, Mr. See:
    BURROUGHS, WILLIAM
        SEWARD
Martin Noll. See:
    BUXBAUM, MARTIN
MARTIN, PATRICIA MILES
    (fl. 1958-67) [American
    author]
    Miska Miles
Martin, Paul. See:
    DEALE, KENNETH
        EDWIN LEE

Martin, Peter. See:
    WATERMAN, NIXON
Martin Pollock. See:
    GARDNER, MAURICE
Martin Porlock. See:
    MACDONALD, PHILIP
Martin, R. J. See:
    MEHTA, RUSTAM
        JEHANGIR
Martin, R. Johnson. See:
    MEHTA, RUSTAM
        JEHANGIR
Martin Redfield. See:
    BROWN, ALICE
MARTIN, RICHARD (1754-1834)
    [Irish lawyer and
    humanitarian]
    Humanity Martin
Martin, Richard. See:
    CREASEY, JOHN
MARTIN, ROBERT BERNARD
    (1918-) [American educator
    and author]
    Robert Bernard
MARTIN, ROBERT LEE (1908-)
    [American author]
    Lee Roberts
Martin, Ross. See:
    ROSENBLATT, MARTIN
Martin Ross. See:
    Herring, Geilles
    MARTIN, VIOLET
        FLORENCE
Martin, Ruth. See:
    RAYNER, CLAIRE
Martin, Sam. See:
    MOSKOWITZ, SAM
Martin Schon. See:
    SCHONGAUER, MARTIN
Martin Scott. See:
    GEHMAN, RICHARD BOYD
MARTIN, SIR THEODORE
    (1816-1909) [Scottish poet
    and biographer]
    Bon Gaultier
Martin the First, King. See:
    VAN BUREN, MARTIN
Martin, Tony. See:
    MORRIS, ALVIN
Martin Toonder. See:
    GROOM, ARTHUR WILLIAM
MARTIN, VIOLET FLORENCE

(1862-1915) [Irish novelist]
Martin Ross
MARTIN, VIOLET FLORENCE.
See also:
Herring, Geilles
MARTIN, WILLIAM (1801-67)
[British writer of children's literature]
Old Chatty Cheerful
Peter Parley
Martincho. See:
EBASSUN, ANTONIO
Martine Carol. See:
MOURER, MARYSE
Martine, Max. See:
AVERY, HENRY M.
MARTINEZ. See:
RIESGO, MANUEL
MARTINEZ Y
MARTINEZ, LOLITA DOLORES
DE (1905-) [Mexican
motion picture actress]
Dolores del Rio
MARTINEZ, OCTAVIO (1934-)
[Spanish bullfighter]
Nacional
MARTINEZ, PEDRO (1932-)
[Spanish bullfighter]
Pedrés
MARTINEZ, ZUVIRÍA GUSTAVO
ADOLFO (1883-)
[Argentine novelist]
Hugo Wast
Martingale, Hawser. See:
SLEEPER, JOHN
SHERBURNE
MARTINI, SIMONE (1283?-
1344) [painter of the
Sienese School]
Di Martino
Martins, Jay. See:
TENER, MARTIN J.
Marty. See:
PAICH, MARTIN LOUIS
Martyn. See also:
MARTIN
Martin
Martyn, Henry. See:
PERRY, MARTIN HENRY
Martyr Abolitionist, The.
See: LOVEJOY, ELIJAH

PARRISH
Martyr Hero, The. See:
BROWN, JOHN
Martyr King, The. See:
HENRY VI
LOUIS XVI
Martyr of Erromango, The. See:
WILLIAMS, JOHN
Martyr of the Renaissance, The.
See: DOLET, ÉTIENNE
Martyr of the Revolution, The
First. See:
SNYDER, CHRISTOPHER
MARTYR, PETER (died 1252)
[Patron saint of the
Inquisition]
Martyr
Martyr, Peter. See:
ANGHIERA, PIETRO
MARTIRE
VERMIGLI, PIETRO
MARTIRE
Martyr President, The. See:
GARFIELD, JAMES ABRAM
LINCOLN, ABRAHAM
Martyr, The. See:
CHARLES I
EDMUND (EADMUND), ST.
EDWARD (EADWARD)
JUSTIN, ST.
Martyr, The Quaker. See:
DYER, MARY
Martyr, The Royal. See:
CHARLES I
EDWARD (EADWARD)
Marvel, Ik. See:
MITCHELL, DONALD GRANT
Marvel, Ike. See:
MITCHELL, DONALD GRANT
Marvel, J. K. See:
MITCHELL, DONALD GRANT
MARVELL, ANDREW (1621-78)
[English poet and satirist]
The British Aristides
Marvell, Holt. See:
MASCHWITZ, ERIC
Marvellous Boy, The. See:
CHATTERTON, THOMAS
Marvin Ingram. See:
INABNETT, MARVIN
MARVIN, JOHN (1897-1944)

[American jazz musician
(guitar, ukulele, singer)]
The Lonesome Singer of
the Air
Johnny Marvin
The Ukulele Ace
MARVIN, JOHN T. (1906-)
[American attorney,
judge and author]
Charles Richards
Marvin, W.R. See:
CAMERON, LOU
MARX, ADOLPH (ARTHUR)
(Harpo). See:
Four Marx Brothers, The
Marx Brothers. See:
Four Marx Brothers, The
MARX, ERICA ELIZABETH
(1909-) [English author]
Robert Manfred
MARX, HERBERT (Zeppo). See:
Four Marx Brothers, The
MARX, JULIUS HENRY
(Groucho). See:
Four Marx Brothers, The
MARX, LEONARD (Chico). See:
Four Marx Brothers, The
MARX, MILTON (1894-) [Ameri-
can actor and actor's agent]
Gummo Marx
MARX, MILTON. See also:
Four Marx Brothers, The
MARY (1542-87) [Queen of
Scotland]
Mary, Queen of Scots
Mary Stuart
The White Queen
Mary. See:
Mairi
Mari
MILES, MAXINE FRANCES
MARY FORBES-
ROBERTSON
MARY I (1516-58) [Queen of
England]
Bloody Mary
Mary Tudor
Mary Adrian. See:
JORGENSEN, MARY VENN
Mary Allerton. See: GOVAN,
CHRISTINE NOBLE
Mary Anne Tate. See:
HALE, ARLENE

Mary Ashley. See:
TOWNSEND, MARY ASHLEY
VAN VOORHIS
Mary Astor. See:
LANGHANKE, LUCILE V.
Mary Bawn. See: WRIGHT,
MARY PAMELA GODWIN
Mary Berwick. See: PROCTOR,
ADELAIDE ANNE
Mary Berwick, Miss. See:
PROCTOR, ADELAIDE ANNE
Mary, Bloody. See:
MARY I
Mary Bodell. See:
PECSOK, MARY BODELL
Mary Brian. See:
DANTZLER, LOUISE
Mary Clavers, Mrs. See:
KIRKLAND, CAROLINE
MATILDA STANSBURY
Mary D. Salter. See:
AINSWORTH, MARY DINS-
MORE SALTER
Mary Dominic, Sister. See:
GALLAGHER, SISTER
MARY DOMINIC
Mary E. Francis. See:
BLUNDELL, MRS. FRANCIS
SWEETMAN
Mary Earl. See:
KING, ROBERT
Mary Elfrieda Winn. See:
SCRUGGS, MARY ELFRIEDA
Mary F.W. Lewis. See: BOND,
MARY FANNING WICKHAM
Mary F. Wickham. See:
BOND, MARY FANNING
WICKHAM
Mary F. Wickham Porcher. See:
BOND, MARY FANNING
WICKHAM
Mary Faid. See:
DUNN, MARY ALICE
Mary Fanning Wickham. See:
BOND, MARY FANNING
WICKHAM
Mary Ford. See:
SUMMERS, COLLEEN
Mary Forrest. See:
FREEMAN, JULIA DEANE
Mary Francis Shura. See:
CRAIG, MARY FRANCIS
Mary Godolphin. See:
AIKIN, LUCY

Mary Hale. See:
 WOOLSEY, MARYHALE
Mary Heathcott. See:
 KEEGAN, MARY HEATH-
 COTT
Mary Henderson. See:
 MAVOR, DR. OSBORNE
 HENRY
Mary, Hercules. See:
 PROMITIS, MARY
Mary, Highland. See:
 CAMPBELL, MARY
 MORISON, MARY
Mary Hunton. See:
 GILZEAN, ELIZABETH
 HOUGHTON BLANCHET
Mary Jane Owen, See:
 BROCKWAY, JENNIE M.
Mary Jerrold. See:
 ALLEN, MARY
Mary Jo Rush. See:
 MATTHEWS, MARY JO
Mary Keith Vincent. See:
 ST. JOHN, WYLLY FOLK
Mary Langdon. See:
 PIKE, MARY HAYDEN
 GREEN
Mary Lavin. See:
 WALSH, MARY
Mary Lou Burley. See:
 SCRUGGS, MARY
 ELFRIEDA
Mary Lou Williams. See:
 SCRUGGS, MARY
 ELFRIEDA
Mary Lou Winn. See:
 SCRUGGS, MARY
 ELFRIEDA
Mary Louise Johnson. See:
 KING, MARY LOUISE
Mary Mapes Dodge. See:
 DODGE, MARY
 ELIZABETH MAPES
Mary Meade. See:
 LOVRIEN, RUTH ELLEN
Mary Merrall. See:
 LLOYD, MARY
Mary Miles Minter. See:
 SHELBY, JULIET
Mary Miller. See:
 NORTHCOTT, WILLIAM
 CECIL

Mary Motley. See:
 DeRENEVILLE, MARY
 MARGARET MOTLEY
 SHERIDAN
Mary of Lorraine. See:
 GUISE, MARY
MARY OF MODENA (1658-1718)
 [Second wife of JAMES II
 of England]
 The Queen of Tears
Mary O'Hara. See:
 STUREVASA, MARY
 O'HARA ALSOP
Mary Orr. See:
 DENHAM, MARY ORR
Mary Parrish. See:
 COUSINS, MARGARET
Mary Pickford. See:
 SMITH, GLADYS MARY
Mary Pickford of this War, The.
 See: KAUMEYER, DOROTHY
Mary Raymond. See:
 KEEGAN, MARY HEATH-
 COTT
Mary Renault. See:
 CHALLANS, MARY
MARY, ST. (c. 15 B.C.-48 A.D.)
 [Mother of JESUS]
 The Blessed Virgin Mary
Mary Stallings. See:
 EVANS, MARY LORRAINE
 STALLINGS
Mary Stuart of Italy, The. See:
 JANE I
Mary, The Blessed Virgin. See:
 MARY, ST.
Mary, Typhoid. See:
 MALLON, MARY
Mary Voyle. See:
 MANNING, ROSEMARY JOY
Mary Westmacott. See:
 MILLER, AGATHA MARY
 CLARISSA
Maryland, A Gentleman of. See:
 BRACKENRIDGE, HUGH
 HENRY
Maryland, The Evil Genius of.
 See: CLAIBORNE,
 WILLIAM
Maryland, The Grand Old Man
 From. See:
 WHYTE, WILLIAM PINKNEY

Maryse Rutledge. See:
    HALE, MARIE LOUISE
    GIBSON
Masaccio. See:
    BARTOLOMEO, MASO DI
    GUIDI, TOMMASO
Masako Matsuno. See:
    KOBAYASHI, MASAKO
    MATSUNO
MASANIELLO (TOMMASO
    ANIELLO) (ANELLO)
    (c.1622-47) [Neapolitan
    insurrectionist; short-time
    ruler of Naples]
The Seven Days' King
Mascara, Red. See:
    MASCARI, JOSEPH ROCCO
MASCARI, JOSEPH ROCCO
    (1922-) [American
    composer]
Red Mascara
MASCHLER, TOM. See:
    Caine, Mark
MASCHWITZ, ERIC (1901-)
    [British novelist]
Holt Marvell
MASCI, GIROLAMO (1227-92)
    [Supreme Pontiff of
    Roman Catholic Church]
Pope Nicholas IV
Mask, The Man in the Iron.
    See: MOODY, WILLIAM
    VAUGHAN
    UNKNOWN
Mason, Adrian. See:
    LEE, REV. ALBERT
Mason, Chuck. See:
    ROWLAND, DONALD
    SYDNEY
MASON, EUDO COLECESTRA
    (1901-) [British
    educator and author]
Otto Maurer
MASON, FRANCIS VAN
    WYCK (1901-) [American
    soldier and author]
Geoffrey Coffin
Frank W. Mason
F. Van Wyck Mason
Van Wyck Mason
Ward Weaver
MASON, FRANCIS VAN WYCK.

See also:
    Coffin, Geoffrey
MASON, LOWELL (1792-1872)
    [American hymn writer]
The Father of American
    Church Music
MASON, MADELINE (1913-)
    [American author and
    lecturer]
David Bartlett
Tyler Mason
MASON, PHILIP (1906-)
    [British civil servant
    and author]
Philip Woodruff
MASON, STEVENS THOMSON
    (1811-43) [American
    politician; Secretary and
    Acting Governor of the Ter-
    ritory of Michigan]
The Boy Governor
Mason, Tally. See:
    DERLETH, AUGUST
    WILLIAM
MASON, WALT (1862-1939)
    [Canadian humorist and
    poet]
The Homer of the Middle
    West
Masonry, The Arch-Priest of
    Anti. See:
    STEVENS, THADDEUS
Massa Linkum. See:
    LINCOLN, ABRAHAM
Massachusettensis. See:
    LEONARD, DANIEL
Massachusetts, A Lady of. See:
    BARRELL, SARAH SAY-
    WARD
Massachusetts Giant, The. See:
    WEBSTER, DANIEL
Massachusetts, The Father of.
    See: WINTHROP, JOHN
Massachusetts Thunderer, The.
    See: WEBSTER, DANIEL
MASSADA, IONE (1899-)
    [English author]
Ione Leigh
MASSARO, SALVATORE (1904-33)
    [American jazz musician
    (guitar)]
Blind Willie Dunn

679

Eddie Lang
Massasoit. See:
    OUSAMEQUIN
    (WOUSAMEQUIN)
MASSÉNA, ANDRÉ (1758-1817)
    [French field marshal]
    Victory's Darling Child
MASSEY, D. CURTIS (1910-)
    [American country music
    singer]
    Curt Massey
Massey, Ilona. See:
    HAJMASSY, ILONA
Massiliensis, Johannes. See:
    CASSIANUS, JOHANNES
MASSILLON, JEAN BAPTISTE
    (1663-1742) [French
    pulpit orator]
    The Cicero of France
    The Peaceful Prelate
MASSINGHAM, HAROLD JOHN
    (1888-) [British author]
    H. J. M.
Masson, Georgina. See:
    JOHNSON, MARION
        GEORGINA WIKELEY
Mast, Jane. See:
    WEST, MAE
Master. See:
    BETTY, WILLIAM
        HENRY WEST
Master Leavitt, Old. See:
    LEAVITT, DUDLEY
Master Little. See:
    MOORE, THOMAS
Master Mind of Mental
    Mystery, The. See:
    DUNNINGER, JOSEPH
Master of Ceremonies, Amer-
    ica's Foremost. See:
    FAY, FRANCIS
        ANTHONY
Master of Ceremonies, The
    Fashion World's Most
    Irrepressible. See:
    CASSINI, OLEG
        LOIEWSKI
Master of English Prose,
    The First. See:
    NORTH, SIR THOMAS
Master of Flémalle. See:
    CAMPIN, ROBERT

Master of Love, The Great.
    See: DANIEL, ARNAUD
    (ARNAUT)
Master of Naturalism, The. See:
    FLAUBERT, GUSTAVE
Master of Paradox. See:
    CHESTERTON, GILBERT
    KEITH
Master of Sentences
    (Magister Sententiarum).
    See: LOMBARD, PETER
Master of Suspense, The
    Cherubic. See:
    HITCHCOCK, ALFRED
    JOSEPH
Master of the Involuntary Scream,
    The Portly. See:
    HITCHCOCK, ALFRED
    JOSEPH
Master of the Sacred Palace.
    See: DOMINIC, ST.
Master of the Swamps. See:
    HATFIELD, BAZIL MUSE
Master of Undergraduate
    Humor. See:
    SHULMAN, MAX
Master Pilot of the Mississippi,
    The. See: CLEMENS,
    SAMUEL LANGHORNE
Master, The (Der Meister). See:
    VON GOETHE, JOHANN
    WOLFGANG
    WIELAND, CHRISTOPHER
    MARTIN
Master, The Old. See:
    GANS, JOE
Master, Word (Lavengro). See:
    BORROW, GEORGE HENRY
MASTERMAN, FRANK EVANS
    (1910-) [American jazz
    musician (leader, singer)]
    Frankie Masters
Masters. See:
    Little Masters
Masters, Frankie. See: MASTER-
    MAN, FRANK EVANS
MASTERS, KELLY R. (1897-)
    [American author]
    Zachary Ball
Masters, William. See:
    COUSINS, MARGARET
Masterson, Whit. See:

Miller, Wade
MASTERSON, WILLIAM BARCLAY
(1853-1921) [American
Indian fighter, gambler,
scout, U. S. marshal and
sports writer]
Bat Masterson
Mata Hari. See:
ZELLE, MAGARETE
GERTRUDE
Match King, The. See:
KREUGER, IVAR
MATCHA, JACK (1919-)
[American newspaperman
and author]
Jackson Mitchel
John Tanner
Matchless Orinda, The. See:
PHILIPS, KATHERINE
MATEO, MIGUEL (1939-)
[Spanish bullfighter]
Miguelin
Matey. See:
VAN BUREN, MARTIN
Mather, Melissa. See:
AMBROS, MELISSA
BROWN
MATHERS, EDWARD POWYS
(1892-) [British
author]
Torquemada
Matheson, Hugh. See:
MACKAY, LEWIS HUGH
MATHESON, SYLVIA ANNE
(1923-) [English
author]
Max Mundy
MATHEW. See also:
MATTHEW
Matthew
MATHEW, THEOBALD (1790-
1856) [Irish temperance
reformer]
Father Mathew
MATHEWS. See also:
MATTHEWS
Matthews
MATHEWS, ALBERT
(1820-1903) [American
miscellaneous writer]
Paul Siegvolk
MATHEWS, CORNELIUS
(1817-89) [American

editor, playwright,
novelist and poet]
Puffer Hopkins
The Late Ben Smith
MATHEWS, EVELYN CRAW
(1906-) [Canadian teacher,
librarian and author]
Nancy Cleaver
MATHEWSON. See also:
MATTHEWSON
MATHEWSON, CHRISTOPHER
(1880-1925) [American
professional baseball
player]
Big Six
Christy Mathewson
Husk
Mathias Acher. See:
BIRNBAUM, NATHAN
Mathilde Blind. See:
COHEN, MATHILDE
MATHIS, JOHN ROYCE (1935-)
[American popular singer]
Johnny Mathis
MATILDA (1102-67) [English
noblewoman; daughter of
HENRY I of England, wife
of GEOFFREY V of Anjou
and mother of HENRY II of
England]
The Empress Maud
The Lady of England
Matilda, Anna. See:
COWLEY, MRS. HANNAH
Matilda Bailey. See:
RADFORD, RUBY LORRAINE
Matilda Hughes. See:
MACLEOD, CHARLOTTE
MATILDA HUGHES
Matilde Verdu. See:
CELA, CAMILO JOSÉ
MATLOCK, JULIAN CLIFTON
(1909-) [American jazz
musician (clarinet)]
Matty Matlock
MATOAKA (1595?-1617)
[American Indian princess;
daughter of POWHATAN]
Pocahontas
Rebecca
MATSON, JAMES RANDEL
(1945-) [American track
and field champion]

Randy Matson
Matsuno, Masako. See:
    KOBAYASHI, MASAKO
    MATSUNO
MATSYS, QUENTIN (c. 1460-
    1530) [Flemish painter]
The Blacksmith of Antwerp
The Flemish Blacksmith
Matt Kinkaid. See:
    ADAMS, CLIFTON
Matt Rockwell. See:
    ROWLAND, DONALD
    SYDNEY
MATTANIAH (fl. 6th cent.
    B.C.) [King of Judah and
    final ruler of the line of
    DAVID]
Zedekiah
MATTHEW [Matthew]. See also:
    MATHEW
Matthew Blood. See:
    DRESSER, DAVIS
Matthew Browne. See:
    RANDS, WILLIAM
    BRIGHTY
MATTHEW, FATHER
    THEOBALD (1790-1856)
    [Irish priest and
    temperance advocate]
The Apostle of Temperance
The Sinner's Friend
Matthew Finch. See:
    FINK, MERTON
Matthew Head. See:
    CANADAY, JOHN EDWIN
Matthew Mark. See:
    BABCOCK, FREDERIC
Matthew Murgatroyd. See:
    JONES, JAMES
    ATHEARN
Matthew, Thomas. See:
    ROGERS, JOHN
MATTHEWS [Matthews]. See
    also: MATHEWS
Matthews, E. Channing. See:
    CHANNING-RENTON,
    LIEUT. ERNEST
    MATTHEWS
MATTHEWS, JAMES
    BRANDER
    [1852-1929) [American
    novelist, essayist, critic
    and playwright]

Brander Matthews
Arthur Penn
MATTHEWS, JOSEPH W.
    (18??-63/64) [American
    politician, Governor of
    Missouri]
The Well-digger
Matthews, Kevin. See:
    FOX, GARDNER
    FRANCIS
MATTHEWS, MARY JO
    (1909-) [American com-
    poser]
Mary Jo Rush
MATTHEWS, STANLEY
    GOODWIN (1924-)
    [Canadian journalist]
    columnist and author]
Mark Goodwin
MATTHEWSON. See also:
    MATHEWSON
MATTHEWSON, WILLIAM
    (fl. 1860) [American pioneer
    scout, buffalo hunter and
    co-founder of Wichita,
    Kansas]
Buffalo Bill
The Buffalo Killer
MATTHIAS I (1442-90)
    [King of Hungary]
The Great
Matty. See:
    MATLOCK, JULIAN
    CLIFTON
MATURE, VICTOR JOHN
    (1916-) [American actor]
Hollywood's No. 1 Glamour
    Boy
The Hunk
MATZO, EMMA (1922-)
    [American motion
    picture actress]
Lizabeth Scott
Maude Adams. See:
    KISKADDEN,
    MAUDE
Maud, The Empress. See:
    MATILDA
MAUDET, CHRISTIAN (1904-)
    [French journalist and
    motion picture writer-
    director]
Christian-Jacque

Maugham, Diana. See:
MARR-JOHNSON,
DIANA MAUGHAM
MAUGHAM, ROBERT CECIL
ROMER (1916-) [British barrister and author]
Robin Maugham
MAUGHAM, WILLIAM
SOMERSET (1874-1965)
[English author and
playwright]
W. Somerset Maugham
Maul of Monks, The. See:
CROMWELL, THOMAS
MAULDIN, WILLIAM
(1921-) [American
cartoonist]
Bill Mauldin
MAULE, HAMILTON BEE
(1915-) [American
journalist and author]
Tex Maule
Mauler, The Manassa. See:
DEMPSEY, WILLIAM
HARRISON
Maung Hauk. See:
HOBBS, CECIL
CARLTON
Maupassant, Guy de. See:
DE MAUPASSANT,
HENRI RENÉ ALBERT
GUY
Maupassant, The American.
See: PORTER:
WILLIAM SYDNEY
Maureen Daly. See:
McGIVERN, MAUREEN
DALY
Maureen O'Hara. See:
BROWN, MAUREEN
FITZSIMONS
Maurer, Otto. See:
MASON, EUDO
COLECESTRA
Maurice. See:
THOMPSON, JAMES
MAURICE
Maurice Barrymore. See:
BLYTHE, HERBERT
MAURICE, DAVID JOHN
KERR (1899-)
[Australian author]

Wunnakyawhtin U Ohn
Ghine
Maurice Elvey. See:
FOLKARD, WILLIAM
Maurice Furnley. See:
WILMOT, FRANK LESLIE
THOMSON
MAURICE, JOHN FREDERICK
DENISON (1805-72) [English
divine and author]
Rusticus
Maurice Silingsby. See:
URNER, NATHAN DANE
Maurice Stevens. See:
WHITSON, JOHN HARVEY
Maurice Templar. See:
GROOM, ARTHUR WILLIAM
Maurice Tourneur. See:
THOMAS, MAURICE
Maurin. See:
RUSSELL, MAURINE
FLETCHER
Maurois, André. See:
HERZOG, ÉMILE SALAMON
WILHELM
Maury. See:
WILLS, MAURICE
MORNING
MAURY, MATTHEW FONTAINE
(1806-73) [American naval
officer, oceanographer
and author]
Harry Bluff
The Pathfinder of the Seas
MAUTNER, JEROME (1913-)
[American composer,
pianist and singer]
Jerry Marlowe
Maverick Post. See:
MAPES, VICTOR
Mavis Areta. See:
WINDER, MAVIS ARETA
Mavis Areta Wynder. See:
WINDER, MAVIS ARETA
MAVOR, DR. OSBORNE HENRY
(1888-1951) [Scottish
dramatist and physician]
James Bridie
Mary Henderson
Mawdsley, Norman. See:
HARGREAVES-MAWDSLEY,
WILLIAM NORMAN

Max. See:
BAER, MAXIMILIAN
ADELBERT
BEERBOHM, SIR
HENRY MAXIMILIAN
RAFFERTY, MAXWELL
LEWIS, JR.
STEINER, MAXIMILIAN
RAOUL
WHITE, CHARLES
WILLIAM
Max Adeler. See:
CLARK, CHARLES
HEBER
Max Brand. See:
FAUST, FREDERICK
SCHILLER
Max Catz. See:
GLASER, MILTON
Max Day. See:
CASSIDAY, BRUCE
BINGHAM
Max, Der. See:
KLEIN-LUCKOW, MAX
Max Edwards. See:
BENJAMIN, CLAUDE
MAX EDWARD
POHLMAN
Max Franklin. See:
DEMING, RICHARD
Max Linder. See:
LEVIELLE, GABRIEL
Max Martine. See:
AVERY, HENRY M.
Max Mundy. See:
MATHESON, SYLVIA
ANNE
Max Nosseck. See:
NORRIS, ALEXANDER
Max O'Rell. See:
BLOUET, PAUL
Max Reiner. See:
CALDWELL, TAYLOR
Max Reinhardt. See:
GOLDMANN, MAX
Max Schmeling. See:
KLEIN-LUCKOW, MAX
Max Stirner. See:
SCHMIDT, KASPAR
Max, The Incomparable. See:
BEERBORM, SIR HENRY
MAXIMILIAN

Max Vernon. See:
KELLOGG, VERNON
LYMAN
Maxie, Madcap. See:
BAER, MAXIMILIAN
ADELBERT
Maxie, Slapsie. See:
ROSENBLOOM, MAX
MAXIM [Maxim]. See also:
Maksim
Maxim Gorky. See:
PESHKOV, ALEKSEI
MAKSIMOVICH
MAXIM, ISAAC (1853-1927)
[American inventor]
Hudson Maxim
MAXIMILIAN I (1459-1519)
[Holy Roman Emperor]
The Last of the Knights
Pochi Danari (The Penniless)
MAXIMILIAN I (1573-1651)
[Duke of Bavaria]
The Great
MAXIMILIAN II (1527-76)
[Holy Roman Emperor]
Delight of Mankind
MAXIMILIAN, FERDINAND
JOSEPH (1832-67) [Emperor
of Mexico]
The Marionette Emperor
Maximilian Münsterberg. See:
NENTWICH, MAX
Maximus Ironmaster. See:
WILKINSON, JOHN DONALD
MAXIMUS, ST. (580-662)
[Byzantine theologian]
The Confessor
Maxine Elliott. See:
DERMOT, JESSIE
MAXTONE GRAHAM, MRS.
JOYCE ANSTRUTHER
(1901-53) [English writer]
Jan Struther
Maxwell. See:
Kenton, Maxwell
Maxwell, Eddie. See:
CHERKOSE, EDWARD
Maxwell, Jack. See:
McKEAG, ERNEST LIONEL
MAXWELL, JAMES CLERK
(1831-79) [Scottish physicist]
The Greatest Theoretical

Physicist of the Nineteenth
Century]
Maxwell, Lois. See:
HOOKER, LOIS
Maxwell MacFee. See:
RENNIE, JAMES ALAN
MAXWELL, MARVEL (1921-72)
[American singer, dancer
and motion picture
actress]
Marilyn Maxwell
MAXWELL, MARY ELIZABETH
BRADDON (1837-1915)
[English novelist, drama-
tist and poet]
Babington White
Maxwell, Ronald. See:
SMITH, RONALD
GREGOR
MAY [May]. See also:
Mae
May, Bernice. See:
CROSS, ZORA BERNICE
MAY
May Britt. See:
WILKENS, MAYBRITT
May Carleton, Cousin. See:
FLEMING, MAY AGNES
May, Edith. See:
DRINKER, ANNA
May, Elaine. See:
BERLIN, ELAINE
MAY, HENRY JOHN (1903-)
[British lawyer and
author]
H. J. Schlosberg
May Hollis Barton. See:
STRATEMEYER,
EDWARD L.
May, Joe. See:
MANDEL, JOSEPH
MAY, KARL FRIEDRICH
(1842-1912) [German
novelist]
Karl Hohenthal
Latreaumont
E. Von Linden
May Robson. See:
ROBISON, MARY
MAY, SAMUEL JOSEPH
(1797-1871) [American
Unitarian clergyman,

humanist and reformer]
The Lord's Chore Boy
May, Sophie. See:
CLARKE, REBECCA
SOPHIA
MAY, WILLIAM (1916-)
[American jazz musician
(trumpet, leader, arranger,
composer)]
Billy May
May Wynne. See: KNOWLES,
MABEL WINIFRED
MAYER, CHARLES LEOPOLD
(1881-) [French author]
Reyam
MAYER, HENRY (1868-   )
[American caricaturist
and author]
Hy
MAYER, JANE ROTHSCHILD.
See: Jaynes, Clare
MAYER, JOHANN ECK (1486-
1543) [German Roman
Catholic theologian]
Johann Eck
MAYFIELD, ANN TODD (1932-)
[American motion picture
actress]
Ann Todd
Mayfield, Julia. See:
HASTINGS, PHYLLIS DORA
HODGE
Mayfield, Millie. See:
HOMES, MARY SOPHIE
SHAW ROGERS
MAYHEW, THOMAS (1592-1682)
[Anglo-American governor;
friend of Indians]
The Patriarch of the Indians
MAYLEM, JOHN (1739-c.1762)
[American poet]
John Phoenix
MAYNARD, HORACE (1814-82)
[American politician;
Congressman from Tennessee]
The Narragansett
MAYNE, ETHEL COLBURN
(-1941) [English journalist,
critic and author]
Frances E. Huntly
MAYNE, WILLIAM JAMES
CARTER. See:

James, Dynely
Mayo, Cass. See:
    STEVENS, CASANDRA
    MAYO
MAYO, CHARLES HORACE
    (1865-1939) [American
    surgeon; co-founder of
    Mayo Clinic]
    Doctor Charlie
Mayo, Margaret. See:
    CLATTEN, LILIAN
Mayo, Mark. See:
    LANE, YOTI
Mayo, Virginia. See:
    JONES, VIRGINIA
MAYO, WILLIAM JAMES
    (1861-1939) [American
    surgeon; co-founder of
    Mayo Clinic]
    Doctor Will
Mayor, The Auctioneer. See:
    SHANK, SAMUEL LEWIS
Mayor, The Boy. See:
    RUSSELL, WILLIAM
    EUSTIS
Mayor, The Indianapolis Potato.
    See: SHANK, SAMUEL
    LEWIS
Mayor, The Labor. See:
    DORE, JOHN FRANCIS
Mayor, The Potato. See:
    SHANK, SAMUEL LEWIS
Mayor, The Veto. See:
    CLEVELAND, STEPHEN
    GROVER
Mayor Von O'Hall. See:
    HALL, ABRAHAM
    OAKEY
Mayoress, Washington's First.
    See: NORTON, MARY
    TERESA
Maypole, The. See:
    SCHULEMBERG,
    ERANGARD MELROSE
    DE
Mayrant, Drayton. See:
    SIMONS, KATHERINE
    DRAYTON MAYRANT
MAYS, WILLIE HOWARD (1931-)
    [American Negro profes-
    sional baseball player]
    Amazing Mays

Buckduck
Willie the Wallop
Maysi, Kadra. See:
    SIMONS, KATHERINE
    DRAYTON MAYRANT
Maysie, Aunt. See:
    JEFFREY-SMITH, MAY
    THORNTON
MAZQUIARÁN, DIEGO
    (1895-1940) [Spanish bull-
    fighter]
    Fortuna
MAZURWSKI, MIKHAIL
    (1909-) [American former
    wrestler; motion picture
    actor]
    Mike Mazurki
MAZZANTINI, LUIS (1856-1926)
    [Spanish bullfighter and
    politician]
    Don Luis Mazzantini
MAZZOLA. See:
    MAZZUOLI (MAZZOLA),
    GIROLAMO FRANCESCO
    MARIA
MAZZUOLI (MAZZOLA),
    GIROLAMO FRANCESCO
    MARIA (1403-40)
    [Italian painter]
    Parmigianino
    Il Parmigiano
Mc. Items so prefixed are listed
    as though spelled "Mac"
Me Too Platt. See:
    PLATT, THOMAS COLLIER
MEAD, EDWIN DOAK (1849-1937)
    [American lecturer and
    author]
    Independent
MEAD, SIDNEY MOKO (1927-)
    [New Zealand author]
    Moko
MEADE, GEORGE GORDON
    (1815-72) [American Civil
    War general officer]
    Four-eyed George
Meade Lux Lewis. See:
    LEWIS, MEADE
Meade, Mary. See:
    LOVRIEN, RUTH ELLEN
MEADOR, JAMES (1912-)
    [American motion picture

actor]
James Craig
Meadowcroft, Enid LaMonte.
    See: WRIGHT,
        ENID MEADOWCROFT
        LaMONTE
Meadowlark. See:
    LEMON, MEADOW
    GEORGE
Meadows Joe, Quaker. See:
    McDOWELL, JOSEPH
Meadows, Peter. See:
    LINDSAY, JACK
Meal and Pumpkins, The Poet
    of Bran. See:
    GRAHAM, SYLVESTER
Mean Mr. Clean, The. See:
    LEONARD, JACK E.
Meander, The Swan of the.
    See: HOMER
MEARNS, DAVID CHAMBERS
    (1899-) [American li-
    brarian and author]
    Farragut Fraddle
Measday, George. See:
    SODERBERG, PERCY
    MEASDAY
MEASE, JOHN (1746-1826)
    [Irish-American Revolu-
    tionary War soldier]
    The Last of the Cocked
    Hats
Measuring Man, The. See:
    DE SALVO, ALBERT H.
Meaux, The Eagle of . See:
    BOSSUET, JACQUES
    BÉNIGNE
MEBANE, JOHN HARRISON
    (1909-) [American
    journalist and author]
    Harold Heartman
Mecca, The Camel-driver of.
    See: MOHAMMED
Meccherino, Il. See:
    BECCAFUMI,
    DOMENICO
Mechanician, The Blind. See:
    STRONG, JOHN
Mechanized Forces, The
    Father of the. See: CHAF-
    FEE, ADNA ROMANZA
Med. See:

FLORY, MEREDITH
IRWIN
Medaro. See:
    NIBBI, GINO
MEDARY, SAMUEL (1801-64)
    [American Democratic
    politician]
    Old Wheel Horse of
    Democracy
Meddler, The. See:
    ROOSEVELT, THEODORE
    TRUMBULL, JOHN
Meddler, The Schemer, an Ally
    of the. See:
    TRUMBULL, JOHN
Meddler, Theodore the. See:
    ROOSEVELT, THEODORE
Mede, Joseph. See:
    GARLAND, DAVID JOHN
Medhurst, Joan. See:
    LIVERTON, JOAN
Medical Association, The Father
    of the American. See:
    DAVIS, NATHAN SMITH
MEDICI, ALESSANDRO
    OTTAVIANO (1535-1605)
    [Supreme Pontiff of
    Roman Catholic Church]
    Pope Leo XI
MEDICI, COSIMO DE' (1389-1464)
    [Italian banker, merchant
    and ruler of Florence]
    Cosimo the Elder
    Pater Patriae (The Father of
    His Country)
MEDICI, COSIMO DE' (1519-74)
    [Italian banker, merchant
    and ruler of Florence]
    Cosimo the Great
MEDICI, GIOVANNI ANGELO
    (1499-1565) [Supreme
    Pontiff of Roman Catholic
    Church]
    Pope Pius IV
MEDICI, GIOVANNI DE' (1475-
    1521) [Supreme Pontiff of
    Roman Catholic Church]
    Pope Leo X
MEDICI, GIULIO DE'
    (1478-1534) [Supreme
    Pontiff of Roman Catholic
    Church]

Pope Clement VII
MEDICI, LORENZO DE' (1449-92)
[Italian banker, merchant
and ruler of Florence]
Lorenzo the Magnificent
MEDICI, LORENZO DE' (1463-
1503) [Italian banker and
merchant]
Lorenzo the Younger
MEDICI, LORENZO DE (1514-
1548) [Italian banker
and merchant]
Lorenzino
MEDICI, PIERO DE' (1416-69)
[Italian banker, merchant
and ruler of Florence]
Piero the Gouty
Medicine Big. See:
KELLY, CLINTON WAYNE
Medicine Man, The Mighty.
See: POWELL, DAVID
FRANK
Medicine, The Father of. See:
HIPPOCRATES
Medill, Robert. See:
McBRIDE, ROBERT
MEDILL
Medium, Margery the Boston.
See: CRANDON, MINA
Medium, The Mother. See:
BENNINGHOFEN, MRS.
ERNEST
Medley, Anne. See:
BORCHARD, RUTH
BERENDSOHN
Medveczky. See:
HATAR, GYOSO VICTOR
JOHN
MEDWICK, JOSEPH M. (1911-)
[American professional
baseball player]
Duckie Wuckie
Mickey
MEEK, ALEXANDER BEAUFORT
(1814-65) [American
politician and educator]
The Father of the Public
Schools of Alabama
MEEK, JOSEPH L. (1810-75)
[American politician and
pioneer settler in Oregon
Territory]

Colonel
Meek, Lois Hayden. See:
STOLZ, LOIS MEEK
Meek, The. See:
FREDERICK II
MEEKE, MRS. MARY (died 1816?)
[British novelist]
Gabrielli
Meeker, Ralph. See:
RATHGEBER, RALPH
MEER, JAN VAN DER
(1628-91) [Dutch painter]
The Elder
Jan Vermeer van Haarlem
MEER, JAN VAN DER
(1656-1705) [Dutch painter]
Jan Vermeer van Haarlem
The Younger
Mees, Steve. See:
FLEXNER, STUART BERG
Meeting, Man of the Town. See:
ADAMS, SAMUEL
Megas. See:
ANTIOCHUS III
MEGERLE, HANS ULRICH
(1644-1709) [German monk,
preacher and satirist]
Abraham-a-Santa Clara
MEGGS, MRS. MARY (died 1691)
[English orange-seller at
the Theatre Royal, London]
Orange Moll
MEHAFFEY, LEROY (1904-)
[American professional
baseball player]
Pop-eye
MEHBOOBKHAN, RAMJANKHAN
(1907-) [Indian motion
picture director]
Mehboob
MEHEMET (MOHAMMED) ALI
(c. 1769-1849) [Viceroy of
Egypt]
The Peter the Great of Egypt
Mehmed Emin Pasha. See:
SCHNITZER, EDUARD
MEHTA, RUSTAM JEHANGIR
(1912-) [Indian author]
Roger Hartmann
R. J. Martin
R. Johnson Martin
Plutonius

MEIBES, JOSEPH (1927-)
[German-American motion
picture actor]
John Ericson
MEIGS, CORNELIA LYNDE
(1884-) [American
educator and author]
Adair Aldon
Meigs, The Hero of Fort. See:
CHRISTY, WILLIAM
Meikle, Clive. See:
BROOKS, JEREMY
Mein, Jenny. See:
GEDDES, JENNY
MEINE, HENRY WILLIAM
(1899-) [American
professional baseball
player]
Heine
Heinrich
Meiring, Desmond. See:
RICE, DESMOND
CHARLES
Meissonier, The American.
See: WATROUS, HARRY
WILSON
Meister. See:
ECKHART (ECCARD)
(ECKARDT), JOHANNES
Meister, Der (The Master). See:
VON GOETHE, JOHANN
WOLFGANG
WIELAND, CHRISTOPHER
MARTIN
MEJÍAS, ANTONIO (1922-)
[Venezuelan bullfighter]
Bienvenida
MEJÍAS, JOSÉ (1914-)
[Spanish bullfighter]
Bienvenida
Pepe
MEJÍAS, JUAN (1936-)
[Spanish bullfighter]
Bienvenida
MEJÍAS, MANOLO (1912-38)
[Spanish bullfighter]
Bienvenida
Mel. See:
GLAZER, MELVIN
OTT, MELVIN THOMAS
PATTON, MELVIN EMERY
STITZEL, MELVILLE J.

TORMÉ, MELVIN
HOWARD
Mel Lewis. See:
SOKOLOFF, MELVIN
Melanchthon. See:
SCHWARZERT, PHILIPP
Melanthon. See:
SCHWARZERT, PHILIPP
MELARO, H. J. M. (1928-)
[American lawyer and
composer]
Speed Melaro
Melba, Nellie. See:
MITCHELL, HELEN PORTER
MELCHIADES. See:
MILTIADES (MELCHIADES)
Melchiades, Pope. See:
MILTIADES (MELCHIADES)
Melchiades, St. See:
MILTIADES (MELCHIADES)
MELI, GIOVANNI (1740-1815)
[Sicilian poet]
The Sicilian Theocritus
Melis, José. See:
GUIU, JOSÉ MELIS
Melissa Hayden. See:
HERMAN, MELISSA
Melissa Mather. See:
AMBROS, MELISSA BROWN
MELL, PATRICK HUES
(1814-88) [American Baptist
clergyman]
The Prince of Parliamentarians
MELLEN, GRENVILLE (1799-
1841) [American poet,
story teller and journalist]
Reginald Reverie
MELLEN, IDA MAY (1877-)
[American aquarist and
author]
Esmeralda de Mar
George Otis
MELLENBRUCH, GILES EDWARD
(1912- [American com-
poser, singer and conductor]
Johnny Giles
Mellers, The King of the. See:
TAYLOR, CHARLES A.
MELLETT, JOHN CALVIN
(1888-) [American author]
Jonathan Brooks
Mellifluous Doctor, The. See:

BERNARD OF
CLAIRVAUX
Melmoth, Courtney. See:
PRATT, SAMUEL JACK-
SON
Melmoth, Sebastian. See:
WILDE, OSCAR FINGAL
O'FLAHERTIE WILLS
Meloney, Franken, joint
pseud. of WILLIAM
BROWN MELONEY (1905-)
and his wife ROSE D.
FRANKEN (1898-) [Amer-
ican novelists and play-
wrights]
Meloney, Franken. See also:
FRANKEN, ROSE D.
(MRS. WILLIAM
BROWN MELONEY)
Melvil. See:
DEWEY, MELVILLE
LOUIS KOSSUTH
MELVILLE, ANDREW (1545-
1622) [Scottish theo-
logian]
The Father of Scottish
Presbytery
Melville, Lewis. See:
BENJAMIN, LEWIS SAUL
Melvyn Douglas. See:
HESSELBERG, MELVYN
Member for Treorky. See:
BOWEN-ROWLANDS,
ERNEST BOWEN
BROWN
Members. See:
Five Members, The
Memorable, The Ever. See:
HALES, JOHN
Memory, The Bard of. See:
ROGERS, SAMUEL
Memphis Bill. See:
TERRY, WILLIAM
HAROLD
Memphis Slim. See:
CHATMAN, PETER
Men. See:
Three Wise Men
Men of Greece, The Seven
Wise. See: Seven
Sages of Greece, The
Men, The King of Brave. See:

HENRY IV
MENA, JUAN DE (1411-56)
[Spanish poet]
The Spanish Ennius
Menander. See:
PAINE, ROBERT TREAT,
JR.
MENANDER (342-290 B.C.)
[Athenian comic poet and
playwright]
The Creator of the New
Comedy
MENCHER, MURRAY (1898-)
[American pianist and
composer]
Ted Murry
MENCKEN, HENRY LOUIS
(1880-1956) [American
editor, lexicographer and
satirist]
Harry
H.L. Mencken
MENDEL [Mendel]. See also:
Mendl
Mendel, Jo. See:
BOND, GLADYS PARKER
MENDEL, JOHANN (1822-84)
[Austrian botanist and
priest]
Gregor
Mendele Mocher Seforim.
See: ABRAMOWITZ,
SHALOM JACOB
MENDELSOHN, OSCAR (1896-)
[Australian chemist and
author]
Oscar Milsen
Mendl. See also:
MENDEL
Mendel
Mendl, Gladys. See:
SCHUTZE, GLADYS
HENRIETTA
MENEDEMUS OF ERETRIA
(fl. 4th cent. B.C.) [Greek
philosopher]
The Eretrian Bull
Menken, Adah Bertha. See:
FUERTES, DOLORES
ADIOS
Menken, Adah Isaacs. See:
FUERTES, DOLORES ADIOS

690

Menlo Park, The Wizard of.
    See: EDISON, THOMAS
    ALVA
Mental Mystery, The Master
    Mind of. See:
    DUNNINGER, JOSEPH
MENTHON. See:
    BERNARD OF MENTHON,
    ST.
Mentor. See:
    URNER, NATHAN DANE
Mentzer. See:
    FISCHART, JOHANN
    BAPTIST
Menzel, Johanna. See:
    MESKILL, JOHANNA
    MENZEL
Mephistopheles of the Ocean,
    The. See:
    SCHLEY, WINFIELD
    SCOTT
Mercator, Gerhardus. See:
    KREMER, GERHARD
Mercedes, El de las (He of
    the Largesse). See:
    HENRY II
Mercenne, The English. See:
    COLLINS, JOHN
MERCER, CECIL WILLIAM
    (1885-1960) [English
    novelist]
    Dornford Yates
MERCER, JESSIE (fl. 1960-66)
    [American columnist and
    author]
    Terry Shannon
MERCER, JOHN H. (1909-)
    [American singer,
    lyric writer and
    recording company
    executive]
    Johnny Mercer
MERCER, MARGARET
    (1791-1846) [American
    author of religious
    articles; founder of
    Sunday Schools]
    The Hannah More of America
Merchant, Andrew Moreton.
    See: FOE, DANIEL
Merchant Evangelist, The. See:
    CRITTENTON, CHARLES

NELSON
Merchant Prince, The. See:
    MORRIS, ROBERT
Merchant, The Beloved. See:
    POLE, MICHAEL DE LA
Merchant, The Silk. See:
    HARIRI, ABU MOHAMMED
    AL KASIM IBN ALI
Mercians, The Lady of the.
    See: AETHELFLAED
MERCURIUS (died 535) [Supreme
    Pontiff of Roman Catholic
    Church]
    Pope John II
Mercury, Modern. See:
    ROOSEVELT, JAMES
Mercutio of Actors, The.
    See: LEWIS, WILLIAM
    THOMAS
Mercy and of Prison Reform,
    The Heaven-sent Angel of.
    See: DIX, DOROTHEA
    LYNDE
Meredith, Arnold. See:
    HOPKINS, KENNETH
Meredith, David William. See:
    MIERS, EARL SCHENCK
Meredith, Nicolete. See:
    STACK, NICOLETE
Meredith, Owen. See:
    LYTTON, LORD (EDWARD
    ROBERT BULWER, 1ST
    EARL OF LYTTON)
Meriel. See:
    FORBES-ROBERTSON,
    MERIEL
    MURIEL
    Muriel
MÉRIMÉE, PROSPER (1803-70)
    [French novelist and
    historian]
    Clara Gazul
MERISI (MERISIO), MICHEL-
    ANGELO (1565-1609)
    [Italian painter]
    Michelangelo de Caravaggio
MERKLE, FREDERICK C.
    (1888-) [American pro-
    fessional baseball player]
    Bonehead
    One of the Gamest Players
    in the Game

MERKLE. See also:
  MARKLE
Merle Oberon. See:
  THOMPSON, ESTELLE
  O'BRIEN MERLE
Merlin. See:
  TENNYSON, ALFRED,
  1ST BARON
  TENNYSON
Merlini, The Great. See:
  RAWSON, CLAYTON
Merlinus Coccaius. See:
  FOLENGO, TEOFILO
Merman, Ethel. See:
  ZIMMERMAN, ETHEL
  AGNES
Merrall, Mary. See:
  LLOYD, MARY
Merrick, David. See:
  MARGULOIS, DAVID
Merrick, Leonard. See:
  MILLER, LEONARD
Merrick, Mark. See:
  RATHBONE, ST. GEORGE
  HENRY
Merridew, Arthur. See:
  GASKOIN, CHARLES
  JACINTH BELLAIRS
MERRILL, JAMES MILFORD
  (1847-1936) [American
  author]
  Wendal Parrish
  Morris Redwing
  Old Timer
Merrill, Judith. See:
  GROSSMAN, JOSEPHINE
  JUDITH
Merrill, P.J. See:
  ROTH, HOLLY
Merrill Staton. See:
  OSTRUS, MERRILL
Merriman, Charles Eustace,
  joint pseud. of WILDER
  DWIGHT QUINT (1863-
  1936) and GEORGE
  TILTON RICHARDSON
  (1863-1938) [American
  journalists and authors]
Merriman, Henry Seton, joint
  pseud. of HUGH STOWELL
  SCOTT (1862-1903) and
  STANLEY JOHN WEYMAN

(1855-1928) [English
  novelists]
Merriman, Henry Seton. See
  also: SCOTT, HUGH STOW-
  ELL
Merritt, E.B. See:
  WADDINGTON, MIRIAM
MERRITT, JAMES (1926-)
  [American jazz musician
  (bass)]
  Jymie
Merriweather, Magnus. See:
  TALBOT, CHARLES
  REMINGTON
Merriwell, Frank. See:
  WHITSON, JOHN HARVEY
Merry Andrew. See:
  BORDE (BOORDE), ANDREW
Merry, Captain, U.S.N. See:
  RYMER, JAMES MALCOLM
Merry, Malcolm J. See:
  RYMER, JAMES MALCOLM
Merry Monarch, The. See:
  CHARLES II
MERRY, ROBERT (1743-1809)
  [American journalist]
  Della Crusca
Merson, Billy. See:
  THOMPSON, WILLIAM HENRY
Merton, Giles. See:
  CURRAN, MONA ELISA
MERTON, THOMAS JAMES
  (1915-68) [French monk,
  priest and author]
  Father M. Louis
MERTZ, BARBARA GROSS
  (1927-) [American historian
  and author]
  Barbara Michaels
Merv. See:
  GRIFFIN, MERVYN EDWARD,
  JR.
Mervyn Thomas. See:
  CURRAN, MONA ELISA
MESERVE, COLONEL ARTHUR
  LIVERMORE (1838-96)
  [American author of dime
  novels]
  Duke Cuyler
  Saco
MESIROW, MILTON (1899-)
  [American jazz musician

(clarinet, saxophone)]
The Ananias of Jazz
Mezz Mesirow
MESKILL, JOHANNA MENZEL
(1930-) [German-
American educator and
author]
Johanna Menzel
MESRITZ, ANDRÉ (1909-)
[British stage and
motion picture actor]
André Morell
Messalina, The Modern. See:
ANHALT-ZERBST,
SOPHIA AUGUSTA
FREDERICA OF
Messenger, Little Billy Cody
the. See:
CODY, WILLIAM
FREDERICK
MESSER, DOCTOR ASA
(1769-1836) [American
educator; president of
Brown University]
The Cunning President
MESSICK, DALIA (1906?-)
[American cartoonist]
Dale Messick
METACOM (METACOMET)
(16??-1676) [Sachem of
the Wampanoaga Indians;
son of MASSASOIT]
King Philip
Pometacom
Metaphysician, The Cornish.
See: DREW, SAMUEL
Metaphysics. See:
ALDEN, HENRY MILLS
Metastasio. See:
TRAPASSI, PIETRO
ANTONIO DOMENICO
BONAVENTURA
Metcalf, George. See:
JOHNSON, GEORGE
METCALF
METCALF, JACK (1717-1810)
[Blind British soldier,
smuggler, stagecoach
driver and engineer]
Blind Jack of
Knaresborough
METCALFE, THOMAS (1780-1855)

[American politician;
Governor of and U.S.
Congressman from Kentucky]
Old Stone Hammer
Metesky, George. See:
HOFFMAN, ABBIE
Methodism in the United States,
The Mother of. See:
HECK, BARBARA RUCKLE
Methodism, The Apostle of.
See: LEE, JESSE
Methodist Agassiz, The. See:
MARCY, OLIVER
Methodist Conference in India,
The Nestor of. See:
BOWEN, GEORGE
METHODIUS (826-85)
[Thessalonian churchman]
The Apostle to the Slavs
St. Methodius
METHODIUS. See also:
Apostles to the Slavs
Methodius, St. See:
Apostles to the Slavs
METHODIUS
METHOLD, KENNETH WALTER
(1931-) [British educator,
publisher and author]
Alexander Kent
Metsanurk, Mait. See:
HUBEL, EDUARD
METZGER, ROSWELL WILLIAM
(1906-) [American pianist
and arranger]
Ros Metzger
Meudon, Le Curé de (The
Parish Priest of Meudon).
See: RABELAIS,
FRANÇOIS
MEULENBELT-LUBER,
HENRIETTA C.A. (1889-)
[Dutch author]
Jet Luber
Meung, Jean de. See:
CLOPINEL, JEAN
Mewburn, Martin. See:
HITCHIN, MARTIN MEWBURN
Mexican Army, The Marion of
the. See:
LANE, JOSEPH
Mexican Spitfire, The. See:
VILLABOS, GUADELOUPE

VELEZ DE
México, Carnicerito de. See:
    GONZÁLEZ, JOSÉ
Mexico, Protector of. See:
    NORTON, JOSHUA A.
Mexico, The Napoleon of. See:
    ITURBIDE, AGUSTÍN
    DE
MEYER, DAVID HAROLD
    (1930-) [American
    actor]
David Janssen
MEYER, DEBORAH
    ELIZABETH (1952-)
    [American swimmer]
Debbie Meyer
MEYER, DR. ALEXANDER
    (fl. 1929) [Russian
    entertainer]
The Prewar Rocking Chair
    Sensation of Russia
MEYER, JACOB (1735-95)
    [American illusionist
    and magician]
Philadelphia
MEYER, JEROME SYDNEY
    (1895-) [American
    editor and author]
S. M. Jennings
Meyer Wallach. See:
    FINKELSTEIN, MEYER
Meyerbeer, Giacomo. See:
    BEER, JAKOB LIEBMANN
MEYNELL, LAURENCE (1899-)
    [English author]
Valerie Baxter
Sidney Bedford
MEYNELL, WILFRID
    (1852-1948) [English
    journalist and biographer]
Jonathan Oldcastle
MEYSENBURG, JANET
    BEECHER (1884-1955)
    [American character
    actress]
Janet Beecher
Mezz. See:
    MESIROW, MILTON
MEZZOFANTI, CARDINAL
    GIUSEPPE (1774-1849)
    [Italian churchman and
    linguist]

The Living Pentecost
The Walking Polyglot
Mia. See:
    FARROW, MARIA DE
    LOURDES VILLIERS
Mia Slavenska. See:
    CORAK, MIA
Michael. See:
    CARVER, RICHARD
    MICHAEL POWER
    Field, Michael
    MICHEL
    Michel
    Michele
    OGDEN, LIEUT. COM-
    MANDER JOHN MICHAEL
    HUBERT
    SHEPLEY-SMITH, MICHAEL
    TERR, MISCHA R.
MICHAEL I (died 845)
    [Byzantine emperor]
Rhangabe
MICHAEL II (died 829)
    [Byzantine emperor]
The Amorian
Michael III (died 867)
    [Byzantine emperor]
The Drunkard
MICHAEL IV (died 1041)
    [Byzantine emperor]
The Paphlagonian
MICHAEL V (died 1042)
    [Byzantine emperor]
The Calker
MICHAEL VI (fl. 11th cent.)
    [Byzantine emperor]
The Warrior
MICHAEL VII (fl. 11th cent.)
    [Byzantine emperor]
Ducas
MICHAEL VIII (1234-82)
    [Byzantine emperor]
Palaeologus
MICHAEL IX (died 1320)
    [Byzantine emperor]
Palaeologus
Michael, Albert. See:
    LYONS, A. NEIL
Michael Angelo. See:
    BUONARROTI, MICHEL-
    ANGELO
Michael Angelo Titmarsh. See:

694

THACKERAY, WILLIAM
MAKEPEACE
Michael Arlen. See:
KOUYOUMDJIAN,
DIKRAN
Michael Bonner. See:
GLASSCOCK, ANNE
BONNER
Michael Brett. See:
TRIPP, MILES
Michael Caine. See:
MICKLEWHITE, MAURICE
JOSEPH
Michael Carey. See:
BURTON, EDWARD J.
Michael Case. See:
HOWARD, ROBERT WEST
Michael Costello. See:
DETZER, KARL
Michael Craig. See:
GREGSON, MICHAEL
Michael Curtiz. See:
KERTESZ, MIHALY
Michael Day. See:
DEMPEWOLFF, RICHARD
FREDERIC
Michael Dunn. See:
MILLER, GARY NEIL
Michael East. See:
WEST, MORRIS LANGLO
Michael Edwards. See:
SLOWITZKY, MICHAEL
Michael Fairless. See:
BARBER, MARGARET
FAIRLESS
Michael Fielding. See:
SCIAPIRO, MICHEL
Michael Gaunt. See:
ROBERTSHAW, JAMES
DENIS
Michael Gold. See:
GRANICH, IRVING
Michael Gorham. See:
FOLSOM, FRANKLIN
BREWSTER
Michael Gould. See:
AYRTON, MICHAEL
Michael Hale. See:
BULLOCK, MICHAEL
Michael Halliday. See:
CREASEY, JOHN
Michael Hamilton. See:

CHETHAM-STRODE,
WARREN
Michael Innes. See:
STEWART, JOHN INNES
MACINTOSH
Michael Ireland. See:
FIGGIS, DARRELL
Michael Jesse. See:
BALDWIN, MICHAEL
Michael Landon. See:
OROWITZ, MICHAEL
Michael Lawrence. See:
LARIAR, LAWRENCE
Michael Milner. See:
COOPER, SAUL
MICHAEL, MOINA (1870?-1944)
[American originator of
Poppy Day]
The Poppy Lady
Michael Phillips. See:
NOLAN, WILLIAM FRANCIS
Michael, Ralph. See:
SHOTTER, RALPH
CHAMPION
Michael Stark. See:
LARIAR, LAWRENCE
Michael Strange. See:
OELRICHS, BLANCHE
MARIE LOUISE
Michael Taaffe. See:
MAGUIRE, ROBERT
AUGUSTINE JOSEPH
Michael Traherne. See:
WATKINS-PITCHFORD,
DENYS JAMES
Michael Underwood. See:
EVELYN, JOHN MICHAEL
Michael Vane. See:
HUMPHRIES, SIDNEY
VERNON
Michael Wells. See:
MULLINS, RICHARD
Michael Whalen. See:
SHOVLIN, JOSEPH
KENNETH
Michael Williams. See:
ST. JOHN, WYLLY FOLK
Michaeles, M. M. See:
GOLDING, MORTON JAY
Michaëlis, Karin. See:
STANGELAND,
KATHARINA MARIE

BECH-BRÖNDUM
Michaels, Barbara. See:
MERTZ, BARBARA
GROSS
Michaels, Dale. See:
RIFKIN, SHEPARD
Michaels, Steve. See:
AVALLONE, MICHAEL
ANGELO, JR.
MICHAELSKA, MARIANNE
(c. 1898-1959) [Polish-
American dancer;
proponent of the shimmy]
The Box Office Girl
Gilda Gray
Miche, Josef. See:
BOCHENSKI, JOSEPH M.
Michel. See:
MICHAEL
Michael
Michele
SIMON, FRANÇOIS
Michel Auclair. See:
VUJOVIC, VLADIMIR
MICHEL, CLAUDE (1738-1814)
[French sculptor]
Clodion
MICHEL, CLÉMENCE LOUISE
(1830-1905) [French
revolutionist]
Louise Michel
Michel Fourest. See:
WYNNE-TYSON,
TIMOTHY JOHN
LYADEN
Michel Mouton. See:
MONTCORBIER,
FRANÇOIS DE
Michelangelo. See:
BUONARROTI,
MICHELANGELO
Michelangelo da Caravaggio.
See: MERISI (MERISIO),
MICHELANGELO
Michelangelo of Music, The.
See: GLÜCK,
CHRISTOPHER
WILLIBALD
Michelangelo of the Lyre, The.
See: PALESTRINA,
GIOVANNI PIERLUIGI
DA
Michelangelo, The French. See:

COUSIN, JEAN
PUGET, PIERRE
Michelangelo, The Spanish. See:
CANO, ALONSO
Michele. See also:
MICHAEL
Michael
MICHEL
Michel
Michele Morgan. See:
ROUSSEL, SIMONE
Micheline Presle. See:
CHASSAGNE, MICHELINE
Michigan Terror, The. See:
HESTON, WILLIAM M.
Michigan, The Boy Geologist of.
See: HOUGHTON,
DOUGLASS
Michigan, The Sweet Singer of.
See: MOORE, JULIA
Mickey. See:
ALPERT, MILTON I.
BLOOM, MILTON
COCHRANE, GORDON
STANLEY
CODIAN, MICHAEL
FINN, NEAL FRANCIS
MEDWICK, JOSEPH M.
PHILLIPS, ALAN
MEYRICK KERR
ROKER, GRANVILLE
WILLIAM
SPILLANE, FRANK
MORRISON
WRIGHT, MARY KATHRYN
Mickey Free. See:
ENTON, DR. HARRY
Mickey McGuire. See:
YULE, JOE, JR.
Mickey Mouse. See:
ELY, WILLIAM HARVEY
JOHNSON
Mickey Rooney. See:
YULE, JOE, JR.
Mickie Compere. See:
DAVIDSON, MICKIE COM-
PERE
MICKLEWHITE, MAURICE JOSEPH
(1933-) [English actor]
Michael Caine
Mid-Victorians, The International
Bad Girl of the. See:
GILBERT, MARIE DOLORES

696

ELIZA ROSANNA
Middle Ages, The Chrysostom
of the. See:
VON REGENSBURG,
BERTHOLD
Middle Ages, The Walter
Scott of the. See:
FROISSART, JEAN
Middle Tennessee, The
Father of. See:
ROBERTSON, JAMES
Middle West, The Homer of.
See: MASON, WALT
Middleton, Arthur. See:
O'BRIEN, EDWARD
J. C. HARRINGTON
MIDDLETON-MURRY, JOHN
(1926-) [British author]
Colin Murry
MIDDLETON, PEGGY YVONNE
(1922-) [Canadian
dancer and motion
picture actress]
Yvonne de Carlo
MIDDLETON, RICHARD
(died 1304) [English
scholastic divine]
The Profound Doctor
(Doctor Profundus)
Midshipman Tom W. Hall.
See:
INGRAHAM, COLONEL
PRENTISS
Midwestern Larry McPhail, A.
See: VEECK, WILLIAM
LOUIS, JR.
MIERS, EARL SCHENCK
(1910-) [American
editor, author and
historian]
David William Meredith
Miff. See:
MOLE, IRVING MILFRED
Mifflin, The Hero of Fort.
See: THAYER, SIMEON
Miggy, Mrs. See:
KRENTEL, MILDRED
WHITE
Mighty Bambino, The. See:
RUTH, GEORGE HERMAN
Mighty Medicine Man, The. See:
POWELL, DAVID FRANK
Mighty Ruler, Very (Genghis

Khan). See:
TEMUJIN
Mighty, The. See:
BOLESLAV I
MIGLIORATI, COSIMO DE
(c. 1336-1406) [Supreme
Pontiff of Roman Catholic
Church]
Pope Innocent VII
Miguelin. See:
MATEO, MIGUEL
Mikan, Baron. See:
BARBA, HARRY
Mike. See:
DI NAPOLI, MARIO
GORMAN, THOMAS
FRANCIS XAVIER
McCLINTOCK, MARSHALL
MONRONEY, ALMER
STILLWELL MIKE
WALLACE, MYRON LEON
Mike, Dr. See:
MIKESELL, WILLIAM
HENRY
Mike Douglas. See:
DOWD, MICHAEL
DELANEY, JR.
Mike Mazurki. See:
MAZURWSKI, MIKHAIL
Mike Moran. See:
ARD, WILLIAM THOMAS
Mike Todd. See:
GOLDBOGEN, AVROM
HIRSCH
MIKESELL, WILLIAM HENRY
(1887-) [American author]
Dr. Mike
Miketta, Bob. See:
MORRIS, ROBERT
Mikhailovich. See:
ALEXEI (ALEXIS)
MIKHAILOVITCH, BORIS
(1895-1963) [Russian-born
producer of American
motion pictures]
Boris Morros
Milan Bach, The. See:
BACH, JOHANN CHRISTIAN
MILBURN, WILLIAM HENRY
(1823-1903) [American
Methodist preacher;
Chaplain of U.S. Senate
and House of Representa-

tives]
The Blind Preacher
Mildred Elizabeth Gillars.
See: SISK,
MILDRED ELIZABETH
Mildred Hark. See:
McQUEEN, MILDRED
HARK
Mildred Lee. See:
SCUDDER, MILDRED
LEE
Mildred Walker. See:
SCHEMM, MILDRED
WALKER
Mildred Waylan. See:
HARRELL, IRENE BURK
Mile-a-Minute Harry. See:
SELFRIDGE, HARRY
GORDON
Miles. See:
MANDER, LIONEL
SITWELL, SIR OSBERT
SOUTHWOLD, STEPHEN
Miles Burton. See:
STREET, CECIL JOHN
CHARLES
MILES, FREDERIC JAMES
(1869-) [British author]
Rangefinder
Miles, John. See:
BICKHAM, JACK MILES
Miles, Lizzie. See:
LANDREAUX, ELIZABETH
MARY
MILES, LUKE (1925-)
[American blues singer]
Long Gone
MILES, MAXINE FRANCES
MARY FORBES-
ROBERTSON (1900?-)
[British aircraft
designer]
Blossom
Mary Miles
Miles, Miska. See:
MARTIN, PATRICIA
MILES
Miles O'Reilly. See:
HALPINE, CHARLES
GRAHAM
Miles Standish, Captain. See:
STANDISH, MILES
(MYLES)

Miles Underwood. See:
GLASSCO, JOHN
Miles, Vera. See:
RALSTON, VERA
MILEY, JAMES (1903-32)
[American jazz musician
(trumpet)]
Bubber Miley
Milford Bard, The. See:
LOFLAND, JOHN
Militant. See:
SANDBURG, CARL AUGUST
Military Academy, The Father
of the United States. See:
THAYER, SYLVANUS
Military Commander of the
State, The Supreme. See:
CHU TEH
Militum, Patricius and Magister.
See: THEODORIC
Milk of Magnesia Phillips. See:
PHILLIPS, ALFRED
NOROTON, JR.
Mill, C.R. See:
CRNJANSKI, MILOS
Mill Boy of the Slashes, The.
See: CLAY, HENRY
MILL, JOHN STUART (1806-73)
[British political econo-
mist and philosopher]
The Logic-chopping Machine
Milland, Ray. See:
TRUSCOTT-JONES,
REGINALD
MILLAR. See also:
MILLER
Miller
MILLAR, KENNETH (1915-)
[American author of
detective stories]
John Macdonald
Ross Macdonald
John Ross Macdonald
MILLAR (MILLER), WILLIAM
(1928-) [Irish-American
actor]
Stephen Boyd
MILLAY, EDNA ST. VINCENT
(1892-1950) [American poet]
Nancy Boyd
Millbank, Captain H.R. See:
ELLIS, EDWARD SYLVES-
TER

Millburn, Cynthia. See:
    BROOKS, ANNE TEDLOCK
MILLENDER, DHARATHULA
    HOOD (1920-) [American
    teacher, librarian and
    author]
    Dolly Millender
MILLER. See:
    MILLAR (MILLER),
    WILLIAM
MILLER, AGATHA MARY
    CLARISSA (1891?-)
    [British author of
    detective stories]
    Agatha Christie
    Mary Westmacott
MILLER, ALTON GLENN
    (1904-44) [American
    jazz musician (trombone,
    arranger, leader)]
    Glenn Miller
Miller, Ann. See:
    COLLIER, LUCY ANN
Miller, Benjamin. See:
    LOOMIS, NOEL MILLER
MILLER, BILL. See:
    Miller, Wade
MILLER, CHARLES (1850-19??)
    [American cowboy, soldier
    and adventurer]
    Bronco Carlos
    Bronco Charlie
MILLER, CINCINNATUS
    HEINE (HEINER)
    (1848-1913) [American
    poet, author and play-
    wright]
    Joaquin Miller
    The Oregon Byron
    The Poet of the Sierras
MILLER, CLARENCE H.
    (1923-) [American
    jazz musician (bass,
    singer)]
    Big Miller
Miller, Eddie "Piano". See:
    LISBONA, EDWARD
MILLER, ERNEST (1897-)
    [American jazz musician
    (trumpet, singer)]
    Punch Miller
MILLER, ESCHAL (1918-)

[American motion picture
    actress]
    Nan Grey
Miller, Eugenia. See:
    MANDELKORN, EUGENIA
    MILLER
MILLER, FLORENCE FENWICK
    (1854-) [British writer
    and lecturer]
    Filomena
Miller, Frank. See:
    LOOMIS, NOEL MILLER
Miller, G.R. See:
    JUDD, FREDERICK
    CHARLES
MILLER, GARY NEIL (1935-)
    [American dwarf motion
    picture actor]
    Michael Dunn
MILLER, GEORGE AMOS
    (1868-) [American Metho-
    dist bishop and author]
    Peggy Ann
MILLER, HARRIET MANN
    (1831-1918) [American
    juvenile writer and
    naturalist]
    Olive Thorne Miller
MILLER, HELEN HILL (1899-)
    [American editor and
    author]
    Helen Hill
MILLER, HOMER VIRGIL
    MILTON (1814-96) [American
    orator]
    The Demosthenes of the
    Mountains
MILLER, JAMES RUSSELL
    (1840-1912) [American
    preacher, author and poet]
    The Modern Bunyan
Miller, John. See:
    SAMACHSON, JOSEPH
MILLER, JOSEPH (1684-1738)
    [English comedian]
    The Father of Jests
    Joe Miller
MILLER, LEONARD (1864-1939)
    [English novelist]
    Leonard Merrick
MILLER, LOWELL OTTO (1889-)
    [American professional base-

699

ball player]
Mooney Miller
Miller, Margaret J. See:
    DALE, MARGARET
    JESSY
Miller, Martha. See:
    IVAN, MARTHA MILLER
    PFAFF
Miller, Martin. See:
    MÜLLER, RUDOLPH
Miller, Mary. See:
    NORTHCOTT, WILLIAM
    CECIL
MILLER, MARY BRITTON
    (1883-) [American
    author]
    Isabel Bolton
MILLER, MRS. HENRY WISE
    (1874-1942) [American
    novelist]
    Alice Duer Miller
MILLER, MITCHELL WILLIAM
    (1911-) [American
    musician, impresario,
    business executive and
    television personality]
    Mitch Miller
MILLER, RICE (c. 1893-1965)
    [American jazz musician
    (singer, harmonica)]
    Sonny Boy Williamson
MILLER, SEYMOUR (1908-)
    [American composer,
    pianist and producer]
    Sy Miller
MILLER, THOMAS (1807-74)
    [English poet and author]
    The Basket-Maker
Miller, Wade
    Whit Masterson
    Dale Wilmer
    joint pseuds. of BOB WADE
    (1920-) and BILL
    MILLER (1920-61) [Amer-
    ican authors of mystery
    novels]
Miller, Warne. See:
    RATHBONE, ST. GEORGE
    HENRY
MILLER, WARNER (1838-1918)
    [American manufacturer
    and politician; Senator
    from New York]

Wood-pulp Miller
MILLER, WILLIAM (1782-1849)
    [American poet]
    The Poet of Low Hampton
MILLER, WILLIAM (1810-72)
    [Scottish poet]
    Laureate of the Nursery
MILLET, JEAN FRANÇOIS
    (1642?-79) [French land-
    scape painter]
    Francisque
MILLET, KADISH (1923-)
    [American composer, pub-
    lisher and music teacher]
    Kay Millet
Millet of America, The. See:
    HIGGINS, EUGENE
MILLETT, NIGEL STANSBURY
    (1904-) [British nobleman
    and author]
    Richard Oke
Millie Mayfield. See:
    HOMES, MARY SOPHIE
    SHAW ROGERS
MILLIGAN, MAURICE MORTON
    (1884-) [American attorney
    and prosecutor]
    Missouri's Tom Dewey
MILLIGAN, TERENCE ALAN
    (1918-) [British comedian,
    playwright and author]
    Spike Milligan
MILLINDER, LUCIUS (1900-)
    [American jazz musician
    (leader)]
    Lucky Millinder
Milliner, The Man. See:
    HENRY III
Millionaire Hobo, The. See:
    HOW, JAMES EADS
Millionaire Sheriff, The. See:
    BAKER, ANDERSON YANCEY
Millionaire, The. See:
    GERRY, PETER GOELET
Millionaire, The Dutch. See:
    PHILIPSE, FREDERICK
Millionaire, The Jolly. See:
    O'BRIEN, WILLIAM
    SHONEY
Millionaire Tramp, The. See:
    HOW, JAMES EADS
MILLMAN. See also:
    Milman

MILLMAN, HARRY (-1937)
[American gangster; leader
of the Purple Gang in
Detroit]
The Lone Wolf of the
Underworld
MILLS, FREDERICK ALLEN
(1869-1948) [American
composer, violinist, pub-
lisher and teacher]
Kerry Mills
MILLS, SAMUEL JOHN
(1783-1818) [American
missionary in Negro
America]
The Father of Foreign
Mission Work in
Christian America
MILLS, WILLIAM R. (1894-)
[American composer,
conductor and pianist]
Billy Mills
Milman. See also:
MILLMAN
Milman, Harry Dubois. See:
CORYELL, JOHN
RUSSELL
MILNER, MARION BLACKETT
(1900-) [British author]
Johanna Field
Milner, Michael. See:
COOPER, SAUL
MILNER, MOSES EMBREE
(1829-76) [American
frontier scout and ad-
venturer]
California Joe
MILNER, THOMAS PICTON
(1822-91) [American
journalist and soldier of
fortune]
Thomas Picton
Paul Preston
Milnes, Single Speech. See:
HOUGHTON, RICHARD
MONCTON MILNES,
1ST BARON
Milo, The English. See:
TOPHAM, THOMAS
MILORADOVITCH, COUNT
MIKHAIL ANDRIEVITCH
(1770-1825) [Russian
general officer]

The Russian Murat
Milsen, Oscar. See:
MENDELSOHN, OSCAR
Milt. See:
JACKSON, MILTON
Milt Rogers. See:
ADELSTEIN, MILTON
MILTIADES (MELCHIADES)
(died 314) [Supreme
Pontiff of Roman Catholic
Church]
Pope Miltiades
Pope Melchiades
St. Miltiades
St. Melchiades
Milton Berle. See:
BERLINGER, MILTON
MILTON, JOHN (1608-74)
[English poet]
The Blind Poet
The British Homer
The Lady of Christ's
Milton Lesser. See:
MARLOWE, STEPHEN
Milton of Germany, The. See:
KLOPSTOCK, FRIEDRICH
GOTTLIEB
Milton Quarterly. See:
CORYELL, JOHN RUSSELL
Milton, The American. See:
LORD, WILLIAM WILBER-
FORCE
Milton, The Anglo-Saxon. See:
CAEDMON (CEDMON)
Milton, The German. See:
KLOPSTOCK, FRIEDRICH
GOTTLIEB
Miltoun, Francis. See:
MANSFIELD, MILBURG
FRANCISCO
Milty, Uncle. See:
BERLINGER, MILTON
Mimi. See:
PERRIN, JEANNIE
ROMMEL, MARILYN
DAYTON
MIMNERMUS (fl. c. 630-600
B.C.) [Greek elegiac poet
of Colophon]
The Smyrnean Poet
Mina Lewiton Simon. See:
LEWITON, MINA
Mince, Johnny. See:

MUENZENBERGER,
JOHN HENRY
MIND, GOTTFRIED (1768-1814)
[Swiss painter]
The Bernese Friendli
The Raphael of Cats
Mind of Mental Mystery, The
Master. See:
DUNNINGER, JOSEPH
Mind, The Copernicus of the.
See: FREUD,
SIGMUND
Mind, The Man With the
Miracle. See:
DUNNINGER, JOSEPH
Mind, The Right Hand. See:
ROBINSON, FRANCES
M.
Mind, The Woman Who Always
Speaks Her. See:
COX-OLIVER, EDNA MAY
MINEO, ATTILIO, (1918-)
[American musician and
publisher]
Art Mineo
Mineralogy, The Father of
American. See:
CLEAVELAND, PARKER
Miniature Petrarch, The. See:
BEMBO, PIETRO
Minier, Nelson. See:
BAKER, LAURA NELSON
STOUTENBURG,
ADRIEN PEARL
Minimo, Duca (The Least of
the Dukes). See:
RAMPAGNETTO,
GAETANO
Minister of Mirth, The Prime.
See: WADE, GEORGE
EDWARD
Minister, The Blind. See:
WOODBRIDGE, TIMOTHY
Minister, The Heaven-sent.
See: PITT, WILLIAM
Minneapolis, The Father of.
See: STEVENS, JOHN H.
Minnesota, The Father of.
See: SIBLEY, HENRY
HASTINGS
Minnesota, The Father of the
University of. See:

PILLSBURY, JOHN
SARGENT
Minnesota's Potato King. See:
SCHROEDER, HENRY
Minnie. See:
MACKAY, MARY
Minnie Maddern Fiske. See:
DAVEY, MARIE AUGUSTA
Minnie Maddern, Little. See:
DAVEY, MARIE AUGUSTA
Minor, Anthropophagus. See:
CONNIFF, JAMES CLIF-
FORD GREGORY
MINSKY, BETTY JANE TOEBE
(1932-) [American author]
Liz Toby
Minstrel, Henry the. See:
BLIND HARRY
Minstrel of the Border, The. See:
SCOTT, SIR WALTER
Minstrel of the English Stage,
The Last. See:
SHIRLEY, JAMES
Minstrel, The Border. See:
SCOTT, SIR WALTER
Minstrel, The Great. See:
SCOTT, SIR WALTER
Minstrelsy, The Father of
American. See:
RICE, THOMAS DART-
MOUTH
Minter, Mary Miles. See:
SHELBY, JULIET
Minto-Cowen, Frances. See:
MUNTHE, FRANCES
Minton, Paula. See:
LITTLE, PAUL H.
MINTON, SHERMAN (1890-)
[American lawyer, poli-
tician and U. S. Senator
from Indiana]
The King of the New Dealers
Shay
Minturn, Edward. See:
JUDSON, EDWARD ZANE
CARROLL
URNER, NATHAN DANE
Minuto. See:
VARGAS, ENRIQUE
Minx of the Movies, The. See:
COMPSON, BETTY
Mirabeau, Barrel. See:

RIQUETI, ANDRÉ
  BONIFACE LOUIS
Mirabeau, Comte de. See:
  RIQUETI, HONORÉ
  GABRIEL
Mirabeau, Marquis de. See:
  RIQUETI, VICTOR
Mirabeau of the Mob, The.
  See: DANTON,
  GEORGES JACQUES
Mirabeau, Vicomte de. See:
  RIQUETI, ANDRÉ
  BONIFACE LOUIS
Mirabilis, Doctor (The Wonder-
  ful Doctor). See:
  BACON, ROGER
Miracle, l'Enfant du. See:
  CHAMBORD, HENRI
  CHARLES DIEUPONNÉ,
  COMTE DE
Miracle Man, The Egyptian.
  See: BEY, RAHMAN
Miracle Mind, The Man With
  the. See:
  DUNNINGER, JOSEPH
Miracle of Nature, The. See:
  CHRISTINA
Miracle of Our Age, The. See:
  SIDNEY (SYDNEY), SIR
  PHILIP
Miranda, Carmen. See:
  CUNHA, MARÍA DE
  CARMO MIRANDA DE
MIRANDA, FRANCISCO DA SÁ
  DE (1495-1558) [Portu-
  guese poet]
  The Portuguese Theocritus
MIRANDA, ROQUE (1799-1843)
  [Spanish bullfighter]
  Rigores
Miriam. See:
  MAKEBA, ZENSI
  MIRIAM
Miriam Bredow. See:
  WOLF, MIRIAM
  BREDOW
Miriam F. Squire. See:
  LESLIE, MIRIAM
  FLORENCE FOLLINE
Miriam Gilbert. See:
  PRESBERG, MIRIAM
  GOLDSTEIN

Miriam Weiss. See:
  SCHLEIN, MIRIAM
Mirth, The Prime Minister of.
  See: WADE, GEORGE
  EDWARD
MIRZA HUSEYN ALI (1817-92)
  [Founder of the Bahai sect]
  Baha Ullah (Splendor of God)
Misanthrope of Athens, The.
  See: TIMON
Mischa Auer. See:
  OUNSKOWSKY, MISCHA
Mischievous Andy. See:
  JACKSON, ANDREW
Miser, The Pinner. See:
  DANCER, DANIEL
Mises, Dr. See:
  FECHNER, GUSTAV
  THEODOR
Miska Miles. See:
  MARTIN, PATRICIA MILES
Miss Ella Vator, By. See:
  SMITH, HARRY ALLEN
Miss Ellen Bogen. See:
  ELLENBOGEN, HENRY
Miss Frances. See:
  HORWICH, FRANCES
  RAPPAPORT
Miss George. See:
  SIDUS, GEORGINA
Miss Leslie. See:
  LESLIE, ELIZA
Miss Mary Berwick. See:
  PROCTOR, ADELAIDE
  ANNE
Miss Mulock. See:
  CRAIK, DINAH MARIA
  MULOCK
Miss Poker Face, Little. See:
  WILLS, HELEN
  NEWINGTON
Miss Read. See:
  SAINT, DORA JESSIE
Miss Roosevelt, Little. See:
  LONGWORTH, ALICE LEE
  ROOSEVELT
Miss Ruth. See:
  DENNIS, RUTH
Miss Tickletoby. See:
  THACKERAY, WILLIAM
  MAKEPEACE
Miss Vaughan. See:

PRITCHARD, HANNAH
Miss Yerrit. See:
TERRY, SARAH BALLARD
Mission work in Christian
America, The Father of
Foreign. See:
MILLS, SAMUEL JOHN
Missionaries, The Grandfather of
the. See:
ROBERTS, ROBERT
RICHFORD
Missionary Bishop of America,
The. See:
DOANE, GEORGE
WASHINGTON
Missions, The Father of Modern.
See: CAREY, WILLIAM
Mississippi College, The Sage
of. See: AVEN,
ALGERNON JASPER
Mississippi, The Father of
Journalism in. See:
MARSCHALK, ANDREW
Mississippi, The Master Pilot
of the. See:
CLEMENS, SAMUEL
LANGHORNE
Mississippi, The Swamp Fox
of. See:
FORREST, NATHAN
BEDFORD
Missouri Kid, The. See:
RUDOLPH, WILLIAM
Missouri, The Father of the
University of. See:
ROLLINS, JAMES SIDNEY
Missouri, The Grand Old Man
of. See:
KIRK, JOHN ROBERT
Missouri, The King of the. See:
MACKENZIE, KENNETH
Missouri, The Man from. See:
TRUMAN, HARRY S
Missouri, The Robin Hood of.
See: JAMES, JESSE
WOODSON
Missouri's Tom Dewey. See:
MILLIGAN, MAURICE
MORTON
Missy. See:
WALKER, WILLIAM
Missy, Little. See:

MOZZEE, PHOEBE ANNE
OAKLEY
Mr. American. See:
TUGWELL, REXFORD GUY
Mr. Anthony. See:
ANTHONY, JOHN J.
Mr. B. See:
ECKSTINE, WILLIAM
CLARENCE
Mr. Bradly. See:
BURROUGHS, WILLIAM
SEWARD
Mr. Broadway. See:
COHAN, GEORGE MICHAEL
Mr. Brown. See:
THACKERAY, WILLIAM
MAKEPEACE
Mr. Charlie. See:
CANNON, CHARLES A.
Mr. Clean, The Mean. See:
LEONARD, JACK E.
Mr. Conny Keyber. See:
FIELDING, HENRY
Mr. Dooley. See:
DUNNE, FINLEY PETER
Mr. Economy. See:
BYRD, HARRY FLOOD
Mr. Five by Five. See:
RUSHING, JAMES ANDREW
Mr. 500. See:
GRANATELLI, ANDREW
Mr. Greenfingers. See:
WALLS, IAN GASCOIGNE
Mr. Inside. See:
BLANCHARD, FELIX
ANTHONY
Mr. Insult. See:
LEONARD, JACK E.
Mr. John. See:
HARBERGER, JOHN PICO
Mr. Kenneth. See:
MARLOWE, KENNETH
Mr. Kisskiss Bangbang. See:
CONNERY, THOMAS
Mr. Malone. See:
GUION, RAYMOND
Mr. Martin. See:
BURROUGHS, WILLIAM
SEWARD
Mr. Music Maker. See:
WELK, LAWRENCE
Mr. New Year's Eve. See:

LOMBARDO, GUY ALBERT
Mr. Outside. See:
DAVIS, GLENN
Mr. Peepers. See:
COX, WALLACE
MAYNARD
Mr. Republican. See:
TAFT, ROBERT
ALPHONSO
Mr. S. T. P. See:
GRANATELLI, ANDREW
Mr. Saturday Night. See:
GLEASON, HERBERT
JOHN
Mr. Smith. See:
LOCKWOOD, RALPH
INGERSOLL
LOUIS-PHILIPPE
Mr. Spec. See:
THACKERAY, WILLIAM
MAKEPEACE
Mr. Television. See:
BERLINGER, MILTON
Mr. Thomas Howard. See:
JAMES, JESSE WOODSON
Mr. Universe. See:
REEVES, STEPHEN
Mr. W. H. See:
HERBERT, WILLIAM
Mr. Wizard. See:
HERBERT, DONALD
JEFFRY
Mr. World. See:
REEVES, STEPHEN
Mr. Yorick. See:
STERNE, LAURENCE
Mistinguett. See:
BOURGEOIS, JEANNE
MARIE
Mistletoe Politician, The.
See: VAN BUREN,
MARTIN
Mistral, Gabriela. See:
ALCAYAGA, LUCILLA
GODOY DE
Mrs. See:
CENTLIVRE, SUSANNAH
GASKELL, ELIZABETH
LEIGHORN STEVENSON
HEMANS, FELICIA
DOROTHEA
Mrs. Anna A. Robie. See:

ROLFE, MARO O.
Mrs. Bloomfield H. Moore.
See: MOORE, CLARA
SOPHIA JESSUP
Mrs. Bloomfield-Moore. See:
MOORE, CLARA SOPHIA
JESSUP
Mrs. Bull. See:
ANN
Mrs. Campbell Praed. See:
PRAED, ROSA CAROLINE
Mrs. Clarissa Packard. See:
GILMAN, CAROLINE
HOWARD
Mrs. Coulson Kernahan. See:
KERNAHAN, JEAN GWYNNE
Mrs. E. J. Richmond. See:
RICHMOND, EUPHEMIA
JOHNSON
Mrs. Elizabeth N. Graham. See:
GRAHAM, FLORENCE
NIGHTINGALE
Mrs. Fairstar. See:
HORNE, RICHARD HENGIST
(HENRY)
Mrs. Fitzherbert. See:
SMYTHE, MARIA ANNE
Mrs. Florice Norton. See:
BRAME CHARLOTTE
MARY
Mrs. Freeman. See:
JENNINGS, SARAH
Mrs. George Archibald. See:
PALMER, ANNA CAMPBELL
Mrs. Georgie Sheldon. See:
DOWNS, SARAH ELIZA-
BETH
Mrs. Grant of Laggan. See:
GRANT, ANNE MACVICAR
Mrs. H. O. Ward. See:
MOORE, CLARA SOPHIA
JESSUP
Mrs. Hemans of America, The.
See: SIGOURNEY, LYDIA
HUNTLEY
Mrs. Henry Jenner. See:
JENNER, KATHERINE LEE
Mrs. Henry Wood. See:
WOOD, ELLEN PRICE
Mrs. Humphry Ward. See:
ARNOLD, MARY AUGUSTA
Mrs. Hunter. See:

BARKER, KATE CLARK
Mrs. Inchbald. See:
INCHBALD, ELIZABETH
SIMPSON
Mrs. James Bond. See:
BOND, MARY FANNING
WICKHAM
Mrs. K. F. Hill. See:
BAER, MRS.
Mrs. Kemper Campbell. See:
CAMPBELL, LITTA
BELLE
Mrs. Leslie Carter. See:
DUDLY, CAROLINE
LOUISE
Mrs. Letitia Booth. See:
RUSSELL, WILLIAM
CLARK
Mrs. Madeline Leslie. See:
BAKER, HARRIETTE
NEWALL WOODS
Mrs. Mark Peabody. See:
VICTOR, MRS. METTA
VICTORIA FULLER
MORSE
Mrs. Markham. See:
PENROSE, ELIZABETH
Mrs. Mary Clavers. See:
KIRKLAND, CAROLINE
MATILDA STANSBURY
Mrs. Miggy. See:
KRENTEL, MILDRED
WHITE
Mrs. Morley. See:
ANN
Mistress of Sophisticated
Slapstick, The. See:
LILLIE, BEATRICE
GLADYS
Mrs. Oldmixon. See:
SIDUS, GEORGINA
Mrs. Partington. See:
SHILLABER, BENJAMIN
PENHALLOW
Mrs. Patrick Campbell. See:
CAMPBELL, BEATRICE
STELLA TANNER
Mrs. Ravenhall. See:
KING, ROBERT
Mrs. Regera Dowdy. See:
GOREY, EDWARD ST.
JOHN

Mrs. Robert Henrey. See:
HENREY, MADELEINE
Mrs. Romilly Fedden. See:
FEDDEN, KATHERINE
WALDO DOUGLAS
Mrs. S. B. Phelps. See:
GRISWOLD, FRANCES
IRENE BURGE
Mrs. Siddons. See:
SIDDONS, SARAH KEMBLE
Mrs. Silence Dogood. See:
FRANKLIN, BENJAMIN
Mrs. Thrale. See:
PIOZZI, HESTER LYNCH
SALUSBURY
Mrs. Willoughby Hodgson See:
HODGSON AGNES
Mitch. See:
MILLER, MITCHELL
WILLIAM
Mitch Hardin. See:
GERRITY, DAVID JAMES
Mitchel, Jackson. See:
MATCHA, JACK
MITCHEL, JOHN PURROY
(1879-1918) [American
politician and investigator]
Young Torquemada
MITCHELL, DR. SILAS WEIR
(1829-1914) [American
physician, novelist and poet]
John Chester
S. Weir Mitchell
MITCHELL, DONALD GRANT
(1822-1908) [American
author]
An Opera-goer
Ik Marvel
Ike Marvel
J. K. Marvel
John Timon
Mitchell, Ewan. See:
JANNER, GREVILLE EWAN
MITCHELL, GORDON B.
(1932-   ) [American jazz
musician (bass)]
Whitey Mitchell
MITCHELL, HELEN PORTER
(1861-1931) [Australian
operatic soprano]
Nellie Melba
MITCHELL, ISAAC (1859-1912)

[American editor and
novelist]
Joseph Nelson
MITCHELL, ISABEL MARY
(1893-) [English author]
Josephine Plain
MITCHELL, JAMES (1926-)
[British actor, educator
and author]
James Munro
MITCHELL, JAMES LESLIE
(1901-35) [Scottish
novelist, archaeologist
and historian]
Lewis Grassic Gibbon
MITCHELL, KEITH MOORE
(1927-) [American
jazz musician (bass,
piano, cello, bass
guitar)]
Red Mitchell
Mitchell, Kerry. See:
WILKES-HUNTER,
RICHARD
MITCHELL, MARGARET JULIA
(1837-1918) [American
actress]
Maggie Mitchell
MITCHELL, ORMSBY
McKNIGHT (1810-62)
[American general
officer and astronomer]
Old Stars
MITCHELL, RICHARD ALLEN
(1930-) [American
jazz musician (trumpet)]
Blue Mitchell
MITCHELL, STEPHEN MIX
(1743-1835) [American
jurist and statesman]
The Stalking Library
MITCHELL, WILLIAM (1879-)
1936) [American general
officer and aviator]
Billy Mitchell
MITCHILL, SAMUEL LATHAM
(1764-1831) [American
scientist and legislator;
Congressman from New
York]
The Nestor of American
Science

MITFORD, JOHN (1782-1831)
[British poet]
Alfred Burton
MITHRIDATES VI (c.131-63 B.C.)
[King of Pontus]
Eupator
Mithridates the Great
Mitton, G.E. See:
SCOTT, GERALDINE EDITH
Mitzi Gaynor. See:
VON GERBER, FRANCESCA
MITZI MARLENE DE
CHARNEY
Mitzie. See:
WELCH, MARILYN
MIX, TOM (1880-1940)
[American motion picture
and radio actor]
The Ralston Straight-shooter
MIZNER, ELIZABETH HOWARD
(1907-) [American educator
and author]
Elizabeth Howard
Mlle. Items so abbreviated are
indexed as though spelled
"Mademoiselle"
MNESARETE (fl. 4th cent. B.C.)
[Athenian courtesan]
Phryne
Mob, The Mirabeau of the. See:
DANTON, GEORGES JACQUES
Mobile Bay, The Hero of. See:
FARRAGUT, DAVID
GLASGOW
MODENA. See:
MARY OF MODENA
Modern Aerial Photography, The
Father of. See:
GODDARD, GEORGE
WILLIAM
Modern Agriculture, The Father
of. See:
YOUNG, ARTHUR
Modern Amphibious Warfare, The
Father of. See:
SMITH, HOLLAND McTYEIRE
Modern Antigone, The. See:
CHARLOTTE, MARIE
THÉRÈSE
Modern Aristophanes, The. See:
FOOTE, SAMUEL
Modern Ballet, The Father of.

See: FOKINE, MICHEL
Modern Baseball, The Father
of. See:
CARTWRIGHT,
ALEXANDER JOY
Modern Bunyan, The. See:
MILLER, JAMES
RUSSELL
Modern Cervantes, The. See:
PEREDA, JOSÉ MARÍA
DE
Modern Chemistry, The Father
of. See:
BOYLE, SIR ROBERT
Modern Drama, The Father
of. See:
IBSEN, HENRIK JOHAN
Modern Fortifications, The
Father of Our. See:
CRAIGHILL, WILLIAM
PRICE
Modern French Songs, The
Father of. See:
PANARD, CHARLES-
FRANÇOIS
Modern Generation's Rudy
Vallee, The. See:
MONROE, VAUGHN
WILTON
Modern Geography, The
Father of. See:
KREMER, GERHARD
Modern Gracchus, The. See:
RIQUETI, HONORÉ
GABRIEL
Modern Greece, The Leonidas
of. See:
BOZZARIS (BOTZARIS),
MARKOS
Modern Literature, The
Alnaschar of. See:
COLERIDGE, SAMUEL
TAYLOR
Modern Madonna Painter, The.
See: CARRIÈRE,
EUGÈNE
Modern Magic, The Father
of. See:
ROBERT-HOUDIN, JEAN
EUGÈNE
Modern Mercury. See:
ROOSEVELT, JAMES

Modern Messalina, The. See:
ANHALT-ZERBST,
SOPHIA AUGUSTA
FREDERICA OF
Modern Missions, The Father
of. See:
CAREY, WILLIAM
Modern Mozart, The. See:
KORNGOLD, ERICH
WOLFGANG
Modern Navy, The Father of
Our. See:
CHANDLER, WILLIAM
EATON
Modern Norwegian Poetry,
The Father of. See:
DASS, PETER
Modern Painting, The Father
of. See:
CIMABUE, GIOVANNI
Modern Philosophy, The Father
of. See:
DESCARTES, RENÉ
Modern Playwright, Germany's
Greatest. See:
HAUPTMANN, GERHART
Modern Pliny, The. See:
GESNER, KONRAD VON
Modern Poetesses, The
Cowper of Our. See:
SOUTHEY, CAROLINE
ANNE BOWLES
Modern Prose Fiction, The
Father of. See:
FOE, DANIEL
Modern Rabelais, The. See:
MAGINN, WILLIAM
Modern Religious World, The.
Joan of Arc of the. See:
UTLEY, ULDINE
Modern Seostris, The. See:
BONAPARTE,
NAPOLEON
Modern Sisyphus, The. See:
WEBSTER, DANIEL
Modern Theory, The Father of.
See: FERMAT, PIERRE DE
Modern Thought, The Columbus
of. See:
EMERSON, RALPH WALDO
Modern Wagner, The. See:
HUMPERDINCK, ENGEL-

BERT
Modernism, The Father of.
    See: CÉZANNE,
    PAUL
    SULLIVAN, LOUIS
    HENRI
Modesty, Virgin. See:
    WILMOT, JOHN
Moffatt, James. See:
    HUGHES, ROBERT J.
MOFFITT, DE LOYCE
    (1906-) [American
    composer, conductor
    and arranger]
Deke Moffitt
MOGRIDGE, GEORGE
    (1787-1854) [English
    miscellaneous writer]
Old Humphrey
Peter Parley
Moguy, Leonide. See:
    MAGUILEVSKY, LEONIDE
Mohair Jack. See:
    GARNER, JOHN NANCE
MOHAMMED (c. 570-632)
    [Arabian prophet; founder of
    the Mohammedan religion]
The Apostle of the Sword
The Camel-driver of Mecca
MOHAMMED (1618-1707)
    [Mogul emperor of
    India]
Alamgir (Conqueror of the
    World)
Aurangzeb (Ornament
    of the Throne)
Aurungzeb (Ornament of
    the Throne)
MOHAMMED. See also:
    MEHEMET (MOHAMMED)
    ALI
    MUHAMMED
MOHAMMED II (c. 1430-81)
    [Sultan of Turkey]
The Conqueror
The Father of Good Works
The Great
MOHAMMED AHMED (c. 1841-85)
    [Mohammedan, pretended
    Mahdi]
The False Prophet
Mohammed Ali. See:

CLAY, CASSIUS MAR-
    CELLUS, JR.
MOHAMMED, MIRZA ALI
    (1819-50) [Indian reformer
    and religious leader]
Bab-ed-din (Gate of
    Righteousness)
Mohammed Pasha. See:
    HOWE, WILLIAM WIRT
Mohawk Valley, The Patriot
    Mother of the. See:
    VAN ALSTINE, MRS.
    MARTIN J.
Mohenesto. See:
    AVERY, HENRY M.
MOHLER, JOHANN ADAM
    (1796-1838) [German
    Catholic historian and
    theologian]
The Catholic Schleiermacher
MOIR, DAVID MACBETH
    (1798-1851) [Scottish phy-
    sician and author]
Delta
Moira Shearer. See:
    KING, MOIRA SHEARER
Mokanna, Al (The Veiled). See:
    DEN ATTA, HAKIM
Moko. See:
    MEAD, SIDNEY MOKO
MOLE, IRVING MILFRED (1898-
    1961) [American jazz
    musician (trombone, leader)]
Miff Mole
MOLÉ, MATHIEU (1584-1656)
    [French statesman]
The Pym of France
MOLESME. See:
    ROBERT DE MOLESME
MOLESWORTH, MARY LOUISA
    (1839-1921) [British
    novelist and writer of
    children's stories]
Ennis Graham
Molière. See:
    POQUELIN, JEAN BAPTISTE
Molière, The English. See:
    O'KEEFFE, JOHN
Molière, The Italian. See:
    GOLDONI, CARLO
Molière, The Spanish. See:
    MORATÍN, LEANDRO

FERNANDEZ DE
MOLINA, RAFAEL (1841-1900)
[Spanish bullfighter]
Lagartijo
Molina, Tirso de. See:
TÉLLEZ, GABRIEL
Molinera, Antonia. See:
CARILLO, ROSITA
FELIX
MOLINSKY, JOAN (1935?-)
[American comedienne]
Joan Rivers
Moll Cutpurse. See:
FRITH, MARY
Moll, Orange. See:
MEGGS, MRS. MARY
Mollie E. Moore Davis. See:
DAVIS, MARY EVELYN
MOORE
Molly. See:
BRETT, MARY
ELIZABETH
STARK, LLOYD CROW
Molly, Captain. See:
McCAULEY, MARY LUD-
WIG HAYS
Molly McGee. See:
JORDAN, MARIAN
DRISCOLL
Molly Pitcher. See:
McCAULEY, MARY
LUDWIG HAYS
Molnár, Ferenc. See:
NEUMANN, FERENC
Molotov, Vyacheslav Mik-
hailovich. See:
SKRYABIN, VYACHESLAV
MIKHAILOVICH
MOLYNEUX, TOM (1784-)
[American Negro pugilist;
world's heavyweight
champion]
Molyneux the Moor
Mon. See:
WALLGREN, MONRAD
CHARLES
Mon Soldat (My Soldier). See:
HENRY IV
Mona Barrie. See:
SMITH, MONA
Monachism, The Father of
Christian. See:
ANTONY (ANTHONY), ST.

Monaco, Il. See:
LORENZO
MONACO, JAMES V. (1885-
1945) [Italian-American
composer and pianist]
Jimmy Monaco
Monahan, Deane. See:
STEELE, JAMES
Monarch of Hampshire, The.
See:
WILLIAMS, ISRAEL
Monarch of Leg Shackles, The.
See: WEISS, EHRICH
(ERIK WEISZ)
Monarch of Mont Blanc, The.
See: SMITH, ALBERT
RICHARD
Monarch of the Prairies, The.
See: CARSON,
CHRISTOPHER
Monarch of Theologians, The.
See: ALEXANDER OF
HALES
Monarch, The Grand. See:
LOUIS XIV
Monarch, The Merry. See:
CHARLES II
Monarque, Le Grand. See:
LOUIS XIV
Monasticism, Founder of
Western. See:
BENEDICT OF NURSIA, ST.
Monasticism, The Founder of
Christian. See:
ANTONY (ANTHONY), ST.
MONCOURGE, ALEXIS (1904-)
[French entertainer and
motion picture actor]
Jean Gabin
MONDELLO, NUNCIO (1912-)
[American jazz musician
(alto saxophone)]
Toots Mondello
Mondor. See:
GIRARD, PHILIPPE
MONDRIAAN, PETER CORNELIS
(1872-1944) [Dutch
abstract painter]
Piet Mondrian
Money Glass, Sound. See:
GLASS, GEORGE CARTER
Money-maker and Hoopla-artist.
See: HIGGINS, ANDREW

JACKSON
Money Smith, Jingle. See:
    SMITH, JAMES MONROE
Money Spencer, Ready. See:
    SPENCER, ELIHU
Moneybag, The (Ivan Kalita).
    See: IVAN I
    DANILOVICH
MONFA, HENRI MARIE
    RAYMOND DE TOULOUSE-
    LAUTREC (1864-1901)
    [French painter, lith-
    ographer and illustrator]
  Toulouse-Lautrec
Monger, Amendment. See:
    ADAMS, SAMUEL
MONGER, IFOR DAVID
    (1908-) [British physician
    and author]
  Peter Mannigan
  Peter Richards
MONGKUT (1804-68) [King of
    Thailand (Siam)]
  Rama IV
Mongo. See:
    SANTAMARIA, RAMÓN
Monica Blake. See:
    MUIR, MARIE
Monica Clynder. See:
    MUIR, MARIE
Monica Hill. See:
    WATSON, JANE WERNER
Monico Delgadillo. See:
    YÁÑEZ, AGUSTÍN
Monig, Christopher. See:
    CROSSEN, KENDELL
    FOSTER
Monk. See:
    HAZEL, ARTHUR
    LEWIS, MATTHEW
    GREGORY
    MONTGOMERY, WILLIAM
    HOWARD
Monk, Alan. See:
    KENDALL, WILLMOORE
Monk, Galdo. See:
    RISELEY, JERRY BURR,
    JR.
MONK, GEORGE (1608-70)
    [Lord Albemarle; English
    nobleman and general
    officer]

  Honest George
  Old George
MONK, HENRY (fl. mid-19th
    cent.) [California stage-
    coach driver]
  Hank Monk
Monk, The. See:
    ALFONSO IV
Monkey, The. See:
    CAMPISTRON, JEAN GALA-
    BERT DE
Monks, The Father of. See:
    ANTONY (ANTHONY), ST.
    ETHELWOLD OF WIN-
    CHESTER
Monks, The Hammer of the. See:
    CROMWELL, THOMAS
Monks, The Maul of. See:
    CROMWELL, THOMAS
Monmouth, Duke of. See:
    SCOTT, JAMES
Monologist, The Boy. See:
    JESSEL, GEORGE
Monomachus. See:
    VLADIMIR II
Monophthalmos (One-Eyed). See:
    ANTIGONUS I
MONRO. See also:
    MONROE
    Monroe
    MUNRO
    Munro
    MUNROE
MONRO, ROBERT HALE (1902-59)
    [British entertainer and
    motion picture actor]
  Sonnie Hale
MONROE [Monroe]. See also:
    MONRO
    MUNRO
    Munro
    MUNROE
MONROE, ELIZABETH KORT-
    RIGHT (1768-1830) [Wife
    of JAMES MONROE, fifth
    President of the United
    States]
  The Beautiful American (La
    Belle Americaine)
MONROE, JAMES (1758-1831)
    [Fifth President of the
    United States]

The Era-of-good-feeling
President
The Last Cocked Hat
MONROE, KEITH (1917-)
[American journalist
and author]
Dale Colombo
Donald Keith
Monroe, Lyle. See:
HEINLEIN, ROBERT
ANSON
Monroe, Marilyn. See:
BAKER (MORTENSEN),
NORMA JEAN
MONROE, VAUGHN WILTON
(1912-) [American
jazz musician (trumpet,
singer, leader)]
The Modern Generation's
Rudy Vallee
MONRONEY, ALMER
STILLWELL MIKE
(1902-) [American
politician; Senator from
Oklahoma]
Mike Monroney
Monsieur de Paris. See:
SANSON, CHARLES
HENRI
Monsieur Le Coq. See:
SIMENON, GEORGES
Monsieur Sans Esprit. See:
FIELDING, HENRY
Monsieur X. See:
PARODI, ALEXANDRE
Monster, The. See:
WILLIAMS, RENWICK
Mont Blanc, The Monarch of.
See: SMITH, ALBERT
RICHMOND
MONTAGU, ELIZABETH
(1720-1800) [English
critic and social leader]
Fidget
MONTAGU, JOHN (1718-92)
[4th Earl of Sandwich]
Jemmy Twitcher
Montagu O'Reilly. See:
ANDREWS, WAYNE
Montague Rockingham. See:
NYE, NELSON CORAL
Montaigne, The American. See:

EMERSON, RALPH WALDO
Montand, Yves. See:
LIVI, YVES (YVO)(IVO)
Montano. See:
ARIAS, BENITO
Montansier, Marguerite. See:
BRUNET, MARGUERITE
MONTBARS (c.1645-)
[French buccaneer]
The Exterminator
Montclair, Dennis. See:
SLADEN, NORMAN ST.
BARBE
MONTCORBIER, FRANÇOIS DE
(1431-146?) [French lyric
poet]
Michael Mouton
François Villon
Montdory. See:
DESGILBERTS,
GUILLAUME
MONTE, GIOVANNI MARIA
CIOCCHI DEL (1487-1555)
[Supreme Pontiff of Roman
Catholic Church]
Pope Julius III
MONTENEGRO, FREY BENITO,
FEYJOO Y (1676-1764)
[Spanish critic, scholar
and Benedictine monk]
The Spanish Addison
MONTES, ANTONIO (1876-1907)
[Spanish bullfighter]
El Sordo
MONTES, FRANCISCO (1805-51)
[Spanish bullfighter]
Paquiro
Montez, Lola. See:
GILBERT, MARIE DOLORES
ELIZA ROSANNA
Montez, María. See:
SILAS, MARÍA DE SANTO
MONTEZUMA I (1390?-1469)
[Aztec emperor of Mexico]
Ilhuicamia (Heavenly Archer)
MONTEZUMA II (1480?-1520)
[Last Aztec Emperor of
Mexico]
Uei Tlatoani (One Who Speaks)
Xocoyotzin (Furious One)
Montfleury. See:
JACOB, ZACHARIE

Montfort, Guy de. See:
JOHNSON, DONALD
McINTOSH
MONTGOMERY, BERNARD
LAW, 1ST VISCOUNT
MONTGOMERY OF
ALAMEIN (1887-)
[British field marshal]
Monty
MONTGOMERY, CHARLES F.
(1930-) [American
jazz musician (piano,
vibraharp, composer)]
Buddy Montgomery
Montgomery, George. See:
LENZ, GEORGE
MONTGOMERY
Montgomery, Gerard. See:
MOULTRIE, JOHN
MONTGOMERY, HENRY, JR.
(1904-) [American
motion picture actor,
director and producer]
Robert Montgomery
MONTGOMERY, JAMES
(1776-1854) [Scottish
poet]
The Bard of Sheffield
MONTGOMERY, JAMES
(1814-71) [Kansas
pioneer and statesman]
The Kansas Hero
MONTGOMERY, JOHN LESLIE
(1925-) [American
jazz musician (guitar)]
Wes Montgomery
Montgomery, L. M. See:
MACDONALD, LUCY
MAUDE MONTGOMERY
Montgomery, Marian. See:
HOLLOWAY, MARIAN
M. RUNNELS
MONTGOMERY, ROBERT
BRUCE (1921-)
[British author of
detective stories]
Edmund Crispin
MONTGOMERY, ROBERT
DOUGLASS (1908-66)
[Canadian stage and
motion picture actor]
Douglass Montgomery

MONTGOMERY, RUTHERFORD
GEORGE (1894-)
[American teacher and
author]
Al Avery
Everitt Proctor
MONTGOMERY, WILLIAM
HOWARD (1921-) [Amer-
ican jazz musician (bass)]
Monk Montgomery
MONTI, LUIGI (1830-1903)
[Italian-American educator,
consul and author]
Samuel Sampleton
Monticello, The Sage of. See:
JEFFERSON, THOMAS
MONTINI, GIOVANNI BATTISTA
(1897-) [Supreme Pontiff
of Roman Catholic Church]
Pope Paul VI
MONTMORENCY. See:
ANNE, DUC DE MONT-
MORENCY
MONTMORENCY-BOUTEVILLE,
HENRI DE (1628-95)
[French marshal; Duc de
Luxembourg]
Le Tapissier de Notre Dame
Montpelier, The Sage of. See:
MADISON, JAMES
MONTPENSIER, ANNE MARIE
LOUISE D'ORLÉANS,
DUCHESSE DE (1627-93)
[French noblewoman; niece
of King LOUIS XIII of
France]
La Grande Mademoiselle
Montross, David. See:
BACKUS, JEAN
Monty. See:
MONTGOMERY, BERNARD
LAW, 1ST VISCOUNT
MONTGOMERY OF
ALAMEIN
WOOLLEY, EDGAR
MONTILLON
Monty Banks. See:
BIANCHI, MARIO
MONVOISON, CATHERINE
(16??-1680) [French
poisoner]
La Voisine

MOODY, JOSEPH (1700-53)
    [American pastor and
    involuntary murderer]
Handkerchief Moody
Moody, The Madonna of Hall.
    See: HALL, MUSA L.
MOODY, WILLIAM VAUGHAN
    (1869-1910) [American
    educator, author and
    playwright]
The Man in the Iron Mask
Moon, At the Sign of the Blue.
    See: LEWIS, DOMINIC
    BEVAN WYNDHAM
Moon-faced Senator from
    Worcester, The. See:
    HOAR, GEORGE
    FRISBIE
Moon, Jack. See:
    ELLIOTT, JOHN R.
Moon Over the Mountain Girl,
    The. See:
    SMITH, KATHRYN
    ELIZABETH
Moondog. See:
    HARDIN, LOUIS THOMAS
Mooney. See:
    MILLER, LOWELL OTTO
MOONEY, CANICE ALBERT
    JAMES (1911-) [Irish
    Catholic priest and
    author]
Cainneach O'Maonaigh
MOONEY, HAROLD (1911-)
    [American composer,
    arranger, and recording
    executive]
Hal Mooney
MOONEY, THOMAS J.
    (1882?-1942) [American
    labor leader]
Tom Mooney
Moonshine. See:
    GATES, JOHN WARNE
Moonshiners, The King of. See:
    GOOCH, WAYNE R.
Moor. See also:
    MOORE
    Moore
    Morr
Moor, Molyneux the. See:
    MOLYNEUX, TOM

Moor, The (Il Moro). See:
    SFORZA, LUDOVICO
MOORE [Moore]. See also:
    Moor
    Morr
MOORE, ANNE PEGG
    (1716-1813) [English imposter]
The Fasting Woman of Tutbury
Moore, Archie. See:
    WRIGHT, ARCHIBALD LEE
Moore, Austin. See:
    MUIR, CHARLES AUGUSTUS
MOORE, BARTHOLOMEW
    FIGURES (1801-78)
    [American attorney]
The Father of the North
    Carolina Bar
Moore, Beryl. See:
    SMITH-WOODS, DOROTHY
    BERYL
MOORE, CLARA SOPHIA JESSUP
    (1824-99) [American author]
Mrs. Bloomfield-Moore
Mrs. Bloomfield H. Moore
Clara Moreton
Mrs. H.O. Ward
Moore, Colleen. See:
    MORRISON, KATHLEEN
Moore, Fenworth. See:
    STRATEMEYER,
    EDWARD L.
MOORE, FRANCIS (1657-1715)
    [English astrologer and
    almanac maker]
Old Moore
Moore, Garry. See: MORFIT,
    THOMAS GARRISON
MOORE, IDORA McCLELLAN
    (1843-1929) [American
    author]
Betsy Hamilton
MOORE, JOHN RICHARD, JR.
    (1925-) [American child
    actor; later author]
Dick Moore
Dickie Moore
MOORE, JOHN TROTWOOD (1858-
    1929) [American editor and
    author]
Trotwood
MOORE, JULIA (1847-1920)
    [American poet]

The Sweet Singer of Michigan
Moore, Kieron. See:
    O'HANRAHAN, KIERON
MOORE-MARRIOTT, GEORGE
    THOMAS (1885-1949)
    [British motion picture
    actor]
    Moore Marriott
MOORE, ROBERT LOWELL, JR.
    (1925-) [American
    television producer and
    author]
    Robin Moore
Moore, Rosalie. See:
    BROWN, ROSALIE
        GERTRUDE MOORE
MOORE, RUSSELL (1913-)
    [American jazz musician
    (trombone)]
    Big Chief
Moore, Terry. See:
    KOFORD, HELEN
MOORE, THOMAS (1779-1852)
    [Irish poet and wit]
    An Irishman
    Thomas Brown the Younger
    Tom Crib
    Master Little
    Thomas Little
    Anacreon Moore
MOORE, WALTER HOMER
    (1844-1917) [American
    churchman]
    The Beloved Dean
MOORE, WILLIAM A. (1924-)
    [American jazz musician
    (tenor saxophone)]
    Brew Moore
MOORE, WILLIAM HENRY
    (1848-1923) [American
    capitalist and railroad
    promoter]
    The Sphinx of the Rock
    Island
MOORHEAD, JAMES KENNEDY
    (1806-84) [American legis-
    lator, canal builder and
    pioneer in telegraphy]
    Old Slackwater
MOORHOUSE, HILDA
    VANSITTART (1908-)
    [British teacher and
    author]

Jane Vansittart
Moorshead, Henry. See:
    PINE, LESLIE GILBERT
Moose. See:
    CHARLAP, MORRIS
    EARNSHAW, GEORGE
Moose, Big. See:
    EARNSHAW, GEORGE
    LIVINGSTON
    WALSH, EDWARD
    AUGUSTIN
Moose, The Bull. See:
    ROOSEVELT, THEODORE
Moose, The Dough. See:
    PERKINS, GEORGE
    WALBRIDGE
MORAES, FRANK ROBERT
    (1907-) [British editor,
    correspondent and author]
    Ariel
Moral. See:
    GOWER, JOHN
    Morel
    Morell
MORAL, JOSÉ ZORRILLAY
    (1817-93) [Spanish play-
    wright]
    The Spoiled Darling of Spanish
    Romanticism
Moralist of the Main, The. See:
    CLEMENS, SAMUEL
    LANGHORNE
Moralist, The Great. See:
    JOHNSON, DR. SAMUEL
Morality, Old. See:
    SMITH, WILLIAM HENRY
Moran and Mack. See:
    Two Black Crows
Moran, George. See:
    Two Black Crows
MORAN, GEORGE C. (189?-1957)
    [American gangster]
    Bugs Moran
Moran, Lord. See:
    WILSON, CHARLES
        McMORAN
Moran, Mike. See:
    ARD, WILLIAM THOMAS
MORATÍN, LEANDRO
    FERNANDEZ DE (1760-1828)
    [Spanish dramatist and poet]
    The Spanish Molière
Moratorium Bill. See:

715

LEMKE, WILLIAM
Moravia, Alberto. See:
    PINCHERLE, ALBERTO
Morchard Bishop. See:
    STONOR, OLIVER
MORDAUNT, MRS. EVELYN
    MAY CLOWES (1877-)
    [English novelist]
    Elinor Mordaunt
    A. Riposte
More, Caroline. See:
    CONE, MOLLY LAMKEN
    STRACHAN, MARGARET
        PITCAIRN
MORE, HANNAH (1745-1835)
    [British poet, playwright
    and religious writer]
    Laureate of the Bluestockings
MORE, HENRY (1614-87)
    [English philosopher]
    The Cambridge Platonist
More of America, The Hannah.
    See: MERCER,
        MARGARET
Moréas, Jean. See:
    PAPADIAMANTOPOULOS,
        IOANNES
MOREHEAD, ALBERT HODGES
    (1909-) [American
    journalist, columnist and
    author]
    Turner Hodges
Morel. See:
    DESCHAMPS, EUSTACHE
    MORAL
    Moral
    Morell
Morel, Dighton. See:
    WARNER, KENNETH
        LEWIS
Moreland. See also:
    MORLAND
Moreland, Peter Henry. See:
    FAUST, FREDERICK
        SCHILLER
Morell. See also:
    MORAL
    Moral
    Morel
Morell, André. See:
    MESRITZ, ANDRÉ
Morenito de Valencia. See:

PUCHOL, AURELIO
MORENO, MANUEL JIMÉNEZ Y
    (1902-) [Spanish bullfighter]
    Chicuelo
Moresby, Louis. See:
    BECK, MRS. LILY MORESBY
        ADAMS
Moret, Neil. See:
    DANIELS, CHARLES N.
Moreton, Andrew, Merchant.
    See: FOE, DANIEL
Moreton, Clara. See:
    MOORE, CLARA SOPHIA
        JESSUP
Moreton, John. See:
    COHEN, MORTON NORTON
Moreton, Lee. See:
    BOUCICAULT, DIONYSIUS
        LARDNER
Moretto Da Brescia. See:
    BONVICINO, ALESSANDRO
Moretto, Il. See:
    BONVICINO, ALESSANDRO
Morey. See:
    BERNSTEIN, MORRIS
Morey, Charles. See:
    FLETCHER, HELEN JILL
MORFIT, THOMAS GARRISON
    (1915-) [American
    comedian, radio and tele-
    vision personality]
    Garry Moore
Morgan, Bruce. See:
    HUESTON, BILLY
Morgan, Dennis. See:
    MORNER, STANLEY
MORGAN, DIANA (1921-)
    [English author]
    Sara Blaine
    Linda Tremaine
Morgan, Emanuel. See:
    Knish, Anne
Morgan, Evans. See:
    DAVIES, LESLIE PURNELL
Morgan, Frank. See:
    WUPPERMAN, FRANCIS
Morgan, Harry. See:
    BRATSBURG, HARRY
Morgan, Henry. See:
    VON OST, HENRY LERNER,
        JR.
MORGAN, HILDA CAMPBELL

(fl. early 20th cent.)
[British novelist]
Hilda Vaughan
Morgan J. Divine, Reverend.
See: BAKER, GEORGE
MORGAN, JOHN HUNT
(1826-64) [American
Confederate guerrilla
leader]
The Raider
MORGAN, LEWIS HENRY
(1818-81) [American
anthropologist]
The Father of American
Anthropology
Morgan, Michele   See:
ROUSSEL, SIMONE
MORGAN, MURRAY (1916-)
[American novelist]
Cromwell Murray
Morgan, Ralph.   See:
WUPPERMAN, RALPH
MORGAN, RUSSELL (1904-69)
[American jazz musician
(trombone, piano, singer,
leader, arranger,
composer)]
Russ Morgan
Morgan, Shubel.   See:
BROWN, JOHN
MORGAN, THOMAS BRUCE
(1926-) [American editor
and author]
Nicholas David
Nicholas Morgan
MORGAN, THOMAS P. (1864-
1929) [American journalist
and author of dime novels]
Tennyson J. Daft
Tom P. Morgan
MORGAN, WILLIAM FORBES
(1879-1937) [American
investment banker and
politician]
The Czar of the Liquor
Industry
The Liquor Czar
MORGANFIELD, McKINLEY
(1915-) [American
jazz musician (singer,
guitar)]
Muddy Waters

Morgannwg, Iolo. See:
WILLIAMS, EDWARD
Morin, Claire. See:
DORE, CLAIRE MORIN
MORISON [Morison]. See also:
MORRISON
Morrison
MORISON, MARY (fl. last part
of 18th cent.) [Sweetheart
of ROBERT BURNS]
Highland Mary
Morison, Patricia. See:
MORRISON, EILEEN
Moritz Julius. See:
BONN, MORITZ JULIUS
MORKOVIN, BORIS VLADIMIR
(1882-) [Russian-American
educator and author]
Bela V. Morkovin
MORLAND. See also:
Moreland
MORLAND, GEORGE (1763-1804)
[English painter]
The English Teniers
Morlay, Gaby. See:
FUMOLEAU, BLANCHE
Morley. See:
COOPER, ALFRED MORTON
Morley, Karen. See:
LINTON, MILDRED
Morley, Mrs. See:
ANN
Mormon Bishop, The. See:
KING, WILLIAM HENRY
Mormons, The Father of the.
See: SMITH, JOSEPH
MORNER STANLEY (1910-)
[American opera singer and
motion picture actor]
Dennis Morgan
Morning Star of Song, The. See:
CHAUCER, GEOFFREY
Morning Star of the Reformation,
The. See:
WICKCLIFFE, JOHN
Moro, Il (The Moor). See:
SFORZA, LUDOVICO
Morr. See also:
Moor
MOORE
Moore
Morr, Skip. See:

717

COOLIDGE, CHARLES
 WILLIAM
MORRA, ALBERTO DI
 (1105/10-87) [Supreme
 Pontiff of Roman
 Catholic Church]
 Pope Gregory VIII
MORRA, EGIDIO (1906-)
 [Italian-American
 composer, trombonist and
 teacher]
 Gene Morra
MORRAH, DAVID WARDLAW,
 JR. (1914-) [American
 humorist]
 Dave Morrah
MORRIS, ALVIN (1913-)
 [American singer, musician
 and actor]
 Tony Martin
 Al Morris
MORRIS, ANTHONY P., JR.
 (1849-) [American
 author of dime novels]
 Nat Newton
MORRIS, BERTDE WAYNE
 (1914-59) [American
 stage and motion picture
 actor]
 Wayne Morris
MORRIS, CHARLES SMITH
 (1833-1922) [American
 historian, compiler and
 author of dime novels]
 Hugh Allen
 J. D. Ballard
 Redmond Blake
 Roland Dare
 S. M. Frazier
 R. R. Inman
 George S. Kaine
 Edward Lytton
 William Murry
 Paul Pastnor
 Jo Pierce
 Paul Preston
 J. H. Southard
 C. E. Tripp
 E. L. Vincent
MORRIS, CHESTER (1901-70)
 [American actor]
 Boston Blackie

Morris, Clara. See:
 MORRISON, CLARA
MORRIS, JOSEPH CHRISTOPHER
 COLUMBUS (1903-)
 [American jazz musician
 (drums)]
 Christopher Columbus
MORRIS, LEONARD CARTER
 (1915-) [American jazz
 musician (trumpet, singer)]
 Skeets Morris
Morris, Peter. See:
 LOCKHART, JOHN GIBSON
Morris Redwing. See:
 MERRILL, JAMES MILFORD
MORRIS, ROBERT (1734-1806)
 [Anglo-American financier]
 Bobby the Cofferer
 Bobby the Treasurer
 The Financier of the American
 Revolution
 The Merchant Prince
 The Patriot Financier
MORRIS, ROBERT (1911-)
 [American composer,
 arranger and teacher]
 Bob Miketta
Morris Rosenfield. See:
 ALTER, MOSHE JACOB
Morris, Ruth. See:
 WEBB, RUTH ENID
 BORLASE MORRIS
MORRIS, SAMUEL (c. 1700-c.
 1770) [American Presby-
 terian clergyman]
 The Father of Presbyterianism
 in Virginia
Morris, Sara. See:
 BURKE, JOHN FREDERICK
MORRIS, TOM (1821-1908)
 [Scottish golfer]
 The Nestor of Golf
MORRISSEY, JOHN (1831-80)
 [Irish-American gambler,
 prize fighter and politician]
 Old Smoke
MORRISON [Morrison]. See also:
 MORISON
 Morison
MORRISON, CLARA (1848-1925)
 [American actress]
 Clara Morris

718

MORRISON, EILEEN (1915-)
[American motion picture
actress]
Patricia Morison
Morrison, Gert W. See:
STRATEMEYER,
EDWARD L.
MORRISON, GEORGE ERNEST
(1862-1920) [Australian
journalist]
Chinese Morrison
MORRISON, JEANETTE (1927-)
[American motion
picture actress]
Janet Leigh
MORRISON, KATHLEEN
(1900-) [American motion
picture actress]
Colleen Moore
MORRISON, MARION MICHAEL
(1907-) [American
motion picture actor]
Duke
John Wayne
MORRISON, RICHARD C.
(1937-) [American
burglar]
The Babbling Burglar
MORRISON, RICHARD JAMES
(1798-1874) [English
astrological almanac
maker]
Zadkiel
MORRISON, THOMAS JAMES
(fl. mid-20th cent.)
[Scottish author]
Alan Muir
MORRISON, VELMA FORD
(1909-) [American
teacher, publisher and
author]
Hildegarde Ford
Morrison, William. See:
SAMACHSON, JOSEPH
MORRISON, WILLIAM RALLS
(1825-1909) [American
politician; Congressman
from Illinois]
Horizontal Bill
Morros, Boris. See:
MIKHAILOVITCH, BORIS
Morrow, Buddy. See:
ZUDEKOFF, MOE

Morrow, Charlotte. See:
KIRWAN, MOLLY MORROW
Morrow, Muni. See:
ZUDEKOFF, MOE
MORSE, ANNE CHRISTENSEN
(1915-) [American author]
Ann Head
Morse, Carol. See:
YEAKLEY, MARJORY HALL
MORSE, CHARLES WYMAN
(1856-1933) [American
business executive]
The Ice King
MORSE, H. CLIFTON (1924-)
[American engineer and
author]
Clifton Fourth
MORSE, JEDIDIAH (1761-1826)
[American geographer and
author]
The Father of American
Geography
MORSE, SAMUEL FINLEY
BREESE (1791-1872)
[American painter and in-
ventor of the magnetic
telegraph]
The Father of the Telegraph
MORSE, THEODORA (1890-1953)
[American song writer]
D.A. Esrom
Dolly Morse
Dorothy Terriss
MORSLEBEN. See:
SUITGER, COUNT OF
MORSLEBEN
Mort. See:
SAHL, MORTON LYON
Mort Herbert. See:
PELOVITZ, MORTON
HERBERT
Mort, Vivian. See:
CROMIE, ALICE HAMILTON
Mortality, Old. See:
PATERSON, ROBERT
MORTENSEN. See:
BAKER (MORTENSEN),
NORMA JEAN
Mortimer. See:
CADE, JOHN
Mortimer, Chapman. See:
CHAPMAN-MORTIMER,
WILLIAM CHARLES

Mortimer, January. See:
GALLICHAN, WALTER M.
MORTIMER, JOHN HAMILTON
(1741-79) [English historical
painter]
The English Salvator Rosa
Mortimer, Peter. See:
ROBERTS, DOROTHY JAMES
Morton, Anthony. See:
CREASEY, JOHN
MORTON, CHARLES (1819-1904)
[English music hall and
variety entertainment
manager]
The Father of the Halls
Morton Cleland. See:
RENNIE, JAMES ALAN
MORTON, HENRY STERLING
(1907-) [American jazz
musician (trombone)]
Benny Morton
Morton, Hugh. See:
McLELLAN, CHARLES
MORTON STEWART
Morton, Jelly Roll. See:
LA MENTHE,
FERDINAND JOSEPH
MORTON, JOHN CAMERON AN-
DRIEU BINGHAM MICHAEL
(1893-) [English author
and journalist]
Beachcomber
Morton, Leah. See:
STERN, ELIZABETH
GERTRUDE
MORTON, OLIVER HAZARD
PERRY THROCK (1823-77)
[American politician;
Congressman from and
Governor of Indiana]
The Devil on Two Sticks
Sitting Bull
Oliver Perry
The War Governor
Morton, Patricia. See:
GOLDING, MORTON JAY
MORTON, SARAH WENTWORTH
APTHORP (1759-1846)
[American poet]
The American Sappho
Philenia
Morton Selten. See:

STUBBS, MORTON
MORTON, THOMAS (fl. 1622-47)
[English fur trader and
playboy]
Thomas Morton of Clifford's
Inn, Gent.
Morton, William. See:
FERGUSON, WILLIAM
BLAIR
MOSCONI, WILLIAM JOSEPH
(1913-) [American
professional billiard player]
Willie Mosconi
MOSCOVITCH, NOEL (c.1905-)
[American motion picture
actor]
Nat Madison
Noel Madison
Mose, The Same Old. See:
WEINBERGER, MOSES
Mose, The Same Young. See:
WEINBERGER, MOSES
MOSEL, GEORGE AULT, JR.
(1922-) [American play-
wright]
Tad Mosel
MOSELEY, ROBERT (1922-)
[American motion picture
actor]
Guy Madison
Moses. See:
Mozis
TUBMAN, HARRIET
Moses Adams. See:
BAGBY, GEORGE WILLIAM
MOSES, ANNA MARY ROBERTSON
(1860-1961) [American
primitive artist]
Grandma Moses
Moses Ben Maimon. See:
MAIMONIDES
MOSES, HILDA (1920-)
[American actress]
Hilda Simms
Moses of America, The. See:
WISE, ISAAC MAYER
Moses, Second (RaMBam). See:
MAIMONIDES
Moses, The Agricultural. See:
TILLMAN, BENJAMIN
RYAN
Moses, The Negro. See:

TUBMAN, HARRIET
Moses, Twentieth Century. See:
CHAPLIN, CHARLES
SPENCER
MOSKOWITZ, SAM (1920-)
[American literary agent,
editor and author]
Sam Martin
MOSLEY, LAWRENCE LEO
(1909-) [American jazz
musician (trombone, slide
saxophone)]
Snub Mosley
Mosquito. See:
MANSON, GEORGE
Mosquitos, Admiral of the.
See: COLUMBUS,
CHRISTOPHER
MOSS, ROBERT ALFRED
(1903-) [British editor
and author]
Nancy Moss
Roberta Moss
Moss Tadrack. See:
CARYL, WARREN
Most Admired Woman, The
World's. See:
ROOSEVELT, ANNA
ELEANOR
Most Conspicuous Contro-
versialist of His Age
The. See:
CHILLINGWORTH,
WILLIAM
Most Faithful King. See:
JOHN V
Most Famous Folk Singer of
his Race, The. See:
WHITE, JOSHUA DANIEL
Most Gracious Majesty, Consort
of Her. See:
ALBERT
Most Helpful Philosopher About
the Business Scene We
Have, The. See:
DRUCKER, PETER
FERDINAND
Most Honorable Order of
Starvation, Knight of The.
See: LIVINGSTON,
WILLIAM
Most Honored Broadcaster,

America's. See:
HARVEY, PAUL
Most Intelligent of American
Sopranos, The. See:
SMITH, PHYLLIS
Most Irrepressible Master of
Ceremonies, The Fashion
World's. See:
CASSINI, OLEG LOIEWSKI
Most Learned Fool in Christen-
dom, The. See:
JAMES I
Most Learned of the Romans,
The. See:
VARRO, MARCUS
TERENTIUS
Most Pulchritudinous
Evangelist, The World's.
See: McPHERSON, AIMEE
SEMPLE
Most Resolute Doctor, The. See:
ST. POURÇAIN, GUILLAUME
DURAND DE
Most Talented Young Composer
in America, The. See:
GOULD, MORTON
Most Thoroughgoing British
Skeptic of the Eighteenth
Century, The. See:
HUME, DAVID
Most Valuable Friend, Wesley's.
See: FLETCHER, JOHN
WILLIAM
MOSTEL, SAMUEL JOE
(1915-) [American actor
and painter]
Zero Mostel
MOTEN, CLARENCE LEMONT
(1916-) [American jazz
musician (bass)]
Benny Moten
Mother. See:
BAILEY, ANNA WARNER
BICKERDYKE, MARY ANN
BALL
CABRINI, MARY FRANCES
CLARKE, SARAH DUNN
JONES, MARY HARRIS
LEE (LEES), ANN
SETON, ELIZABETH ANN
BAYLEY
SHIPTON, URSULA

SOUTHIEL
Mother Ann. See:
LEE (LEES), ANN
Mother Medium, The. See:
BENNINGHOFEN, MRS.
ERNEST
Mother of a Thousand Daughters,
The. See:
AGNEW, ELIZA
Mother of All the Doughboys,
The. See:
SCHUMANN-HEINK,
MME. ERNESTINE
Mother of All the Russians,
The Little. See:
ANHALT-ZERBST, SOPHIA
AUGUSTA FREDERICA OF
Mother of Believers, The. See:
AYESHA
Mother of Detective Stories,
The. See: GREEN,
ANNA KATHARINE
Mother of Everybody's Children,
The Second. See:
ABBOTT, GRACE
Mother of Methodism in the
United States, The. See:
HECK, BARBARA RUCKLE
Mother of Peoples, The. See:
MARGUERITE OF FRANCE
Mother of Thanksgiving, The. See:
HALE, SARAH JOSEPHA
Mother of the American Legion,
The. See:
SCHUMANN-HEINK,
MME. ERNESTINE
Mother of the Confederacy,
The. See:
LAW, SALLIE CHAPMAN
GORDON
Mother of the Gridiron Club,
The Father and Nursing.
See: CARSON, JOHN
MILLER
Mother of the Kindergarten,
The. See:
BLOW, SUSAN
ELIZABETH
Mother of the Mohawk Valley, The
Patriot. See: VAN
ALSTINE, MRS.
MARTIN J.
Mother of the Red Cross, The.

BARTON, CLARISSA
HARLOWE
Mother of the Strip Tease, The.
See: DENNIS, RUTH
Mother Raymond de Jesus. See:
DION, SISTER RAYMOND
DE JESUS
Mother Ross. See:
DAVIES, CHRISTIAN
MOTIER, MARIE JEAN PAUL
ROCH YVES GILBERT
(1757-1834) [French
statesman and general
officer]
The French Gamecock
Grandison Cromwell
Marquis de Lafayette
Motion Picture Industry, The
Dynamo of the Italian. See:
LAURENTIS, DINO DE
Motion Picture Industry, The
Garibaldi of the Italian.
See: LAURENTIS, DINO DE
Motion Picture Industry, The
Kingfish of the Italian. See:
LAURENTIS, DINO DE
MOTLEY, ARTHUR HARRISON
(1900-) [American pub-
lisher, business executive
and public speaker]
Red Motley
Motley Manners. See:
DUGANNE, AUGUSTINE
JOSEPH HICKEY
Motley, Mary. See:
DeRENEVILLE, MARY
MARGARET MOTLEY
SHERIDAN
Motordom, The Genius of. See:
FORD, HENRY
MOTT, JAMES WHEATON (1883-
1945) [American lawyer and
politician; congressman
from Oregon]
Tonguepoint Mott
MOTT, LUCRETIA (1793-1880)
[American preacher and
abolitionist]
The Advance Agent of
Emancipation
The Invincible Warrior in
Righteous Causes

722

The Flower of Quakerism
The Sweet-spirited
    Advocate of Justice, Love
    and Humanity
MOTTE-GUYON, JEANNE
    MARIE BOUVIER DE LA
    (1648-1717) [French
    mystic]
Madame Guyon
MOTTOLA, ANTHONY
    CHARLES (1918-)
    [American composer,
    conductor and guitarist]
Tony Mottola
MOTTRAM, RALPH HALE
    (1883-) [English novelist]
J. Marjoram
MOULTRIE, JOHN (1799-1874)
    [British poet]
Gerard Montgomery
Mount, Lindsay of the. See:
    LINDSAY (LYNDSAY),
    SIR DAVID
Mount, The Bard of Rydal. See:
    WORDSWORTH, WILLIAM
Mount Vernon, The Sage of.
    See: WASHINGTON,
    GEORGE
Mountain, Burns of the Green.
    See: EASTMAN,
    CHARLES GAMAGE
Mountain Evangelist, The. See:
    JONES, SAMUEL PORTER
Mountain Giant, The White.
    See: CRAWFORD,
    ETHAN ALLEN
Mountain Girl, The Moon Over
    the. See:
    SMITH, KATHRYN
    ELIZABETH
Mountain, The Hero of King's.
    See: CLEVELAND,
    BENJAMIN
Mountain, The Old Man of the.
    See: HASAN-IBN-AL-
    SABBAH
Mountains, The Apostle of
    the Rocky. See:
    DE SMET, PETER JOHN
Mountains, The Demosthenes of
    the. See:
    MILLER, HOMER VIRGIL

MILTON
Mountains, The Emperor of the.
    See: PETER
Mountains, The Nestor of the
    Rocky. See:
    CARSON, CHRISTOPHER
Mountains, The Patriarch of the.
    See: CRAWFORD, ABEL
MOURER, MARYSE (1922-67)
    [French motion picture
    actress]
Martine Carol
Mouse. See:
    RANDOLPH, IRVING
Mouse, Mickey. See:
    ELY, WILLIAM HARVEY
    JOHNSON
Mouth, Cicero's. See:
    POT, PHILIPPE
Mouthed, Golden. See:
    CHRYSOSTOM, ST. JOHN
    GALLOWAY, CHARLES
    BETTS
Mouthpiece, The Great. See:
    FALLON, WILLIAM J.
Mouton, Michel. See:
    MONTCORBIER, FRANÇOIS
    DE
MOUTON, ROBERT L. (1892-)
    [American horticulturist and
    politician; representative
    from Louisiana]
Marine Bob
The Louisiana Ram
Movement, Peter-the-Hermit of
    the Abolitionist. See:
    LUNDY, BENJAMIN
Movement, The Dean of the
    American Labor. See:
    FURUSETH, ANDREW
Movies, Queen of the. See:
    SMITH, GLADYS MARY
Movies, The Grand Old Lady of
    the. See: KOERBER,
    LEILA
Movies, The Minx of the. See:
    COMPSON, BETTY
MOWATT, ANNA CORA OGDEN
    RITCHIE (1819-70)
    [American playwright,
    actress and novelist]
Helen Berkley

Henry C. Browning
Isabel
Mowbray, J. P. See:
WHEELER, ANDREW
CARPENTER
Moxie. See:
WHITNEY, MOXAM
MOYERS, BILLY DON (1934-)
[White House press
secretary]
Bill D. Moyers
Mozart, The Modern. See:
KORNGOLD ERICH
WOLFGANG
MOZART, WOLFGANG
AMADEUS (1756-91)
[Austrian composer]
The Raphael of Music
Mozis. See also:
MOSES
Moses
Mozis Addums. See:
BAGBY, GEORGE
WILLIAM
Mozo, El (The Younger). See:
HERRERA, FRANCISCO
MOZZEE, PHOEBE ANNE
OAKLEY (1860-1926)
[American markswoman
and expert rifle shot]
Little Missy
Annie Oakley
Little Sure Shot
Mr. Names prefixed by this
abbreviation are indexed
as though spelled
"Mister"
Mrs. Names prefixed by this
abbreviation are indexed
as though spelled
"Mistress"
MUDDOCK, JOYCE EMERSON
PRESTON (1843-1934)
[English novelist and
traveler]
Dick Donovan
Muddy. See:
RUEL, HEROLD D.
Muddy Waters. See: MORGAN-
FIELD, McKINLEY
Mude, O. See:
GOREY, EDWARD ST. JOHN

Mudsill. See:
HAMMOND, JAMES HENRY
MUELLER. See:
MÜLLER (MUELLER),
FRIEDRICH
MUENZENBERGER, JOHN HENRY
(1912-) [American jazz
musician (clarinet, saxo-
phones)]
Johnny Mince
MUGGERIDGE, EDWARD JAMES
(1830-1904) [Anglo-American
photographer]
Eadweard Muybridge
Muggsy. See:
SPANIER, FRANCIS
JOSEPH
MUHAMMAD. See also:
MOHAMMED
MUHAMMAD, ZAHIR UD-DIN
(1483-1530) [First of the
great Moguls of India]
Baber (Babur) (Tiger)
MUHLENBERG, JOHN PETER
GABRIEL (1746-1807)
[American general officer]
Devil Pete
Muir, Alan. See:
MORRISON, THOMAS JAMES
MUIR, BARBARA KENRICK
GOWING (1908-) [British
editor and author]
Barbara Kaye
MUIR, CHARLES AUGUSTUS
(fl. 1925-64) [British author]
Austin Moore
Muir, Jane. See:
PETRONE, JANE MUIR
Muir, Jean. See:
FULLERTON, JEAN MUIR
MUIR, KENNETH ARTHUR
(1907-) [British educator
and author]
Mark Finney
MUIR, MARIE (1904-)
[British author]
Monica Blake
Monica Clynder
Jean Scott
MUIR, PERCIVAL HORACE
(1894-) [American
antiquarian bookseller and

bibliographer]
Percy Muir
Percy H. Muir
MULCAHY, LUCILLE
BURNETT (1918-)
[American librarian and
author]
Helen Hale
MULDOON, WILLIAM (1846-
1933) [American profes-
sional boxer, commis-
sioner and promoter]
The Czar of Boxing
The Father of American
Boxing
The Iron Duke
The Old Roman
The Solid Man
Mule. See:
HAAS, GEORGE W.
HOLLEY, MAJOR
QUINCY, JR.
WATSON, MILTON
Mule, Seven. See:
BARNUM, WILLIAM
HENRY
Muley. See:
DOUGHTON, ROBERT L.
Muley Malack. See:
NOAH, MORDECAI
MANUEL
MULFORD, PRENTICE
(1834-91) [American
journalist, hermit and
author]
Dogberry
MULLANY, PATRICK FRANCIS
(1847-93) [Irish-American
churchman, educator and
author]
Brother Azarias
MULLENGER, DONNA (1921-)
[American television and
motion picture actress]
Donna Reed
Müller, Billex. See:
ELLIS, EDWARD
SYLVESTER
MÜLLER, CHARLES GEORGE
(1897-) [American news-
paperman and author]
Charles Geoffrey

MÜLLER, FRITZ (1821-97)
[German zoologist]
The Prince of Observers
MÜLLER, HAROLD (1901-62)
[American football player]
Brick Muller
MÜLLER, JOHANNES (1436-76)
[German mathematician and
astronomer]
Regiomontanus
Müller, Maler. See:
MULLER (MUELLER),
FRIEDRICH
MÜLLER (MUELLER),
FRIEDRICH (1749-1825)
[German poet, painter and
engraver]
Maler Müller
MÜLLER, RUDOLPH (1899-)
Czechoslovakian motion
picture actor]
Martin Miller
MULLIGAN, GERALD JOSEPH
(1927-) [American jazz
musician (baritone saxo-
phone, composer, arranger
and leader)]
Gerry Mulligan
Jeru
Mullins, Ann. See:
DALLY, ANN MULLINS
MULLINS, RICHARD (1926-)
[American author]
Michael Wells
Mulock, Miss. See:
CRAIK, DINAH MARIA
MULOCK
Multatuli. See:
DEKKER, EDUARD DOUWES
Mun. See:
LEAF, MUNRO
MÜNCH-BELLINGHAUSEN,
ELIGIUS FRANZ JOSEPH,
REICHFRIEHERR VON
(1806-71) [Austrian drama-
tist]
Friedrich Halm
MÜNCH, CHARLES (1891-)
[French orchestra leader]
France's Greatest Conductor
Münchausen of the West, The.
See: CROCKETT, DAVID

MÜNCHAUSEN, KARL
    FRIEDRICH HIERONYMUS,
    BARON VON (1720-97)
    [German soldier; probable
    author of book of tall
    tales]
    Baron Münchhausen
Mundy, Max. See:
    MATHESON, SYLVIA ANNE
Mundy, Sue. See:
    CLARK, M. JEROME
Munger, Al. See:
    UNGER, MAURICE ALBERT
Mungo, St. See:
    KENTIGERN
Muni Morrow. See:
    ZUDEKOFF, MOE
Muni, Paul. See:
    WEISENFREUND, MUNI
Muni, Sakya. See:
    GAUTAMA SIDDHARTHA
Municipal Government, The
    Father of the City
    Manager Plan of. See:
    CHILDS, RICHARD
    SPENCER
MUNN, FRANK (1895-1953)
    [American radio singer
    and recording artist]
    The Golden Voice of Radio
MUÑOZ, FERMÍN (1882-1914)
    [Spanish bullfighter]
    Corchaito
MUNRO [Munro]. See also:
    MONRO
    MONROE
    Monroe
    MUNROE
MUNRO, BERNICE HALE
    (1899-) [British revue
    artist and motion
    picture actress]
    Binnie Hale
Munro, C.K. See:
    MACMULLEN, CHARLES
    KIRKPATRICK
Munro, Christy. See:
    TAVES, ISABELLA
MUNRO, HECTOR HUGH
    (1870-1916) [Scottish
    novelist and short story
    writer]

Saki
Munro, James. See:
    CAVE, RODERICK GEORGE
    JAMES MUNRO
    MITCHELL, JAMES
MUNROE. See also:
    MONRO
    MONROE
    Monroe
    MUNRO
    Munro
MUNROE, ELIZABETH LEE
    (1910-) [American teacher
    and poet]
    Lisa Grenelle
MUNSON, MARY LOU EASLEY
    (1935-) [American teacher
    and author]
    Lou Munson
Munson, Ona. See:
    WOLCOTT, ONA
Münsterberg, Maximilian. See:
    NENTWICH, MAX
MUNTHE, FRANCES (1915-)
    [British author]
    Frances Cowen
    Frances Minto-Cowen
MURAD (AMURATH) I
    (1319-89) [Sultan of Turkey]
    Khudavendighiar
MURAIRE, JULES (1883-1946)
    [French actor and
    comedian]
    Raimu
MURAT, JOACHIM (1771- 1815)
    [French marshal and King
    of Naples]
    Beau Sabreur (Handsome
    Swordsman)
    The Dandy King
    King Franconi
    The Theatrical King
Murat of America, The. See:
    WHEAT, CHATHAM
    ROBERDEAU
Murat of the Union Army, The.
    See: LOGAN, JOHN
    ALEXANDER
Murat, The Russian. See:
    MILORADOVITCH, COUNT
    MIKHAEL ANDRIEVITCH
Murderer, The Brides in the

Bath. See:
SMITH, GEORGE JOSEPH
Murderer, The Ragged Stranger.
See: WANDERER, CARL
MURFIN, JANE. See:
Martin, Allan Langdon
MURFREE, MARY NOAILLES
(1850-1922) [American
novelist]
Charles Egbert Craddock
R. Emmett Dembry
Murgatroyd, Matthew. See:
JONES, JAMES
ATHEARN
MURIEL [Muriel]. See also:
Meriel
Muriel A. Schwartz. See:
ELIOT, THOMAS
STEARNS
Muriel Angelus. See:
FINDLAY, MURIEL A.
MURIEL, JOHN (1909-)
[English author]
Simon Dewes
John Lindsey
Muriel Stafford. See:
SAUER, MURIEL
STAFFORD
Murieta, Joaquin. See:
CARILLO, JOAQUIN
Murnau, F.W. See:
PLUMPE, FRIEDRICH W.
Murnau, Friedrich. See:
PLUMPE, FRIEDRICH W.
MURPHY, CHARLES FRANCIS
(1858-1924) [American
politician and Tammany
Hall official]
Silent Charley
MURPHY, FRANCIS (1836-1907)
[Irish-American
temperance advocate]
The Apostle of Temperance
MURPHY, FRANK (1893-1949)
[American statesman;
Attorney General of the
United States and As-
sociate Justice of United
States Supreme Court]
Frank the Just
The New Deal's Tom Dewey
MURPHY, LYLE (1908-)

[American jazz musician
(composer, arranger, saxo-
phone)]
Spud Murphy
MURPHY, MABEL ANSLEY
(1870-) [American author]
Anne S. Lee
MURPHY, MELVIN E. (1915-)
[American jazz musician
(trombone, trumpet, mello-
phone, leader, composer,
arranger, singer)]
Turk Murphy
MURRAY [Murray]. See also:
MURRY
Murry
Murray, Adrian. See:
CURRAN, MONA ELISA
MURRAY, ALMA (1854-1945)
[English actress]
The Poetic Actress Without a
Rival
Murray, Arthur. See:
TEICHMAN, ARTHUR
MURRAY
Murray, Cromwell. See:
MORGAN, MURRAY
MURRAY, DONALD PATRICK
(1929-) [American actor]
Don Murray
Murray, Edna. See:
ROWLAND, DONALD
SYDNEY
MURRAY, GEORGE GILBERT
AIMÉ (1866-1957) [American
classical scholar and author]
The Foremost Greek Scholar
of Our Time
Murray Goodman. See:
SCHACHT, ALEXANDER
Murray Hill. See:
HOLLIDAY, ROBERT
CORTES
MURRAY, JAMES ARTHUR
(1937-) [American jazz
musician (drums)]
Sunny Murray
MURRAY, JOHN (1741-1815)
[British-American Uni-
versalist clergyman]
The Father of American
Universalism

The Father of Universalism
in America
MURRAY, JOHN (1778-1843)
[English publisher]
The Anak of Publishers
The Emperor of the West
MURRAY, JOHN (1923-)
[American author]
Robert Combs
MURRAY, JUDITH SARGENT
STEVENS (1751-1820)
[American playwright,
poet and essayist]
Constantia
Murray Leinster. See:
JENKINS, WILLIAM
FITZGERALD
Murray, Lieut. See:
BALLOU, MATURIN
MURRAY
Murray, Louis. See:
FUCHS, MURRAY LOUIS
Murray, Mae. See:
KOENIG, MARIE
ADRIENNE
MURRAY, NICHOLAS (1802-61)
[Irish controversialist and
author]
Kirwan
Murray Rumsey. See:
RUMSHINSKY, MURRAY
Murray, Sinclair. See:
SULLIVAN, EDWARD ALAN
MURRAY, THOMAS JEFFERSON
(1894-) [American
politician; U.S. representa-
tive from Tennessee]
Tom Murray
MURRAY, WILLIAM HENRY
(1869-) [American
farmer and politician;
Governor of Oklahoma]
Alfalfa Bill Murray
Cockle-bur Bill
The Sage of Tishomingo
MURRAY, WILLIAM HENRY
HARRISON (1840-1904)
[American Congregational
clergyman, sportsman
and author]
Adirondack
MURRELL, ELSIE KATHLEEN

(1883-) [English author]
E.K. Seth-Smith
MURRONE, PIETRO
ANGELARI DA (1215-94)
[Supreme Pontiff of Roman
Catholic Church]
Pope Celestine V
MURRY [Murry]. See also:
MURRAY
Murray
Murry, Colin. See:
MIDDLETON-MURRY, JOHN
MURRY, KATHLEEN BEAU-
CHAMP (1888-1923)
[New Zealand author]
Katherine Mansfield
Murry, Ted. See:
MENCHER, MURRAY
Murry, William. See:
MORRIS, CHARLES SMITH
Muscles. See:
WANER, LLOYD JAMES
Muscovy General, The. See:
DALYELL (DALZELL),
THOMAS
Muse of Cumberland. See:
BLAMIRE, SUSANNA
Muse of Greece, The. See:
XENOPHON
Muse, The Attic. See:
XENOPHON
Muse, The Scian. See:
SIMONIDES
Muse, The Tenth. See:
BRADSTREET, ANNE
DUDLEY
CRUZ, JUANA INÉS DE LA
DESHOULIÈRES,
ANTOINETTE DU LIGIER
DE LA GARDE
SCUDÉRI, MADELEINE DE
UNKNOWN
Museum, The Father of The. See:
BICKMORE, ALBERT
SMITH
Mushafir, Kartikeya Skylar. See:
TIKEKAR, SHRIPAD
RAMCHANDRA
Musheed Karweem. See:
POWELL, EDWARD
STEPHEN, SR.
MUSIAL, STANLEY FRANK (1920-)

[American professional
baseball player]
Stan Musial
Stan the Man
Music Composers, The Dean
of America's Show. See:
KERN, JEROME DAVID
Music Maker, Mr. See:
WELK, LAWRENCE
Music-maker, The Red-
headed. See:
HALL, WENDELL WOODS
Music, The Dandy of Country.
See: DEAN, JIMMY RAY
Music, The Dean of American.
See: DAMROSCH,
WALTER JOHANNES
Music, The Dean of American
Popular. See:
WHITEMAN, PAUL
Music, The Father of. See:
PALESTRINA, GIOVANNI
PIERLUIGI
Music, The Father of American
Church. See:
MASON, LOWELL
Music, The Father of American
Orchestral. See:
GRAUPNER, JOHANN
CHRISTIAN GOTTLIEB
Music, The Father of Anglican
Church. See:
PURCELL, HENRY
Music, The Father of English
Cathedral. See:
TALLIS, THOMAS
Music, The Father of Greek. See:
TERPANDER
Music, The Father of
Orchestral. See:
HAYDN, FRANZ JOSEPH
Music, The Hercules of. See:
GLÜCK, CHRISTOPHER
WILLIBALD
Music, The Michelangelo of.
See: GLUCK,
CHRISTOPHER WILLI-
BALD
Music, The Prince of. See:
PALESTRINA, GIOVANNI
PIERLUIGI
Music, The Racine of. See:
SACCHINI, MARIE-

GASPARD
Music, The Raphael of. See:
MOZART, WOLFGANG
AMADEUS
Music, The Savior of Church.
See: PALESTRINA,
GIOVANNI PIERLUIGI
Music, The Thomas Jefferson
of Folk. See:
SEEGER, PETER
Music, The Wizard of Word.
See: POE, EDGAR ALLAN
Musical Corn, The King of. See:
WELK, LAWRENCE
Musical Small-coal Man, The.
See: BRITTON, THOMAS
MUSICK, JOHN ROY (1848-1901)
[American journalist and
author]
Benjamin Broadaxe
Musick, The Father of. See:
BYRD (BIRDE), WILLIAM
Musketeer. See:
BARKER, ARTHUR JAMES
Musketeer, The Fourth. See:
DUMAS, ALEXANDRE
ULLMAN, JULIUS
Musketeers. See:
Three Musketeers, The
MUSKETT, NETTA (1893-)
[English author]
Anne Hill
MUSLIH-UD-DIN (1184?-1291)
[Persian poet]
The Oriental Catullus
Saadi
Sadi
MUSSET, LOUIS CHARLES
ALFRED DE (1810-57)
[French poet and playwright]
Alfred de Musset
The French Byron
MUSSOLINI, BENITO (1883-1945)
[Italian dictator]
Il Duce
MUSSULLI, HENRY W. (1917-)
[American jazz musician
(alto and baritone saxophones)]
Boots Mussulli
Mustang, The Gray. See:
FRÉMONT, JOHN CHARLES
Mutt. See:
ENS, JEWEL

Mutt, Papa. See:
CAREY, THOMAS
Muybridge, Eadweard. See:
MUGGERIDGE, EDWARD
JAMES
My-book, Doctor. See:
ABERNETHY, JOHN
My Little Portuguese. See:
BROWNING, ELIZABETH
BARRETT
My Soldier (Mon Soldat). See:
HENRY IV
My Uncle, The Nephew of. See:
SWEENEY, PETER BARR
Myconius, Oswald. See:
GEISHUSLER, OSWALD
Myers, Harriet Kathryn. See:
WHITTINGTON, HARRY
MYLES. See:
STANDISH, MILES
(MYLES)
Myles, Devera. See:
ZUCKER, DOLORES MAE
BOLTON
Myles na Gopaleen. See:
O'NUALLAIN, BRIAN
Myra Brown. See:
COOK, MYRA B.
Myra Buttle. See:
PURCELL, VICTOR
Myrna Loy. See:
WILLIAMS, MYRNA
Myron. See:
HOLMES, ABIEL
Myron, Paul. See:
LINEBARGER, PAUL
MYRON WENTWORTH
Myrtle, Lewis. See:
HILL, GEORGE CANNING
Mystery Man of Europe, The.
See: ZACHARIAS,
BASIELEIOS
Mystery, The Master Mind
of Mental. See:
DUNNINGER, JOSEPH
Mystery Writers in English
and Probably in Any
Language, The Doyen of.
See: STOUT, REX
TODHUNTER
Mysticism, The Father of
Western. See:

BERNARD OF CLAIRVAUX

N

N. I. Edson. See:
DENISON, MARY ANDREWS
N. N. See:
PENNELL, ELIZABETH
N. Ognev. See:
ROSANOV, MIKHAIL
GRIGORIEVICH
N. P. See:
WILLIS, NATHANIEL
PARKER
N. R. A. Czar, The. See:
JOHNSON, HUGH SAMUEL
N. R. A., The Crack-Down Czar
of the. See:
JOHNSON, HUGH SAMUEL
N. Shchedrin. See:
SALTYKOV, MIKHAIL
EVGRAFOVICH
NABOKOV, VLADIMIR
(VLADIMIROVICH) (1899-)
[Russian educator and
author]
V. Sirin
NABORS, JAMES THURSTON
(1932-) [American television
entertainer]
Jim Nabors
Nacella Young. See:
TATE, VELMA
Nacional. See:
MARTÍNEZ, OCTAVIO
Nacional II. See:
ANNLÓ, JUAN
NACK, JAMES M. (1809-79)
[American poet]
The Deaf and Dumb Poet
Nadia Gray. See:
KUJNIR-HERESCU, NADIA
Nadia Nerina. See:
JUDD, NADINE
NADIR, SHAH (1688-1747) [King
of Persia]
The Conqueror
Nadir, William. See:
DOUGLASS, WILLIAM
Naftali, Ch. See:
BRANDWEIN, CHAIM

NAFTALI
NAGELE, ANTON (1876-)
[German educator and
author]
Stauffer Clavell
Nails, Old Silver. See:
STUYVESANT, PETER
NAIRNE, CAROLINA
OLIPHANT (1766-1845)
[Scottish poet]
The Flower of Strathearn
NAISMITH [Naismith]. See also:
NASMYTH
NAISMITH, DR. JAMES A.
(1861-1939) [Canadian-
American professor of
physical education;
originator of the game
of basketball]
The Father of Basketball
Naismith, Laurence. See:
JOHNSON, LAWRENCE
Naldi, Nita. See:
DOOLEY, ANITA DONNA
NAMATH, JOSEPH WILLIAM
(1943-) [American pro-
fessional football player]
Broadway Joe
Joe Namath
Joe Willie
Namby Pamby. See:
PHILIPS, AMBROSE
Name, The Girl With the
Ginger Snap. See:
PITTS, ZASU
NAMIK, MEHMED
(1840-88) [Turkish poet,
writer and patriot]
Kemal Bey
NAMOVICZ, GENE INYART
(1927-) [American
librarian and author]
Gene Inyart
Nan. See:
SHIPLEY, NANCY E.
Nan Asquith. See:
PATTINSON, NANCY
EVELYN
Nan, Brandy. See:
ANN
Nan Fairbrother. See:
McKENZIE, NAN

Nan Gilbert. See:
GILBERTSON, MILDRED
GEIGER
Nan Grey. See:
MILLER, ESCHAL
Nana Sahib. See:
PANTH, BRAHMIN DUNDHU
NANCE, WILLIS (1913-)
[American jazz musician
(violin, cornet, singer)]
Ray Nance
Nancy. See:
FAULKNER, ANNE IRVIN
MOSS, ROBERT ALFRED
SEWARD, ANNA
Nancy Bartlett. See:
STRONG, CHARLES
STANLEY
Nancy Boyd. See:
MILLAY, EDNA ST.
VINCENT
Nancy Bruff. See:
GARDNER, NANCY BRUFF
Nancy Cleaver. See:
MATHEWS, EVELYN CRAW
Nancy Dudley. See:
COLE, LOIS DWIGHT
Nancy Hartwell. See:
CALLAHAN, CLAIRE WALLIS
Nancy Paschal. See:
TROTTER, GRACE VIOLET
Nancy Richard West. See:
WESTPHAL, WILMA ROSS
Nancy Sherman. See:
ROSENBERG, NANCY
SHERMAN
Nancy Telfair. See:
DuBOSE, LOUISE JONES
Nancy Walker. See:
SWOYER, ANNA MYRTLE
NANDAKUMAR, PREMA
(1939-) [Indian translator
and author]
Aswin
Nanette Fabray. See:
FABARES, NANETTE
NANN, NICHOLAS T. (1928-)
[American musician and
composer]
Nick Mann
Nannerella. See:
MAGNANI, ANNA

NANTON, JOSEPH
(1904-48) [American
jazz musician (trombone)]
Tricky Sam Nanton
Nap. See:
LAJOIE, NAPOLEON
Lombard, Nap
NAPIER-CLAVERING, ALAN
(1903-) [British
motion picture actor]
Alan Napier
Napier, Diana. See:
ELLIS, MOLLY
NAPIER, JOHN (1550-1617)
[Scottish nobleman,
astronomer and mathe-
matician]
The Father of Logarithms
NAPIER, PRISCILLA (1908-
[English author]
Penelope Hunt
Eve Stewart
NAPIER, SIR CHARLES
(1786-1860) [British
admiral]
Black Charlie
NAPJUS, ALICE JAMES
(1913-) [American
educator and author]
James Napjus
Naples, The Parthenope of.
See: VIDA, MARCO
GIROLAMO
Napoleon I. See:
BONAPARTE, NAPOLEON
Napoleon II. See:
BONAPARTE, NAPOLEON
FRANÇOIS CHARLES
JOSEPH
Napoleon III. See:
BONAPARTE, CHARLES
LOUIS NAPOLEON
Napoleon, Little. See:
BRUMBAUGH, CARL
Napoleon, Little Mac the
Young. See:
McCLELLAN, GEORGE
BRINTON
Napoleon, Louis. See:
BONAPARTE, CHARLES
LOUIS NAPOLEON
Napoleon of Crime, The. See:

WORTH, ADAM
Napoleon of Gas, The. See:
ADDICKS, JOHN EDWARD
O'SULLIVAN
Napoleon of Luzon, The. See:
MacARTHUR, DOUGLAS
Napoleon of Mexico, The. See:
ITURBIDE, AGUSTÍN
DE
Napoleon of Oratory, The. See:
PITT, WILLIAM
Napoleon of Peace, The. See:
LOUIS PHILIPPE
Napoleon of Protection, The.
See: McKINLEY,
WILLIAM
Napoleon of Slavery, The. See:
CALHOUN, JOHN CALD-
WELL
Napoleon of the California Bar,
The. See:
DELMAS, DELPHIN
MICHAEL
Napoleon of the Drama, The.
See: BUNN, ALFRED
ELLISTON, ROBERT
WILLIAM
Napoleon of the North, The. See:
COMSTOCK, PETER
Napoleon of the Pacific, The.
See: KAMEHAMEHA I
Napoleon of the Stump, The. See:
POLK, JAMES KNOX
Napoleon of the Turf, The. See:
JOHNSON, WILLIAM
RANSOM
Napoleon, Prince. See:
BONAPARTE, JOSEPH
CHARLES PAUL
Napoleon, The Little. See:
BEAUREGARD, PIERRE
GUSTAVE TOUTANT
Nappy. See:
LAMARE, HILTON
Nares, Owen. See:
RAMSAY, OWEN NARES
Narragansett, The. See:
MAYNARD, HORACE
Nasby, Petroleum V. See:
LOCKE, DAVID ROSS
Nasby, Reverend Petroleum
Vesuvius. See:

LOCKE, DAVID ROSS
NASCIMENTO, EDSON
ARANTES DO (1940-)
[Brazilian soccer player]
Pelé
NASELI, ALBERTO (fl. 1568-83)
[Italian actor]
Zan Ganassa
Nash, Daniel. See:
LOADER, WILLIAM
REGINALD
NASH, FRANK (189?-1933)
[American bank robber]
George Nash
Jelly Nash
NASH (NASHE), THOMAS
(1567-1601) [British
pamphleteer, dramatist
and novelist]
Pasquil
NASH, RICHARD (1674-1762)
[English dandy, gambler
and master of ceremonies
at Bath]
Beau Nash
The King of Bath
Nash, Simon. See:
CHAPMAN, RAYMOND
Nasir, Alcofribas. See:
RABELAIS, FRANÇOIS
NASMYTH. See also:
NAISMITH
Naismith
NASMYTH, PATRICK (PETER)
(1787-1831) [Scottish
landscape painter]
The Scotch Hobbema
NASON, LEONARD HASTINGS
(1895-) [American
author and verse writer]
Steamer
NASSAU-DILLENBURG,
COUNT LOUIS OF
(1538-74) [Brother of
WILLIAM OF ORANGE]
The Bayard of the Nether-
lands
Nassau Street, The Antiquarian
of. See:
GOWANS, WILLIAM
Nast, Elsa Ruth. See:
WATSON, JANE WERNER

NAST, THOMAS (1840-1902)
[American political cari-
caturist and illustrator]
Our Best Recruiting Sergeant
Nat. See:
ABELSON, NATHAN
FARBER, NATHANIEL C.
GOODWIN, NATHANIEL
CARL
GOULD, NATHANIEL
MADISON, NATHANIEL
JOSEPH
SHILKRET, NATHANIEL
Nat, Fighting. See:
FITZ-RANDOLPH,
NATHANIEL
Nat Karta. See:
NORWOOD, VICTOR GEORGE
CHARLES
Nat King Cole. See:
COLES, NATHANIEL ADAMS
Nat Madison. See:
MADISON, NATHANIEL
JOSEPH
MOSCOVITCH, NOEL
Nat Newton. See:
MORRIS, ANTHONY P., JR.
Nat Ridley, Jr. See:
STRATEMEYER,
EDWARD L.
Nat Woods. See:
STRATEMEYER,
EDWARD L.
Natalie Wood. See:
GURDIN, NATASHA
NATHAN, DANIEL. See:
Queen, Ellery
Nathan Hale of the South, The.
See: DAVIS, SAM
Nathanael West. See:
WEINSTEIN, NATHAN
Nathaniel. See:
FIELD, NATHAN
Nathaniel Dring. See:
McBROOM, R. CURTIS
Natick Cobbler, The. See:
WILSON, HENRY
Nation, Acting Governor of the
English. See:
CAXTON, WILLIAM
NATION, CARRY AMELIA
MOORE (1846-1911)

[American temperance
agitator]
The Lady With the Hatchet
National Guard of New York, The
Father of the. See:
PHISTERER, FREDERICK
National Pastime, The Czar of
the. See:
LANDIS, KENESAW
MOUNTAIN
National Road, The Father of
the. See:
CLAY, HENRY
Nationalist School of Composition,
The Father of the Czech.
See: SMETANA,
BEDŘICH
Nation's Hostess, The. See:
MADISON, DOROTHY
PAYNE TODD
Nations, The Beloved Man of
the Four. See:
HAWKINS, BENJAMIN
Nations, The Savior of the.
See: WELLINGTON,
ARTHUR WELLESLEY,
1ST DUKE OF
Native of America, A. See:
PARKE, JOHN
NATONEK, HANS (1892-)
[German editor and author]
Nek
Natty. See:
DOMINIQUE, ANATIE
Natural History, The Father
of English. See:
RAY (WRAY), JOHN
Naturalism, The Master of. See:
See: FLAUBERT,
GUSTAVE
Naturalist, The Blind. See:
HUBER, FRANÇOIS
Naturalist, The Poet. See:
THOREAU, HENRY
DAVID
Nature, The Miracle of. See:
CHRISTINA
Nature, The Painter of. See:
BELLEAU, REMI
Nature, The Priest of. See:
NEWTON, SIR ISAAC
Nature, The Prose Homer of

Human. See:
FIELDING, HENRY
NAUTA, RENICUS DOWE (1869-)
[Dutch educator and author]
Navita
NAVARRE. See:
MARGARET OF NAVARRE
Navarre, Henry of. See:
BLAINE, JAMES
GILLESPIE
HENRY IV
WATTERSON, HENRY
Navarre of the American
Revolution, The. See:
BUTLER, THOMAS
NAVARRO, THEODORE (1923-50)
[American jazz musician
(trumpet)]
Fats Navarro
NAVASKY, VICTOR S. See:
Hirsch, William Randolph
Navigation, The Father of
British Inland. See:
EGERTON, FRANCIS
Navigation, The Father of
Steamboat. See:
FULTON, ROBERT
Navigator, Henry the. See:
HENRY
Navigator, Prince Henry the.
See: HENRY
Navita. See:
NAUTA, RENICUS DOWE
Navy, The Chesterfield of the.
See: LE ROY, WILLIAM
EDGAR
Navy, The Father of Our
Modern. See:
CHANDLER, WILLIAM
EATON
Navy, The Father of the
American. See:
ADAMS, JOHN
BARRY, COMMODORE JOHN
HUMPHREYS, JOSHUA
Navy, The Father of the English.
See: HENRY VIII
Navy, The Founder of the
American. See:
PAUL, JOHN
Nay. See also:
NEY

Nay
Ney, Richard Yea and. See:
RICHARD I
Nazi, Robert le. See:
ROBERT, GEORGE
ACHILLE MARIE-
JOSEPH
NAZIANZUS. See:
GREGORY OF
NAZIANZUS, ST.
Neagle, Anna. See:
ROBERTSON, MARJORIE
Neal. See:
Neil
NEILL
Neill
THOMAS, CORNELIUS
DICKINSON
Neal, Harry. See:
BIXBY, JEROME
LEWIS
Neal, Hilary. See:
NORTON, OLIVE
MARION
NEAL, JOHN (1793-1876)
[American editor,
novelist and poet]
Jehu O'Cataract
Somebody, M.D.C., 1817
NEAL, PATSY LOUISE
(1926-) [American
actress]
Patricia Neal
NEARING, ELIZABETH
CUSTER (1900-)
[American novelist]
Sue McVeigh
NEBERROTH, HAROLD
(1909-53) [American
motion picture actor]
Alan Curtis
Nebraska, The Kid Sheriff of.
See: WEDGWOOD,
EDGAR A.
Neck. See also:
Nek
Neck, Old Tu'key. See:
STILLWELL, JOSEPH
WARREN
Necktie, Red. See:
WEARIN, OTHA DONNER
Ned. See:

HANLON, EDWARD HUGH
HARRIGAN, EDWARD
SHUTER, EDWARD
WARD, EDWARD
Ned Buntline. See:
JUDSON, EDWARD ZANE
CARROLL
Ned, Durable. See:
KALBFUS, EDWARD
CLIFFORD
Ned Hunter, Lieut. See:
ELLIS, EDWARD
SYLVESTER
Ned St. Myer. See:
STRATEMEYER,
EDWARD L.
Ned Sparling. See:
SENARENS, LUIS PHILIP
Ned Tent. See:
DENNETT, HERBERT
VICTOR
Ned Warren. See:
MANNING, WILLIAM
HENRY
Neff, Hildegarde. See:
KNEF, HILDEGARDE
Negri, Pola. See:
CHALUPEK, APPOLONIA
Negro, America's One-eyed
Jewish. See:
DAVIS, SAMMY, JR.
Negro Moses, The. See:
TUBMAN, HARRIET
Negro Novelist, The First
American. See:
CHESNUTT, CHARLES
WADDELL
Negro Sappho, The. See:
WHEATLEY, PHYLLIS
Negus. See:
THEODORE II
Nehemiah, The American. See:
WINTHROP, JOHN
Neil. See:
LAWRENCE, CORNELIUS C.
NEAL
Neal
NEILL
Neill
Neil Bell. See:
SOUTHWOLD, STEPHEN
Neil Collen. See:

LEE, LINCOLN
Neil Gordon. See:
    MACDONELL, ARCHIBALD
    GORDON
Neil MacNeil. See:
    BALLARD, WILLIS
    TODHUNTER
Neil Moret. See:
    DANIELS, CHARLES N.
Neil, Ross. See:
    HARWOOD, ISABELLA
Neil Webb. See:
    ROWLAND, DONALD
    SYDNEY
NEILL [Neill]. See also:
    NEAL
    Neal
    Neil
Neill Graham. See:
    DUNCAN, WILLIAM MUR-
    DOCH
NEILL, THOMAS HEWSON
    (1826-85) [American Civil
    War general officer]
    Beau Neill
Neilson. See also:
    NELSON
    Nelson
Neilson, Lilian Adelaide. See:
    BROWN, ELIZABETH ANN
NEILY, HARRY (1881-)
    [American sporting editor]
    The Skillful Neily (El
    Neily Manoso)
    Señor Neilly
Nek. See:
    Neck
    NATONEK, HANS
NELHAMS, TERENCE (1940-)
    [British singer and
    motion picture actor]
    Adam Faith
Nell. See:
    GWYN (GWYNNE),
    ELEANOR
Nell Chenault. See:
    SMITH, LINELL NASH
Nell Speed. See:
    SAMPSON, EMMA SPEED
Nellie. See:
    FOX, JACOB NELSON
Nellie Blessing Eyster. See:

EYSTER, PENELOPE ANNA
    MARGARETTA BLESSING
Nellie Bly. See:
    SEAMAN, ELIZABETH
    COCHRANE
Nellie Grahame. See:
    DUNNING, ANNIE KETCHUM
Nellie Melba. See:
    MITCHELL, HELEN PORTER
Nellie, Pretty Witty. See:
    GWYN (GWYNNE),
    ELEANOR
NELSON [Nelson]. See also:
    Neilson
Nelson, Baby Face. See:
    GILLIS, LESTER M.
NELSON, DOLOREZ
    ALEXANDRIA (1929-)
    [American jazz musician
    (singer)]
    Lorez Alexandria
NELSON, ERIC HILLIARD
    (1940-) [American singer
    and actor]
    Rickey Nelson
Nelson, Gene. See:
    BERG, GENE
Nelson, George. See:
    GILLIS, LESTER M.
NELSON, HORATIO, VISCOUNT
    NELSON (1758-1805)
    [English admiral]
    The Embodiment of Sea Power
    The Hero of a Hundred Fights
    The Hero of the Nile
    Lord Nelson
Nelson, Joseph. See:
    MITCHELL, ISAAC
NELSON, KNUTE (1843-1923)
    [American politician;
    governor of and United
    States senator from
    Minnesota]
    The Little Corporal
    The Little Giant of Alexandria
    The Little Norwegian
NELSON, LOUIS DELISLE (1885-
    1949) [American jazz
    musician (clarinet)]
    Big Eye Louis Nelson
Nelson, Marguerite. See:
    FLOREN, LEE

NELSON, MICHAEL HARRING-
TON (1921-) [British
author]
Henry Stratton
Nelson Minier. See:
BAKER, LAURA NELSON
STOUTENBURG, ADRIEN
PEARL
NELSON, OSWALD GEORGE
(1906-) [American
orchestra leader; radio
and television actor]
Ozzie Nelson
NELSON, PEGGY LOU
SNYDER (190?-)
[American singer, radio
and television actress]
Harriet Hilliard
Nelson Percival. See:
RYMER, JAMES
MALCOLM
Nelson, Sandy. See:
EGNATZIK, JOSEPH
NELSON, WILLIAM (1824-62)
[American Civil War
general officer]
Bull Nelson
Dad Nelson
Neltze Blanchan. See:
DOUBLEDAY, NELTZE
DE GRAFF
Nemesis. See:
HARRIS, SIR CHARLES
ALEXANDER
Nemesis, The Cherry-trees.
See: JENCKES,
VIRGINIA ELLIS
Nemo. See:
BROWNE, HABLOT
KNIGHT
NENTWICH, MAX (1868-)
[German author]
Maximilian Münsterberg
Nephew of My Uncle, The.
See: SWEENEY,
PETER BARR
Nephew of the Almighty. See:
BROTHERS, RICHARD
Nerina, Nadia. See:
JUDD, NADINE
Nero of Germany, The. See:
WENCESLAUS IV

Nero of the North, The. See:
CHRISTIAN II
Nerval, Gerard de. See:
LABRUNIE, GERARD
Nesbit, Edith. See:
BLAND, MRS. HUBERT
Nesbit, Troy. See:
FOLSOM, FRANKLIN
BREWSTER
NESMITH, ROBERT I. (1891-)
[American businessman and
author]
Captain Jafah Clarke
Nest, The Hero of the Hornet's.
See: PRENTISS, BENJAMIN
MAYBERRY
NESTOR (1056-1114) [Russian
monk and historian]
The Father of Russian History
Nestor Ironside. See:
STEELE, SIR RICHARD
Nestor of American Botany,
The. See:
DARLINGTON, WILLIAM
Nestor of American Science,
The. See:
MITCHILL, SAMUEL
LATHAM
SILLIMAN, BENJAMIN
Nestor of Congregationalism, The.
See: BACON, LEONARD
Nestor of Europe, The. See:
LEOPOLD I
Nestor of Golf, The. See:
MORRIS, TOM
Nestor of the Chemical Revolu-
tion, The. See:
BLACK, JAMES
Nestor of the German-American
Journalists, The. See:
PREETORIUS, EMIL
Nestor of the Hampden County
Bar, The. See:
BATES, WILLIAM GELSTON
Nestor of the Methodist Confer-
ence in India, The. See:
BOWEN, GEORGE
Nestor of the Patriots, The. See:
HAWLEY, JOSEPH
Nestor of the Rocky Mountains,
The. See:
CARSON, CHRISTOPHER

Netherlands, The Apostle of
the. See:
ARMAND, ST.
Netherlands, The Bayard of
the. See:
NASSAU-DILLENBURG,
COUNT LOUIS OF
NETTL, JOHN PETER (1926-68)
[German educator and
author]
Paul Norwood
NEUBAUER, WILLIAM ARTHUR
(1916-) [American
author]
William Arthur
Christine Bennett
Norman Bligh
Ralph Carter
Joan Garrison
Jan Hathaway
Rebecca Marsh
Norma Newcom'ɔ
Gordon Semple
NEUMANN, FERENC (1878-
1952) [Hungarian play-
wright and novelist]
Ferenc Molnár
Nevada Commoner, The. See:
JONES, JOHN PERCIVAL
Never Fail. See:
BURNS, WILLIAM JOHN
Never-Made-Good Crack
Downs, King of the. See:
JOHNSON, HUGH SAMUEL
Never Sleeps, The Chief Who.
See: WAYNE, ANTHONY
NEVERS, ERNEST A. (1902-)
[American football
player]
Ernie Nevers
NEVIL (NEVILLE), RICHARD
(c.1428-71) [Earl of
Warwick]
The King-maker
The Last of the Barons
Nevil Shute. See:
NORWAY, NEVIL SHUTE
NEVILL, CECILY (fl. 15th cent.)
[Mother of EDWARD
IV of England]
The White Rose of Raby
NEVILLE. See:

NEVIL (NEVILLE), RICHARD
NEVILLE, BARBARA ALISON
BOODSON (1935-)
[British nurse and author]
Edward Candy
Neville, Lee. See:
RICHARDS, LELA HORN
NEVINS, JOSEPH ALLAN
(1890-) [American editor,
educator, historian and
author]
Allan Nevins
New America, Cromwell of.
See: ADAMS, SAMUEL
New Comedy, The Creator of
the. See:
ARISTOPHANES
MENANDER
New Deal, Crown Prince of the.
See: ROOSEVELT, JAMES
New Deal, The Author of the.
See: BURKE, EDWARD
RAYMOND
New Deal, The Babe Ruth of the.
See: JOHNSON, HUGH
SAMUEL
New Dealers, The King of the.
See: MINTON, SHERMAN
New Deal's Tom Dewey, The.
See: MURPHY, FRANK
New England, Burns of. See:
EASTMAN, CHARLES
GAMAGE
New England Cicero, The. See:
WEBSTER, DANIEL
New England Clergy, The
Patriarch of the. See:
NOTT, SAMUEL
New England Commerce, The
Father of. See:
ALLERTON, ISAAC
New England States, Columella
of the. See:
LOVELL, JOHN, JR.
New England, The Busby of. See:
LOWELL, JOHN
New England, The Congregational
Pope of. See:
BACON, LEONARD
New England, The Father of. See:
ENDICOTT, JOHN
New England, The Hero of. See:

STANDISH, MILES
(MYLES)
New England, The Patriarch of.
See: COTTON, JOHN
New England, The Poet
Laureate of. See:
WHITTIER, JOHN
GREENLEAF
New England, The Voice of.
See: FROST, ROBERT
LEE
New France, The Father of.
See: CHAMPLAIN,
SAMUEL DE
New Hampshire Demosthenes,
The. See:
WEBSTER, DANIEL
New Jersey, Despot-in-Chief
in and over the Rising
State of. See:
LIVINGSTON, WILLIAM
New Jersey, Extraordinary
Chancellor of the Rising
State of. See:
LIVINGSTON, WILLIAM
New Jersey, The Father of the
Free School System in.
See: CUTLER,
AUGUSTUS WILLIAM
New Jersey, The Samuel
Adams of. See:
FISHER, HENDRICK
New Orleans, The Hero of. See:
JACKSON, ANDREW
New Philopator (Loving his
Father). See:
PTOLEMY VII
New World, The Liberator of
the. See:
FRANKLIN, BENJAMIN
New Year's Eve, Mr. See:
LOMBARDO, GUY
ALBERT
New York, A Citizen of. See:
DUNLAP, WILLIAM
New York Bar, The Father of
the. See:
JONES, SAMUEL
New York City's Official
Greeter of Famous People.
See: WHALEN, GROVER
ALOYSIUS

New York State Boxing Bill,
The Father of the. See:
WALKER, JAMES JOHN
New York, The Father of Con-
crete Roads in. See:
GREENE, FREDERICK
STUART
New York, The Father of
Greater. See:
GREEN, ANDREW HASWELL
New York, The Father of Pres-
byterianism in the State of.
See: McNISH, GEORGE
New York, The Father of the
Bar of the State of. See:
VAN VECHEN, ABRAHAM
New York, The Father of the
National Guard of. See:
PHISTERER, FREDERICK
New York, The First Citizen of.
See: McINTYRE, OSCAR
ODD
New York, The Mad Poet of. See:
CLARKE, McDONALD
New York, The Playboy of. See:
WALKER, JAMES JOHN
New York Turf, The Father of
the. See:
DE LANCEY, JAMES
NEWBERGER, GABRIEL F.
(c. 1867-1939) [American
poet]
The Poet of the Ozarks
Newbury, Jack of. See:
WINCHCOMB, JOHN
NEWBY, ERIC (1919-)
[British author]
James Parker
Newcomb, Norma. See:
NEWBAUER, WILLIAM
ARTHUR
NEWCOMBE, DONALD (1926-)
[American professional
baseball player]
Don Newcombe
NEWCOMEN, MATTHEW. See:
Smectymnuus
NEWELL, CHARLES MARTIN
(1821-187?) [American
novelist]
Captain Robert Barnacle
NEWELL, PETER (1862-1924)

[American humorist,
writer and illustrator]
Sheaf Hershey
NEWELL, ROBERT (1807-69)
[American pioneer in
Oregon]
Doc
Doctor
NEWELL, ROBERT HENRY
(1836-1901) [American
editor, humorist and
poet]
Orpheus C. Kerr
Newell, Roy. See:
RAYMOND, HAROLD
NEWELL
Newfane, The Hermit of. See:
BROWN, DAVID
NEWHART, GEORGE ROBERT
(1929-) [American
comedian]
Bob Newhart
NEWMAN, DAVID (1933-)
[American jazz
musician (alto and tenor
saxophone)]
Fathead Newman
NEWMAN, JOHN. See:
Johns, Kenneth
NEWMAN, LEONARD HUGH
(1909-) [English author]
The Butterfly Farmer
Newman, Margaret. See:
POTTER, MARGARET
NEWMAN
Newman of America, The. See:
HEWITT, AUGUSTINE
FRANCIS
Newman, Richard Brinsley.
See: GIFFORD,
FRANKLIN KENT
News Man, The Danbury. See:
BAILEY, JAMES MONT-
GOMERY
Newspaper, America's One-man.
See: WINCHEL, WALTER
Newspaper Woman, The First
American. See:
CROLY, JANE
CUNNINGHAM
Newspapers, The Father of
American. See:

HARRIS, BENJAMIN
NEWTON, DWIGHT BENNETT
(1916-) [American writer]
Dwight Bennett
Clement Hardin
Ford Logan
Dan Temple
Newton, Francis. See:
HOBSBAWN, ERIC JOHN
ERNEST
NEWTON, HENRY JOTHAM
(1823-95) [American in-
ventor in the field of
photography]
The Father of the Dry Plate
Process in America
Newton, Nat. See:
MORRIS, ANTHONY P., JR.
NEWTON, RICHARD HEBER
(1840-1914) [American
Protestant clergyman and
theologian]
Heber Newton
NEWTON, SIR ISAAC (1642-1727)
[English mathematician and
natural philosopher]
The Priest of Nature
NEY [Ney]. See also:
Nay
NEY, MICHEL (1769-1815)
[Cavalry marshal under
NAPOLEON I]
Bravest of the Brave
Marshal Ney
Ney of the Confederacy. See:
CHEATHAM, BENJAMIN
FRANKLIN
NEYLAND, GENERAL ROBERT
REESE, JR. (1892-)
[American football coach]
Football's Greatest Coach
Niagara Power, The Father of.
See: RANKINE, WILLIAM
BIRCH
NIBBI, GINO (1896-) [Italian art
dealer, critic and author]
Medaro
Niblo, Fred. See:
NOBILE, FEDERICO
NIC SHIUBHLAIGH, MAIRE
(-1958) [Irish actress]
Maire Price

Nicator. See:
    DEMETRIUS II
    SELEUCUS I
NICHOLAS (died 867) [Supreme
    Pontiff of Roman Catholic
    Church]
    The Great
    Pope Nicholas I
    St. Nicholas
Nicholas. See:
    NICOLAUS
    Nikolaus
    MORGAN, THOMAS
    BRUCE
NICHOLAS I (1796-1855) [Czar
    of Russia]
    The Iron Czar
    The Iron Emperor
Nicholas II, Pope. See:
    GERHARD OF BURGUNDY
Nicholas III, Pope. See:
    ORSINI, GIOVANNI
    GAETANO
Nicholas IV, Pope. See:
    MASCI, GIROLAMO
Nicholas V, Pope. See:
    PARENTUCELLI, TOM-
    MASO
Nicholas Blake. See:
    DAY-LEWIS, CECIL
Nicholas Carter. See:
    CORYELL, JOHN
    RUSSELL
    DAVIS, FREDERICK
    WILLIAM
    DEY, FREDERICK VAN
    RENSSELAER
    JENKS, GEORGE
    CHARLES
    SAWYER, EUGENE
    TAYLOR
Nicholas David. See:
    MORGAN, THOMAS
    BRUCE
Nicholas, Don. See:
    DE COLLIBUS,
    NICHOLAS
NICHOLAS, JOE (1883-)
    [American jazz
    musician (cornet,
    clarinet)]
    Wooden Joe Nicholas

Nicholas Ray. See:
    KIENZLE, RAYMOND
    NICHOLAS
Nicholas, St. See:
    NICHOLAS
    NICOLAUS, ST.
Nicholas Silver. See:
    FAUST, FREDERICK
    SCHILLER
Nicholas Tooley. See:
    WILKINSON, NICHOLAS,
NICHOLS, DALE WILLIAM
    (1904-) [American painter,
    illustrator and author]
    Willem de Polman
Nichols, Dave. See:
    FROST, HELEN
NICHOLS, ERNEST LORING
    (1905-65) [American jazz
    musician (trumpet, leader)]
    Red Nichols
NICHOLS, GEORGE HERBERT
    FOSDIKE (1883-) [British
    army officer, journalist and
    author]
    Quex
NICHOLS, JOHN CONOVER
    (1896-1945) [American
    politician; congressman from
    Oklahoma]
    Oklahoma Jack
Nichols, Scott. See:
    SCORTIA, THOMAS
    NICHOLAS
NICHOLSON. See also:
    NICOLSON
NICHOLSON, ELIZA JANE
    POITEVENT HOLBROOK
    (1849-96) [American news-
    paper proprieter and poet]
    Pearl Rivers
NICHOLSON, MARGARET BEDA
    LARMINIE (1924-)
    [British author]
    Margaret Yorke
NICHOLSON, SIR WILLIAM
    NEWZAM PRIOR. See:
    Beggarstaff, J. and W.
Nick. See:
    BOLIN, NICOLAI P.
    CASTLE, NICHOLAS
    LA ROCCA, DOMINICK

JAMES
NANN, NICHOLAS T.
ROSSI, NICHOLAS LOUIS,
JR.
Nick Adams. See:
ADAMSHOCK, NICHOLAS
Nick Carter. See:
CARTER, VINCENT
CORYELL, JOHN RUSSELL
DAVIS, FREDERICK
WILLIAM
DEY, FREDERICK VAN
RENSSELAER
HARBAUGH, THOMAS
CHALMERS
JENKS, GEORGE CHARLES
SAWYER, EUGENE
TAYLOR
Nick Jerret. See:
BERTOCCI, NICHOLAS
Nick Lucas. See:
LUCANESE, NICK
Nick of the Bribery Bank,
Emperor. See:
BIDDLE, NICHOLAS
Nick Parkyakarkas. See:
EINSTEIN, HARRY
Nick Travis. See:
TRAVASCIO, NICHOLAS
ANTHONY
NICOL. See also : NICOLL
NICOL, ERIC PATRICK (1919-)
[Canadian author]
Jabez
Nicolai. See:
KASATKIN, IVAN
Nicolai Lenin. See: ULYANOV,
VLADIMIR ILYICH
NICOLAS, JEAN (1740-1823)
[French politician]
The Tartuffe of the Revolution
NICOLAUS. See also:
NICHOLAS
Nicholas
Nikolaus
NICOLAUS, ST. (fl. c. 300
A.D.) [Saint of the Greek
Church; patron saint of Rus-
sia and of boys, thieves,
mariners and virgins]
The Boy Bishop
St. Nicholas

Santa Claus
Santa Klaus
Nicole Courcel. See:
ANDRIEUX, NICOLE
Nicolete Meredith. See:
STACK, NICOLETE
NICOLL. See also:
NICOL
NICOLL, SIR WILLIAM
ROBERTSON (1851-1923)
[Scottish theologian and
editor]
Claudius Clear
NICOLSON. See also:
NICHOLSON
NICOLSON, ADELA FLORENCE
(1865-1904) [English poet]
Laurence Hope
Niece, Uncle Sam's Favorite.
See: KAUMEYER, DOROTHY
NIELSEN, HELEN BERNIECE
(1918-) [American author]
Kris Giles
Nielsen, Virginia. See:
McCALL, VIRGINIA
NIELSEN
Night, Mr. Saturday. See:
GLEASON, HERBERT JOHN
Nightclub Queen, The. See:
GUINAN, MARY LOUISE
CECELIA
NIGHTINGALE, FLORENCE
(1820-1910) [English nurse,
hospital reformer and
humanitarian]
The Lady With the Lamp
Nightingale of the Southern
Army, The Florence. See:
TRADER, ELLA KING
NEWSOM
Nightingale, The Italian. See:
CATALANI, ANGELICA
Nightingale, The Swedish. See:
LIND, JOHANNA MARIA
Nightingales, The Four. See:
Four Marx Brothers, The
Nightmare of Europe, The. See:
BONAPARTE, NAPOLEON
Nikolaus. See also:
NICHOLAS
Nicholas
NICOLAUS

Nikolaus Lenau. See:
    VON STREHLENAU,
    NIKOLAUS NIEMBSCH
Nikolaus of Flue. See:
    LÖWENBRUGGER,
    NIKOLAUS
Nil Admirari, Esq. See:
    SHELTON, FREDERICK
    WILLIAM MAY
Nile, The Hero of the. See:
    NELSON, HORATIO,
    VISCOUNT NELSON
Niles Chignon. See:
    LINGEMAN, RICHARD
    ROBERTS
Nimrod. See:
    APPERLEY, CHARLES
    JAMES
Nina. See:
    RHOADES, CORNELIA
    HARSEN
Nina Bawden. See:
    KARK, NINA MARY
    MABEY
Nina Simone. See:
    WAYMON, EUNICE
    KATHLEEN
Nine-to-five Pro, A. See:
    BEARD, FRANK
Nineteenth Century, The Colos-
    sus of the. See:
    BONAPARTE, NAPOLEON
Nineteenth Century, The Greatest
    Theoretical Physicist of
    the. See:
    MAXWELL, JAMES
    CLERK
Ninette de Valois. See:
    STANNUS, EDRIS
NINIAN, ST. (fl. c. 400)
    [British missionary]
    The Apostle of the Picts
Nininger, The Sage of. See:
    DONNELLY, IGNATIUS
Niño de la Eterna Sonrisa.
    See: TORRES, EMILIO
Niño de la Palma. See:
    ORDÓÑEZ, CAYETANO
Niño de Tomares. See:
    TORRES, EMILIO
Ninon de Lenclos. See:
    LENCLOS, ANNE
Nirmala-Kumara Vasu. See:

BOSE, NIRMAL KUMAR
NISBET, GEORGE (1836-1926)
    [French slave dealer on the
    Red Sea Coast]
    Osman Digna
Nita Naldi. See:
    DOOLEY, ANITA DONNA
NITTI, FRANK (1885-1932)
    [Italian-American racketeer;
    member of gang headed by
    ALPHONSE CAPONE]
    The Enforcer
NIVEN, LAURENCE VAN COTT
    (1938-) [American author]
    Larry Niven
NIXON, RICHARD MILHAUS
    (1913-) [Thirty-seventh
    President of the United
    States]
    Tricky Dick
No. Items so prefixed are in-
    dexed as though spelled
    "Number"
Noah, Father. See:
    WELLES, GIDEON
NOAH, MORDECAI MANUEL
    (1785-1851) [American
    playwright and essayist]
    Muley Malack
    Major Noah
Noah Nuff. See:
    BELLAW, AMERICUS
    WELLINGTON
Noah, Uncle. See:
    BROOKS, NOAH
NOBILE, FEDERICO (1874-1948)
    [American motion picture
    director]
    Fred Niblo
NOBLE, JOHN AVERY (1892-1944)
    [Hawaiian orchestra leader
    and composer]
    Johnny Noble
Noble, The. See:
    ALFONSO IX
    CHARLES III
    FREDERICK WILLIAM
Noblest Roman of Them All, The.
    See:
    McMILLIN, BENTON
    THURMAN, ALLAN GRAN-
    BERRY
Noch Vaster (Even Firmer).

743

See: STEENDAM,
JACOB
NOCK, ALBERT JAY (-1945)
[American editor and
author]
Journeyman
NOÉ, AMÉDÉE DE (1819-79)
[French caricaturist]
Cham (Ham)
Noel Ames. See:
BARROWS, MARJORIE
Noel de Vic Beamish. See:
BEAMISH, ANNE
O'MEARA DE VIC
Noel Dunbar, Dr. See:
INGRAHAM, COLONEL
PRENTISS
NOEL, LUCIEN (1897-)
[French motion picture
comedian]
Noel-Noel
Noel Madison. See:
MOSCOVITCH, NOEL
NOKES, JAMES (died c. 1692)
[English actor]
Nurse Nokes
Nolan, Brian. See:
O'NUALLAIN, BRIAN
NOLAN, GEORGE (1904-)
[Irish-American motion
picture actor]
George Brent
NOLAN, JEANNETTE COVERT
(fl. 1914-61) [American
reporter, novelist and
biographer]
Caroline Tucker
NOLAN, WILLIAM FRANCIS
(1928-) [American car-
toonist, actor and writer]
Frank Anmar
F. E. Edwards
Michael Phillips
Nolde, Emil. See:
HANSEN, EMIL
Noll. See:
CROMWELL, OLIVER
NOLL, LOU BARKER
(1927-) [American edu-
cator, poet and writer]
Bink Noll
Noll, Martin. See:

BUXBAUM, MARTIN
Noll, Old. See:
CROMWELL, OLIVER
Nominalium, Princeps. See:
OCKHAM (OCCAM),
WILLIAM OF
Noname. See:
SENARENS, LUIS PHILIP
Nonpareil, The. See:
KELLY, JOHN
NOONE, JAMES (1895-1944)
[American jazz musician
(clarinet)]
Jimmie Noone
Nora Jackson. See:
TENNANT, NORA JACKSON
Nora K. Strange. See:
STANLEY, NORA KATHLEEN
BEGBIE
Nora Kaye. See:
KOREFF, NORA
Norah Lee. See:
BARSTOW, NORAH LEE
HAYMOND
Norbert, W. See:
WIENER, NORBERT
NORBURY, THE EARL OF (died
1831) [Chief Justice of Com-
mon Pleas in Ireland]
The Hanging Judge
Norcross, John. See:
CONROY, JOHN WESLEY
Norden, Charles. See:
DURRELL, LAWRENCE
GEORGE
Noreen Mack. See:
O'FLYNN, HONORIA
Norell, Norman. See:
LEVINSON, NORMAN
Norfolk Boy, The. See:
PORSON, RICHARD
Norfolk, Jack of. See:
HOWARD, SIR JOHN
Norfolk, The Jockey of. See:
HOWARD, SIR JOHN
Norford Scott. See:
ROWLAND, DONALD
SYDNEY
Norm. See:
VAN BROCKLIN, NORMAN
WELCH, NORMAN A.
Norma Hodgson. See:

744

RUSSELL, NORMA HULL
LEWIS
Norma Newcomb. See:
NEUBAUER, WILLIAM
ARTHUR
Norma Paul Ruedi. See:
AINSWORTH, NORMA
Norman. See:
Edwards, Norman
Norman A. King. See:
TRALINS, S. ROBERT
NORMAN, ALEXANDER VESEY
BETHUNE (1930-)
[British museum curator
and author]
Vesey Norman
Norman Angell. See:
LANE, RALPH NORMAN
ANGELL
Norman Angell, Sir. See:
LANE, RALPH NORMAN
ANGELL
Norman Bligh. See:
NEUBAUER, WILLIAM
ARTHUR
Norman Brainerd. See:
FULLER SAMUEL
RICHARD, JR.
Norman D. Kerr. See:
SIEBER, SAM DIXON
Norman D. Spencer. See:
FACTOR, JOHN
Norman Davis. See:
LUCAS, CHRISTOPHER
NORMAN
Norman Deane. See:
CREASEY, JOHN
Norman Edward Mace Smith. See:
SHERATON, NEIL
Norman Foster. See:
HOEFFER, NORMAN
Norman Galway. See:
GENTRY, BYRON B.
Norman, James. See:
SCHMIDT, JAMES
NORMAN
Norman, Joe. See:
HEARD, JOSEPH
NORMAN
Norman Kerry. See:
KAISER, ARNOLD
Norman Mansfield. See:

GLADDEN, EDGAR
NORMAN
Norman Mawdsley. See:
HARGREAVES-MAWDSLEY,
WILLIAM NORMAN
Norman Norell. See:
LEVINSON, NORMAN
Norman, Robert. See:
GARDNER, MAURICE
Norman, William the. See:
WILLIAM I
Normand, Mabel. See:
FORTESCUE, MABEL
Normandy, The Gem of. See:
AELFGIFA, EMMA
Normannus. See:
TONNIES, FERDINAND
JULIUS
Norrey. See also:
DILCOCK, NOREEN
Norrey Ford. See:
DILCOCK, NOREEN
Norreys Connell. See:
O'RIORDAN, CONAL
O'CONNELL
NORRIS, ALEXANDER (1902-)
[Polish stage actor; later
motion picture actor and
director]
Max Nosseck
NORRIS, BENJAMIN FRANKLIN
(1870-1902) [American
novelist]
Frank Norris
NORRIS, GEORGE WILLIAM
(1861-1944) [American
politician; congressman
from Nebraska]
The Dean of the Liberals
The Father of Public Utility
Regulation
The Greek Purist
The Father of the Twentieth
Amendment to the Consti-
tution
NORRIS, REV. JOHN (1657-1711)
[English platonist]
The English Plato
North, Alexander of the. See:
CHARLES XII
North, André. See:
NORTON, ALICE MARY

North, Andrew. See:
NORTON, ALICE MARY
North Carolina Bar, The
Father of the. See:
MOORE, BARTHOLOMEW
FIGURES
North Carolina, The Father of
Rural Credit in. See:
HILL, JOHN SPRUNT
North Carolina, The Father of
the University of. See:
DAVIE, WILLIAM
RICHARDSON
North Carolina, The Samuel
Adams of. See:
HARNETT, CORNELIUS
North, Charles W. See:
BAUER, ERWIN A.
North, Christopher. See:
WILSON, JOHN
North, David's Harp of the.
See: WALLIN, JOHAN
OLOF
NORTH, FREDERICK, 2D
EARL OF GUILFORD
(1732-92) [British states-
man and Prime Minister]
Lord North
North, Gil. See:
HORNE, GEOFFREY
NORTH, GRACE MAY (1876-)
[American author]
Carol Norton
North, Ingoldsby. See:
URNER, NATHAN DANE
NORTH, JOHN RINGLING
(1903-) [American circus
impresario and executive]
The Greatest Showman Since
Barnum
North, Leigh. See:
PHELPS, ELIZABETH
STEWART
North, Nero of the. See:
CHRISTIAN II
North, Sheree. See:
BETHEL, DAWN
NORTH, SIR THOMAS
(1535?-1601?) [English
translator and writer]
The First Master of English
Prose

North, The Addison of the.
See: MACKENZIE,
HENRY
North, The Apostle of the. See:
ANSAGAR (ANSCHARIUS)
GILPIN, BERNARD
North, The Ariosto of the. See:
SCOTT, SIR WALTER
North, The Cock of the. See:
GEORGE, DUKE OF
GORDON
North, The Great Magician of
the. See:
SCOTT, SIR WALTER
North, The Great Wizard of the.
See: ANDERSON, JOHN
HENRY
North, The Lion of the. See:
GUSTAVIUS II
North, The Madman of the. See:
CHARLES XII
North, The Magician of the. See:
HAMANN, JOHANN GEORG
SCOTT, SIR WALTER
North, The Magnus of the. See:
HAMANN, JOHANN GEORG
North, The Man from the. See:
HOBMAN, JOSEPH BURTON
North, The Napoleon of the. See:
COMSTOCK, PETER
North, The Nero of the. See:
CHRISTIAN II
North, The Quixote of the. See:
CHARLES XII
North, The Semiramis of the.
See: ANHALT-ZERBST,
SOPHIA AUGUSTA
FREDERICA OF
MARGARET
North, The Star of the. See:
GUSTAVUS II
North, The Wizard of the. See:
SCOTT, SIR WALTER
Northamptonshire Peasant Poet.
See: CLARE, JOHN
Northcote, Peter. See:
BOULTING, SYDNEY
NORTHCOTT, WILLIAM CECIL
(1902-) [British Congre-
gational clergyman and
author]
Mary Miller

Northern Addison, The. See:
MACKENZIE, HENRY
Northern Herodotus, The. See:
STURLESON, SNORRE
Northland, The Silver Fox of
the. See:
BIERMAN, BERNARD
WILLIAM
Northumbrian Gentleman, The.
See: TEGNER, HENRY
STUART
Northwest, The Father of the
Old. See:
CASS, LEWIS
NORTON, ALICE MARY
(fl. 1938-67) [American
librarian and author]
André North
Andrew North
Norton, Carol. See:
NORTH, GRACE MAY
NORTON, JOSHUA A. (1819-80)
[Demented San Francisco
resident; imagined
himself a nobleman]
Emperor Norton
Protector of Mexico
NORTON, MARY TERESA
(1875-) [American poli-
tician; congresswoman
from New Jersey]
Washington's First
Mayoress
Norton, Mrs. Florice. See:
BRAME, CHARLOTTE
MARY
NORTON, OLIVE MARION
(1913-) [Scottish author]
Hilary Neal
Bess Norton
Kate Norway
Norton, Sybil. See:
COURNOS, HELEN SYBIL
NORTON
NORVILLE, KENNETH (1908-)
[American jazz musician
(vibraharp, xylophone,
leader)]
Red Norvo
Norvo, Red. See:
NORVILLE, KENNETH
Norway, Kate. See:

NORTON, OLIVE
MARION
NORWAY, NEVIL SHUTE
(1899-1960) [British author]
Nevil Shute
Norway, The Fair Maid of. See:
MARGARET
Norwegian Poetry, The Father
of Modern. See:
DASS, PETER
Norwegian, The Little. See:
NELSON, KNUTE
Norwich, Taylor of. See:
BORROW, GEORGE HENRY
Norwood, Paul. See:
NETTL, JOHN PETER
NORWOOD, VICTOR GEORGE
CHARLES (1920-)
[British author]
Coy Banton
Shane V. Baxter
Clay Brand
Jim Bowie
Walt Cody
Shayne Colter
Wes Corteen
Clint Dangerfield
Johnny Dark
Vince Destry
Doone Fargo
Wade Fisher
G. Gearing-Thomas
Mark Hampton
Hank Janson
Nat Karta
Whip McCord
Brett Rand
Brad Regan
Shane Russell
Rondo Shane
Jim Tressidy
Nose, Golden. See:
BRAHE, TYCHO
Nosey. See:
CROMWELL, OLIVER
WELLINGTON, ARTHUR
WELLESLEY, 1ST
DUKE OF
Nosseck, Max. See:
NORRIS, ALEXANDER
Nostradamus. See:
NOTRE-DAME, MICHEL DE

Nostradamus, The Portuguese.
See: BANDARRA,
GONÇALO ANNES
Notre Dame, Le Tapissier de.
See: MONTMORENCY-
BOUTEVILLE, HENRI
DE
Notre Dame, The Rock of. See:
ROCKNE, KNUTE KENNETH
NOTREDAME, MICHEL DE
(1503-66) [French
physician and astrologer]
Nostradamus
NOTT, HENRY JUNIUS (1797-
1837) [American humorist
and educator]
Jeremiah Hopkins
NOTT, SAMUEL (1754-1852)
[American clergyman
and educator]
The Patriarch of the New
England Clergy
Nottingham Poet, The. See:
BAILEY, PHILIP JAMES
Nottingham, The Boy Poet of.
See: WHITE, HENRY
KIRKE
NOUE, FRANÇOIS DE LA
(1531-91) [Huguenot leader]
Bras de Fer
NOURSE, ALAN EDWARD
(1928-) [American author]
Al Edwards
Nova Scotia, The Whitfield of.
See: ALLINE, HENRY
Novak, Joseph. See:
KOSINSKI, JERZY
NIKODEM
NOVAK, MARILYN PAULINE
(1933-) [American
actress]
Kim Novak
Novalis (Fallow Land). See:
HARDENBERG, FRIEDRICH
LEOPOLD, BARON VON
Novanglus. See:
ADAMS, JOHN
Novarro, Ramón. See:
SAMANIEGOES, RAMÓN
Novel, The Father of the
English. See:
FIELDING, HENRY

Novel, The Father of the His-
torical. See:
SCOTT, SIR WALTER
Novel, The Founder of the
English Domestic. See:
RICHARDSON, SAMUEL
Novel, The Homer of the. See:
SCOTT, SIR WALTER
Novelist, M.O. Rolfe, The
Detective. See:
ROLFE, MARO O.
Novelist, M. O'Rolfe, the
Irish. See:
ROLFE, MARO O.
Novelist, The First American
Negro. See:
CHESNUTT, CHARLES
WADDELL
Novelists, The Dean of Con-
temporary English. See:
FORSTER, EDWARD
MORGAN
Novelists, The Hogarth of. See:
FIELDING, HENRY
Novelists, The Salvator Rosa of
British. See:
RADCLIFFE, ANN WARD
NOVELLA, RITA (1920-)
[Mexican singer, dancer
and motion picture actress]
Donna Drake
Rita Rio
NOVELLO, EUGENE (1912-)
[American composer]
Gene Novello
Novello, Ivor. See:
DAVIES, IVOR NOVELLO
NOWELL, ALEXANDER
(c. 1507-1602) [English
ecclesiastic]
Bottled Beer
NUBIN, ROSETTA (1910-)
[American jazz musician
(singer, guitar)]
Sister Rosetta Tharpe
NUCERA, MARISA LONETTE
(1959-) [American poet]
Marisa
Nuff, Noah. See:
BELLAW, AMERICUS
WELLINGTON
NUGENT, JAMES. See:

Jim-Jim Crowd, The
NUGENT, JOHN PEER (1930-)
[American correspondent
and author]
Barry Exall
Nui (The Great). See:
KAMEHAMEHA I
Nullifier, The Great. See:
CALHOUN, JOHN
CALDWELL
No. 1, Adelphi Terriss. See:
LEWIN, WILLIAM
CHARLES JAMES
No. 1 Boatbuilder, America's.
See: HIGGINS,
ANDREW JACKSON
No. 1 Glamour Boy, Holly-
wood's. See:
MATURE, VICTOR JOHN
No. 1 Industrial Architect, The
World's. See:
KAHN, ALBERT
No. 1 Innkeeper, The. See:
HILTON, CONRAD
NICHOLSON
No. 1, Public Enemy. See:
DILLINGER, JOHN
HERBERT
GILLIS, LESTER M.
No. 1, World Citizen. See:
DAVIS, GARRY
NUMKENA, ANTHONY
(1936-) [American
motion picture actor]
Earl Holliman
Nun of Dülmen, The. See:
EMMERICH, ANNA
KATHARINA
Nun of Kent, The. See:
BARTON, ELIZABETH
Nun, The Portuguese. See:
ALCOFORADO,
MARIANNA
Nuneaton, The Oracle of. See:
SIMPSON, THOMAS
NUÑEZ DE ARCE, GASPAR
(1834-1903) [Spanish
poet, dramatist and
statesman]
The Spanish Tennyson
NUNN, WILLIAM CURTIS
(1908-)

[American educator and
author]
Will Curtis
Ananias Twist
Nunquam. See:
BLATCHFORD, ROBERT
Nuraini. See:
SIM, KATHARINE
THOMASSET
Nurk Twins, The, stage name
of JOHN LENNON (1940-)
and PAUL McCARTNEY
(1942-) [Liverpudlian
singing and instrumental
group]
Nurk Twins, The. See also:
Beatles, The
NURMI, PAAVO (1897-)
[Finnish long distance
runner; Olympic champion]
The Flying Finn
Nurse. See:
NOKES, JAMES
Nurse of Danville, The Student.
See: BURCHARD,
SAMUEL DICKINSON
Nursery, The Laureate of the.
See: MILLER, WILLIAM
RANDS, WILLIAM
BRIGHTY
NURSIA. See:
BENEDICT OF NURSIA,
ST.
Nursing Mother of the Gridiron
Club, The Father and. See:
CARSON, JOHN MILLER
Nutt, Commodore. See:
McNUTT, GEORGE
WASHINGTON MORRISON
NUTTER, WILLIAM H. (1875-
1941) [American author
and journalist]
Halliday Witherspoon
NUVOLARI, TAZIO (1892-1953)
[Italian motorcycle and
automobile racing driver]
Il Maestro
The Flying Mantuan
NYE, EDGAR WILSON
(1850-96) [American
humorist]
Bill Nye

NYE, JAMES WARREN
(1814-76) [American
politician; congressman
from Nevada]
Gray Eagle
NYE, NELSON CORAL
(1907-) [American
writer of Western novels]
Clem Colt
Drake C. Denver
Montague Rockingham
Nye Tredgold. See:
TRANTER, NIGEL
Nym Crinkle. See:
WHEELER, ANDREW
CARPENTER
Nyren, Dorothy. See:
CURLEY, DOROTHY
NYREN

O

O' Birds. See:
BURROUGHS, JOHN
O. E. See:
RÖLVAAG, OLE
EDVART
O. H. Leslie. See:
SLESAR, HENRY
O. Henry. See:
PORTER, WILLIAM
SYDNEY
O. Henry Girl, The. See:
AYRES, AGNES
O. J. See:
SIMPSON, ORENTHAL
JAMES
O. K. See:
KELLY, JONATHAN
FALCONBRIDGE
O. M. See:
HALL, OAKLEY
MAXWELL
O. Mude. See:
GOREY, EDWARD ST.
JOHN
O. O. See:
McINTYRE, OSCAR ODD
O. O. Green. See:
DURGNAT, RAYMOND
ERIC

O SIOCHAIN, PADRAIG
AUGUSTINE (1905-) [Irish
journalist, editor and
author]
Patrick Augustine Sheehan
O, The Big. See:
ROBERTSON, OSCAR
PALMER
O. W. L. (Oh Wonderful Love),
Servant of the Lord. See:
GRAHAM, JAMES
Oak George, Live. See:
LAW, GEORGE
Oakey, Elegant. See:
HALL, ABRAHAM OAKEY
Oakie, Jack. See:
OFFIELD, LEWIS D.
Oakland, Vivian. See:
ANDERSON, VIVIAN
Oakley, Annie. See:
MOZZEE, PHOEBE ANNE
OAKLEY
OAKLEY, ERIC GILBERT
(1916-) [British editor
and author]
Peter Capon
Grapho
Paul Gregson
Oaksmith, Elizabeth. See:
SMITH, ELIZABETH
OAKES
OASTLER, RICHARD (1789-
1861) [English reformer]
The Factory King
OAKES, TITUS (1649-1705)
[English conspirator and
perjurer]
The Savior of His Country
Obediah Skinflint. See:
HARRIS, JOEL CHANDLER
Obedient Servant, Your. See:
WELLES, GEORGE ORSON
OBEE, LOIS (1909-) [British
stage and motion picture
actress]
Sonia Dresdel
Oberholtzer, Peter. See:
BRANNON, WILLIAM T.
Oberon. See:
HAWTHORNE, NATHANIEL
Oberon, Merle. See:
THOMPSON, ESTELLE

O'BRIEN MERLE
OBICI, AMEDEO (1877-1947)
[Italian-American
pioneer in the peanut
industry]
The Peanut King
Objector, The Great. See:
HOLMAN, WILLIAM
STEELE
Oboe, Peter. See:
JACOBS, WALTER
DARNELL
O'Brian, Frank. See:
GARFIELD, BRIAN
WYNNE
O'Brian, Hugh. See:
KRAMPKE, HUGH
O'Brien, Dave. See:
BARCLAY, DAVID
O'Brien, Dean D. See:
BINDER, OTTO OSCAR
O'BRIEN, EDWARD J.C.
HARRINGTON (1890-1941)
[American editor]
Arthur Middleton
O'Brien, Flann. See:
O'NUALLAIN, BRIAN
O'BRIEN, FLORENCE ROMA
MUIR (1891-1930)
[English novelist]
Romer Wilson
O'BRIEN, JANE (1918-)
[American motion
picture actress]
Jane Bryan
O'BRIEN, JOHN (1836-87)
[American actor and
comedian]
John T. Raymond
O'BRIEN, JOHN V. (1836-89)
[American circus
entrepreneur]
Pogey O'Brien
O'Brien, Marianne. See:
JUDD, MARY ANN
O'BRIEN, WILLIAM JOSEPH,
JR. (1899-) [American
actor]
Pat O'Brien
O'BRIEN, WILLIAM SHONEY
(1826-78) [American
banker and capitalist]

The Jolly Millionaire
Observer, Veteran. See:
MANSFIELD, EDWARD
DEERING
Observers, The Prince of. See:
MÜLLER, FRITZ
O'CAROLAN, TURLOCH (1670-
1738) [Irish wandering
minstrel]
The Orpheus of the Green
Isle
O'Casey, Sean. See:
CASEY, JOHN
O'Cataract, Jehu. See:
NEAL, JOHN
OCCAM. See:
OCKHAM (OCCAM),
WILLIAM OF
Occidente, Maria del. See:
BROOKS, MARIA GOWEN
Ocean Sea, Admiral of the. See:
COLUMBUS, CHRISTOPHER
Ocean, The Mephistopheles of
the. See:
SCHLEY, WINFIELD
SCOTT
Ocean, The Prose Homer of the
Great. See:
RUSSELL, WILLIAM
CLARK
Ocean, The Shepherd of the.
See: RALEIGH, SIR
WALTER
OCHS,* ADOLPH SIMON (1858-
1935) [American newspaper
publisher]
The Builder of Chattanooga
The Watchdog of Central Park
Ochus. See:
ARTAXERXES II
DARIUS II
OCKHAM (OCCAM), WILLIAM
OF (c.1300-49) [English
scholastic philosopher]
Doctor Invincibilis
The Invincible Doctor
Princeps Nominalium
The Singular Doctor
Venerabilis Inceptor
The Venerable Initiator
O'CONNELL, DANIEL (1775-
1847) [Irish political

751

leader]
The Liberator
O'CONNELL, DANIEL J.
    (1874-) [Irish-
    American detective]
Hard Rock
O'CONNOR, ALMA (1927-)
    [American television and
    motion picture actress]
Ann Gillis
O'Connor, Frank. See:
    O'DONOVAN, MICHAEL
O'CONNOR, JOHN WOOLF
    (1902-) [American edu-
    cator and author]
Jack O'Connor
O'Connor, Liam. See:
    LIDDY, JAMES DANIEL
    REEVES
O'Connor, Patrick. See:
    WIBBERLEY, LEONARD
    PATRICK O'CONNOR
O'CONNOR, THOMAS POWER
    (1848-1929) [Irish
    journalist and nationalist
    leader]
    The Father of the House of
    Commons
    Tay Pay
Octave Thanet. See:
    FRENCH, ALICE
ODA OF LAGERY (1042-99)
    [Supreme Pontiff of
    Roman Catholic Church]
Pope Urban II
O'DANIEL, WILBERT LEE
    (1890-1969) [American
    politician; Governor of
    Texas]
Pappy O'Daniel
O'DAY, CAROLINE GOODWIN
    (1875-1943) [American
    politician; Democratic
    representative at large
    from New York State]
The White House Pet
O'Day, Dawn. See:
    PARIS, DAWN
Odd. See:
    McINTYRE, OSCAR ODD
Ode, The Prince of the. See:
    RONSARD, PIERRE DE

O'DEA, ANNE CALDWELL
    (1867-1936) [American
    author, actress, and
    singer]
Anne Caldwell
Odell, Gill, joint pseud. of
    TRAVISS GILL (1891-)
    and CAROL ODELL
    (-) [British authors]
ODELL, JONATHAN (1737-
    1818) [American loyalist,
    satirist, physician and
    missionary]
    Camillo Querno, Poet
    Laureate to the Congress
Odem, J. See:
    RUBIN, JACOB A.
ODESCALCHI, BENEDICT
    (1611-89) [Supreme Pontiff
    of Roman Catholic Church]
Pope Innocent XI
Odetta. See:
    HOLMES, ODETTA
O'Dhu, Fergus. See:
    TROTTER, CANON JOHN
    CRAWFORD
Odile Versois. See:
    POLIAKOFF-BAIDAROV,
    MARINA DE
O'Donnell, Cathy. See:
    STEELY, ANN
O'DONOVAN, MICHAEL
    (1903-) [Irish writer]
Frank O'Connor
O'Donovan, P. M. See:
    PEACOCK, THOMAS LOVE
O'DOUL, FRANK JOSEPH
    (1897-) [American pro-
    fessional baseball player]
Lefty O'Doul
O'Dowd, Cornelius. See:
    LEVER, CHARLES JAMES
O'Dubh, Cathal. See:
    DUFF, CHARLES ST.
    LAWRENCE
Oecolampadius, Johannes. See:
    HUSSGEN, JOHANNES
OELRICHS, BLANCHE MARIE
    LOUISE (1890-1950)
    [American poet, playwright,
    and actress]
Michael Strange

O'FARRILL, ARTURO (1921-)
[Cuban composer of jazz
music]
Chico
Office Girl, The Box. See:
MICHAELSKA, MARIANNE
Office, The Father of the
Patent. See:
RUGGLES, JOHN
Officer, The Intelligence. See:
JAMES, LIONEL
Officer X, Flying. See:
BATES, HERBERT ERNEST
Official Greeter of Famous
People, New York City's
Official. See:
WHALEN, GROVER
ALOYSIUS
OFFIELD, LEWIS D. (1903-)
[American vaudevillian
and motion picture actor]
Jack Oakie
O'FIENNE, SEAN (1895-)
[Irish-American motion
picture director]
John Ford
O'Finn, Thaddeus. See:
McGLOIN, JOSEPH
THADDEUS
O'FLYNN, HONORIA (1909-)
[Irish composer]
Noreen Mack
OGDEN, LIEUT. COMMANDER
JOHN MICHAEL HUBERT
(1923-) [English naval
officer and author]
Michael Ogden
OGDEN, ROBERT (1746-1826)
[American lawyer]
The Honest Lawyer
Ogden, Ruth. See:
IDE, FRANCES OTIS
OGDEN
Ogdred Weary. See:
GOREY, EDWARD ST.
JOHN
Ogilvy, Gavin. See:
BARRIE, SIR JAMES
MATTHEW
OGLESBY, RICHARD JAMES
(1824-99) [American
politician; governor of

Illinois]
Farmers' Dick
Uncle Dick
OGLETHORPE, JAMES EDWARD
(1696-1785) [English
philanthropist and colonist;
founder of the colony, now
state, of Georgia]
Lord Oglethorpe
OGNALL, LEOPOLD HORACE
(1908-) [Canadian author]
Harry Carmichael
Hartley Howard
Ognev, N. See:
ROSANOV, MIKHAIL
GRIGORIEVICH
O'Gorman Mahon, The. See:
MAHON, CHARLES JAMES
PATRICK
O'GRADY, FRANCIS DOMINIC
(1909-) [Australian civil
servant and author]
Frank O'Grady
O'Grady, Rohan. See:
SKINNER, JUNE O'GRADY
Ogre, The Corsican. See:
BONAPARTE, NAPOLEON
O'Hall, Mayor Von. See:
HALL, ABRAHAM OAKEY
O'Hanlon, George. See:
RICE, GEORGE
O'HANRAHAN, KIERON (1925-)
[Irish stage and motion
picture actor]
Kieron Moore
O'Hara, Dale. See:
GILLESE, JOHN PATRICK
O'HARA, JOHN HENRY (1905-)
[American author]
Francey Delaney
John O'Hara
The Voice of the Hangover
Generation
O'Hara, Kevin. See:
CUMBERLAND, MARTEN
O'Hara, Mary. See:
STUREVASA, MARY
O'HARA ALSOP
O'Hara, Maureen. See:
BROWN, MAUREEN
FITZSIMONS
O'HIGGINS, HYACINTH HAZEL

(1922-) [British stage
and motion picture actress]
Hy Hazell
Ohio Gong, The. See:
ALLEN, WILLIAM
Ohio Labor, The Father of. See:
CROSSER, ROBERT
Ohio Roscius, The. See:
LYON, LOUIS
Ohio, The Father of the Public
School System in. See:
RICE, HARVEY
Ohio, The Gentle Shepherd of.
See: GROSVENOR,
CHARLES HENRY
Ohio, The Idol of. See:
McKINLEY, WILLIAM
Ohio, The Snapping Turtle of
the. See:
FINK, MIKE
Ohio University, The Father of.
See: CUTLER, MANASSEH
Ohio's Ace Investigator. See:
SLATER, ORA E.
Ohiyesa. See:
EASTMAN, CHARLES
ALEXANDER
Ohon. See:
BARBA, HARRY
Oil King, The Standard. See:
ROCKEFELLER, JOHN
DAVISON
Oil Marland, Hot. See:
MARLAND, ERNEST
WHITWORTH
Oke, Richard. See:
MILLETT, NIGEL
STANSBURY
O'Keefe, Dennis. See:
FLANAGAN, EDWARD
O'KEEFE, LESTER (1896-)
[American composer and
actor]
Tom Form
O'KEEFFE, JOHN (1747-1833)
[Irish dramatist]
The English Molière
O'KELLY, PATRICK (1754-1835)
[Irish poet]
Bard O'Kelly
O'Key. See: RADWANSKI,
PIERRE ARTHUR

Oklahoma Jack. See:
NICHOLS, JOHN CONOVER
Oklahoma's Yodeling Cowboy.
See: AUTRY, GENE
ORVON
Ol'. See also:
Old
Ol' Arkansas. See:
WARNECKE, LONNIE
Ol' Redhead, The. See:
BARBER, WALTER LANIER
OLAF (died 1024) [King of
Sweden]
The Lap King
OLAF I (969-1000) [King of
Sweden]
Olaf Tryggvesson
OLAF I (died 1095) [King of
Denmark]
Hunger
OLAF II (955?-1030) [King of
Norway and Sweden]
Olaf Haraldsson
St. Olaf
OLAF III (died 1093) [King of
Norway]
Olaf Haraldsson
Olaf Kyrre (The Quiet)
OLAF IV (1100?-15) [King of
Norway]
Olaf Magnusson
OLAF SITRICSON (died 981)
[King of Northumbria and
of Dublin]
Olaf the Red
OLANDER, JOAN LUCILLE
(1933-) [American motion
picture actress]
Mamie Van Doren
OLCOTT, JOHN SIDNEY
(1873-1949) [Irish-Canadian
motion picture director]
Sidney Olcott
Old. See:
CROME, JOHN
CUYP, JACOB GERRITS
MOORE, FRANCIS
OL'
PARR, THOMAS
Old Abe. See:
LINCOLN, ABRAHAM

Old Ace of Spades. See:
  LEE, ROBERT EDWARD
Old Agamemnon. See:
  CARRINGTON, EDWARD
Old Alcalde, The. See:
  ROBERTS, ORAN MILO
Old Allegheny. See:
  COLSTON, RALEIGH
  EDWARD
Old Alphabet. See:
  BEAUREGARD, PIERRE
  GUSTAVE TOUTANT
Old Andy. See:
  JOHNSON, ANDREW
Old Aristides. See:
  BICKNELL, JOSHUA
Old Bachelor, An. See:
  CURTIS, GEORGE
  WILLIAM
Old Bags. See:
  SCOTT, JOHN
Old Bald. See:
  PRESTON, JOHN THOMAS
  LEWIS
Old Bandanna. See:
  THURMAN, ALLAN
  GRANBERRY
Old Bard, Scio's Blind. See:
  HOMER
Old Bard, The Blind. See:
  HOMER
Old Beeswax. See:
  SEMMES, RAPHAEL
Old Ben Wade. See:
  WADE, BENJAMIN
  FRANKLIN
Old Billy. See:
  SHERMAN, WILLIAM
  TECUMSEH
Old Blizzards. See:
  LORING, WILLIAM WING
Old Block, The. See:
  DELANO, ALONZO
Old Blood and Guts. See:
  PATTON, GEORGE
  SMITH, JR.
Old Bona Fide. See:
  LOUIS XIV
Old Boney. See:
  BONAPARTE, NAPOLEON
Old Bore. See:
  BEAUREGARD, PIERRE

GUSTAVE TOUTANT
Old Bory. See:
  BEAUREGARD, PIERRE
  GUSTAVE TOUTANT
Old Boy in Specs, The. See:
  DAVIS, MATHEW
  LIVINGSTON
Old Brains, See:
  HALLECK, HENRY WAGER
Old Broadbrim. See:
  RATHBONE, ST. GEORGE
  HENRY
Old Brown of Ossawatomie. See:
  BROWN, JOHN
Old Buck. See:
  BUCHANAN, JAMES
Old Buena Vista. See:
  TAYLOR, ZACHARY
Old Bullion. See:
  BENTON, THOMAS HART
Old Cap Collier. See:
  IRON, NATHANIEL COL-
  CHESTER
  SAWYER, EUGENE TAYLOR
Old Captain Ezekiel. See:
  GREELEY, EZEKIEL
Old Chapultepec. See:
  SCOTT, WINFIELD
Old Chatty Cheerful. See:
  MARTIN, WILLIAM
Old Chickamauga. See:
  STEEDMAN, JAMES
  BARRETT
Old Chief. See:
  CLAY, HENRY
Old Chinook. See:
  WISE, HENRY ALEXANDER
Old Club. See:
  COLSTON, RALEIGH
  EDWARD
Old Clubby. See:
  COLSTON, RALEIGH
  EDWARD
Old Cockeye. See:
  BUTLER, BENJAMIN
  FRANKLIN
Old Colonel, The. See:
  ARNHEIM, GUS
Old Commoner, The. See:
  STEVENS, THADDEUS
Old Coon, The Same. See:
  CLAY, HENRY

Old Creepy. See:
    KARPOVIECZ, FRANCIS
    ALBIN
Old Davy. See:
    TWIGGS, DAVID
    EMANUEL
Old Denmark. See:
    FEBIGER, CHRISTIAN
Old Dessauer, The (Der
    Alte Dessauer). See:
    LEOPOLD
Old Detective, The. See:
    ROLFE, MARO O.
Old Dog, The. See:
    BARTLETT, FREDERICK
    ORIN
Old Double Dome. See:
    BRISBANE, ARTHUR
Old Douro. See:
    WELLINGTON, ARTHUR
    WELLESLEY, 1ST
    DUKE OF
Old Dreadnaught. See:
    BOSCAWEN, EDWARD
Old Dutch Cleanser. See:
    BLANKENBURG, RUDOLPH
Old Eight to Seven. See:
    HAYES, RUTHERFORD
    BIRCHARD
Old Figgers. See:
    GROSVENOR, CHARLES
    HENRY
Old Flintlock. See:
    HANSON, ROGER
    WEIGHTMAN
Old Forty-eight Hours. See:
    DOUBLEDAY, ABNER
Old Fox, The. See:
    GRIFFITH, CLARK
    WASHINGTON, GEORGE
Old Frank. See:
    CHEATHAM, BENJAMIN
    FRANKLIN
Old Fuss and Feathers. See:
    SCOTT, WINFIELD
Old George. See:
    MONK, GEORGE
Old Gimlet Eye. See:
    BUTLER, SMEDLEY
    DARLINGTON
Old Gimpy. See:
    EVANS, ROBLEY
    DUNGLISON

Old Granny. See:
    HARRISON, WILLIAM
    HENRY
Old Grog. See:
    VERNON, EDWARD
Old Grover. See:
    CLEVELAND, STEPHEN
    GROVER
Old Hickory. See:
    JACKSON, ANDREW
Old Hoss. See:
    STEPHENSON, JACKSON
    RIGGS
Old Humbug. See:
    BENTON, THOMAS HART
Old Humphrey. See:
    MOGRIDGE, GEORGE
Old Iron Pants. See:
    JOHNSON, HUGH SAMUEL
Old Jack. See:
    JACKSON, THOMAS
    JONATHAN
Old Jeb. See:
    STUART, JAMES EWELL
    BROWN
Old John W. See:
    HEISMAN, JOHN WILLIAM
Old Jube. See:
    EARLY, JUBAL ANDERSON
Old Jubilee. See:
    EARLY, JUBAL ANDERSON
Old Kill Devil. See:
    FREEMAN, AUSTIN
Old Lady, Chicago's Grand. See:
    HUDLUN, ANNA
    ELIZABETH
Old Lady of Opera, The Grand.
    See: SCHUMANN-HEINK,
    MME. ERNESTINE
Old Lady of the Movies, The
    Grand. See:
    KOERBER, LEILA
Old Lefthander, The. See:
    SANDERS, JOSEPH L.
Old Line Whig. See:
    WILLIAMS, JAMES
Old Lion of Athens, The Grim.
    See: GROSVENOR,
    CHARLES HENRY
Old Lion, The. See:
    ROOSEVELT, THEODORE
Old Maestro, The. See:
    ANZELEVITZ, BERNARD

Old Man Eloquent. See:
ADAMS, JOHN QUINCY
COLERIDGE, SAMUEL
TAYLOR
CUSTIS, GEORGE
WASHINGTON PARKE
ISOCRATES
Old Man Eloquent of the Senate,
The. See:
HOAR, GEORGE FRISBIE
Old Man from Maryland, The
Grand. See:
WHYTE, WILLIAM
PINCKNEY
Old Man, Hollywood's Grand.
See: BLYTHE, LIONEL
Old Man of Alexandria, The
Grand. See:
DUNN, EMMETT CLARKE
Old Man of Football, The
Grand. See:
STAGG, AMOS ALONZO
Old Man of Labor, The Grand.
See: GOMPERS,
SAMUEL
Old Man of Missouri, The
Grand. See:
KIRK, JOHN ROBERT
Old Man of Scio's Rocky
Isle, The Blind. See:
HOMER
Old Man of the Gridiron, The.
See: KENNEALLY,
GEORGE V.
Old Man of the Mountain, The.
See: HASAN-IBN-AL-
SABBAH
Old Man of the Screen, The
Grand. See:
ROBERTS, THEODORE
"Old Man River," Football's.
See: STAGG, AMOS
ALONZO
Old Man, The. See:
ALEXANDER, WILLIAM
ANDERSON
KALBFUS, EDWARD
CLIFFORD
Old Man, The Bad. See:
EARLY, JUBAL ANDERSON
Old Man, The (Der Alte). See:
ADENAUER, KONRAD
Old Man, The Grand. See:

FRANKLIN, BENJAMIN
GLADSTONE, WILLIAM
EWART
PITT, WILLIAM
SAVAGE, GEORGE MARTIN
Old Man, The Union's Grand.
See: SAVAGE, GEORGE
MARTIN
Old Master. See:
LEAVITT, DUDLEY
Old Master, The. See:
GANS, JOE
Old Morality. See:
SMITH, WILLIAM HENRY
Old Mortality. See:
PATERSON, ROBERT
Old Mose, The Same. See:
WEINBERGER, MOSES
Old Noll. See:
CROMWELL, OLIVER
Old Northwest, The Father of
the. See:
CASS, LEWIS
Old One Wing. See:
MARTIN, JAMES GREEN
Old Ossawatomie. See:
BROWN, JOHN
Old Palma (Palma Vecchio). See:
PALMA, JACOPO
Old Pancake. See:
COMSTOCK, HENRY
TOMPKINS PAIGE
Old Pap Safety. See:
THOMAS, GEORGE
HENRY
Old Parlez. See:
COLSTON, RALEIGH
EDWARD
Old Pete. See:
LONGSTREET, JAMES
Old Phil. See:
THOMPSON, PHILIP
BURTON, SR.
Old Polly. See:
COLSTON, RALEIGH
EDWARD
Old Possum. See:
ELIOT, THOMAS STEARNS
Old Pretender, The. See:
STUART, JAMES FRANCIS
EDWARD
Old Prob. See:
ABBE, CLEVELAND

Old Probabilities. See:
  ABBE, CLEVELAND
Old Professor, The. See:
  KYSER, JAMES KING
    KERN
Old Public Functionary. See:
  BUCHANAN, JAMES
Old Put. See:
  PUTNAM, ISRAEL
Old Q. See:
  DOUGLAS, WILLIAM
Old Ranger. See:
  REYNOLDS, JOHN
Old Reliable. See:
  CARLSON, JULES
  THOMAS, GEORGE
    HENRY
Old Rock. See:
  BENNING, HENRY
    LEWIS
Old Roman, The. See:
  BENTON, THOMAS HART
  COMISKEY, CHARLES
    ALBERT
  MULDOON, WILLIAM
  THURMAN, ALLAN
    GRANBERRY
Old Rosey. See:
  ROSECRANS, WILLIAM
    STARKE
Old Rough and Ready. See:
  TAYLOR, ZACHARY
Old Round About. See:
  CLEVELAND, BENJAMIN
Old Rowley. See:
  CHARLES II
Old Saddlebags. See:
  McDONALD, JOSEPH
    EWING
Old Sanitary. See:
  YEATMAN, JAMES
Old Settler, The. See:
  LYMAN, ALBERT
    ROBISON
Old Silver Leg. See:
  STUYVESANT, PETER
Old Silver Nails. See:
  STUYVESANT, PETER
Old Sink or Swim. See:
  ADAMS, JOHN
Old Sir Henry. See:

  VANE, SIR HENRY
Old Slackwater. See:
  MOORHEAD, JAMES
    KENNEDY
Old Slow Trot. See:
  THOMAS, GEORGE
    HENRY
Old Smoke. See:
  MORRISSEY, JOHN
Old Spades. See:
  LEE, ROBERT EDWARD
Old Spex. See:
  SMITH, FRANCIS
    HENNEY
Old Stager. See:
  ADAMS, WILLIAM
    TAYLOR
Old Stars. See:
  MITCHELL, ORMSBY
    McKNIGHT
Old Stone Hammer. See:
  METCALFE, THOMAS
Old Straight. See:
  STEWART, ALEXANDER
    PETER
Old Swamp Fox, The. See:
  MARION, FRANCIS
Old Tecumseh. See:
  SHERMAN, WILLIAM
    TECUMSEH
Old, The. See:
  GORM
  HAAKON IV HAAKONSSON
Old Three Stars. See:
  GRANT, HIRAM
    ULYSSES
Old Tige. See:
  ANDERSON, GEORGE
    THOMAS
Old Timer. See:
  MERRILL, JAMES
    MILFORD
Old Tip. See:
  HARRISON, WILLIAM
    HENRY
Old Tippecanoe. See:
  HARRISON, WILLIAM
    HENRY
Old Titanic Earth-son, The.
  See:
  WEBSTER, DANIEL

Old Tom. See:
 JACKSON, THOMAS
 JONATHAN
Old Tomcat of the Keys, The.
 See: ZURKE,
 ROBERT
Old Tomorrow. See:
 MACDONALD, SIR JOHN
 ALEXANDER
Old Trouper, The. See:
 KOERBER, LEILA
Old Tu'key Neck. See:
 STILWELL, JOSEPH
 WARREN
Old Tush. See:
 DAVIES, CHARLES
Old Tycoon, The. See:
 PRICE, STERLING G.
Old 'un
 Young 'un, joint pseuds.
 of FRANCIS ALEXANDER
 DURIVAGE (1814-81) and
 GEORGE P. BURNHAM
 (-) [American novelists
 and playwrights]
Old Usufruct. See:
 TILDEN, SAMUEL JONES
Old Veto. See:
 CLEVELAND, STEPHEN
 GROVER
 HUMPHREYS, BENJAMIN
 GRUBB
 JOHNSON, ANDREW
Old Viking, The. See:
 FURUSETH, ANDREW
Old War Horse, Lee's. See:
 LONGSTREET, JAMES
Old War Horse of Reform,
 The. See:
 BLANKENBURG, RUDOLPH
Old War Horse, The. See:
 COOK, PHILIP
 DEVIN, THOMAS CASIMIR
Old Wheel-horse of Democracy.
 See: MEDARY, SAMUEL
Old Whiskers. See:
 WILES, GREENBURY F.
Old White Hat. See:
 GREELEY, HORACE
Old Wicked. See:
 GODFREY, HOLLEN
Old Woman, The Chief. See:
 STEVENS, THADDEUS

Old Zach. See:
 TAYLOR, ZACHARY
Old Zeb. See:
 WEAVER, ZEBULON
Oldcastle, Jonathan. See:
 MEYNELL, WILFRID
OLDCASTLE, SIR JOHN
 (1377?-1417) [English
 Lollard leader and
 Protestant martyr]
 Baron Cobham
 The Good Lord Cobham
OLDEN, CHARLES (c.1909-)
 [British violinist and
 music-hall entertainer]
 Ted Ray
OLDFIELD, CLAUDE HOUGHTON
 (fl. early 20th cent.)
 [British chartered ac-
 countant, civil servant and
 writer]
 Claude Houghton
OLDFIELD, NANCE (1683-1730)
 [English actress]
 Anne Oldfield
Oldfield, Peter. See:
 BARTLETT, VERNON
OLDHAM, JOHN (1653-83)
 [English satirical poet]
 The English Juvenal
Oldmixon, Mrs. See:
 SIDUS, GEORGINA
Oldschool, Oliver, Esq. See:
 DENNIE, JOSEPH
Oldstyle, Jonathan. See:
 IRVING, WASHINGTON
Oldstyle, Jonathan, Gent. See:
 IRVING, WASHINGTON
Oldstyle, Oliver. See:
 PAULDING, JAMES KIRKE
Ole. See:
 OLSEN, JOHN SIGURD
Ole Luk-oie. See:
 SWINTON, SIR ERNEST
 DUNLOP
O'Leary, Chester F. See:
 KUEHNELT-LEDDIHN,
 ERIK RITTER VON
OLESON. See also:
 OLSEN
 OLSON
OLESON, JOHN (c.1908-)
 [Canadian-born Norwegian

motion picture actor]
John Qualen
Olive Baxter. See:
EASTWOOD, HELEN
Olive Douglas. See:
BUCHAN, ANNA
Olive Green. See:
REED, MYRTLE
Olive Pratt Raynor. See:
ALLEN, CHARLES
GRANT BLAIRFINDIE
Olive, Princess. See:
SERRES, MRS. OLIVIA
WILMOT
Olive Thorne Miller. See:
MILLER, HARRIET
MANN
OLIVEIRA, JOAO DONATO DE
(1934-) [Brazilian jazz
musician (piano, trombone,
accordion, composer)]
Joao Donato
OLIVEN, FRITZ (1874-)
[German lawyer and
author]
Rideamus
Oliver. See:
OLIVIER
Olivier
ONIONS, GEORGE OLIVER
OPDYCKE, JOHN BAKER
Oliver Bronson. See:
ROWLAND, DONALD
SYDNEY
Oliver, Edna May. See:
COX-OLIVER, EDNA MAY
OLIVER, ELI L. (1899-)
[Vice-president of Labor's
Nonpartisan League]
Kiss-of-death Oliver
Oliver Fleming. See:
MACDONALD, PHILIP
Oliver, George. See:
ONIONS, GEORGE OLIVER
Oliver Goldsmith of America, The.
See: TAYLOR, BENJAMIN
FRANKLIN
Oliver Gordon. See:
EMERSON, HENRY OLIVER
Oliver, Jane. See:
REES, HELEN CHRISTINA
EASSON EVANS

OLIVER, JOSEPH (1885-1938)
[American jazz musician
(cornet, leader)]
King Oliver
Oliver Lee Clifton. See:
RATHBONE, ST. GEORGE
HENRY
Oliver, Mark. See:
TYLER-WHITTLE,
MICHAEL SIDNEY
OLIVER, MELVIN JAMES
(1910-) [American jazz
musician (composer,
leader, arranger, singer,
trumpet)]
Sy Oliver
Oliver Oldschool, Esq. See:
DENNIE, JOSEPH
Oliver Oldstyle. See:
PAULDING, JAMES
KIRKE
Oliver Optic. See:
ADAMS, WILLIAM TAY-
LOR
Oliver Optic, M. D. See:
ADAMS, WILLIAM TAYLOR
Oliver Pangbourne. See:
ROCKEY, HOWARD
Oliver Patterson. See:
ROWLAND, DONALD
SYDNEY
Oliver Perry. See:
MORTON, OLIVER HAZARD
PERRY THROCK
Oliver Sandys. See:
EVANS, MARGUERITE
FLORENCE HELENE
OLIVER, THOMAS N. (1904-)
[American professional
baseball player]
Rebel
Oliver Thurston. See:
FLANDERS, HENRY
Oliver, Vic. See:
VON SAMEK, VICTOR
Olivia Rangely. See:
KANTO, PETER
Olivia Vernon. See:
BRONTË, ANNE
OLIVIER [Olivier]. See also:
OLIVER
Oliver

Olivier Henry. See:
PORTER, WILLIAM
SYDNEY
OLIVIER, SIR LAURENCE
(1907-) [English actor,
director and producer]
The Present Champion of
the English Theater
Oll. See:
COOMES, OLIVER
Olmedo, Alex. See:
RODRÍGUEZ, ALEJANDRO
OLMEDO Y
Olmsted, Charlotte. See:
KURSH, CHARLOTTE
OLMSTED
Olney, The Bard of. See:
COWPER, WILLIAM
OLSEN. See also:
OLESON
OLSON
OLSEN, JOHN EDWARD
(1925-) [American
editor, correspondent
and author]
Jack Olsen
Jonathan Rhoades
OLSEN, JOHN SIGURD (1892-
1965) [Norwegian-
American vaudeville and
motion picture comedian]
Ole Olsen
OLSEN, THEODORE VICTOR
(1932-) [American author]
Joshua Stark
Christopher Storm
OLSON. See also:
OLESON
OLSEN
OLSON, ANN-MARGRET (1941-)
[Swedish-American motion
picture actress]
Ann-Margret
OLSON, HENRY RUSSELL
(1913-) [American
musician]
Henry Russell
OLSON, ROBERT G. (1913-)
[American composer]
Jon Roberts
Glenn Rollins
OLT. See also:
Ault

OLT, ARISZTID. See:
BLASKO, BELA LUGOSI
O'MAHONEY, JACQUES
(1919-) [American motion
picture actor]
Jock Mahoney
Omahundro, J.B. See:
INGRAHAM, COLONEL
PRENTISS
O'Malley, C. See:
LEVER, CHARLES JAMES
O'Malley, Kevin. See:
HOSSENT, HARRY
O'MALLEY, MARY DOLLING
SANDERS, LADY
O'MALLEY (1889-) [English
novelist]
Ann Bridge
OMAN, CAROLA MARY ANIMA
(1897-) [British
biographer and writer]
C. Lenanton
Carola Oman
O'Maonaigh, Cainneach. See:
MOONEY, CANICE ALBERT
JAMES
OMAR I (died 644) [Caliph
of the Mussulmans]
Commander of the Faithful
The Emperor of Believers
OMAR KHAYYAM (1025-1123)
[Persian author and mathe-
matician]
The Tentmaker
Omar Pasha. See:
LATAS, MICHAEL
Omar Sharif. See:
SHALHOUB, MICHAEL
Omnipotent, The. See:
BERNARD, PIERRE A.
Omnium, Jacob. See:
HIGGINS, MATTHEW
JAMES
OMOHUNDRO, JOHN B.
(-1880) [American Indian
Scout, frontiersman and
showman]
Texas Jack
O'More, Peggy. See:
BLOCKLINGER, PEGGY
O'MORE
Ona Munson. See:
WOLCOTT, ONA

O'Nair, Mairi. See:
   EVANS, CONSTANCE
   MAY
Ondra, Anny. See:
   ONDRAKOVA, ANNY
ONDRAKOVA, ANNY (1903-)
   [Polish silent motion
   picture actress]
   Anny Ondra
One. See also:
   'un
One-armed Devil, The. See:
   KEARNY, PHILIP
One-armed Phil. See:
   KEARNY, PHILIP
One Behind the Throne Greater
   Than the Throne Itself.
   See: STUART, JOHN
One-eyed Jewish Negro,
   America's. See:
   DAVIS, SAMMY, JR.
One-eyed (Monophthalmos). See:
   ANTIGONUS I
One, Furious (Xocoyotzin). See:
   MONTEZUMA II
One-legged Governor, The.
   See: STUYVESANT,
   PETER
One-man Hit Parade, The
   Army's. See:
   LOESSER, FRANK
   HENRY
One-man Newspaper, America's.
   See: WINCHEL,
   WALTER
One-man Patriot. See:
   FISH, HAMILTON, JR.
One-man Trust Company, The.
   See: WILSON, CHARLES
   MOSEMAN
One of America's Greatest
   Inventors. See:
   BOYDEN, SETH
One of the Barclays. See:
   OTIS, MRS. HARRISON
   GRAY (ELIZA HEN-
   DERSON BORDMAN)
One of the Gamest Players in
   the Game. See:
   MERKLE, FREDERICK C.
One of the People. See:
   HOPKINSON, FRANCIS

One of the People (Achad
   Ha-am). See:
   GINZBERG, ASCHER
One of the Supreme Colorists of
   the World. See:
   TURNER, JOSEPH MAL-
   LORD WILLIAM
One Speech. See:
   LEE, JOSHUA BRYAN
One, The Great. See:
   BEBAN, GARY JOSEPH
   GLEASON, HERBERT
   JOHN
One, The Other (l'Autre). See:
   BONAPARTE,
   NAPOLEON
One Who Remembers (Háfiz).
   See: SHAMS UN-DIN
   MOHAMMED
One Who Speaks (Uei Tlatoani).
   See: MONTEZUMA II
One Wing, Old. See:
   MARTIN, JAMES GREEN
O'NEALE, MARGARET L.
   (1796-1879) [American
   author]
   Peggy Eaton
   Peggy O'Neale
O'Neil, The. See:
   TYRONE, HUGH O'NEIL
O'Neill, C. M. See:
   WILKES-HUNTER,
   RICHARD
O'NEILL, CHARLES (1821-93)
   [American politician;
   congressman from Penn-
   sylvania]
   The Father of the House
O'Neill, Egan. See:
   LININGTON, ELIZABETH
O'Neill, Maire. See:
   ALLGOOD, MAIRE
O'Neill, Peggy. See:
   EATON, MARGARET
   O'NEILL
O'NEILL, ROSE CECIL (1874-)
   [American illustrator;
   creator of the Kewpie doll]
   O'Neill Latham
Ongar, The Taylors of. See:
   TAYLOR, ISAAC
ONIONS, GEORGE OLIVER

(1873-1961) [English novelist]
George Oliver
Oliver Onions
ONIONS, MRS. GEORGE
OLIVER (1878-)
[English novelist]
Berta Ruck
Onlooker. See:
GRANGE, CYRIL
O'Nolan, Brian. See:
O'NUALLAIN, BRIAN
Onoto Watanna. See:
BABCOCK, WINNIFRED
EATON
Onslow Stevens. See:
STEVENSON, ONSLOW
FORD
O'NUALLAIN, BRIAN (1911-66)
[Irish civil servant,
journalist and author]
George Knowall
Myles na Gopaleen
Brian Nolan
Flann O'Brien
Brian O'Nolan
Onze, Jan. See:
HOFMEYR, JAN
HENDRIK
Oom. See:
BERNARD, PIERRE A.
Oom Paul. See:
KRUGER, STEPHANUS
JOHANNES PAULUS
Oomph Girl, The. See:
SHERIDAN, CLARA
LOU
OPDYCKE, JOHN BAKER
(1878-) [American
author]
Oliver Opdyke
Opera-goer, An. See:
MITCHELL, DONALD
GRANT
Opera, The Grand Old Lady of.
See: SCHUMANN-HEINK,
MME. ERNESTINE
OPIE, JOHN (1761-1807)
[English portrait and
historical painter]
The Cornish Wonder
OPITZ, MARTIN (1597-1639)

[German writer and poet]
The Dryden of Germany
The Father of German Poetry
Opium-Eater, The English. See:
DE QUINCEY, THOMAS
OPPENHEIM, EDWARD PHIL-
LIPS (1866-1946) [English
novelist]
E. Phillips Oppenheim
Anthony Partridge
The World's Most Prolific
and Popular Writer of
Thrillers
OPPENHEIM, JILL (1940-)
[American motion picture
actress]
Jill St. John
OPPENHEIMER, JOEL LESTER
(1930-) [American produc-
tion manager and author]
Aquarian
Optic, Oliver. See:
ADAMS, WILLIAM
TAYLOR
Optic, Oliver, M.D. See:
ADAMS, WILLIAM
TAYLOR
Oracle of Denmark, The. See:
VON BERNSTORFF,
COUNT JOHANN
HARTWIG ERNST
Oracle of Nuneaton, The. See:
SIMPSON, THOMAS
Oracle of the Church, The.
See: BERNARD OF
CLAIRVAUX
Oram Eflor. See:
ROLFE, MARO O.
Oram Eflor, Colonel. See:
ROLFE, MARO O.
Oram R. McHenry, Colonel.
See: ROLFE, MARO O.
Orange Industry, The Father of
the Florida. See:
HARRIS, JAMES ARM-
STRONG
Orange Juice. See:
SIMPSON, ORENTHAL
JAMES
Orange King, The. See:
HARRIS, JAMES ARM-
STRONG

Orange Moll. See:
 MEGGS, MRS. MARY
Orange Peel. See:
 PEEL, SIR ROBERT
Orange, William of. See:
 WILLIAM III
Orator. See:
 HENLEY, JOHN
 HUNT, HENRY
Orator of Free Dirt, The.
 See: JULIAN,
 GEORGE WASHINGTON
Orator of Lamoille, The Silver-
 tongued. See:
 SHAW, HOWARD ELWIN
Orator of Secession, The. See:
 YANCEY, WILLIAM
 LOWNDES
Orator of South Carolina, The
 Eagle. See:
 CALHOUN, JOHN
 CALDWELL
Orator of Tennessee, The
 Eagle. See:
 HENRY, GUSTAVUS
 ADOLPHUS
Orator of the Human Race,
 The. See:
 CLOOTZ, JEAN BAP-
 TISTE DU VAL DE
 GRÂCE
Orator of the Platte, The Boy.
 See: BRYAN, WILLIAM
 JENNINGS
Orator of the South, The
 Silver-tongued. See:
 BAKER, ALPHEUS
Orator, The Boy. See:
 LEE, JOSHUA BRYAN
Orator, The Eagle. See:
 HENRY, GUSTAVUS
 ADOLPHUS
 STOKES, WILLIAM
 BRICKLY
Orator, The Hoosier. See:
 ORTON, HARLOW S.
Orator, The Silver-tongued.
 See: BELL, JOSHUA FRY
 BRYAN, WILLIAM JEN-
 NINGS
 DOUGHERTY, DANIEL
 KIRKPATRICK, JOHN
 MILTON

ROLLINS, JAMES
 SIDNEY
Orator, The Stocking-foot. See:
 McKINLEY, WILLIAM
Orators, The Homer of. See:
 CHRYSOSTOM, ST. JOHN
Orators, The Prince of. See:
 DEMOSTHENES
Oratory, The Napoleon of. See:
 PITT, WILLIAM
Orazio Gentileschi. See:
 LOMI, ORAZIO
ORBACH, JEROME (1935-)
 [American actor]
 Jerry Orbach
Orbis, Restitutor (Restorer of
 the Empire). See:
 AURELIANUS, LUCIUS
 DOMITIUS
Orcagna. See:
 CIONE, ANDREA DI
Orchards, The Patron Saint of
 American. See:
 CHAPMAN, JOHN
Orchestral Music, The Father
 of. See:
 HAYDN, FRANZ JOSEPH
Orchestral Music, The Father
 of American. See:
 GRAUPNER, JOHANN
 CHRISTIAN GOTTLIEB
Orchid Man, The. See:
 CARPENTIER, GEORGES
ORCZY, EMMUSKA (1865-1947)
 [English novelist and
 playwright]
 Baroness Orczy
Order of Starvation, Knight of
 the Most Honorable. See:
 LIVINGSTON, WILLIAM
ORDÓÑEZ, CAYETANO
 (1904-) [Spanish bull-
 fighter]
 Niño de la Palma
ORDÓÑEZ, CAYETANO (1928-)
 [Spanish bullfighter]
 Niño de la Palma
O'REED, MAGGIE TERESA
 (1916-) [American
 comedienne, actress and
 singer]
 Martha Raye
Oregon Byron, The. See:

MILLER, CINCINNATUS
HEINE (HEINER)
Oregon, The Apostle of. See:
BLANCHET, FRANCIS
HERBERT
O'REILLY, MARY M. (1865-
19??) [American Assistant
Director of the Mint]
The Sweetheart of the
Treasury
O'Reilly, Miles. See:
HALPINE, CHARLES
GRAHAM
O'Reilly, Montagu. See:
ANDREWS, WAYNE
O'Rell, Max. See:
BLOUET, PAUL
ORFILA, MATHIEU JOSEPH
BONAVENTURE (1787-)
[Spanish chemist and
doctor]
The Father of Toxicology
ORGAN, JOHN (1925-)
[British author and
illustrator]
Graham Ashley
Desmond Farrell
Organ, The Poet of the. See:
CRAWFORD, JESSE
Organized Alumni Work at
Fisk University, The
Father of. See:
PROCTOR, HENRY HUGH
Organized Charity, The Apostle
of. See:
VINCENT DE PAUL
Organizer of Victory, The. See:
CARNOT, LAZARE-
NICHOLAS MARGUERITE
Oriental Catullus, The. See:
MUSLIH-UD-DIN
ORIGEN (ORIGENES) (c.185-
c.253) [Christian writer,
teacher and theologian]
Admantius (The Man of
Steel)
Original Bathing Girl, The. See:
STEADMAN, VERA
Original Glamour Girl, The.
See: GOODMAN,
THEODOSIA
Original Radio Girl, The. See:
DE LEATH, VAUGHN

Orinda, The Matchless. See:
PHILIPS, KATHERINE
O'RIORDAN, CONAL
O'CONNELL (1874-1948)
[Irish novelist and play-
wright]
Norreys Connell
Orlando. See:
HOLLAND, EDWIN CLIF-
FORD
Orleans, The Bastard of. See:
DUNOIS, JEAN
Orleans, The Hero of New. See:
JACKSON, ANDREW
Orleans, The Maid of (La
Pucelle d'Orléans). See:
JOAN OF ARC, ST.
(JEANNE D'ARC)
ORME, EVE (1894-)
[Irish author]
Irene Day
Orme, Rowan. See:
ROWAN-HAMILTON,
SYDNEY ORME
Ormiston, Roberta. See:
FLETCHER, ADELE
WHITLEY
Ormsbee, David. See:
LONGSTREET, STEPHEN
Ormund, Frederic. See:
DEY, FREDERICK VAN
RENSSELAER
Ornament of the Throne
(Aurangzeb). See:
MOHAMMED
Ornament of the Throne
(Aurungzeb). See:
MOHAMMED
Ornamental Gardening, The
Father of Horticulture and.
See: HENDERSON, PETER
Ornithologists, The Father of.
See: EDWARDS, GEORGE
ORNITZ, SAM. See:
Hollywood Ten, The.
ORNSTEIN, RICHARD
(1880-) [German motion
picture director]
Richard Oswald
O'Rolfe, M., The Irish Novelist.
See: ROLFE, MARO O.
OROWITZ, MICHAEL (1937-)
[American television and

motion picture actor]
Michael Landon
Orphan of the Temple, The.
See: CHARLOTTE,
MARIE THÉRÈSE
Orpheus C. Kerr. See:
NEWELL, ROBERT
HENRY
Orpheus of Highwaymen, The.
See: GAY, JOHN
Orpheus of the Green Isle, The.
See: O'CAROLAN,
TURLOCH
Orr, Mary. See:
DENHAM, MARY ORR
ORR, ROBERT (1948-)
[Canadian professional
hockey player]
Bobby Orr
ORRICO, CARMEN (1935-)
[American model and
motion picture actor]
John Saxon
Orrin Primm, Brother. See:
WILLETT, BROTHER
FRANCISCUS
Orris. See:
INGELOW, JEAN
ORRMONT, ARTHUR (1922-)
[American editor and
author]
Anson Hunter
ORSINI, GIACINTO BOBONI
(c. 1106-98) [Supreme
Pontiff of Roman
Catholic Church]
Pope Celestine III
ORSINI, GIOVANNI GAETANO
(1210/20-80) [Supreme
Pontiff of Roman Catholic
Church]
Pope Nicholas III
ORSINI, PIETRO FRANCESCO
(1649-1730) [Supreme
Pontiff of Roman Catholic
Church]
Pope Benedict XIII
Orson. See:
WELLES, GEORGE
ORSON
Orson Bean. See:
BURROWS, DALLAS

FREDERICK
Orson Gouge. See:
LARNER, JEREMY
ORSZÁGH, PAVOL (1849-1921)
[Slovak poet]
Hviezdoslav
ORTEGA, ANTHONY ROBERT
(1928-) [American jazz
musician (saxophone,
clarinet, flute)]
Batman
Tony
Orth, Richard. See:
GARDNER, RICHARD
Orthodoxy, Champion of. See:
PUSEY, EDWARD
BOUVERIE
Orthodoxy, The Father of. See:
ATHANSIUS, ST.
ORTON, ARTHUR (1834-98)
[English perjurer; claimant
to baronetcy and estates in
Hampshire]
Thomas Castro
Sir Roger Charles
Tichborne
ORTON, HARLOW S. (1817-95)
[American orator]
The Hoosier Orator
ORTUÑO, EMILIO (1937-)
[Spanish bullfighter]
Jumillano
Orwell. See:
SMITH, WALTER CHAL-
MERS
Orwell, George. See:
BLAIR, ERIC
ORY, EDWARD (1886-)
[American jazz musician
(trombone, leader, com-
poser)]
Kid Ory
Osander. See:
ALLEN, BENJAMIN
OSBORN, LAUGHTON (c. 1800-
78) [American poet and
playwright]
Charles Erskine White, D. D.
OSBORNE, CHARLES HUMFREY
CAULFIELD (1891-)
[British educator and
writer]

C. Humfrey
Osborne, David. See:
SILVERBERG, ROBERT
OSBORNE, DOROTHY GLADYS
YEO (1917-) [British
artist and author]
Gladys Armour
OSBORNE, GEORGE O.
(1845-1926 [Warden
of New Jersey State
Prison]
The Father of Prison Reform
in the United States
OSBOURNE, SAMUEL LLOYD
(1868-1947) [English
novelist and playwright]
Lloyd Osbourne
Oscar. See:
Oskar
WILDE, OSCAR FINGAL
O'FLAHERTIE WILLS
Oscar A. Gwynne. See:
ELLIS, EDWARD SYLVES-
TER
Oscar, Henry. See:
WALE, HENRY
Oscar Milsen. See:
MENDELSOHN, OSCAR
Oscar of the Waldorf. See:
TSCHIRKY, OSCAR MICHEL
Osey, Herr N. See:
WEISS, EHRICH (ERIK
WEISZ)
OSGOOD, FRANCES SARGENT
LOCKE (1811-50) [American
poet]
Florence
O'Shea, Sean. See:
TRALINS, S. ROBERT
Osiander, Andreas. See:
HOSEMANN, ANDREAS
Oskar. See:
LENZ, HEINRICH OSKAR
Oscar
Oskar Werner. See:
BSCHLIESSMAYER, OSKAR
JOSEPH
Osma Couch Gallinger. See:
TOD, OSMA GALLINGER
Osman Digna. See:
NISBET, GEORGE
OSMAN (OTHMAN) I (1259-1326)

[Founder of the Ottoman
Empire]
The Victorious
OSMUN, THOMAS EMBLEY
(1826-) [American
Orthoëpist]
Alfred Ayres
Ossawatomie Brown. See:
BROWN, JOHN
Ossawatomie, Old. See:
BROWN, JOHN
Ossawatomie, Old Brown of.
See: BROWN, JOHN
Ossip Schubin. See:
KIRSCHNER, ALOISIA
OSTRANDER, ISABEL
(1883-1924) [American
novelist]
Robert Fox Chipperfield
David Fox
Douglas Grant
OSTROW, SAMUEL (1911-)
[American composer]
Sammy Ostrow
OSTRUS, MERRILL (1919-)
[American composer and
musician]
Merrill Staton
O'SULLIVAN [O'Sullivan]. See
also: SULLIVAN
Sullivan
O'SULLIVAN, DENIS PATRICK
TERENCE JOSEPH
(1906-) [American jazz
musician (piano)]
Joe Sullivan
O'SULLIVAN, DENNIS (1818-
1907) [American Civil War
soldier; intimate friend of
ULYSSES S. GRANT]
The Penny Plug
O'SULLIVAN, EUGENE (1892-)
[British musical comedy
and motion picture actor]
Gene Gerrard
O'SULLIVAN, RAYMOND
(1947-) [Irish singer of
popular songs]
Gilbert O'Sullivan
O'Sullivan, Seumas. See:
STARKEY, JAMES
SULLIVAN

Oswald A. Gwynne. See:
ELLIS, EDWARD
SYLVESTER
Oswald Frederick. See:
SNELLING, OSWALD
FREDERICK
Oswald Myconius. See:
GEISHUSLER, OSWALD
Oswald, Richard. See:
ORNSTEIN, RICHARD
OTEY, JAMES HARVEY
(1800-63) [American
Protestant clergyman]
The Good Bishop
Other One, The (l'Autre). See:
BONAPARTE,
NAPOLEON
Othere. See:
WINDSOR-GARNETT,
JOHN RAYNHAM
OTHMAN. See:
OSMAN (OTHMAN) I
Otis Criblecoblis. See:
DUKINFIELD, WILLIAM
CLAUDE
Otis, George. See:
MELLEN, IDA MAY
Otis, James. See:
KALER, JAMES OTIS
OTIS, MRS. HARRISON GRAY
(ELIZA HENDERSON
BORDMAN) (1796-1873)
[American author]
One of the Barclays
O'Toole, Rex. See:
TRALINS, S. ROBERT
O'Toole, Terence. See:
OTWAY, CAESAR
Otranto, The Duke of. See:
MANOLESCO, GEORGE
Otreb, Rudolf. See:
FLUDD (FLUD), ROBERT
OTT, MELVIN THOMAS (1908-
58) [American professional
baseball player]
Mel Ott
Ott, Peter. See:
VON HILDEBRAND,
DIETRICH
OTTAVIANO (938?-64) [Supreme
Pontiff of Roman
Catholic Church]
The Boy Pope

Pope John XII
OTTESEN, THEA TAUBER
(1913-) [Hungarian
teacher and author]
Bank-Jensen
OTTO I (912-73) [Emperor and
King of Germany and Duke
of Saxony; Holy Roman
Emperor]
The Great
OTTO II (955-83) [Emperor and
King of Germany and Holy
Roman Emperor]
The Red
OTTO III (980-1002)
[Emperor of Germany and
Holy Roman Emperor]
The Wonder of the World
OTTO IV (1174?-1218) [Emperor
of Germany]
Otto of Brunswick
Otto Goldschmidt, Madame. See:
LIND, JOHANNA MARIA
Otto Maurer. See:
MASON, EUDO COLE-
CESTRA
OTTO OF BAMBERG (1060-
1139) [German churchman
and missionary]
The Apostle of Pomerania
Otto Von Homberg. See:
GEISE, DR. OTTO
OTTOBONI, PIETRO (1610-91)
[Supreme Pontiff of
Roman Catholic Church]
Pope Alexander VIII
OTWAY, CAESAR (1780-1842)
[Irish miscellaneous
writer]
Terence O'Toole
Ouida. See:
RAMÉE, MARIE LOUISE
DE LA
OUNSKOWSKY, MISCHA
(1905-67) [Russian-born
motion picture comedian]
Mischa Auer
Our Battle Laureate. See:
BROWNELL, HENRY
HOWARD
Our Best Recruiting Sergeant.
See: NAST, THOMAS
Our Bob. See:

REYNOLDS, ROBERT
RICE
TAYLOR, ROBERT LOVE
Our Chet. See:
ARTHUR, CHESTER
ALAN
Our Dramatic Poets, The
Horace of. See:
SHAKESPEARE, WILLIAM
Our Fritz (Unser Frits). See:
FREDERICK WILLIAM
Our Grover. See:
CLEVELAND, STEPHEN
GROVER
Our Modern Fortifications, The
Father of. See:
CRAIGHILL, WILLIAM
PRICE
Our Patrick Henry. See:
KOLB, REUBEN
FRANCIS
Our Talisman. See:
LIPPARD, GEORGE
Our Time, The Foremost
Greek Scholar of. See:
MURRAY, GEORGE
GILBERT AIMÉ
OURSLER, CHARLES FULTON
(1893-1952) [American
author, editor and play-
wright]
Anthony Abbott
Fulton Oursler
OURSLER, WILLIAM CHARLES
(1913-) [American
author]
Gale Gallager
Will Oursler
OUSAMEQUIN (WOUSAMEQUIN)
(died 1661) [chief of the
Wampanoaga Indians]
Massasoit
Outdoor Girl of the Films, The.
See: VALLI, VIRGINIA
Outdoors, The Bishop of All.
See: JACKSON, SHELDON
OUTRAM, SIR JAMES
(1803-61) [British general
officer]
The Bayard of India
Outremer, D' (From Overseas).
See: LOUIS IV
OUTREMEUSE, JEAN D'. See:

Mandeville, Jehan de
(Sir John)
Outside, Mr. See:
DAVIS, GLENN
Over the Mountain Girl, The
Moon. See:
SMITH, KATHRYN
ELIZABETH
OVERHOLSER, WAYNE D.
(1906-) [American author]
John S. Daniels
Lee Leighton
Wayne Roberts
Dan J. Stevens
Joseph Wayne
Overland Three, The. See:
Golden Gate Trinity, The
Overseas, From (D'Outremer).
See: LOUIS IV
OVERTON, RICHARD (fl.
1642-63) [English
pamphleteer and satirist]
Martin Marpriest
Ovid Demaris. See:
DESMARAIS, OVIDE E.
Ovid, The French. See:
BELLAY, JOACHIM DU
Owen Aherne. See:
CASSILL, RONALD
VERLIN
Owen, Bill. See:
ROWBOTHAM, BILL
Owen Fox. See:
FARMER, BERNARD
JONES
Owen Fox Jerome. See:
FRIEND, OSCAR JEROME
OWEN, FRANK. See:
Cato
Owen Hall. See:
DAVIS, JAMES
Owen, Hugh. See:
FAUST, FREDERICK
SCHILLER
Owen Innsley. See:
JENNISON, LUCIA
OWEN, JOHN (1560?-1622?)
[English author of Latin
epigrams]
The British Martial
Little Owen the Epigrammaker
Owen, John Pickard. See:
BUTLER, SAMUEL

OWEN, MARVIN JAMES
(1908-) [American
professional baseball
player]
Freck
Owen, Mary Jane. See:
BROCKWAY, JENNIE M.
Owen Meredith. See:
LYTTON, LORD (EDWARD
ROBERT BULWER,
1ST EARL OF LYT-
TON)
Owen Nares. See:
RAMSAY, OWEN NARES
OWEN, STEPHEN JOSEPH
(1898-) [American foot-
ball coach]
Big Steve
Steve Owen
OWENS, CLARENCE B.
(1885-) [American
professional baseball
umpire]
Brick
OWENS, JAMES CLEVELAND
(1914-) [American Negro
track star]
Jesse Owens
Owl. See:
RUSSELL, WILLIAM
HENRY
Owl, Sebastian. See:
THOMPSON, HUNTER
STOCKTON
Owl, The. See:
GARNER, JOHN NANCE
Owlglass, Dr. See:
BLAICH, HANS ERICH
Owlglass (Howleglass). See:
EULENSPIEGEL (ULEN-
SPIEGEL), TILL
Owney. See:
MADDEN, OWEN
Owney the Killer. See:
MADDEN, OWEN
Owski. See:
DINGELL, JOHN DAVID
Ox, Dumb. See:
AQUINAS, ST. THOMAS
OXBERRY, WILLIAM
(1784-1824) [English
printer, poet, publisher,

publican and player]
Five P's
Oxenham, John. See:
DUNKERLEY, WILLIAM
ARTHUR
Oxford, A Gentleman of. See:
SHELLEY, PERCY
BYSSHE
Oxford, A Graduate of. See:
RUSKIN, JOHN
Oxford, Jane. See:
WILLIAMS, ELMA MARY
Oy-vik. See:
HOLMVIK, OYVIND
Oz. See:
ROBERTSON, OSCAR
PALMER
Ozarks, The Poet Entertainer of
the. See:
LUCEY, THOMAS ELMORE
Ozarks, The Poet of the. See:
NEWBERGER, GABRIEL F.
Ozy. See:
ROSSET, BENJAMIN
CHARLES
Ozzie. See:
NELSON, OSWALD
GEORGE

P

P.B., John Fitzvictor. See:
SHELLEY, PERCY BYSSHE
P.B., Jonathan Fiske. See:
SHELLEY, PERCY BYSSHE
P.D. See:
BALLARD, WILLIS TOD-
HUNTER
HAUGHTON, PERCY
DUNCAN
P. de Fletin. See:
FIELDEN, THOMAS
PERCEVAL
P.F. See:
FRENEAU, PHILIP
MORIN
P.G. See:
WODEHOUSE, PELHAM
GRENVILLE
P.J. Merrill. See:
ROTH, HOLLY

P.K. See:
ROSEGGER, PETER
P.L. Jacob, Bibliophile.
See: LACROIX,
PAUL
P.M. See:
MACGILLIVRAY, JAMES
PITTENDRIGH
P.M. O'Donovan. See:
PEACOCK, THOMAS LOVE
P-Shaw. See:
SHAW, GEORGE
BERNARD
P.T. Selbit. See:
TIBBLES, PERCY
THOMAS
P. Thorne. See:
SMITH, MRS. MARY
PRUDENCE WELLS
P.V. Barrington. See:
BARLING, MURIEL
VERE MANT
P.W. Silvanus. See:
STRASSER, BERNARD
PAUL
P's, Five. See:
OXBERRY, WILLIAM
Pa-he-haska. See:
CODY, WILLIAM
FREDERICK
Pabst, G.W. See:
WILHELM, GEORG
Pace, Peter. See:
BURNETT, DAVID
PACELLI, EUGENIO MARIA
GIUSEPPE GIOVANNI
(1876-1958) [Supreme
Pontiff of Roman Catholic
Church]
Pope Pius XII
PACHTER, HENRY MAXIMILIAN
(1907-) [German-
American educator and
author]
Henry Rabasseire
Pacific Coast, The Silver-
tongued Spellbinder of the.
See:
DELMAS, DELPHIN
MICHAEL
Pacific Cyclone, The. See:
SMITH, HOLLAND

McTYEIRE
Pacific Slope, The Wild Humor-
ist of the. See:
CLEMENS, SAMUEL
LANGHORNE
Pacific, The. See:
FREDERICK III
PEDRO II
Pacific, The Napoleon of the.
See: KAMEHAMEHA I
Pacificator, The Great. See:
CLAY, HENRY
COCHRANE, CLARK
BETTON
Packard, Mrs. Clarissa. See:
GILMAN, CAROLINE
HOWARD
PACKER, JOY PETERSEN
(1905-) [South African
journalist and author]
Lady Packer
Paco Camino. See:
CAMINO, FRANCISCO
Pacorro. See:
ANTÓN, FRANCISCO
Padraic. See:
PEARSE, PATRICK HEN-
RY
Padre, Star-Man's. See:
PATRICK, JOHNSTONE
GILLESPIE
Padrone, Il. See:
SINATRA, FRANCIS
ALBERT
Padua, Anthony of. See:
FERDINAND
Padua, The Swan of. See:
ALGAROTTI, COUNT
FRANCESCO
PAETL, ERICH (1875-)
[German editor and author]
Erich Her
Pagan, Kristian. See:
SEBELIEN, JOHN ROBERT
FRANCIS
PAGANELLI, BERNARDO (died
1153) [Supreme Pontiff of
Roman Catholic Church]
Pope Eugene III
PAGE [Page]. See also:
PAIGE
Paige

771

Page, Eileen. See:
HEAL, EDITH
PAGE, EVELYN. See:
Scarlett, Roger
Page, G. S. See:
GALBRAITH, GEORGIE
STARBUCK
Page, Gale. See:
RUTTER, SALLY
PAGE, GROVER, JR.
(1918-) [American
librarian and author]
K. K. McGinnis
Page, H. A. See:
JAPP, ALEXANDER HAY
PAGE, JOHN (1744-1808)
[American Revolutionary
patriot and governor of
Virginia]
John Partridge
PAGE, JOHN ARTHUR (1910-)
[American radio announcer
and motion picture actor]
Robert Paige
PAGE, JOSEPH FRANCIS
(1917-) [American
professional baseball
player]
Joe Page
PAGE, KIRBY (1890-1957)
[American churchman,
evangelist and pacifist]
The Itinerant Evangelist
for Peace
Page, Lorna. See:
ROWLAND, DONALD
SYDNEY
PAGE, ORAN (1908-54)
[American jazz musician
(trumpet)]
Hot Lips Page
Page, Patti. See:
FOWLER, CLARA ANN
Page, Stanton. See:
FULLER, HENRY BLAKE
Pageants, The Painter of. See:
CAGLIARI (CALIARI),
PAOLO
Paget, Debra. See:
GRIFFIN, DEBRALEE
PAGET, VIOLET (1856-1935)
[English aesthetic
philosopher, critic and

novelist]
Vernon Lee
Pagnanelli, George. See:
DEROUNIAN, ARTHUR
Pahaska. See:
CODY, WILLIAM
FREDERICK
Pai Ta-shun. See:
PETERSON, FREDERICK
PAICH, MARTIN LOUIS (1925-)
[American composer,
conductor and arranger]
Marty Paich
PAIGE [Paige]. See also:
PAGE
Page
PAIGE, ELBRIDGE GERRY (1816-
59) [American humorist]
Dow, Jr.
Paige, Janis. See:
JADEN, DONNA MAE
PAIGE, LEROY ROBERT
(1904?-) [American
Negro professional base-
ball player]
Satchel Paige
Paige, Robert. See:
PAGE, JOHN ARTHUR
PAIKOWSKI, FRANCISZEK
ANDZEJ (1916-) [Polish-
American tennis player]
Frank Parker
PAINE [Paine]. See also:
PAYNE
Payne
Paine, J. Lincoln. See:
KRAMISH, ARNOLD
PAINE, LAUREN (1916-)
[American author]
Will Benton
Mark Carrel
PAINE, ROBERT TREAT, JR.
(1773-1811) [American
editor, orator and poet]
Menander
PAINE, THOMAS (1737-1809)
[Anglo-American political
writer]
Forester
Humanus
Painter of Loneliness, The. See:
HOPPER, EDWARD
Painter of Nature, The. See:

BELLEAU, REMI
Painter of Pageants, The. See:
   CAGLIARI (CALIARI),
   PAOLO
Painter of Presidents, The. See:
   STUART, GILBERT
Painter of Presidents, The
   Portrait. See:
   STUART, GILBERT
Painter of the Graces, The.
   See: APPIANO,
   ANDREA
Painter, The Faultless. See:
   VANNUCCHI, ANDREA
   DOMENICO D'AGNOLO
   DI FRANCESCO DI
   LUCA
Painter, The Learned. See:
   LEBRUN, CHARLES
Painter, The Modern Madonna.
   See: CARRIÈRE,
   EUGÈNE
Painter, The Shadow
   (Skiagraphos). See:
   APOLLODORUS
Painters, The Anacreon of.
   See: ALBANI (ALBANO),
   FRANCESCO
Painters, The Juvenal of. See:
   HOGARTH, WILLIAM
Painters, The King of. See:
   PARRHASIUS
Painters, The King of the
   Flower. See:
   DE LONGPRÉ, PAUL
Painters, The Prince of. See:
   APELLES
   PARRHASIUS
Painting, The Father of
   Modern. See:
   CIMABUE, GIOVANNI
Painting, The Founder of Scene.
   See: AGATHARCOS
Painting, The Scott of. See:
   GILBERT, SIR JOHN
Painting, The Thunderbolt of.
   See: ROBUSTI, JACOPO
Pair, The Interwoven. See:
   Happiness Boys, The
PAIVA, DJANIRA (1914-)
   [Brazilian artist]
   Djanira
Palace, Master of the Sacred.

See: DOMINIC, ST.
Palace, The Pet of the. See:
   STRATTON, CHARLES
   SHERWOOD
Palaeologus. See:
   JOHN V (or VI)
   JOHN VII
   JOHN VIII
   MANUEL II
   MICHAEL VIII
   MICHAEL IX
Palance, Jack. See:
   PALANUIK, WALTER
PALANUIK, WALTER (1920-)
   [American stage and
   motion picture actor]
   Jack Palance
Pale Horse, Death on a. See:
   WIRZ, CAPTAIN HENRY
PALENTHORPE-TODD,
   RICHARD ANDREW
   (1919-) [Irish actor]
   Richard Todd
PALESTRANT, SIMON S.
   (1907-) [American artist,
   educator and author]
   Stephen Edwards
   S. P. Stevens
   Paul E. Strand
PALESTRINA, GIOVANNI
   PIERLUIGI DA (c. 1524-
   94) [Italian musician]
   The Father of Music
   The Michelangelo of the Lyre
   The Prince of Music
   The Savior of Church Music
Palestrina, The English. See:
   GIBBONS, ORLANDO
PALFREY, SARAH HAMMOND
   (1823-) [American
   novelist and poet]
   E. Foxton
Palinurus. See:
   CONNOLLY, CYRIL
   VERNON
Palladianism, The High Priest
   of English. See:
   BOYLE, RICHARD
Palladio, The English. See:
   JONES, INIGO
PALLANTE, ALADDIN AB-
   DULLAH (1913-70) [Amer-
   ican jazz musician (violin,

singer, comedian)]
Aladdin

PALMA, JACOPO (c.1480-
1528) [Venetian artist]
Il Vecchio (The Elder)
Palma Vecchio (Old Palma)

PALMA, JACOPO (1544-
1628) [Venetian artist]
Il Giovane (The Younger)
Palma Giovane (Young
Palma)

Palma, Niño de la. See:
ORDÓÑEZ, CAYETANO

PALMER, ANNA CAMPBELL
(1854-1928) [American
author]
Mrs. George Archibald

Palmer Bend. See:
PUTNAM, GEORGE
PALMER

PALMER, CLAUDE (1893-)
[British character
actor]
Claude Allister

PALMER, DANIEL DAVID
(1845-1913) [Founder of
the Palmer School of
Chiropractic]
Fish Palmer

PALMER, ELSIE PAVITT
(1922-) [American
educator and author]
Peter Palmer

Palmer, Gregg. See:
LEE, PALMER

PALMER, JAMES SHEDDEN
(1810-67)
[American Civil War
admiral]
Piecrust Palmer

PALMER, JAYNE (1930-1967)
[American motion picture
actress]
Jayne Mansfield

PALMER, JOHN (1728-68)
[English actor]
Gentleman Palmer

PALMER, JOHN LESLIE
(1885-1944) [English
author]
Christopher Haddon

PALMER, JOHN LESLIE. See

also:
Beeding, Francis

PALMER, JOHN WILLIAMSON
(1825-1906) [American
editor and miscellaneous
writer]
John Coventry

Palmer, Lilli. See:
HARRISON, MARIA LILLI
PEISER

Palmer, Lynde. See:
PEEBLES, MARY
LOUISE

PALMER, STUART (1905-)
[American author of
detective stories]
Jay Stewart

PALMERSTON, HENRY JOHN
TEMPLE, 3RD VISCOUNT
(1784-1865) [British
statesman]
Firebrand Palmerston
Pam

Palo Alto, The Hermit Author
of. See:
HOOVER, HERBERT CLARK

Palsgrave, Goodman. See:
FREDERICK V

Palsgrave, Goody. See:
STUART, ELIZABETH

Paltenghi, Madeleine. See:
ANDERSON, MADELEINE
PALTENGHI

PALUDAN-MULLER, FREDERIK
(1809-76) [Danish poet]
Fritz

Pam. See:
PALMERSTON, HENRY
JOHN TEMPLE, 3RD
VISCOUNT

Pamby, Namby. See:
PHILIPS, AMBROSE

Pamela Barrington. See:
BARLING, MURIEL VERE
MANT

"Pamela," By the Author of.
See: RICHARDSON,
SAMUEL

Pamela Wynne. See:
SCOTT, WINIFRED MARY

Pampas, The Wild Bull of the.
See: FIRPO, LUIS ANGEL

Pamphili. See:
EUSEBIUS OF CAESAREA
PAMPHILI, GIOVANNI BATTISTA
(1574-1655) [Supreme
Pontiff of Roman Catholic
Church]
Pope Innocent X
Pan, Peter. See:
BARTIER, PIERRE
Pan, The Great. See:
AROUET, FRANÇOIS
MARIE
Panama. See:
FRANCIS, DAVID ALBERT
PANARD, CHARLES-
FRANÇOIS (1694-1765)
[French performer and
song writer]
The Father of Modern
French Songs
Panavision Kid, The. See:
BOWERING, GEORGE
Pancake, Old. See:
COMSTOCK, HENRY
TOMPKINS PAIGE
Pancho. See:
GONZALES, RICHARD
ROSQUELLAS, ADOLFO
SNYDER, FRANK J.
Pancho Segura. See:
CANO, FRANCISCO
SEGURA
Pancho Villa. See:
ARANGO, DOROTEO
Panchón. See:
GONZÁLES, FRANCISCO
PANCOAST, ASA (1905-)
[American composer
and organist]
Ace Pancoast
PANCONCELLI-CALZIA,
GIULIO (1878-)
[Italian educator and
author]
G. P. C.
PANDEL, TED (1935-)
[American pianist and
composer]
Praxiteles
Pangbourne, Oliver. See:
ROCKEY, HOWARD
PANIKKAR, KÁVALAM MADHAVA

(1895-) [Indian educator,
editor and author]
Chanakya
Kerala Putra
PANOWSKI, EILEEN THOMP-
SON (1920-) [American
radiochemistry technician
and author]
Eileen Thompson
Pansy. See:
ALDEN, ISABELLA MAC-
DONALD
PANTALÉON, JACQUES
(died 1264) [Supreme
Pontiff of Roman Catholic
Church]
Pope Urban IV
PANTH, BRAHMIN DUNDHU
(c. 1820-c. 1859) [Indian
rebel]
Nana Sahib
Pants. See:
ROWLAND, CLARENCE H.
Pants, Old Iron. See:
JOHNSON, HUGH
SAMUEL
Paoli, Betty. See:
GLÜCK, BARBARA
ELIZABETH
Paolo, Fra (Brother Paul). See:
SARPI, PIETRO (PAOLO)
Paolo Uccello. See:
DONO, PAOLO DE
Paolo Veronese. See:
CAGLIARI (CALIARI),
PAOLO
Paolotto, Fra. See:
GHISLANDI, FRA VITTORE
Paor, Risteard de. See:
POWER, RICHARD
Pap. See:
Pop
Pops
PRICE, STERLING G.
THOMAS, GEORGE HENRY
Pap Safety, Old. See:
THOMAS, GEORGE HENRY
Papa. See:
CELESTIN, OSCAR
HAYDN, FRANZ JOSEPH
LAINE, GEORGE VITELLE
Papa Doc. See:

DUVALIER, DR.
FRANÇOIS
Papa Jac. See:
ASSUNTO, JACOB
Papa Mutt. See:
CAREY, THOMAS
Papa, Tallulah's. See:
BANKHEAD, WILLIAM
BROCKMAN
PAPADIAMANTOPOULOS,
IOANNES (1856-1910)
[French poet, born in
Athens]
Jean Moréas
PAPALEO, ANTHONY (1928-)
[American actor]
Anthony Franciosa
PAPARESCHI, GREGORIO
(died 1143) [Supreme
pontiff of Roman Catholic
Church]
Pope Innocent II
Papuans, Apostle to the. See:
ABEL, CHARLES
WILLIAM
PAPE, DONNA LUGG (1930-)
[American journalist,
verse writer and author]
D.L. Pape
Paper King, The. See:
LAW, JOHN
Paphlagonian, The. See:
MICHAEL IV
Pappy. See:
O'DANIEL, WILBERT
LEE
Paprika. See:
HOLMVIK, OYVIND
Paprika from Hungary, The Hot.
See: BANKY, VILMA
Paquiro. See:
MONTES, FRANCISCO
Paracelsus, Philippus
Aureolus. See:
VON HOHENHEIM,
THEOPHRASTUS
BOMBASTUS
Parade, The Army's One-man
Hit. See:
LOESSER, FRANK HENRY
Paradox, Master of. See:
CHESTERTON, GILBERT
KEITH

Paragon, Peter the. See:
SWEENEY, PETER BARR
Paratrooper Pet, The. See:
KAUMEYER, DOROTHY
Parcieux, Chevalier de. See:
RIVAROL (RIVAROLI),
ANTOINE
PARÉ, AMBROISE (1517-90)
[French surgeon]
The Father of French Surgery
PARENTUCELLI, TOMMASO
(1397-1455) [Supreme
Pontiff of Roman Catholic
Church]
Pope Nicholas V
PARES, MARION STAPYLTON
(1914-) [British author]
Judith Campbell
PARGETER, EDITH MARY
(1913-) [British author
and translator]
Ellis Peters
PARHAM, CHARLES VALDEZ
(1913-) [American jazz
musician (bass)]
Truck Parham
PARIS, DAWN (1918-)
[American motion picture
actress]
Dawn O'Day
Anne Shirley
Paris, Monsieur de. See:
SANSON, CHARLES
HENRI
PARISH, MARGARET HOLT
(1937-) [American librar-
ian and author]
Margaret Holt
Parish Priest of Meudon, The
(Le Curé de Meudon). See:
RABELAIS, FRANÇOIS
Park Avenue, The Imperial Pea-
cock of. See:
BONAPARTE, CHARLES
JOSEPH
Park Ludlow. See:
BROWN, THERON
Park, The Sage of Gramercy.
See: TILDEN, SAMUEL
JONES
Park, The Squire of Hyde. See:
ROOSEVELT, FRANKLIN
DELANO

Park, The Watchdog of Central.
See: OCHS, ADOLPH
SIMON
Park, The Wizard of Menlo.
See: EDISON, THOMAS
ALVA
Parke, Harry. See:
EINSTEIN, HARRY
PARKE, JOHN (1754-89) [American poet and soldier]
A Native of America
Parker, Bill. See:
PARSONS, WILLIAM
Parker Bonner. See:
BALLARD, WILLIS TOD-
HUNTER
PARKER, CECELIA (c.1935-)
[American model and
motion picture actress]
Suzy Parker
Parker, Cecil. See:
SCHWABE, CECIL
PARKER, CHARLES (1920-55)
[American jazz musician
(alto saxophone)]
Bird
Charlie Parker
Yardbird
PARKER, DOROTHY ROTHS-
CHILD (1893-1967)
[American author, play-
wright and critic]
Constant Reader
Dorothy Parker
PARKER, ERIC (1870-)
[British author and
journalist]
Cheviot of the Field
PARKER, FRANCIS JAMES
(1913-) [American
professional baseball
player]
Salty
Parker, Frank. See:
PAIKOWSKI, FRANCISZEK
ANDZEJ
PARKER, HENRY TAYLOR
(1867-1934) [American
drama critic and news-
paper correspondent]
H. T. P.
Parker, James. See:

NEWBY, ERIC
PARKER, JOHN HENRY
(1866-) [American
officer in Spanish-Amer-
ican war]
Gatling Gun Parker
PARKER, RAYMOND KLEIN
(1913-) [American pro-
fessional football coach]
Buddy Parker
The Top Football Coach in
America
Parker, Seth. See:
LORD, PHILLIPS HAYNES
Parker, Willard. See:
VAN EPS, WORSTER
PARKINSON, JOHN (1567-1650)
[British herbalist]
Botanicus Regius Primarius
Parkyakarkus. See:
EINSTEIN, HARRY
Parkyakarkas. Nick. See:
EINSTEIN, HARRY
Parley, Peter. See:
GOODRICH, SAMUEL
GRISWOLD
KETTELL, SAMUEL
MARTIN, WILLIAM
MOGRIDGE, GEORGE
Parlez, Old. See:
COLSTON, RALEIGH
EDWARD
Parliamentarian, The. See:
LUCE, ROBERT
Parliamentarians, The Prince
of. See:
MELL, PATRICK HUES
Parliamentary Procedure. See:
CANNON, CLARENCE
Parlin, John. See:
GRAVES, JOHN PARLIN
Parmigianino. See:
MAZZUOLI (MAZZOLA),
GIROLAMO FRANCESCO
MARIA
Parmigiano, Il. See:
MAZZUOLI (MAZZOLA),
GIROLAMO FRANCESCO
MARIA
Parnassus, The Lawgiver of.
See: BOILEAU-DES-
PRÉAUX, NICHOLAS

Parnassus, The Restorer of.
See: VALDÉS, JUAN
MELENDEZ
Parnassus, The Solon of. See:
BOILEAU-DESPRÉAUX,
NICHOLAS
PARNELL, CHARLES STEWART
(1846-91) [Irish statesman]
The Uncrowned King of
Ireland
PARNELL, THOMAS FREDER-
ICK (1862-1957) [English
ventriloquist]
The Father of Variety
Fred Russell
PARODI, ALEXANDRE
(1901-) [French
delegate to United
Nations Security Council]
Monsieur X
Parody, The Father of. See:
HIPPONAX
PARR, THOMAS (1483?-1635)
[Shropshire farm servant,
said to have lived to the
age of 152 years]
Old Parr
PARRA, AUGUSTÍN (1924-)
[Spanish bullfighter]
Parrita
PARRHASIUS (fl. c.400 B.C.)
[Greek painter]
The King of Painters
The Prince of Painters
Parricide, The. See:
JOHN (JOHANNES) OF
SWABIA
Parricide, the Beautiful. See:
CENCI, BEATRICE
PARRIS, JOHN (1917-)
[English author]
Alison Lascelles
Parrish, Mary. See:
COUSINS, MARGARET
Parrish, Wendal. See:
MERRILL, JAMES
MILFORD
Parrita. See:
PARRA, AUGUSTÍN
PARRY, HUGH JONES
(1916-) [Anglo-American
sociologist and author]
James Cross

Parry, John. See:
WHELPTON, GEORGE
ERIC
Parsley Peel. See:
PEEL, SIR ROBERT
Parson. See:
BROWNLOW, WILLIAM
GANNAWAY
HOBSON, RICHMOND
PEARSON
WEEMS, MASON LOCKE
Parson Lot. See:
KINGSLEY, REV. CHARLES
Parson of Bennington Fields,
The Fighting. See:
ALLEN, REVEREND
THOMAS
Parson, The Fighting. See:
ALLEN, REVEREND
THOMAS
BALCH, BENJAMIN
BROWNLOW, WILLIAM
GANNAWAY
DEWEY, JEDEDIAH
JONES, JOHN WILLIAM
KELLEY, DAVID CAMP-
BELL
SWALLOW, SILAS COM-
FORT
Parson, The Soldier. See:
CALDWELL, JAMES
Parson, The Sporting. See:
RUSSELL, JOHN
Parson, The Warrior. See:
THURSTON, CHARLES
MYNN
Parson, The Welsh. See:
DAVIS, JAMES JOHN
Parson's Emperor. See:
CHARLES IV
PARSONS, LOUELLA (1893-)
[American Hollywood
gossip columnist]
Lolly
PARSONS, MRS. ELSIE WORTH-
INGTON CLEWS (1875-1941)
[American anthropologist
and writer]
John Main
Parsons, Tom. See:
MACPHERSON, THOMAS
GEORGE
PARSONS, WILLIAM (1933-)

[American composer and
singer]
Bill Parker
PARTCH, VIRGIL FRANKLIN
(1916-) [American
cartoonist]
Vip
Parthenope of Naples, The.
See: VIDA, MARCO
GIROLAMO
Particular, Pertinax. See:
WATKINS, TOBIAS
Partington, F.H. See:
YOXALL, HARRY
WALDO
Partington, Mrs. See:
SHILLABER, BENJAMIN
PENHALLOW
Partisan of Independence. See:
ADAMS, JOHN
PARTON, SARA PAYSON WIL-
LIS (1811-72) [American
author]
Fanny Fern
Partridge, Anthony. See:
OPPENHEIM, EDWARD
PHILLIPS
Partridge, John. See:
PAGE, JOHN
Partridge, Kathleen. See:
WOODERIDGE, KATHLEEN
MABEL
Party of California, The Father
of the Union. See:
VAN DYKE, WALTER
Party, The Father of the
Republican. See:
COLE, AMBROSE N.
Party, The Goliath of His. See:
BAYARD, JAMES
ASHETON
Parvez (The Victorious). See:
KHOSRAU II
Parvus (The Little). See:
JOHN OF SALISBURY
Pascale. See:
PETIT, ANNE-MARIE
PASCHAL (died 824) [Supreme
Pontiff of Roman Catholic
Church]
Pope Paschal I
St. Paschal

Paschal II, Pope. See:
BIEDA, RANIERI DA
Paschal, Nancy. See:
TROTTER, GRACE VIOLET
Pasha. See:
ALI
CAPLI, ERDOGAN
GLUBB, SIR JOHN BAGOT
GORDON, CHARLES
GEORGE
HICKS, WILLIAM
HOBART-HAMPDEN,
AUGUST CHARLES
KEMAL, MUSTAFA
(MUSTAPHA)
Pasha, Emin. See:
SCHNITZER, EDUARD
Pasha, Ismet. See:
INÖNÜ, ISMET
Pasha, Mehmed Emin. See:
SCHNITZER, EDUARD
Pasha, Mohammed. See:
HOWE, WILLIAM WIRT
Pasha, Omar. See:
LATAS, MICHAEL
Pasquil. See:
NASH (NASHE), THOMAS
Pasquin. See:
ALLEN, PAUL
Pasquin, Anthony. See:
WILLIAMS, JOHN
Pasquin Petronius. See:
RILEY, ISAAC
Pasquino. See:
McLAUGHLIN, JAMES
FAIRFAX
Pass, Joe. See:
PASSALAQUA, JOSEPH
ANTHONY
Pass, The Father of the Forward.
See: HEISMAN, JOHN
WILLIAM
PASSALAQUA, JOSEPH
ANTHONY (1929-) [Amer-
ican jazz musician (guitar)]
Joe Pass
Pasternak, K.F. See:
KRASZEWSKI, JÓZEF
IGNACY
Pastime, The Czar of the
National. See:
LANDIS, KENESAW

MOUNTAIN
Pastnor, Paul. See:
    MORRIS, CHARLES
    SMITH
Pastor. See:
    RUSSELL, CHARLES
    TAZE
PASTOR, ANTONIO (1837-1908)
    [American music-hall
    manager]
    Tony Pastor
Pastor Felix. See:
    LOCKHART, ARTHUR
    JOHN
Pastor of the Poor, The.
    See: COX, JAMES R.
Pastor, Tony. See:
    PASTOR, ANTONIO
    PASTRITTO, ANTONIO
PASTOR, VICENTE   (1879-
    died after 1918) [Spanish
    bullfighter]
    Chico de la Blusa
PASTRITTO, ANTONIO (1907-)
    [American jazz musician
    (singer, leader, tenor
    saxophone)]
    Tony Pastor
Pasture, Rogelet de la. See:
    WEYDEN, ROGIER
    VAN DER
Pasture, Roger de la. See:
    WEYDEN, ROGIER VAN
    DER
Pat. See:
    BALLARD, FRANCIS
    DRAKE
    BOONE, CHARLES
    EUGENE
    BROWN, EDMUND
    GERALD
    CONROY, PATRICK
    DOMINIC
    CRAWFORD, CLIFFORD
    RANKIN
    HINGLE, MARTIN
    PATTERSON
    JONES, VIRGIL CAR-
    RINGTON
    LAWLOR, PATRICK
    ANTHONY
    MALONE, PERCY LAY

O'BRIEN, WILLIAM
    JOSEPH, JR.
    SUZUKI, CHIYOKO
Pat Beauchamp. See:
    WASHINGTON, MARGUERITE
    BEAUCHAMP
Pat Beauchamp Washington. See:
    WASHINGTON, MARGUERITE
    BEAUCHAMP
Pat Haynes. See:
    McKEAG, ERNEST LIONEL
Pat Maloney. See:
    MARKUN, PATRICIA
    MALONEY
Patch, Wally. See:
    VINICOMBE, WALTER
Patent Office, The Father of the.
    See: RUGGLES, JOHN
Pater Patriae (The Father of His
    Country). See:
    CICERO, MARCUS
    TULLIUS
    HADRIAN (ADRIAN)
    MEDICI, COSIMO DE'
PATERSON [Paterson]. See also:
    PATTERSON
    Patterson
PATERSON, ANDREW BARTON
    (1864-1941) [Australian
    journalist and poet]
    Banjo
Paterson, Anne. See:
    EINSELEN, ANNE F.
Paterson, Huntley. See:
    LUDOVICI, ANTHONY
    MARIO
PATERSON, ROBERT (1715-
    1801) [Scottish stonecutter]
    Old Mortality
PATERSON, WILLIAM ROMAINE
    (1870-) [Scottish author]
    Benjamin Swift
Path, Bright (Wa-Tho-Huck).
    See: THORPE, JAMES
    FRANCIS
Pathfinder of the Seas, The.
    See: MAURY, MATTHEW
    FONTAINE
Pathfinder, The. See:
    FRÉMONT, JOHN CHARLES
Patience Hartman. See:
    ZAWADSKY, PATIENCE

780

PATMAN, WRIGHT (1893-)
[American farmer and
lawyer; congressman
from Texas]
Anti-chain-store Patman
The Father of the Bonus
Patriae, Amicus. See:
WISE, JOHN
Patriae, Pater (The Father of
His Country). See:
CICERO, MARCUS
TULLIUS
HADRIAN (ADRIAN)
MEDICI, COSIMO DE'
Patriarch of Columbia, The.
See: TAYLOR, THOMAS
Patriarch of Ferney, The. See:
AROUET, FRANÇOIS
MARIE
Patriarch of New England, The.
See: COTTON, JOHN
Patriarch of the Hills, The. See:
CRAWFORD, ABEL
Patriarch of the Indians, The.
See: MAYHEW, THOMAS
Patriarch of the Mountains,
The. See:
CRAWFORD, ABEL
Patriarch of the New England
Clergy, The. See:
NOTT, SAMUEL
Patriarch of the Spanish
Theater, The. See:
ENCINA (ENZINA),
JUAN DEL
Patrice, Ann. See:
GALBRAITH, GEORGIE
STARBUCK
Patricia. See:
NEAL, PATSY LOUISE
Patricia Charters. See:
CARLON, PATRICIA
BERNARDETTE
Patricia Curtis. See:
CARLON, PATRICIA
BERNARDETTE
Patricia Denning. See:
WILLIS, CORINNE
DENNENY
Patricia Lynn. See:
WATTS, MABEL PIZZEY
Patricia Morison. See:

MORRISON, EILEEN
Patricia Morton. See:
GOLDING, MORTON JAY
Patricia Roc. See:
RIESE, FELICIA
Patricia Wilde. See:
WHITE, PATRICIA
LORRAIN-ANN
Patrician of the Romans. See:
PEPIN (PIPPIN) III
Patricio Marroquin. See:
MARKUN, PATRICIA
MALONEY
Patricius and Magister Militum.
See: THEODORIC
Patrick. See:
Quentin, Patrick
WELCH, GEORGE PATRICK
Patrick Augustine Sheehan. See:
O SIOCHAIN, PADRAIG
AUGUSTINE
Patrick Balfour. See:
KINROSS, PATRICK LORD
Patrick Campbell, Mrs. See:
CAMPBELL, BEATRICE
STELLA TANNER
Patrick Downe. See:
LASCELLES, WALTER
Patrick, Gail. See:
FITZPATRICK, MARGARET
Patrick Henry Brown. See:
BROWN, EDMUND GERALD
Patrick Henry, Our. See:
KOLB, REUBEN FRANCIS
Patrick, John. See:
GOGGAN, JOHN PATRICK
PATRICK, JOHNSTONE GIL-
LESPIE (1918-) [Scottish
Presbyterian minister and
author]
Luke Forward
Star-Man's Padre
Patrick, Keats. See:
KARIG, WALTER
Patrick, Leal. See:
STONE, PATTI
Patrick, Lilian. See:
KEOGH, LILIAN GILMORE
Patrick O'Connor. See:
WIBBERLEY, LEONARD
PATRICK O'CONNOR
Patrick, Q., joint pseud. of

MARTHA MOTT KELLEY
(191?-) and RICHARD
WILSON WEBB (191?-)
[American authors of
detective stories]
Patrick, Q. See also:
Quentin, Patrick
WEBB, RICHARD WILSON
PATRICK, ST. (389?-463)
[English-Irish churchman]
The Apostle of Ireland
Succat
Patriot Financier, The. See:
MORRIS, ROBERT
Patriot King, The. See:
ST. JOHN, HENRY
Patriot Mother of the Mohawk
Valley, The. See:
VAN ALSTINE, MRS.
MARTIN J.
Patriot of Humanity, The. See:
GRATTAN, HENRY
Patriot, One-Man. See:
FISH, HAMILTON, JR.
Patriot Printer of 1776, The.
See: BRADFORD,
WILLIAM
Patriots, The Nestor of the.
See: HAWLEY, JOSEPH
Patron Saint of American
Orchards, The. See:
CHAPMAN, JOHN
Patsy. See:
SCARRY, PATRICIA
MURPHY
PATTEN. See also:
PATTON
PATTEN, GEORGE WASHINGTON
(1808-82) [American
poet and Union Army
soldier]
The Poet Laureate of the
Army
PATTEN, WILLIAM GILBERT
(1866-1945) [American
writer of dime novels and
juvenile literature]
Herbert Bellwood
Wyoming Bill
Harry Dangerfield
Gordon MacLaren
Gil Patten

Gilbert Patten
Julian St. Dare
Burt L. Standish
William West Wilding
PATTERSON [Patterson]. See
also: PATERSON
Paterson
PATTERSON, ELEANOR
MEDILL (1884-1948)
[American newspaper editor
and owner]
Cissie Patterson
PATTERSON, HENRY (1929-)
[British educator and
author]
Martin Fallon
Hugh Marlowe
Harry Patterson
Patterson, Jane. See:
BRITTON, MATTIE LULA
COOPER
Patterson, Oliver. See:
ROWLAND, DONALD
SYDNEY
Patti. See also:
Patty
Patti, Black. See:
JONES, SISSIERRETTA
JOYNER
Patti Page. See:
FOWLER, CLARA ANN
PATTINSON, NANCY EVELYN
(1909-) [English author]
Nan Asquith
PATTISON, DOROTHY WYNDLOW
(1832-78) [English
philanthropist]
Sister Dora
PATTON. See also:
PATTEN
PATTON, GEORGE SMITH, JR.
(1885-1945) [American
general officer]
Old Blood and Guts
PATTON, JOHN (1936-)
[American jazz musician
(organ)]
Big John
PATTON, MELVIN EMERY
(1924-) [American
athlete]
Mel Patton

Patty. See:
    DUKE, ANNA MARIE
    PATRICIA
    Patti
Patty Lee. See:
    CAREY, ALICE
PAUFICHET, JULES (1883-
    1951) [French motion
    picture actor]
    Jules Berry
Paul. See:
    DELAROCHE, HIPPOLYTE
    GAUGUIN, EUGÈNE
        HENRI PAUL
    PAOLO
    Pol
    SAUL
    SCOFIELD, DAVID
    SWINGS, POLIDORE F. F.
    VINCENT DE PAUL
PAUL (died 767) [Supreme
    Pontiff of Roman Catholic
    Church]
    Pope Paul I
    St. Paul
Paul II, Pope. See:
    PIETRO, BARBO
Paul III, Pope. See:
    FARNESE, ALESSANDRO
Paul IV, Pope. See:
    CARAFFA, GIAMPIETRO
Paul V, Pope. See:
    BORGHESE, CAMILLO
Paul VI, Pope. See:
    MONTINI, GIOVANNI
        BATTISTA
Paul Allyn. See:
    SCHOSBERG, PAUL A.
Paul Annixter. See:
    STURTZEL, HOWARD
        ALLISON
Paul Ash. See:
    ASCHENBRENNER, PAUL
Paul, Auren. See:
    URIS, AUREN
Paul Bell. See:
    CHORLEY, HENRY
        FOTHERGILL
Paul Bern. See:
    LEVY, PAUL
Paul, Brother (Fra Paolo). See:
    SARPI, PIETRO (PAOLO)

Paul Creyton. See:
    TROWBRIDGE, JOHN
        TOWNSEND
Paul, Daniel. See:
    KESSEL, LIPMANN
Paul de Mar. See:
    FOLEY, PEARL
Paul Dupont. See:
    FREWIN, LESLIE RONALD
Paul E. Strand. See:
    PALESTRANT, SIMON S.
Paul Éluard. See:
    GRINDAL, EUGENE
Paul, Emily. See:
    EICHER, ETHEL
        ELIZABETH
Paul Fort. See:
    STOCKTON, FRANCIS
        RICHARD
Paul French. See:
    ASIMOV, ISAAC
Paul Gavarni. See:
    CHEVALIER, SULPICE
        GUILLAUME
Paul Gilbert. See:
    MACMAHON, PAUL
Paul Gosslet. See:
    LEVER, CHARLES JAMES
Paul Grayson. See:
    DEMPSEY, JAMES E.
Paul Gregory. See:
    LENHART, JASON GREGORY
Paul Gregson. See:
    OAKLEY, ERIC GILBERT
Paul Haggard. See:
    LONGSTREET, STEPHEN
Paul Henreid. See:
    VON HERNREID, PAUL
Paul, Hugo. See:
    LITTLE, PAUL H.
Paul Hunter. See:
    WEAVER, BERTRAND
Paul J. Prescott. See:
    IRONS, LETTIE ARTLEY
Paul James. See:
    WARBURG, JAMES PAUL
Paul, Jean. See:
    RICHTER, JOHANN PAUL
        FRIEDRICH
PAUL, JOHN (1747-92) [Scottish-
    American naval hero]
    The Bayard of the Sea

The Founder of the American
Navy
John Paul Jones
Paul, John. See:
    WEBB, CHARLES HENRY
Paul Jones of the South. See:
    SEMMES, RAPHAEL
Paul Kapp. See:
    HARDT, RICHARD
Paul King. See:
    DRACKETT, PAUL
Paul Klenovsky. See:
    WOOD, SIR HENRY
        JOSEPH
Paul, Les. See:
    POLFUS, LESTER
Paul Lukas. See:
    LUKACS, PAL
Paul Marsh. See:
    HOPKINS, KENNETH
Paul Martens. See:
    SOUTHWOLD, STEPHEN
Paul Martin. See:
    DEALE, KENNETH EDWIN
        LEE
PAUL, MAURY HENRY BIDDLE
    (1890-1942) [American
    journalist and society
    editor]
    Cholly Knickerbocker
Paul Muni. See:
    WEISENFREUND, MUNI
Paul Myron. See:
    LINEBARGER, PAUL
        MYRON WENTWORTH
Paul Norwood. See:
    NETTL, JOHN PETER
Paul, Oom. See:
    KRUGER, STEPHANUS
        JOHANNES PAULUS
Paul Pastnor. See:
    MORRIS, CHARLES
        SMITH
Paul Potter. See:
    CONGDON, CHARLES
        TABER
Paul Prendergast. See:
    LEIGH, PERCIVAL
Paul Preston. See:
    COOPER, ALFRED
        BENJAMIN
    MILNER, THOMAS

    PICTON
    MORRIS, CHARLES SMITH
Paul Rayson. See:
    JENNINGS, LESLIE NELSON
Paul Revere. See:
    ABARBANELL, JACOB
        RALPH
Paul, St. See:
    SAUL
Paul, St. Vincent de. See:
    VINCENT DE PAUL
Paul Schultze. See:
    LANGER, ALFONS
Paul Sheriff. See:
    SHOUVALOV, PAUL
Paul Siegvolk. See:
    MATTHEWS, ALBERT
Paul Somers. See:
    WINTERTON, PAUL
Paul Stacey. See:
    SAVILL, ROY
Paul Tabor. See:
    TABORI, PAUL
Paul the Deacon. See:
    PAULUS DIACONUS
Paul Thomas. See:
    MANN, THOMAS
Paul, William. See:
    EICHER, ETHEL ELIZA-
        BETH
Paula. See:
    LITTLE, PAUL H.
Paula Minton. See:
    LITTLE, PAUL H.
Paula Prentiss. See:
    RAGUSA, PAULA
Paula Raymond. See:
    WRIGHT, PAULA RAMONA
PAULDING, JAMES KIRKE
    (1779-1860) [American
    author]
    Oliver Oldstyle
PAULDING, JAMES KIRKE. See
    also: Langstaff,
        Launcelot
Paule Croset. See:
    CORDAY, PAULA
Pauline Welch. See:
    BODENHEIM, HILDA
        MORRIS
PAULO. See:
    PAUL

Paul
Pol
SARPI, PIETRO
    (PAULO)
Paulson, Jack. See:
    JACKSON, CAARY PAUL
PAULUS DIACONUS (fl. 8th
    cent.) [Lombard his-
    torian and monk]
Paul the Deacon
Paunch, Fat (Physcon). See:
    PTOLEMY VII (or VIII
    or IX)
Pauper et Ignotus. See:
    THATCHER, JOHN
    WELLS
Pausanias, The British. See:
    CAMDEN, WILLIAM
Pautuxie. See:
    DAVIES, MARY CAROLYN
PAVAGEAU, ALCIDE (1888-)
    [American jazz musician
    (bass)]
Slow Drag
Pavan, Marisa. See:
    PIERANGELI, ANNA
    MARIA
PAVIA. See:
    PETER OF PAVIA
Pavlova, Dainty Baby June
    the Pocket-Sized. See:
    HOVICK, JUNE
Pawnee Bill. See:
    LILLIE, MAJOR
    GORDON W.
Pawnees, The White Chief
    of The. See:
    LILLIE, MAJOR
    GORDON W.
Pax. See:
    CHOLMONDELEY, MARY
Paxinou, Katina. See:
    CONSTANTOPOULOS,
    KATINA
Paxton, Dr. John. See:
    LAWTON, SHERMAN
    PAXTON
Paxton, Jack. See:
    LAWTON, SHERMAN
    PAXTON
Paxton, Philip. See:
    HAMMETT, SAMUEL

ADAMS
PAXTON, THOMAS R. (1937-)
    [American composer and
    singer]
Tom Paxton
Pay, Tay. See:
    O'CONNOR, THOMAS
    POWER
Paye, Robert. See:
    LONG, MRS. GABRIELLE
    MARGARET VERE CAMP-
    BELL
PAYNE [Payne]. See also:
    PAINE
    Paine
PAYNE, DONALD GORDON
    (1924-) [British editor and
    author]
Ian Cameron
Donald Gordon
James Vance Marshall
Payne, Harold. See:
    KELLY, GEORGE C.
PAYNE, PERCIVAL (1935-)
    [American jazz musician
    (drums)]
Sonny Payne
Pea, Swee'. See:
    STRAYHORN, WILLIAM
PEABODY, ELIZABETH
    PALMER (1804-94) [Amer-
    ican educator]
The Grandmother of Boston
Peabody, Mrs. Mark. See:
    VICTOR, MRS. METTA
    VICTORIA FULLER
    MORSE
Peace. See:
    LUDLOW, LOUIS LEON
Peace, The Apostle of. See:
    LADD, WILLIAM
Peace, The Father of. See:
    DORIA, ANDREA
Peace, The Founder of. See:
    BENEDICT OF NURSIA,
    ST.
Peace, The Itinerant Evangelist
    for. See:
    PAGE, KIRBY
Peace, The Napoleon of. See:
    LOUIS PHILIPPE
Peace, The Prince of the. See:

GODOY, MANUEL DE
Peaceful Prelate, The. See:
    MASSILLON, JEAN
    BAPTISTE
Peaceful, The. See:
    EDGAR (EADGAR)
Peacemaker, Great. See:
    GRANT, HIRAM
    ULYSSES
Peacemaker, The. See:
    CHANNING, WILLIAM
    ELLERY
    EDWARD VII
    IRENAEUS, ST.
Peach, The. See:
    DEPEW, CHAUNCEY
    MITCHELL
Peach, The Georgia. See:
    COBB, TYRUS
    RAYMOND
Peaches. See:
    HYNES, FRANCES
    HEENAN
Peacock of Park Avenue, The
    Imperial. See:
    BONAPARTE, CHARLES
    JOSEPH
Peacock Senator, The. See:
    CONKLING, ROSCOE
PEACOCK, THOMAS LOVE
    (1785-1866) [English
    poet and novelist]
    P.M. O'Donovan
    Peter Peppercorn
Peak, The Apostle of the. See:
    BAGSHAW, WILLIAM
Peanut King, The. See:
    GWALTNEY, PEMBROKE
    DECATUR
    OBICI, AMEDEO
Peanut Man, The. See:
    CARVER, DR. GEORGE
    WASHINGTON
Peanuts. See:
    HOLLAND, HERBERT
    LEE
    HUCKO, MICHAEL
    ANDREW
PEARCE [Pearce]. See also:
    Peerce
    PIERCE
    Pierce

Pearce, Guy. See:
    PILLEY, CHARLES
PEARCE, RICHARD ELMO
    (1909-) [American editor
    and author]
    Dick Pearce
Pearl, Eric. See:
    ELMAN, RICHARD MARTIN
Pearl, Irene. See:
    GUYONVARCH, IRENE
    CECILIA
Pearl Lang. See:
    LACK, PEARL
PEARL, LEO J. (1907-)
    [American musician]
    Lee Pearl
Pearl of Ireland, The. See:
    BRIDGET, ST.
Pearl of York, The. See:
    CLITHEROW, MARGARET
    MIDDLETON
Pearl Rivers. See:
    NICHOLSON, ELIZA JANE
    POITEVENT HOLBROOK
PEARSE, PATRICK HENRY
    (1879-1916) [Irish educator,
    writer and patriot]
    Padraic Pearse
PEARSON, COLUMBUS CALVIN
    (1932-) [American jazz
    musician (piano, composer)]
    Duke Pearson
PEARSON, EDMUND LESTER
    (1880-1937) [American
    editor, bibliographer, li-
    brarian and authority on
    murder]
    The Librarian
PEARSON, ELIPHALET (1752-
    1826) [American educator]
    Elephant
PEARY, MARIE AHNIGHITO
    (1893-) [Daughter of the
    Arctic explorer ROBERT
    EDWIN PEARY]
    The Snow Baby
Peasant. See:
    BRUEGHEL (BREUGHEL),
    PIETER
Peasant Bard, The. See:
    BURNS, ROBERT
    CANNING, JOSIAH DEAN

Peasant of the Danube, The.
    See: LEGENDRE, LOUIS
Peasant Poet, Northampton-
    shire. See:
    CLARE, JOHN
Peasant Pope, The. See:
    SARTO, GIUSEPPE
    MELCHIORRE
PECCI, GIOACCHINO VINCENZO
    (1810-1903) [Supreme
    Pontiff of Roman Catholic
    Church]
    Pope Leo XIII
PECHEY, ARCHIBALD THOMAS
    (1876-) [British author
    and dramatist]
    Valentine
PECK, ELLEN (fl. 1867-75)
    [American author]
    Cuyler Pine
PECK, GEORGE WASHINGTON
    (1817-59) [American
    journalist and music critic]
    Cantrell A. Bigly
PECK, GEORGE WILBUR
    (1840-1916) [American
    governor, editor and
    author]
    Terence McGrant
PECK, WILLIAM HENRY
    (1830-92) [American
    educator and novelist]
    Mahlon A. Brown
Peckham, Richard. See:
    HOLDEN, RAYMOND
    PECKHAM
Pecos, The Law West of the.
    See: BEAN, ROY
PECSOK, MARY BODELL
    (1919-) [American author]
    Mary Bodell
Pedant, Deliberate. See:
    ELIOT, THOMAS STEARNS
PEDERSEN, CARL (1897-)
    [Danish singer and motion
    picture actor]
    Carl Brisson
PEDERSEN, KNUT (1859-1952)
    [Norwegian writer]
    Knut Hamsun
PEDLER, ANNE I. STAFFORD
    (1901-) [English
    author]

Anne Stafford
Pedrés. See:
    MARTÍNEZ, PEDRO
PEDRO I (1320-67) [King of
    Portugal]
    The Judiciary
    The Severe
PEDRO II (1648-1706) [King of
    Portugal]
    The Pacific
PEDRO III (1239-85) [King of
    Aragon]
    The Great
PEDRO IV (1319-87) [King of
    Aragon]
    The Ceremonious
PEDRO (PETER) (1334-69)
    [King of Castile and Léon]
    Pedro el Cruel
    Peter the Cruel
Pee Wee. See:
    ERWIN, GEORGE
    HUNT, WALTER
    REESE, HAROLD HENRY
    RUSSELL, CHARLES
    ELLSWORTH
    SPITELARA, JOSEPH T.
PEEBLES, MARY LOUISE
    (1833-1915) [American
    author]
    Lynde Palmer
PEEL, HAZEL MARY (1930-)
    [British horsewoman and
    author]
    Hayman
Peel, Lady. See:
    LILLIE, BEATRICE GLADYS
PEEL, SIR ROBERT (1750-1830)
    [English calico printer]
    Parsley Peel
PEEL, SIR ROBERT (1788-1850)
    [English statesman]
    Orange Peel
Peepers, Mr. See:
    COX, WALLACE MAYNARD
Peerce. See also:
    PEARCE
    Pearce
    PIERCE
    Pierce
Peerce, Jan. See:
    PERELMAN, JACOB
    PINCUS

Peerless Leader, The. See:
  CHANCE, FRANK LeROY
Peeslake, Gaffer. See:
  DURRELL, LAWRENCE
  GEORGE
Peg. See:
  LYNCH, MARGARET
  PEGLER, JAMES
  WESTBROOK
  WOFFINGTON,
  MARGARET
Peggy. See:
  ARNOLD, MARGARET
  SHIPPEN
  ASHCROFT, EDITH
  MARGARET EMILY
  CASS, MARY MARGARET
  CHAMBERS, MARGARET
  ADA EASTWOOD
  HOFFMANN, MARGARET
  JONES
  O'NEALE, MARGARET L.
  VAN PRAAGH, MARGARET
  WAGNER, MARGARET D.
Peggy Ann. See:
  MILLER, GEORGE AMOS
Peggy Craig. See:
  KREIG, MARGARET B.
Peggy Dow. See:
  VARNADOW, PEGGY
Peggy Eaton. See:
  O'NEALE, MARGARET L.
Peggy Gaddis. See:
  DERN, PEGGY GADDIS
Peggy Lee. See:
  ENGSTROM, NORMA
  DOLORES (JEAN)
Peggy O'More. See:
  BLOCKLINGER, PEGGY
  O'MORE
Peggy O'Neill. See:
  EATON, MARGARET
  O'NEILL
Peggy, Pothouse. See:
  EATON, MARGARET
  O'NEILL
PEGLER, JAMES WESTBROOK
  (1894-1969) [American
  journalist, newspaper
  columnist and author]
  Peg
  Westbrook Pegler

PELAGIUS (died 561) [Supreme
  Pontiff of Roman Catholic
  Church]
  Pope Pelagius I
PELAGIUS (died 590) [Supreme
  Pontiff of Roman Catholic
  Church]
  Pope Pelagius II
PELAYO, LUIS (fl. 1st half
  20th cent.) [Spanish taxi
  driver and heckler at bull-
  fights]
  Ronquillo (Little Hoarse One)
Pelé. See:
  NASCIMENTO, EDSON
  ARANTES DO
Peleg Arkwright. See:
  PROUDFIT, DAVID LAW
PELHAM, JOHN (1838-63)
  [American Confederate
  Civil War officer]
  The Boy Major
  Gallant Pelham
PELLEGRINI, CARLO (1838-89)
  [Italian caricaturist]
  Ape
PELOVITZ, MORTON HERBERT
  (1925-   ) [American jazz
  musician (bass, composer)]
  Mort Herbert
Pelvis, The. See:
  PRESLEY, ELVIS ARON
PEMBERTON, ISRAEL (1715-79)
  [American Quaker merchant
  and philanthropist]
  The King of the Quakers
  King Wampum
Pembury, Bill. See:
  GROOM, ARTHUR WILLIAM
Pen. See also:
  PENN
  Penn
  Penne
Pen of the Congress, The Hand
  and. See:
  THOMPSON, CHARLIE
Pen of the Revolution, The. See:
  JEFFERSON, THOMAS
PENA, ROBERTO COLLAZO
  (1916-   ) [Cuban composer,
  author and pianist]
  Bobby Collazo

Pencil. See:
SOWDEN, SIR WILLIAM
JOHN
Pendennis, Arthur. See:
THACKERAY, WILLIAM
MAKEPEACE
Pender, Lex. See:
PENDOWER, JACQUES
Pender, Marilyn. See:
PENDOWER, JACQUES
Pendleton, Conrad. See:
KIDD, WALTER E.
PENDLETON, GEORGE HUNT
(1825-89) [American
politician]
The Father of Civil Service
Reform
Gentleman George
PENDOWER, JACQUES
(1899-) [British civil
servant and author]
Tom Curtis
Penn Dowers
T.C.H. Jacobs
Thomas Curtis Hicks Jacobs
Lex Pender
Marilyn Pender
Anne Penn
Penelope Hunt. See:
NAPIER, PRISCILLA
Penfeather, Amabel. See:
COOPER, SUSAN
FENIMORE
Penholder. See:
EGGLESTON, EDWARD
PENIAKOFF, VLADIMIR (1897-
1951) [Russian soldier
and author]
Popski
PENKETHMAN (PINKETHMAN),
WILLIAM (died 1725)
[English comedian]
The Idol of the Rabble
Pinkey
Penklub. See:
LANGE, CARL GUSTAV
ALBERT
Penman of the American
Revolution, The. See:
DICKINSON, JOHN
Penn. See:
Pen

Penne
PERRINE, WILLIAM
SMITH, RICHARD PENN
Penn, Anne. See:
PENDOWER, JACQUES
Penn, Arthur. See:
MATTHEWS, JAMES
BRANDER
Penn, Christopher. See:
LAWLOR, PATRICK
ANTHONY
Penn Dowers. See:
PENDOWER, JACQUES
Penn Shirley. See:
CLARKE, SARAH J.
PENN, WILLIAM (1644-1718)
[British colonizer in
America]
The Father of Pennsylvania
Penne. See also:
Pen
PENN
Penn
Penne, Agile. See:
AIKEN, ALBERT W.
PENNELL, ELIZABETH
(1855-1936) [American
author]
A Greedy Woman
N. N.
Penner, Joe. See:
PINTER, JOSEPH
Penniless, The (Pochi Danari).
See: MAXIMILIAN I
Penniman, Major. See:
DENISON, CHARLES
WHEELER
Pennington, Penny. See:
GALBRAITH, GEORGIE
STARBUCK
Pennington, Stuart. See:
GALBRAITH, GEORGIE
STARBUCK
Pennot, Reverend Peter. See:
ROUND, WILLIAM
MARSHALL FITTS
Pennsylvania Farmer, The. See:
DICKINSON, JOHN
Pennsylvania Politics, The Czar
of. See:
CAMERON, SIMON
Pennsylvania, The Father of.

See: PENN, WILLIAM
Pennsylvania, The Father of the
    Public School System of.
    See: WOLF, GEORGE
Penny Pennington. See:
    GALBRAITH, GEORGIE
    STARBUCK
Penny Plug, The. See:
    O'SULLIVAN, DENNIS
Penny Singleton. See:
    McNULTY, DOROTHY
PENROSE, ELIZABETH
    (1780-1837) [British
    writer of children's
    literature]
  Mrs. Markham
Penrose, Margaret. See:
    STRATEMEYER,
    EDWARD L.
Pentecost, The Living. See:
    MEZZOFANTI, CARDINAL
    GIUSEPPE
People. See:
    Golden Calves of the
      People, The
People, Father of the (Père
    du Peuple). See:
    LOUIS XII
People, Friend of the (l'Ami
    du Peuple). See:
    MARAT, JEAN PAUL
People, New York City's
    Official Greeter of
    Famous. See:
    WHALEN, GROVER
    ALOYSIUS
People, One of the. See:
    HOPKINSON, FRANCIS
People, One of the (Achad
    Ha-am). See:
    GINZBERG, ASCHER
People, The Apostle of
    Quiet. See:
    YOUNG, EMILY HILDA
People, The Father of the.
    See: CHRISTIAN III
People, The Friend of the.
    See: JEFFERSON,
    THOMAS
People, The Man of the. See:
    FOX, CHARLES JAMES
    HENRY, PATRICK

JEFFERSON, THOMAS
LINCOLN, ABRAHAM
People, The Poet of the Common.
    See: RILEY, JAMES
    WHITCOMB
People, The Tribune of the.
    See: ADAMS, SAMUEL
    BRIGHT, JOHN
People's Artist of the Republic.
    See: IPPOLITOV-IVANOV,
    MIKHAIL MIKHAILOVICH
People's Attorney, The. See:
    BRANDEIS, LOUIS DEM-
    BITZ
People's Author, The. See:
    CLEMENS, SAMUEL
    LANGHORNE
People's Friend, The. See:
    GORDON, WILLIAM
People's Laureate, The. See:
    RILEY, JAMES WHITCOMB
People's Lawyer, The. See:
    BRANDEIS, LOUIS
    DEMBITZ
People's President, The. See:
    CLEVELAND, STEPHEN
    GROVER
    JACKSON, ANDREW
Peoples, The Mother of. See:
    MARGUERITE OF FRANCE
People's Will, The. See:
    PITT, WILLIAM
People's William, The. See:
    PITT, WILLIAM
Pep. See:
    YOUNG, LEMUEL FLOYD
Pepe. See:
    MEJÍAS, JOSÉ
Pepe-Hillo. See:
    DELGADO, JOSÉ
Pepete. See:
    RODRÍGUEZ, JOSÉ
Pepete III. See:
    GALLEGO, JOSÉ
Pepin, Little King. See:
    CHANNING, WILLIAM
    ELLERY
PEPIN (PIPPIN) III (c. 714-68)
    [Carolingian King of the
    Franks]
  Patrician of the Romans
  The Short

Pepper. See:
ADAMS, PARK
AUSTIN, JAMES PHILIP
MARTIN, JOHNNY LEONARD
Pepper Box. See:
BARTELL, RICHARD
Pepper Box, Peter. See:
FESSENDEN, THOMAS
GREEN
PEPPER, CURTIS G. (1920-)
[American writer for
television and films]
Curtis Bill Pepper
PEPPER, J.H. (fl. mid 19th
cent.) [English director
of Royal Polytechnic
Institute]
Professor
Pepper, Joan. See:
WETHERELL-PEPPER,
JOAN ALEXANDER
Peppercorn, Peter. See:
PEACOCK, THOMAS
LOVE
Pepperpod, Pip. See:
STODDARD, CHARLES
WARREN
Pepys in Essex. See:
TOMPKINS, HERBERT
WINCKWORTH
Pepys, Puritan. See:
SEWALL, SAMUEL
PEPYS, SAMUEL (1633-1703)
[English politician and
diarist]
The Prince of Gossips
Per Aëra. See:
BOOTHBY, FREDERICK
LEWIS MAITLAND
Per Mare. See:
BOOTHBY, FREDERICK
LEWIS MAITLAND
Percival G---. See:
IRVING, PETER
PERCIVAL, JOHN (1779-1862)
[American naval officer]
Mad Jack
Percival, Nelson. See:
RYMER, JAMES
MALCOLM
Percival Pickering. See:
STIRLING, ANNA MARIA

DIANA WILHELMINA
PICKERING
Percival, Vincent. See:
BONNER, CAREY
Percy. See:
MUIR, PERCIVAL
HORACE
Percy, Charles Henry.
See: SMITH, DODIE
Percy, Florence. See:
AKERS, ELIZABETH
CHASE
Percy H. Muir. See:
MUIR, PERCIVAL HORACE
Percy Marshall. See:
YOUNG, PERCY
MARSHALL
Percy of the House, The Harry.
See: WISE, HENRY
ALEXANDER
PERCY, SIR HENRY (1364-1403)
[English military leader]
Hotspur
PERCY, SIR HENRY (1564-1632)
[9th Earl of Northumber-
land]
The Wizard Earl
Perdida, Fair. See:
ROBINSON, MRS. MARY
DARBY
Perdita. See:
ROBINSON, MRS. MARY
DARBY
père. See:
DUMAS, ALEXANDRE
Père. See:
MARQUETTE, JACQUES
Père du Peuple (Father of the
People). See:
LOUIS XII
Père Duchesne, Le. See:
HÉBERT, JACQUES RENÉ
Père Hyacinthe. See:
LOYSON, CHARLES
Père Joseph (Father Joseph).
See: TREMBLAY,
FRANÇOIS LE CLERC
DU
PEREDA, JOSÉ MARÍA DE
(1833-1906) [Spanish
novelist]
The Modern Cervantes

Peregrine. See:
    DEUTSCHER, ISAAC
Peregrine Pickle. See:
    UPTON, GEORGE
    PUTNAM
PEREGRINUS, PETRUS
    (fl. 13th cent.) [French
    scientist and soldier]
    Peter de Mariacourt
    Peter the Pilgrim
PEREIRA, D. NUNO ÁLVAREZ
    (1360-1431) [First con-
    stable of Portugal]
    The Portuguese Cid
PEREIRA, HAROLD BERTRAM
    (1890-) [British
    journalist and author]
    Hussaini Muhammad Askari
    Mabel Yeates
Perelman, Cultured. See:
    SHULMAN, MAX
PERELMAN, JACOB PINCUS
    (1904-) [American
    singer]
    Jan Peerce
PERETTI, FELICE (1521-90)
    [Supreme Pontiff of
    Roman Catholic Church]
    Pope Sixtus V
Perfect Cure, The. See:
    STEAD, JAMES HENRY
Perfect Fool, The. See:
    LEOPOLD, ISAIAH
    EDWIN
Perfect Prince, The. See:
    JOHN II
Perfect Publisher, The. See:
    KNOPF, ALFRED A.
Perfect, The. See:
    JOHN II
PERGA. See:
    APOLLONIUS OF PERGA
PERIANDER. See:
    Seven Sages of Greece,
    The
Perier, François. See:
    PILU, FRANÇOIS
Period, The Greatest Writer
    of the Restoration. See:
    DRYDEN, JOHN
PERKINS, CHARLES NELSON
    (1936-) [Australian

civil rights activist and
    social welfare director]
    Australia's Martin Luther King
Perkins, Eli. See:
    LANDON, MELVILLE DE
    LANCEY
Perkins, Faith. See:
    BRAMER, JENNIE
    PERKINS
PERKINS, FRANCES (1882-1965)
    [American public official;
    Secretary of Labor under
    President FRANKLIN
    DELANO ROOSEVELT]
    Fearless Francess
    The Loquatious Linguist Whom
    Labor Loves
    The Liberal Politician
PERKINS, GEORGE DOUGLAS
    (1840-1914) [American
    editor and politician;
    congressman from Iowa]
    Uncle George
PERKINS, GEORGE WALBRIDGE
    (1862-1920) [American
    banker and politician]
    The Dough Moose
PERKINS, JUSTIN (1805-69)
    [American Congregationalist
    missionary to Persia]
    The Apostle of Persia
PERKINS, THOMAS HANDASYD
    (1764-1854) [American
    merchant; personal friend
    of DANIEL WEBSTER]
    Long Tom Perkins
Perley. See:
    POORE, BENJAMIN PER-
    LEY
Perpetual Adolescent of American
    Poetry, The. See:
    POUND, EZRA LOOMIS
Perpetual Candidate, The. See:
    CLEVELAND, STEPHEN
    GROVER
Perpetual Secretary, The. See:
    THOMPSON, CHARLIE
PERREAU-SAUSSINE, GHISLAINE
    (1941-) [American motion
    picture actress]
    Gigi Perreau
PERREN. See:

PETERS (PERRERS)
(PIERCE) (PERREN),
ALICE
PERRERS. See:
PETERS (PERRERS)
(PIERCE) (PERREN),
ALICE
PERRIN, JEANNINE (1926-)
[American jazz musician
(singer, piano)]
Mimi
PERRINE, WILLIAM (fl. 1896-
1921) [American news-
paper columnist]
Penn
Perron, General. See:
AULLIER, PIERRE
Perry. See:
COMO, PIERINO
Perry, Captain William B.
See:
BROWN, WILLIAM
PERRY
PERRY, CLAIR WILLARD
(1887-) [American
author]
Clay Perry
Perry, Edgar A., See:
POE, EDGAR ALLAN
PERRY, FREDERICK JOHN
(1909-) [English tennis
player]
Fred Perry
Perry, Harry Dennies. See:
INGRAHAM,
COLONEL PRENTISS
PERRY, LINCOLN (1902-)
[American Negro motion
picture comedian]
Stepin Fetchit
Perry Lindsay. See:
DERN, PEGGY
GADDIS
PERRY, MARTIN HENRY
(1903-) [English author]
Henry Martyn
Perry, Oliver. See: MORTON
OLIVER HAZARD
PERRY THROCK
PERRY, OLIVER HAZARD
(1785-1819) [American
naval officer]
The Hero of Lake Erie

Perse. See also:
PERSSE
Perse, Saint-John. See:
LEGER, MARIE-RENÉ
ALEXIS SAINT-LEGER
Persecutor, The. See:
RAWSON, EDWARD
Perseus, Peter. See:
THACKERAY, WILLIAM
MAKEPEACE
PERSHING, JOHN JOSEPH
(1860-1958) [American
general officer; Chief of
A.E.F. and Chief of Staff]
Black Jack Pershing
Persia, The Anacreon of. See:
SHAMS UD-DIN
MOHAMMED
Persia, The Apostle of. See:
PERKINS, JUSTIN
Persia, The Homer of. See:
MANSUR, ABDUL QASIM
(HASAN)
Persis. See:
HAIME, AGNES IRVINE
CONSTANCE ADAMS
Person of Honour, A. See:
SOUTHLAND, T.
SWIFT, JONATHAN
Person of Quality, A. See:
SWIFT, JONATHAN
Personne. See:
FONTAINE, FELIX
GREGORY DE
PERSONS, TRUMAN
STRECKFUS (1924-)
[American author]
Truman Capote
Perspicuous Doctor, The Plain
and. See:
BURLEIGH (BURLEY),
WALTER
PERSSE. See also:
Perse
PERSSE, ISABELLA AUGUSTA
(1852-1932) [Irish play-
wright and author]
Lady Augusta Gregory
Perth, The Fair Maid of. See:
GLOVER, CATHERINE
Pertinax Particular. See:
WATKINS, TOBIAS
Peru, The Apostle of. See:

BARCENA (BARZENA),
ALONSO DE
Perucho. See:
GARCÍA, FRANCISCO
Perugino (The Peruvian). See:
VANNUCCI, PIETRO
Peruvian, The (Perugino). See:
VANNUCCI, PIETRO
Pesarese, Il. See:
CANTARINI, SIMONE
Pesaro, The Swan of. See:
ROSSINI, GIOACHINO
ANTONIO
PESHKOV, ALEKSI MAKSIMO-
VICH (1868-1936) [Russian
novelist]
Maxim Gorky
Pet Marjorie. See:
FLEMING, MARGARET
Pet of the Palace, The. See:
STRATTON, CHARLES
SHERWOOD
Pet, The Paratrooper. See:
KAUMEYER, DOROTHY
Pet, The Petticoat. See:
VAN BUREN, MARTIN
Pet, The White House. See:
O'DAY, CAROLINE
GOODWIN
Pete. See:
ALEXANDER, GROVER
CLEVELAND
BROWN, JAMES OSTEND
CANDOLI, WALTER
JOSEPH
FOX, ERVIN
LONGSTREET, JAMES
MANION, CLYDE
JENNINGS
PIERPONT, HARRY
ROZELLE, ALVAN RAY
SEEGER, PETER
Pete, Devil. See:
MUHLENBERG, JOHN
PETER GABRIEL
Pete, Hard-headed. See:
STUYVESANT, PETER
Pete Jolly. See:
CERAGIOLI, PETER A.
Pete La Rocca. See:
SIMS, PETER
Pete, Little. See:

FUNG JING TOY
Pete, Old. See:
LONGSTREET, JAMES
Pete, Pistol. See:
MARAVICH, PETER
Pete Williams. See:
FAULKNOR, CLIFFORD
VERNON
Peter. See:
DALZEL, JOB PATRICK
PALMER, ELSIE PAVITT
PEDRO (PETER)
Stevens, Peter
TARENTAISE, PETER OF
PETER (died c. 64) [Apostle of
JESUS CHRIST; first
Supreme Pontiff of Roman
Catholic Church]
Kepha (Petros) (Rock)
Pope Peter
St. Peter
Simon
Simon Peter
PETER (c. 1050-c. 1115) [French
monk; leader of the First
Crusade]
Peter of Amiens
Peter the Hermit
PETER (fl. 1812) [Calabrian
robber chief]
The Emperor of the Mountains
PETER I (1672-1725) [Czar of
Russia]
Peter the Great
PETER I (1844-1921) [King of
Serbia and King of the
Serbs, Croats and
Slovenes]
Karageorgevich
PETER III (1728-62) [Czar
of Russia]
Pĕtr Feodorovich
Peter Arno. See:
PETERS, CURTIS ARNOUX
Peter Ash. See:
HAUCK, LOUISE PLATT
Peter Atall, Esq. See:
WALN, ROBERT
Peter Bannon. See:
DURST, PAUL
Peter Boylston. See:
CURTIS, GEORGE TICKNOR

Peter Brand. See:
    LARSEN, ERLING
Peter Cagney. See:
    WINTER, BEVIS
Peter Canisius Van Lierde.
    See: VAN LIERDE,
    JOHN
Peter Capon. See:
    OAKLEY, ERIC
    GILBERT
Peter Chambers. See:
    PHILLIPS, DENNIS
    JOHN ANDREW
Peter Chester. See:
    PHILLIPS, DENNIS
    JOHN ANDREW
Peter Cheyney. See:
    SOUTHOUSE-CHEYNEY,
    REGINALD EVELYN
    PETER
Peter Collinson. See:
    HAMMETT, SAMUEL
    DASHIELL
Peter Coon. See:
    BERNARD, PIERRE A.
Peter Cotes. See:
    BOULTING, SYDNEY
Peter Crumpet. See:
    BUCKLEY, FERGUS
    REID
Peter Curtis. See:
    LOFTS, NORAH
    ROBINSON
Peter Darien. See:
    BASSETT, WILLIAM
    B.K.
Peter Dawson. See:
    FAUST, FREDERICK
    SCHILLER
Peter de Mariacourt. See:
    PEREGRINUS, PETRUS
Peter de Morny. See:
    WYNNE-TYSON, ESME
Peter Farmer. See:
    LLOYD, JOHN
    IVESTER
Peter Fenwick. See:
    HOLMES, PETER
    FENWICK
Peter Gordon. See:
    WILKES-HUNTER,
    RICHARD

Peter Graves. See:
    ARNESS, PETER
Peter Grievous, Esq. See:
    HOPKINSON, FRANCIS
Peter Hardin. See:
    VACZEK, LOUIS
Peter, Headstrong. See:
    STUYVESANT, PETER
Peter Henry Moreland. See:
    FAUST, FREDERICK
    SCHILLER
Peter Hermanns. See:
    BRANNON, WILLIAM T.
Peter Lind Hayes. See:
    LIND, JOSEPH CONRAD
Peter Locke. See:
    McCUTCHAN, JOHN
    WILSON
Peter, Long. See:
    AARTSEN, PETER
Peter Loring. See:
    SHELLABARGER, SAMUEL
Peter Lum. See:
    CROWE, BETTINA LUM
Peter Maitland. See:
    MACGILLIVRAY, JAMES
    PITTENDRIGH
Peter Malin. See:
    CONNOR, PATRICK
    REARDON
Peter Malloch. See:
    DUNCAN, WILLIAM MURDOCH
Peter Mannigan. See:
    MONGER, IFOR DAVID
Peter Manton. See:
    CREASEY, JOHN
Peter Martin. See:
    WATERMAN, NIXON
Peter Martyr. See:
    ANGHIERA, PIETRO
    MARTIRE
    MARTYR, PETER
    VERMIGLI, PIETRO
    MARTIRE
Peter Meadows. See:
    LINDSAY, JACK
Peter Morris. See:
    LOCKHART, JOHN GIBSON
Peter Mortimer. See:
    ROBERTS, DOROTHY
    JAMES
Peter Northcote. See:

BOULTING, SYDNEY
Peter Oberholtzer. See:
    BRANNON, WILLIAM T.
Peter Oboe. See:
    JACOBS, WALTER
    DARNELL
Peter of Mantua. See:
    GUARNIERI, PIETRO
    GIOVANNI
PETER OF PAVIA (died 984)
    [Supreme Pontiff of
    Roman Catholic Church]
    Pope John XIV
Peter of Venice. See:
    GUARNIERI, PIETRO
Peter Oldfield. See:
    BARTLETT, VERNON
Peter Ott. See:
    VON HILDEBRAND,
    DIETRICH
Peter Pace. See:
    BURNETT, DAVID
Peter Pan. See:
    BARTIER, PIERRE
Peter Parley. See:
    GOODRICH, SAMUEL
    GRISWOLD
    KETTELL, SAMUEL
    MARTIN, WILLIAM
    MOGRIDGE, GEORGE
Peter Paul Turner. See:
    JEFFERY, GRANT
Peter Pennot, Reverend. See:
    ROUND, WILLIAM
    MARSHALL FITTS
Peter Pepper Box. See:
    FESSENDEN, THOMAS
    GREEN
Peter Peppercorn. See:
    PEACOCK, THOMAS
    LOVE
Peter Perseus. See:
    THACKERAY, WILLIAM
    MAKEPEACE
Peter Pindar. See:
    WOLCOT, JOHN
Peter Pinto. See:
    BERNE, ERIC LENNARD
Peter Plymley. See:
    SMITH, SYDNEY
Peter Porcupine. See:
    COBBETT, WILLIAM

Peter Query. See:
    TUPPER, MARTIN
    FARQUHAR
Peter Quince. See:
    DAY, GEORGE HAROLD
    DEXTER, TIMOTHY
    STORY, ISAAC
Peter Rabbit. See:
    LONG, WILLIAM JOSEPH
Peter Reynolds. See:
    HORROCKS, PETER
Peter Richards. See:
    MONGER, IFOR DAVID
Peter Saya. See:
    PETERSON, ROBERT
    EUGENE
Peter Shelley. See:
    DRESSER, DAVIS
Peter Stirling. See:
    STERN, DAVID
Peter Storme. See:
    STERN, PHILIP VAN
    DOREN
Peter the Cruel. See:
    PEDRO (PETER)
Peter the Great of Egypt, The.
    See: MEHEMET
    (MOHAMMED) ALI
Peter the Hermit. See:
    PETER
Peter the Hermit of the Abolition-
    ist Movement. See:
    LUNDY, BENJAMIN
Peter the Paragon. See:
    SWEENEY, PETER BARR
Peter the Pilgrim. See:
    PEREGRINUS, PETRUS
PETER THE WILD BOY (17??-
    85) [German foundling
    "discovered in a wood near
    Hamelin walking on his
    hands and feet and living
    like an animal"]
    The Wild Boy
Peter Underhill. See:
    SODERBERG, PERCY
    MEASDAY
Peter Vernon. See:
    HUDDLESTON, SISLEY
Peter Warlock. See:
    HESELTINE, PHILIP
    ARNOLD

Peter Whitney. See:
ENGLE, PETER KING
PETERMAN, ROBERTA
(1930-) [American
singer]
Roberta Peters
Peters, Caroline. See:
BETZ, EVA KELLY
PETERS, CURTIS ARNOUX
(1904-68) [American
cartoonist]
Curt Arno
Peter Arno
PETERS, DONALD L. (1925-)
[American photographer,
teacher and author]
Leslie Peters
Peters, Ellis. See:
PARGETER, EDITH MARY
PETERS, HUGH (c. 1598-
1660) [English Puritan
clergyman]
The Pulpit Buffoon
PETERS, JANE (1908-42)
[American motion picture
actress]
Carole Lombard
Peters, Lawrence. See:
DAVIES, LESLIE
PURNELL
PETERS (PERRERS) (PIERCE)
(PERREN), ALICE (fl.
14th cent.) [Mistress of
EDWARD III of England]
The Lady of the Sun
PETERS, ROBERT LOUIS
(1925-) [American
author]
Lewis Peters
Peters, Roberta. See:
PETERMAN, ROBERTA
Peters, S. H. See:
PORTER, WILLIAM
SYDNEY
Peters, S. T. See:
BRANNON, WILLIAM T.
Peters, Susan. See:
CARNAHAN, SUZANNE
PETERSON, CORINNA (1923-)
[English author]
Corinna Cochrane
PETERSON, FREDERICK

(1859-1938) [American
neurologist and poet]
Pai Ta-shun
Peterson, James. See:
ZEIGER, HENRY ANTHONY
PETERSON, ROBERT EUGENE
(1928-) [American clergy-
man and author]
Peter Saya
PETIOT DANIEL-ROPS, HENRY
(1901-) [French author]
Daniel-Rops
PETIT, ANNE-MARIE (1938-)
[French motion picture
actress]
Pascale Petit
Petit Caporal, Le (The Little
Corporal). See:
BONAPARTE, NAPOLEON
Petit Homme Rouge, Le. See:
VIZETELLY, ERNEST
ALFRED
Peto. See:
WHITE, JAMES DILLON
Peto, James. See:
WHITE, JAMES DILLON
Pëtr Feodorovich. See:
PETER III
PETRARCH (FRANCESCO
PETRARCA) (1304-74)
[Italian poet and scholar]
The Father of Humanism
PETRARCH (FRANCESCO
PETRARCA). See also:
Great Triumvirate of Italian
Literature, The
Immortal Four of Italy, The
Petrarch of Spain, The. See:
VEGA, GARCILASSO DE LA
Petrarch, The English. See:
SIDNEY (SYDNEY), SIR
PHILIP
Petrarch, The Female. See:
LEWIS, ESTELLE ANNA
BLANCHE ROBINSON
Petrarch, The French. See:
AUBANEL, THÉODORE
Petrarch, The Miniature. See:
BEMBO, PIETRO
Petrarch, The Spanish. See:
VEGA, GARCILASSO DE LA
Petrel, Stormy. See:

CHANDLER, WILLIAM
EATON
Petri Kettenfeier. See:
ROSEGGER, PETER
PETRI, OLAUS (OLAF) (1493-
1552) [Swedish reformer]
The Luther of Sweden
Petroleum V. Nasby. See:
LOCKE, DAVID ROSS
Petroleum Vesuvius Nasby,
Reverend. See:
LOCKE, DAVID ROSS
PETRONE, JANE MUIR
(1929-) [American
author]
Jane Muir
Petronius, Pasquin. See:
RILEY, ISAAC
Petros (Kepha) (Rock). See:
PETER
Petrovitch. See:
ALEXEI (ALEXIS)
Petrus de Alliaco. See:
AILLY, PIERRE D'
Petticoat. See:
ALLEN, WILLIAM
Petticoat Pet, The. See:
VAN BUREN, MARTIN
PETTY, WILLIAM (1623-87)
[English physician, stat-
istician, political econo-
mist and inventor]
The Universal Genius
Peuple, l'Ami du (The Friend
of the People). See:
MARAT, JEAN PAUL
Peuple, Père du (Father of the
People). See:
LOUIS XII
Pezet, Dr. F. See:
ZAUNER, FRANZ PAUL
PEZZA, MICHELE (1760-1806)
[Italian robber and
Bourbon partisan leader]
Fra Diavolo (Brother
Devil)
Pfaal, Hans. See:
POE, EDGAR ALLAN
PFIRMAN, CHARLES H.
(1891-) [American
professional baseball
umpire]
Cy

PFOUTZ, SHIRLEY ECLOV
(1922-) [American author]
Shirley Eclov
PHAREZ, BRANSBY WILLIAM
(1870-1961) [English
music-hall performer]
Bransby Williams
Pharisee, The Academic. See:
BONAPARTE, CHARLES
JOSEPH
Pharaoh. See:
SANDERS, FARRELL
PHELPS, ELIZABETH STEWART
(18??-1920) [American
author]
Leigh North
PHELPS, ELIZABETH STUART
(1815-52) [American
author]
H. Trusta
Phelps, Frederic. See:
McCULLEY, JOHNSTON
Phelps, Mrs. S.B. See:
GRISWOLD, FRANCES
IRENE BURGE
Phenomenal Presiding Elder, The.
See: WILSON, JOHN
ALFRED BAYNUM
Phidias, The French. See:
GOUJON, JEAN
PIGALLE, JEAN BAPTISTE
Phil. See:
BARLING, PHILIP
BRETON, PHILLIPPE
DIKE, PHILIP LATIMER
RIZZUTO, PHILIP FRANCIS
STONG, PHILIP DUFFIELD
Phil Brito. See:
COLOMBRITO, PHILIP
Phil Kearny, Dashing. See:
KEARNY, PHILIP
Phil, Little. See:
SHERIDAN, PHILIP HENRY
THOMPSON, PHILIP
BURTON, JR.
Phil, Old. See:
THOMPSON, PHILIP
BURTON, SR.
Phil, One-armed. See:
KEARNY, PHILIP
Phil Silvers. See:
SILVERSMITH, PHILIP
Phil, Sleepy. See:

KNOX, PHILANDER CHASE
Phil Squires. See:
    BARKER, S. OMAR
Phil Stanley. See:
    IND, ALLISON
Philadelphia. See:
    MEYER, JACOB
Philadelphia, A Citizen of. See:
    CAREY, MATHEW
Philadelphia, A Lady of. See:
    BOTSFORD, MARGARET
Philadelphia, The Father of
    Greater. See:
    BULLITT, JOHN
    CHRISTIAN
Philadelphia's Jean Valjean.
    See: BURKE, WILLIAM
Philadelphus. See:
    ATTALUS II
Philadelphus (The Brotherly).
    See: PTOLEMY II
Philander Doesticks, P. B.,
    Q. K. See:
    THOMSON, MORTIMER
    NEAL
Philenia. See:
    MORTON, SARAH
    WENTWORTH APTHORP
Philidor. See:
    DANICAN, FRANÇOIS
    ANDRÉ
Philip. See:
    MAGNUS-ALLCROFT,
    SIR PHILIP
PHILIP (fl. 1st cent. A.D.)
    [Deacon and preacher of
    the early Christian
    church]
    The Evangelist
PHILIP (1180?-1208) [Holy
    Roman Emperor and
    King of Germany]
    Philip of Swabia
PHILIP (1342-1404) [Founder of
    the last ducal house of
    Burgundy]
    The Bold
PHILIP (1396-1467) [Duke of
    Burgundy]
    The Good
PHILIP I (204-49) [Roman
    emperor]
    The Arabian

PHILIP I (1478-1506) [King of
    Castile]
    The Handsome
PHILIP II (382-336 B.C.)
    [King of Macedon]
    Philip of Macedon
PHILIP II (1165-1223)
    [King of France]
    Philip Augustus
PHILIP III (1245-85) [King of
    France]
    The Bold
PHILIP IV (1268-1314) [King of
    France]
    The Fair
PHILIP V (1294?-1322) [King of
    France]
    The Tall
PHILIP V (1683-1746) [King of
    Spain]
    Philip Baboon
Philip A. Bartlett. See:
    STRATEMEYER,
    EDWARD L.
Philip Ben. See:
    BARLING, PHILIP
Philip Dorn. See:
    VAN DUNGEN, FRITZ
Philip Embey. See:
    PHILIPP, ELLIOT ELIAS
Philip Francis. See:
    LOCKYER, ROGER
PHILIP, JOHN (1775-1851)
    [English Congregational
    missionary to South Africa]
    The Liberator of Africa
Philip Kent. See:
    BULMER, HENRY KENNETH
Philip, King. See:
    METACOM (METACOMET)
PHILIP OF HESSE (1504-67)
    [Landgrave of Hesse]
    The Magnanimous
Philip Paxton. See:
    HAMMETT, SAMUEL
    ADAMS
Philip Quilibet. See:
    POND, GEORGE EDWARD
Philip St. Clair. See:
    HOWARD, MUNROE
Philip Slingsby. See:
    WILLIS, NATHANIEL
    PARKER

Philip Spring. See:
DOBSON, E. PHILIP
Philip the King. See:
MARSTON, PHILIP
BOURKE
Philip Weston. See:
DE FILIPPI, AMEDEO
Philip Woodruff. See:
MASON, PHILIP
PHILIPP, ELLIOT ELIAS
(1915-) [British
physician and author]
Philip Embey
Victor Tempest
Philipp Galen. See:
LANGE, ERNST PHILIPP
KARL
Philippa Shore. See:
HOLBECHE, PHILIPPA
JACK
PHILIPPE. See:
LOUIS PHILIPPE
Philippe Égalité. See:
JOSEPH, LOUIS
PHILIPPE
Philippe, The American Louis.
See: FILLMORE,
MILLARD
PHILIPPI, JOHANNES (c. 1506-
56) [German historian]
Johannes Sleidanus
The Protestant Livy
Philippi, Mark. See:
BENDER, ARNOLD
Philippus Aureolus Paracelsus.
See: VON HOHENHEIM,
THEOPHRASTUS
BOMBASTUS
PHILIPS, AMBROSE
(1675?-1749) [English
poet and dramatist]
Namby Pamby
PHILIPS, KATHERINE (c. 1634-
64) [English poet]
An English Sappho
The Matchless Orinda
PHILIPS, MARDIN WILSON
(1806-89) [American
author, reformer and
agriculturist]
Log Hall Philips
The Sage of Log Hall

Philips, Thomas. See:
DAVIES, LESLIE PURNELL
PHILIPSE, FREDERICK (1626-
1702) [Dutch-American
millionaire]
The Dutch Millionaire
PHILLIPS, ALAN MEYRICK
KERR (1916-) [British
soldier, government of-
ficial and author]
Mickey Phillips
PHILLIPS, ALFRED NOROTON,
JR. (1894-) [American
manufacturer and politician;
congressman from Con-
necticut]
Milk of Magnesia Phillips
PHILLIPS-BIRT, DOUGLAS
(1920-) [British naval
architect and author]
Argus
David Hextall
Douglas Hogarth
PHILLIPS, DAVID GRAHAM
(1867-1911) [American
novelist]
John Graham
PHILLIPS, DENNIS JOHN
ANDREW (1924-)
[British author]
Peter Chambers
Peter Chester
Phillips, Esther. See:
JONES, ESTHER MAY
Phillips, Jack. See:
SANDBURG, CARL AUGUST
Phillips, John. See:
MARQUAND, JOHN
PHILLIPS
PHILLIPS, JOSEPH EDWARD
(1915-) [American jazz
musician (tenor saxophone)]
Flip Phillips
Phillips, Mark, joint pseud. of
LAURENCE MARK JANIFER
(fl. 1959-63) and RANDALL
GARRETT (fl. 1959-63)
[American authors]
Phillips, Mark. See also:
JANIFER, LAURENCE
MARK
PHILLIPS, MAURICE JACK

800

(1914-) [American
editor and author]
Mac Phillips
Phillips, Michael. See:
    NOLAN, WILLIAM
    FRANCIS
PHILLIPS, PAULINE ESTHER
    FRIEDMAN (1918-)
    [American newspaper
    columnist and author]
Abigail Van Buren
Dear Abby
Poppo
Phillips Rogers. See:
    IDELL, ALBERT E.
Phillips, Steve. See:
    WHITTINGTON, HARRY
PHILLIPS, TULLY MARSHALL
    (1864-1943) [American
    stage and motion picture
    actor]
Tully Marshall
PHILLIPS, WALTER SHELLEY
    (1867-1940) [American
    artist and writer]
El Comancho
Wi-chash-ta-Ish-nah-nah
PHILLPOTTS, EDEN
    (1862-1960) [English
    novelist and dramatist]
Harrington Hext
Philly Joe. See:
    JONES, JOSEPH
    RUDOLPH
PHILO JUDAEUS (c. 20 B.C. -
    after 40 A.D.) [Hellenistic
    Jewish philosopher of
    Alexandria]
The Jewish Plato
Philo of Alexandria
Philo of Alexandria. See:
    PHILO JUDAEUS
Philodicaius. See:
    YOUNG, THOMAS
Philomath. See:
    FRANKLIN, BENJAMIN
Philometor. See:
    ATTALUS III
    DEMETRIUS III
    PTOLEMY VI
Philomusus. See:
    LOCHER, JACOB

Philopator (Loving his Father).
    See: PTOLEMY IV
Philopator Neos Dionysos.
    See: PTOLEMY XI
Philopator, New (Loving his
    Father). See:
    PTOLEMY VII
Philopator Philometer Caesar.
    See: PTOLEMY XIV
Philopatrius. See:
    DOVE, DAVID JAMES
PHILOPOEMEN (c. 252-183 B.C.)
    [General officer of the
    Achaena League]
The Last of the Greeks
Philosophe des Dames, Le. See:
    CARO, ELME MARIE
Philosopher About the Business
    Scene We Have, The Most
    Helpful. See:
    DRUCKER, PETER FERD-
    INAND
Philosopher, America's Fore-
    most Speculative. See:
    WEISS, PAUL
Philosopher of China, The. See:
    CONFUCIUS
Philosopher of Democracy, The.
    See: JEFFERSON, THOMAS
Philosopher of Ferney, The. See:
    AROUET, FRANÇOIS
    MARIE
Philosopher of Librarianship.
    See: RANGANATHAN,
    SHIYALI RAMAMRITA
Philosopher of Malmesbury, The.
    See: HOBBES, THOMAS
Philosopher of Sans Souci, The.
    See: FREDERICK II
Philosopher of the Arabs, The.
    See: KINDI, AL (ABU
    YŪSUF YA IQUB IBN-
    ISHAQ AL-KINDI)
Philosopher of Wimbledon, The.
    See: HORNE, JOHN
Philosopher, The. See:
    BENTHAM, JEREMY
    CONSTANTINE
    EDWARD (EADWARD)
    LEO VI
    SENECA, MARCUS LUCIUS
    ANNAEUS

SORRELL, VICTOR
GARLAND
Philosopher, The Chelsea. See:
CARLYLE, THOMAS
Philosopher, The Cowboy. See:
ROGERS, WILLIAM PENN
ADAIR
Philosopher, The Dark. See:
HERACLITUS
Philosopher, The First Russian.
See: SOLOVIEV,
VLADIMIR
Philosopher, The Laughing.
See: DEMOCRITUS
Philosopher, The Political. See:
SMITH, THOMAS VERNON
Philosopher, The Unknown. See:
ST. MARTIN, LOUIS-
CLAUDE DE
Philosopher, The Weeping. See:
HERACLITUS
Philosophers, The God of all.
See: CICERO, MARCUS
TULLIUS
Philosophers, The Homer of. See:
ARISTOCLES
Philosophers, The Prince of.
See: ARISTOCLES
Philosophy. See:
SMITH, THOMAS
VERNON
Philosophy, Founder of the
Utilitarian School of. See:
CUMBERLAND, RICHARD
Philosophy, The Father of. See:
BACON, ROGER
VON HALLER, ALBRECHT
Philosophy, The Father of
Modern. See:
DESCARTES, RENÉ
Philosophy, The Father of
Roman. See:
CICERO, MARCUS TULLIUS
Philosophy, The Founder of
the Critical. See:
KANT, IMMANUEL
Philroye, Humphrey. See:
STEELE, SIR RICHARD
Phineas Beck. See:
CHAMBERLAIN, SAMUEL
Phinn E. Lapide. See:
LAPIDE, PINCHAS E.

PHIPPS, JOYCE (1910-   )
[British comedienne and
motion picture actress]
Joyce Grenfell
Phipps, Margaret. See:
TATHAM, LAURA ESTHER
Phipson, Joan. See:
FITZHARDINGE, JOAN
MARGARET
PHISTERER, FREDERICK
(1836-1909) [German-
American politician; active
in establishing New York
state militia]
The Father of the National
Guard of New York
Phiz. See:
BROWNE, HABLOT KNIGHT
Phlogobombos, Terentius. See:
JUDAH, SAMUEL BEN-
JAMIN HELBERT
Phoebus. See:
GASTON
Phoenix, John. See:
DERBY, GEORGE HORATIO
MAYLEM, JOHN
Phonograph, The Father of the.
See: EDISON, THOMAS
ALVA
Photography, The Father of.
See: TALBOT, WILLIAM
HENRY FOX
Photography, The Father of
Modern Aerial. See:
GODDARD, GEORGE
WILLIAM
Phra. See:
ARNOLD, EDWIN LESTER
Phrasemaker. See:
WILSON, THOMAS
WOODROW
Phryne. See:
MNESARETE
Phyllis Ann Carter. See:
EBERLE, IRMENGARDE
Phyllis Calvert. See:
BICKLE, PHYLLIS
Phyllis Curtin. See:
SMITH, PHYLLIS
Phyllis Fairbanks. See:
LANDESBERG,
PHYLLIS G.

Phyllis Kirk. See:
    KIRKEGAARD, PHYLLIS
Phyllis Richards. See:
    AUTY, PHYLLIS
Physcon (Fat Paunch). See:
    PTOLEMY VII (or VIII
    or IX)
Physician, The Beloved. See:
    LUKE, ST.
Physician, The Good. See:
    HIGBEE, CHESTER
    GOSS
Physician's Physician, The.
    See: DA COSTA,
    JACOB MENDEZ
Physicians, The Prince of.
    See: AVICENNA
Physicist of the Nineteenth
    Century, The Greatest
    Theoretical. See:
    MAXWELL, JAMES
    CLERK
Physick and Astronomy,
    Student in. See:
    AMES, NATHANIEL
PHYSICK, PHILIP SYNG
    (1768-1857) [American
    surgeon]
    The Father of American
    Surgery
Physics, The Father of
    American Experimental.
    See: ROOD, OGDEN
    NICHOLAS
Physiography, The Father of
    the Science of. See:
    DAVIS, WILLIAM MORRIS
Physiology, The Father of.
    See: VON HALLER,
    ALBRECHT
Physiology, The Father of
    Experimental. See:
    GALEN
Piaf, Edith. See:
    GASSION, EDITH
    GIOVANNA
Pianner Kid, The. See:
    LOPEZ, VINCENT
"Piano" Miller, Eddie. See:
    LISBONA, EDWARD
PIATT, JOHN JAMES. See:
    Wedded Poets, The.

PIATT, SARAH MORGAN BRYAN.
    See: Wedded Poets, The
Picasso, Fashion's. See:
    BALENCIAGA, CRISTOBAL
PICASSO, PABLO RUIZ Y
    (1881-) [Spanish painter
    and sculptor]
    The Father of Cubism
PICCOLIMINI, ENEA SILVIO
    DE (1405-64) [Supreme
    Pontiff of Roman Catholic
    Church]
    Pope Pius II
    Aeneas Silvius
PICCOLOMINI, FRANCESCO
    TODESCHINI DE' (1439-
    1503) [Supreme Pontiff of
    Roman Catholic Church]
    Pope Pius III
Pickelherring. See:
    REYNOLDS, ROBERT
PICKENS, ANDREW (1739-1817)
    [American general officer]
    Skyagunsta
    The Wizard of Tomassee
Pickens, Slim. See:
    LINDLEY, LOUIS BERT
Pickering, Percival. See:
    STIRLING, ANNA MARIA
    DIANA WILHELMINA
    PICKERING
Pickford, Gladys. See:
    SMITH, GLADYS MARY
Pickford, Mary. See:
    SMITH, GLADYS MARY
Pickford of this War, The Mary.
    See: KAUMEYER, DOROTHY
Pickle, Peregrine. See:
    UPTON, GEORGE PUTNAM
Pickle the Spy. See:
    MACDONNELL, ALASTAIR
    RUADH
PICKLES, MABEL ELIZABETH
    (1902-) [British
    teacher, musician and
    author]
    Elizabeth Burgoyne
Pickwick. See:
    DICKENS, CHARLES JOHN
    HUFFAM
Picton, Thomas. See:
    MILNER, THOMAS PICTON

Picts, The Apostle of the.
See: NINIAN, ST.
Picture Industry, The Dynamo
of the Italian Motion.
See: LAURENTIS, DINO
DE
Picture Industry, The Garibaldi of
the Italian Motion. See:
LAURENTIS, DINO DE
Picture Industry, The Kingfish
of the Italian Motion. See:
LAURENTIS, DINO DE
Picture-maker's Picture-maker.
See: CAPRA, FRANK
Picturesque Explorer of the
United States, The. See:
LANMAN, CHARLES
Pie. See:
TRAYNOR, HAROLD JOSEPH
Piecrust. See:
PALMER, JAMES
SHEDDEN
Pied Piper of Contentment,
The. See:
COUÉ, ÉMILE
Pier Angeli. See:
PIERANGELI, ANNA
MARIA
PIERALISI, VIRNA (1937-)
[Italian motion picture
actress]
Virna Lisi
PIERANGELI, ANNA MARIA
(1932-) [Italian motion
picture actress]
Pier Angeli
Marisa Pavan
PIERCE. See:
PEARCE
Pearce
Peerce
PETERS (PERRERS)
(PIERCE) (PERREN),
ALICE
PIERCE, FRANKLIN (1804-69)
[Fourteenth President of
the United States]
Handsome Frank
Purse
Pierce, Jo. See:
MANNING, WILLIAM
HENRY

MORRIS, CHARLES
SMITH
PIERCE, JOHN ROBINSON
(1910-) [American
scientist and author]
J. J. Coupling
PIERCE, JOSEPH DE
LACROIS (1904-)
[American jazz musician
(trumpet, cornet)]
Dede
Pierce, Katherine. See:
ST. JOHN, WYLLY FOLK
Pierce Pungent. See:
POWELL, THOMAS
Piermarini. See:
MARCHESE, MALACRIDA
Piero Della Francesca. See:
FRANCHESI, PIERO DEI
Piero di Lorenzo. See:
COSIMO, PIERO DI
Piero the Gouty. See:
MEDICI, PIERO DE'
PIERPONT, HARRY (1906-34)
[American bank robber
and outlaw]
Pete
Pierre, Abbé. See:
GROUÈS, HENRI ANTOINE
Pierre Chenal. See:
COHEN, PIERRE
Pierre Coalfleet. See:
DAVISON, FRANK CYRIL
Pierre Costello. See:
HOSKEN, ERNEST CHARLES
HEATH
Pierre Dufour. See:
LACROIX, PAUL
Pierre d'Urstelle. See:
DORST, JEAN PIERRE
Pierre Fresnay. See:
LAUDENBACH, PIERRE-
JULES
Pierre Hamp. See:
BOURILLON, PIERRE
Pierre le Grand. See:
FRANÇOIS, PIERRE
Pierre Loti. See:
VIAUD, LOUIS MARIE
JULIEN
Pierre Norman Connor. See:
CONNOR, REV. JOSEPH P.

Pierre-Paul Prud'hon. See:
    PRUDON, PIERRE
Pierrot. See:
    ARNOLD, GEORGE
Piers Anthony. See:
    JACOB, PIERS
        ANTHONY DILLING-
        HAM
Piet Mondrian. See:
    MONDRIAAN, PIETER
        CORNELIS
Piet, Tony. See:
    PIETRUSZKA, ANTHONY
        FRANCIS
Pieter the Elder. See:
    BRUEGHEL (BREUGHEL),
        PIETER
    BURMAN (BURMANN),
        PIETER
Pieter the Younger. See:
    BRUEGHEL (BREUGHEL),
        PIETER
    BURMAN (BURMANN),
        PIETER
Pietism, The Father of.
    See: SPENER,
        PHILIPP JAKOB
PIETRO, BARBO (1417-71)
    [Supreme Pontiff of
    Roman Catholic Church]
    Pope Paul II
PIETRO, GUIDO DI
    (1387-1455) [Italian
    Dominican friar and
    painter of religious sub-
    jects]
    Fra Angelico
    Giovanni da Fiesole
Pietro Laurati. See:
    LORENZETTI, PIETRO
PIETRUSZKA, ANTHONY
    FRANCIS (1907-)
    [American professional
    baseball player]
    Tony Piet
    Tony the Silent
    Whitey
Pieux, Le (The Pious). See:
    LOUIS I
Piffoël, Doctor. See:
    DUDEVANT, AMANDINE
        AURORE LUCIE
        DUPIN, "BARONNE"

Pig Iron. See:
    KELLEY, WILLIAM
        DARRAGH
PIGALLE, JEAN BAPTISTE
    (1714-85) [French sculptor]
    The French Phidias
PIGNATELLI, ANTONIO
    (1615-1700) [Supreme
    Pontiff of Roman Catholic
    Church]
    Pope Innocent XII
PIKE, ALBERT (1809-91)
    [American lawyer, soldier
    and author]
    Casca
PIKE, MARY HAYDEN GREEN
    (1824-1908) [American novelist]
    Mary Langdon
    Sydney A. Story, Jr.
Pike, Robert L. See:
    FISH, ROBERT L.
PILCHER, ROSAMUNDE (1924-)
    [British author]
    Jane Fraser
Pilgrim, Anne. See:
    ALLAN, MABEL ESTHER
Pilgrim Bard, The. See:
    CUMMINGS, SCOTT
Pilgrim, David. See:
    Beeding, Francis
Pilgrim, Derel. See:
    KANTO, PETER
Pilgrim, Peter the. See:
    PEREGRINUS, PETRUS
Pilgrim, Symus the. See:
    COBB, SYLVANUS, JR.
Pilio, Gerone. See:
    WHITFIELD, JOHN
        HUMPHREYS
Pilkington, Cynthia. See:
    HORNE, CYNTHIA MIRIAM
Pillar of the Constitution, The.
    See: WEBSTER, DANIEL
Pillar of the Doctors, The. See:
    CHAMPEAUX, GUILLAUME
        DE
Pillar Saints, The Father of the.
    See: STYLITES, SIMEON
PILLEY, CHARLES (1885-)
    [British barrister and
    author]
    Guy Pearce
PILLSBURY, JOHN SARGENT

(1828-1901) [American
milling executive and
politician; Governor of
Minnesota]
The Father of the University
of Minnesota
Pilnyak, Boris. See:
VOGAU, BORIS
ANDREYEVICH
Pilot, A Fighter. See:
JOHNSON, HUGH
ANTHONY STEPHEN
Pilot in the World, Bar None,
The Greatest. See:
BALCHEN, BERNT
Pilot of the Mississippi, The
Master. See:
CLEMENS, SAMUEL
LANGHORNE
Pilot that Weathered the Storm,
the. See:
PITT, WILLIAM
Pilot, The Lightning. See:
BIXBY, HORACE EZRA
PILU, FRANÇOIS (1919-)
[French motion picture
actor]
François Perier
Pinchbeck Lyre. See:
SASSOON, SIEGFRIED
LORAINE
PINCHERLE, ALBERTO
(1907-) [Italian author]
Alberto Moravia
PINCKNEY, CHARLES
(1757-1824) [American
statesman; Governor of
South Carolina]
Blackguard Charlie
PINDAR (c. 552-443 B.C.)
[Greek lyric poet]
The Dircaean Swan
The Theban Bard
The Theban Eagle
The Theban Garden Swan
The Theban Lyre
Pindar, Peter. See:
WOLCOT, JOHN
Pindar, The British. See:
GRAY, THOMAS
Pindar, The French. See:
DINEMANDY (DORAT),
JEAN

Pindar, The Italian. See:
CHIABRERA, GABRIELLO
Pindare, Lebrun. See:
LEBRUN, PONCE-DENIS
ECOUCHARD
Pine, Cuyler. See:
PECK, ELLEN
PINE, LESLIE GILBERT
(1907-) [British editor
and author]
Henry Moorshead
Pine, Tall. See:
SIBLEY, HENRY HASTINGS
Pineapple King, The Hawaiian.
See: DOLE, JAMES
DRUMMOND
Pines, Walker in the. See:
SIBLEY, HENRY HASTINGS
Pinetop. See:
SMITH, CLARENCE
Pink Whiskers. See:
LEWIS, JAMES
HAMILTON
PINKERTON, ALLAN (1819-84)
[Scottish-American
detective]
The Eye
PINKERTON, WILLIAM A.
(1846-1923) [American
detective]
Big Bill Pinkerton
PINKETHMAN. See:
PENKETHMAN (PINKETH-
MAN), WILLIAM
Pinkey. See:
HARGRAVE, WILLIAM
McKINLEY
PENKETHMAN (PINKETH-
MAN), WILLIAM
WHITNEY, ARTHUR
CARTER
Pinky. See:
HARRINGTON, FRANCIS C.
TOMLIN, TRUMAN
VIDACOVICH, I. J.
Pinner Miser, The. See:
DANCER, DANIEL
Pinocchio. See:
JAMES, CORNELIUS
PINTARD, JOHN (1759-1844)
[Founder of the Massachu-
setts Historical Society]
The Father of Historical

Societies in America
PINTER, HAROLD (1930-   )
[English playwright]
David Baron
PINTER, JOSEPH (1904-41)
[Hungarian-American
radio comedian]
Joe Penner
PINTO, FERÑAO MENDES
(c.1509-83) [Portuguese
adventurer and traveler]
The Prince of Liars
PINTO, JACQUELINE HARRIS
(1927-   ) [English
author]
Jacqueline Blairman
Pinto, Peter. See:
BERNE, ERIC LENNARD
Pinturicchio. See:
BETTI, BERNARDINO DI
PINZA, FORTUNATO (1893-
1957) [Italian opera singer
and motion picture actor]
Ezio Pinza
Pious. See also:
PIUS
Pius
Pious John. See:
WANAMAKER, JOHN
Pious Schoolmaster of Skippack,
The. See:
DOCK, CHRISTOPHER
Pious, The. See:
ALBERT IV
ALBRECHT
EDWARD VI
FREDERICK III
LOTHAIR I
LOUIS VII
ROBERT II
WILLIAM I
Pious, The (Le Pieux). See:
LOUIS I
PIOZZI, HESTER LYNCH
SALUSBURY (1741-1821)
[English writer; close
friend of DR.
SAMUEL JOHNSON]
Mrs. Thrale
Pip Pepperpod. See:
STODDARD, CHARLES
WARREN
Pipe-Line. See:

DISNEY, WESLEY ERNEST
Piper Laurie. See:
JACOBS, ROSETTA
Piper of Contentment, The Pied.
See: COUÉ, ÉMILE
Piper, Roger. See:
FISHER, JOHN
Piper, The (Auletes). See:
PTOLEMY XI
PIPER, WILLIAM THOMAS, SR.
(1881-1970) [American
aviation magnate]
The Henry Ford of Aviation
Pipes. See:
WHISTLER, GEORGE
WASHINGTON
PIPPIN. See:
PEPIN (PIPPIN) III
Pirate of the Gulf, The. See:
LAFITTE, JEAN
PISANO, ANDREA (1270-1349)
[Italian sculptor]
Andrea de Pontedera
Pistoia, Cino da. See:
SIGHIBULDI, GUITTONCINO
DEI
Pistol Pete. See:
MARAVICH, PETER
Pistoleers, The Prince of. See:
HICKOCK, JAMES BUTLER
Pit, The Bottomless. See:
PITT, WILLIAM
PITATI, BONIFAZIO DI
(1487-1553) [Italian Renais-
sance painter]
Bonifazio Veneziano
Bonifazio Veronese
PITCHER, EVELYN GOODENOUGH
(1915-   ) [American edu-
cator and author]
Evelyn Goodenough
PITCHER, GLADYS (1890-   )
[American educator, editor,
musician and author]
Betsy Adams
Barbara Wentworth
Ann Weston
Pitcher, Molly. See:
McCAULEY, MARY
LUDWIG HAYS
Pitchfork. See:
TILLMAN, BENJAMIN
RYAN

Pitchfork Ben. See:
TILLMAN, BENJAMIN
RYAN
Pitt, Jeremy. See:
WYNNE-TYSON,
TIMOTHY JON
LYADEN
Pitt Stadium, The Father of.
See: HAMILTON,
ALFRED REED
Pitt, The American. See:
STEVENS, THADDEUS
PITT, WILLIAM (1708-78)
[English statesman; Earl
of Chatham]
The British Cicero
The Distressed Statesman
The Elder Pitt
The Grand Old Man
The Great Commoner
The Napoleon of Oratory
The People's Will
The People's William
PITT, WILLIAM (1759-1806)
[English statesman]
The Bottomless Pit
The Heaven-sent Minister
The Pilot that Weathered the
Storm
The Younger Pitt
PITT, WILLIAM. See also:
Wondrous Three, The
PITTACUS. See:
Seven Sages of Greece,
The
PITTMAN, KEY (1872-1940)
[American miner,
politician and senator
from Nevada]
The Voice of Silver
PITTS, ZASU (1898-1963)
[American motion picture
actress]
The Girl With the Ginger
Snap Name
Pittsburgh Candy King, The.
See: CLARK, DAVID
LYTLE
Pittsburgh, The Father of.
See: WASHINGTON,
GEORGE
Pittsfield, The Sage of. See:
DAWES, HENRY LAURENS

PIUS [Pius]. See also:
Pious
PIUS (died c. 155) [Supreme
Pontiff of Roman Catholic
Church]
Pope Pius I
St. Pius
Pius II, Pope. See:
PICCOLOMINI, ENEA SIL-
VIO DE
Pius III, Pope. See:
PICCOLOMINI, FRANCES-
CO TODESCHINI DE'
Pius IV, Pope. See:
MEDICI, GIOVANNI
ANGELO
Pius V, Pope. See:
GHISLIERI, MICHELE
Pius VI, Pope. See:
BRASCHI, GIOVANNI
ANGELO
Pius VII, Pope. See:
CHIARMONTI, LUIGI
BARNABA
Pius VIII, Pope. See:
CASTIGLIONE, FRANCES-
CO XAVERIO
Pius IX, Pope. See:
FERRETTI, GIOVANNI
MARIA MASTAI
Pius X, Pope. See:
SARTO, GIUSEPPE
MELCHIORRE
Pius XI, Pope. See:
RATTI, ACHILLE AM-
BROGIO DAMIANO
Pius XII, Pope. See:
PACELLI, EUGENIO
MARIA GIUSEPPE
GIOVANNI
Pius, St. See:
GHISLIERI, MICHELE
PIUS
SARTO, GIUSEPPE
MELCHIORRE
PIXÉRÉCOURT, GUILBERT DE
(1773-1844) [French
dramatic author]
The Corneille of the
Boulevard(s)
The Shakespeare of the
Boulevard(s)
Pixie Hungerford. See:

BRINSMEAD, HESBA FAY
PIZARRO, FRANCISCO (1475-
1541) [Spanish conqueror
of Peru]
El Conquistador (The
Conqueror)
PLACE, MARIAN TEMPLETON
(1910-) [American
author]
Dale White
R.D. Whitinger
Plaidy, Jean. See:
HIBBERT, ELEANOR
BURFORD
Plain and Perspicuous Doctor,
The. See:
BURLEIGH (BURLEY),
WALTER
Plain, Josephine. See:
MITCHELL, ISABEL
MARY
Plains, The Champion Buffalo
Hunter, of the. See:
CODY, WILLIAM
FREDERICK
Plan, The Father of the
Townsend. See:
TOWNSEND, FRANCIS
EVERETT
Plant Doctor, The. See:
CARVER, DR. GEORGE
WASHINGTON
PLANT, HENRY BRADLEY
(1819-99) [American
railroad builder and
industrialist in Florida]
The King of Florida
Plant Wizard, The. See:
BURBANK, LUTHER
PLANTAGENET, LADY EDITH
(fl. 12th cent.) [Kinswoman
of RICHARD COEUR DE
LION]
The Fair Maid of Anjou
Plastic Historian, The. See:
DAVIDSON, JO
Plastics, The Father of
British. See:
SWINBURNE, SIR JAMES,
9TH BARONET
Plate Glass Industry, The
Father of the. See:
FORD, JOHN BAPTISTE

Plate, The Fashion. See:
LEWIS, JAMES HAMILTON
PLATH, SYLVIA (1932-63)
[American editor, educator
and author]
Victoria Lucas
Plato. See:
ARISTOCLES
Plato of the Eighteenth Century,
The. See:
AROUET, FRANÇOIS MARIE
Plato, The English. See:
NORRIS, REV. JOHN
Plato, The German. See:
JACOBI, FRIEDRICH
HEINRICH
Plato, The Jewish. See:
PHILO JUDAEUS
Plato, The Puritan. See:
HOWE, JOHN
Platonic Puritan, The. See:
HOWE, JOHN
Platonist, The. See:
TAYLOR, THOMAS
Platonist, The Cambridge. See:
MORE, HENRY
PLATOV, MATVEI IVANOVICH,
COUNT (1757-1818)
[Russian soldier and noble-
man]
Hetman of the Cossacks of
the Don
PLATT, THOMAS COLLIER (1833-
1910) [American politician;
congressman from New York]
Easy Boss Platt
Me Too Platt
Platte, The Boy Orator of the.
See: BRYAN, WILLIAM
JENNINGS
Playboy of New York, The. See:
WALKER, JAMES JOHN
Playboy, The. See:
REYNOLDS, ROBERT RICE
Playboy, The Congressional.
See: ZIONCHECK,
MARION A.
Player, The World's Greatest
Alto Saxophone. See:
DORSEY, JAMES
Players in the Game, One of
the Gamest. See:
MERKLE, FREDERICK C.

Playfair, I. See:
WILDE, OSCAR FINGAL
O'FLAHERTIE WILLS
Playwright, America's First
Professional. See:
DUNLAP, WILLIAM
Playwright, Germany's
Greatest Modern. See:
HAUPTMANN, GERHART
Playwright, The First Harvard.
See: CROWNE, JOHN
Pleasant Gardens Joe. See:
McDOWELL, JOSEPH
PLEASANTS, JOHN HAMPDEN
(1797-1846) [American
journalist and editor]
The Bayard of the Press
Pleasure, King. See:
BEEKS, CLARENCE
PLEMIANNIKOW, ROGER
VADIM (1928-)
[French motion picture
writer-director]
Roger Vadim
Pleydell, Susan. See:
SENIOR, ISABEL JANET
COUPER
Plick et Plock. See:
SIMENON, GEORGES
PLIMSOLL, SAMUEL
(1824-98) [English social
reformer]
The Sailor's Friend
Pliny. See:
SECUNDUS, GAIUS
PLINIUS
SECUNDUS, GAIUS PLINI-
US CAECILIUS
Pliny, The Modern. See:
GESSNER, KONRAD VON
Pliny the Youngest. See:
WILSON, STANLEY
KIDDER
Plock, Plick et. See:
SIMENON, GEORGES
Plon-Plon. See:
BONAPARTE, JOSEPH
CHARLES PAUL
Plotter, The. See:
FERGUSON, ROBERT
Plough, Alpha of the. See:
GARDINER, ALFRED
GEORGE

Plow 'em Under Wallace. See:
WALLACE, HENRY AGARD
Plowboy, The Delaware. See:
BIGGS, BENJAMIN
THOMAS
Plowboy, The Tennessee. See:
ARNOLD, RICHARD
EDWARD
Plowman, A Heaven-taught. See:
BURNS, ROBERT
Pluche, Jeames de la. See:
THACKERAY, WILLIAM
MAKEPEACE
PLUFF, BARBARA LITTLEFIELD
(1926-) [American author
of juvenile fiction]
Barbara Clayton
Plug, The Penny. See:
O'SULLIVAN, DENNIS
Plum. See:
WARNER, SIR PELHAM
WODEHOUSE, PELHAM
GRENVILLE
Plumb, Beatrice. See:
HUNZICKER, BEATRICE
PLUMB
Plumed Knight. See:
BLAINE, JAMES GIL-
LESPIE
Plumed Knight of the Confederacy,
The. See:
STUART, JAMES EWELL
BROWN
PLUMPE, FRIEDRICH W.
(1889-1931) [German
motion picture director]
F.W. Murnau
Friedrich Murnau
Plupy. See:
SHUTE, HENRY AUGUSTUS
PLUTARCH (c.46-c.120)
[Greek historian, essayist
and biographer]
The Cheronean Sage
Plutarch of France, The. See:
LE VAYER, FRANÇOIS DE
LA MOTHE
Plutarch, The Hollywood. See:
DIETERLE, WILHELM
Plutonius. See:
MEHTA, RUSTAM
JEHANGIR
Plymley, Peter. See:

SMITH, SYDNEY
POAGUE, WILLIAM ROBERT
    (1899-   ) [American edu-
    cator and politician;
    congressman from Texas]
The Professor
Pocahontas. See:
    MATOAKA
Pochi Danari (The Penniless).
    See: MAXIMILIAN I
Pocket-Sized Pavlova, Dainty
    Baby June the. See:
    HOVICK, JUNE
Poe, Edgar. See:
    LEVINE, PHILIP
POE, EDGAR ALLAN (1809-49)
    [American poet, critic,
    short story writer and
    editor]
A Bostonian
By a Bostonian
Eddie
Israfel
Edgar A. Perry
Hans Pfaal
Quarles Quicken
Henri le Reunêt
The Wizard of Word Music
Poet. See:
    CLOSE, JOHN
Poet Bunn, The. See:
    BUNN, ALFRED
Poet Entertainer of the Ozarks,
    The. See:
    LUCEY, THOMAS ELMORE
Poet Laureate of California,
    The. See:
    COOLBRITH, IDA DONNA
    McGROARTY, JOHN
    STEVEN
Poet Laureate of New England,
    The. See:
    WHITTIER, JOHN
    GREENLEAF
Poet Laureate of the Army,
    The. See:
    PATTEN, GEORGE
    WASHINGTON
Poet Laureate of the Con-
    federacy, The. See:
    TIMROD, HENRY
Poet Laureate of the South, The.

See: HAYNE, PAUL
    HAMILTON
Poet Laureate to the Congress,
    Camillo Querno. See:
    ODELL, JONATHAN
Poet Naturalist, The. See:
    THOREAU, HENRY DAVID
Poet, Northamptonshire Peasant.
    See: CLARE, JOHN
Poet of Bran Meal and Pumpkins,
    The. See:
    GRAHAM, SYLVESTER
Poet of Broadway, The Mad. See:
    CLARKE, McDONALD
Poet of California, The Mad. See:
    KENDALL, W.S.
Poet of Charleston, The. See:
    HAYNE, PAUL HAMILTON
Poet of Childhood, The. See:
    FIELD, EUGENE
Poet of Despair, The. See:
    THOMSON, JAMES
Poet of Inverurie, The Weaver.
    See: THOM, WILLIAM
Poet of Low Hampton, The. See:
    MILLER, WILLIAM
Poet of New York, The Mad.
    See: CLARKE,
    McDONALD
Poet of Nottingham, The Boy.
    See: WHITE, HENRY
    KIRKE
Poet of Reason, The. See:
    BOILEAU-DESPRÉAUX,
    NICHOLAS
Poet of the American Revolution,
    The. See:
    FRENEAU, PHILIP MORIN
Poet of the Common People, The.
    See: RILEY, JAMES
    WHITCOMB
Poet of the Commonplace, The.
    See: LONGFELLOW,
    HENRY WADSWORTH
Poet of the Confederacy, The.
    See: RYAN, ABRAM
    JOSEPH
Poet of the Damned, The. See:
    ALIGHIERI, DURANTE
Poet of the Excursion, The. See:
    WORDSWORTH, WILLIAM
Poet of the Golden Gate, The.

See: KIRCHOFF,
THEODORE
Poet of the Organ, The. See:
CRAWFORD, JESSE
Poet of the Ozarks, The. See:
NEWBERGER, GABRIEL F.
Poet of the Shenandoah Valley,
The. See:
LUCAS, DANIEL
BEDINGER
Poet of the Sierras, The. See:
MILLER, CINCINNATUS
HEINE (HEINER)
Poet of Violence, The. See:
CHANDLER, RAYMOND
Poet Sportsman, The. See:
McLELLAN, ISAAC
Poet, The Ayrshire. See:
BURNS, ROBERT
Poet, The Backwoods, See:
BERRYHILL, S. NEWTON
Poet, The Banker. See:
ROGERS, SAMUEL
STEDMAN, EDMUND
CLARENCE
Poet, The Barber. See:
BOÉ, JACQUES
Poet, The Birmingham. See:
FREETH, JOHN
Poet, The Blind. See:
GROTO, LUIGI
MILTON, JOHN
Poet, The Children's. See:
ANDERSEN, HANS
CHRISTIAN
LONGFELLOW, HENRY
WADSWORTH
RILEY, JAMES WHITCOMB
Poet, The Cumberland. See:
WORDSWORTH, WILLIAM
Poet, The Deaf and Dumb. See:
NACK, JAMES M.
Poet, The Domestic. See:
COWPER, WILLIAM
Poet, The Ephesian. See:
HIPPONAX
Poet, The Evolution. See:
CARRUTH, WILLIAM
HERBERT
Poet, The First American.
See: STEENDAM,
JACOB
Poet, The French. See:

RONSARD, PIERRE DE
Poet, The Ghetto. See:
WINCHEVSKY, MORRIS
Poet, The Good Gray. See:
WHITMAN, WALTER
Poet, The Hoosier. See:
RILEY, JAMES WHITCOMB
Poet, The Lancashire. See:
WAUGH, EDWIN
Poet, The Mad. See:
CLARKE, MacDONALD
LEE, NATHANIEL
Poet, The Manchester. See:
SWAIN, CHARLES
Poet, The Nottingham. See:
BAILEY, PHILIP JAMES
Poet, The Poet's. See:
SPENSER, EDMUND
Poet, The Postman. See:
CAPERN, EDWARD
Poet, The Puritan. See:
WHITTIER, JOHN
GREENLEAF
Poet, The Quaker. See:
BARTON, BERNARD
WHITTIER, JOHN GREEN-
LEAF
Poet, The Small-beer. See:
FITZGERALD, WILLIAM
THOMAS
Poet, The Smyrnean. See:
MIMNERMUS
Poet, The Squab. See:
DRYDEN, JOHN
Poet, The Sunrise. See:
LANIER, SIDNEY
Poet, The Tramp. See:
KEMP, HIBBARD
Poet, The Tuscan. See:
ARIOSTO, LUDOVICO
Poet, The Water. See:
TAYLOR, JOHN
Poet Who Wrote in Sanscrit, The
Greatest. See:
BHARTRIHARI
(BHARTRHARI)
Poète Lacrymal, The. See:
BOUILLY, JEAN NICOLAS
Poetess, The Quaker. See:
LIPPINCOTT, MARTHA
SHEPARD
Poetesses, The Cowper of Our
Modern. See:

SOUTHEY, CAROLINE
ANNE BOWLES
Poetic Actress Without a
Rival, The. See:
MURRAY, ALMA
Poetry and History, The
Father of Scottish. See:
BARBOUR, JOHN
Poetry, The Father of. See:
HOMER
Poetry, The Father of
American Ballad. See:
HEWITT, JOHN HENRY
(HILL)
Poetry, The Father of Bur-
lesque. See:
HIPPONAX
Poetry, The Father of Dutch.
See: VAN MAERLANT,
JAKOB DE COSTER
Poetry, The Father of English.
See: CHAUCER,
GEOFFREY
Poetry, The Father of Epic.
See: HOMER
Poetry, The Father of German.
See: OPITZ, MARTIN
Poetry, The Father of Italian.
See: FREDERICK II
Poetry, The Father of Modern
Norwegian. See:
DASS, PETER
Poetry, The Father of Roman.
See: ENNIUS, QUINTUS
Poetry, The Perpetual Adoles-
cent of American. See:
POUND, EZRA LOOMIS
Poetry, The Prince of
Spanish. See:
VEGA, GARCILASSO
DE LA
Poets. See:
Wedded Poets, The
Poets in his Time, The Prince
of. See:
SPENSER, EDMUND
Poet's Poet, The. See:
SPENSER, EDMUND
Poets, The Father of American.
See: BRYANT,
WILLIAM CULLEN
Poets, The Father of Dutch.

See: VAN MAERLANT,
JAKOB DE COSTER
Poets, The Father of Flemish.
See: VAN MAERLANT,
JAKOB DE COSTER
Poets, The Flower of. See:
CHAUCER, GEOFFREY
Poets, The Homer of Our
Dramatic. See:
SHAKESPEARE, WILLIAM
Poets, The Horace of Our
Dramatic. See:
SHAKESPEARE, WILLIAM
Poets, The Prince of. See:
HOMER
SPENSER, EDMUND
POGANY, WILLIAM ANDREW
(1882-) [Hungarian-
American artist and
illustrator]
Willy Pogany
Pogey. See:
O'BRIEN, JOHN V.
Point, The Hero of Stony.
See: WAYNE,
ANTHONY
Pointed Arrow, The. See:
JACKSON, ANDREW
POIRE, EMMANUEL
(1858-1909) [French
caricaturist]
Caran d'Ache
Poison, Big. See:
WANER, PAUL GLEE
Poison Ivy. See:
ANDREWS, IVY PAUL
Poison, Little. See:
WANER, LLOYD JAMES
Poison Twins, The, joint nick-
name of LLOYD JAMES
WANER (1906-) and his
brother, PAUL GLEE
WANER (1903-) [American
professional baseball
players]
Poison Twins, The. See also:
WANER, LLOYD JAMES
WANER, PAUL GLEE
Poisoner, The. See:
WU, LADY
POITIERS. See:
HILARY OF POITIERS

Poker Alice Tubbs. See:
    TUBBS, ALICE
Poker Charley. See:
    FARWELL, CHARLES
    BENJAMIN
Poker Face. See:
    GARNER, JOHN NANCE
Poker Face, Little Miss. See:
    WILLS, HELEN
    NEWINGTON
Pol. See:
    PAUL
    Paul
    PAULO
    SWINGS, POLIDORE F.F.
Pola Negri. See:
    CHALUPEK, APPOLONIA
POLE, MICHAEL DE LA
    (fl. early 14th cent.)
    [London merchant;
    afterwards Lord Chan-
    cellor and Earl of Suffolk
    The Beloved Merchant
POLE, REGINALD (1500-58)
    [British churchman]
    Cardinal of England
POLFUS, LESTER (1916-)
    [American jazz
    musician (guitar)]
    Les Paul
Polgar. See:
    KUBELIK, JAN
POLIAKOFF-BAIDAROV,
    MARINA DE (1938-   )
    [French motion
    picture actress]
    Odile Versois
    Marina Vlady
Police Captain Howard. See:
    SENARENS, LUIS PHILIP
Police, The Scourge of the
    District. See:
    BLANTON, THOMAS
    LINDSAY
Policy King, The. See:
    ADAMS, ALBERT J.
Policy, The Father of the
    Protective. See:
    CLAY, HENRY
Polidoro da Caravaggio. See:
    CALDARA, POLIDORO
Poliorcetes (Besieger of Cities).

See: DEMETRIUS I
POLITELLA, DARIO (1921-)
    [American journalist,
    educator and author]
    Tony Granite
    David Stewart
Politian. See:
    AMBROGINI, ANGELO
Political Philosopher, The. See:
    SMITH, THOMAS VERNON
Political Savior of Virginia,
    The. See:
    WALKER, GILBERT
    CARLTON
Politician, The Liberal. See:
    PERKINS, FRANCES
Politician, The Mistletoe. See:
    VAN BUREN, MARTIN
Politicians, The Admirable
    Crichton of Our City. See:
    HALL, ABRAHAM OAKEY
Politics, The Czar of Pennsyl-
    vania. See:
    CAMERON, SIMON
Politics, The Schoolmaster in.
    See: WILSON, THOMAS
    WOODROW
Politicus. See:
    KULSKI, WLADYSLAW
    WSZEBOR
Poliuto. See:
    WILKIE, FRANC BANGS
Poliziano. See:
    AMBROGINI, ANGELO
Poljanski, Hristo Andonov. See:
    ANDONOV-POLJANSKI,
    HRISTO
POLK, JAMES KNOX (1795-1849)
    [Eleventh President of the
    United States]
    The First Dark Horse
    The Napoleon of the Stump
    Young Hickory
POLK, LEONIDAS (1806-64)
    [American Confederate
    general officer and Protes-
    tant Episcopal bishop]
    The Fighting Bishop
Pollard, Snub. See:
    FRASER, HAROLD
Pollock, Martin. See:
    GARDNER, MAURICE

Pollux. See:
    Castor and Pollux of
    Georgia, The
Polly. See:
    MARK, PAULINE DAHLIN
    THOMSON, MARY AGNES
Polly Hill. See:
    HUMPHREYS, MARY
    EGLANTYNE HILL
Polly Hobson. See:
    EVANS, JULIA RENDEL
Polly, Old. See:
    COLSTON, RALEIGH
    EDWARD
Polly the Weaver. See:
    JOHNSON, MARY
    McDONOUGH
Polly Ward. See:
    POLUSKI, BYNO
Polman, Willem de. See:
    NICHOLS, DALE WILLIAM
Polo. See:
    BARNES, PAUL D.
Polonius. See:
    FITZGERALD, EDWARD
POLUSKI, BYNO (1908-)
    [British-born motion
    picture actress]
    Polly Ward
Polyglot, The Walking. See:
    MEZZOFANTI, CARDINAL
    GIUSEPPE
Polyphemus of Literature, The.
    See: JOHNSON, DR.
    SAMUEL
POMBAL, MARQUES DE,
    SEBASTIAO JOSE DE
    CARVALHO E MELLO
    (1699-1782) [Portuguese
    diplomat and statesman]
    The Great Marquis
Pomerania, The Apostle of.
    See: OTTO OF BAMBERG
Pomeranus. See:
    BUGENHAGEN, JOHANN
Pomeroy, Florence Mary. See:
    POWLEY, FLORENCE
    MARY POMEROY
Pomeroy, Hub. See:
    CLAASSEN, HAROLD
POMEROY, MARCUS MILLS
    (1833-96) [American

journalist, printer and
    politician]
    Brick Pomeroy
POMEROY, SAMUEL CLARKE
    (1816-91) [American
    politician; senator from
    Kansas]
    Subsidy Pomeroy
Pometacom. See:
    METACOM (METACOMET)
Pomfret, Baron. See:
    DAME, LAWRENCE
Pommer, Dr. See:
    BURGENHAGEN, JOHANN
POMPADOUR, MARQUISE DE,
    JEANNE ANTOINETTE
    POISSON, MME. LENOR-
    MAND D'ETOILES (1721-
    64) [Mistress of King
    LOUIS XV of France]
    Madame Pompadour
POMPEO, JOHN ANTHONY
    (1934-) [American jazz
    musician (drums, vibra-
    phone, timbales)]
    John Rae
POMPEY, GNAEUS POMPEIUS
    MAGNUS (106-48 B.C.)
    [Roman general officer and
    consul]
    Pompey the Great
POMPEY, SEXTUS POMPEIUS
    MAGNUS (75-35 B.C.)
    [Roman general officer]
    The Younger
POND, FREDERICK EUGENE
    (1856-1925) [American
    editor and writer on field
    sports]
    Will Wildwood
POND, GEORGE EDWARD
    (1837-99) [American editor
    and author]
    Philip Quilibet
Pond, The Sage of Walden. See:
    THOREAU, HENRY DAVID
Pondiac. See:
    PONTIAC
Poningoe. See:
    SMITH, FRANCIS SHUBAEL
PONS, ALICE JOSEPHINE
    (1904-) [French-

American opera singer]
Lily Pons
PONSONBY, DORIS ALMON
(fl. 1946-63) [English
author]
Doris Rybot
PONSONBY, MISS SARAH
(1755-1831) [Irish recluse]
Lady of the Vale
Maid of Llangollen
PONTE, GIACOMO DA
(1510-92) [Venetian
painter]
Jacopo Bassano
Ponte, Lorenzo Da. See:
CONEGLIANO, EMANUELE
Ponteach. See:
PONTIAC
Pontedera, Andrea de. See:
PISANO, ANDREA
PONTI, DIANA DA (fl. 1582-
1605) [Italian actress]
Lavinia
PONTIAC (c. 1720-69)
[American Indian chief]
Pondiac
Ponteach
PONTIAN (PONTIANUS) (died
235) [Supreme Pontiff
of Roman Catholic Church]
Pope Pontian (Pontianus)
St. Pontian (Pontianus)
Pontiff of Bullfighting, The.
See: GOMEZ, JOSE
Pontormo, Jacopo da. See:
CARRUCCI, JACOPO
Pony Bob. See:
HASLAM, ROBERT
Pony Express Rider, Wild Bill
the. See:
CODY, WILLIAM
FREDERICK
Poole, Vivian. See:
JAFFE, GABRIEL
VIVIAN
POOLE, WILLIAM (183?-55)
[American butcher and
prize fighter]
Bill the Butcher
Butcher Bill Poole
POOR, AGNES BLAKE
(-1922) [American
author]

Dorothy Prescott
Poor Little Rich Girl, The. See:
VANDERBILT, GLORIA
Poor Man's Counsellor, The.
CLARK, ABRAHAM
Poor Man's Friend, The. See:
COUZENS, JAMES
Poor Man's Priest, The. See:
DOLLING, FATHER
RICHARD RADCLYFFE
Poor Richard. See:
FRANKLIN, BENJAMIN
Poor, Santa Claus of the
Manchester. See:
CHENEY, SOPHIE H.
Poor Scholar, The. See:
REID, CAPTAIN MAYNE
Poor, The Father of the. See:
GILPIN, BERNARD
Poor, The Pastor of the. See:
COX, JAMES R.
POORE, BENJAMIN PERLEY
(1820-87) [American news-
paper correspondent, editor
and miscellaneous writer]
Perley
Pop. See:
Pap
Pops
WARNER, GLENN SCOBEY
ZUKOR, ADOLPH
Pop-eye. See:
MEHAFFEY, LEROY
Pope Adeodatus I. See:
DEUSDEDIT
Pope Adeodatus II. See:
ADEODATUS
Pope Adrian I. See:
ADRIAN
Pope Adrian II. See:
ADRIAN
Pope Adrian III. See:
ADRIAN
Pope Adrian IV. See:
BREAKSPEAR, NICKOLAS
Pope Adrian V. See:
FIESCHI, OTTOBONO
Pope Adrian VI. See:
DEDEL, ADRIAN
Pope Agapetus I. See:
AGAPETUS
Pope Agapetus II. See:
AGAPETUS

Pope Agatho. See:
AGATHO
POPE, ALEXANDER (1688-1744)
[English poet]
The Bard of Twickenham
The English Horace
Bob Short
Pope Alexander I. See:
ALEXANDER
Pope Alexander II. See:
BAGGIO, ANSELMO DA
Pope Alexander III. See:
BANDINELLI, ROLAND
Pope Alexander IV. See:
CONTI, RINALDO
Pope Alexander V. See:
CANDIA, PIETRO DI
Pope Alexander VI. See:
BORGIA, RODRIGO
Pope Alexander VII. See:
CHIGI, FABIO
Pope Alexander VIII. See:
OTTOBONI, PIETRO
Pope Anacletus. See:
ANACLETUS (ANEN-
CLETUS) (CLETUS)
Pope Anastasius I. See:
ANASTASIUS
Pope Anastasius II. See:
ANASTASIUS
Pope Anastasius III. See:
ANASTASIUS
Pope Anastasius IV. See:
SUBARRA, CORRADO
DELLA
Pope Anicetus. See:
ANICETUS
Pope Anterus. See:
ANTERUS
Pope Benedict I. See:
BENEDICT
Pope Benedict II. See:
BENEDICT
Pope Benedict III. See:
BENEDICT
Pope Benedict IV. See:
BENEDICT
Pope Benedict V. See:
BENEDICT
Pope Benedict VI. See:
BENEDICT
Pope Benedict VII. See:

BENEDICT
Pope Benedict VIII. See:
BENEDICT
Pope Benedict IX. See:
BENEDICT
Pope Benedict X. See:
JOHN, COUNT OF
TUSCULUM
Pope Benedict XI. See:
BOCCASINI , NICCOLO
Pope Benedict XII. See:
FORNIER, JACQUES
Pope Benedict XIII. See:
ORSINI, PIETRO
FRANCESCO
Pope Benedict XIV. See:
LAMBERTINI, PROSPERO
Pope Benedict XV. See:
CHIESA, GIACOMO DELLA
Pope Boniface I. See:
BONIFACE
Pope Boniface II. See:
BONIFACE
Pope Boniface III. See:
BONIFACE
Pope Boniface IV. See:
BONIFACE
Pope Boniface V. See:
BONIFACE
Pope Boniface VI. See:
BONIFACE
Pope Boniface VII. See:
BONIFACE
Pope Boniface VIII. See:
CAETANI, BENEDETTO
Pope Boniface IX. See:
TOMACELLI, PIETRO
Pope Caius. See:
CAIUS
Pope Callistus I. See:
CALLISTUS
Pope Callistus II. See:
GUY OF BURGUNDY
Pope Callistus III. See:
BORGIA, ALONSO
Pope Celestine I. See:
CELESTINE
Pope Celestine II. See:
CASTELLO, GUIDO DI
Pope Celestine III. See:
ORSINI, GIACINTO
BOBONI

Pope Celestine IV. See:
CASTIGLIONE,
GOFFREDO
Pope Celestine V. See:
MURRONE, PIETRO
ANGELARI DA
Pope Clement I. See:
CLEMENT
Pope Clement II. See:
SUITGER, COUNT OF
MORSLEBEN
Pope Clement III. See:
SCOLARI, PAOLO
Pope Clement IV. See:
FOULQUES, GUY LE
GROS
Pope Clement V. See:
GOT, BERTRAND DE
Pope Clement VI. See:
ROGER, PIERRE
Pope Clement VII. See:
MEDICI, GIULIO DE'
Pope Clement VIII. See:
ALDOBRANDINI,
IPPOLITO
Pope Clement IX. See:
ROSPIGLIOSI, GIULIO
Pope Clement X. See:
ALTIERI, EMILIO
Pope Clement XI. See:
ALBANI, GIAN
FRANCESCO
Pope Clement XII. See:
CORSINI, LORENZO
Pope Clement XIII. See:
REZZONICO, CARLO
DELLA TORRE
Pope Clement XIV. See:
GANGANELLI,
GIOVANNI
Pope Conon. See:
CONON
Pope Constantine I. See:
CONSTANTINE
Pope Cornelius. See:
CORNELIUS
Pope Damasus I. See:
DAMASUS
Pope Damasus II. See:
COUNT POPPO OF
BAVARIA
Pope Deusdedit I. See:
DEUSDEDIT

Pope Dionysius. See:
DIONYSIUS
Pope Donus. See:
DONUS
Pope Eleutherus. See:
ELEUTHERUS
Pope Eugene I. See:
EUGENE
Pope Eugene II. See:
EUGENE
Pope Eugene III. See:
PAGANELLI, BERNARDO
Pope Eugene IV. See:
CONDULMER, GABRIELE
Pope Eusebius. See:
EUSEBIUS
Pope Eutychian. See:
EUTYCHIAN
Pope Evaristus. See:
EVARISTUS
Pope Fabian. See:
FABIAN
Pope Felix I. See:
FELIX
Pope Felix II. See:
FELIX
Pope Felix III. See:
FELIX
Pope Felix IV. See:
FELIX
Pope Formosus. See:
FORMOSUS
Pope Gelasius I. See:
GELASIUS
Pope Gelasius II. See:
CONIUOLO, GIOVANNI
Pope Gregory I. See:
GREGORY
Pope Gregory II. See:
GREGORY
Pope Gregory III. See:
GREGORY
Pope Gregory IV. See:
GREGORY
Pope Gregory V. See:
GREGORY
Pope Gregory VI. See:
GRATIANUS, JOHANNES
Pope Gregory VII. See:
HILDEBRAND
Pope Gregory VIII. See:
MORRA, ALBERTO DI

Pope Gregory IX. See:
UGOLINO, COUNT OF
SEGNI
Pope Gregory X. See:
VISCONTI, TEOBALDO
Pope Gregory XI. See:
BEAUFORT, PIERRE
ROGER DE
Pope Gregory XII. See:
CARRARIO, ANGELO
Pope Gregory XIII. See:
BUONCOMPAGNI, UGO
Pope Gregory XIV. See:
SFONDRATI, NICCOLO
Pope Gregory XV. See:
LUDOVISI, ALESSANDRO
Pope Gregory XVI. See:
CAPPELLARI, BAR-
TOLOMMEO ALBERTO
Pope Hilary. See:
HILARY
Pope Honorius I. See:
HONORIUS
Pope Honorius II. See:
SCANNABECCHI,
LAMBERTO
Pope Honorius III. See:
SAVELLI, CENCIO
Pope Honorius IV. See:
SAVELLI, GIACOMO
Pope Hormisdas. See:
HORMISDAS
Pope Innocent I. See:
INNOCENT
Pope Innocent II. See:
PAPARESCHI, GREGORIO
Pope Innocent III. See:
SEGNI, LOTHAIR OF
Pope Innocent IV. See:
FIESCHI, SINIBALDI
Pope Innocent V. See:
TARENTAISE, PETER OF
Pope Innocent VI. See:
AUBERT, ETIENNE
Pope Innocent VII. See:
MIGLIORATI, COSIMO DE
Pope Innocent VIII. See:
CIBO, GIOVANNI
BATTISTA
Pope Innocent IX. See:
FACCHINETTI, GIOVANNI
ANTONIO

Pope Innocent X. See:
PAMPHILI, GIOVANNI
BATTISTA
Pope Innocent XI. See:
ODESCALCHI, BENEDICT
Pope Innocent XII. See:
PIGNATELLI, ANTONIO
Pope Innocent XIII. See:
CONTI, MICHELANGELO
POPE, JANE (1742-1818) [English
actress]
Lively Pope
Pope Joan. See:
JOAN
Pope John I. See:
JOHN
Pope John II. See:
MERCURIUS
Pope John III. See:
JOHN
Pope John IV. See:
JOHN
Pope John V. See:
JOHN
Pope John VI. See:
JOHN
Pope John VII. See:
JOHN
Pope John VIII. See:
JOAN
JOHN
Pope John IX. See:
JOHN
Pope John X. See:
JOHN
Pope John XI. See:
JOHN
Pope John XII. See:
OTTAVIANO
Pope John XIII. See:
JOHN
Pope John XIV. See:
PETER OF PAVIA
Pope John XV. See:
JOHN
Pope John XVII. See:
JOHN
Pope John XVIII. See:
JOHN
Pope John XIX. See:
JOHN
Pope John XXI. See:

GIULIANI, PETER
   REBULI
Pope John XXII. See:
   D'EUSE, JACQUES
Pope John XXIII. See:
   RONCALLI, ANGELO
   GIUSEPPE
Pope Julius I. See:
   JULIUS
Pope Julius II. See:
   ROVERE, GIULIANO
   DELLA
Pope Julius III. See:
   MONTE, GIOVANNI
   MARIA CIOCCHI DEL
Pope Landus. See:
   LANDUS
Pope Leo I. See:
   LEO
Pope Leo II. See:
   LEO
Pope Leo III. See:
   LEO
Pope Leo IV. See:
   LEO
Pope Leo V. See:
   LEO
Pope Leo VI. See:
   LEO
Pope Leo VII. See:
   LEO
Pope Leo VIII. See:
   LEO
Pope Leo IX. See:
   BRUNO, COUNT OF
   EGISHEIM-DAGSBURG
Pope Leo X. See:
   MEDICI, GIOVANNI DE'
Pope Leo XI. See:
   MEDICI, ALESSANDRO
   OTTAVIANO
Pope Leo XII. See:
   GENGA, ANNIBALE
   SERMATTEI DELLA
Pope Leo XIII. See:
   PECCI, GIOACCHINO
   VINCENZO
Pope Liberius. See:
   LIBERIUS
Pope Linus. See:
   LINUS
Pope Lucius I. See:
   LUCIUS

Pope Lucius II. See:
   CACCIANEMICI, GHERARDO
Pope Lucius III. See:
   ALLUCINGOLI, UBALDO
Pope Marcellinus. See:
   MARCELLINUS
Pope Marcellus I. See:
   MARCELLUS
Pope Marcellus II. See:
   SPANNOCHI, MARCELLO
   CERVINI DEGLI
Pope Marcus. See:
   MARCUS
Pope Marinus I. See:
   MARINUS
Pope Marinus II. See:
   MARINUS
Pope Martin I. See:
   MARTIN
Pope Martin II. See:
   MARINUS
Pope Martin III. See:
   MARINUS
Pope Martin IV. See:
   BRION, SIMON DE
Pope Martin V. See:
   COLONNA, ODDONE
Pope Melchiades. See:
   MILTIADES (MELCHIADES)
Pope Miltiades. See:
   MILTIADES (MELCHIADES)
Pope Nicholas I. See:
   NICHOLAS
Pope Nicholas II. See:
   GERHARD OF BURGUNDY
Pope Nicholas III. See:
   ORSINI, GIOVANNI
   GAETANO
Pope Nicholas IV. See:
   MASCI, GIROLAMO
Pope Nicholas V. See:
   PARENTUCELLI, TOMMASO
Pope of Catholic Action, The.
   See: SARTO, GIUSEPPE
   MELCHIORRE
Pope of New England, The
   Congregational. See:
   BACON, LEONARD
Pope Paschal I. See:
   PASCHAL
Pope Paschal II. See:
   BIEDA, RANIERI DA
Pope Paul I. See:

PAUL

Pope Paul II. See:
PIETRO, BARBO
Pope Paul III. See:
FARNESE, ALESSANDRO
Pope Paul IV. See:
CARAFFA, GIAMPIETRO
Pope Paul V. See:
BORGHESE, CAMILLO
Pope Paul VI. See:
MONTINI, GIOVANNI
BATTISTA
Pope Pelagius I. See:
PELAGIUS
Pope Pelagius II. See:
PELAGIUS
Pope Peter. See:
PETER
Pope Pius I. See:
PIUS
Pope Pius II. See:
PICCOLIMINI, ENEA
SILVIO DE
Pope Pius III. See:
PICCOLOMINI, FRAN-
CESCO TODESCHINI DE'
Pope Pius IV. See:
MEDICI, GIOVANNI
ANGELO
Pope Pius V. See:
GHISLIERI, MICHELE
Pope Pius VI. See:
BRASCHI, GIOVANNI
ANGELO
Pope Pius VII. See:
CHIARMONTI, LUIGI
BARNABA
Pope Pius VIII. See:
CASTIGLIONE, FRAN-
CESCO XAVERIO
Pope Pius IX. See:
FERRETTI, GIOVANNI
MARIA MASTAI
Pope Pius X. See:
SARTO, GIUSEPPE
MELCHIORRE
Pope Pius XI. See:
RATTI, ACHILLE
AMBROGIO DAMIANO
Pope Pius XII. See:
PACELLI, EUGENIO
MARIA GIUSEPPE
GIOVANNI

Pope Pontian (Pontianus). See:
PONTIAN (PONTIANUS)
Pope Romanus. See:
ROMANUS
Pope, Rome's Greatest. See:
GREGORY
Pope Sabinian. See:
SABINIAN
Pope Sergius I. See:
SERGIUS
Pope Sergius II. See:
SERGIUS
Pope Sergius III. See:
SERGIUS
Pope Sergius IV. See:
SERGIUS
Pope Severinus. See:
SEVERINUS
Pope Silverius. See:
SILVERIUS
Pope Simplicius. See:
SIMPLICIUS
Pope Siricius. See:
SIRICIUS
Pope Sisinnius. See:
SISINNIUS
Pope Sixtus I. See:
SIXTUS
Pope Sixtus II. See:
SIXTUS
Pope Sixtus III. See:
SIXTUS
Pope Sixtus IV. See:
ROVERE, FRANCESCO
DELLA
Pope Sixtus V. See:
PERETTI, FELICE
Pope Soter (Soterus). See:
SOTER (SOTERUS)
Pope Stephen I. See:
STEPHEN
Pope Stephen II. See:
STEPHEN
Pope Stephen III. See:
STEPHEN
Pope Stephen IV. See:
STEPHEN
Pope Stephen V. See:
STEPHEN
Pope Stephen VI. See:
STEPHEN
Pope Stephen VII. See:
STEPHEN

Pope Stephen VIII. See:
STEPHEN
Pope Stephen IX. See:
STEPHEN
Pope Stephen X. See:
FREDERICK OF LORRAINE
Pope Sylvester I. See:
SYLVESTER
Pope Sylvester II. See:
SYLVESTER
Pope Sylvester III. See:
SYLVESTER
Pope Symacchus. See:
SYMACCHUS
Pope Telesphorus. See:
TELESPHORUS
Pope, The. See:
SINATRA, FRANCIS
ALBERT
Pope, The Boy. See:
OTTAVIANO
Pope, The Peasant. See:
SARTO, GIUSEPPE
MELCHIORRE
Pope, The Protestant. See:
CORSINI, LORENZO
Pope Theodore I. See:
THEODORE
Pope Theodore II. See:
THEODORE
Pope Urban I. See:
URBAN
Pope Urban II. See:
ODA OF LAGERY
Pope Urban III. See:
CRIVELLI, UBERTO
Pope Urban IV. See:
PANTALEON, JACQUES
Pope Urban V. See:
GRIMORD, GUILLAUME DE
Pope Urban VI. See:
PRIGNANO,BARTOLOMMEO
Pope Urban VII. See:
CASTAGNA, GIAMBAT-
TISTA
Pope Urban VIII. See:
BARBERINI, MAFFEO
Pope Valentine. See:
VALENTINE
Pope Victor I. See:
VICTOR
Pope Victor II. See:

GEBHARD, COUNT OF
HIRSCHBERG
Pope Victor III. See:
DESIDERIUS, PRINCE OF
BENEVENTO
Pope Vigilius. See:
VIGILIUS
Pope Vitalian. See:
VITALIAN
Pope Zachary. See:
ZACHARY
Pope Zephyrinus. See:
ZEPHYRINUS
Pope Zosimus. See:
ZOSIMUS
POPESCU, CHRISTINE PULLEIN-
THOMPSON (1930-)
[British author]
Christine Keir
Christine Pullein-Thompson
Poppo. See:
PHILLIPS, PAULINE
ESTHER FRIEDMAN
POPPO OF BAVARIA. See:
COUNT POPPO OF
BAVARIA
Poppy Lady, The. See:
MICHAEL, MOINA
Pops. See:
ARMSTRONG, DANIEL
LOUIS
FOSTER, GEORGE MURPHY
Pap
Pop
SNOWDEN, ELMER
CHESTER
WHITEMAN, PAUL
Popski. See:
PENIAKOFF, VLADIMIR
Popular Music, The Dean of
American. See:
WHITEMAN, PAUL
Popular Writer of Thrillers,
The World's Most Prolific
and. See:
OPPENHEIM, EDWARD
PHILLIPS
Populism, The Intellectual Giant
of. See:
ALLEN, WILLIAM VINCENT
POQUELIN, JEAN BAPTISTE
(1622-73) [French play-

wright and actor]
The Anatomist of Humanity
The French Aristophanes
Molière
Porcher, Mary F. Wickham.
    See: BOND, MARY
        FANNING WICKHAM
Porcupine, Peter. See:
    COBBETT, WILLIAM
Porlock, Martin. See:
    MACDONALD, PHILIP
Porphyry. See:
    MALCHUS
PORSON, RICHARD (1759-1808)
    [English classical scholar
    and authority on Greek]
Devil Dick
The Norfolk Boy
Port, Wymar. See:
    JUDY, WILL
Porta, Baccio della. See:
    FATTORINO, BARTOLOM-
        MEO DI PAGOLO DEL
Porte Crayon. See:
    STROTHER, DAVID
        HUNTER
Porter, Alvin. See:
    ROWLAND, DONALD
        SYDNEY
PORTER, HAROLD EVERETT
    (1887-1936) [American
    novelist, short story
    writer and dramatist]
Holworthy Hall
Porter, Kathryn. See:
    SWINFORD, BETTY JUNE
        WELLS
PORTER, LINN BOYD (1851-
    1916) [American author]
Albert Ross
Porter, Mark. See:
    LECKIE, ROBERT HUGH
PORTER, MRS. ELEANOR
    HODGMAN (1868-1920)
    [American novelist and
    short story writer]
Eleanor Stewart
PORTER, WILLIAM SYDNEY
    (1862-1910) [American
    short story writer]
The American Maupassant
James L. Bliss
Howard Clark

T. B. Dowd
O. Henry
Olivier Henry
S. H. Peters
Bill Porter
PORTER, WILLIAM TROTTER
    (1809-58) [American
    editor and journalist]
York's Tall Son
Portly Master of the Involuntary
    Scream, The. See:
    HITCHCOCK, ALFRED
        JOSEPH
Portrait Painter of Presidents,
    The. See:
    STUART, GILBERT
Portugal, The Homer of. See:
    CAMOENS, LUIZ DE
Portugal, The Livy of. See:
    BARROS, JOAO DE
Portuguese Apollo, The. See:
    DE CAMOENS, LUIZ
Portuguese Cid, The. See:
    PEREIRA, D. NUNO
        ALVAREZ
Portuguese Drama, The Father
    of. See:
    VICENTE, GIL
Portuguese Horace, The. See:
    FERREIRA, ANTONIO
Portuguese Livy, The. See:
    BARROS, JOAO DE
Portuguese Mars, The. See:
    ALBUQUERQUE, AFFONSO
        D'
Portuguese, My Little. See:
    BROWNING, ELIZABETH
        BARRETT
Portuguese Nostradamus, The.
    See: BANDARRA,
        GONÇALO ANNES
Portuguese Nun, The. See:
    ALCOFORADO, MARIANNA
Portuguese Theocritus, The. See:
    MIRANDA, FRANCISCO DA
        SA DE
Portuguese Titian, The. See:
    COELLO, ALONSO SANCHEZ
Posey. See:
    JENKINS, FREDDY
POSEY, ALEXANDER LAWRENCE
    (1873-1908) [Creek Indian
    editor and poet]

Chinnubbie Harjo
Possum, Old. See:
    ELIOT, THOMAS
        STEARNS
Post, A.H. See:
    BADGER, JOSEPH E.,
        JR.
Post, Maverick. See:
    MAPES, VICTOR
POSTL, KARL ANTON
    (1793-1864) [Austrian-
    American novelist and
    travel writer]
Charles Sealsfield
Charles Sidons
Postman Poet, The. See:
    CAPERN, EDWARD
Postman, The Bideford. See:
    CAPERN, EDWARD
POSTON, CHARLES DEBRILL
    (1825-1902) [American
    explorer and author]
The Father of Arizona
POSTON, THOMAS (1927-)
    [American actor]
Tom Poston
POT, PHILIPPE (1428-94)
    [Prime Minister of
    LOUIS XI of France]
Cicero's Mouth
Potato. See:
    VALDEZ, CARLOS
Potato Hill, The Sage of. See:
    HOWE, EDGAR WATSON
Potato King, Minnesota's. See:
    SCHROEDER, HENRY
Potato Mayor, The. See:
    SHANK, SAMUEL LEWIS
Potato Mayor, The Indianapolis.
    See: SHANK, SAMUEL
        LEWIS
Potato Quixote. See:
    ALCOTT, AMOS BRONSON
Potato, The Aroostook. See:
    BREWSTER, RALPH
        OWEN
Pothouse Peggy. See:
    EATON, MARGARET
        O'NEILL
Potiphar, joint pseud. of
    GEORGE ANTHONY HERN
    (1916-) and J. F.

MARRACK (-) [English
    editors and authors]
Potsy. See:
    CLARK, GEORGE
POTTEN, HENRY THOMAS
    (1867-) [British Congre-
    gational minister and
    author]
Hibernia
POTTER, GEORGE WILLIAM, JR.
    (1930-) [American author]
E. L. Withers
POTTER, MARGARET NEWMAN
    (1926-) [British editor
    and author]
Anne Betteridge
Margaret Newman
Potter, Paul. See:
    CONGDON, CHARLES TABER
Potteries, The Father of the.
    See: WEDGEWOOD,
        JOSIAH
POTTLE, GILBERT EMERY
    BEMSLEY (1875-)
    [American playwright and
    novelist]
Gilbert Emery
Emery Bemsley Pottle
Emery Pottle
POTTS, HARRY (1869-1913)
    [English music-hall
    performer]
Harry Fragson
POTTS, JAMES HENRY (1848-)
    [Deaf American churchman
    and orator]
The Deafman Eloquent
Poughkeepsie Seer, The. See:
    DAVIES, ANDREW JACKSON
Poum et Zette. See:
    SIMENON, GEORGES
POUND, EZRA LOOMIS (1885-)
    [American poet, critic and
    propagandist]
William Atheling
The Perpetual Adolescent of
    American Poetry
Alfred Venison
Poussin, Gaspar. See:
    DUGHET, GASPAR
Poussin, The English. See:
    COOPER, RICHARD

POWELL, CLIVE (1943-)
[English jazz musician
(organ, singer, leader)]
Georgie Fame
POWELL, DAVID FRANK
(1857-) [American
physician and army
surgeon]
Fancy Frank
The Mighty Medicine Man
The Surgeon Scout
The White Beaver
POWELL, EARL (1924-)
[American jazz musician
(piano)]
Bud Powell
POWELL, EVERARD STEPHEN,
SR. (1907-) [American
jazz musician
(clarinet, alto saxophone)]
Musheed Karweem
Rudy Powell
Powell, Frank. See:
INGRAHAM, COLONEL
PRENTISS
POWELL, GORDON (1922-)
[American jazz musician
(drums)]
Specs Powell
Powell I. Ford. See:
DEMPSEY, JAMES E.
POWELL, JAMES ROBERT
(1814-83) [American pioneer
developer of Birmingham,
Alabama]
The Duke of Birmingham
Powell, Jane. See:
BURCE, SUZANNE
POWELL, JOHN STEPHEN
(1857-1921) [American
judge in Philippine Islands]
Big Judge Powell
POWELL, RANSOM T. (fl. 1862-
65) [American Union Civil
War drummer boy; prisoner
at Andersonville prison]
Red Cap
POWELL, RICHARD EWING
(1904-63) [American actor
and singer]
Dick Powell
Powell, Richard Stillman. See:

BARBOUR, RALPH HENRY
POWELL, TALMAGE (1920-)
[American author]
Jack McCready
POWELL, THOMAS (1809-87)
[American poet, dramatist
and journalist]
Diogenes
Pierce Pungent
Ernest Trevor
Power, Apostle of Light and. See:
LIEB, JOHN WILLIAM
Power of God, The Supreme.
See: SIMON MAGUS
POWER, RICHARD (1928-)
[Irish civil servant,
lecturer and author]
Risteard de Paor
Power, The Dynamo of. See:
ROOSEVELT, THEODORE
Power, The Embodiment of Sea.
See: NELSON, HORATIO,
VISCOUNT NELSON
Power, The Father of Niagara.
See: RANKINE, WILLIAM
BIRCH
Powers, Anne. See:
SCHWARTZ, ANNE POWERS
Powers, George. See:
INFIELD, GLENN BERTON
Powers, Margaret. See:
HEAL, EDITH
Powers Tracy. See:
WARD, DONALD G.
POWLES, MATILDA ALICE
(1864-1952) [English
comedienne]
Lady de Frece
Vesta Tilley
POWLEY, FLORENCE MARY
POMEROY (1892-)
[British educator and
author]
Florence Mary Pomeroy
POWYS, THEODORE FRANCIS
(1875-1953) [English author]
T. F. Powys
Poyntz, Launce. See:
WHITTAKER, FREDERICK
Pozo, Chano. See:
GONZALES, LUCIANO
POZO, FRANCISCO (1915-)

825

[Cuban jazz musician
(bongos, conga, timbales)]
Chino Pozo
PRAED, ROSA CAROLINE
(1851-1935) [Australian
author]
Mrs. Campbell Praed
Prairies, The Monarch of the.
See: CARSON,
CHRISTOPHER
Praisegod Barebones. See:
BARBON, PRAISEGOD
Praize, Ann. See:
BLEWETT, DOROTHY
EMILIE
PRAJADHIPOK (1893-1941)
[King of Thailand (Siam)]
Rama VII
Pratap Roy Ramala. See:
BHOSALE,
YESHWANTRAO P.
PRATHER, RICHARD SCOTT
(1921-) [American author]
David Knight
Douglas Ring
PRATT, AGNES EDWARDS
ROTHERY (1888-)
[American author]
Agnes Rothery
PRATT, DANIEL (1809-87)
[American traveler,
lecturer and eccentric]
The Great American
Traveler
PRATT, DENNIS (1897-)
[British opera singer
and motion picture actor]
Dennis King
PRATT, ELIZA ANNA FARMAN
(1837-1907) [American
editor and author]
Ella Farman
PRATT, JOHN (1931-) [British
naval officer and author]
John Winton
PRATT, SAMUEL JACKSON
(1749-1814) [English
actor and playwright]
Courtney Melmoth
PRATT, THEODORE (1901-)
[American novelist]
Timothy Brace

PRATT, WILLIAM HENRY
(1887-1969) [British stage
and motion picture actor]
Boris Karloff
Praxiteles. See:
PANDEL, TED
Prays, The Woman Who Always.
See: DUCHESNE, ROSE
PHILIPPINE
Pre-Adamite. See:
HOAR, GEORGE FRISBIE
Pre-Raphaelite, The American.
See: STILLMAN, WILLIAM
JAMES
Preacher, Lay. See:
DENNIE, JOSEPH
Preacher of Los Angeles, The.
Boy. See:
IRONSIDE, HENRY ALLAN
Preacher President, The. See:
GARFIELD, JAMES ABRAM
Preacher, The. See:
SHORT, DEWEY
Preacher, The Banished. See:
WILLIAMS, ROGER
Preacher, The Blind. See:
MILBURN, WILLIAM HENRY
WADDELL, JAMES
Preacher, The Boy. See:
FURMAN, RICHARD
KENNEDY, CRAMMOND
LIPSCOMB, ANDREW AD-
GATE
Preacher, The Chartist. See:
KINGSLEY, REV. CHARLES
Preacher, The Glorious. See:
CHRYSOSTOM, ST. JOHN
Preacher, The Hunter. See:
LYNN, BENJAMIN
Preacher, The Unfair. See:
BARROW, ISAAC
Preacher to the Largest Congre-
gation in the United States,
A Lay. See:
BOK, EDWARD WILLIAM
Preachers, The King of. See:
BOURDALONE, LOUIS
Preaching Woman, The. See:
SPRAGUE, ACHSA W.
PREBBLE, JOHN EDWARD
CURTIS (1915-) [British
journalist and author]

John Curtis
PREBBLE, MARJORIE MARY
    CURTIS (1912-) [British
    businesswoman and
    author]
  Ann Compton
  Denise Conway
  Marjorie Curtis
Precious Warrior (Chinghiz Khan).
    See: TEMUJIN
Precious Warrior
    (Chinghiz Khan).
    See:
    TEMUJIN
Precious Warrior (Jenghiz
    Khan). See:
    TEMUJIN
Preedy, George. See:
    LONG, MRS. GABRIELLE
    MARGARET VERE
    CAMPBELL
PREETORIUS, EMIL (1827-1905)
    [German-American
    journalist and publicist]
  The Nestor of the
    German-American
    Journalists
Prelate, The Fighting. See:
    SPENSER, HENRY
Prelate, The Peaceful. See:
    MASSILLON, JEAN BAP-
    TISTE
Premier. See:
    BLAINE, JAMES
    GILLESPIE
Premier Air Woman, America's.
    See: PUTNAM AMELIA
    EARHART
Premont, Brother Jeremy.
    See:
    WILLETT, BROTHER
    FRANCISCUS
Prendergast, Paul. See:
    LEIGH, PERCIVAL
PRENTISS, BENJAMIN
    MAYBERRY (1819-1901)
    [American Civil War
    general officer]
  The Hero of the Hornet's
    Nest
Prentiss, Karl. See:
    PURDY, KEN WILLIAM

Prentiss, Paula. See:
    RAGUSA, PAULA
Pres. See:
    YOUNG, LESTER WILLIS
PRESBERG, MIRIAM GOLDSTEIN
    (1919-) [American author]
  Miriam Gilbert
Presbyterianism in the State of
    New York, The Father of.
    See: McNISH, GEORGE
Presbyterianism in Virginia,
    The Father of. See:
    MORRIS, SAMUEL
Presbyterianism, The St.
    Francis of. See:
    MAKEMIE, FRANCIS
Presbytery, The Father of
    Scottish. See:
    MELVILLE, ANDREW
Prescot, Julian. See:
    BUDD, JOHN
Prescott, Dorothy. See:
    POOR, AGNES BLAKE
Prescott, Paul J. See:
    IRONS, LETTIE ARTLEY
Present Champion of the English
    Theater, The. See:
    OLIVIER, SIR LAURENCE
Preserver, The (Soter). See:
    ANTIOCHUS I
    ATTALUS I
    DEMETRIUS I
    PTOLEMY I
    PTOLEMY VIII
President, An Accidental. See:
    FILLMORE, MILLARD
President de facto, The. See:
    HAYES, RUTHERFORD
    BIRCHARD
President Maker, The. See:
    CLAY, HENRY
President, The Accidental. See:
    ADAMS, JOHN QUINCY
    TYLER, JOHN
President, The Bachelor. See:
    BUCHANAN, JAMES
President, The Centennial. See:
    HARRISON, BENJAMIN
President, The Cunning. See:
    MESSER, DOCTOR ASA
President, The Dark Horse. See:
    HAYES, RUTHERFORD

BIRCHARD
President, The Dude. See:
  ARTHUR, CHESTER
  ALAN
President, The Emancipation.
  See: LINCOLN,
  ABRAHAM
President, The Era-of-good-
  feeling. See:
  MONROE, JAMES
President, The Farmer. See:
  HARRISON, WILLIAM
  HENRY
  WASHINGTON, GEORGE
President, The Fraud. See:
  HAYES, RUTHERFORD
  BIRCHARD
President, The Martyr. See:
  GARFIELD, JAMES ABRAM
  LINCOLN, ABRAHAM
President, The People's. See:
  CLEVELAND, STEPHEN
  GROVER
  JACKSON, ANDREW
President, The Preacher. See:
  GARFIELD, JAMES
  ABRAM
President, The Sectional. See:
  LINCOLN, ABRAHAM
President, The Surveyor. See:
  WASHINGTON, GEORGE
President, The Tanner. See:
  GRANT, HIRAM
  ULYSSES
President, The Teacher. See:
  GARFIELD, JAMES ABRAM
President, The Trust-busting.
  See: ROOSEVELT,
  THEODORE
President, The Veto. See:
  CLEVELAND, STEPHEN
  GROVER
  JOHNSON, ANDREW
President, The Wool-carder.
  See: FILLMORE,
  MILLARD
Presidents, The Adviser of.
  See: BARUCH, BERNARD
  MANNES
Presidents, The Painter of.
  See: STUART, GILBERT
Presidents, The Portrait

Painter of. See:
  STUART, GILBERT
Presiding Elder, The Phenomenal.
  See: WILSON, JOHN
  ALFRED BAYNUM
Presland, John. See:
  BENDIT, GLADYS
  WILLIAMS
Presle, Micheline. See:
  CHASSAGNE, MICHELINE
PRESLEY, ELVIS ARON
  (1935-) [American singer
  and actor]
  The Hillbilly Cat
  The Pelvis
Press Agent, The Great Left-
  Handed. See:
  MAILS, WALTER
Press, The Bayard of the. See:
  PLEASANTS, JOHN
  HAMPDEN
Prestidigitateur, The Eminent.
  See: CARTER, CHARLES
  J.
Presto, Fa (Hurry Up). See:
  GIORDANO, LUCA
Preston, George F. See:
  WARREN, JOHN BYRNE
  LEICESTER
Preston Graham, Lieut. See:
  INGRAHAM, COLONEL
  PRENTISS
PRESTON, JAMES (1913-)
  [Australian author]
  Ronald James
Preston, James. See:
  UNETT, JOHN
PRESTON, JOHN THOMAS
  LEWIS (fl. 1861-65)
  [American educator and
  Civil War general officer]
  Old Bald
Preston, Paul. See:
  COOPER, ALFRED
  BENJAMIN
  MILNER, THOMAS PICTON
  MORRIS, CHARLES SMITH
Preston, Richard. See:
  LINDSAY, JACK
Preston Sturges. See:
  BIDEN, EDMOND P.
PRESTOPNIK, IRVING (1912-49)

[American jazz musician
(clarinet)]
Irving Fazola
Pretender, The. See:
CLEVELAND STEPHEN
GROVER
Pretender, The Old. See:
STUART, JAMES
FRANCIS EDWARD
Pretender, The Young. See:
STUART, CHARLES
EDWARD LOUIS
PHILIP CASIMIR
Pretoria and Waterford, Roberts
of Kandahar. See:
ROBERTS, FREDERICK
SLEIGH
Pretorius, Hertha. See:
KOUTS, HERTHA PRE-
TORIUS
Prettiest Carmen on Record,
The. See:
SWARTHOUT, GLADYS
Prettiest Three-million-dollar
Corporation with Freckles
in America, The. See:
VON KAPPELHOFF,
DORIS
Pretty Boy. See:
FLOYD, CHARLES ARTHUR
Pretty, Violet. See:
STROSS, MRS. RAYMOND
Pretty, Witty Nellie. See:
GWYN (GWYNNE),
ELEANOR
Préville. See:
DUBUS, PIERRE-LOUIS
PREVOST, ANTOINE
FRANÇOIS (1697-1763)
[French churchman and
novelist]
The Abbé Prévost
Prévost d'Exiles
Prevost, Marie. See:
DUNN, MARIE BICKFORD
Prewar Rocking Chair Sensa-
tion of Russia, The. See:
MEYER, DR. ALEXANDER
Price, Benton. See:
WILSON, ROGER C.
Price, Dennis. See:
ROSE-PRICE, DENNISTOUN

FRANKLYN JOHN
PRICE, FRANCIS WILSON
(1895-) [American Pres-
byterian clergyman and
author]
Frank W. Price
PRICE, FRANK J. (1860-1939)
[American journalist and
author]
Faulkner Conway
PRICE, GEORGE (1910-)
[British Baptist minister
and educator]
Rhys Price
Price, Jennifer. See:
HOOVER, HELEN
DRUSILLA BLACKBURN
Price, Maire. See:
NIC SHIUBHLAIGH, MAIRE
PRICE, STERLING G. (1809-69)
[American Civil War
general officer]
Dad
The Old Tycoon
Pap
Price, Walter. See:
WILSON, ROGER C.
Prichard, Katharine Susannah.
See: THROSSELL,
KATHARINE SUSANNAH
PRICHARD
Pride of the Rockies, The. See:
DEVLAN, EUGENE
PRIDGETT, GERTRUDE
MALISSA NIX (1886-1939)
[American Negro blues
singer]
Ma Rainey
Priest of Anti-Masonry, The Arch.
See: STEVENS, THADDEUS
Priest of English Palladianism,
The High. See:
BOYLE, RICHARD
Priest of Meudon, The Parish
(Le Curé de Meudon). See:
RABELAIS, FRANÇOIS
Priest of Nature, The. See:
NEWTON, SIR ISAAC
Priest of the Constitution, The
High. See:
BAYARD, JAMES ASHETON
Priest, The Glacier. See:

829

HUBBARD, FATHER
   BERNARD ROSECRANS
Priest, The Mad. See:
   BALL, JOHN
Priest, The Red. See:
   VIVALDI, ANTONIO
PRIESTLEY, JOHN BOYNTON
   (1894-) [English
   novelist, playwright and
   essayist]
   J.B. Priestley
Priests, The Scourge of the.
   See: FAREL, GUILLAUME
PRIGNANO, BARTOLOMMEO
   (1318-89) [Supreme
   Pontiff of Roman Catholic
   Church]
   Pope Urban VI
PRILEY, MARGARET HUBBARD
   (1909-) [American author]
   Margaret Ann Hubbard
Primarius, Botanicus Regius.
   See: PARKINSON, JOHN
Prime Minister of Mirth, The.
   See: WADE, GEORGE
   EDWARD
Primm, Brother Orrin. See:
   WILLETT, BROTHER
   FRANCISCUS
Prince. See:
   LASHA, WILLIAM B.
Prince Albert. See:
   ALBERT
Prince Arthur. See:
   ARTHUR, CHESTER ALAN
Prince Charley. See:
   GALLOWAY, CHARLES
   BETTS
Prince Charlie, Bonny. See:
   STUART, CHARLES
   EDWARD LOUIS
   PHILIP CASIMIR
Prince Charming. See:
   FAROUK I
Prince Cheng. See:
   SHIH HUANG TI
Prince Ching. See:
   SHIH HUANG TI
Prince Henry the Navigator.
   See: HENRY
PRINCE, HUGH DENHAM
   (1906-60) [American

musician]
Hughie Prince
Prince John. See:
   BEAUREGARD, PIERRE
   GUSTAVE TOUTANT
   VAN BUREN, JOHN
Prince Lahovary, His Highness.
   See: MANOLESCO, GEORGE
Prince Napoleon. See:
   BONAPARTE, JOSEPH
   CHARLES PAUL
Prince of Alchemy, The. See:
   RUDOLF (RUDOLPH) II
Prince of America, The. See:
   TODD, JOHN PAYNE
Prince of American Letters, The.
   See: IRVING, WASHINGTON
Prince of Ancient Comedy, The.
   See: ARISTOPHANES
Prince of Artists, The. See:
   DURER, ALBRECHT
Prince of Baseball, The Clown.
   See: SCHACHT, ALEXANDER
Prince of Basketball, The Clown.
   See: LEMON, MEADOW
   GEORGE
PRINCE OF BENEVENTO. See:
   DESIDERIUS, PRINCE OF
   BENEVENTO
Prince of Coxcombs, The. See:
   JOSEPH, CHARLES
Prince of Cricketers, The Black.
   See: RANJITSINHJI,
   PRINCE
Prince of Destruction, The. See:
   TIMUR LENK
Prince of Diplomatists, The.
   See: TALLEYRAND-PERI-
   GORD, CHARLES
   MAURICE DE
Prince of Erie. See:
   FISK, JAMES, JR.
Prince of Flatworkers, The.
   See: BURKE, WILLIAM
Prince of Gossips, The. See:
   PEPYS, SAMUEL
Prince of Gourmets, The. See:
   BRILLAT-SAVARIN,
   ANTHELME
Prince of Grammarians, The.
   See: DYSCOLUS,
   APOLLONIUS

Prince of Humbugs. See:
BARNUM, PHINEAS
TAYLOR
Prince of Humorists, The.
See: CLEMENS,
SAMUEL LANGHORNE
Prince of Interviewers, The.
See: SENIOR, NASSAU
WILLIAM
Prince of Journalists, The.
See: GREELEY, HORACE
Prince of Knickerbocker, The.
See: KNICKERBOCKER,
HERMAN
Prince of Liars, The. See:
PINTO, FERNÃO MENDES
Prince of Mail Contractors,
The. See:
REESIDE, JAMES
Prince of Music, The. See:
PALESTRINA, GIOVANNI
PIERLUIGI
Prince of Observers, The. See:
MÜLLER, FRITZ
Prince of Orators, The. See:
DEMOSTHENES
Prince of Painters, The.
See: APELLES
PARRHASIUS
Prince of Parliamentarians, The.
See: MELL, PATRICK
HUES
Prince of Philosophers, The.
See: ARISTOCLES
Prince of Physicians, The.
See: AVICENNA
Prince of Pistoleers, The.
See: HICKOCK, JAMES
BUTLER
Prince of Poets in his Time,
The. See:
SPENSER, EDMUND
Prince of Poets, The. See:
HOMER
SPENSER, EDMUND
Prince of Princes, The. See:
GEORGE IV
Prince of Publishers, The. See:
TONSON, JACOB
Prince of Schaghticoke, The.
See: KNICKERBOCKER,
HERMAN
Prince of Scholastics. See:

AQUINAS, ST. THOMAS
Prince of Showmen. See:
BARNUM, PHINEAS
TAYLOR
Prince of Spanish Poetry, The.
See: VEGA,
GARCILASSO DE LA
Prince of Story-tellers, The.
See: BOCCACCIO,
GIOVANNI
Prince of the Air, The. See:
WEISS, EHRICH (ERIK
WEISZ)
Prince of the Humanists, The.
See: GERHARDS, GER-
HARD (GEERT GEERTS)
Prince of the New Deal, Crown.
See: ROOSEVELT, JAMES
Prince of the Ode, The. See:
RONSARD, PIERRE DE
Prince of the Peace, The. See:
GODOY, MANUEL DE
Prince of the Sonnet, The. See:
BELLAY, JOACHIM DU
Prince of Thieves, The. See:
MANOLESCO, GEORGE
Prince of Viana. See:
CHARLES IV
PRINCE OF WALES. See:
EDWARD, PRINCE OF
WALES
Prince of Wit and Wisdom, The.
See: ROGERS, WILLIAM
PENN ADAIR
PRINCE RUPERT (1619-82)
[Nephew of CHARLES I of
England]
The Mad Cavalier
Prince Rupert of the Confederacy,
The. See:
STUART, JAMES EWELL
BROWN
Prince, The. See:
JUDAH I
Prince, The Black. See:
EDWARD, PRINCE OF
WALES
Prince, The Crown. See:
McADOO, WILLIAM GIBBS
Prince, The Merchant. See:
MORRIS, ROBERT
Prince, The Perfect. See:
JOHN II

Prince, The Red. See:
FREDERICK-CHARLES,
PRINCE
Prince, The Sailor. See:
GEORGE V
Prince Titi. See:
FREDERICK LOUIS
Princeps Nominalium. See:
OCKHAM (OCCAM),
WILLIAM OF
Princes, The Beau of. See:
GEORGE IV
Princes, The Prince of. See:
GEORGE IV
Princes, The Scourge of. See:
ARETINO, PIETRO
Princess Alice. See:
LONGWORTH, ALICE
LEE ROOSEVELT
Princess Olive. See:
SERRES, MRS. OLIVIA
WILMOT
Princeton, The Sage of. See:
CLEVELAND, STEPHEN
GROVER
ROOSEVELT, THEODORE
Principle, The Father of the
Short Ballot. See:
CHILDS, RICHARD
SPENCER
PRING-MILL, ROBERT
DUGUID FORREST
(1924-) [British linguist,
editor and author]
Robert Duguid
Pringle, Eileen. See:
BISBEE, AILEEN
PRINGLE, JOHN (1895-1936)
[American motion picture
actor]
John Gilbert
Pringle-Pattison, Andrew
Seth. See:
SETH, ANDREW
Printer of 1776, The Patriot.
See: BRADFORD,
WILLIAM
Printer, The Learned. See:
BOWYER, WILLIAM
Printing, The Father of. See:
GENSFLEISCH, JOHAN
Printing, The Father of English.

See: CAXTON, WILLIAM
Printing, The Historian of. See:
AMES, JOSEPH
Prior, James. See:
KIRK, JAMES PRIOR
Prior, S. See:
GALT, JOHN
Prison Reform in the United
States, The Father of. See:
OSBORN, GEORGE O.
Prison Reform, The Heaven-sent
Angel of Mercy and of.
See: DIX, DOROTHEA
LYNDE
Prisoner of Chillon, The. See:
BONNIVARD, FRANÇOIS
DE
Prisoner of Ham, The. See:
BONAPARTE, CHARLES
LOUIS NAPOLEON
Prisoner of the Vatican, The.
See: FERRETTI, GIO-
VANNI MARIA MASTAI
Prisoner's Friend, The. See:
BEAL, ABRAHAM
Prisons, The Angel of the. See:
TUTWILER, JULIA
STRUDWICK
PRITCHARD, HANNAH (1711-68)
[English actress]
Miss Vaughan
PRITKIN, RON (1920-)
[American composer and
conductor]
Ron Terry
Private Eddie Fisher. See:
FISHER, EDWIN JACK
Private John. See:
ALLEN, JOHN MILLS
Private T. E. Shaw. See:
LAWRENCE, THOMAS
EDWARD
Private's Gary Cooper, The Buck.
See: MacARTHUR,
DOUGLAS
Pro, A Nine-to-five. See:
BEARD, FRANK
Prob, Old. See:
ABBE, CLEVELAND
Probabilities, Old. See:
ABBE, CLEVELAND
Probationer, The Scottish. See:

DAVIDSON, THOMAS
Procedure, Parliamentary. See:
    CANNON, CLARENCE
Process in America, The Father
    of the Dry Plate. See:
    NEWTON, HENRY
    JOTHAM
PROCOPIUS, ANDREW (died
    1434) [Hussite leader]
    The Great
PROCTOR, ADELAIDE ANNE
    (1825-64) [English poet]
    Mary Berwick
    Miss Mary Berwick
PROCTOR, BRYAN WALLER
    (1787-1874) [British poet
    and barrister]
    Barry Cornwall
Proctor, Everitt. See:
    MONTGOMERY, RUTHER-
    FORD GEORGE
PROCTOR, HENRY HUGH
    (1868-1933) [American
    Negro Clergyman]
    The Father of Organized
    Alumni Work at Fisk
    University
PROCTOR, MARY (fl. early
    20th cent.) [British
    astronomer, author and
    lecturer]
    The Lady of the Stars
Prodigy of France, The. See:
    BUDE (BUDAEUS),
    GUILLAUME
Prodigy of Learning, The. See:
    HAHNEMANN, CHRISTIAN
    SAMUEL FREDERICK
Prodigy, The American. See:
    SAUVOLLE, LE MOINE
Prodigy, The Infant. See:
    MANTLE, MICKEY
    CHARLES
Producer, The Boy. See:
    THALBERG, IRVING
    GRANT
Producers, The Barnum of
    Broadway. See:
    MARGULOIS, DAVID
Prof. See:
    Professor
    Professor, The

WEAVER, MONTE MORTON
Professional English Biographer,
    The First. See:
    WALTON, IZAAK
Professional Playwright,
    America's First. See:
    DUNLAP, WILLIAM
Professional Thief, The. See:
    UNKNOWN
Professor. See:
    PEPPER, J. H.
    Prof
    Professor, The
    WILSON, THOMAS
    WOODROW
Professor Bunker C. Hill. See:
    ABEL, ALAN IRWIN
Professor Gildersleeve. See:
    URNER, NATHAN DANE
Professor, The. See:
    COLONNA, GERARD
    CRANDALL, MILTON
    POAGUE, WILLIAM ROBERT
    Prof
    Professor
Professor, The American. See:
    FELTON, CORNELIUS
    CONWAY
Professor, The Old. See:
    KYSER, JAMES KING KERN
Professor Wilden-Hart, By. See:
    WILDEN-HART, BERNARD
    JOHN
PROFFITT, JOSEPHINE MOORE
    (1914-) [American author
    and composer]
    Sylvia Dee
Profile, The Great. See:
    BLYTHE, JOHN
Profound Doctor, The (Doctor
    Profundus). See:
    BRADWARDINE, THOMAS
    MIDDLETON, RICHARD
Profundus, Doctor (The
    Profound Doctor). See:
    BRADWARDINE, THOMAS
    MIDDLETON, RICHARD
Prohibition, The Apostle of. See:
    HILL, WALTER BARNARD
Prohibition, The Father of. See:
    DOW, NEAL
Prolific and Popular Writer of

Thrillers, The World's Most.
See: OPPENHEIM,
EDWARD PHILLIPS
PROMITIS, MARY (fl. 1928)
[American marathon
dancer]
Hercules Mary
Prophet of Romanticism, The.
See: HARDENBERG,
FRIEDRICH LEO-
POLD, BARON VON
Prophet of the Revolution, The.
See: HENRY, PATRICK
Prophet of the Syrians, The.
See: SYRUS, EPHRAEM
Prophet, The Dumb. See:
CLEVELAND, STEPHEN
GROVER
Prophet, The False. See:
MOHAMMED AHMED
Prophet, The Stuffed. See:
CLEVELAND, STEPHEN
GROVER
Prophet, The Weeping. See:
SEWALL, JOSEPH
Prose Fiction, The Father of
Modern. See:
FOE, DANIEL
Prose Homer of Human Nature,
The. See:
FIELDING, HENRY
Prose Homer of the Great
Ocean, The. See:
RUSSELL, WILLIAM
CLARK
Prose, The Bard of. See:
BOCCACCIO, GIOVANNI
Prose, The Father of
American. See:
IRVING, WASHINGTON
Prose, The Father of English.
See: ASCHAM, ROGER
Prose, The Father of Greek.
See: HERODOTUS
Prose, The Father of Italian.
See: BOCCACCIO,
GIOVANNI
Prose, The First Master of
English. See:
NORTH, SIR THOMAS
Prose, The Solon of French.
See: BALZAC, JEAN

LOUIS GUEZ DE
Prose Writers, The Spenser of
English. See:
TAYLOR, JEREMY
Prosperity's Advance Agent. See:
McKINLEY, WILLIAM
Protection, The Napoleon of.
See: McKINLEY,
WILLIAM
Protective Policy, The Father
of the. See:
CLAY, HENRY
Protector and Defender of the
Kingdom. See:
JOHN OF LANCASTER
Protector of England, Lord.
See: CROMWELL, OLIVER
CROMWELL, RICHARD
Protector of Mexico. See:
NORTON, JOSHUA A.
Protector of the Indians, The.
See: LAS CASAS,
BARTOLOME DE
Protestant Duke, The. See:
SCOTT, JAMES
Protestant Livy, The. See:
PHILIPPI, JOHANNES
Protestant Pope. See:
CORSINI, LORENZO
Proteus. See:
STEINMETZ, KARL
AUGUST RUDOLF
Proteus Echo, Esq. See:
FRANKLIN, BENJAMIN
Protomartyr of the Scottish
Reformation, The. See:
HAMILTON, PATRICK
Proud Duke of Somerset, The.
See: SEYMOUR,
CHARLES, 6TH DUKE
OF SOMERSET
Proud, Tarquin the. See:
TARQUINIUS SUPERBUS,
LUCIUS
Proud, The. See:
ALBERT
Proud World, Censor of the.
See: ARETINO, PIETRO
PROUDFIT, DAVID LAW
(1842-97) [American author]
Peleg Arkwright
Prout, Father. See:

834

MAHONY, FRANCIS
SYLVESTER
Provençals, The Juvenal of
the. See:
CARDINAL, PIERRE
PROVINE, JOHN WILLIAM
(1866-1942) [American
educator]
Dutchy Provine
Prud'hon, Pierre-Paul. See:
PRUDON, PIERRE
PRUDON, PIERRE (1758-1823)
[French historical and
portrait painter]
Pierre-Paul Prud'hon
Prus, Boleslaw. See:
GLOWACKI,
ALEXANDER
Prussians, The Apostle of the.
See: ADELBERT
BRUNO, ST.
Pryde, Anthony. See:
WEEKES, AGNES
RUSSELL
PRYDE, JAMES. See:
Beggarstaff, J. and W.
Psalm Singer. See:
ADAMS, SAMUEL
Psalmanazar, George. See:
UNKNOWN
Psappho. See:
UNKNOWN
Psychiatry, The Father of
American. See:
RUSH, BENJAMIN
Pteleon. See:
GRIEVE, CHRISTOPHER
MURRAY
PTOLEMY I (c.367-283 B.C.)
[King of Egypt]
Soter (The Preserver)
PTOLEMY II (309-246 B.C.)
[King of Egypt]
Philadelphus (The Brotherly)
PTOLEMY III (c.282-221 B.C.)
[King of Egypt]
Euergetes (Benefactor)
PTOLEMY IV (c.244-203 B.C.)
[King of Egypt]
Philopator (Loving his
Father)
PTOLEMY V (c.210-181 B.C.)
[King of Egypt]

Epiphanes (The Illustrious)
PTOLEMY VI (c.186-145 B.C.)
[King of Egypt]
Philometor
PTOLEMY VII (or VIII or IX)
(c.184-116 B.C.) [King
of Egypt]
Euergetes II (Benefactor)
Physcon (Fat Paunch)
PTOLEMY VII (161-144 B.C.)
[King of Egypt]
New Philopator (Loving his
Father)
PTOLEMY VIII (died 81 B.C.)
[King of Egypt]
Lathyrus
Soter II (The Preserver)
PTOLEMY IX (died 88 B.C.)
[King of Egypt]
Alexander I
PTOLEMY X (c.105-80 B.C.)
[King of Egypt]
Alexander II
PTOLEMY XI (c.95-51 B.C.)
[King of Egypt]
Auletes (The Piper)
Philopator Neos Dionysos
PTOLEMY XII (c.61-48 B.C.)
[King of Egypt; brother
and husband of CLEOPATRA]
Dionysos
PTOLEMY XIV (47-30 B.C.)
[King of Egypt]
Philopator Philometer Caesar
Cesarion
PTOLEMY KERAUNOS (died 279
B.C.) [King of Macedonia]
The Thunderbolt
Pu-Yi, Henry. See:
HSUAN T'UNG
Public Enemy No. 1. See:
DILLINGER, JOHN HER-
BERT
GILLIS, LESTER M.
Public Functionary, Old. See:
BUCHANAN, JAMES
Public School System in Ohio,
The Father of the. See:
RICE, HARVEY
Public School System of
Pennsylvania, The Father
of the. See:
WOLF, GEORGE

Public School System, The
Father of the English. See:
WYKEHAM (WICKHAM),
WILLIAM OF
Public Schools of Alabama,
The Father of the.
See: MEEK,
ALEXANDER BEAUFORT
Public Utility Regulation, The
Father of. See:
NORRIS, GEORGE
WILLIAM
Publican, Samuel the. See:
ADAMS, SAMUEL
Publisher, The Perfect. See:
KNOPF, ALFRED A.
Publishers, The Anak of. See:
MURRAY, JOHN
Publishers, The Prince of.
See: TONSON, JACOB
Publius, joint pseud. of
ALEXANDER HAMILTON
(1757-1804), JOHN JAY
(1745-1829) and JAMES
MADISON (1751-1836)
[American statesmen and
authors of articles in
The Federalist]
Publius. See also:
HAMILTON, ALEXANDER
MADISON, JAMES
Pucelle d'Orleans, La (The
Maid of Orleans). See:
JOAN OF ARC, ST.
(JEANNE D'ARC)
PUCHOL, AURELIO (1914-53)
[Spanish bullfighter]
Morenito de Valencia
Puck of Commentators, The.
See: STEEVENS,
GEORGE
PUDDICOMBE, ANNE
ADALISA (1836-1908)
[English novelist]
Allen Raine
Puddler Jim. See:
DAVIS, JAMES JOHN
Pudge. See:
HEFFELFINGER,
WILLIAM W.
PUENTE, ERNEST, JR.
(1925-) [American

jazz musician (leader,
vibraharp, timbales, piano,
alto saxophone)]
Tito Puente
Puffer Hopkins. See:
MATHEWS, CORNELIUS
Pug. See:
ISMAY, HASTINGS
LIONEL, 1ST BARON
PUGET, PIERRE (1622-94)
[French painter, sculptor,
engineer and architect]
The French Michelangelo
PUGH, MARSHALL MORRISON
(fl. mid-20th cent.)
[Scottish author]
Pugh
Pulchritudinous Evangelist,
The World's Most. See:
McPHERSON, AIMEE
SEMPLE
Pullein-Thompson, Christine.
See: POPESCU, CHRIS-
TINE PULLEIN-
THOMPSON
Pullein-Thompson, Diana. See:
FARR, DIANA PULLEIN-
THOMPSON
PULLING, CHRISTOPHER
ROBERT DRUCE (1893-)
[British barrister, police
commissioner, lecturer and
author]
Christopher Druce
Pulpit Buffoon, The. See:
PETERS, HUGH
Pulps, King of the. See:
FAUST, FREDERICK
SCHILLER
Pulu. See:
TIGLATH-PILESER III
Pumpernickel. See:
WEINSTEIN, SOL
Pumpkins, The Poet of Bran
Meal and. See:
GRAHAM, SYLVESTER
Punch. See:
MILLER, ERNEST
Punch, T in. See:
THORP, JOSEPH PETER
Pungent, Pierce. See:
POWELL, THOMAS

Punjab, The Lion of the.
    See: RANJIT SINGH
PUNNETT, IVOR McCAULEY
    (1927-) [English
    author]
  Guy Bruce
  Roger Simons
Punning. See:
    BYLES, MATHER
Punteret. See:
    SANZ, JOAQUIN
PURCELL, HENRY (1658-95)
    [English musician and
    composer]
  The Father of Anglican
    Church Music
PURCELL, VICTOR (1896-)
    [British civil servant
    and author]
  Myra Buttle
PURDOM, THOMAS E.
    (1936-) [American
    author]
  Tom Purdom
PURDY, KEN WILLIAM
    (1913-) [American
    author]
  Karl Prentiss
Pure, Simon. See:
    SWINNERTON, FRANK
    ARTHUR
Pure, The. See:
    BAFFO
Purist, The Great. See:
    NORRIS, GEORGE
    WILLIAM
Puritan, College. See:
    SHERMAN, JOHN
Puritan Pepys. See:
    SEWALL, SAMUEL
Puritan Plato, The. See:
    HOWE, JOHN
Puritan Poet, The. See:
    WHITTIER, JOHN
    GREENLEAF
Puritan, The. See:
    ABBOT, GEORGE
Puritan, The Platonic. See:
    HOWE, JOHN
Puritans, The Last of the.
    See: ADAMS, SAMUEL
PURNELL, WILLIAM (1915-65)

[American jazz musician
    (drums)]
  Keg
Purse. See:
    PIERCE, FRANKLIN
PUSEY, EDWARD BOUVERIE
    (1800-82) [English
    divine and ecclesiastical
    writer]
  Champion of Orthodoxy
Push-'em-up. See:
    LAZZERI, ANTHONY
    MICHAEL
Pushful Joe. See:
    CHAMBERLAIN, JOSEPH
PUSHKIN, ALEXANDER
    (1799-1837) [Russian poet]
  The Russian Byron
Pussyfoot. See:
    JOHNSON, WILLIAM
    EUGENE
Put, Old. See:
    PUTNAM, ISRAEL
PUTNAM, AMELIA EARHART
    (1898-1937?) [American
    aviatrix]
  America's Premier Air
    Woman
  Amelia Earhart
Putnam, Eleanor. See:
    BATES, ARLO
    BATES, HARRIET
    LEONORA VOSE
PUTNAM, GEORGE PALMER
    (1887-) [American pub-
    lisher and author]
  Palmer Bend
PUTNAM, ISRAEL (1718-90)
    [American Revolutionary
    War general officer]
  Old Put
  Wolf Putnam
Putnam, J. Wesley. See:
    DRAGO, HENRY SINCLAIR
Putnam Weale. See:
    SIMPSON, BERTRAM
    LENOX
Putra, Kerala. See:
    PANIKKAR, KAVALAM
    MADHAVA
PYESHKOV, ALEXEI
    MAXIMOVICH (1868-1936)

[Russian playwright]
Maxim Gorki
PYLE, ERNEST TAYLOR
(1900-45) [American
journalist]
Ernie Pyle
PYM, JOHN (1584-1643)
[English parliamentary
leader]
King Pym
PYM, JOHN. See also:
Five Members, The
Pym of France, The. See:
MOLÉ, MATHIEU
PYTHAGORAS (c. 582-c. 500
B.C.) [Greek philosopher
and mathematician]
The Sage of Samos
The Samian Sage

Q

Q. See:
QUILLER-COUCH, SIR
ARTHUR THOMAS
Q., Dorothy. See:
HOLMES, OLIVER
WENDELL
Q.E.D. See:
UNKNOWN
Q.K. Philander Doesticks, P.B.
See: THOMSON,
MORTIMER NEAL
Q, Old. See:
DOUGLAS, WILLIAM
Q. Patrick. See:
Patrick, Q.
Quentin, Patrick
WEBB, RICHARD WILSON
Quacks, The Autocrat of the.
See: HEADLEY, JOEL
TYLER
Quad. See also:
Quod
Quad, M. See:
LEWIS, CHARLES
BERTRAND
Quaid-i-azam (Great Leader).
See: JINNAH,
MOHAMMED ALI
Quaker Dolly. See:

MADISON, DOROTHY
PAYNE TODD
Quaker Martyr, The. See:
DYER, MARY
Quaker Meadows Joe. See:
McDOWELL, JOSEPH
Quaker Poet, The. See:
BARTON, BERNARD
WHITTIER, JOHN
GREENLEAF
Quaker Poetess, The. See:
LIPPINCOTT, MARTHA
SHEPARD
Quaker Soldier, The. See:
BIDDLE, CLEMENT
Quaker, The Fighting. See:
GREENE, NATHANAEL
WANTON, JOHN
Quakeress, The Fair. See:
LIGHTFOOT, HANNAH
Quakerism, The Flower of.
See: MOTT, LUCRETIA
Quakers, The King of the. See:
PEMBERTON, ISRAEL
Qualen, John. See:
OLESON, JOHN
Quality. See:
WOOD, VIOLET
Quality, A Lady of. See:
BAGNOLD, ENID
Quality, A Person of. See:
SWIFT, JONATHAN
Quarles Quicken. See:
POE, EDGAR ALLAN
Quarreler, The. See:
LOUIS X
Quarterly, Milton. See:
CORYELL, JOHN
RUSSELL
QUEDENS, EUNICE (1912-)
[American actress and
comedienne]
Eve Arden
Queen. See:
King and Queen of Hos-
pitality, The
MARIE OF RUMANIA
Queen Alice. See:
LONGWORTH, ALICE LEE
ROOSEVELT
Queen Bess, Good. See:
ELIZABETH I

Queen Dick. See:
CROMWELL, RICHARD
Queen Dolly. See:
MADISON, DOROTHY
PAYNE TODD
Queen Dowager, The. See:
MADISON, DOROTHY
PAYNE TODD
Queen, Ellery
Ellery Queen, Jr.
Barnaby Ross
joint pseuds. of DANIEL
NATHAN (Frederic
Dannay) (1905-) and
MANFRED BENNINGTON
LEE (1905-71) [writers
of detective and mystery
stories]
Queen Margot. See:
MARGARET OF VALOIS
Queen Marie. See:
MARIE OF RUMANIA
Queen Marie of Hollywood. See:
KOERBER, LEILA
Queen of Bohemia, The. See:
McELHENEY, JANE
Queen of Hearts, The. See:
STUART, ELIZABETH
Queen of Jazz, The. See:
ABUZA, SOPHIE
SCRUGGS, MARY
ELFRIEDA
Queen of Queens, The. See:
CLEOPATRA
Queen of Scots. See:
MARY
Queen of Song, The. See:
CATALANI, ANGELICA
Queen of Tears, The. See:
MARY OF MODENA
Queen of Technicolor, The.
See: BROWN, MAUREEN
FITZSIMONS
Queen of the Cowgirls, The.
See: SMITH, FRANCES
OCTAVIA
Queen of the English Stage,
The. See: BROWN,
ELIZABETH ANN
Queen of the Folk Singers, The.
See: BAEZ, JOAN
Queen of the Gospel Song. See:

JACKSON, MAHALIA
Queen of the Gypsies, The. See:
ADAMS, ROSE
Queen of the Movies. See:
SMITH, GLADYS MARY
Queen of the Rosewater Ad-
ministration, The. See:
GREENHOW, ROSE O'NEAL
Queen of the Silent Serials,
The. See:
WHITE, PEARL
Queen of the Vampires, The. See:
GOODMAN, THEODOSIA
Queen of the West, The. See:
SMITH, FRANCES
OCTAVIA
Queen Sarah. See:
JENNINGS, SARAH
Queen, The Bandit. See:
STARR, BELLE
Queen, The Little. See:
ISABELLA OF VALOIS
Queen, The Nightclub. See:
GUINAN, MARY LOUISE
CECELIA
Queen, The Snow. See:
STUART, ELIZABETH
Queen, The Virgin. See:
ELIZABETH I
Queen, The White. See:
MARY
Queen, The Winter. See:
STUART, ELIZABETH
Queens, The Queen of. See:
CLEOPATRA
Queensberry, The Duke of. See:
DOUGLAS, WILLIAM
Queensberry, The Marquis of.
See: DOUGLAS, JOHN
SHOLTO
Quentin, Patrick
Q. Patrick
Jonathan Stagge, joint
pseuds. of RICHARD WIL-
SON WEBB (191?-) and
HUGH CALLINGHAM
WHEELER (1913-) [Amer-
ican authors of detective
stories]
Quentin, The Eagle. See:
ROOSEVELT, QUENTIN
Querno, Poet Laureate to the

Congress, Camillo. See:
ODELL, JONATHAN
Query, Peter. See:
TUPPER, MARTIN
FARQUHAR
QUESNAY DE BEAUREPAIRE,
JULES (1837-1923)
[French jurist and writer]
Jules de Glouvet
QUESNAY, FRANÇOIS (1694-
1774) [French
physician and economist]
The European Confucius
Quetzalcóatl (The Fair God).
See: CORTÉS, HERNÁN
Quex. See:
NICHOLS, GEORGE
HERBERT FOSDIKE
Quick, Double. See:
HOLLINGSWORTH,
JAMES H.
Quicken, Quarles. See:
POE, EDGAR ALLAN
Quicksilver Bob. See:
FULTON, ROBERT
Quiet People, The Apostle of.
See: YOUNG, EMILY
HILDA
Quiet, The (Olaf Kyrre). See:
OLAF III
QUIEVREUX, JEAN-FRANÇOIS
(1926-) [French jazz
musician]
Jef Gilson
Quilibet, Philip. See:
POND, GEORGE EDWARD
Quill. See:
GRANGE, CYRIL
QUILLER-COUCH, SIR ARTHUR
THOMAS (1863-1944)
[English scholar and
man of letters]
Q.
QUILLINAN, DOROTHY
WORDSWORTH (1804-47)
[English author]
Dora Wordsworth
QUIN [Quin]. See also:
QUINN
Quin, Dan. See:
LEWIS, ALFRED HENRY
QUIN, JAMES (1693-1766)

[English actor]
The Whitfield of the Stage
Quince, Peter. See:
DAY, GEORGE HAROLD
DEXTER, TIMOTHY
STORY, ISAAC
QUINCY, JOSIAH (1772-1864)
[American Revolutionary
leader; educator, Mayor
of Boston and congressman
from Massachusetts]
King Josiah the First
QUINLAN, STERLING C.
(1916-) [American radio
official and author]
Red Quinlan
QUINN. See also:
QUIN
Quin
QUINN, JAMES ALOYSIUS
(18??-1924) [American
politician, active in
Chicago]
Hot Stove Jimmy
QUINT, WILDER DWIGHT. See:
Merriman, Charles Eustace
Quintero, Álvarez, joint pseud.
of JOAQUÍN QUINTERO
(1873-1944) and his brother
SERAFÍN QUINTERO (1871-
1938) [Spanish playwrights].
Also known as The Brothers
Quintero.
Quintilian, The French. See:
HARPE, JEAN FRANÇOIS
DE LA
Quirinus. See:
ROMULUS
Quist, Felicia. See:
HOBSON, LAURA
ZAMETKIN
Quixote of the Jerseys, Don. See:
LIVINGSTON, WILLIAM
Quixote of the North, The. See:
CHARLES XII
Quixote, Potato. See:
ALCOTT, AMOS BRONSON
Quiz. See:
CASWALL, E.
Quod. See also:
Quad
Quod, John. See:

IRVING, JOHN TREAT
QUOIREZ, FRANÇOISE (1935-
) [French author]
Françoise Sagan
Quousque. See:
    ATKINS, FREDERICK
    ANTHONY

R

R.A. Wilson. See:
    KING, ROBERT
R.A. Woodrook. See:
    COWLISHAW, RANSON
R. Alcon. See:
    BRONTË, EMILY JANE
R. Austin Freeman. See:
    FREEMAN, RICHARD
    AUSTIN
R.C. Carton. See:
    CRITCHETT, RICHARD
    CLAUDE
R.C.H. See:
    SWEENEY, CHARLES
R.D. Whitinger. See:
    PLACE, MARIAN
    TEMPLETON
R. Emmett Dembry. See:
    MURFREE, MARY
    NOAILLES
R.F.K. See:
    KENNEDY, ROBERT
    FRANCIS
R.G. See:
    CHOATE, GWEN
    PETERSON
R.H. Jayne, Lieut. See:
    ELLIS, EDWARD
    SYLVESTER
R. Hunt Wilby. See:
    EYSTER, WILLIAM
    REYNOLDS
R.J. Cristy. See:
    DE CRISTOFORO, R.J.
R.J. Martin. See:
    MEHTA, RUSTAM
    JEHANGIR
R. Johnson Martin. See:
    MEHTA, RUSTAM
    JEHANGIR
R. Kraselchik. See:

DYER, CHARLES
R.L.S. See:
    STEVENSON, ROBERT
    LOUIS BALFOUR
R. Laugier. See:
    CUMBERLAND, MARTEN
R.M. Hawthorne, Captain. See:
    ELLIS, EDWARD
    SYLVESTER
R.M. Krapp. See:
    ADAMS, ROBERT MARTIN
R. Patrick Ward. See:
    HOLZAPFEL, RUDOLF
    PATRICK
R.R. Inman. See:
    MORRIS, CHARLES
    SMITH
R.R.R. See:
    RUSK, ROBERT
    ROBERTSON
R.R. Winter. See:
    WINTERBOTHAM, RUSSELL
    ROBERT
R. Von Einseidel. See:
    TETZNER, MARTHA
    HELENE
R.W. See:
    CAMPBELL, ROSEMAE
    WELLS
R. Welldon Finn. See:
    FINN, REGINALD PATRICK
    ARTHUR
RAABE, WILHELM (1831-1910)
    [German novelist]
Jakob Corvinus
Rabasseire, Henry. See:
    PACHTER, HENRY
    MAXIMILIAN
Rabbit. See:
    HODGES, JOHN
    CORNELIUS
    McNAIR, DONALD ERIE
    MARANVILLE, WALTER
    JAMES VINCENT
Rabbit, Peter. See:
    LONG, WILLIAM JOSEPH
Rabble, The Idol of the. See:
    PENKETHMAN (PINKETH-
    MAN), WILLIAM
RABE, FLORENCE (c.1890-1954)
    [American businesswoman,
    lawyer and motion picture

actress]
Florence Bates
RABELAIS, FRANÇOIS
(1495-1553) [French
humorist and author]
Le Curé de Meudon
(The Parish Priest of
Meudon)
The Father of Ridicule
Alcofribas Nasir
Rabelais of Germany, The.
See: FISCHART,
JOHANN BAPTIST
Rabelais, The English. See:
AMORY, THOMAS
STERNE, LAURENCE
SWIFT, JONATHAN
Rabelais, The Modern. See:
MAGINN, WILLIAM
Rabinowitsch, Lydia. See:
KAMPNER, LYDIA
RABINOWITSCH
RABINOWITZ, JEROME
(1918-) [American
choreographer, director
and producer]
Jerome Robbins
RABINOWITZ (RABINOVITZ),
SOLOMON J. (1859-1916)
[Yiddish short-story
writer and journalist]
Shalom Aleichem
Raby, The White Rose of.
See: NEVILL, CECILY
Race, That Singular Splendor
of the Italian. See:
ALIGHIERI, DURANTE
Race, The Most Famous Folk
Singer of His. See:
WHITE, JOSHUA
DANIEL
Race, The Orator of the Human.
See: CLOOTZ, JEAN
BAPTISTE DU VAL DE
GRÂCE
Rachel, Aunt. See:
JACKSON, RACHEL
DONELSON
Rachel Bennett. See:
HILL, MARGARET OHLER
RACINE, JEAN BAPTISTE
(1639-99) [French

dramatist and poet]
The Virgil of the French
Drama
Racine, Le Singe de. See:
CAMPISTRON, JEAN
GALABERT DE
Racine of Italy, The. See:
TRAPASSI, PIETRO
ANTONIO DOMENICO
BONAVENTURA
Racine of Music, The. See:
SACCHINI, MARIE-
GASPARD
Rackham Holt. See:
HOLD, MARGARET VAN
VECHTEN SAUNDERS
RACKHAM, JOHN (16??-1720)
[British pirate]
Calico Jack
RADCLIFFE, ANN WARD
(1764-1823) [British
novelist]
The Salvator Rosa of
British Novelists
Radclyffe. See:
HALL, MARGUERITE
RADCLYFFE
RADEBAUGH, ROY (1910-60)
[American motion picture
actor]
Richard Cromwell
RADETZSKY VON RADETZ,
COUNTESS BERTHA
LEONARZ DE HARDING
(1902-) [German author]
Bertita Harding
RADFORD, RUBY LORRAINE
(1891-) [American edu-
cator and author]
Matilda Bailey
Marcia Ford
Radio Broadcasting, The Father
of. See:
DAVIS, HARRY PHILLIPS
Radio Girl, The Original. See:
DE LEATH, VAUGHN
Radio, The Father of. See:
FOREST, LEE DE
Radio, The Golden Voice of.
See: MUNN, FRANK
Radio, The Magic Fingers of.
See: DUCHIN, EDWIN FRANK

Radio, The Voice of the. See:
STEFAN, KARL
Radio's Own Statue of Liberty.
See: SMITH, KATHRYN
ELIZABETH
RADOCCHIA, EMILIO JOSEPH
(1932-) [American jazz
musician (vibraharp,
composer)]
Emil Richards
RADWANSKI, PIERRE
ARTHUR (1903-)
[Polish anthropologist
and author]
Al-Van-Gar
Chochlik
O'Key
Rae, John. See:
POMPEO, JOHN
ANTHONY
Rafe. See:
GIBBS, RAPHAEL
SANFORD
Raffaello. See:
SANTI (SANZIO),
RAFFAELLO
Rafferty, Chips. See:
GOFFAGE, JOHN
RAFFERTY, MAXWELL
LEWIS, JR. (1917-)
[California State
Superintendent of
Public Instruction]
Max Rafferty
RAFTOR, CATHERINE
(1711-85) [English
actress]
Kitty Clive
Ragged Lawyer, The. See:
GROVER, MARTIN
Ragged Stranger Murderer,
The. See:
WANDERER, CARL
Ragged Stranger, The. See:
RYAN, EDWARD
JOSEPH
RAGLIN, ALVIN (1917-)
[American jazz
musician (bass)]
Junior Raglin
RAGONESE, DON (1920-)
[American composer,

singer and musician]
Don Rodney
Ragtime Composers, The King
of the. See:
JOPLIN, SCOTT
Ragtime Jimmy. See:
DURANTE, JAMES
FRANCIS
RAGUSA, PAULA (c. 1939-)
[American motion picture
actress]
Paula Prentiss
RAI, DEWAN BAHADUR
DEWAN JAMIAT (1861-)
[Indian government official
and author]
A.D.B.
Raider, The. See:
MORGAN, JOHN HUNT
Rail Splitter, The. See:
LINCOLN, ABRAHAM
Railroad King, The. See:
GOULD, JASON
Railroads, The Father of. See:
COOPER, PETER
Railway King, The. See:
CORNING, ERASTUS
HUDSON, GEORGE
Raimond. See also:
RAYMOND
Raymond
Raimond, C.E. See:
ROBINS, ELIZABETH
RAIMONDI, MARCANTONIO
(1475?-1534?) [Italian
Renaissance line engraver]
Marcantonio
Raimu. See:
MURAIRE, JULES
Rain No Mo' Man, The Ain't
Gonna. See:
LEE, EDWARD D.
Rainbow, Beautiful (Wah-Kat-Yu-
Ten). See:
BEAUCHAMP, WILLIAM
MARTIN
Raine, Allen. See:
PUDDICOMBE, ANNE
ADALISA
Rainey, Ma. See:
PRIDGETT, GERTRUDE
MALISSA NIX

Rainham, Thomas. See:
BARREN, CHARLES
Rainy-Day Smith. See:
SMITH, JOHN THOMAS
RAIS (RETZ), GILLES DE
(1404?-40) [Soldier
Marshal of France and
mass murderer]
Bluebeard
Rajah. See:
HORNSBY, ROGERS
RAKOSI, CARL (1903-)
[Hungarian-American
social worker and
author]
Callman Rawley
RALEIGH, SIR WALTER
(1552-1618) [English
statesman and scholar]
The Shepherd of the Ocean
Raley Brien. See:
McCULLEY, JOHNSTON
Raley, Rowiena. See:
McCULLEY, JOHNSTON
Ralf Harolde. See:
WIGGER, RALF
HAROLDE
Ralph. See:
HAMMOND INNES, RALPH
MACGREGOR, JOHN
RELPH
Ralph Carter. See:
NEUBAUER, WILLIAM
ARTHUR
Ralph Connor. See:
GORDON, CHARLES
WILLIAM
Ralph Iron. See:
SCHREINER, OLIVE
EMILIE ALBERTINA
Ralph, Jessie. See:
CHAMBERS, JESSIE
RALPH
Ralph Kelly. See:
GEIS, DARLENE
STERN
Ralph Meeker. See:
RATHGEBER, RALPH
Ralph Michael. See:
SHOTTER, RALPH
CHAMPION
Ralph Morgan. See:

WUPPERMAN, RALPH
Ralph Ringwood. See:
HYNES, CAPTAIN
ALFRED D.
Ralph Royal. See:
ABARBANELL, JACOB
RALPH
Ralph, Uncle. See:
SHAW, RALPH ROBERT
Ralston, Jan. See:
DUNLOP, AGNES MARY
ROBERTSON
Ralston Straight-shooter, The.
See: MIX, TOM
RALSTON, VERA (1929-)
[American television and
motion picture actress]
Vera Miles
Ram. See:
HALL, MINOR
Ram, The Louisiana. See:
MOUTON, ROBERT L.
Rama. See:
GUPTA, RAM CHANDRA
Rama I. See:
BUDDHA YOD FA, P'RA
Rama II. See:
BUDDHA LOES-LA, P'RA
Rama III. See:
CHESDA
Rama IV. See:
MONGKUT
Rama V. See:
CHULALONGKORN
Rama VI. See:
VAJIRAVUDH
Rama VII. See:
PRAJADHIPOK
Rama VIII. See:
MAHIDOL, ANANTA
Rama IX. See:
ADULYADEJ, BHUMIBIL
Ramala, Pratap Roy. See:
BHOSALE, YESHWANTRAO
P.
RaMBam (Second Moses). See:
MAIMONIDES
Rambler. See:
THATCHER, JOHN WELLS
RAMÉE, MARIE LOUISE DE LA
(1839-1908) [English
novelist]

Ouida
Ramel, Walter. See:
    DE LA MARE, WALTER
    JOHN
RAMENGHI, BARTOLOMMEO
    (1484-1542) [Italian
    painter]
Bagnacavallo
RAMÍREZ, ALFONSO (1916-)
    [Mexican bullfighter]
El Calesero
Ramón de las Cuevas. See:
    HARRINGTON, MAX
    RAYMOND
Ramón Lacroix. See:
    McKEAG, ERNEST
    LIONEL
Ramón Novarro. See:
    SAMANIEGOES, RAMÓN
Ramona Graham. See:
    COOK, RAMONA GRAHAM
RAMPAGNETTO, GAETANO
    (1863-1938) [Italian
    author, poet, playwright
    and soldier]
Duca Minimo (The Least of
    the Dukes)
Gabriele d'Annunzio
Rampo, Edogawa. See:
    HIRAI, TARO
RAMSAY [Ramsay]. See also:
    RAMSEY
RAMSAY, ALLAN (1686-1758)
    [Scottish poet]
The Scottish Theocritus
RAMSAY, ANDREW MICHAEL
    (1686-1743) [Scottish
    author]
Chevalier de Ramsay
Ramsay, Fay. See:
    EASTWOOD, HELEN
Ramsay, Guthrie. See:
    BOWRAN, JOHN GEORGE
RAMSAY, OWEN NARES
    (1888-1943) [British
    matinee idol and silent
    motion picture actor]
Owen Nares
Ramsbottom, Dorothea Julia.
    See: THACKERAY,
    WILLIAM MAKEPEACE
Ramsbottom Horsely. See:

BERNE, ERIC LENNARD
RAMSES III (1198-67 B.C.)
    [King of Egypt]
Rhampsinitus
RAMSEY. See also:
    RAMSAY
    Ramsay
RAMSEY, ALEXANDER
    (1754-1824) [Anglo-Amer-
    ican physician]
The Caliban of Science
RAMSKILL, VALERIE PATRICIA
    ROSKAMS (fl. 1947-64)
    [British journalist and
    author]
Carole Brooke
RAMSPECK, ROBERT
    (1930-35) [American
    politician; representative
    from Georgia]
The Guardian of the Civil
    Service
Ramy Allison White. See:
    STRATEMEYER,
    EDWARD L.
Rand Allison. See:
    McCORMICK, WILFRED
Rand, Brett. See:
    NORWOOD, VICTOR
    GEORGE CHARLES
RANDALL [Randall]. See also:
    Randle
RANDALL, ANTHONY (1924-)
    [American actor]
Tony Randall
Randall, Clay. See:
    ADAMS, CLIFTON
Randall, Janet. See:
    YOUNG, JANET RANDALL
Randall, Jean. See:
    HAUCK, LOUISE PLATT
Randall, Robert. See:
    SILVERBERG, DAVID
Randall, Rona. See:
    SHAMBROOK, RONA
Randi, Don. See:
    SCHWARTZ, DON
Randle. See also:
    RANDALL
    Randall
Randle, Frank. See:
    McEVOY, ARTHUR

845

RANDOLPH. See:
    FITZRANDOLPH,
    NATHANIEL
Randolph Churchill, Lord. See:
    CHURCHILL, RANDOLPH
    HENRY SPENCER
RANDOLPH, EVELYN ST.
    LEGER (fl. early 20th
    cent.) [British author]
    Evelyn St. Leger
Randolph, Geoffrey. See:
    ELLIS, EDWARD
    SYLVESTER
RANDOLPH, IRVING
    (1909-) [American
    jazz musician (trumpet)]
    Mouse
RANDOLPH, JOHN (1773-1833)
    [American politician and
    orator]
    Jack the Giant-killer
    John Randolph of Roanoke
    Little David
    The Man with the Sling
Randolph Johnson. See:
    RASLEY, JOHN M.
Randolph, Lieut. J.H. See:
    ELLIS, EDWARD
    SYLVESTER
Randolph Scott. See:
    CRANE, RANDOLPH
Random, Alan. See:
    KAY, ERNEST
RANDS, WILLIAM BRIGHTY
    (1823-82) [English mis-
    cellaneous and juvenile
    writer]
    Matthew Browne
    Henry Holbeach
    The Laureate of the
    Nursery
    T. Talker
Randy. See:
    MATSON, JAMES RANDEL
    TURPIN, RANDOLPH
    VAN HORNE, HARRY
        RANDALL
    WESTON, RANDOLPH E.
Raney, Sue. See:
    CLAUSSEN, RAELENE
    SUE
RANGANATHAN, SHIYALI

RAMAMRITA (1892-)
    [Indian librarian, mathe-
    matician, educator and
    author]
    Philosopher of Librarianship
Rangefinder. See:
    MILES, FREDERIC
    JAMES
Rangely, E.R. See:
    KANTO, PETER
Rangely, Olivia. See:
    KANTO, PETER
Ranger, Ken. See:
    CREASEY, JOHN
Ranger, Old. See:
    REYNOLDS, JOHN
RANJIT SINGH (1780-1839)
    [Sikh ruler of Lahore]
    The Lion of the Punjab
RANJITSINHJI, PRINCE
    (1872-1933) [Indian
    maharaja]
    The Black Prince of
    Cricketers
RANKIN, JOHN ELLIOTT
    (1882-) [American
    lawyer and politician;
    congressman from
    Mississippi]
    T.V.A. Rankin
RANKINE, WILLIAM BIRCH
    (1858-1905) [American
    founder of hydroelectric
    plant at Niagara Falls]
    The Father of Niagara Power
RANN, JOHN (died 1744)
    [English highwayman]
    Sixteen-string Jack
RANSFORD, OLIVER (1914-)
    [British anesthetist and
    author]
    John Wylcotes
RANSOM, JAY ELLIS (1914-)
    [American editor, writer
    and correspondent]
    Henry T. Adams
Raoul de Liancourt. See:
    WINGENBACH, CHARLES
    EDWARD
RAPELA, MANUEL MEJÍAS Y
    (1885-) [Spanish bull-
    fighter]

Bienvienida
Raphael. See:
   SANTI (SANZIO),
   RAFAELLO
RAPHAEL, FREDERIC
   MICHAEL. See:
   Caine, Mark
Raphael, Jay. See:
   JOSEPHS, RAY
Raphael of Cats, The. See:
   MIND, GOTTFRIED
Raphael of England, The. See:
   REYNOLDS, SIR
   JOSHUA
Raphael of Holland, The. See:
   VON HEEMSKERK
   (HEMSKERK), MARTIN
Raphael of Music, The. See:
   MOZART, WOLFGANG
   AMADEUS
Raphael, The Flemish. See:
   DE VRIENDT, FRANS
   FLORIS
Raphael, The French. See:
   LE SUEUR, EUSTACHE
Raphaelite, The American Pre-.
   See: STILLMAN,
   WILLIAM JAMES
Rapid Robert. See:
   FELLER, ROBERT
   WILLIAM ANDREW
RAPP, JOHANN GEORG (1757-
   1847) [German religious
   reformer; founder of
   the Harmonists]
   George Rapp
Rappahannock, The Drummer
   Boy of the. See:
   HENDERSHOT, ROBERT
   HENRY
Rare Ben Jonson. See:
   JONSON, BENJAMIN
Rascal Freneau, That. See:
   FRENEAU, PHILIP
   MORIN
RASH, DORA EILEEN AGNEW
   WALLACE (1897-) [Brit-
   ish educator and author]
   Doreen Wallace
RASLEY, JOHN M. (1913-)
   [American composer and
   conductor]

Randolph Johnson
RASPUTIN, GREGORY
   EFIMOVICH (1871-1916)
   [Russian peasant monk]
   The Holy Devil
Rat. See:
   THOMAS, FRANK WILLIAM
Rat, Red. See:
   McDANIEL, IRA C.
Ratatöskr. See:
   BLAICH, HANS ERICH
RATHBONE, ST. GEORGE
   HENRY (1854-1938)
   [American dime novelist
   and author of boys' books]
   A Private Detective
   Harrison Adams
   Major Andy Burton
   Herbert Carter
   Oliver Lee Clifton
   Dash Dale
   Duke Duncan
   Ward Edwards
   Aleck Forbes
   Jack Howard
   Lieut. Keene
   John Prentice Langley
   W.B. Lawson
   Col. Lawrence Leslie
   Marline Manly
   Mark Merrick
   Warne Miller
   Old Broadbrim
   Alex Robertson, M.D.
   Harry St. George
   Jack Sharpe
   Gordon Stewart
RATHGEBER, RALPH (1920-)
   [American stage and
   motion picture actor]
   Ralph Meeker
Rationalism, The Father of
   German. See:
   SEMLER, JOHANN SALOMO
RATOFF, GREGORY (1893-)
   [Russian-American motion
   picture director and actor]
   Gregory the Great
RATTI, ACHILLE AMBROGIO
   DAMIANO (1857-1939)
   [Supreme Pontiff of Roman
   Catholic Church]

Pope Pius XI
Rattray, Simon. See:
  TREVOR, ELLESTON
Rau, Santha Rama. See:
  BOWERS, SANTHA RAMA
    RAU
Raucourt. See:
  SAUCEROTTE,
    FRANÇOISE-MARIE
    ANTOINETTE JOSÈPHE
Rault, Walter. See:
  GORHAM, MAURICE
    ANTHONY CONEYS
Ravenhall, Mrs. See:
  KING, ROBERT
Rawley, Callman. See:
  RAKOSI, CARL
RAWLINSON, THOMAS (1681-
  1725) [English book and
  manuscript collector]
  Tom Folio
RAWSON, CLAYTON (1906-)
  [American magician,
  editor and author]
  The Great Merlini
RAWSON, EDWARD (1615-93)
  [Anglo-American
  secretary of Boston
  Colony; persecutor of
  Quakers]
  The Persecutor
Ray. See:
  BLOCH, RAYMOND A.
  Bob and Ray
  BOLGER, RAYMOND
    WALLACE
  BRADBURY, RAY
    DOUGLAS
  BRYANT, RAPHAEL
  NANCE, WILLIS
  Raye
  SCHALK, RAYMOND
    WILLIAM
  SLATTERY,
    RAYMOND PAUL
Ray Abrams. See:
  ABRAMSON, RAYMOND
Ray, Aldo. See:
  daRE, ALDO
Ray Anthony. See:
  ANTONINI, RAYMOND
Ray Carter. See:
  KRUMBEIN, MAURICE

Ray Charles. See:
  ROBINSON, RAY CHARLES
RAY, DANNY (1934-)
  [American jazz musician
  (conga drums)]
  Big Black
Ray, Irene. See:
  SUTTON, RACHEL IRENE
    BEEBE
RAY, JOHN (1627-1705)
  [English naturalist and
  author]
  The Father of English Botany
RAY, JOHN ALVIN (1927-)
  [American singer and
  composer]
  Johnnie Ray
Ray Lorning. See:
  BRALY, MALCOLM
Ray Milland. See:
  TRUSCOTT-JONES,
    REGINALD
Ray, Nicholas. See:
  KIENZLE, RAYMOND
    NICHOLAS
Ray, René. See:
  CREESE, IRENE
RAY, ROBERT J. (1919-)
  [American violinist and
  composer]
  Buddy Ray
Ray, Ted. See:
  OLDEN, CHARLES
RAY, TERRY (1915-)
  [American motion picture
  actress]
  Ellen Drew
Ray, Uncle. See:
  COFFMAN, RAMON
    PEYTON
Ray, Wesley. See:
  GAULDEN, RAY
RAY (WRAY), JOHN
  (1627?-1705) [English
  naturalist, educator and
  clergyman]
  The Father of English
    Natural History
Ray Z. Bixby. See:
  TRALINS, S. ROBERT
RAYBURN, SAMUEL TALIAFER-
  RO (1882-1961)
  [American

848

lawyer and politician;
U.S. representative from
Texas]
Sam Rayburn
Raye. See also:
RAY
Ray
Raye, Carol. See:
CORKREY, KATHLEEN
Raye, Don. See:
WILHOITE, DONALD
MACRAE, JR.
Raye, Martha. See:
O'REED, MAGGIE
TERESA
Raymond. See:
DYER, CHARLES
Raimond
Raymond Cordy. See:
CORDIAUX, RAYMOND
Raymond de Jesus, Mother.
See: DION, SISTER
RAYMOND DE JESUS
Raymond Dyer, C. See:
DYER, CHARLES
Raymond, Gene. See:
GUION, RAYMOND
RAYMOND, HAROLD NEWELL
(1884-1957) [American
composer and publisher]
Roy Newell
Raymond, Ida. See:
TARDY, MARY T.
Raymond, John T. See:
O'BRIEN, JOHN
Raymond, Mary. See:
KEEGAN, MARY
HEATHCOTT
Raymond, Paula. See:
WRIGHT, PAULA
RAMONA
RAYMOND, RENÉ (1906-   )
[English novelist]
James Hadley Chase
Raymond, Robert. See:
ALTER, ROBERT
EDMOND
Raymond Russell. See:
FEARING, LILIAN
BLANCHE
Raymond Scott. See:
WARNOW, HARRY

Raymond Sperry, Jr. See:
STRATEMEYER,
EDWARD L.
Raymond Stone. See:
STRATEMEYER,
EDWARD L.
RAYMOND, WALTER (1852-   )
[British author]
Tom Cobleigh
RAYNAL, GUILLAUME THOMAS
FRANÇOIS (1713-96)
[French author]
Abbé Raynal
Rayne, Alan. See:
TOBIN, JAMES EDWARD
RAYNER, CLAIRE (1931-   )
[British author]
Sheila Brandon
Berry Chetwynd
Ann Lynton
Ruth Martin
Isobel Saxe
Raynor, Olive Pratt. See:
ALLEN, CHARLES GRANT
BLAIRFINDIE
Rayson, Paul. See:
JENNINGS, LESLIE
NELSON
Razaf, Andy. See:
RAZAFKERIEFO, ANDREA
PAUL
RAZAFKERIEFO, ANDREA
PAUL (1895-   ) [American
lyric writer]
Andy Razaf
REA, JOHN HUNTINGDON
(1909-   ) [American motion
picture actor]
John Ridgeley
Read, Miss. See:
SAINT, DORA JESSIE
Reade, Hamish. See:
GRAY, SIMON
Reade, Regina. See:
RICHARDSON, RANDELL
Reader, Constant. See:
PARKER, DOROTHY
ROTHSCHILD
Ready Money. See:
SPENCER, ELIHU
Ready, Old Rough and. See:
TAYLOR, ZACHARY

Real McCoy, The. See:
    McCOY, CAPTAIN
        WILLIAM
    SELBY, NORMAN
Realism, The Father of. See:
    HOWELLS, WILLIAM
        DEAN
REANEY, JAMES CRERAR
    (1926-   ) [Canadian
    author]
    Spoonbill
Reardon. See:
    CONNOR, PATRICK
        REARDON
Reason, The Poet of. See:
    BOILEAU DESPRÉAUX,
        NICHOLAS
Rebak, H. See:
    BAKER, HENRY
Rebecca. See:
    ANDREWS, CICILY
        ISABEL
    FÉLIX, RACHEL
    MATOAKA
Rebecca Marsh. See:
    NEUBAUER, WILLIAM
        ARTHUR
Rebecca Scarlett. See:
    BURT, KATHERINE
        NEWLIN
Rebecca West. See:
    FAIRFIELD, CECILY
        ISABEL
Rebel. See:
    OLIVER, THOMAS N.
Rebel Governor, The. See:
    TRUMBULL, JONATHAN
Rebel of Salem, The. See:
    WILLIAMS, ROGER
Rebel of Seventh Avenue, The.
    See: CASSINI, OLEG
        LOIEWSKI
Rebel, The Enchanting. See:
    FUERTES, DOLORES
        ADIOS
Rebel, The Virginia. See:
    BACON, NATHANIEL
Rebel, Unreconstructed. See:
    GLASS, GEORGE CARTER
Recalde, Íñigo López de. See:
    LOYOLA, IGNATIUS OF,
        ST. (ÍÑIGO DE OÑEZ

    Y LOYOLA)
RÉCAMIER, JEANNE FRANÇOISE
    JULIE ADÉLAÏDE BERNARD
    (1777-1849) [French beauty
    and society leader]
    Madame Récamier
Reclamation, The Father of.
    See: WISNER, EDWARD
Record, The Prettiest Carmen
    on. See:
    SWARTHOUT, GLADYS
Recruiting Sergeant, Our Best.
    See: NAST, THOMAS
Red. See:
    ALLEN, HENRY, JR.
    AUERBACH, ARNOLD
        JACOB
    BARBER, WALTER LANIER
    BLAIK, EARL HENRY
    CALLENDER, GEORGE
    COOLIDGE, JOHN CALVIN
    GARLAND, WILLIAM M.
    GRANGE, HAROLD EDWARD
    HALLOWAY, JAMES L.
    HOLT, ISAAC
    KELLY, THOMAS RAY-
        MOND
    LEWIS, HARRY SINCLAIR
    McKENZIE, WILLIAM
    MITCHELL, KEITH MOORE
    MOTLEY, ARTHUR
        HARRISON
    NICHOLS, ERNEST LORING
    QUINLAN, STERLING C.
    RICHARDS, CHARLES
    SCHOENDIENST, ALBERT
        FRED
    SKELTON, RICHARD
        BERNARD
    SMITH, WALTER WELLES-
        LEY
Red Baron, The. See:
    VON RICHTHOFEN, BARON
        MANFRED
Red Baron, The Bloody. See:
    VON RICHTHOFEN, BARON
        MANFRED
Red, Big. See:
    LITTLE, MALCOLM
Red Buttons. See:
    SCHWATT, AARON
Red Cap. See:

POWELL, RANSOM T.
Red Cross Knight, The.
  See: GEORGE, ST.
Red Cross, The Mother of the.
  See: BARTON,
    CLARISSA HARLOWE
Red Dean, The. See:
  JOHNSON, HEWLETT
Red Douglas, The. See:
  DOUGLAS, ARCHIBALD
  DOUGLAS, GEORGE
Red Eminence (Éminence Rouge).
  See: RICHELIEU, DUC
    DE, ARMAND JEAN
    DU PLESSIS
Red Fox. See:
  JACKSON, WILLIAM
    HICKS
Red Fox of Kinderhook, The.
  See: VAN BUREN,
    MARTIN
Red Fox, The. See:
  HAZELTON, JAMES
  JEFFERSON, THOMAS
Red Godfrey, The Warbling
  Banjoist. See:
  GODFREY, ARTHUR
    MICHAEL
Red Head, The. See:
  BOW, CLARA
  GODFREY, ARTHUR
    MICHAEL
  Redhead
Red-headed Music Maker, The.
  See: HALL, WENDELL
    WOODS
Red-headed Booster of the
  Rockies, The. See:
  BELFORD, JAMES
    BURNS
Red-hot Mammas, The Last
  of the. See:
  ABUZA, SOPHIE
RED JACKET (c.1758-1830)
  [Seneca Indian chief]
  Sa-go-ye-wat-he
Red King, The. See:
  WILLIAM II
Red Knight of Germany, The.
  See: VON RICHTHOFEN,
    BARON MANFRED
Red, Little. See:

BARTON, DAVID
Red Mascara. See:
  MASCARI, JOSEPH ROCCO
Red Necktie. See:
  WEARIN, OTHA DONNER
Red Norvo. See:
  NORVILLE, KENNETH
Red, Olaf the. See:
  OLAF SITRICSON
Red Priest, The. See:
  VIVALDI, ANTONIO
Red Prince, The. See:
  FREDERICK-CHARLES,
    PRINCE
Red Rat. See:
  McDANIEL, IRA C.
Red Reeder, Colonel. See:
  REEDER, RUSSELL P., JR.
Red River Dave. See:
  McENERY, DAVID
Red Robert (Rob Roy). See:
  MACGREGOR, ROBERT
Red Rodney. See:
  CHUDNICK, ROBERT
Red Rose, The Knight of the.
  See: TAYLOR, ALFRED
    ALEXANDER
Red, Rufus the. See:
  WILLIAM II
Red, Sonny. See:
  KYNER, SYLVESTER
Red, The. See:
  AMADEUS VII
  CONRAD
  ERIC
  OTTO II
Red, The. (Ivan Krasny).
  See: IVAN II
Redbarn Wash. See:
  SHAW, GEORGE BERNARD
Redbeard. See:
  FREDERICK I
Redd, Vi. See:
  GOLDBERG, ELVIRA REOD
REDDAWAY, WILLIAM BRIAN
  (1913-) [British economist
  and author]
  Academic Investor
Redeemed Captive, The. See:
  WILLIAMS, JOHN
Redfield Martin. See:
  BROWN, ALICE

Redhead. See also:
    Red Head
Redhead, The Ol'. See:
    BARBER, WALTER
    LANIER
Redingote Grise. See:
    BONAPARTE,
    NAPOLEON
REDMAN, BEN RAY (1896-)
    [American editor and
    author]
    Jeremy Lord
Redmayne, Barbara. See:
    HOWE, MURIEL
Redmond Blake. See:
    AIKEN, ALBERT W.
    MORRIS, CHARLES
    SMITH
REDONDO, JOSÉ (1818-53)
    [Spanish bullfighter]
    El Chiclanero
Redway Grode. See:
    GOREY, EDWARD ST.
    JOHN
REDWINE, WILBUR (1926-)
    [American composer and
    pianist]
    Skip Redwine
Redwing, Morris. See:
    MERRILL, JAMES
    MILFORD
REECE, ALPHONSO SON
    (1931-) [American
    jazz musician
    (trumpet)]
    Dizzy Reece
REED [Reed]. See also:
    REID
    Reid
REED, ALEXANDER WYCLIF
    (1908-) [New Zealand
    publisher and author]
    Harlequin
Reed, Donna. See:
    MULLENGER, DONNA
Reed, Eliot, joint pseud.
    of ERIC AMBLER
    (1909-) [English author]
    and CHARLES RODDA
    (1891-) [Australian
    author]
Reed, Eliot. See also:

RODDA. CHARLES
REED, ELIZABETH STEWART
    (1914-) [American
    journalist and author]
    Elizabeth Grey Stewart
REED, ISOBEL (1893-)
    [British stage and motion
    picture actress]
    Isobel Elsom
Reed, Jean. See:
    HOVICK, JUNE
REED, LILLIAN CRAIG
    (1932-) [American news-
    paperwoman and author]
    Kit Reed
REED, MYRTLE (1874-1911)
    [American author]
    Olive Green
REED, THOMAS BRACKETT
    (1839-1902) [American
    politician; Congressman
    from Maine]
    Biddy
    Czar Reed
    The Terrible Turk
REEDER, RUSSELL P., JR.
    (1902-) [American
    soldier and author]
    Colonel Red Reeder
REES, HELEN CHRISTINA
    EASSON EVANS
    (1903-) [British Red
    Cross official and author]
    Jane Oliver
Reese. See:
    MARKEWICH, MAURICE
REESE, HAROLD HENRY
    (1919-) [American pro-
    fessional baseball player]
    Pee Wee Reese
REESIDE, JAMES (1789-1842)
    [Scottish-American business-
    man and mail contractor]
    The Land Admiral
    The Prince of Mail Contractors
Reeve, Joel. See:
    COX, WILLIAM R.
REEVES, MARIAN CALHOUN
    LAGARÉ (c.1854-)
    [American author]
    Fadette
REEVES, STEPHEN (1926-)

[American physical culturist and motion picture actor]
Ercole
Steve Reeves
Shape
Mr. Universe
Mr. World
Reform Governor, The. See:
CLEVELAND, STEPHEN
GROVER
Reform in the United States, The
Father of Prison. See:
OSBORNE, GEORGE O.
Reform, The Father of. See:
CARTWRIGHT, JOHN
Reform, The Father of Civil
Service. See:
JENCKES, THOMAS ALLEN
PENDLETON, GEORGE
HUNT
Reform, The Heaven-sent
Angel of Mercy and of
Prison. See:
DIX, DOROTHEA LYNDE
Reform, The Old War Horse of.
See: BLANKENBURG,
RUDOLPH
Reformation, Intellectual Father
of the. See:
GERHARDS, GERHARD
(GEERT GEERTS)
Reformation, The Apostle of
the Scottish. See:
KNOX, JOHN
Reformation, The Elijah of the
French. See:
FAREL, GUILLAUME
Reformation, The Fénelon of
the. See:
ARNDT, JOHN
Reformation, The Luther of
the Early Temperance.
See: HEWIT, NATHANIEL
Reformation, The Morning Star
of the. See:
WICKLIFFE, JOHN
Reformation, The Protomartyr
of the Scottish. See:
HAMILTON, PATRICK
Reformed Church in America,
The Father of the Dutch.
See: LIVINGSTON,
JOHN HENRY

Reformer of the Laws (Lagoböter).
See: MAGNUS VI
Reformer, The First Scotch. See:
HAMILTON, PATRICK
Reg. See:
BUTLER, REGINALD COT-
TRELL
MANNING, REGINALD WEST
Regan, Brad. See:
NORWOOD, VICTOR GEORGE
CHARLES
Regardant, Villain. See:
TOZER, BASIL JOHN
JOSEPH
Regency, The Wizard of The
Albany. See:
VAN BUREN, MARTIN
Regent, The Good. See:
STUART, JAMES
Regera Dowdy, Mrs. See: GOREY,
EDWARD ST. JOHN
Regester, Seeley. See: VICTOR,
MRS. METTA VICTORIA
FULLER MORSE
Regina Reade. See:
RICHARDSON, RANDELL
Reginald. See:
DE KOVEN, HENRY LOUIS
REGINALD
Reginald Bliss. See:
WELLS, HERBERT GEORGE
Reginald Denny. See:
DAYMORE, REGINALD
LEIGH
Reginald Irving. See:
JOHNSTON, SIR REGINALD
FLEMING
Reginald Reverie. See:
MELLEN, GRENVILLE
Regiomontanus. See:
MÜLLER, JOHANNES
Regius Primarius, Botanicus.
See: PARKINSON, JOHN
Régnier. See:
TOUSEZ, FRANÇOIS
JOSEPH PIERRE
RÉGNIER, MATHURIN (1573-
1613) [French satirical
poet]
The Father of French Satire
Regulation, The Father of Public
Utility. See:
NORRIS, GEORGE WILLIAM

Rehan, Ada. See:
  CREHAN, ADA
Rehn, Viktoria. See:
  KOHN-BEHRENS,
    CHARLOTTE
Rei Lavrador (Farmer King).
  See: DINIZ (DENIS)
Reichstadt, Duke of. See:
  BONAPARTE, NAPOLEON
    FRANÇOIS CHARLES
    JOSEPH
REID [Reid]. See also:
  REED
  Reed
Reid, Ann Alexander. See:
  MARLOW, MRS. LOUIS
REID, CAPTAIN MAYNE (1818-
  83) [Irish-American
  frontiersman, school-
  teacher and author]
  The Poor Scholar
Reid, Christian. See:
  TIERNAN, FRANCES
    CHRISTINE FISHER
REID, FRANCES PUGH (1910-)
  [American educator and
  author]
  Marian Allison
REID, JOHN COWIE (1916-)
  [New Zealand educator,
  broadcaster and author]
  Caliban
REID, PATRICIA (1925-)
  [American actress]
  Kim Stanley
REID, WHITELAW (1837-1912)
  [American journalist,
  diplomat and historian]
  Agate
REILING, NETTY (1900-)
  [German novelist]
  Anna Seghers
Reilly. See also:
  RILEY
  Riley
Reilly, William K. See:
  CREASEY, JOHN
Reincarnated Troubadour, The.
  See: SEEGER, PETER
Reindeer. See:
  KILLEFER, WILLIAM
Reine, La Bonne. See:

FRANCE, CLAUDE DE
Reiner, Max. See:
  CALDWELL, TAYLOR
REINFELD, FRED (1910-64)
  [American chess expert and
  writer on the subject]
  Edward Young
REINHARDT, JEAN BAPTISTE
  (1910-53) [Belgian gypsy
  guitarist]
  Django Reinhardt
Reinhardt, Max. See:
  GOLDMANN, MAX
REISNER, CHARLES (1887-1962)
  [American motion picture
  director]
  Chuck Reisner
REIZENSTEIN, ELMER LEOPOLD
  (1892-1967) [American
  playwright]
  Elmer Rice
Réjane. See:
  RÉJU, GABRIELLE-
    CHARLOTTE
RÉJU, GABRIELLE-CHARLOTTE
  (1857-1920) [French actress]
  Réjane
Reliable, Old. See:
  CARLSON, JULES
  THOMAS, GEORGE HENRY
Religious World, The Joan of
  Arc of the Modern. See:
  UTLEY, ULDINE
Reling, Jan. See:
  DAVIS, HORACE BANCROFT
RELPH. See also:
  RALPH
RELPH, HARRY (1868-1928)
  [English music-hall
  comedian]
  Little Tich
REMARK, ERICH PAUL
  (1897-1970) [German novelist]
  Erich Maria Remarque
Remarque, Erich Maria. See:
  REMARK, ERICH PAUL
Rembrandt. See:
  VAN RIJN (RYN), REM-
    BRANDT HARMESZ
    (HARMENZOON)
Remembers, One Who (Háfiz). See:
  SHAMS UN-DIN MOHAMMED

REMICK, LEE (1935-) [American actress]
America's Answer to Brigitte Bardot
Remus, Uncle. See:
HARRIS, JOEL CHANDLER
RENA, HENRY (1900-49) [American jazz musician (trumpet, leader)]
Kid Rena
Renaissance, The Martyr of the. See:
DOLET, ÉTIENNE
Renaldo, Duncan. See:
DUNCAN, RENAULT RENALDO
Renault, Mary. See:
CHALLANS, MARY
RENÉ I (1408/9-80) [Duke of Anjou and King of Naples]
Le Bon Roi René
The Good
René Clair. See:
CHOMETTE, RENÉ
René, Gros. See:
DU PARC, RENÉ BERTHELOT
René Laroche. See:
McKEAG, ERNEST LIONEL
René, Le Bon Roi. See:
RENÉ I
René Ray. See:
CREESE, IRENE
Renée Adorée. See:
FONTE, JEANNE DE LA
Renée Houston. See:
GRIBBIN, KATHERINA HOUSTON
Renegade, The Great. See:
GIRTY, SIMON
Renier, Elizabeth. See:
BAKER, BETTY DOREEN FLOOK
Renner, A. M. See:
GATTERMANN, EUGEN LUDWIG
Rennie, Christopher. See:
AMBROSE, ERIC
RENNIE, JAMES ALAN (1899-) [Scottish author]
Morton Cleland
Boone Denver

Maxwell Mac Fee
Renou. See:
ROUSSEAU, JEAN-JACQUES
Renshaw Stretton. See:
DYER, CHARLES
Renton, Julia. See:
COLE, MARGARET ALICE
RENTZEL, DELOS WILSON (1909-) [U. S. government and aviation industry official]
Del Rentzel
Repealer, The Great. See:
BARTON, BRUCE
Reproach, The Knight Without. See: BARBAZAN, ARNAULD GUILHELM DE
Reproach, The Knight Without Fear and Without. See:
BAYARD, PIERRE DU TERRAIL, CHEVALIER DE
Reptiles, The King of. See:
VILLE, BERNARD GERMAIN ÉTIENNE DE LA
Republic, People's Artist of the. See: IPPOLITOV-IVANOV, MIKHAIL MIKHAILOVICH
Republic, The Father of the Chinese. See:
SUN YAT-SEN
Republic, The Heir of the. See:
BONAPARTE, NAPOLEON
Republic, The Schoolmaster of the. See:
WEBSTER, NOAH
Republican Blair, Black. See:
BLAIR, FRANCIS PRESTON, JR.
Republican, Mr. See:
TAFT, ROBERT ALPHONSO
Republican Party, The Father of the. See:
COLE, AMBROSE N.
Republican, The Black. See:
BLAIR, FRANCIS PRESTON, JR.
RESNICK, LEON (1923-) [American composer and violinist]
Lee Resnick

Resolute Doctor, The. See:
BACONTHORPE (BACON)
(BACHO), JOHN
Resolute Doctor, The Most.
See: ST. POURÇAIN,
GUILLAUME DURAND
DE
Resolute John Florio. See:
FLORIO, JOHN
(GIOVANNI)
RESTIF, NICHOLAS EDME
(1734-1806) [French
printer and writer]
Restif de la Bretonne
The French Defoe
Restitutor Orbis (Restorer of
the Empire). See:
AURELIANUS, LUCIUS
DOMITIUS
Restoration Period, The
Greatest Writer of the.
See: DRYDEN, JOHN
Restorer, Elijah the. See:
DOWIE, JOHN ALEXANDER
Restorer of Parnassus, The.
See: VALDÉS, JUAN
MELENDEZ
Restorer of the Empire
(Restitutor Orbis). See:
AURELIANUS, LUCIUS
DOMITIUS
Retla, Robert. See:
ALTER, ROBERT EDMOND
Retlaw, S.P. See:
STEINHAUSER, WALTER
PHILIP
Retner, Beth A., See:
BROWN, BETH
Rett Winwood. See: COREY,
FRANCIS ADELBERT
RETZ, See:
RAIS (RETZ), GILLES DE
Reuben, Genial. See:
KOLB, REUBEN FRANCIS
REUCHLIN, JOHANN (1455-1522)
[German humanist and pro-
moter of Hebrew studies]
Capnio
Kapnio
Reunét, Henri le. See:
POE, EDGAR ALLAN
Reunion, The Hero of. See:

SMITH, HENRY BOYNTON
REURSLAG, GUURTJE JOHANNA
HENDRIKA (1886-)
[Dutch educator and author]
J. Riemens-Reurslag
Reval, Jacques. See:
LAVER, JAMES
Rev. XII, The Woman of. See:
SOUTHCOTT, JOANNA
Revere, Paul. See:
ABARBANELL, JACOB
RALPH
Reverend Charles James Grimble.
See: ELIOT, THOMAS
STEARNS
Reverend James Steward. See:
TRUMBULL, HENRY
Reverend Major J. Divine.
See: BAKER, GEORGE
Reverend Morgan J. Divine.
See: BAKER, GEORGE
Reverend Peter Pennot. See:
ROUND, WILLIAM
MARSHALL FITTS
Reverend Petroleum Vesuvius
Nasby. See:
LOCKE, DAVID ROSS
Reverie, Reginald. See:
MELLEN, GRENVILLE
Reverte, La. See:
RODRÍGUEZ, AUGUSTÍN
Revival, The Hymnist of the
English. See:
WESLEY, CHARLES
Revolution, The Amazon of the.
See:
TERWAGNE, ANNE JOSEPH
Revolution, The Bayard of the.
See: LAURENS, GEORGE
Revolution, The Brain of the.
See: ADAMS, SAMUEL
Revolution, The Cato of the.
See: BLAND, RICHARD
Revolution, The Circe of the.
See: ROLAND DE LA
PLATIÈRE, JEANNE
MANON PHILIPON
Revolution, The Day-star of the.
See: HAMILTON, ANDREW
Revolution, The Father of the
American. See:
ADAMS, SAMUEL

Revolution, The Father of
the Russian. See:
ULYANOV, VLADIMIR
ILYICH
Revolution, The Fighting
Surgeon of the.
DOWNER, ELIPHALET
Revolution, The Financier of
the American. See:
MORRIS, ROBERT
Revolution, The First Martyr of
the. See:
SNYDER, CHRISTOPHER
Revolution, The Lafayette of
the Greek. See:
HOWE, SAMUEL
GRIDLEY
Revolution, The Little Grand-
mother of the Russian.
See: BRESHKOVSKY,
CATHERINE
Revolution, The Navarre of the
American. See:
BUTLER, THOMAS
Revolution, The Nestor of the
Chemical. See:
BLACK, JAMES
Revolution, The Pen of the.
See: JEFFERSON,
THOMAS
Revolution, The Penman of the
American. See:
DICKINSON, JOHN
Revolution, The Poet of the
American. See:
FRENEAU, PHILIP
MORIN
Revolution, The Prophet of
the. See:
HENRY, PATRICK
Revolution, The Scribe of the.
See: JEFFERSON,
THOMAS
Revolution, The Sword of the.
See: WASHINGTON,
GEORGE
Revolution, The Tartuffe of the.
See:
NICOLAS, JEAN
Revolution, The Voice of the.
See: HENRY, PATRICK
Rex Gordon. See:

HOUGH, STANLEY BEN-
NETT
Rex Harrison. See:
CAREY, REGINALD
Rex Ingram. See:
FITCHCOCK, REX
Rex Lode. See:
GOLDSTEIN, WILLIAM
ISAAC
Rex O'Toole. See:
TRALINS, S. ROBERT
Rex Toole. See:
TRALINS, S. ROBERT
Rex Welldon Finn. See:
FINN, REGINALD PATRICK
ARTHUR
Rex Windsor. See:
ARMSTRONG, DOUGLAS
ALBERT
Rey, Alvino. See:
McBURNEY, ALBERT
REY, HANS AUGUSTO (1898-)
[German businessman,
illustrator and author]
Uncle Gus
Reyam. See:
MAYER, CHARLES
LEOPOLD
REYES, FERNANDO DE LOS
(1930-) [Mexican bull-
fighter]
El Callao
REYES, FRANCISCO VEGA DE
LOS (1903-31) [Spanish
bullfighter]
Gitanillo de Triana
REYES, RAFAEL VEGA DE LOS
(1915-) [Spanish
bullfighter]
Gitanillo de Triana II
REYNOLDS, ALBERT PIERCE
(1919-) [American pro-
fessional baseball player]
Allie Reynolds
REYNOLDS, CHARLES
ALEXANDER (1842-76)
[American hunter, guide
and scout]
Lonesome Charley
REYNOLDS, HELEN MARY
GREENWOOD CAMPBELL
(1884-) [Canadian writer

and illustrator]
Helen Dickson
Dickson Reynolds
REYNOLDS, JOHN (1788-1865)
[American scout in
War of 1812]
Old Ranger
REYNOLDS, JOHN CROMWELL
(1810-49) [American
surgeon in Mexican War]
The Fighting Doctor
REYNOLDS, MARIE FRANCES
(1932-) [American
actress and television
personality]
Debbie Reynolds
Reynolds, Marjorie. See:
GOODSPEED, MARJORIE
Reynolds, Peter. See:
HORROCKS, PETER
REYNOLDS, ROBERT (fl. 1610-
40) [English comedian]
Pickelherring
REYNOLDS, ROBERT RICE
(1884-) [American
politician, senator from
North Carolina]
Our Bob
The Playboy
REYNOLDS, SIR JOSHUA
(1723-92) [English portrait
painter]
The Raphael of England
REZZONICO, CARLO DELLA
TORRE (1693-1769) [Supreme
Pontiff of Roman Catholic
Church]
Pope Clement XIII
Rhampsinitus. See:
RAMSES III
Rhangabe. See:
MICHAEL I
RHEM, CHARLES FLINT
(1903-) [American pro-
fessional baseball
player]
Shad
Rheticus. See:
VON LAUCHEN, GEORG
JOACHIM
Rhetorician, The. See:
SENECA, MARCUS

LUCIUS ANNAEUS
RHETT, ROBERT BARNWELL
(1800-76) [American
secessionist advocate]
The Father of Secession
RHOADES [Rhoades]. See also:
RHODES
Rhodes
Roads
RHOADES, CORNELIA HARSEN
(1863-1940) [American
author of children's books]
Nina Rhoades
Rhoades, Jonathan. See:
OLSEN, JOHN EDWARD
Rhode. See also:
Road
Rhode, Austen. See:
FRANCIS, BASIL HOSKINS
Rhode Island, The Father of.
See: CLARKE, JOHN
Rhode, John. See:
STREET, CECIL JOHN
CHARLES
Rhode, Winslow. See:
ROE, FREDERIC GORDON
Rhodes. See:
ANDRONICUS OF RHODES
RHOADES
Rhoades
Roads
RHODES, JAMES LAMAR
(1927-) [American
professional baseball
player]
Dusty Rhodes
RHODES, JOHN GORDON
(1907-) [American
professional baseball
player]
Dusty Rhodes
Rhodes (Roads), The King of.
See: MACADAM, JOHN
LOUDON
Rhonda Fleming. See:
LOUIS, MARILYN
Rhondo Shane. See:
NORWOOD, VICTOR GEORGE
CHARLES
Rhymer, The Corn-law. See:
ELLIOTT, EBENEZER
Rhymer, Thomas the. See:

LEARMOUNT, THOMAS,
OF ERCILDOUNE
Rhymour of Ercildoune,
Thomas. See:
LEARMOUNT, THOMAS,
OF ERCILDOUNE
Rhys. See:
PRICE, GEORGE
Ribbonson. See also:
ROBINSON
Robinson
Ribbonson, Horatio. See:
SHAW, GEORGE
BERNARD
RIBERA, JUSEPE DE
(1588-1656) [Spanish
painter and etcher]
Lo Spagnoletto (The Little
Spaniard
Ricardo Cortez. See:
KRANZ, JACOB
Ricardo, Don. See:
RIDGELY, RICHARD
Rice, Dan. See:
McLAREN, DANIEL
RICE, DANIEL (1822-1900)
[American circus clown]
The King of American .
Clowns
The Shakespeare Clown
RICE, DESMOND CHARLES
(1924-) [British
author]
Desmond Meiring
RICE, DOROTHY MARY
(1913-) [Irish author of
books for children]
Dorothy Borne
Dorothy Vicary
Rice, Elinor. See:
HAYS, ELINOR RICE
Rice, Elmer. See:
REIZENSTEIN, ELMER
LEOPOLD
RICE, GEORGE (1917-)
[American stage and
motion picture actor]
George O'Hanlon
RICE, GRANTLAND
(1880-1954) [American
sports writer]
Granny

RICE, HARVEY (1800-91)
[American politician and
public school advocate]
The Father of the Public
School System in Ohio
RICE, THOMAS DARTMOUTH
(1808-60) [American actor
and minstrel]
The Father of American
Minstrelsy
Rich, Barbara. See:
JACKSON, LAURA RIDING
RICH, BERNARD (1917-)
[American jazz musician
(drums, leader, singer)]
Buddy Rich
Baby Traps
Rich, Fugger the. See:
FUGGER, JAKOB II
Rich Girl, The Poor Little. See:
VANDERBILT, GLORIA
Rich, Jakob the. See:
FUGGER, JAKOB II
RICH, JOHN (1692-1761)
[English theater manager
and harlequin]
The Father of Harlequins
RICH, PENELOPE DEVEREUX
(fl. late 16th cent.)
[Loved by SIR PHILIP
SIDNEY[
Stella
Rich, Robert. See:
TRUMBO, DALTON
RICH, ROBERT FLEMING
(1883-) [American
politician; congressman
from Pennsylvania]
Woolly Bob
Rich, The (Dives). See:
CRASSUS, MARCUS
LICINIUS
Richard. See:
THORPE, ROLLO SMOLT
WAGNER, WILHELM
RICHARD
RICHARD (died 1173) [Scottish
theologian, teacher and
mystic]
Richard of St. Victor
RICHARD I (died 996) [Duke of
Normandy]

The Fearless
RICHARD I (1157-99) [King
   of England]
   Coeur de Lion (The Lion
      Hearted)
   Richard Coeur de Lion
   Richard Yea and Nay
RICHARD II (died 1027) [Duke
   of Normandy]
   The Good
RICHARD III (1452-85) [King
   of England]
   The Boar
   Crookback
   Crouchback
Richard A. Lawrence. See:
   LEOPOLD, NATHAN F.
Richard A. Stone. See:
   STRATEMEYER,
      EDWARD L.
Richard Allen. See:
   MARKOWITZ, RICHARD
Richard Arlen. See:
   VAN MATTIMORE,
      RICHARD
Richard Barnum. See:
   STRATEMEYER,
      EDWARD L.
Richard Benson. See:
   COOPER, SAUL
Richard Bowood. See:
   DANIELL, ALBERT
      SCOTT
Richard Bracefield. See:
   WOOLLEY, EDWARD
      MOTT
Richard Bridgman. See:
   DAVIES, LESLIE
      PURNELL
Richard Brinsley Newman.
   See: GIFFORD,
      FRANKLIN KENT
Richard Burton. See:
   JENKINS, RICHARD
Richard Carle. See:
   CARLETON, CHARLES
      NICHOLS
Richard Cromwell. See:
   RADEBAUGH, ROY
Richard Cummings. See:
   GARDNER, RICHARD
Richard Dehan. See:

GRAVES, CLOTILDE INEZ
   AUGUSTA MARY
Richard Denning. See:
   DENNINGER, LOUIS A.
Richard Dix. See:
   BRIMMER, ERNEST
Richard Evans. See:
   KUNITZ, RICHARD E.
Richard Falcon.
   See: SHAPIRO, SAMUEL
Richard Fisguill. See:
   WILSON, RICHARD HENRY
Richard Foster. See:
   CROSSEN, KENDELL
      FOSTER
Richard Greaves. See:
   McCUTCHEON, GEORGE
      BARR
Richard Gump. See:
   GUCKENHEIMER, DR.
      FRITZ
Richard Harris Barham. See:
   INGOLDSBY, THOMAS
Richard Hayward. See:
   KENDRICK, BAYNARD
      HARDWICK
Richard Haywarde. See:
   COZZENS, FREDERICK
      SWARTWOUT
Richard Hull. See:
   SAMPSON, RICHARD
      HENRY
Richard Jeremy. See:
   FOX, CHARLES
Richard Jocelyn. See:
   CLUTTERBUCK, RICHARD
Richard Keverne. See:
   HOSKEN, CLIFFORD
Richard Kinver. See:
   VOGEL, HARRY
      BENJAMIN
Richard Llewellyn. See:
   LLOYD, RICHARD DOYLE
      VIVIAN LLEWELLYN
Richard Lyte. See:
   WHELPTON, GEORGE
      ERIC
Richard Marsten. See:
   HUNTER, EVAN
Richard Martin. See:
   CREASEY, JOHN
Richard of Ely. See:

FITZNEALE, RICHARD
Richard Oke. See:
MILLETT, NIGEL
STANSBURY
Richard Orth. See:
GARDNER, RICHARD
Richard Oswald. See:
ORNSTEIN, RICHARD
Richard Peckham. See:
HOLDEN, RAYMOND
PECKHAM
Richard, Poor. See:
FRANKLIN, BENJAMIN
Richard Preston. See:
LINDSAY, JACK
Richard Rock. See:
MAINPRIZE, DON
Richard Saunders. See:
FRANKLIN, BENJAMIN
Richard Stillman Powell.
See: BARBOUR, RALPH
HENRY
Richard Surrey. See:
BROOKER, BERTRAM
Richard Todd. See:
PALENTHORPE-TODD,
RICHARD ANDREW
Richard Tucker. See:
TICKER, REUBEN
Richard W. Hinton. See:
ANGOFF, CHARLES
Richard Wallace. See:
IND, ALLISON
Richard Wayne. See:
DECKER, DUANE
Richard Weda. See:
DALLWITZ-WEGNER,
RICHARD VON
Richard Wegner. See:
DALLWITZ-WEGNER,
RICHARD VON
Richards, Allen. See:
ROSENTHAL, RICHARD A.
RICHARDS, CHARLES
(1912-) [American
jazz musician (piano)]
Red Richards
Richards, Charles. See:
MARVIN, JOHN T.
Richards, Clay. See:
CROSSEN, KENDELL
FOSTER

Richards, Cliff. See:
WEBB, HAROLD
Richards, Duane. See:
HURLEY, VIC
Richards, Emil. See:
RADOCCHIA, EMILIO
JOSEPH
Richards, Francis, joint pseud.
of FRANCES LOUISE
LOCKRIDGE (-) and her
husband RICHARD LOCK-
RIDGE (1898-) [American
writers of mystery stories]
Richards, Frank. See:
HAMILTON, CHARLES
Richards, Harvey D. See:
SAINSBURY, NOEL
EVERINGHAM
Richards, Johnny. See:
CASCALES, JOHN
RICHARDS, LELA HORN
(1870-) [American
author]
Lee Neville
Richards, Peter. See:
MONGER, IFOR DAVID
Richards, Phyllis. See:
AUTY, PHYLLIS
RICHARDS, RONALD CHARLES
WILLIAM (1923-)
[British printer and
author]
K. Allen Saddler
RICHARDS, THOMAS ADDISON
(1829-1900) [American
landscape painter]
The Doughty of the South
RICHARDS, VINCENT (1903-)
[American tennis player,
commissioner and business-
man]
Vinnie Richards
RICHARDSON, ANTHONY (1899-)
[English author]
Thomas Stewart Currie
RICHARDSON, CLAIBORNE F.
(1929-) [American
composer]
Claibe Richardson
RICHARDSON, GEORGE TILTON.
See: Merriman, Charles
Eustace

RICHARDSON, HENRIETTA
(1870-1946) [Australian
novelist]
Henry Handel Richardson
RICHARDSON, ISRAEL BUSH
(1815-62) [American
general officer]
Fighting Dick
RICHARDSON, RANDELL
(1921-　) [American
singer]
Regina Reade
Rosalind Rogers
RICHARDSON, ROBERT
CLINTON, JR. (1935-　)
[American professional
baseball player]
Bobby Richardson
RICHARDSON, SAMUEL
(1689-1761) [English
novelist]
By the Author of "Pamela"
The Founder of the English
Domestic Novel
Richelieu. See:
ROBINSON, WILLIAM
ERIGENA
RICHELIEU, DUC DE,
ARMAND JEAN DU
PLESSIS (1585-1642)
[French cardinal and
statesman]
Éminence Rouge (Red
Eminence)
Cardinal Richelieu
Richie. See:
GOLDBERG, RICHARD
RICKEY
Richmal Crompton. See:
LAMBURN, RICHMAL
CROMPTON
RICHMAN, ABRAHAM SAMUEL
(1921-　) [American
jazz musician (tenor
saxophone, clarinet,
flute)]
Boomie Richman
RICHMOND, EUPHEMIA
JOHNSON (1825-　)
[American novelist]
Effie Johnson
Mrs. E.J. Richmond

Richmond, George. See:
BRISTER, RICHARD
Richmond, Grace. See:
MARSH, JOHN
Richmond, Henry, Earl of.
See: HENRY VII
Richmond, Kane, See:
BOWDITCH, FREDERICK W.
RICHTER, JOHANN PAUL
FRIEDRICH (1763-1825)
[German novelist]
Jean Paul
RICHTHOFEN. See:
VON RICHTHOFEN, BARON
MANFRED
Rick. See also:
Riq
Rick Holmes. See:
HARDWICK, RICHARD
HOLMES, JR.
Rick Walters. See:
ROWLAND, DONALD
SYDNEY
RICKARD, GEORGE LEWIS
(1871-1929) [American
prize fight promoter]
Tex Rickard
RICKENBACKER, EDWARD
VERNON (1890-　)
[American automobile
racer, military aviator,
manufacturer and airline
executive]
Ace of Aces
Eddie Rickenbacker
Rickert, Corinne Holt. See:
SAWYER, CORINNE HOLT
RICKERTS, HELEN (1923-　)
[American model and
motion picture actress]
Helena Carter
Rickey. See:
NELSON, ERIC HILLIARD
Richie
RICKEY, WESLEY BRANCH
(1881-1965) [American
professional baseball player
and executive]
The Brain
Branch Rickey
RIDDELL, CHARLOTTE ELIZA
LAWSON (1832-1906)

862

[English novelist]
F. G. Trafford
Riddell, John. See:
    FORD, COREY
RIDDLE, R. RICHARD (1936-)
    [American composer]
Dick Riddle
RIDDLE, THOMAS WILKINSON
    (1886-) [British
    clergyman and author]
T. W. R.
Rideamus. See:
    OLIVEN, FRITZ
Rider, Rough. See:
    ROOSEVELT, THEODORE
Rider, Wild Bill the Pony
    Express. See:
    CODY, WILLIAM
    FREDERICK
RIDGE, JOHN ROLLIN (1827-67)
    [American Cherokee
    Indian editor and poet]
Yellow Bird (Chees-quat-a-
    law-ny)
Ridgeley, John. See:
    REA, JOHN HUNTINGDON
Ridgely. See:
    TORRENCE, FREDERICK
    RIDGELY
RIDGELY, RICHARD (1910-)
    [American musician and
    composer]
Don Ricardo
Ridgway, Jason. See:
    MARLOWE, STEPHEN
Ridicule, The Father of. See:
    RABELAIS, FRANÇOIS
Riding, Laura. See:
    JACKSON, LAURA RIDING
Ridley, Nat, Jr. See: STRATE-
    MEYER, EDWARD L.
RIDSTE, FRANCES (1919-48)
    [American motion
    picture actress]
Carole Landis
Riemens-Reurslag, J. See:
    REURSLAG, GUURTJE
    JOHANNA HENDRIKA
RIENZI, COLA DI (c. 1313-54)
    [Italian patriot and
    political reformer]
The Last of the Romans

The Last of the Tribunes
RIESE, FELICIA (1918-)
    [British stage and motion
    picture actress]
Patricia Roc
RIESGO, MANUEL MARTÍNEZ Y
    (1855-1937) [Spanish bull-
    fighter]
Agujetas
Riff, Charles. See:
    EMBREE, CHARLES, JR.
RIFKIN, SHEPARD (1918-)
    [American editor and
    author]
Dale Michaels
Rifle, The Father of the
    Automatic. See:
    BROWNING, JOHN MOSES
Rift, Valerie. See:
    BARTLETT, MARIE SWAN
RIGAUD, HYACINTHE (1659-1743)
    [French portrait painter]
The French Van Dyck
Right-angled, Tri-angled
    Thurman. See:
    THURMAN, ALLAN
    GRANBERRY
Right Cross. See:
    ARMSTRONG, PAUL
Right Hand Mind, The. See:
    ROBINSON, FRANCES M.
Righteous Causes, The Invincible
    Warrior in. See:
    MOTT, LUCRETIA
Righteousness, Gate of (Bab-ed-din).
    See: MOHAMMED, MIRZA
    ALI
Rights, The Father of States'.
    See: CALHOUN, JOHN
    CALDWELL
Rigores. See:
    MIRANDA, ROQUE
RIGSBY, HOWARD (1909-)
    [American editor and author]
Mark Howard
Vechel Howard
RIKHOFF, JAMES C. (1931-)
    [American public relations
    manager and author]
Jim Cornwall
Joe Fargo
Alan Kincaid

RILEY [Riley]. See also:
  Reilly
RILEY, ISAAC (fl. late 17th
  cent.) [American pub-
  lisher]
  Pasquin Petronius
RILEY, JAMES WHITCOMB
  (1849-1916) [American
  poet, lecturer and reader
  of poetry]
  The Burns of America
  The Children's Poet
  The Hoosier Poet
  Benjamin F. Johnson of
  Boone
  The People's Laureate
  The Poet of the Common
  People
Riley of the South, The. See:
  STANTON, FRANK LEBBY
Riley, Tex. See:
  CREASEY, JOHN
RILEY, WILLIE (1866-)
  [British author]
  W. Rye Leigh
RIMBAUD, JEAN NICOLAS
  ARTHUR (1854-91) [French
  poet]
  Arthur Rimbaud
RIMINI. See:
  GREGORY OF RIMINI
Rimmer, W.J. See:
  ROWLAND, DONALD
  SYDNEY
RINES, JOSEPH (1902-)
  [American composer and
  musician]
  Joe Rines
Ring. See:
  LARDNER, RINGGOLD
  WILMER
Ring, Douglas. See:
  PRATHER, RICHARD
  SCOTT
Ringbolt, Captain. See:
  CODMAN, JOHN
RINGLING, JOHN (1866-1936)
  [American circus
  owner]
  The Circus King
Ringo, Johnny. See:
  KEEVIL, HENRY JOHN

Ringo Starr. See:
  Beatles, The
  STARKEY, RICHARD
Ringwood, Ralph. See:
  HYNES, CAPTAIN ALFRED
  D.
Rinn, Der Mann Vom. See:
  SPECKBACHER, JOSEPH
Rio, Dolores del. See:
  MARTÍNEZ, LOLITA
  DOLORES DE
Rio, Rita. See:
  NOVELLA, RITA
RIORDAN, IRENE (c.1906-)
  [American motion picture
  and television actress]
  Irene Ryan
Rios, Tere. See:
  VERSACE, MARIE TERESA
  RIOS
Rip. See:
  CONNALLY, GEORGE
  WALTER
  TORN, ELMORE
  VAN WINKLE, HAROLD E.
Riposte, A. See:
  MORDAUNT, MRS. EVELYN
  MAY CLOWES
Ripper. See:
  COLLINS, JAMES ANTHONY
Ripper, Jack the. See:
  UNKNOWN
Riq. See:
  ATWATER, RICHARD
  Rick
RIQUETI, ANDRÉ BONIFACE
  LOUIS (1754-92) [French
  soldier and politician]
  Barrel-Mirabeau
  Vicomte de Mirabeau
RIQUETI, HONORÉ GABRIEL
  (1749-91) [French orator
  and revolutionary leader]
  Comte de Mirabeau
  The Hurricane
  The Modern Gracchus
RIQUETI, VICTOR (1715-89)
  [French political economist]
  The Friend of Man
  Marquis de Mirabeau
Risdon, Elizabeth. See:
  EVANS, ELIZABETH

Rise up William Allen. See:
ALLEN, WILLIAM
RISELEY, JERRY BURR, JR.
(1920-) [American
attorney and author]
Galdo Monk
Rising State of New Jersey,
Despot-in-Chief in and
over the. See:
LIVINGSTON, WILLIAM
Rising State of New Jersey,
Extraordinary Chancellor
of the. See:
LIVINGSTON, WILLIAM
Risteard de Paor. See:
POWER, RICHARD
RISTER, CARL COKE
(1889-1955) [Australian
author and historian]
James Marshall
Rita. See:
CORDAY, PAULA
HUMPHREYS, ELIZA
MARGARET
Rita Hayworth. See:
CANSINO, MARGARITA
CARMEN
RITA, JOE DE. See:
Stooges, The Three
Rita Rio. See:
NOVELLA, RITA
RITTER, WOODWARD (1907-)
[American motion
picture cowboy and
Western music singer]
Tex Ritter
Rival of Sappho, The. See:
LEWIS, ESTELLE
ANNA BLANCHE
ROBINSON
Rival, The Poetic Actress
Without a. See:
MURRAY, ALMA
RIVAROL (RIVAROLI),
ANTOINE (1753-1801)
[French wit and writer]
Chevalier de Parcieux
Comte de Rivarol
River," Football's "Old Man.
See: STAGG, AMOS
ALONZO
River School of American

Artists, Founder of the
Hudson. See:
COLE, THOMAS
Rivera, Diego. See:
RODRÍGUEZ DIEGO MARÍA
CONCEPCIÓN JUAN
NEPOMUCENTO ESTANIS-
LAO DE LA ROVERA Y
BARRIENTOS ACOSTA Y
Rivers, Joan. See:
MOLINSKY, JOAN
Rivers, Larry. See:
GROSSBERG, YITZROCH
LOIZA
Rivers, Pearl. See:
NICHOLSON, ELIZA JANE
POITEVENT HOLBROOK
Riverside, John. See:
HEINLEIN, ROBERT ANSON
Rives, Amélie. See:
TROUBETZKOY, PRINCESS
AMÉLIE RIVES
Rives, Leigh. See:
SEWARD, WILLIAM WARD,
JR.
Rivet. See:
McCLINTIC, JAMES V.
RIVIERE, WILLIAM ALEXANDER
(1916-) [American guide
and author]
Bill Riviere
RIXEY, EPPA, JR. (1891-)
[American professional
baseball player]
Jephtha
RIZZO, ANTHONY (1937-)
[American guitarist]
Bob Rizzo
RIZZUTO, PHILIP FRANCIS
(1918-) [American pro-
fessional baseball player]
Phil Rizzuto
Ro Tae-yong. See:
RUTT, RICHARD
ROACH, JOHN (1813-87) [Irish-
American shipbuilder]
The Father of Iron Ship-
building in America
Road. See also:
Rhode
Road, The Father of the National.
See: CLAY, HENRY

Roads. See also:
RHOADES
Rhoades
RHODES
Rhodes
Roads, Good. See:
CARTWRIGHT, WILBURN
KING, CYRUS MURDOCK
Roads in New York, The
Father of Concrete. See:
GREENE, FREDERICK
STUART
Roads (Rhodes), The King of.
See: MACADAM, JOHN
LOUDON
Roads, The Colossus of the.
See: HARRIMAN,
EDWARD H.
Roads, The Father of Good.
See: SPROUL, WILLIAM
CAMERON
Roanoke, John Randolph of. See:
RANDOLPH, JOHN
ROARK, GARLAND (1904-)
[American drugstore
executive and author]
George Garland
Rob Donn. See:
MACKAY, ROBERT
Rob Roy (Red Robert). See:
MACGREGOR, ROBERT
ROBB, JOHN S. (fl. 1847)
[American humorist]
Solitaire
Robber, The. See:
EDWARD IV
Robbie of the Codes. See:
ROBINSON, FRANCES M.
Robbins. See also:
ROBINS
Robins
Robbins, Harold. See:
RUBIN, HAROLD
Robbins, Jerome. See:
RABINOWITZ, JEROME
Robe, White. See:
ROBERTS, JOHN
ROBERDS, FRED A. (1941-)
[American composer,
singer and actor]
Smokey Roberds
Robert. See:

MONTGOMERY, HENRY,
JR.
UNKNOWN
ROBERT I (died 1035) [Duke of
Normandy]
Robert the Devil
ROBERT I (1274-1329) [King of
Scotland]
Robert the Bruce
ROBERT II (970?-1031) [King
of France]
Robert the Pious
ROBERT II (1054?-1134)
[Eldest son of WILLIAM
THE CONQUEROR]
Curt-hose
Curtmantle
ROBERT II (c. 1316-90) [King of
Scotland]
The Steward
Robert Alda. See:
D'ABRUZZA, ALPHONSO
Robert Alton. See:
HART, ROBERT ALTON
Robert Arnold Conrad. See:
HART, MOSS
Robert Arthur. See:
ARTHAUD, ROBERT
FEDER, R.H.
Robert B. Wright. See:
BRUCE, ROBERT
Robert Barclay Dillingham. See:
FOULKE, WILLIAM
DUDLEY
Robert Barnacle, Captain. See:
NEWELL, CHARLES
MARTIN
Robert Bernard. See:
MARTIN, ROBERT
BERNARD
Robert Blake. See:
DAVIES, LESLIE PURNELL
Robert Bracefield. See:
WOOLEY, EDWARD MOTT
Robert Carlton. See:
HALL, RAYMOND RUSH
Robert Carroll. See:
ALPERT, HOLLIS
Robert Combs. See:
MURRAY, JOHN
Robert Crane. See:
ROBERTSON, FRANK

CHESTER
Robert D. Andrews. See:
    ANDREWS, CHARLES
    ROBERT DOUGLAS
    HARDY
Robert de Brunne. See:
    MANNYNG, ROBERT
ROBERT DE MOLESME (c. 1028-
    1111) [French churchman;
    founder of the Cistercian
    Order]
    Robert of Champagne
    Robert of Citeaux
Robert Douglas. See:
    ANDREWS, CHARLES
    ROBERT DOUGLAS
    HARDY
    FINLAYSON, ROBERT
    DOUGLAS
Robert Dudley. See:
    BALDWIN, JAMES
Robert Duguid. See:
    PRING-MILL, ROBERT
    DUGUID FORREST
Robert Forio. See:
    WEISS, IRVING J.
Robert Forsythe. See:
    CRICHTON, KYLE SAMUEL
Robert Franz. See:
    KNAUTH, ROBERT
Robert, Friedrich. See:
    EHLERS, FRIEDRICH
    ROBERT
ROBERT, GEORGES ACHILLE
    MARIE-JOSEPH (1875-)
    [French former High
    Commissioner of Martinique
    and Guadeloupe]
    Robert le Nazi
Robert Greene. See:
    DEINDORFOR, ROBERT
    GREENE
Robert Guillaume. See:
    SNEDDON, ROBERT
    WILLIAM
Robert Harbinson. See:
    BRYANS, ROBERT
    HARBINSON
ROBERT-HOUDIN, JEAN
    EUGÈNE (1805-71) [French
    illusionist and magician]
    The Father of Modern Magic

Robert Hutton. See:
    WINNE, ROBERT BRUCE
Robert Irving. See:
    ADLER, IRVING
Robert Joffrey. See:
    KHAN, ABDULLAH JAFFER
    ANVER BEY
Robert Keiser. See:
    KING, ROBERT
Robert Kingsley. See:
    CLARKE, JOHN CAMPBELL
Robert Kole. See:
    KOLODIN, ROBERT
Robert L. Pike. See:
    FISH, ROBERT L.
ROBERT, LAWRENCE WOOD,
    JR. (1887-) [American
    construction engineer and
    politician]
    Chip
Robert Lowery. See:
    HANKE, ROBERT LOWERY
Robert McLeod. See:
    KNOX, WILLIAM
Robert Manfred. See:
    MARX, ERICA ELIZABETH
Robert Markham. See:
    AMIS, KINGSLEY
Robert Medill. See:
    McBRIDE, ROBERT
    MEDILL
Robert Norman. See:
    GARDNER, MAURICE
Robert of Anjou, Charles. See:
    CHARLES I
Robert of Carobert, Charles.
    See: CHARLES I
Robert Orr Chipperfield. See:
    OSTRANDER, ISABEL
Robert Paige. See:
    PAGE, JOHN ARTHUR
Robert Paye. See:
    LONG, MRS. GABRIELLE
    MARGARET VERE
    CAMPBELL
Robert Randall. See:
    SILVERBERG, ROBERT
Robert, Rapid. See:
    FELLER, ROBERT WILLIAM
    ANDREW
Robert Raymond. See:
    ALTER, ROBERT EDMOND

Robert, Red (Rob Roy). See:
MACGREGOR, ROBERT
Robert Retla. See:
ALTER, ROBERT EDMOND
Robert Rich. See:
TRUMBO, DALTON
Robert, Ruby. See:
FITZSIMMONS, ROBERT
PROMETHEUS
Robert S. Tralins. See:
TRALINS, S. ROBERT
Robert Sencourt. See:
GEORGE, ROBERT
ESMONDE GORDON
Robert Shayne. See:
DAWE, ROBERT SHAEN
Robert Slender, Stocking
Weaver. See:
FRENEAU, PHILIP
MORIN
Robert Steel. See:
WHITSON, JOHN HARVEY
Robert Sterling. See:
HART, WILLIAM STER-
LING
Robert Street. See:
THOMAS, GORDON
Robert Taylor. See:
BRUGH, SPANGLER
ARLINGTON
Robert Tibber. See:
FRIEDMAN, EVE
ROSEMARY TIBBER
Robert Timsol. See:
BIRD, FREDERIC
MAYER
Robert Traver. See:
VOELKER, JOHN
DONALDSON
Robert, Uncle. See:
LEE, ROBERT EDWARD
Robert W. Hamilton. See:
STRATEMEYER,
EDWARD L.
Robert Warwick. See:
BIEN, ROBERT TAYLOR
Robert Wells. See:
WELSCH, ROGER LEE
Robert Whistlecraft, William
and. See:
FRERE, JOHN HOOKHAM
Robert Willey. See:

LEY, WILLY
Roberta. See:
MOSS, ROBERT ALFRED
Roberta Carr. See:
ROBERTS, IRENE
Roberta Courtland. See:
DERN, PEGGY GADDIS
Roberta Ormiston. See:
FLETCHER, ADELE
WHITLEY
Roberta Peters. See:
PETERMAN, ROBERTA
Roberts, Anthony. See:
WATNEY, JOHN BASIL
ROBERTS, BRIGHAM HENRY
(1857-1933) [Morman
church leader]
The Defender of the Faith
ROBERTS, C. LUCKEYTH
(1893-) [American com-
poser and musician]
Luckey Roberts
Roberts, Captain. See:
HOBART-HAMPDEN,
AUGUST CHARLES
ROBERTS, CAPTAIN BAR-
THOLOMEW (1682-1722)
[Welsh pirate]
Black Bart
ROBERTS, CARL ERIC
BECHOFER (1894-)
[English author and
biographer]
Ephesian
ROBERTS, CECIL EDRIC
MORINGTON (1892-)
[English novelist, short
story writer and dramatist]
Russell Beresford
Seer
ROBERTS, DOROTHY JAMES
(1903-) [American author]
Peter Mortimer
ROBERTS, ERIC (1914-)
[British writer and broad-
caster]
Robin
ROBERTS, FREDERICK SLEIGH
(1832-1914) [English
general officer]
Roberts of Kandahar, Pre-
toria and Waterford

ROBERTS, IRENE (1926-)
[British author]
Roberta Carr
Elizabeth Harle
I. Roberts
Ivor Roberts
Iris Rowland
Roberts, Jim. See: BATES,
    BARBARA SNEDEKER
ROBERTS, JOHN (fl. 1883-
    1929) [American missionary
    to Shoshoni Indians]
White Robe
Roberts, Jon. See:
    OLSON, ROBERT G.
Roberts, Julian. See:
    BARDENS, DENNIS
        CONRAD
Roberts, Lee. See:
    MARTIN, ROBERT LEE
Roberts, McLean. See:
    MACHLIN, MILTON
        ROBERT
ROBERTS, ORAN MILO
    (1815-98) [American
    soldier, statesman and
    jurist]
The Old Alcalde
ROBERTS, ROBERT RICHFORD
    (1778-1843) [American
    Methodist Episcopal
    missionary]
The Grandfather of the Mis-
    sionaries
ROBERTS, THEODORE (1861-
    1928) [American motion
    picture actor]
Dad
The Grand Old Man of the
    Screen
ROBERTS, THOMAS WILLIAM
    (1856-1931) [Australian
    painter]
Tom Roberts
Roberts, Tom. See:
    ROBERTS, THOMAS
        WILLIAM
    THOMAS, ROBERT
        MURRAY
Roberts, Virginia. See:
    DEAN, NELL MARR
Roberts, Wayne. See:

OVERHOLSER, WAYNE D.
ROBERTSHAW, JAMES
    DENIS (1911-) [English
    author]
Michael Gaunt
Robertson, Alex, M.D. See:
    RATHBONE, ST. GEORGE
        HENRY
ROBERTSON, CLIFFORD
    PARKER, 3D (1925-)
    [American actor]
Cliff Robertson
ROBERTSON, CONSTANCE
    NOYES (1897-)
    [American novelist]
Dana Scott
Robertson, E. Arnot. See:
    TURNER, EILEEN
        ARBUTHNOT ROBERT-
        SON
ROBERTSON, FRANK CHESTER
    (1890-) [American
    writer of Western
    stories]
Robert Crane
Frank Chester Field
King Hill
Robertson, Helen. See:
    EDMISTON, HELEN JEAN
        MARY
Robertson, Ignatius Loyola. See:
    KNAPP, SAMUEL
        LORENZO
ROBERTSON, JAMES
    (1742-1814) [American
    pioneer in the development
    of Nashville, Tennessee]
The Father of Middle
    Tennessee
ROBERTSON, JAMES B.
    (1910-) [American com-
    poser and country music
    singer]
Texas Jim
ROBERTSON, JAMES LOGIE
    (1846-1922) [Scottish poet]
Hugh Halliburton
ROBERTSON, JOHN WYLIE
    (1889-1966) [American
    motion picture actor]
Wylie Watson
ROBERTSON, KEITH (1914-)

[American author]
Carlton Keith
Robertson MacDougall. See:
MAIR, GEORGE
BROWN
ROBERTSON, MARJORIE
(1908-) [British dancer
and motion picture actress]
Anna Neagle
ROBERTSON, OSCAR PALMER
(1938-) [American Negro
basketball player]
The Big O
Oz
ROBERTSON, THOMAS
ANTHONY (1897-)
[American agriculturist,
business executive and
author]
Don Tomasito
Robertus de Fluctibus. See:
FLUDD (FLUD), ROBERT
ROBESPIERRE, FRANÇOIS-
JOSEPH MAXIMILIEN
ISIDORE DE (1759-94)
[French revolutionary
leader]
The Incorruptible
The Sea-Green Incorruptible
Robespierre Marat Fitzthunder.
See: SHAW, GEORGE
BERNARD
Robey, George. See:
WADE, GEORGE
EDWARD
Robie, Mrs. Anna A. See:
ROLFE, MARO O.
Robin. See:
ARMIN, ROBERT
BRYANS, ROBERT
HARBINSON
MAUGHAM, ROBERT
CECIL ROMER
MOORE, ROBERT
LOWELL, JR.
ROBERTS, ERIC
Robin Bluestring. See:
WALPOLE, SIR ROBERT
Robin Hood of Missouri, The.
See: JAMES, JESSE
WOODSON
Robin Hood of the Forest, The.

See: ALLEN, ETHAN
Robin Hood of the Sierras. See:
CARILLO, JOAQUIN
ROBINS [Robins]. See also:
Robbins
ROBINS, ELIZABETH (1866-1952)
[American novelist, play-
wright, critic and actress]
C.E. Raimond
Robins, Rollo. See:
ELLIS, EDWARD
SYLVESTER
Robins, Seelin. See:
ELLIS, EDWARD
SYLVESTER
ROBINSON [Robinson]. See also:
Ribbonson
ROBINSON, ANNIE DOUGLAS
GREEN (1842-)
[American author]
Marian Douglas
ROBINSON, CHAILLE PAYNE
(fl. 1947-65) [American
author]
Jean Kirby
Kathleen Robinson
Robinson Crusoe. See:
ANDERSON, JAMES
Robinson, Edward G. See:
GOLDENBERG, EMANUEL
ROBINSON, EDWIN MEADE
(1878-1946) [American
editor and journalist]
Ted Robinson
ROBINSON, ELIZABETH
CAMERON (fl. 1928-65)
[American educator, editor
and author]
Elizabeth Cameron
Elizabeth Clemons
ROBINSON, FAYETTE LODAWICK
(1818-84) [American circus
impresario]
Yankee Robinson
ROBINSON, FRANCES M.
(1906-) [American secretary
to GENERAL HUGH S.
JOHNSON, N.R.A. ad-
ministrator]
The Right Hand Mind
Robbie of the Codes
ROBINSON, FREDERICK JOHN

(1782-1859) [English
nobleman and statesman]
Goosey Goderich
ROBINSON, JACK ROOSEVELT
(1919-) [American pro-
fessional baseball player]
Jackie Robinson
ROBINSON, JOAN MARY
GALE THOMAS (fl.1953-60)
[British author and
illustrator]
Joan Gale Thomas
Robinson, John Philo. See:
CRIPPEN, DR. HAWLEY
HARVEY
Robinson, Madeleine. See:
SVOBDA, MADELEINE
ROBINSON, MARY (fl. late
18th cent.) [English
girl, deceived by JOHN
HATFIELD, forger]
The Beauty of Buttermere
ROBINSON, MRS. MARY
DARBY (1758-1800)
[English actress,
novelist and poet]
Fair Perdida
Perdita
ROBINSON, MRS. THÉRÈSE
ALBERTINE (1797-1870)
[German-American
author]
Talvi
ROBINSON, RAY CHARLES
(1932-) [American jazz
musician (singer, piano,
composer, organ, alto
saxophone)]
Ray Charles
ROBINSON, SOLON (1803-80)
[American pioneer,
agriculturist and author]
The King of the Squatters
Robinson, Sugar Ray. See:
SMITH, WALKER, JR.
ROBINSON, WILLIAM
(1878-1949) [American
Negro tap dancer and
entertainer]
Bojangles
Bill Robinson
ROBINSON, WILLIAM
ELLSWORTH

(18??-1918) [American
illusionist and magician]
Chung Ling Soo
ROBINSON, WILLIAM ERIGENA
(1814-92) [Irish-American
journalist and writer]
Richelieu
ROBINSON, WILLIAM STEVENS
(1818-76) [American
editor and letter writer]
Gilbert
Warrington
ROBINSON, WILLIAM WHEELER
(1918-) [American editor
and author]
Bill Robinson
ROBISON, MARY (1865-1942)
[Australian-American
actress]
May Robson
Robot, The Boy. See:
FISCHER, ROBERT JAMES
Robson, May. See:
ROBISON, MARY
Robson, Stuart. See:
STUART, HENRY ROBSON
ROBUSTI, JACOPO (1518-94)
[Venetian painter]
Il Furioso
The Thunderbolt of Painting
Tintoret
Tintoretto
Roc, Patricia. See:
RIESE, FELICIA
Rocca, Pete la. See:
SIMS, PETER
Roche, A.K. See:
KAPLAN, BOCHE
Roche, John. See:
LE ROI, DAVID DE
ROCHE
ROCHE, MARGARET ELEANOR
(1917-) [American radio
and television commentator]
Maggi McNellis
Rochester. See:
ANDERSON, EDDIE
Rock. See:
ROCKNE, KNUTE
KENNETH
Rock, Hard. See:
O'CONNELL, DANIEL J.

Rock Hudson. See:
FITZGERALD, ROY
Rock Island, The Sphinx of
the. See:
MOORE, WILLIAM
HENRY
Rock (Kepha) (Petros). See:
PETER
Rock of Chicamauga, The.
See: THOMAS, GEORGE
HENRY
Rock of Notre Dame, The.
See: ROCKNE, KNUTE
KENNETH
Rock, Old. See:
BENNING, HENRY
LEWIS
Rock, Richard. See:
MAINPRIZE, DON
ROCKEFELLER, JOHN
DAVISON (1839-1937)
[American capitalist and
philanthropist]
John D.
The Standard Oil King
ROCKEY. See also:
Rocky
ROCKEY, HOWARD (1886-1934)
[American novelist]
Ronald Bryce
Oliver Pangbourne
Rockies, The Daniel Boone of
the. See:
BRIDGER, JAMES
Rockies, The Pride of the.
See: DEVLAN, EUGENE
Rockies, The Red-headed
Rooster of the. See:
BELFORD, JAMES
BURNS
Rocking Chair Sensation of
Russia, the Prewar. See:
MEYER, DR. ALEXANDER
Rockingham, Montague. See:
NYE, NELSON CORAL
ROCKNE, KNUTE KENNETH
(1888-1931) [American
football coach]
Rock
The Rock of Notre Dame
Rocks. See:
STONE, FREDERICK

MATHER
Rockwell, Matt. See:
ROWLAND, DONALD
SYDNEY
Rockwood, Roy. See:
STRATEMEYER,
EDWARD L.
Rocky. See:
ROCKEY
STONE, JOHN THOMAS
Rocky Isle, The Blind Old
Man of Scio's. See:
HOMER
Rocky Lane. See:
ALBERSHART, HARRY
Rocky Marciano. See:
MARCHEGIANO, ROCCO
FRANCIS
Rocky Mountains, The Apostle
of the. See:
DE SMET, PETER JOHN
Rocky Mountains, The Nestor
of the. See:
CARSON, CHRISTOPHER
Rod. See:
GILBERT, RODRIGUE
GABRIEL
LAVER, RODNEY GEORGE
STEIGER, RODNEY
STEPHEN
Rod Caley. See:
ROWLAND, DONALD
SYDNEY
Rod Cameron. See:
COX, ROD
Rod La Rocque. See:
LA ROUR, RODERICK LA
ROCQUE DE
RODD, KYLIE TENNANT
(1912-) [Australian book-
man and author]
Kylie Tennant
RODDA, CHARLES (1891-)
[Australian journalist and
author]
Gavin Holt
Gardner Low
RODDA, CHARLES. See also:
Reed, Eliot
RODDEY, PHILIP DALE
(1820-97) [American
merchant and Confederate

872

general officer]
The Swamp Fox of the
Tennessee Valley
Roddy. See:
McDOWALL, RODERICK
ANDREW
RODEHEAVER, HOMER ALLAN
(1880-1956) [American
evangelist, trombonist,
hymn writer and publisher]
Rodey
RODERICK (fl. c. 710) [Last
ruler of the West-Gothic
kingdom of Spain]
The Last of the Goths
Rodey. See:
RODEHEAVER, HOMER
ALLAN
Rodgers. See also:
ROGERS
Rogers
Rodgers, Frank. See:
INFIELD, GLENN
BERTON
Rodman, Emerson. See:
ELLIS, EDWARD
SYLVESTER
Rodman, Maia. See:
WOJCIECHOWSKA, MAIA
Rodney, Bob. See:
RODRIGO, ROBERT
Rodney Bullingham. See:
SLADEN, NORMAN ST.
BARBE
Rodney, Don. See:
RAGONESE, DON
Rodney, Red. See:
CHUDNICK, ROBERT
Rodolphus Agricola. See:
HUYSMANN, ROELOF
RODRIGO, ROBERT (1928-)
[British sports writer,
script writer and editor]
Bob Rodney
RODRÍGUEZ. See:
SÁNCHEZ, MANUEL
RODRÍGUEZ Y
RODRÍGUEZ, ALEJANDRO
OLMEDO Y (1936-)
[Peruvian tennis player]
Alex Olmedo
RODRÍGUEZ, AUGUSTIN

(c. 1880-19??) [Spanish
bullfighter; fought as a
woman]
La Reverte
María Salomé
RODRÍGUEZ, DIEGO MARÍA
CONCEPCIÓN JUAN
NEPOMUCENTO ESTANISLAO
DE LA RIVERA Y BAR-
RIENTOS ACOSTA Y
(1886-) [Mexican artist]
Diego Rivera
RODRÍGUEZ, FRANCISCO
HERRERA (1783-1820)
[Spanish bullfighter]
Curro Guillén
RODRÍGUEZ, JOAQUIN (1729-
c. 1800) [Spanish bullfighter]
Costillares
RODRÍGUEZ, JOAQUIN
(1903-) [Spanish bull-
fighter]
Cagancho
RODRÍGUEZ, JOSÉ (1824-62)
[Spanish bullfighter]
Pepete
RODRÍGUEZ, JOSÉ (1867-99)
[Spanish bullfighter]
Pepete
RODRÍGUEZ, JUAN A.
(1935-) [Puerto Rican
professional golfer]
Chi Chi
RODRÍGUEZ, MANUEL
(1883-1923) [Spanish
bullfighter]
Manolete
RODRÍGUEZ, RAFAEL. See:
Three Musketeers, The
ROE, EDWARD PAYSON
(1838-88) [American
author]
E. P. Roe
ROE, FREDERIC GORDON
(1894-) [British author]
Criticus
F. G. R.
Uncle Gordon
Winslow Rhode
Roe, Harry Mason. See:
STRATEMEYER,
EDWARD L.

ROE, MARY ABIGAIL
  (c.1840-) [American
  author]
  C.M. Cornwall
ROEBUCK, JOHN ARTHUR
  (1801-79) [English
  politician]
  Tear 'em
ROETER, ADA (1906-)
  [American pianist and
  composer]
  Ada Rubin
Roffe. See:
  ERICSON, ROLF
Rog. See:
  TOUHY, ROGER
Rogelet de la Pasture. See:
  WEYDEN, ROGIER VAN
  DER
Roger. See:
  Scarlett, Roger
Roger Barlow. See:
  LECKIE, ROBERT HUGH
Roger Bax. See:
  WINTERTON, PAUL
Roger, Black. See:
  TOUHY, ROGER
Roger Bontemps. See:
  COLLERYE, ROGER DE
Roger Capel. See:
  SHEPPARD, LANCELOT
  CAPEL
Roger Charles Tichborne, Sir.
  See: ORTON, ARTHUR
Roger de Coverley, Sir. See:
  ADDISON, JOSEPH
  SEWALL, JONATHAN
Roger de la Pasture. See:
  WEYDEN, ROGIER VAN
  DER
Roger Fuller. See:
  TRACY, DONALD FISKE
Roger Harris. See:
  WILSON, ROGER HARRIS
  LEBUS
Roger Hartmann. See:
  MEHTA, RUSTAM
  JEHANGIR
Roger, Jolly. See:
  BRADFIELD, ROGER
Roger Lewis. See:
  ZARCHY, HARRY

Roger-Maxe de la Glannege. See:
  LEGMAN, GERSHON
ROGER, PIERRE (1291-1352)
  [Supreme Pontiff of Roman
  Catholic Church]
  Pope Clement VI
Roger Piper. See:
  FISHER, JOHN
Roger Simons. See:
  PUNNETT, IVOR
  McCAULEY
Roger Starbuck. See:
  COMSTOCK, AUGUSTUS
Roger Vadim. See:
  PLEMIANNIKOW, ROGER
  VADIM
Roger Valentine. See:
  DUKE, DONALD NORMAN
ROGER, VICTORIANO
  (1898-1936) [Spanish bull-
  fighter]
  Valencia II
ROGERS [Rogers]. See also:
  Rodgers
ROGERS, CHARLES (1904-)
  [American motion picture
  actor and dance orchestra
  leader]
  America's Boyfriend
  Buddy Rogers
Rogers, Ginger. See:
  McMATH, VIRGINIA
  KATHERINE
ROGERS, HENRY HUTTLESTON
  (1840-1909) [American
  capitalist]
  Hell Hound Rogers
ROGERS, JOHN (c.1500-55)
  [English Lutheran reformer
  and martyr]
  Thomas Matthew
Rogers, Lee. See:
  WILSON, ROGER C.
Rogers, Milt. See:
  ADELSTEIN, MILTON
ROGERS, MILTON M. (1924-)
  [American jazz musician
  (composer, trumpet, flugel-
  horn, leader)]
  Shorty Rogers
Rogers, Phillips. See:
  IDELL, ALBERT E.

Rogers, Rosalind. See:
RICHARDSON, RANDELL
Rogers, Roy. See:
SLYE, LEONARD
ROGERS, SAMUEL (1762-1855)
[English poet]
The Banker-Poet
The Bard of Memory
ROGERS, TIMOTHY LOUIS
AIVERUM (1915-)
[American composer,
singer and comedian]
Timmie Rogers
Rogers, Wade. See:
MADLEE, DOROTHY
HAYNES
ROGERS, WILLIAM PENN
ADAIR (1879-1935)
[American humorist,
actor and author]
The Ambassador of Good
Will
The Cherokee Kid
The Cowboy Philosopher
The Man Who Can Say
Anything and Make
Everybody Like it
The Prince of Wit and
Wisdom
Will Rogers
Rohan O'Grady. See:
SKINNER, JUNE
O'GRADY
ROHE, VERA-ELLEN
WESTMEYR (1927-)
[American singer,
dancer and motion
picture actress]
Vera-Ellen
Rohmer. See also:
Romer
Rohmer, Sax. See:
WADE (WARDE), ARTHUR
SARSFIELD
Roi Soleil, Le (The Sun King).
See: LOUIS XIV
ROKER, GRANVILLE
WILLIAM (1932-)
[American jazz musician
(drums)]
Mickey Roker
Roland. See:

KIRK, RONALD T.
ROWLAND
Rowland
Roland Dare. See:
MORRIS, CHARLES SMITH
ROLAND DE LA PLATÌERE,
JEANNE MANON
PHILIPON (1754-93) [French
revolutionist and writer]
The Circe of the Revolution
Madame Roland
Roland, Gilbert. See:
ALONSO, LUIS ANTONIO
DAMASO DE
Roland, The Roman. See:
SICINIUS DENATUS
Roland Vane. See:
McKEAG, ERNEST LIONEL
Rolf Boldrewood. See:
BROWNE, THOMAS
ALEXANDER
ROLFE, FREDERICK WILLIAM
SERAFINO AUSTIN
LEWIS MARY (1860-1913)
[British eccentric,
novelist and historian]
Baron Corvo
ROLFE, MARO O. (1852-1925)
[American journalist,
historian and novelist]
A Civil War Captain
Colonel Oram Eflor
Colonel Oram R. McHenry
Oram Eflor
The Detective Novelist, M.O.
Rolfe
M. O'Rolfe, The Irish Novelist
Mrs. Anna A. Robie
Sergeant Rolfe
A.W. Rolker
The Old Detective
The Young Detective
Rolker, A.W. See:
ROLFE, MARO O.
Rollie. See:
CULVER, ROLLAND
PIERCE
Rollins, Glenn. See:
OLSON, ROBERT G.
ROLLINS, JAMES SIDNEY
(1812-88) [American
orator and sponsor of the

University of Missouri]
The Father of the University
of Missouri
The Silver-tongued Orator
ROLLINS, KATHLEEN. See:
Debrett, Hal
ROLLINS, MRS. ELLEN
CHAPMAN HOBBS
(1831-81) [American
author]
E.H. Arr
ROLLINS, THEODORE WALTER
(1929-) [American jazz
musician (tenor saxo-
phone, composer)]
Sonny Rollins
Rollo Robins. See:
ELLIS, EDWARD
SYLVESTER
Roloff. See:
BENY, WILFRED ROY
RÖLVAAG, OLE EDVART
(1876-1931) [Norwegian
novelist]
O.E. Rölvaag
Romaine, David. See:
BOHME, DAVID M.
ROMAINE, LAWRENCE B.
(1900-) [American
rhymester, editor and
author]
The Weathercock
Romaine, Linton. See:
LEE, REV. ALBERT
Romains, Jules. See:
FARIGOULE, LOUIS-
HENRI JEAN
Roman Achilles, The. See:
SICINIUS DENATUS
Roman Hippocrates, The. See:
CELSUS, AULUS
CORNELIUS
Roman Literature, The Father
of. See:
ENNIUS, QUINTUS
Roman of Them All, The
Grandest. See:
McMILLIN, BENTON
Roman of Them All, The
Noblest. See:
McMILLIN, BENTON
THURMAN, ALLAN

GRANBERRY
Roman Philosophy, The Father
of. See:
CICERO, MARCUS TULLIUS
Roman Poetry, The Father of.
See: ENNIUS, QUINTUS
Roman Roland, The. See:
SICINIUS DENATUS
Roman Satire, The Father of.
See: LUCILIUS, CAIUS
Roman, The Old. See:
BENTON, THOMAS HART
COMISKEY, CHARLES
ALBERT
MULDOON, WILLIAM
THURMAN, ALLAN
GRANBERRY
Romance, The Genius of. See:
HAWTHORNE, NATHANIEL
Romano, Enotrio. See:
CARDUCCI, GIOSUE
Romano, Giulio. See:
CACCINI, GIULIO
Romans, Patrician of the.
See: PEPIN (PIPPIN) III
Romans, The Last of the. See:
RIENZI, COLA DI
Romans, The Most Learned of
the. See:
VARRO, MARCUS
TERENTIUS
Romanticism, The Prophet of.
See: HARDENBERG,
FRIEDRICH LEOPOLD,
BARON VON
Romanticism, The Spoiled
Darling of Spanish. See:
MORAL, JOSÉ ZORRILLAY
ROMANUS (died 897) [Supreme
Pontiff of Roman Catholic
Church]
Pope Romanus
ROMANUS, AGAEDIUS, OF
COLONNA (c. 1247-1316)
[Scholastic philosopher,
general of the Augustine
order]
Doctor Fundatissimus
Romanus, Hercules. See:
COMMODUS, LUCIUS
AELIUS AURELIUS
ROMBERG, SIGMUND

(1887-1951) [Hungarian-
American composer]
The American Successor to
Johann Strauss
Rome, King of. See:
BONAPARTE, NAPOLEON
FRANÇOIS CHARLES
JOSEPH
Rome, Stewart. See:
RYOTT, SEPTIMUS
WILLIAM
Rome, The Shield of. See:
VERRUCOSUS, QUINTUS
FABIUS MAXIMUS
Rome, The Sword of. See:
MARCELLUS (MARCUS
CLAUDIUS)
Rome, The Third Founder of.
See: CAIUS MARIUS
Romer. See:
Rohmer
WILSON, FLORENCE
ROMA MUIR
Romer Wilson. See:
O'BRIEN, FLORENCE
ROMA MUIR
Romero, Gary. See:
CATSOS, NICHOLAS A.
Rome's Greatest Pope. See:
GREGORY
Romilly Fedden, Mrs. See:
FEDDEN, KATHERINE
WALDO DOUGLAS
ROMMEL, ERWIN JOHANNES
EUGEN (1891-1944) [Ger-
man field marshal]
The Desert Fox
ROMMEL, MARILYN DAYTON
(fl. 1963) [American
journalist and author]
Mimi Rommel
Romney Brent. See:
LARRALDE, ROMULO
Romney, Edana. See:
RUBENSTEIN, EDANA
ROMULUS (fl. 753-716 B.C.)
[Legendary founder and
first King of Rome]
Quirinus
Romy Schneider. See:
ALBACH-RETTY,
ROSEMARIE

Ron Archer. See:
WHITE, THEODORE
EDWIN
Ron Terry. See:
PRITKIN, RON
Rona Randall. See:
SHAMBROOK, RONA
Ronald. See:
FIRBANK, ARTHUR
ANNESLEY RONALD
Ronald Bryce. See:
ROCKEY, HOWARD
Ronald Fraser. See:
TILTMAN, RONALD
FRANK
Ronald James. See:
PRESTON, JAMES
Ronald Maxwell. See:
SMITH, RONALD GREGOR
Ronald Scott Thorn. See:
WILKINSON, RONALD
Ronald Squire. See:
SQUIRL, RONALD
Ronald Welch. See:
FELTON, RONALD OLIVER
RONAN, THOMAS MATTHEW
(1907-) [Australian
farmer and author]
Tom Ronan
RONCALLI, ANGELO GIUSEPPE
(1881-1963) [Supreme
Pontiff of Roman Catholic
Church]
Pope John XXIII
Rondo, Father. See:
DAVAUX, J.B.
Ronny Lee. See:
LEVENTHAL, RONALD
Ronquillo (Little Hoarse One).
See: PELAYO, LUIS
RONSARD, PIERRE DE
(1524-85) [French poet]
The French Poet
The Prince of the Ode
Rooan Hurkey. See:
HOLZAPFEL, RUDOLF
PATRICK
ROOD, OGDEN NICHOLAS
(1831-1902) [American
physicist and researcher]
The Father of American Ex-
perimental Physics

Rooney. See:
 LEE, WILLIAM
  HENRY FITZHUGH
Rooney, Mickey. See:
 YULE, JOE, JR.
ROOSEVELT, ANNA ELEANOR
 (1884-1962) [American
 humanitarian and author;
 wife of President
 FRANKLIN DELANO
 ROOSEVELT]
Eleanor
The World's Most Admired
 Woman
ROOSEVELT, FRANKLIN
 DELANO (1882-1945)
 [Thirty-second President
 of the United States]
The Boss
F.D.
F.D.R.
That Man in the White House
The Houdini in the White
 House
The Squire of Hyde Park
The Sphinx
ROOSEVELT, FRANKLIN
 DELANO. See also:
Big Three, The
ROOSEVELT, JAMES (1907-)
 [Eldest son of President
 FRANKLIN DELANO
 ROOSEVELT]
The Crown Prince of the
 New Deal
Modern Mercury
Son Jimmy
Roosevelt, Little Miss. See:
 LONGWORTH, ALICE LEE
  ROOSEVELT
ROOSEVELT, QUENTIN
 (1897-1918) [American
 aviator; son of Presi-
 dent THEODORE
 ROOSEVELT]
Quentin the Eagle
Roosevelt Sykes. See:
 BEY, ROOSEVELT SYKES
ROOSEVELT, THEODORE
 (1858-1919) [Twenty-sixth
 President of the United
 States]

The Bull Moose
The Driving Force
The Dynamo of Power
Four Eyes
Great White Chief
The Happy Warrior
Haroun-al-Roosevelt
The Hero of San Juan Hill
The Man on Horseback
The Meddler
The Old Lion
Rough Rider
The Sage of Princeton
Teddy Roosevelt
Telescope Teddy
Theodore the Meddler
The Trust-buster
The Trust-busting President
The Typical American
Rooster of the Rockies, The
 Red-headed. See:
 BELFORD, JAMES BURNS
Rooster, The Great Thundering.
 See: JOHNSON, HUGH
  SAMUEL
Rope Maker, The Beautiful
 (La Belle Cordière). See:
 LABÉ, LOUISE
ROPER, DANIEL CALHOUN
 (1867-1943) [American
 lawyer and politician]
The Chief Executioner
ROPES, ARTHUR REED (1859-
 1933) [English musical
 comedy librettist]
Adrian Ross
ROQUER, EMMA DE (1858-
 1942) [French-Spanish
 dramatic soprano]
Emma Calvé
The Singing Duse
Rory Calhoun. See:
 DURGIN, FRANCIS
  TIMOTHY
Ros. See:
 METZGER, ROSWELL
  WILLIAM
 ROSS
 Ross
 Russ
Rosa. See:
 JEFFREY, ROSA GRIFFITH

VERTNER JOHNSON

Rosa Anderson. See:
  KAULITZ-NIEDECK,
    ROSA
Rosa of British Novelists, The
    Salvator. See:
  RADCLIFFE, ANN WARD
Rosa, The English Salvator.
    See: MORTIMER, JOHN
    HAMILTON
Rosalie. See:
  BROWN, ROSALIE
    GERTRUDE MOORE
Rosalie Moore. See:
  BROWN, ROSALIE
    GERTRUDE MOORE
Rosalind Erskine. See:
  LONGRIGG, ROGER
    ERSKINE
Rosalind Rogers. See:
  RICHARDSON, RANDELL
Rosalyn Cohen. See:
  HIGGINS, ROSALYN
    COHEN
Rosamond. See also:
  Rosamund
  Rosimund
Rosamund Fair. See:
  CLIFFORD, ROSAMOND
Rosamund. See also:
  Rosamond
  Rosimond
Rosamund John. See:
  JONES, NORA R.
ROSANOV, MIKHAIL
  GRIGORIEVICH (1888-)
  [Russian author]
  N. Ognev
Roscius. See:
  BURBAGE, RICHARD
Roscius, The African. See:
  ALDRIDGE, IRA
Roscius, The English. See:
  BETTERTON, THOMAS
  GARRICK, DAVID
Roscius, The French. See:
  BARON (BOYRON),
    MICHEL
  TALMA, FRANÇOIS
    JOSEPH
Roscius, The Infant. See:
  BETTY, WILLIAM

HENRY WEST

Roscius, The Irish. See:
  BARRY, SPRANGER
Roscius, The Ohio. See:
  LYON, LOUIS
Roscius, The Scottish. See:
  JOHNSTON, HENRY
    ERSKINE
Roscius, The Young. See:
  BETTY, WILLIAM HENRY
    WEST
Roscoe, Charles. See:
  ROWLAND, DONALD
    SYDNEY
ROSE, A. McGREGOR (1846-98)
  [Scotch-Canadian journalist]
  A. M. R. Gordon
Rose, Alex. See:
  ROYZ, OLESH
Rose, Billy. See:
  ROSENBERG, WILLIAM
    SAMUEL
ROSE, CAMILLE DAVIED
  (1893-) [American editor
  and author]
  Camille Davied
Rose, Florella. See:
  CARLSON, VADA F.
ROSE, GEORGE (1817-82)
  [English humorous writer]
  Arthur Sketchley
Rose, Hilary. See:
  MACKINNON, CHARLES ROY
Rose Hobart. See:
  KEEFER, ROSE
Rose, Irving. See:
  BROWNE, ERNEST D.
Rose Kennedy. See:
  VICTOR, MRS. METTA
    VICTORIA FULLER
    MORSE
Rose of Raby, The White. See:
  NEVILL, CECILY
ROSE, PETER DE. See:
  Sweethearts of the Air
ROSE-PRICE, DENNISTOUN
  FRANKLYN JOHN (1915-)
  [British stage and motion
  picture actor]
  Dennis Price
Rose, Sammy the. See:
  ROSENMAN, SAMUEL
    IRVING

879

Rose Sharon. See:
GROSSMAN, JOSEPHINE
JUDITH
Rose, The. See:
ROSENMAN, SAMUEL
IRVING
Rose, The Knight of the Red.
See: TAYLOR, ALFRED
ALEXANDER
Rose, The Knight of the White.
See: TAYLOR, ROBERT
LOVE
Rose, Tokyo. See:
D'AQUINO, IVA IKUKO
TOGURI
ROSE, WALTER (1913-)
[American jazz musician
(piano, leader)]
Wally Rose
Rose Young. See:
HARRIS, MARION ROSE
YOUNG
ROSECRANS, WILLIAM
STARKE (1819-98) [American
Civil War general officer]
Old Rosey
Rosedale, Ivan. See:
DITMAS, FRANCIS IVAN
LESLIE
ROSEGGER, PETER (1843-1918)
[Austrian poet and
novelist]
P.K.
Petri Kettenfeier
Rosemary. See:
Davis, Rosemary L.
Rosemary Manning. See:
COLE, MARGARET
ALICE
ROSEN, ALBERT LEONARD
(1925-) [American
professional baseball
player]
Al Rosen
ROSENBACH, ABRAHAM
SIMON WOLF (1876-1952)
[American dealer in
and authority on rare books
and manuscripts]
Dr. Rosenbach
ROSENBAUM, BORGE (1909-)
[Danish pianist and

comedian]
Victor Borge
The Unmelancholy Dane
ROSENBERG, GEORGE (1864-
1936) [German-American
composer]
George Rosey
ROSENBERG, NANCY SHERMAN
(1931-) [American author]
Nancy Sherman
ROSENBERG, WILLIAM
SAMUEL (1899-1966)
[American theatrical pro-
ducer, song writer and
shorthand expert]
Billy Rose
ROSENBLATT, MARTIN (1920-)
[American vaudeville,
television and motion
picture actor]
Ross Martin
ROSENBLOOM, MAX (c.1903-)
[American professional
boxer; later motion picture
actor]
Slapsie Maxie
ROSENFIELD, LOUIS ZARA
(1910-) [American author]
Louis Zara
Rosenfield, Morris. See:
ALTER, MOSHE JACOB
ROSENMAN, SAMUEL IRVING
(1896-) [American jurist
and politician]
The Rose
Sammy the Rose
ROSENTHAL, RICHARD A.
(1925-) [American editor
and author]
Allen Richards
Rosetta Tharpe, Sister. See:
NUBIN, ROSETTA
ROSEVEAR, JOHN (1936-)
[American advertising
consultant and author]
Jim Circus
ROSEWALL, KENNETH R.
(1934-) [Australian tennis
player]
Ken Rosewall
Rosewater Administration, The
Queen of the. See:

GREENHOW, ROSE
    O'NEAL
Rosey. See also:
    Rosy
Rosey, George. See:
    ROSENBERG, GEORGE
Rosey, Old. See:
    ROSECRANS, WILLIAM
    STARKE
Rosimond. See:
    LA ROZE, CLAUDE
    Rosamond
    Rosamund
Rosina Land. See:
    HASTINGS, PHYLLIS
    DORA HODGE
ROSKOLENKO, HARRY
    (1907-) [American
    author]
    Colin Ross
Rosny, J.H., the Elder. See:
    BOËX, JOSEPH HENRY
    HONORE
Rosny, J.H., The Younger. See:
    BOËX, SERAPHIN JUSTIN
    FRANÇOIS
Rosny, Joseph Henri, joint
    pseud. of JOSEPH HENRI
    HONORÉ BOËX (1856-
    1940) and his brother
    SÉRAPHIN JUSTIN
    FRANÇOIS BOËX (1859-
    1948) [French novelists]
Rosny, Joseph Henri. See also:
    BOËX, JOSEPH HENRI
    HONORÉ
    BOËX, SÉRAPHIN JUSTIN
    FRANÇOIS
ROSOFSKY, BARNEY (1909-67)
    [American professional
    boxer; world's lightweight
    champion]
    Barney Ross
ROSPIGLIOSI, GIULIO
    (1600-69) [Supreme Pontiff
    of Roman Catholic Church]
    Pope Clement IX
ROSQUELLAS, ADOLFO
    (1900-) [Argentine-
    American orchestra
    leader, violinist and
    composer]

    Pancho
ROSS [Ross]. See also:
    Ros
    Russ
Ross, Adrian. See:
    ROPES, ARTHUR REED
Ross, Aircraftsman. See:
    LAWRENCE, THOMAS
    EDWARD
Ross, Albert. See:
    PORTER, LINN BOYD
Ross, Annie. See:
    SHORT, ANNABELLE
Ross, Barnaby. See:
    Queen, Ellery
Ross, Barney. See:
    ROSOFSKY, BARNEY
Ross Beckman. See:
    DEY, FREDERICK VAN
    RENSSELAER
ROSS, CHARLES HENRY
    (1842?-97) [English artist
    and author]
    Boswell Butt, Esq.
    Ally Sloper
Ross, Colin. See:
    ROSKOLENKO, HARRY
ROSS, EULALIE STEINMETZ
    (1910-) [American librar-
    ian and compiler]
    Eulalie Steinmetz
ROSS, GERTRUDE MARY
    (1889-1957) [English
    music-hall actress]
    Gertie Gitana
Ross Hunter. See:
    FUSS, MARTIN
Ross, Ivan T. See:
    ROSSNER, ROBERT
Ross, John. See:
    COOWESCOOWE
    (KOOWESKOOWE)
Ross, Katherine. See:
    WALTER, DOROTHY BLAKE
ROSS, KEITH (1899-1960)
    [American motion picture
    actor]
    Ian Keith
ROSS, LANCELOT PATRICK
    (1906-) [American tenor]
    Lanny Ross
Ross, Leonard Q. See:

ROSTEN, LEO CALVIN
Ross Macdonald. See:
    MILLAR, KENNETH
Ross, Martin. See:
    Herring, Geilles
    MARTIN, VIOLET
    FLORENCE
Ross Martin. See:
    ROSENBLATT, MARTIN
Ross, Mother. See:
    DAVIES, CHRISTIAN
Ross Neil. See:
    HARWOOD, ISABELLA
Ross, Shirley. See:
    GAUNT, BERNICE
Ross, Sutherland. See:
    CALLARD, MAURICE
    FREDERICK THOMAS
Ross, The Man of. See:
    KYRLE, JOHN
ROSSER, THOMAS LAFAYETTE
    (1836-1910) [American
    Civil War general officer]
    The Savior of the Valley
ROSSET, BENJAMIN CHARLES
    (1910-) [Irish author]
    Ozy
ROSSETTI, CHRISTINA
    GEORGINA (1830-94)
    [English poet]
    Ellen Alleyn
ROSSETTI, GABRIEL CHARLES
    DANTE (1828-82) [English
    poet and painter]
    Dante Gabriel Rossetti
Rossetti, Gabriele. See:
    CITERIORE, VASTO
    ABRUZZO
ROSSI, NICHOLAS LOUIS, JR.
    (1924-) [American com-
    poser and author]
    Nick Rossi
ROSSINI, GIOACHINO ANTONIO
    (1792-1868) [Italian
    operatic composer]
    The Swan of Pesaro
Rossiter, Will. See:
    WILLIAMS, W.R.
ROSSNER, ROBERT (1932-)
    [American educator and
    author]
    Ivan T. Ross

ROSSON, HAROLD (1895-)
    [American cinematographer]
    Hal Rosson
ROSTEN, LEO CALVIN
    (1908-) [American
    economist, author and
    humorist]
    Leonard Q. Ross
Rostrevor, George. See:
    HAMILTON, GEORGE
    ROSTREVOR
Rosy. See:
    McHARGUE, JAMES
    EUGENE
    Rosey
Rotarius. See:
    KEREKES, TIBOR
Roth, Alexander. See:
    DUNNER, JOSEPH
ROTH, HOLLY (-1964)
    [American journalist and
    author]
    K. G. Ballard
    P. J. Merrill
Rothery, Agnes. See:
    PRATT, AGNES
    EDWARDS ROTHERY
Rothko, Mark. See:
    ROTHKOVICH, MARCUS
ROTHKOVICH, MARCUS
    (1903-) [Russian artist]
    Mark Rothko
Rotundity, His. See:
    ADAMS, JOHN
Rouchefoucauld-Chamfort, La.
    See: CHAMFORT,
    NICOLAS SÉBASTIAN
    ROCH
Rouge, Éminence (Red Eminence).
    See: RICHELIEU, DUC DE,
    ARMAND JEAN DU
    PLESSIS
Rouge, Le Petit Homme. See:
    VIZETELLY, ERNEST
    ALFRED
Rough. See:
    CARRIGAN, WILLIAM F.
Rough and Ready, Old. See:
    TAYLOR, ZACHARY
Rough Rider. See:
    ROOSEVELT, THEODORE
Round About, Old. See:

CLEVELAND, BENJAMIN
Round House George. See:
    LEHMAN, GEORGE
Round Man, The Little. See:
    BUTTS, JAMES
    WALLACE, JR.
Round Table, The Knight of
    Our. See:
    AEGIDIUS OF ASSISI
Round Top, The Hero of
    Little. See:
    CHAMBERLAIN, JOSHUA
    LAWRENCE
ROUND, WILLIAM MARSHALL
    FITTS (1845-1906)
    [American journalist, prison
    reformer and novelist]
Reverend Peter Pennot
Roundsman of the Lord, The.
    See: COMSTOCK,
    ANTHONY
ROUSSEAU, HENRY JULIEN
    FÉLIX (1844-1910)
    [French painter]
Le Douanier
ROUSSEAU, JEAN-JACQUES
    (1712-78) [Swiss-French
    philosopher]
Citizen of Geneva
Renou
ROUSSEL, SIMONE (1920-)
    [French motion picture
    actress]
Michele Morgan
ROVERE, FRANCESCO
    DELLA (1414-84)
    [Supreme Pontiff of Roman
    Catholic Church]
Pope Sixtus IV
ROVERE, GIULIANO DELLA
    (1443-1513) [Supreme
    Pontiff of Roman Catholic
    Church]
Pope Julius II
Row, The Dean of Cotton.
    See: DOUGHTY, JAMES P.
Row, The Founder of Rum.
    See: McCOY, CAPTAIN
    WILLIAM
ROWAN-HAMILTON, SYDNEY
    ORME (1877-) [British
    justice, critic, play-

wright and author]
Rowan Orme
Rowboat. See:
    JOHNSON, JOHN MONROE
ROWBOTHAM, BILL (1914-)
    [British dance orchestra
    musician; later motion
    picture actor]
Bill Owen
ROWE, LINWOOD THOMAS
    (1912-) [American
    professional baseball
    player]
Schoolboy Rowe
ROWE, MARGARET KEVIN
    (1920-) [Australian
    Catholic nun and author]
Sister Teresa Margaret
Rowe, Saville. See:
    SCOTT, CLEMENT
    WILLIAM
ROWE, VIVIAN CLAUDE
    (1902-) [British author]
Charles Hooton
Rowena Lee. See:
    BARTLETT, MARIE SWAN
Rowiena Raley. See:
    McCULLEY, JOHNSTON
Rowing, The Grandfather of Yale.
    See: SHEFFIELD,
    GEORGE ST. JOHN
Rowland. See:
    Roland
    THOMAS, STANLEY
    POWERS ROWLAND
ROWLAND-BROWN, LILIAN
    (1863-) [British author]
Rowland Grey
ROWLAND, CLARENCE H.
    (1879-) [American
    professional baseball
    manager]
Pants Rowland
ROWLAND, DONALD SYDNEY
    (1928-) [British author of
    action novels]
Annette Adams
Jack Bassett
Hazel Baxter
Helen Berry
Lewis Brant
Alison Bray

William Brayce
Oliver Bronson
Chuck Buchanan
Rod Caley
Wesley Craille
John Dryden
Freda Fenton
Charles Field
Burt Kroll
Helen Langley
Henry Lansing
Harvey Lant
Irene Lynn
Hank Madison
Chuck Mason
Stuart McHugh
Edna Murray
Lorna Page
Oliver Patterson
Alvin Porter
W.J. Rimmer
Matt Rockwell
Charles Roscoe
Norford Scott
Bart Segundo
Frank Shaul
Clinton Spurr
J.D. Stevens
Kay Talbot
Will Travers
Rick Walters
Neil Webb
Rowland, Iris. See:
    ROBERTS, IRENE
Rowland Thirlmere. See:
    WALKER, JOHN
Rowland Welch. See: DAVIES,
    LESLIE PURNELL
Rowland Wright. See:
    WELLS, CAROLYN
ROWLANDS, JOHN (1841-1904)
    [British explorer and
    journalist]
    Sir Henry Morton Stanley
ROWLES, JAMES GEORGE
    (1918-) [American
    composer and pianist]
    Jimmy Rowles
Rowley, Old. See:
    CHARLES II
Rowley, Thomas. See:
    CHATTERTON, THOMAS

Roxey. See:
    CROUCH, JACK
    ALBERT
Roy. See:
    ELDRIDGE, DAVID ROY
ROY, EWELL PAUL (1929-)
    [American economist and
    author]
    Victor Bonnette
    Ernest Lemoine
Roy, Lee. See:
    ANTHONY, LEO
Roy, Liam. See: SCARRY,
    PATRICIA MURPHY
Roy Newell. See:
    RAYMOND, HAROLD
    NEWELL
Roy, Ramala Pratap. See: BHO-
    SALE, YESHWANTRAO P.
Roy, Rob. (Red Robert). See:
    MACGREGOR, ROBERT
Roy Rockwood. See:
    STRATEMEYER,
    EDWARD L.
Roy Rogers. See:
    SLYE, LEONARD
Roy Wells. See:
    DOWNEY, RAYMOND
    JOSEPH
Royal. See also:
    ROYALL
Royal Highness. See:
    ALBERT
Royal Martyr, The. See:
    CHARLES I
    EDWARD (EADWARD)
Royal, Ralph. See:
    ABARBANELL, JACOB
    RALPH
Royaliste Boucher, Le. See:
    LASSERAN-HASSENCOME,
    SEIGNEUR DE
    MONTLUC
ROYALL. See also:
    Royal
ROYALL, ANNE NEWPORT
    (1769-1854) [American
    writer, traveler and
    controversialist]
    Godless Anne Royall
Royce, Ashley A. See:
    HAWTHORNE, NATHANIEL

ROYZ, OLESH (1898-)
[Polish-American
labor union official]
Alex Rose
Roz. See:
ABISCH, ROSLYN KROOP
RUSSELL, ROSALIND
ROZELLE, ALVAN RAY
(1926-) [American
sports executive]
Pete Rozelle
Rubber Arm. See:
CONNALLY, GEORGE
WALTER
Rubber King, The. See:
HARTER, DOW WATTERS
Rube. See:
FISHER, REUBEN
GOLDBERG, REUBEN
LUCIUS
MARQUARDT, RICHARD
W.
WADDELL, GEORGE
EDWARD
WALBERG, GEORGE
Rubén Darío. See:
SARMIENTO, FÉLIX
RUBÉN GARCÍA
RUBENSTEIN, EDANA (1919-)
[South African-born
motion picture actress]
Edana Romney
Rubin, Ada. See:
ROETER, ADA
RUBIN, HAROLD (1912-)
[American novelist]
Harold Robbins
RUBIN, JACOB A. (1910-)
[Austrian journalist,
editor and author]
J. Odem
RUBINOFF, DAVID (1897-)
[Russian-American
violinist and orchestra
leader]
Dave Rubinoff
RUBINSTEIN, HELENA
(1871?-1965) [Polish-
American beauty culture
executive]
Madame Helena Rubinstein
Rubio de Bostón, El. See:

TUCK, PORTER
Rubrouck (William of
Ruysbroeck). See:
RUBRUQUIS, GUILLAUME
RUBRUQUIS, GUILLAUME
(c.1220-c.1293)
[French medieval missionary
and writer]
William of Ruysbroeck
(Rubrouck)
Ruby. See:
BRAFF, REUBEN
Ruby Robert. See:
FITZSIMMONS, ROBERT
PROMETHEUS
Ruck, Berta. See:
ONIONS, MRS. GEORGE
OLIVER
RUDERMAN, SEYMOUR
GEORGE (1926-) [American
song lyricist and editor]
Rudy
Rudi. See: BLESH,
RUDOLPH PICKETT
HOLZAPFEL, RUDOLF
PATRICK
Rudy
Ruedi
Rudi, Mad. See:
HESS, RUDOLF
Rudolf. See:
FRIML, CHARLES
RUDOLF
Rudolf Otreb. See:
FLUDD, (FLUD),
ROBERT
RUDOLF (RUDOLPH) II
(1552-1612) [Emperor of
the Holy Roman Empire]
The German Trismegistus
The Prince of Alchemy
RUDOLPH. See:
RUDOLF (RUDOLPH) II
Rudolph Guglielmi. See:
D'ANTONGUOLLA,
RODOLPHO ALFONZO
RAFAELO PIERRE
FILIBERT GUGLIEL-
MO DI VALENTIN
Rudolph Valentino. See:
D'ANTONGUOLLA,
RODOLPHO ALFONZO

RAFAELO PIERRE
FILIBERT GUGLIEL-
MO DI VALENTIN
RUDOLPH, WILLIAM (18??-
-1905) [American bank
robber and criminal]
Bill
Charles Gorney
The Missouri Kid
Rudy. See:
POWELL, EVERARD
STEPHEN, SR.
RUDERMAN, SEYMOUR
GEORGE
Rudi
Ruedi
VALLEE, HUBERT
PRIOR
Rudy Vallee, The Modern
Generation's. See:
MONROE, VAUGHN
WILTON
Rudyard. See:
KIPLING, JOSEPH
RUDYARD
Ruedi. See also:
Rudi
Rudy
Ruedi, Norma Paul. See:
AINSWORTH, NORMA
RUEL. See also:
RULE
Rule
RUEL, HEROLD D. (1896-)
[American professional
baseball player]
Muddy Ruel
Ruffle, The. See:
TEGNER, HENRY
STUART
RUFFNER, WILLIAM
HENRY (1824-1908)
[American clergyman
and educator]
The Horace Mann of the
South
Rufus Hamilton. See:
GILLMORE, RUFUS
HAMILTON
Rufus Learsi. See:
GOLDBERG, ISRAEL
Rufus the Red. See:

WILLIAM II
Rufus, William. See:
WILLIAM II
Rugby, Arnold of. See:
ARNOLD, THOMAS
RUGG, WILLIAM AUGUSTUS
(1789-1828) [English
actor]
Handsome Conway
William Augustus Conway
RUGGLES, BENJAMIN
(1783-1857) [American
politician; Congressman
from Ohio]
The Wheel Horse of the
Senate
RUGGLES, JOHN (1789-1874)
[American politician;
congressman from Maine]
The Father of the Patent
Office
RUIZ, ANTONIO (1783-1860)
[Spanish bullfighter]
El Sombrerero (The Hat-
maker)
RUIZ-CAMINO, CARLOS
(1920-) [Mexican bull-
fighter]
Carlos Arruza
RULE [Rule]. See also:
RUEL
RULE, JAMES S. (1896-)
[American composer,
pianist and singer]
Jimmy Rule
Rule Jones, Golden. See:
JONES, SAMUEL MILTON
Ruler, Hard. See:
HAROLD III
Ruler of the British
(Bretwalda). See:
ETHELBERT
(AETHELBERT)
(AEDILBERCT)
Ruler, Very Mighty (Genghis
Khan) See:
TEMUJIN
RULFS, HELEN (c.1905-)
[American motion picture
actress]
Helen Vinson
Rum Row, The Founder of. See:

McCOY, CAPTAIN
WILLIAM
Rum Runners, The King of.
See: McCOY, CAPTAIN
WILLIAM
Ruman, Sig. See:
RUMANN, SIEGFRIED
RUMANIA. See:
MARIE OF RUMANIA
RUMANN, SIEGFRIED
(c. 1884-1967) [German
motion picture actor]
Sig Ruman
RUMBOLD-GIBBS, HENRY
ST. JOHN CLAIR
(fl. mid-20th cent.)
[English author, painter
and explorer]
Henry Gibbs
Simon Harvester
Rumer Godden. See:
FOSTER, MRS.
LAURENCE
Rumsey, Murray. See:
RUMSHINSKY, MURRAY
RUMSHINSKY, MURRAY
(1907-) [American
musician]
Murray Rumsey
Run Forever. See:
KOLB, REUBEN
FRANCIS
Runaway Slaves, Attorney
General for. See:
CHASE, SALMON
PORTLAND
Runners, The King of Rum.
See: McCOY, CAPTAIN
WILLIAM
Runnymede. See:
DISRAELI, BENJAMIN,
1ST EARL OF
BEACONSFIELD
RUNYON, ALFRED DAMON
(1884-1946) [American
author and journalist]
Damon Runyon
RUNYON, CHARLES W.
(1928-) [American
editor, correspondent
and author]
Mark West

RUPERT. See:
PRINCE RUPERT
Rupert Chute. See:
CLEVELAND, PHILIP
JEROME
Rupert of Debate, The. See:
LORD STANLEY
Rupert of the Confederacy, The
Prince. See:
STUART, JAMES EWELL
BROWN
RUPERT, RAPHAEL RUDOLPH
(1910-) [Hungarian law-
yer and author]
Istvan Tatray
RUPPERT, CHARLES (1914-)
[American motion picture
actor]
Charles Drake
RUPPERT, JACOB, SR.
(1867-1939) [American
brewer, soldier, politician
and baseball club owner]
The Colonel
Four Straight Jake
Jake Ruppert
Rural Credit in North Carolina,
The Father of. See:
HILL, JOHN SPRUNT
Rural Free Delivery, The
Father of. See:
BUTLER, MARION
RUSH, BENJAMIN (1745-1813)
[American physician;
signer of the Declaration of
Independence]
The Father of American
Psychiatry
Rush, Mary Jo. See:
MATTHEWS, MARY JO
RUSHING, JAMES ANDREW
(1903-) [American jazz
musician (singer)]
Mr. Five by Five
Jimmy Rushing
RUSIN, IRVING (1911-)
[American jazz musician
(tenor saxophone)]
Babe Rusin
RUSK, JEREMIAH McLAIN
(1830-93) [American
politician; Secretary of

Agriculture]
Uncle Jerry
RUSK, ROBERT ROBERTSON
(1879-) [Scottish
lecturer and author]
R.R.R.
RUSKIN, JOHN (1819-1900)
[English author, art
critic and social reformer]
A Graduate of Oxford
J.R.
Russ. See:
CASE, RUSSELL D.
COLUMBO,
RUGGIERO DE
RUDOLPHO
GARCIA, RUSSELL
HENEGAR, RUSSELL DALE
MORGAN, RUSSELL
Ros
ROSS
Ross
TAYLOR, CHARLES
R.S.
Russ Kidd. See:
DONSON, CYRIL
Russell, Albert. See:
BIXBY, JEROME LEWIS
Russell Beresford. See:
ROBERTS, CECIL EDRIC
MORINGTON
RUSSELL-BROWN, CLAUDIA
ANNA (1911-) [British
singer and musical
satirist]
Anna Russell
RUSSELL, CHARLES ELLS-
WORTH (1906-69)
[American jazz musician
(clarinet)]
Pee Wee Russell
RUSSELL, CHARLES TAZE
(1852-1916) [American
religious leader]
Pastor Russell
RUSSELL, DILLON (1920-)
[American jazz
musician (bass)]
Curly Russell
Russell, Fred. See:
PARNELL, THOMAS
FREDERICK

RUSSELL, GEORGE WILLIAM
(1867-1935) [Irish writer]
AE
Aeon
Russell, Henry. See:
OLSON, HENRY RUSSELL
Russell, J. See:
BIXBY, JEROME LEWIS
RUSSELL, JOHN (1795-1883)
[British curate and
sportsman]
Jack
The Sporting Parson
RUSSELL, JOHN (1885-)
[American explorer and
author]
Luke Thrice
RUSSELL, JOSEPH (1719-1804)
[American merchant and
shipowner]
The Duke
Russell, Lillian. See:
LEONARD, HELEN LOUISE
RUSSELL, LORD JOHN (1792-
1878) [English statesman,
author and orator]
Finality John
Russell, Lucy May. See:
CORYELL, JOHN RUSSELL
RUSSELL, MAURINE FLETCHER
(1899-) [American
educator and author]
Maurin Russell
RUSSELL, NORMA HULL
LEWIS (1902-)
[British librarian and
author]
Norma Hodgson
Russell, Raymond. See:
FEARING, LILIAN
BLANCHE
RUSSELL, ROSALIND (1912-)
[American actress]
Roz Russell
Russell, Shane. See:
NORWOOD, VICTOR
GEORGE CHARLES
RUSSELL, SIDNEY KEITH
(1914-) [American com-
poser]
Bob Russell
RUSSELL, WILLIAM CLARK

(1844-1911) [English
writer of sea stories]
Mrs. Letitia Booth
The Prose Homer of the
Great Ocean
W. Clark Russell
A Seafarer
RUSSELL, WILLIAM EUSTIS
(1857-96) [American poli-
tician; Mayor of Cam-
bridge, Mass. at the
age of 28]
The Boy Mayor
Billie the Kid
RUSSELL, WILLIAM HENRY
(1802-73) [American
politician and California
pioneer]
Owl Russell
Russell Williams. See:
WHITSON, JOHN HARVEY
RUSSELL, WINIFRED BRENT
(fl. 1926-36)
[American poet and short
story writer]
Virginia Stait
Russia, The Himmler of. See:
BERIA, LAVRENTI
PAVLOVICH
Russia, The Prewar Rocking
Chair Sensation of. See:
MEYER, DR. ALEXANDER
Russian Byron, The. See:
PUSHKIN, ALEXANDER
Russian History, The Father of.
See: NESTOR
Russian Lion, The. See:
HACKENSCHMIDT, GEORGE
Russian Livy, The. See:
KARAMZIN, NICHOLAS
MIKHAELOVITCH
Russian Murat, The. See:
MILORADOVITCH, COUNT
MIKHAEL ANDRIEVITCH
Russian Philosopher, The
First. See:
SOLOVIEV, VLADIMIR
Russian Revolution, The
Father of the. See:
ULYANOV, VLADIMIR
ILYICH
Russian Revolution, The Little

Grandmother of the. See:
BRESHKOVSKY, CATHERINE
Russian Voltaire, The. See:
SOUMAROKOV, ALEXANDRE
PETROVITCH
Russians, The Little Mother of
All the. See:
ANHALT-ZERBST, SOPHIA
AUGUSTA FREDERICA
OF
RUSSO, GIUSEPPE LUIGI
(1884-) [Italian educator
and author]
Joseph Louis Russo
Rustic Bard, The. See:
DINSMOOR, ROBERT
Rusticus. See:
JENKINS, MacGREGOR
MAURICE, JOHN FREDER-
ICK DENISON
Rusty. See:
GILL, RALPH
Ruth. See:
BARROWS, MARJORIE
Ruth A. Hill. See:
VIGUERS, RUTH HILL
Ruth Ainsworth. See:
GILBERT, RUTH GALIARD
AINSWORTH
Ruth Carson. See:
BUGBEE, RUTH CARSON
Ruth Dixon. See:
BARROWS, MARJORIE
RUTH, GEORGE HERMAN (1894-
1948) [American professional
baseball player]
Babe Ruth
The Bambino
The Idol of the American Boy
The Mighty Bambino
The Sultan of Swat
Ruth Gordon. See:
JONES, RUTH
Ruth Martin. See:
RAYNER, CLAIRE
Ruth, Miss. See:
DENNIS, RUTH
Ruth Morris. See:
WEBB, RUTH ENID
BORLASE MORRIS
Ruth of the New Deal, The Babe.
See: JOHNSON, HUGH

SAMUEL
Ruth Ogden. See:
  IDE, FRANCES OTIS
  OGDEN
Ruth St. Denis. See:
  DENNIS, RUTH
Ruth Uhl. See:
  FRANK, RUTH VERD
RUTHER, WYATT (1923-)
  [American jazz musician
  (bass)]
  Bull Ruther
Rutherford, Douglas. See:
  McCONNELL, JAMES
  DOUGLAS RUTHERFORD
RUTHERFORD, JOSEPH
  FRANKLIN (1869-1942)
  [American lawyer and
  churchman; president of
  Jehovah's Witnesses]
  Judge Rutherford
Rutherford, Mark. See:
  WHITE, WILLIAM HALE
Rutland, Arthur. See:
  ADCOCK, ARTHUR ST.
  JOHN
RUTLEDGE, EDWARD WILLIAM
  (1906-) [British
  Roman Catholic priest
  and author]
  Dom Denys Rutledge
Rutledge, Marice. See:
  HALE, MARIE LOUISE
  GIBSON
Rutledge, Maryse. See:
  HALE, MARIE LOUISE
  GIBSON
RUTT, RICHARD (1925-)
  [British Church of
  England priest and writer]
  Ro Tae-yong
RUTTER, SALLY (c.1918-)
  [American motion picture
  actress]
  Gale Page
Ruy Traube. See:
  TRALINS, S. ROBERT
Ruysbroeck, William of
  (Rubrouck). See:
  RUBRUQUIS, GUILLAUME
Ruzé. See:
  COIFFIER, ANTOINE

Ruzzante. See:
  BEOLCO, ANGELO
RYALL, WILLIAM BOLITHO
  (1891-1930) [British
  journalist and miscel-
  laneous writer]
  William Bolitho
RYAN [Ryan]. See also:
  RYUN
RYAN, ABRAM JOSEPH
  (1840-86) [American poet
  and Roman Catholic
  churchman]
  Father Ryan
  The Poet of the Confederacy
RYAN, EDWARD JOSEPH (18??-
  -1920) [Victim of CARL
  WANDERER, American
  murderer]
  The Ragged Stranger
RYAN, EDWARD JOSEPH. See
  also: WANDERER, CARL
Ryan, Irene. See:
  RIORDAN, IRENE
Rybot, Doris. See:
  PONSONBY, DORIS ALMON
Rydal Mount, The Bard of. See:
  WORDSWORTH, WILLIAM
Rydell, Forbes, joint pseud. of
  DELORES STANTON
  FORBES (1923-) and
  HELEN B. RYDELL (-)
  [American authors]
Rydell, Forbes. See also:
  FORBES, DELORIS
  STANTON
Ryerson, Lowell. See:
  VAN ATTA, WINFRED
  LOWELL
RYLE, JOHN (1817-18??)
  [Anglo-American silk
  manufacturer]
  The Father of the Silk
  Industry
RYMER, JAMES MALCOLM
  (1814?-84) [English author
  of dime novels]
  Bertha T. Bishop
  J.D. Conroy
  Malcolm J. Errym
  Captain Merry, U.S.N.
  Malcolm J. Merry

Nelson Percival
Septimus R. Urban
RYOTT, SEPTIMUS WILLIAM
(1886-1965) [British
stage matinée idol and
motion picture actor]
Stewart Rome
RYUN. See also:
RYAN
Ryan
RYUN, JAMES RONALD
(1947-) [American
middle distance
runner]
Jim Ryun
RYWELL, MARTIN (1905-)
[American editor and
author]
Taylor Hemingway
Deane Sears
RZEWUSKI, COUNT HENRYK
(1791-1866) [Polish
novelist]
J. Bejla

S

S. Anna Lewis. See:
LEWIS, ESTELLE ANNA
BLANCHE ROBINSON
S. B. Phelps, Mrs. See:
GRISWOLD, FRANCES
IRENE BURGE
S. D. See:
BURNFORD, SHEILA
PHILIP COCHRANE A
AVERY
S. F. Welty. See:
WELTY, SUSAN F.
S. H. Peters. See:
PORTER, WILLIAM
SYDNEY
S. Howell. See:
STYLES, FRANK
SHOWELL
S. J. H. See:
HALE, SARAH JOSEPHA
S. M. Frazier. See:
MORRIS, CHARLES
SMITH
S. M. Jennings. See:

MEYER, JEROME SYDNEY
S. M. Tenneshaw. See:
BEAUMONT, CHARLES
S. P. Stevens. See:
PALESTRANT, SIMON S.
S. Prior. See:
GALT, JOHN
S. S. Scott, Major. See:
HARBAUGH, THOMAS
CHALMERS
S. S. Smith. See:
WILLIAMSON, THAMES
ROSS
S. S. Van Dine. See:
WRIGHT, WILLARD
HUNTINGTON
S. T. P., Mr. See:
GRANATELLI, ANDREW
S. T. Peters. See:
BRANNON, WILLIAM T.
S. Weir Mitchell. See:
MITCHELL, DR. SILAS
WEIR
S. Z. Sakall. See:
SZAKALL, EUGENE GERO
Sa-go-ye-wat-he. See:
RED JACKET
Saadi. See:
MUSLIH-UD-DIN
Sabalkanski (Crosser of the
Balkans). See:
DIEBITSCH, HANS KARL
FRIEDRICH, COUNT
SABATH, ADOLPH JOACHIM
(1866-1952) [Bohemian-
American politician;
congressman from Illinois]
The Dean of the House
Sabiad. See:
WHITE, STANHOPE
SABINI, JOHN ANTHONY
(1921-) [American career
diplomat and author]
John Anthony
SABINIAN (died 606) [Supreme
Pontiff of Roman Catholic
Church]
Pope Sabinian
Sabio, El (The Learned). See:
FERDINAND VI
Sabio, El (The Wise). See:
ALFONSO X

Sabra Holbrook. See:
 ERICKSON, SABRA
 ROLLINS
Sabreur, Beau (Handsome
 Swordsman). See:
 MURAT, JOACHIM
Sabu. See:
 DASTAGIR, SABU
SACAJAWEA (SACAGAWEA)
 (c. 1786-c. 1812) [Shoshone
 Indian woman; guide on
 Lewis and Clark expedi-
 tion]
 The Bird Woman
SACCHINI, MARIE-GASPARD
 (1734-86) [Italian com-
 poser]
 The Racine of Music
Sacha. See:
 CARNEGIE, RAYMOND
 ALEXANDER
Sachem. See:
 HILLHOUSE, WILLIAM
Sachem of Tammany Hall, The.
 See: KELLY, JOHN
 TWEED, WILLIAM MARCY
Sacheverell Smith. See:
 DARLING, WILLIAM
 YOUNG
SACHEVERELL, WILLIAM
 (1638-91) [English
 politician]
 The First Whig
SACHS, ALBERT LOUIS
 (1935-) [South African
 attorney and author]
 Albie Sachs
SACHS, HANS (1494-1576)
 [German poet, minnesinger
 and shoemaker]
 The Laureate of the Gentle
 Craft
SACHS, NELLY (1891-)
 [German poet and
 dramatist]
 Leonie
Saco. See:
 MESERVE, COLONEL
 ARTHUR LIVERMORE
Sacred Palace, Master of the.
 See: DOMINIC, ST.
Sacrobosco, Johannes de.

See: HOLYWOOD, JOHN
Sad Sam. See:
 JONES, SAMUEL POUND
Saddle Star, The World's Top
 Boots-and-. See:
 SLYE, LEONARD
Saddle, The Wizard of the. See:
 FORREST, NATHAN
 BEDFORD
Saddlebags, Old. See:
 McDONALD, JOSEPH
 EWING
Saddler, K. Allen. See:
 RICHARDS, RONALD
 CHARLES WILLIAM
SADE, COMTE DONATIEN
 ALPHONSE FRANÇOIS DE
 (1740-1814) [French
 soldier and author,
 notorious for his sexual
 perversion]
 Marquis de Sade
Sadi. See:
 MUSLIH-UD-DIN
Sadik Hakim. See:
 THORNTON, ARGONNE
 DENSE
Safeguard, Union. See:
 GRANT, HIRAM ULYSSES
Safety, Old Pap. See:
 THOMAS, GEORGE HENRY
Sagan, Françoise. See:
 QUOIREZ, FRANÇOISE
Sage, Anna. See:
 CUMPANAS, ANA
Sage de la Grande Armée, Le.
 See:
 DROUOT, ANTOINE, COMTE
Sage, Juniper, joint pseud. of
 EDITH THATCHER HURD
 (1910-) and MARGARET
 WISE BROWN (-)
 [American authors]
Sage of America, The. See:
 FRANKLIN, BENJAMIN
Sage of Anacostia, The. See:
 BAILEY, FREDERICK
 AUGUST WASHINGTON
Sage of Ashland, The. See:
 CLAY, HENRY
 LEE, HENRY
Sage of Auburn, The. See:

SEWARD, WILLIAM
HENRY
Sage of Chappaqua, The. See:
GREELEY, HORACE
Sage of Chelsea, The. See:
CARLYLE, THOMAS
Sage of Concord, The. See:
ALCOTT, AMOS BRONSON
EMERSON, RALPH WALDO
Sage of Emporia, The. See:
WHITE, WILLIAM ALLEN
Sage of Gramercy Park, The.
See: TILDEN, SAMUEL
JONES
Sage of Greystone, The. See:
TILDEN, SAMUEL JONES
Sage of Happy Valley, The.
See: TAYLOR, ALFRED
ALEXANDER
Sage of Hickory Hill, The.
See: WATSON, THOMAS
EDWARD
Sage of Kinderhook, The.
See: VAN BUREN,
MARTIN
Sage of Lindenwald, The.
See: VAN BUREN,
MARTIN
Sage of Log Hall, The. See:
PHILIPS, MARDIN
WILSON
Sage of McDuffie, The. See:
WATSON, THOMAS
EDWARD
Sage of Mississippi College,
The. See:
AVEN, ALGERNON
JASPER
Sage of Monticello, The. See:
JEFFERSON, THOMAS
Sage of Montpelier, The.
See: MADISON, JAMES
Sage of Mount Vernon, The.
See: WASHINGTON,
GEORGE
Sage of Nininger, The. See:
DONNELLY, IGNATIUS
Sage of Pittsfield, The. See:
DAWES, HENRY
LAURENS
Sage of Potato Hill, The. See:
HOWE, EDGAR

WATSON
Sage of Princeton, The. See:
CLEVELAND, STEPHEN
GROVER
ROOSEVELT, THEODORE
Sage of Samos, The. See:
PYTHAGORAS
Sage of Sinnissippi, The. See:
LOWDEN, FRANK ORREN
Sage of Springfield, The. See:
LINCOLN, ABRAHAM
Sage of the Hermitage, The.
See: JACKSON, ANDREW
Sage of the Verduga Hills, The.
See: McGROARTY, JOHN
STEVEN
Sage of Tishomingo, The. See:
MURRAY, WILLIAM
HENRY
Sage of Uvalde, The. See:
GARNER, JOHN NANCE
Sage of Walden Pond, The.
See: THOREAU, HENRY
DAVID
Sage of Walpole, The. See:
BIRD, FRANCIS
WILLIAM
Sage of Wheatland, The. See:
BUCHANAN, JAMES
Sage, The Aquinian. See:
JUVENAL
Sage, The Ascraean. See:
HESIOD
Sage, The Bactrian. See:
ZOROASTER
Sage, The Cheronean. See:
PLUTARCH
Sage, The Ligurian. See:
AULUS PERSIUS FLACCUS
Sage, The Samian. See:
PYTHAGORAS
Sage, The Silver. See:
THOMAS, JOHN WILLIAM
ELMER
Sage, The Sockless. See:
SIMPSON, JERRY
Sages of Greece. See:
Seven Sages of Greece, The
Sagest of the Usurpers, The.
See: CROMWELL, OLIVER
Sagittarius. See:
SCHÜTZ, HEINRICH

Sah-nee-weh. See:
    HENDRICKS, NAMÉE
Sahib, Nana. See:
    PANTH, BRAHMIN
      DUNDHU
Sahib Shihab. See:
    GREGORY, EDMUND
SAHL, MORTON LYON
    (1927-) [Canadian
    comedian]
  Mort Sahl
Saidie. See:
    WILLIAMS, SARAH
Sailor. See:
    KELLY, ALVIN
    SAYLER
Sailor Kid, The. See:
    LONDON, JOHN GRIFFITH
Sailor King, The. See:
    WILLIAM IV
Sailor Prince, The. See:
    GEORGE V
Sailor William. See:
    WILLIAM IV
Sailor's Friend, The. See:
    PLIMSOLL, SAMUEL
    WESTON, AGNES
SAINSBURY, NOEL
    EVERINGHAM (1884-)
    [American author]
  Harvey D. Richards
  Dorothy Wayne
SAINT. Those not indexed
    below may be found listed
    under their respective
    surnames.
SAINT. See:
    ADELBERT
    ADEODATUS
    ADRIAN
    AGAPETUS
    AGATHO
    ALBAN, ST.
    ALBERTUS MAGNUS,
      SAINT, COUNT OF
      BOLLSTÄDT
    ALEXANDER
    ANACLETUS (ANENCLETUS)
      (CLETUS)
    ANASTASIUS
    ANASTASIUS, ST.
    ANGILBERT, ST.

ANICETUS
ANTERUS
ANTONY (ANTHONY), ST.
AQUINAS, ST. THOMAS
ARMAND, ST.
ATHANASIUS, ST.
AUGUSTINE (AUSTIN), ST.
BASIL, ST.
BECKET, THOMAS À
BEDE (BEDA) (BAEDA),
  ST.
BENEDICT
BENEDICT OF NURSIA, ST.
BERNARD OF CLAIRVAUX
BERNARD OF MENTHON,
  ST.
BONIFACE
BRIDGET, ST.
BRUNO (BRUN), ST.
BRUNO, ST.
CAEDMON (CEDMON), ST.
CAIUS
CALLISTUS
CELESTINE
CHRISTOPHER, ST.
CHRYSOSTOM, ST. JOHN
CLEMENT
CLOTILDA
COLUMBA, ST.
COLUMBAN (COLUMBANUS),
  ST.
CORNELIUS
CYRIL OF ALEXANDRIA,
  ST.
DAMASUS
DENIS (DENYS), ST.
DEUSDEDIT
DIONYSIUS
DIONYSIUS OF
  ALEXANDRIA, ST.
DOMINIC, ST.
EDMUND (EADMUND), ST.
ELEUTHERUS
EPIPHANIUS, ST.
EUGENE
EUSEBIUS
EUTYCHIAN
EVARISTUS
FABIAN
FELIX
GELASIUS
GEORGE, ST.

GERTRUDE OF HELFTA,
ST.
GREGORY
GREGORY OF ARMENIA,
ST.
GREGORY OF NAZIANZUS,
ST.
HENRY II
HILARY
HORMISDAS
HUBERT, ST.
HYGINUS
IGNATIUS OF
ANTIOCH, ST.
INNOCENT
IRENAEUS, ST.
JAMES THE GREATER,
ST.
JOAN OF ARC, ST.
(JEANNE D'ARC)
JOHN
JOHN THE EVANGELIST,
ST.
JULIUS
JUSTIN, ST.
LEO
LINUS
LOUIS IX
LOYOLA, IGNATIUS OF,
ST. (IÑIGO DE OÑEZ
Y LOYOLA)
LUCIUS
LUKE, ST.
MARCELLINUS
MARCELLUS
MARCUS
MARTIN
MARY, ST.
MAXIMUS, ST.
METHODIUS
MILTIADES (MELCHIADES)
NICOLAUS, ST.
NINIAN, ST.
PASCHAL
PATRICK, ST.
PETER
PONTIAN (PONTIANUS)
SERGIUS
SILVERIUS
SIMPLICIUS
SIRICIUS
SIXTUS

SOTER (SOTERUS)
STEPHEN
STEPHEN I
SYLVESTER
SYMACCHUS
TELESPHORUS
URBAN
VICTOR
VINCENT DE PAUL
VITALIAN
VLADIMIR I
WENCESLAUS
ZACHARY
ZEPHRYNUS
ZOSIMUS
St. Albert the Great. See:
ALBERTUS MAGNUS,
SAINT, COUNT OF
BOLLSTÄDT
St. Aloysius. See:
GONZAGA, LUIGI
St. Alphonsus. See:
LIGOURI, ALPHONSUS
St. Anthony, The First Citizen
of. See:
STEELE, FRANKLIN
St. Antony of Egypt. See:
ANTONY (ANTHONY), ST.
St. Augustine. See:
AUGUSTINUS, AURELIUS
St. Basil. See:
BASIL, ST.
SPENCE, SIR BASIL
UNWIN
St. Bernadette. See:
SOUBIROUS, MARIE
BERNARDE
St. Bonaventura. See:
FIDANZA, GIOVANNI DI
St. Boniface. See:
WINFRID (WYNFRITH)
St. Briavels, James. See:
WOOD, JAMES PLAYSTED
ST. BRUNO, ALBERT
FRANCIS (1909-)
[Australian journalist,
soldier and author]
Frank Bruno
ST. CLAIR, BYRD HOOPER
(1905-) [American
librarian and author]
Byrd Hooper

St. Clair, Philip. See:
HOWARD, MUNROE
St. Clair, Victor. See:
BROWNE, GEORGE
WALDO
St. Cyr, Cyprian. See:
BERNE, ERIC
LENNARD
St. Cyril. See:
Apostles to the Slavs
CONSTANTINE
St. Dare, Julian. See:
PATTEN, WILLIAM
GILBERT
St. Denis le Cadet See:
ALLEN, PAUL
SAINT-DENIS, MICHEL
JACQUES (1897-) [French
theatrical producer,
actor and author]
Jacques Duchesne
St. Denis, Ruth. See:
DENNIS, RUTH
SAINT, DORA JESSIE
(1913-) [English author]
Miss Read
St. Francis of Assisi. See:
BERNARDONE,
GIOVANNI FRANCESCO
St. Francis of Presbyterianism,
The. See:
MAKEMIE, FRANCIS
St. George, Harry. See:
RATHBONE, ST. GEORGE
HENRY
St. George, The Chevalier de.
See: STUART, JAMES
FRANCIS EDWARD
Saint-Germain, La Sibylle
du Faubourg. See:
LENORMAND, MARIE
ANNE ADÉLAÏDE
St. Gregory, See:
GREGORY
HILDEBRAND
ST. GREGORY OF ARMENIA.
See: GREGORY OF
ARMENIA, ST.
St. Gregory of Tours. See:
FLORENTIUS, GEORGIUS
St. Guillaume de Gellone.
See: GUILLAUME

D'ORANGE
ST. JACQUES, BERTRAND
HARDOUIN (1600-48)
[French actor]
Guillot-Gorju
St. James. See:
STRANG, JAMES JESSE
St. Jerome. See:
EDMUNDS, GEORGE
FRANKLIN
ST. JOHN. See:
CHRYSOSTOM, ST. JOHN
ST. JOHN, AL (1893-1963)
[American motion picture
actor]
Fuzzy St. John
St. John, Beth. See:
JOHN, ELIZABETH
BEAMAN
St. John, Betta. See:
STREIDLER, BETTY
St. John de Crèvecoeur. See:
CRÈVECOEUR, MICHEL-
GUILLAUME JEAN
DE
St. John, Dick. See:
GOSTING, RICHARD
ST. JOHN, HENRY (1678-1751)
[English statesman and
political writer]
The Patriot King
Viscount Bolingbroke
St. John, J. Hector. See:
CRÈVECOEUR, MICHEL-
GUILLAUME JEAN DE
St. John, Jill. See:
OPPENHEIM, JILL
St. John, John. See:
SALE, RICHARD
St. John of the Cross. See:
ÁLVAREZ, JUAN DE
YAPES Y
ST. JOHN, PERCY BOLLING-
BROKE (1821-89)
[English author of dime
novels]
Henry L. Boone
J. T. Brougham
Harry Cavendish
J. L. Freeman
Lady Esther Hope
Captain McKeen

Warren St. John
Saint-John Perse. See:
    LEGER, MARIE-RENÉ
    ALEXIS SAINT-LEGER
St. John Terrell. See:
    ECCLES, GEORGE
    CLINTON, JR.
St. John the Divine. See:
    JOHN THE EVANGELIST,
    ST.
ST. JOHN, WILLIAM POPE
    (1848-97) [American
    banker; advocate of free
    coinage of gold and
    silver]
    The Apostle of Free Coinage
    for Silver
ST. JOHN, WYLLY FOLK
    (1908-) [American
    journalist and author]
    Eleanor Fox
    Eve Larson
    Katherine Pierce
    Mary Keith Vincent
    Michael Williams
St. Kayne, Humphrey. See:
    CRAWFURD, OSWALD
St. Laurence, A. See:
    FELKIN, ALFRED
    LAURENCE
St. Leger, Evelyn. See:
    RANDOLPH, EVELYN
    ST. LEGER
St. Leo. See:
    BRUNO, COUNT OF
    EGISHEIM-DAGSBURG
    LEO
ST. MARTIN, LOUIS-CLAUDE
    DE (1743-1805) [French
    mystical philosopher]
    The Unknown Philosopher
St. Melchiades. See:
    MILTIADES (MELCHIADES)
St. Methodius. See:
    Apostles to the Slavs
St. Mox, E. S. --A U. S.
    Detective. See:
    ELLIS, EDWARD
    SYLVESTER
St. Mungo. See:
    KENTIGERN
St. Myer, Ned. See:

STRATEMEYER,
    EDWARD L.
St. Nicholas. See:
    NICHOLAS
    NICOLAUS, ST.
Saint of American Orchards,
    The Patron. See:
    CHAPMAN, JOHN
St. Patrick's, The Dean of.
    See: SWIFT, JONATHAN
St. Paul. See:
    SAUL
St. Pius. See:
    GHISLIERI, MICHELE
    PIUS
    SARTO, GIUSEPPE
    MELCHIORRE
ST. POURÇAIN, GUILLAUME
    DURAND DE (died c. 1333)
    [French bishop]
    The Most Resolute Doctor
St. Simeon. See:
    STYLITES, SIMEON
St. Soterus. See:
    SOTER (SOTERUS)
St. Stephen, The British. See:
    ALBAN, ST.
St. Teresa. See:
    TERESA OF AVILA
Saint, The. See:
    HENRY II
Saint, The (El Santo). See:
    FERDINAND III
Saint, The Seraphic. See:
    BERNARDONE, GIOVANNI
    FRANCESCO
St. Thomas à Becket. See:
    BECKET, THOMAS À
ST. THOMAS AQUINAS. See:
    AQUINAS, ST. THOMAS
St. Thomas of London. See:
    BECKET, THOMAS À
St. Victor, Richard of. See:
    RICHARD
St. Vincent de Paul. See:
    VINCENT DE PAUL
St. Vivant, M. See:
    BIXBY, JEROME LEWIS
St. Vrain, Major E. L. See:
    MANNING, WILLIAM
    HENRY
Sainte-Beuve of English Criticism,

The. See:
ARNOLD, MATTHEW
SAINT-MARIE, BEVERLY
(1942?-) [Canadian
Indian singer and com-
poser]
Buffy
Saintleger. See:
LEGER, MARIE-RENÉ
ALEXIS SAINT-LEGER
Saints, The Father of the
Pillar. See:
STYLITES, SIMEON
Sakall, S.Z. See:
SZAKALL, EUGENE
GERO
Saki. See:
MUNRO, HECTOR HUGH
Saks, Elmer Eliot. See:
FAWCETT, FRANK
DUBREZ
Sakya Muni. See:
GAUTAMA, SIDDHARTHA
Sal. See:
MAGLIE, SALVATORE
ANTHONY
Salaam, Liaqat Ali. See:
CLARKE, KENNETH
SPEARMAN
Salamatullah. See:
ULLAH, SALAMAT
SALE, CHARLES PARTLOW
(1885-1935) [American
actor, humorist and
author]
Chic Sale
SALE, RICHARD (1911-)
[American author]
John St. John
SALEEBY, CALEB WILLIAMS
(1878-) [British
physician and author]
Crusader
Lens
Salem, The Rebel of. See:
WILLIAMS, ROGER
Sales, Soupy. See:
HINES, MILTON
Salian, The. See:
CONRAD II
SALINGER, JEROME DAVID
(1919-) [American

author]
J.D. Salinger
SALISBURY. See:
JOHN OF SALISBURY
SALSBURY
Sallie Bingham. See:
ELLSWORTH, SALLIE
BINGHAM
Sally, Axis. See:
SISK, MILDRED ELIZABETH
ZUCCA, RITA LOUISE
Sally Forrest. See:
FEENEY, KATHARINE
SCULLY
Sally Gray. See:
STEVENS, CONSTANCE
Sally Jackson. See:
KELLOGG, JEAN
Sally Pratt McLean. See:
GREENE, SARAH PRATT
McLEAN
Salomé, María. See:
RODRÍGUEZ, AUGUSTÍN
SALOMONS, JEAN-PIERRE
(1909-) [French actor]
Jean-Pierre Aumont
SALSBURY. See also:
SALISBURY
SALSBURY, NATE (1888-)
[American humorist and
author]
Baron Ireland
Salten, Felix. See:
SALZMANN, FELIX
Salter, Mary D. See:
AINSWORTH, MARY
DINSMORE SALTER
Salty. See:
PARKER, FRANCIS JAMES
SALTYKOV, MIKHAIL
EVGRAFOVICH (1826-89)
[Russian writer]
N. Shchedrin
SALVATIERRA, JUAN MARÍA
DE (1648-1717) [Italian
Jesuit priest; founder of
missions along California
coast]
The Apostle of California
Salvator Rosa of British
novelists, The. See:
RADCLIFFE, ANN WARD

Salvator Rosa, The English.
See: MORTIMER,
JOHN HAMILTON
SALZMANN, FELIX (1881-1945)
[Hungarian-Viennese
novelist and playwright]
Felix Salten
Sam. See:
ALLEN, MARION C.
BYRD, SAMUEL
ARMANIE
GRANT, HIRAM ULYSSES
HOUSTON, SAMUEL
JONES, SAMUEL PORTER
LEVENSON, SAMUEL
RAYBURN, SAMUEL
TALIAFERRO
WOLCHOK, SAMUEL
WOOD, SAMUEL
GROSVENOR
YORTY, SAMUEL
WILLIAM
Sam Allison. See:
LOOMIS, NOEL MILLER
Sam Bowie. See:
BALLARD, WILLIS
TODHUNTER
Sam Browne. See:
SMITH, RONALD
GREGOR
Sam, Buckskin. See:
HALL, MAJOR SAMUEL
STONE
Sam Collins. See:
VAGG, SAMUEL
Sam Curzon. See:
KRASNEY, SAMUEL A.
Sam Jackson. See:
TRUMBO, DALTON
Sam Martin. See:
MOSKOWITZ, SAM
Sam, Sad. See:
JONES, SAMUEL
POUND
Sam Slick. See:
HALLIBURTON, THOMAS
CHANDLER
Sam Slick, Jr. See:
HAMMETT, SAMUEL
ADAMS
Sam, Slippery. See:
TILDEN, SAMUEL JONES

Sam, Soapy. See:
WILBERFORCE, SAMUEL
Sam Spit. See:
SCHNECK, STEPHEN
Sam the Maltster. See:
ADAMS, SAMUEL
Sam, Tricky. See:
NANTON, JOSEPH
Sam, Uncle. See:
GRANT, HIRAM ULYSSES
WILSON, SAMUEL
Sam, Wahoo. See:
CRAWFORD, SAMUEL EARL
SAMACHSON, JOSEPH (1906-)
[American chemist,
educator and author]
John Miller
William Morrison
SAMANIEGOES, RAMÓN
(1899-1968) [Mexican
motion picture actor]
Ramón Novarro
Same Old Coon, The. See:
CLAY, HENRY
Same Old Mose, The. See:
WEINBERGER, MOSES
Same Young Mose, The. See:
WEINBERGER, MOSES
Samian Sage, The. See:
PYTHAGORAS
Sammy. See:
BENSKIN, SAMUEL
LERNER, SAMUEL M.
OSTROW, SAMUEL
SNEAD, SAMUEL JACKSON
Sammy Casque. See:
DAVIS, SYDNEY
CHARLES HOUGHTON
Sammy, Slinging. See:
BAUGH, SAMUEL ADRIAN
Sammy Snead, Slamming. See:
SNEAD, SAMUEL JACKSON
Sammy the Rose. See:
ROSENMAN, SAMUEL
IRVING
Samos, The Sage of. See:
PYTHAGORAS
SAMOSATA. See:
LUCIAN OF SAMOSATA
Sampleton, Samuel. See:
MONTI, LUIGI
SAMPSON, EMMA SPEED

(1868-) [American
author]
Nell Speed
SAMPSON, RICHARD HENRY
(1896-) [English
mystery story writer]
Richard Hull
SAMSON, GEORGE ALEXANDER
GIBB (1858-1918) [English
actor and theater manager]
Sir George Alexander
Samson, The British. See:
TOPHAM, THOMAS
Samuel Adams of New Jersey,
The. See:
FISHER, HENDRICK
Samuel Adams of North
Carolina, The. See:
HARNETT, CORNELIUS
Samuel Cutler. See:
FOLSOM, FRANKLIN
BREWSTER
Samuel Falkland. See:
HEIJERMANS
(HEYERMANS), HERMAN
Samuel Goldwyn. See:
GOLDFISH, SAMUEL
Samuel Jeake, Jr. See:
AIKEN, CONRAD POTTER
Samuel Marchbanks. See:
DAVIES, ROBERTSON
Samuel Sampleton. See:
MONTI, LUIGI
Samuel the Publican. See:
ADAMS, SAMUEL
SAMUEL, YESHUE (1907-)
[Syrian churchman
and author]
Athanasius Y. Samuel
San Juan Hill, The Hero of.
See: ROOSEVELT,
THEODORE
San Simeon, The Lord of.
See: HEARST,
WILLIAM RANDOLPH
Sanborn, B.X. See:
BALLINGER, WILLIAM
SANBORN
SÁNCHEZ, ANTONIO (1831-95)
[Spanish bullfighter]
El Tato (Baby Brother)
SÁNCHEZ, MANUEL RODRÍGUEZ

Y (1917-47) [Spanish bull-
fighter]
Manolete
SÁNCHEZ, SALVADOR (1844-98)
[Spanish bullfighter]
Frascuelo
SANCHO II (died 1072) [King of
Castile]
The Strong
SANCHO III (fl. early 11th cent.)
[King of Navarre]
The Great
Sanction. See:
JOHNSTON, SIR REGINALD
FLEMING
Sand, George. See:
DUDEVANT, AMANDINE
AURORE LUCIE DUPIN,
"BARONNE"
Sand, Jules. See:
DUDEVANT, AMANDINE
AURORE LUCIE DUPIN
"BARONNE"
SANDEAU, JULES
Sand Lot Agitator, The. See:
KEARNEY, DENIS
SANDBURG, CARL AUGUST
(1878-1967) [American
author]
Militant
Jack Phillips
Charles A. Sandburg
SANDEAU, JULES (1811-83)
[French author]
Jules Sand
Sandel, Cora. See:
FABRICIUS, SARA
SANDERS [Sanders]. See also:
SAUNDERS
Saunders
SANDERS, DANIEL JACKSON
(fl. 1891-1907) [American
Negro Presbyterian clergy-
man, editor and educator]
Zeus
SANDERS, ED (1939-)
[American editor,
publisher, singer and
author]
Black Hobart
SANDERS, FARRELL (1940-)
[American jazz musician

900

(tenor saxophone)]
Pharaoh
SANDERS, JOSEPH L.
(1896-1965) [American
jazz musician (piano,
composer, singer,
leader)]
The Old Lefthander
Joe Sanders
Sanders, Kent. See:
WILKES-HUNTER,
RICHARD
SANDERS, THOMAS (1904-)
[British motion picture
Actor]
Tom Conway
Sanders, Winston P. See:
ANDERSON, POUL
WILLIAM
Sandor, Jean. See:
SIMENON, GEORGES
SANDOZ, MARI SUSETTE
(1901-66) [American
educator and author]
Mari Macumber
Sandra Dallas. See:
ATCHISON, SANDRA
DALLAS
Sandra Dee. See:
DOUVAIN, SANDRA
SANDRO, BENOZZO DI LESE
DI (1420-98) [Florentine
painter]
Benozzo Gozzoli
Sandro Botticelli. See:
FILIPEPI, ALESSANDRO
DI MARIANO DEI
Sandrocottus. See:
CHANDRA GUPTA
(CHANDRA GUPTA
MAURYA)
SANDS, LEO GEORGE
(1912-) [American
business executive and
author]
Lee Craig
Jack Helmi
SANDS, THOMAS ADRIAN
(1937-) [American
composer, singer and
actor]
Tommy Sands

Sandy. See:
DENNIS, SANDRA DALE
FELDSTEIN, SAUL
GRISWOLD, A. MINER
HERRING, ARTHUR L.
KOUFAX, SANFORD
VANCE, JOSEPH ALBERT
Sandy Nelson. See:
EGNATZIK, JOSEPH
Sandys, George Windle.
See: CRAWFURD, OSWALD
Sandys, Oliver. See:
EVANS, MARGUERITE
FLORENCE HELENE
SANGER, EDWARD (1882-1956)
[British stage and motion
picture actor]
Holmes Herbert
SANGER, GEORGE. See:
Lord
SANGER, JOHN. See:
Lord
SANICOLA, HENRY W. (1915-)
[American composer]
Hank Sanicola
Sanitary, Old. See:
YEATMAN, JAMES
SANNAZARO, JACOPO
(1458-1530) [Italian poet
and humanist]
Actius Syncerus
The Christian Virgil
Sans Esprit, Monsieur. See:
FIELDING, HENRY
Sans Souci, The Philosopher of.
See: FREDERICK II
Sanscrit, The Greatest Poet
Who Wrote in. See:
BHARTRIHARI
(BHARTRHARI)
SANSON, CHARLES HENRI (fl.
late 18th cent.) [French
executioner officiated
at death of LOUIS XVI]
Monsieur de Paris
Sansovino. See:
CONTUCCI, ANDREA
TATTI, JACOPO
Sansterre. See:
JOHN I
Santa Clara, Abraham-a. See:
MEGERLE, HANS ULRICH

Santa Claus. See:
    COLEMAN, LEIGHTON
    NICOLAUS, ST.
Santa Claus of the Manchester
    Poor. See:
    CHENEY, SOPHIE H.
Santa Klaus. See:
    NICOLAUS, ST.
SANTAMARIA, RAMÓN (1922-)
    [Cuban jazz musician
    (leader, Latin percussion
    instruments)]
    Mongo Santamaria
Santayana, George. See:
    BORRAS, JORGE
    AUGUSTÍN NICOLAS
    RUIZ DE SANTAYANA Y
Santee, Collier. See:
    FLEXNER, STUART BERG
Santha Rama Rau. See:
    BOWERS, SANTHA
    RAMA RAU
SANTI (SANZIO), RAFFAELLO
    (1843-1520) [Italian
    Renaissance painter]
    Raffaello
    Raphael
Santo, El (The Saint). See:
    FERDINAND III
SANZ, JOAQUIN (1853-88)
    [Spanish bullfighter]
    Punteret
SANZIO. See:
    SANTI (SANZIO),
    RAFAELLO
SAPIENS (BADONICUS),
    GILDAS (516?-70?) [Welsh
    historian]
    Gildas the Wise
SAPOR II (fl. 4th cent. A.D.)
    [King of Persia]
    The Great
Sapper. See:
    McNEILE, HERMAN
    CYRIL
Sapphira. See:
    BARBER, MARY
Sappho. See:
    UNKNOWN
Sappho, An English. See:
    PHILIPS, KATHERINE
Sappho of Toulouse, The. See:

ISAURE, CLÉMENCE
Sappho, The American. See:
    MORTON, SARAH WENT-
    WORTH APTHORP
Sappho, The English. See:
    LANDON, LETITIA ELIZA-
    BETH
Sappho, The French. See:
    SCUDÉRI, MADELEINE DE
Sappho, The Negro. See:
    WHEATLEY, PHILLIS
Sappho, The Rival of. See:
    LEWIS, ESTELLE ANNA
    BLANCHE ROBINSON
Sappho, The Scotch. See:
    COCKBURN, CATHERINE
    TROTTER
Sara Blaine. See:
    MORGAN, DIANA
Sara, Colonel Delle. See:
    AIKEN, ALBERT W.
Sara Linden. See:
    BARTLETT, MARIE SWAN
Sara Morris. See:
    BURKE, JOHN FREDERICK
Sarah. See:
    FELIX, SOPHIE
Sarah Anna Lewis. See:
    LEWIS, ESTELLE ANNA
    BLANCHE ROBINSON
Sarah Bernhardt. See:
    BERNARD, HENRIETTE
    ROSINE
Sarah Grand. See:
    McFALL, FRANCES
    ELIZABETH CLARK
Sarah Kilpatrick. See:
    UNDERWOOD, MARVIS
    EILEEN
Sarah, Queen. See:
    JENNINGS, SARAH
Sarah Stafford Smith. See:
    SMITH, DOROTHY
    STAFFORD
Sarah, The Divine. See:
    BERNARD, HENRIETTE
    ROSINE
Sarah Verney. See:
    HOLLOWAY, BRENDA
    WILMAR
Saratoga, The Hero of. See:
    GATES, HORATIO

Sarbievius, Casimir. See:
SARBIEWSKI, MACIEJ
KAZIMIERZ
SARBIEWSKI, MACIEJ
KAZIMIERZ (1595-1640)
[Polish poet]
Casimir Sarbievius
Sardanapalus. See:
ASHURBANIPAL
Sardanapalus of Germany, The.
See: WENCESLAUS IV
SARDELLA, EDWARD A.
(1928-) [American com-
poser]
Ed Sardella
SARG, ANTHONY FREDERICK
(1882-1942) [American
artist, author and pup-
peteer]
Tony Sarg
Sarge. See:
CONNALLY, GEORGE
WALTER
SARGENT, LUCIUS MANLIUS
(1786-1867) [American
miscellaneous writer and
temperance advocate]
Amgis
Sigma
SARMIENTO, FELIX RUBÉN
GARCÍA (1867-1916)
[Nicaraguan poet]
Rubén Darío
SARNOFF, JANYC (1928-)
[American musician]
Jan Sarnoff
Sarong Girl, The. See:
KAUMEYER, DOROTHY
SAROYAN, WILLIAM (1908-)
[American author and
playwright]
Sirak Goryan
SARPI, PIETRO (PAULO)
(1552-1623) [Venetian
historian]
Fra Paolo (Brother Paul)
Servita
SARRUF, ALEXANDER
(1908-) [Egyptian
motion picture actor]
Alex D'Arcy
Sarto, Andrea del. See:

VANNUCCHI, ANDREA
DOMENICO D'AGNOLO
DI FRANCESCO DI
LUCA
Sarto, Ben. See:
FAWCETT, FRANK
DUBREZ
SARTO, GIUSEPPE MELCHIORRE
(1835-1914) [Supreme
Pontiff of Roman Catholic
Church]
The Peasant Pope
Pope Pius X
The Pope of Catholic Action
St. Pius
Sash, Leon. See:
SHASH, LEON ROBERT
Sashun, Sigma. See:
SASSOON, SIEGFRIED
LORAINE
SASS, GEORGE HERBERT
(1845-1908) [American
lawyer and author]
Barton Gray
Sassone, Il. See:
HASSE, JOHANN ADOLF
SASSOON, SIEGFRIED LORAINE
(1886-1967) [English poet,
author and soldier]
Saul Kane
Pinchbeck Lyre
Sigma Sashun
Satchel. See:
PAIGE, LEROY ROBERT
Satchmo. See:
ARMSTRONG, DANIEL
LOUIS
Satire, The Father of. See:
ARCHILOCHUS
Satire, The Father of French.
See: REGNIER, MATHURIN
Satire, The Father of Roman.
See: LUCILIUS, CAIUS
Satirist, A Bludgeon. See:
HOPKINS, DR. LEMUEL
Satirist, The First English.
See: HALL, JOSEPH
Satterly, Weston. See:
SUNNERS, WILLIAM
SATTERWHITE, COLLEN GRAY
(1920-) [American jazz
musician (trombone, com-

poser, arranger)]
Tex Satterwhite
Saturday Night, Mr. See:
    GLEASON, HERBERT
    JOHN
Satyr, The. See:
    CHARLES II
SAUCEROTTE, FRANÇOISE-
    MARIE ANTOINETTE
    JOSÈPHE (1756-1815)
    [French actress]
Raucourt
SAUER. See also:
    SOWER
SAUER, JOSEPH (c. 1908-)
    [American motion picture
    actor]
Joseph Sawyer
SAUER, MURIEL STAFFORD
    (fl. 1943-63) [American
    graphologist and author]
Muriel Stafford
SAUL (died c. 67) [Christian
    missionary and theologian]
The Apostle of the Gentiles
Paul
Saul of Tarsus
St. Paul
Saul Kane. See:
    SASSOON, SIEGFRIED
    LORAINE
Saulsbury Triumvirate, The,
    joint nickname of ELI
    SAULSBURY (1817-93),
    GOVE SAULSBURY (1815-
    81) and WILLARD
    SAULSBURY (1820-92)
    [Brothers; American
    lawyers and holders of
    public offices in
    Delaware]
SAUNDERS [Saunders]. See also:
    SANDERS
    Sanders
Saunders, Caleb. See:
    HEINLEIN, ROBERT
    ANSON
Saunders, David. See:
    SONTUP, DANIEL
SAUNDERS, HILARY AIDAN
    ST. GEORGE. See:
    Beeding, Francis
Saunders, Ione. See:

COLE, MARGARET
    ALICE
Saunders, Richard. See:
    FRANKLIN, BENJAMIN
SAUVOLLE, LE MOINE
    (c. 1617-1701) [French-
    Canadian Governor of
    Louisiana]
The American Prodigy
Savage, Blake. See:
    GOODWIN, HAROLD
    LELAND
SAVAGE, GEORGE MARTIN
    (1849-1938) [American
    educator; President
    Emeritus of Union Univer-
    sity]
The Grand Old Man
The Union's Grand Old Man
Savage, The White. See:
    GIRTY, SIMON
Savant, The Blind. See:
    GORE, THOMAS PRYOR
SAVELLI, CENCIO (died 1227)
    [Supreme Pontiff of
    Roman Catholic Church]
Pope Honorius III
SAVELLI, GIACOMO (died
    1287) [Supreme Pontiff
    of Roman Catholic Church]
Pope Honorius IV
SAVILL, ROY (1921-)
    [English author]
Paul Stacey
Saville Rowe. See:
    SCOTT, CLEMENT
    WILLIAM
Savior of Church Music, The.
    See: PALESTRINA,
    GIOVANNI PIERLUIGI DA
Savior of His Country, The. See:
    OATES, TITUS
    WASHINGTON, GEORGE
Savior of Society, The. See:
    BONAPARTE, CHARLES
    LOUIS NAPOLEON
Savior of the Arts, The. See:
    SIROVICH, WILLIAM
    IRVING
Savior of the Constitution, The.
    See: BLOOM, SOL
Savior of the DuPonts. See:
    DU PONT, ALFRED IRÉNÉE

904

Savior of the Nations, The. See:
WELLINGTON, ARTHUR
WELLESLEY, 1ST
DUKE OF
Savior of the Valley, The.
See: ROSSER, THOMAS
LAFAYETTE
Savior of Virginia, The
Political. See:
WALKER, GILBERT
CARLTON
Savoy, Anne. See:
BROOKS, ANNE SOOY
Sawdust Caesar. See:
GOERING, HERMANN
WILHELM
SAWTREY, WILLIAM
(died 1401) [Lollard,
burned at the stake in
Smithfield]
The First Victim in England
SAWYER, CORINNE HOLT
(fl. 1944-66) [American
educator, editor and
author]
Corinne Holt Rickert
SAWYER, EDWIN MILBY
(1910-) [American
baseball club
manager]
Eddie Sawyer
SAWYER, EUGENE TAYLOR
(1846-1924) [American
author of dime novels]
Nicholas Carter
Nick Carter
Old Cap Collier
Sawyer, John. See:
FOLEY, CEDRIC JOHN
Sawyer, Joseph. See:
SAUER, JOSEPH
Sawyer, Mark. See:
GREENHOOD, CLARENCE
DAVID
Sax Rohmer. See:
WADE (WARDE), ARTHUR
SARSFIELD
Saxe, Burton. See:
SIKES, WILLIAM WIRT
Saxe Holm. See:
JACKSON, HELEN MARIA
FISKE HUNT
Saxe, Isobel. See:

RAYNER, CLAIRE
SAXE, MAURICE, COMTE DE
(1696-1750) [Polish
nobleman and soldier]
Marshal de Saxe
Saxie. See:
DOWELL, HORACE KIRBY
SAXO, GRAMMATICUS
(c. 1140-1206) [Danish
chronicler]
The Scholar
SAXON, GLADYS RELYEA
(fl. 1942-55) [American
author]
M. Borden
Marion Seyton
Saxon, John. See:
ORRICO, CARMEN
Saxon, The. See:
LOTHAIR II
Saxons, The Last of the. See:
HAROLD II
Saxophone Player, The World's
Greatest Alto. See:
DORSEY, JAMES
SAY, THOMAS (1787-1834)
[American conchologist,
entomologist and zoölogist]
The Father of American
Conchology
The Father of American
Descriptive Entomology
The Father of American
Entomology
The Father of American
Zoölogy
Saya, Peter. See:
PETERSON, ROBERT
EUGENE
SAYERS, DOROTHY LEIGH
(1893-1957) [English play-
wright and author of detec-
tive stories]
Johanna Leigh
SAYLER. See also:
Sailor
SAYLER, HARRY LINCOLN
(1863-1913) [American
writer of boys' books]
Ashton Lamar
Gordon Stuart
Elliott Whitney
SBARBARO, TONY (1897-)

[American jazz musician
(drums)]
Tony Spargo
Scaeva. See:
STUART, ISAAC WILLIAM
SCALA, FLAMINIO (fl. 1600-
21) [Italian dramatist]
Flavio
Scala, Gia. See:
SCOGLIO, GIOVANNA
Scanderbeg. See:
CASTRIOTA, GEORGE
SCANNABECCHI, LAMBERTO
(died 1130) [Supreme
Pontiff of Roman Catholic
Church]
Pope Honorius II
Scapin, Jupiter. See:
BONAPARTE, NAPOLEON
Scaramuccio. See:
LAWRENCE, WILLIAM
JOHN
Scarface. See:
CAPONE, ALPHONSE
Scarlett, Rebecca. See:
BURT, KATHERINE
NEWLIN
Scarlett, Roger, joint
pseud. of DOROTHY
BLAIR (-) and
EVELYN PAGE (1902-)
[American authors]
SCARPA, SALVATORE (1918-)
[American composer and
conductor]
Don Donson
Scarred, The (Le Belafré). See:
FRANÇOIS DE LORRAINE
HENRI I
SCARRY, PATRICIA
MURPHY (1924-)
[Canadian actress and
radio and television
writer]
Liam Roy
Patsy Scarry
Scat Man. See:
CROTHERS, SHERMAN
Scene Painting, The Founder of.
See: AGATHARCOS
SCHACHT, ALEXANDER
(1894-) [American base-
ball comedian, author and

restaurateur]
The Clown Prince of Baseball
Murray Goodman
Al Schacht
SCHAEFER, HAROLD HERMAN
(1925-) [American com-
poser and arranger]
Hal Schaefer
Schaghticoke, The Prince of.
See: KNICKERBOCKER,
HERMAN
SCHAKOVSKOY, PRINCESS
ZINAIDA (1906-)
[Russian journalist, poet,
correspondent and author]
Jacques Croise
SCHALK, RAYMOND WILLIAM
(1892-1970) [American
professional baseball
player]
Cracker
Ray Schalk
SCHANFIELD, LEWIS MAURICE
(1867-1941) [American
comedian; member of
vaudeville team of Weber
and Fields]
Lew Fields
SCHAREIN, ARTHUR OTTO
(1906-) [American pro-
fessional baseball player]
Scoop
SCHARY, ISIDORE (1905-)
[American motion picture
writer and producer]
Dore Schary
SCHAUFFLER, HENRY ALBERT
(1837-1905) [Congregational
clergyman; missionary in
American midwest]
The Apostle to the Slavs
SCHEFFLER, JOHANNES
(1624-77) [German
churchman, physician and
writer]
Angelus Silesius
Schemer, an Ally of the Meddler,
The. See:
TRUMBULL, JOHN
SCHEMM, MILDRED WALKER
(1905-) [American
educator and author]
Mildred Walker

SCHERR, MARIE (fl. 1926-31)
[American author]
Marie Cher
Schicklgrüber, Adolf. See:
HITLER, ADOLF
SCHIFF, SYDNEY (18??-1944)
[English novelist]
Stephen Hudson
SCHIFRIN, BORIS (1932-)
[Argentinian jazz
musician (piano)]
Lalo
SCHILSKY, AUSTIN (1897-)
[British stage and
motion picture actor]
Austin Trevor
SCHINDLER, RAYMOND C.
(1882-1959) [American
detective]
A Great Detective
SCHITTENHELM, GISELE
EVE (1906-)
[German motion picture
actress]
Brigitte Helm
Schlacter, Susan. See:
THALER, SUSAN
Schlamme, Martha. See:
HAFTEL, MARTHA
SCHLEE, VALENTINA
NICHOLAEVNA SANINA
(1904-) [Russian-
American fashion designer
and dressmaker]
Valentina
Schleiermacher, The Catholic.
See: MOHLER, JOHANN
ADAM
SCHLEIN, MIRIAM (1926-)
[American author]
Miriam Weiss
SCHLESINGER, BRUNO
(1876-1962) [German
orchestra conductor]
Bruno Walter
SCHLETZ, ELKE (1940-)
[German motion picture
actress]
Elke Sommer
SCHLEY, WINFIELD SCOTT
(1839-1911) [American
admiral; Spanish-
American war hero]

The Mephistopheles of the
Ocean
Schlosberg, H.J. See:
MAY, HENRY JOHN
SCHLUDERPACHERU, HERBERT
CHARLES ANGELO
KUCHACEVICH ZE (1917-)
[Czech motion picture
actor]
Herbert Lom
Schmeling, Max. See:
KLEIN-LUCKOW, MAX
SCHMIDT, EDUARD (1890-1966)
[German writer]
Kasimir Edschmid
SCHMIDT, JAMES NORMAN
(1912-) [American
educator and author]
James Norman
SCHMIDT, KASPAR (1806-56)
[German anarchistic
writer]
Max Stirner
SCHMITZ, ETTORE (1861-1928)
[Italian fiction writer]
Italo Svevo
SCHNECK, STEPHEN (1933-)
[American entertainer and
author]
Ben Bite
Mack Fite
Larry Kite
James Knight
Jams Lite
Sam Spit
SCHNEIDER, ABRAM
LEOPOLDOVICH (1917-)
[Russian-American
theatrical producer]
Alan Schneider
SCHNEIDER, GUENTHER
(1890-1956) [American
motion picture actor]
Edward Arnold
SCHNEIDER, ISIDOR (1896-)
[Polish-American poet
and novelist]
I.S.
Schneider, Romy. See:
ALBACH-RETTY,
ROSEMARIE
SCHNITTER. See:
SNEIDER (SCHNITTER),

JOHANNES
SCHNITTKIND, HENRY
THOMAS (1888-   )
[Lithuanian-American
Author]
Henry Thomas
SCHNITZER, EDUARD
(1840-92) [German
explorer and administrator
in Africa]
Emin Pasha
Mehmed Emin Pasha
Schnozzola. See:
DURANTE, JAMES
FRANCIS
SCHOENBERG, ALFRED
(1868-1949) [German-
American vaudeville
comedian and entertainer]
Al Shean
SCHOENDIENST, ALBERT
FRED (1923-) [American
baseball manager]
Red Schoendienst
SCHOENFELD, WILLIAM C.
(1893-) [American com-
poser, conductor and
arranger]
Lowell Blake
Hugh Conrad
Scholar, Henry the (Henry
Beauclerc). See:
HENRY I
Scholar of Our Time, The
Foremost Greek. See:
MURRAY, GEORGE
GILBERT AIMÉ
Scholar of the Georgia Bar, The
See: HILL, WALTER
BARNARD
Scholar, The. See:
SAXO, GRAMMATICUS
Scholar, The Poor. See:
REID, CAPTAIN MAYNE
Scholastic Doctor, The. See:
ANSELM OF LAON
Scholastic, The. See:
EPIPHANIUS, ST.
Scholastics, Prince of. See:
AQUINAS, ST. THOMAS
Scholefield, Edmund O. See:
BUTTERWORTH, WILLIAM

EDMUND III
SCHOLLANDER, DONALD
ARTHUR (1946-) [American
Olympic swimming champion]
Don Schollander
Schon, Martin. See:
SCHONGAUER, MARTIN
SCHONFIELD, HUGH JOSEPH
(1901-) [British author,
editor and translator]
Hegesippus
SCHONGAUER, MARTIN
(1445?-91) [German
engraver and painter]
Hipsch Martin
Hubsch Martin
Martin Schon
School Education, The Father of
the System of Common.
See: TREADWELL, JOHN
School of American Artists,
Founder of the Hudson River.
See: COLE, THOMAS
School of Composition, The
Father of the Czech
Nationalist. See:
SMETANA, BEDŘICH
School of Philosophy, Founder
of the Utilitarian. See:
CUMBERLAND, RICHARD
School System in New Jersey,
The Father of the Free.
See: CUTLER, AUGUSTUS
WILLIAM
School System in Ohio, The Father
of the Public. See:
RICE, HARVEY
School System of Pennsylvania,
The Father of the Public.
See: WOLF, GEORGE
School System, The Father of the
English Public. See:
WYKEHAM (WICKHAM),
WILLIAM OF
School System, The Father of the
Free. See: ENGLISH,
JAMES EDWARD
Schoolboy. See: ROWE,
LINWOOD THOMAS
Schoolmaster in Politics, The.
See: WILSON, THOMAS
WOODROW

Schoolmaster of Skippack, The
Pious. See:
DOCK, CHRISTOPHER
Schoolmaster of the Republic,
The. See:
WEBSTER, NOAH
Schoolmaster to America, The.
See: WEBSTER,
NOAH
Schoolmen, The Last of the.
See: BIEL (BYLL),
GABRIEL
MAJOR (MAIR), JOHN
SUAREZ, FRANCISCO
Schools of Alabama, The
Father of the Public. See:
MEEK, ALEXANDER
BEAUFORT
SCHOONOVER, GLORIA JEAN
(1928-) [American
singer and motion pic-
ture actress]
Gloria Jean
SCHOPENHAUER, FELIX
BEGLIO (1925-43) [Mexi-
can born bullfighter]
Felix Guzmán
SCHOPFER, JEAN (1868-1931)
[Swiss-French
novelist, playwright and
historian]
Claude Anet
SCHOSBERG, PAUL A. (1938-)
[American journalist and
author]
Paul Allyn
SCHREINER, OLIVE EMILIE
ALBERTINA (1855-1920)
[South African author]
Ralph Iron
SCHRIFT, SHIRLEY (1922-)
[American vaudeville,
stage and motion picture
actress]
Shelley Winters
SCHROEDER, HENRY (1855-
1928) [German-American
agriculturist]
Minnesota's Potato King
Schubin, Ossip. See:
KIRSCHNER, ALOISIA
SCHUBLE, HENRY

GEORGE, JR.
(1908-) [American
professional baseball
player]
Heinie Schuble
SCHULEFAND, RICHARD
(c. 1929-) [American
comedian and motion pic-
ture actor]
Dick Shawn
SCHULEMBERG, ERANGARD
MELROSE DE (died 1743)
[Duchess of Kendal;
mistress of GEORGE I of
England]
The Maypole
SCHULMERICH, EDWARD WES-
LEY (1902-)
[American college football
and professional baseball
player]
Ironhorse
Schultz, Dutch. See:
FLEGENHEIMER, ARTHUR
SCHULTZ, JAMES WILLARD
(1869-) [American
author]
Ap-i-juni
SCHULTZE, CARL EMIL
(1866-1939) [American
cartoonist; creator of
"Foxy Grandpa"]
Bunny
Schultze, Paul. See:
LANGER, ALFONS
SCHUMANN-HEINK, MME.
ERNESTINE (1861-1936)
[German-American operatic
contralto]
The Grand Old Lady of Opera
The Mother of All the Dough-
boys
The Mother of the American
Legion
Schura. See:
KOLLONTAY,
ALEXANDRA
SCHÜTZ, HEINRICH (1585-1672)
[German composer]
Sagittarius
SCHUTZE, GLADYS
HENRIETTA

(1881-) [English
novelist]
Henrietta Leslie
Gladys Mendl
SCHUYLER, PHILIP JOHN
(1733-1804) [American
Revolutionary War
general officer]
The Great Eye
Schuyler Staunton. See:
BAUM, LYMAN FRANK
SCHWABE, CECIL (1897-)
[British motion picture
actor]
Cecil Parker
SCHWANBECK, KARL ADAM
(1845-95) [American
soldier, Indian fighter
and diplomat]
Charles Adams
SCHWARTZ, WILBUR (1914-)
[American musician,
composer and arranger]
Don Swan
SCHWARTZ, ANNE POWERS
(1913-) [American
author]
Anne Powers
SCHWARTZ, BERNARD
(1925-) [American
actor]
Tony Curtis
SCHWARTZ, DON (1937-)
[American jazz musician
(piano, harpsichord,
organ)]
Don Randi
SCHWARTZ, FRANCES. See:
Sylvin, Francis
SCHWARTZ, JOOST WILLEM
VAN DER POORTEN
(1858-1915) [Dutch
novelist and short story
writer]
Maarten Maartens
Schwartz, Muriel A. See:
ELIOT, THOMAS
STEARNS
SCHWARTZ, RICHARD
(1928-) [American
jazz musician (trumpet,
arranger, leader)]

Dick Sutton
SCHWARZERT, PHILIPP
(1497-1560) [German
religious reformer and
scholar; collaborator with
MARTIN LUTHER]
Melanchthon
Melanthon
The Teacher of Germany
SCHWATT, AARON (1919-)
[American vaudeville,
television and motion pic-
ture comic]
Red Buttons
Schweppervescence, The Em-
bodiment of. See:
WHITEHEAD, WALTER
EDWARD
SCHWERIN, COUNT KURT
CHRISTOPH (1684-1757)
[German general officer]
The Little Marlborough
SCHWICHTENBERG, WILBUR
(1912-) [American jazz
musician (trombone)]
Will Bradley
SCIACCA, ANTHONY (1921-)
[American jazz musician
(clarinet, saxophone, piano,
composer, arranger)]
Tony Scott
Scian Muse, The. See:
SIMONIDES
SCIAPIRO, MICHEL (1891-1962)
[Russian composer, con-
ductor and violinist]
Michael Fielding
SCICOLONE. See:
VILLANI (SCICOLONE),
SOPHIA
Science Fiction, The Father of.
See: VERNE, JULES
Science of Anthropology, The
Founder of the. See:
BLUMENBACH, JOHANN
FRIEDRICH
Science of Physiography, The
Father of. See:
DAVIS, WILLIAM MORRIS
Science, The Caliban of. See:
RAMSEY,
ALEXANDER

Science, The Dean of American. See: CATTELL, JAMES McKEEN

Science, The Nestor of American. See: MITCHILL, SAMUEL LATHAM SILLIMAN, BENJAMIN

Sciences, The Father of the Brooklyn Institute of Arts and. See: HEALY AARON AUGUSTUS

Scientific Witness, The Ideal. See: SPILSBURY, SIR BERNARD HENRY

Scio's Blind Old Bard. See: HOMER

Scio's Rocky Isle, The Blind Old Man of. See: HOMER

SCIPIO AFRICANUS, PUBLIUS CORNELIUS (237-183 B.C.) [Roman general; hero of the Second Punic War]
Scipio the Elder

SCOBEY, ROBERT (1916-63) [American jazz musician (trumpet, leader)]
Bob Scobey

SCOFIELD, DAVID (1922-) [British actor]
Paul Scofield

SCOGLIO, GIOVANNA (1936-) [Italian motion picture actress]
Gia Scala

SCOLARI, PAOLO (died 1187) [Supreme Pontiff of Roman Catholic Church]
Pope Clement III

Scoop. See: SCHAREIN, ARTHUR OTTO

Scoops. See: CARRY, GEORGE DORMAN

Scorpion Stanley. See: LORD STANLEY

SCORTIA, THOMAS NICHOLAS (1926-) [American chemist and author]
Artur R. Kurz
Gerald McDow
Scott Nichols

SCOT. See also: SCOTT Scott

SCOT, ALEXANDER (1525?-84) [Scottish poet]
The Scottish Anacreon

Scotch Hobbema, The. See: NASMYTH, PATRICK (PETER)

Scotch Reformer, The First. See: HAMILTON, PATRICK

Scotch Sappho, The. See: COCKBURN, CATHERINE TROTTER

Scotland, The Scourge of. See: EDWARD I

Scotland, The Uncrowned King of. See: DUNDAS, HENRY

Scots, Mary, Queen of. See: MARY

Scots, Queen of. See: MARY

Scots, The Apostle of the. See: KNOX, JOHN

Scots, The Hammer of the. See: EDWARD I

SCOTT [Scott]. See also: SCOT

SCOTT, ADAM, OF TUSHIELAW (died 1529) [Scottish robber]
The King of the Border
The King of Thieves

SCOTT, ADRIAN. See: Hollywood Ten, The

Scott, Anthony. See: DRESSER, DAVIS

SCOTT, ARTHUR BUDD (1890-1949) [American jazz musician (guitar, banjo, singer)]
Bud Scott

Scott Brady. See: TIERNEY, GERALD

Scott Campbell. See:

911

DAVIS, FREDERICK
WILLIAM
SCOTT, CLEMENT WILLIAM
(1841-1904) [English
dramatic critic and
playwright]
John Doe
Saville Rowe
SCOTT, CORA ANNETT PEPI-
TONE (1931-) [American
author of books for
children]
Cora Annett
Scott, Dan. See:
BARKER, S. OMAR
STRATEMEYER,
EDWARD L.
Scott, Dana. See:
ROBERTSON, CONSTANCE
NOYES
SCOTT, EVELYN (1893-)
[American poet and
author]
E. Souza
Scott, Frances V. See:
WING, FRANCES SCOTT
SCOTT, GERALDINE EDITH
(fl. late 19th, early
20th cent.) [British
author]
G. E. Mitton
Scott, Gordon. See:
WERSCHKUL, GORDON M.
SCOTT, HUGH STOWELL
(1862-1903) [English
novelist]
Henry Seton Merriman
SCOTT, HUGH STOWELL.
See also:
Merriman, Henry Seton
SCOTT, JAMES (1649-85)
[Claimant to the British
throne]
James Crofts
Duke of Monmouth
James Fitzroy
The Little Duke
The Protestant Duke
Scott, Jane. See:
McELFRESH, ELIZABETH
ADELINE
Scott, Jean. See:

MUIR, MARIE
SCOTT, JOHN (1751-1838) [1st
Earl of Eldon; Lord
Chancellor of England]
Old Bags
Scott, Kerry. See:
SWANSON, HAROLD
NORLING
Scott, Lizabeth. See:
MATZO, EMMA
Scott, Major S. S. See:
HARBAUGH, THOMAS
CHALMERS
Scott, Martin. See:
GEHMAN, RICHARD BOYD
SCOTT, MICHAEL (c. 1175-
c. 1230) [Scottish scholar
and astrologer]
The Wondrous Wizard
Scott Nichols. See:
SCORTIA, THOMAS
NICHOLAS
Scott, Norford. See:
ROWLAND, DONALD
SYDNEY
Scott of Belgium, The Walter.
See: CONSCIENCE,
HENDRICK
Scott of Painting, The. See:
GILBERT, SIR JOHN
Scott of the Middle Ages, The
Walter. See:
FROISSART, JEAN
SCOTT, PETER DALE (1929-)
[Canadian educator and
author]
Adam Greene
John Sproston
Scott, Randolph. See:
CRANE, RANDOLPH
Scott, Raymond. See:
WARNOW, HARRY
SCOTT, ROBERT W. (1937-)
[American musician and
composer]
Bobby Scott
SCOTT, ROBERT WALTER
(1861-1929) [American
politician and agriculturist]
Farmer Bob
Farmer Bob Scott
SCOTT, SIR WALTER (1771-1832)

[Scottish poet, novelist, historian and editor]
The Ariosto of the North
The Black Hussar of Literature
The Border Minstrel
By the Author of "Waverley"
Jedediah Cleisbotham
Captain Clutterbuck
The Father of the Historical Novel
The Great Magician
The Great Magician of the North
The Great Minstrel
The Great Unknown
The Homer of the Novel
The Magician
The Magician of the North
Malachi Malagrowth
The Minstrel of the Border
The Shirra
Laurence Templeton
The Wizard
The Wizard of the North
Scott, The American. See:
COOPER, JAMES FENIMORE
Scott, The Southern. See:
ARIOSTO, LUDOVICO
SCOTT, THOMAS JEFFERSON (1912-) [American composer and ballad singer]
The American Troubadour
Tom Scott
Scott, Tommy. See:
WOODWARD, THOMAS JONES
Scott, Tony. See:
SCIACCA, ANTHONY
Scott, Warwick. See:
TREVOR, ELLESTON
SCOTT, WINFIELD (1786-1866) [American general officer]
The Hero of Chippewa
Old Chapultepec
Old Fuss and Feathers
SCOTT, WINIFRED MARY (fl. early 20th cent.) [British novelist]
Pamela Wynne

Scottish Anacreon, The. See:
SCOT, ALEXANDER
Scottish Boanerges, The, joint nickname of JAMES ALEXANDER HALDANE (1768-1851) [Scottish preacher], and his brother ROBERT HALDANE (1764-1842) [Scottish philanthropist and theological writer]
Scottish Chaucerians, The Last of the. See:
LINDSAY (LYNDSAY), SIR DAVID
Scottish Hogarth, The. See:
ALLAN, DAVID
Scottish Homer, The. See:
WILKIE, WILLIAM
Scottish Poetry and History, The Father of. See:
BARBOUR, JOHN
Scottish Presbytery, The Father of. See:
MELVILLE, ANDREW
Scottish Probationer, The. See:
DAVIDSON, THOMAS
Scottish Reformation, The Apostle of the. See:
KNOX, JOHN
Scottish Reformation, The Proto-martyr of the. See:
HAMILTON, PATRICK
Scottish Roscius, The. See:
JOHNSTON, HENRY ERSKINE
Scottish Solomon, The. See:
JAMES I
Scottish Teniers, The. See:
WILKIE, SIR DAVID
Scottish Theocritus, The. See:
RAMSAY, ALLAN
Scotty. See:
MACGREGOR, IRVINE T.
Scotus, Johannes. See:
ERIGENA, JOHANNES SCOTUS
Scotus Viator. See:
SETON-WATSON, ROBERT WILLIAM
Scourge of England, The Hammer and. See:
WALLACE, SIR WILLIAM

Scourge of God, The. See:
    ATTILA (ETZEL)
    (ETHELE)
Scourge of Grammer, The. See:
    JACOB, GILES
Scourge of Homer, The
    (Homeromastix). See:
    ZOILUS
Scourge of Princes, The. See:
    ARETINO, PIETRO
Scourge of Scotland, The.
    See: EDWARD I
Scourge of the District Police,
    The. See:
    BLANTON, THOMAS
    LINDSAY
Scourge of the Priests, The.
    See: FAREL,
    GUILLAUME
Scourge of the Swastika, The.
    See: HIMMLER,
    HEINRICH
Scout, Bill Cody the. See:
    CODY, WILLIAM
    FREDERICK
Scout, The Surgeon. See:
    POWELL, DAVID FRANK
Scouts, The Last of the Great.
    See: CODY, WILLIAM
    FREDERICK
SCOVILLE, JOSEPH ALFRED
    (1815-64) [American
    journalist and novelist]
    Walter Barrett
    Manhattan
Scream, The Portly Master of
    the Involuntary. See:
    HITCHCOCK, ALFRED
    JOSEPH
Screen, The First Lady of
    the. See:
    GUICHE, LILLIAN DE
Screen, The Grand Old Man
    of the. See:
    ROBERTS, THEODORE
Screen, The Mansfield of the.
    See: WALTHALL,
    HENRY B.
Screen, The Siren of the.
    See: WEST, MAE
Screeno. See:
    BAILEY, HOWARD HENRY

Screen's Bad Girl, The. See:
    WEST, MAE
Screen's Greatest Lover, The.
    See: D'ANTONGUOLLA,
    RODOLPHO ALFONZO
    RAFAELO PIERRE
    FILIBERT GUGLIELMO
    DI VALENTIN
Scribble, Loquacious, Esq. See:
    HAMILTON, DR.
    ALEXANDER
Scribbler. See:
    SOWDEN, SIR WILLIAM
    JOHN
Scribe, Long. See:
    DOWLING, VINCENT
Scribe of the Revolution, The.
    See: JEFFERSON,
    THOMAS
Scribe, The. See:
    EZRA (EZDRAS)
Scribe, The City-Items. See:
    COWDRICK, JESSE C.
Scriblerus Secundus. See:
    FIELDING, HENRY
SCRUGGS, MARY ELFRIEDA
    (1910-) [American jazz
    musician (composer, ar-
    ranger, leader, piano)]
    Mary Lou Burley
    Mary Lou Williams
    Mary Elfrieda Winn
    Mary Lou Winn
    The Queen of Jazz
SCUDDER, MILDRED LEE
    (1908-) [American author]
    Mildred Lee
SCUDÉRI, MADELEINE DE
    (1607-71) [French poet and
    novelist]
    The French Sappho
    The Tenth Muse
Sculptor of American History,
    The. See:
    KELLY, JAMES EDWARD
Sculptors, The Dean of United
    States. See:
    DAVIDSON, JO
Sculpture, The Correggio of.
    See: GOUJON, JEAN
Sculpture, The Van Dyck of.
    See: COYSEVOX, ANTOINE

Se-baptist, The. See:
SMITH, JOHN
Sea, Admiral of the Ocean.
See: COLUMBUS,
CHRISTOPHER
Sea Devil, The. See:
VON LUCKNER, COUNT
FELIX
Sea-Green Incorruptible, The.
See: ROBESPIERRE,
FRANÇOIS-JOSEPH
MAXIMILIAN ISIDORE
DE
Sea King's Daughter, The.
See: ALEXANDRA,
CAROLINE MARIE
CHARLOTTE LOUISA
JULIA
Sea-Lion. See:
BENNETT, GEOFFREY
MARTIN
Sea Power, The Embodiment
of. See:
NELSON, HORATIO, VIS-
COUNT NELSON
Sea, The Abraham Lincoln of
The. See:
FURUSETH, ANDREW
Sea, The Bayard of the. See:
PAUL, JOHN
Seafarer, A. See:
RUSSELL, WILLIAM
CLARK
Sealsfield, Charles. See:
POSTL, KARL ANTON
SEAMAN, ELIZABETH
COCHRANE (1867-1922)
[American journalist]
Nellie Bly
SEAMAN, SYLVIA S. See:
Sylvin, Francis
Sean. See:
CONNERY, THOMAS
Sean Gregory. See:
HOSSENT, HARRY
Sean O'Casey. See:
CASEY, JOHN
Sean O'Shea. See:
TRALINS, S. ROBERT
Search, Edward. See:
TUCKER, ABRAHAM
Search, John. See:

WHATELY, RICHARD
Searcher, The. See:
FLUDD (FLUD), ROBERT
Searchlight. See:
FRANK, WALDO DAVID
SEARCY, GEORGE (George
Moran). See:
Two Black Crows
SEARING, LAURA CATHERINE
REDDEN (1840-1923)
[American journalist and
author]
Howard Glyndon
SEARLE, JOYCE COLLINS
(1930-) [American jazz
musician (piano, singer)]
Joyce Collins
Sears, Deane. See:
RYWELL, MARTIN
SEARS, EDWARD I. (1819-76)
[Irish-American author
and editor]
H. W. Chevalier
SEARS, ISAAC (1729-86)
[American merchant and
Revolutionary War
politician]
King Sears
Seas, The Pathfinder of the. See:
MAURY, MATTHEW
FONTAINE
Seattle's Sensational Son. See:
ZIONCHECK, MARION A.
SEAVER, GEORGE THOMAS
(1944-) [American pro-
fessional baseball player]
Tom Seaver
SEBASTIAN (1554-78) [King of
Portugal]
The Madman
Sebastian Cash. See:
SMITHELLS, ROGER
WILLIAM
Sebastian Cauliflower. See:
SELDES, GILBERT VIVIAN
Sebastian, Lee. See:
SILVERBERG, ROBERT
Sebastian Melmoth. See:
WILDE, OSCAR FINGAL
O'FLAHERTIE
WILLS
Sebastian Owl. See:

THOMPSON, HUNTER
STOCKTON
SEBELIEN, JOHN ROBERT
FRANCIS (1858-) [Danish
educator and author]
Kristian Pagan
Secession, The Father of. See:
RHETT, ROBERT
BARNWELL
Secession, The Orator of. See:
YANCEY, WILLIAM
LOWNDES
Second Aristotle, The. See:
ACHILLINI, ALESSANDRO
Second Charlemagne, The.
See: CHARLES V
Second Dauphin, The. See:
LOUIS
Second, Henry. See:
HARRISON, HENRY
SNYDOR
Second John. See:
ADAMS, JOHN QUINCY
Second Moses (RaMBam). See:
MAIMONIDES
Second Mother of Everybody's
Children, The. See:
ABBOTT, GRACE
Second Shakespeare, The. See:
MARLOWE, CHRISTOPHER
Second Solomon, The. See:
JAMES I
Second Washington, The. See:
CLAY, HENRY
Second William Jennings
Bryan, The. See:
LEE, JOSHUA BRYAN
Secondsight, Solomon. See:
McHENRY, JAMES
Secondthoughts, Solomon. See:
KENNEDY, JOHN
PENDLETON
Secretary Lethington. See:
MAITLAND OF LETHING-
TON, WILLIAM
Secretary, The Perpetual. See:
THOMPSON, CHARLIE
Secretary, The Singing. See:
McCABE, CHARLES
CARDWELL
Secrets of 82 Nations, The
Curator of. See:

HAMMARSKJÖLD, DAG
HJALMAR CARL AGNE
Sectional President, The. See:
LINCOLN, ABRAHAM
SECUNDUS, GAIUS PLINIUS
(c. 23-79) [Roman states-
man, soldier and author]
The Elder
Pliny
SECUNDUS, GAIUS PLINIUS
CAECILIUS (62-113)
[Roman orator and author]
Pliny
The Younger
Secundus, Scriblerus. See:
FIELDING, HENRY
Sedan, The Man of. See:
BONAPARTE, CHARLES
LOUIS NAPOLEON
Sedges, John. See:
BUCK, PEARL
SYDENSTRICKER
SEDGMAN, FRANCIS ARTHUR
(1927-) [Australian
tennis player]
Frank Sedgman
SEDGWICK, JOHN (1813-64)
[American general officer]
Uncle John
Seditious Jesuit, The. See:
CAMPION, EDMUND
SEDLEY, SIR CHARLES
(1639?-1701) [English
poet, wit and dramatist]
The Tibullus of His Age
SEDLEY, WILLIAM HENRY
(1806-72) [Anglo-American
actor]
William Henry Sedley-Smith
SEDRIC, EUGENE PAUL
(1907-63) [American jazz
musician (clarinet, tenor
saxophone)]
Gene Sedric
Honey Bear
Seebord, G.E. See:
SODERBERG, PERCY
MEASDAY
SEEDS, ROBERT I. (1908-)
[American professional
baseball player]
Suitcase

SEEGER, PETER (1919-)
[American folk singer,
folk lorist and musician]
America's Tuning Fork
Pete Seeger
The Reincarnated Troubadour
The Thomas Jefferson of
Folk Music
Seeley Regester. See:
VICTOR, MRS. METTA
VICTORIA FULLER
MORSE
Seelin Robins. See:
ELLIS, EDWARD
SYLVESTER
Seer. See:
ROBERTS, CECIL EDRIC
MORINGTON
Seer of Wellesley Hills, The.
See: BABSON, ROGER
WARD
Seer, The. See:
AVEN, ALGERNON
JASPER
Seer, The Great. See:
JOHNSON, DR. SAMUEL
Seer, The Poughkeepsie. See:
DAVIES, ANDREW
JACKSON
SEFERIADES, GIORGOS
STYLIANOU (1900-   )
[Greek lawyer and
author]
George Seferis
Seferis, George. See:
SEFERIADES, GIORGOS
STYLIANOU
Seforim, Mendele Mocher.
See: ABRAMOWITZ,
SHALOM JACOB
Seghers, Anna. See:
REILING, NETTY
SEGNI. See:
UGOLINO, COUNT OF
SEGNI
SEGNI, LOTHAIR OF (1160/61-
1216) [Supreme Pontiff
of Roman Catholic
Church]
Pope Innocent III
Segundo, Bart. See:
ROWLAND, DONALD

SYDNEY
Segura, Francisco. See:
CANO, FRANCISCO
SEGURA
Segura, Pancho. See:
CANO, FRANCISCO
SEGURA
SEID, RUTH (1913-)
[American editor and
author]
Jo Sinclair
Seifert, Elizabeth. See:
GASPAROTTI, ELIZABETH
SEIFERT
SEIGNOBOSC, FRANÇOISE
(1897-1961) [French author
and illustrator of juvenile
literature]
Françoise
Sekely, Steve. See:
SZEKELY, ISTVAN
SEKULOVICH, MLADEN (1914-)
[American actor]
Karl Malden
Selbit, P.T. See:
TIBBLES, PERCY THOMAS
SELBY, NORMAN (1873-1940)
[American professional
boxer; world's welterweight
champion]
Kid McCoy
The Real McCoy
Selden, George. See:
THOMPSON, GEORGE
SELDEN
SELDES, GILBERT VIVIAN
(1893-1970) [American
journalist, critic and
author]
Lucien Bluphocks
Sebastian Cauliflower
Foster Johns
Vivian Shaw
SELDON-TRUSS, LESLIE
(1892-) [British author]
George Selmark
Seldon Truss
SELEUCUS I (c.358-280 B.C.)
[King of the Seleucidae]
Nicator
SELEUCUS II (c.247-226 B.C.)
[King of the Seleucidae]

917

Callinicus
SELFRIDGE, HARRY GORDON
(1864-1947) [Anglo-Amer-
ican merchant prince]
Mile-a-Minute Harry
Selim. See:
WOODWORTH, SAMUEL
SELIM II (died 1574)
[Sultan of Turkey]
The Sot
SELKIRK, JAMES BROWN
(1832-1904) [Scottish
poet]
J.B.
SELL, HILDEGARDE
LORETTA (1906-)
[American singer and
entertainer]
The First Lady of Supper
Clubs
Hildegarde
The Incomparable Hildegarde
SELLERS, ISAIAH (c.1802-64)
[American author and
Mississippi River pilot]
Mark Twain
SELLERS, JOHN B. (1924-)
[American composer and
singer]
Brother John Sellers
Selmark, George. See:
SELDON-TRUSS, LESLIE
Selten, Morton. See:
STUBBS, MORTON
SELVAGGIO, JOHN R. (1937-)
[American musician and
singer]
Johnny Carlo
Semiramis of the North, The.
See: ANHALT-ZERBST,
SOPHIA AUGUSTA
FREDERICA OF
MARGARET
SEMLER, JOHANN SALOMO
(1725-91) [German
Protestant theologian,
critic and church historian]
The Father of German
Rationalism
SEMMES, RAPHAEL (1809-77)
[American Confederate
naval officer]

Old Beeswax
Paul Jones of the South
SEMPLE, DUGALD (1884-)
[Scottish author, lecturer
and naturalist]
Wheelhouse
Semple, Gordon. See:
NEUBAUER, WILLIAM
ARTHUR
SENARENS, LUIS PHILIP
(1863-1939) [American
author of dime novels]
Kit Clyde
W.J. Earle
Noname
Police Captain Howard
Ned Sparling
Senate, The Beau Brummel of
the. See:
LEWIS, JAMES HAMILTON
Senate, The Cato of the. See:
WHITE, HUGH LAWSON
WRIGHT, SILAS
Senate, The Cicero of the British
See: CANNING, GEORGE
Senate, The Croesus of the.
See: COUZENS, JAMES
Senate, The Lion of the. See:
BORAH, WILLIAM EDGAR
Senate, The Old Man Eloquent
of the. See:
HOAR, GEORGE FRISBIE
Senate, The Wheel Horse of
the. See:
RUGGLES, BENJAMIN
Senator. See:
GRIMES, BURLEIGH A.
Senator from Worcester, The
Moon-faced. See:
HOAR, GEORGE FRISBIE
Senator, The Cowboy. See:
ASHURST, HENRY
FOUNTAIN
Senator, The Peacock. See:
CONKLING, ROSCOE
Senator, The Silent. See:
STURGEON, DANIEL
Sencourt, Robert. See:
GEORGE, ROBERT
ESMONDE GORDON
SENECA, LUCIUS ANNAEUS
(c. 5 B.C.-65 A.D.) [Roman

philosopher and statesman]
The Younger
SENECA, MARCUS LUCIUS ANNA-
EUS (c. 54 B.C.-39 A.D.)
[Roman rhetorician]
The Elder
The Philosopher
The Rhetorician
Seneca, The Christian. See:
HALL, JOSEPH
Seneca, The English. See:
HALL, JOSEPH
SENIOR, ISABEL JANET
COUPER SYME (fl. 1959-64)
[British pianist and author]
Susan Pleydell
SENIOR, NASSAU WILLIAM
(1790-1864) [British
economist]
The Prince of Interviewers
SENNETT, MACK (1880-1960)
[American producer of
silent slapstick motion
picture comedies]
Father Goose
The King of Comedy
Señor Neily. See:
NEILY, HARRY
Sensation of Russia, The Prewar
Rocking Chair. See:
MEYER, DR. ALEXANDER
Sensational Son, Seattle's.
See: ZIONCHECK,
MARION A.
Sentences, Master of (Magister
Sententiarum). See:
LOMBARD, PETER
Sententiarum, Magister
(Master of Sentences). See:
LOMBARD, PETER
Sentimental Gentleman of
Swing, The. See:
DORSEY, THOMAS
Sentimental Gentleman, The.
See: DORSEY, THOMAS
Sentinel. See:
BOGART, WILLIAM
HENRY
Seostris, The Corsican. See:
BONAPARTE, NAPOLEON
Seostris, The Modern. See:
BONAPARTE, NAPOLEON

Sepia. See:
HOLMVIK, OYVIND
Septimus R. Urban. See:
RYMER, JAMES MALCOLM
URNER, NATHAN DANE
Sepulcher, Baron and Defender
of the Holy. See:
GODFREY OF BOUILLON
Sepulcher, Defender of the Holy.
See: GODFREY OF BOUILLON
Sequoyah. See:
GUESS (GIST), GEORGE
Seraphic Doctor, The. See:
FIDANZA, GIOVANNI DI
Seraphic Saint, The. See:
BERNARDONE, GIOVANNI
FRANCESCO
Seraphicus, Doctor. See:
JOHN OF FIDANZA
Sergeant. See:
ROLFE, MARO O.
Serjeant
YORK, ALVIN CULLUM
Sergeant, Our Best Recruiting.
See: NAST, THOMAS
Sergei Bielyi. See:
HOLLO, ANSELM
SERGIUS (died 701) [Supreme
Pontiff of Roman Catholic
Church]
Pope Sergius I
St. Sergius
SERGIUS (died 847) [Supreme
Pontiff of Roman Catholic
Church]
Pope Sergius II
SERGIUS (died 911) [Supreme
Pontiff of Roman Catholic
Church]
Pope Sergius III
SERGIUS (died 1012) [Supreme
Pontiff of Roman Catholic
Church]
Pope Sergius IV
Serials, The Queen of the Silent.
See: WHITE, PEARL
Serjeant. See:
SARGENT, LUCIUS MANLIUS
Sergeant
TALFOURD, SIR THOMAS
NOON
Serranito. See:
GONZÁLEZ, HILARIO

SERRES, MRS. OLIVIA WILMOT (1772-1834) [English impostor]
Princess Olive
Serrifile, F.O.O. See:
HOLMES, WILLIAM KERSLEY
Serry Wood. See:
FREEMAN, GRAYDON LA VERNY
Servant of the Lord O.W.L. (Oh Wonderful Love). See:
GRAHAM, JAMES
Servant, Your Obedient. See:
WELLES, GEORGE ORSON
Service, Dr. See:
ISENDAHL, WALTHER
Service Reform, The Father of Civil. See:
JENCKES, THOMAS ALLEN
PENDLETON, GEORGE HUNT
Service, The Guardian of Civil. See: RAMSPECK, ROBERT
Serving Knight, The. See:
McCONNELL, JOHN PRESTON
Servita. See:
SARPI, PIETRO (PAOLO)
Sessue. See:
HAYAKAWA, KINTARO
Sesyle Joslin. See:
HINE, SESYLE JOSLIN
SETANTA (died c.2 A.D.) [Irish pagan warrior and national hero]
The Achilles of the Gael
Cu Cullin
Cuchulain
SETARO, PETER D. (1924-) [American author and composer]
Larry Baxter
Sete, Bola. See:
ANDRADA, DJALMA DE
SETH, ANDREW (1856-1931) [Scottish philosophical writer and educator]
Andrew Seth Pringle-Pattison
Seth Parker. See:
LORD, PHILLIPS HAYNES

Seth-Smith, E.K. See:
MURRELL, ELSIE KATHLEEN
Setis, Keal. See:
STILES, EZRA CLARKE
SETON, ELIZABETH ANN BAY-LEY (1774-1821) [American Catholic churchwoman; founder of Sisters of Charity]
Mother Seton
Seton, Ernest Thompson. See:
THOMPSON, ERNEST SETON
SETON-WATSON, ROBERT WILLIAM (1879-) [British author]
Scotus Viator
Settle, Edith. See:
ANDREWS, WILLIAM LINTON
SETTLE, ELKANAH (1648-1724) [British playwright]
Doeg
Settlements, Father of Social. See: TOYNBEE, ARNOLD
Settler, The Old. See:
LYMAN, ALBERT ROBISON
Seumas O. Ceithearnaigh. See:
CARNEY, THOMAS PATRICK
Seumas O'Sullivan. See:
STARKEY, JAMES SULLIVAN
Seuss, Dr. See:
GEISEL, THEODOR SEUSS
Seven Days' King, The. See:
MASANIELLO (TOMMASO ANIELLO) (ANELLO)
Seven Mule. See:
BARNUM, WILLIAM HENRY
Seven, Old Eight to. See:
HAYES, RUTHERFORD BIRCHARD
Seven Sages of Greece, The
The Seven Wise Men of Greece, collective nicknames of BIAS (fl. middle of 6th cent. B.C.); CHILO (CHILON) (fl. early 6th cent. B.C.); CLEOBULUS (died c.560 B.C.); PERI-ANDER (died 585 B.C.); PITTACUS (c.651-c.569 B.C.); SOLON (c.638-c.559

B.C.) and THALES (c. 640-
c. 546 B.C.) [Greek
statesmen]
1776, The Patriot Printer of.
See: BRADFORD,
WILLIAM
Seventh Avenue, The Rebel of.
See: CASSINI, OLEG
LOIEWSKI
'77, The Hero of. See:
HAYES, RUTHERFORD
BIRCHARD
Several Hands, By. See:
BEHN, MRS. APHRA
Severe, The. See:
PEDRO I
SEVERINSEN, CARL H.
(1927-) [American jazz
musician (trumpet,
leader)]
Doc Severinsen
SEVERINUS (died 640) [Supreme
Pontiff of Roman Catholic
Church]
Pope Severinus
Severn, David. See:
UNWIN, DAVID STORR
SEVERN, WILLIAM IRVING
(1914-) [American news
editor and author]
Bill Severn
Sewell, Arthur. See:
WHITSON, JOHN HARVEY
SEWALL, JONATHAN (1728-96)
[American lawyer, loyalist
and author]
Sir Roger de Coverley
SEWALL, JOSEPH (1688-1769)
[American Methodist
clergyman and pulpit
orator]
The Weeping Prophet
SEWALL, SAMUEL (1652-1730)
[British merchant, printer,
diarist and magistrate]
Puritan Pepys
SEWARD, ANNA (1747-1809)
[English poet]
The Swan of Litchfield
Nancy Seward
Seward D. Lisle. See: ELLIS,
EDWARD SYLVESTER

SEWARD, JOHN NEIL (1924-)
[American businessman and
author]
Jack Seward
SEWARD, WILLIAM HENRY
(1801-72) [American
politician; governor of and
senator from New York;
Secretary of State]
The Sage of Auburn
SEWARD, WILLIAM WARD, JR.
(1913-) [American educator
and author]
Leigh Rives
SEWELL, JAMES LUTHER
(1901-) [American baseball
club manager]
Luke Sewell
Sewing Machine, The Father of
the. See:
HOWE, ELIAS
SEYMOUR, CHARLES, 6TH
DUKE OF SOMERSET
(1662-1748) [British
statesman]
The Proud Duke of Somerset
Seymour, James. See:
CUNNINGHAM, JAMES
Seyton, Marion. See:
SAXON, GLADYS RELYEA
SFONDRATI, NICCOLÒ (1535-91)
[Supreme Pontiff of Roman
Catholic Church]
Pope Gregory XIV
SFORZA, LUDOVICO (1451-1508)
[Italian ruler of Milan]
Il Moro (The Moor)
Sforza (Stormer of Cities). See:
ATTENDOLO, MUZIO
Shabazz, Malik El. See:
LITTLE, MALCOLM
Shackles, The Monarch of Leg.
See: WEISS, EHRICH
(ERIK WEISZ)
Shackleton, C.C. See:
ALDISS, BRIAN WILSON
Shad. See:
COLLINS, LESTER
RALLINGSTON
RHEM, CHARLES FLINT
Shadow. See:
WILSON, ROSSIERE

Shadow Painter, The
    (Skiagraphos). See:
    APOLLODORUS
SHAFTSBURY, ASHLEY-
    COOPER, ANTHONY, 1ST
    EARL OF. See:
    Cabal, The
Shahcoolen. See: KNAPP,
    SAMUEL LORENZO
SHAHN, BENJAMIN
    (1898-) [Lithuanian-
    American artist]
    The American Hogarth
    Ben Shahn
Shake. See:
    KEANE, ELLSWORTH
    McGRANAHAN
Shakespeare Clown, The. See:
    RICE, DANIEL
Shakespeare of Divines, The.
    See: TAYLOR, JEREMY
Shakespeare of Germany, The.
    See: VON KOTZEBUE,
    AUGUST FREDERICK
    FERDINAND
Shakespeare of the Boulevard(s),
    The. See:
    PIXÉRÉCOURT, GUILBERT
    DE
Shakespeare, The French. See:
    CORNEILLE, PIERRE
Shakespeare, The Hoosier. See:
    GRAY, FINLY HUTCHINSON
Shakespeare, The Second. See:
    MARLOWE, CHRISTOPHER
Shakespeare, The Sister of.
    See: BAILLIE, JOANNA
Shakespeare, The Welsh. See:
    WILLIAMS, EDWARD
SHAKESPEARE, WILLIAM
    (1564-1616) [English play-
    wright, poet, theater
    manager and actor]
    The Bard of All Time
    The Bard of Avon
    The Homer of Our Dramatic
    Poets
    The Horace of our Dramatic
    Poets
    The Immortal Bard
    Sweet Swan of Avon
SHALHOUB, MICHAEL (1932-)

[Egyptian actor]
    Omar Sharif
Shalom Aleichem. See:
    RABINOWITZ (RABINOVITZ),
    SOLOMON J.
SHAMBROOK, RONA (fl. mid-
    20th cent.) [English author]
    Rona Randall
SHAMS UD-DIN MOHAMMED (fl.
    14th cent.) [Persian lyric
    poet, divine, grammarian
    and philosopher]
    The Anacreon of Persia
    Hâfiz (One Who Remembers)
Shane. See also:
    Shayne
Shane Douglas. See:
    WILKES-HUNTER, RICHARD
Shane, John. See:
    DURST, PAUL
Shane, Rhondo. See:
    NORWOOD, VICTOR
    CHARLES GEORGE
Shane Russell. See:
    NORWOOD, VICTOR GEORGE
    CHARLES
Shane V. Baxter. See:
    NORWOOD, VICTOR GEORGE
    CHARLES
Shanghai Bill. See:
    HICKOCK, JAMES BUTLER
SHANK, CLIFFORD EVERETT, JR.
    (1926-) [American jazz
    musician (flute, saxophones,
    composer)]
    Bud Shank
SHANK, SAMUEL LEWIS
    (1872-1927) [American
    lecturer, actor and
    politician; Mayor of
    Indianapolis]
    The Auctioneer Mayor
    The Indianapolis Potato Mayor
    The Potato Mayor
Shannon. See:
    GARST, DORIS SHANNON
Shannon, Dell. See:
    LININGTON, ELIZABETH
Shannon, Terry. See:
    MERCER, JESSIE
Shanty. See:
    HOGAN, JAMES FRANCIS

Shanwa. See:
    HAARER, ALEC ERNEST
Shao-Yang, Lin. See:
    JOHNSTON, SIR REGINALD
Shape. See:
    REEVES, STEPHEN
SHAPIRO, SAMUEL (1927-)
    [American educator and
    author]
    Richard Falcon
SHAPPIRO, HERBERT ARTHUR
    (fl. 1941-69) [American
    journalist, playwright and
    author]
    Burt Arthur
    Herbert Arthur
    Arthur Herbert
Sharif, Omar. See:
    SHALHOUB, MICHAEL
Sharkey. See:
    BONANO, JOSEPH
SHARKEY, JOHN MICHAEL
    (1931-) [American
    editor and author]
    Jack Sharkey
Sharman. See also:
    SHERMAN
    Sherman
Sharman, Maisie. See:
    BOLTON, MAISIE
    SHARMAN
Sharon Leslie. See:
    LUSTER, SHIRLEY
Sharon, Rose. See:
    GROSSMAN, JOSEPHINE
    JUDITH
SHARP, HAROLD SPENCER
    (1909-) [American librar-
    ian, educator, army
    officer and author]
    Big Hal
    Hal
    Heine
    The Little Colonel
Sharp Knife, The. See:
    JACKSON, ANDREW
Sharp, Luke. See:
    BARR, ROBERT
Sharp, Margery. See:
    CASTLE, MRS.
    GEOFFREY L.
SHARP, MARJORIE BARNHILL

ZEHR (1914-)
    [American librarian, teach-
    er and editor]
    Marge
    Zehrzy-Wehrzy
Sharp, Sidney. See:
    MAPES, VICTOR
SHARP, WILLIAM (1856?-1905)
    [Scottish poet and man of
    letters]
    Fiona Macleod
    H. P. Siwäarmill
Sharpe, C. See:
    HOUGH, CLARA SHARPE
Sharpe, Jack. See:
    RATHBONE, ST. GEORGE
    HENRY
    SHARPE, JOHN RUFUS III
SHARPE, JOHN RUFUS III
    (1909-) [American com-
    poser]
    Jack Sharpe
SHARROCK, MARIAN EDNA
    DORMITZER (1897-)
    [American author]
    M.A. Dormie
SHASH, LEON ROBERT
    (1922-) [American jazz
    musician (accordion,
    vibraphone, guitar)]
    Leon Sash
SHAUGHNESSY, CLARK DANIEL
    (1892-1970) [American foot-
    ball coach]
    Soup
Shaul, Frank. See:
    ROWLAND, DONALD SYD-
    NEY
SHAUTE, JOSEPH BENJAMIN
    (1900-) [American
    professional baseball
    player]
    Lefty Shaute
SHAVER, FLOYD HERBERT
    (1905-) [American
    composer, dancer and
    pianist]
    Buster Shaver
Shaw, Artie. See:
    ARSHAWSKY, ARTHUR
Shaw, Barton. See:
    DRUMMOND, PATRICK

HAMILTON

SHAW, GEORGE BERNARD
(1856-1950) [Irish
journalist, playwright,
critic and wit]
Corno di Bassetto
Robespierre Marat
Fitzthunder
G. B. Larking
G. B. S.
P-Shaw
Horatio Ribbonson
Bernard Shaw
Redbarn Wash
SHAW, HENRY WHEELER
(1818-85) [American
humorist]
Josh Billings
Uncle Esek
SHAW, HOWARD ELWIN
(1827-1924) [American
politician, timber
land owner and manufac-
turer]
The Silver-tongued Orator
of Lamoille
Shaw, Jane. See:
EVANS, JEAN BELL
SHAW
SHAW, JOHN (1778-1809)
[American physician and
poet]
Ithacus
Shaw-nee-aw-kee (The Silver
Man). See:
KINZIE, JOHN
Shaw, Private T. E. See:
LAWRENCE, THOMAS
EDWARD
SHAW, RALPH ROBERT (1907-)
[American librarian,
author, inventor and
educator]
The Great Shaw
Himself
Uncle Ralph
Shaw, Susan. See:
SLOOTS, PATSY
Shaw, Victoria. See:
ELPHICK, JEANETTE
Shaw, Vivian. See:
SELDES, GILBERT VIVIAN

SHAW, WILLIAM SMITH (1778-
1826) [American librarian]
Athenaeum Shaw
Shawn, Dick. See:
SCHULEFAND, RICHARD
SHAWN, EDWIN MYERS
(1891-) [American
dancer and choreographer]
Ted Shawn
Shay. See:
MINTON, SHERMAN
Shayne. See also:
Shane
Shayne Colter. See:
NORWOOD, VICTOR
GEORGE CHARLES
Shayne, Gordon. See:
WINTER, BEVIS
Shayne, Robert. See:
DAWE, ROBERT SHAEN
Shchedrin, N. See:
SALTYKOV, MIKHAIL
EVGRAFOVICH
She-Wolf of France, The. See:
ISABELLA OF FRANCE
She-Wolf, The. See:
LINCOLN, MARY TODD
SHEA, JOHN GERALD (1906-)
[American editor and
author]
Jack Fitzgerald
Sheaf Hershey. See:
NEWELL, PETER
SHEAHAN, HENRY BESTON
(1888-) [Writer of
children's stories]
Henry B. Beston
Henry Beston
Shean, Al. See:
SCHOENBERG, ALFRED
Shearer, Moira. See:
KING, MOIRA SHEARER
Shearing, Joseph. See:
LONG, MRS. GABRIELLE
MARGARET VERE CAMP-
BELL
SHEAROUSE, FLORINE W.
(1898-) [American
lyricist]
Florine Ashby
Sheehan, Patrick Augustine. See:
O SIOCHAIN, PADRAIG

AUGUSTINE
SHEEN, FULTON JOHN
(1895-) [Roman
Catholic clergyman,
educator and author]
Bishop Sheen
SHEETS, FREDERICK HILL
(1859-1928) [American
clergyman]
The Happy Warrior
SHEFFIELD, GEORGE ST.
JOHN (1842-1924)
[American rowing coach
and promoter at Yale
University]
The Grandfather of Yale
Rowing
Sheffield, The Bard of. See:
MONTGOMERY, JAMES
Sheik-al-Jebal. See:
HASAN-IBN-AL-SABBAH
SHEIL, LILY (c.1908-)
[Anglo-American
journalist and writer]
Sheilah Graham
The Last of the Unholy Trio
Sheila Brandon. See:
RAYNER, CLAIRE
Sheila Greenwald. See:
GREEN, SHEILA ELLEN
Sheila Stuart. See:
BAKER, MARY GLADYS
Sheilah Graham. See:
SHEIL, LILY
Shek, Chiang Kai. See:
CHIANG CHUNG-CHENG
SHEKLES, GAIL (1918-)
[American stage and
motion picture actor]
Craig Stevens
SHELBY, JULIET (1902-)
[American silent motion
picture actress]
Mary Miles Minter
Shelby's Man of Faith. See:
ANTHONY, JOHN ALSTON
Sheldon, Ann. See:
STRATEMEYER,
EDWARD L.
Sheldon, George E. See:
STAHL, LEROY
Sheldon Leonard. See:

BERSHAD, SHELDON
Sheldon, Mrs. Georgie. See:
DOWNS, SARAH
ELIZABETH
SHELLABARGER, SAMUEL
(1888-1954) [American
educator and author]
John Esteven
Peter Loring
Shelland. See:
BRADLEY-BIRT, FRANCIS
BRADLEY
SHELLEY, PERCY BYSSHE
(1792-1822) [English poet]
Jonathan Fiske, P.B.
John Fitzvictor, P.B.
A Gentleman of Oxford
Mad Shelley
Shelley, Peter. See:
DRESSER, DAVIS
Shelley Winters. See:
SCHRIFT, SHIRLEY
Shelly. See:
MANNE, SHELDON
SHELTON [Shelton]. See also:
SKELTON
SHELTON, FREDERICK
WILLIAM MAY (1815-81)
[American Episcopal
clergyman, humorist and
essayist]
Nil Admirari, Esq.
Shelton, Lola. See:
KLAUE, LOLA SHELTON
SHEN YEN-PING (1896-)
[Chinese author]
Mao-Tun
Shenandoah Valley, The Poet of.
See: LUCAS, DANIEL
BEDINGER
SHEPARD, BENJAMIN HENRY
JESSE FRANCIS
(1848-1927) [Anglo-
American musician and
author]
Francis Grierson
Shepard, Hazel. See:
SMITH, HELEN AINSLIE
SHEPARD, MORGAN VAN ROER-
BACH (1865/77-)
[American editor, writer
and publisher]

John Martin
Shepard, William. See:
    WALSH, WILLIAM
    SHEPARD
Shepherd, Gordon. See:
    BROOK-SHEPHERD,
    GORDON
Shepherd, John. See:
    BALLARD, WILLIS
    TODHUNTER
Shepherd Lord, The. See:
    CLIFFORD, HENRY DE
Shepherd of Ohio, The Gentle.
    See: GROSVENOR,
    CHARLES HENRY
Shepherd of the Ocean, The.
    See: RALEIGH, SIR
    WALTER
SHEPHERD, ROBERT HENRY
    WISHART (1888-)
    [Scottish Presbyterian
    clergyman and author]
Henry Wishart
Shepherd, The Ettrick. See:
    HOGG, JAMES
Shepherd, The Gentle. See:
    GRENVILLE, GEORGE
Shepherd Tom. See:
    HAZARD, THOMAS
    ROBINSON
SHEPLEY-SMITH, MICHAEL
    (1907-61) [British stage
    and motion picture actor]
Michael Shepley
SHEPPARD, HUGH RICHARD
    LAWRIE (1880-1937)
    [Anglican pacifist and
    divine]
Dick Sheppard
SHEPPARD, JOHN (1702-24)
    [English criminal]
Jack Sheppard
SHEPPARD, LANCELOT CAPEL
    (1906-) [British educator,
    translator and author]
Roger Capel
SHEPPARD, MORRIS (1875-
    1941) [American politician;
    senator from Texas and
    advocate of prohibition]
The Father of the Eighteenth
    Amendment

SHEPPERD, JOHN (1907-)
    [American stage and
    motion picture actor]
Shepperd Strudwick
Sheraskevski, Boris. See:
    BROWN, JOHN J.
SHERATON, NEIL (1914-)
    [English author]
Norman Edward Mace Smith
Sheree North. See:
    BETHEL, DAWN
SHERIDAN, CLARA LOU
    (1915-67) [American
    motion picture actress]
The Oomph Girl
Ann Sheridan
SHERIDAN, LADY HELEN
    SELINA (1807-67) [Irish
    poet; Countess of Gifford]
Impulsia Gushington
SHERIDAN, LIONEL ASTOR
    (1927-) [British lawyer,
    educator and author]
Lee Ang Shoy
SHERIDAN, PHILIP HENRY
    (1831-88) [American Civil
    War general officer]
The Jack of Clubs
Little Phil
SHERIDAN, RICHARD BRINSLEY
    (1751-1816) [Irish play-
    wright and politician]
Sherry
Sheriff. See:
    BLAKE, JOHN FRED
    HARRIS, DAVID STANLEY
    LEE, HAL BURNHAM
Sheriff of Nebraska, The Kid.
    See: WEDGWOOD,
    EDGAR A.
Sheriff, Paul. See:
    SHOUVALOV, PAUL
Sheriff, The Buffalo. See:
    CLEVELAND, STEPHEN
    GROVER
Sheriff, The Millionaire. See:
    BAKER, ANDERSON YANCEY
SHERMAN [Sherman]. See also:
    Sharman
Sherman, Allan. See:
    COPELON, ALLAN
SHERMAN, ELEANOR RAE

(1929-) [American model,
illustrator, interior
decorator and author]
Ellie Rae Fleuridas
Sherman, Elizabeth. See:
FRISKEY, MARGARET
RICHARDS
SHERMAN, FRANK DEMPSTER
(1860-1916) [American
poet, architect, mathema-
tician and genealogist]
Felix Carmen
Sherman, Joan. See:
DERN, PEGGY GADDIS
SHERMAN, JOHN (1613-85)
[Anglo-American
clergyman]
College Puritan
SHERMAN, JOHN (1823-1900)
[American politician;
congressman from Ohio]
The Great Financier
Sherman, Nancy. See:
ROSENBERG, NANCY
SHERMAN
SHERMAN, ROGER (1721-93)
[American legislator]
The Learned Shoemaker
SHERMAN, WILLIAM TECUMSEH
(1820-91) [American Civil
War general officer]
The Great Marcher
Mad Tom
Old Billy
Old Tecumseh
Uncle Billy
Sherock, Shorty. See:
CHEROCK, CLARENCE
FRANCIS
Sherry. See:
SHERIDAN, RICHARD
BRINSLEY
Sherwood Bonner. See:
MACDOWELL, KATHERINE
SHERWOOD BONNER
SHERWOOD, JOSEPHINE
(1884-1957) [American
stage and motion
picture actress]
Josephine Hull
SHERWOOD, MARGARET
POLLOCK (1864-1955)

[American author and
educator]
Elizabeth Hastings
SHERWOOD, MARY ELIZABETH
WILSON (1826-1903)
[American novelist and
short story writer]
M. E. W. S.
Shibli Bagarag. See:
LAWLOR, PATRICK
ANTHONY
Shield of Rome, The. See:
VERROCOSUS, QUINTUS
FABIUS MAXIMUS
SHIELDS, GEORGE OLIVER
(1846-1925) [American
editor and author]
Coquina
SHIELDS, WILLIAM JOSEPH
(1888-1961) [Irish stage
and motion picture actor]
Barry Fitzgerald
Shih, Chiang Chieh. See:
CHIANG CHUNG-CHENG
SHIH HUANG TI (259-210 B.C.)
[Ruler of the Chinese
feudal state of Tsin]
The First Emperor
Prince Cheng
Prince Ching
Shihab, Sahib. See:
GREGORY, EDMUND
SHILKRET, NATHANIEL
(1895-) [American com-
poser, clarinetist and
conductor]
Nat Shilkret
SHILLABER, BENJAMIN PEN-
HALLOW (1814-90) [Amer-
ican humorist, journalist
and poet]
Mrs. Partington
SHILLARD-SMITH, CHRISTINE
WETHERILL (1910-)
[American fashion designer]
Tina Leser
Shingle, Solomon. See:
BELLAW, AMERICUS
WELLINGTON
Ship-Building, The Father of.
See: DICKIE, GEORGE
WILLIAM

Shipbuilding in America, The.
Father of Iron. See:
ROACH, JOHN
SHIPLEY, NANCY E. (fl. mid-
20th cent.) [Scottish
author]
Nan Shipley
Shipmaster, American. See:
CODMAN, JOHN
SHIPTON, URSULA SOUTHIEL
(1488-c.1560) [English
witch]
Mother Shipton
Shipwreck. See:
KELLY, ALVIN
Shipyard Bunyan, The. See:
HIGGINS, ANDREW
JACKSON
Shirley. See:
SHURLY
SKELTON, SIR JOHN
Shirley, Anne. See:
PARIS, DAWN
Shirley Booth. See:
FORD, THELMA BOOTH
Shirley Camper. See:
SOMAN, SHIRLEY
Shirley, Dame. See:
CLAPPE, LOUISE
AMELIA KNAPP
Shirley Eclov. See:
PFOUTZ, SHIRLEY
ECLOV
SHIRLEY, JAMES (1596-1666)
[English playwright]
The Last Minstrel of the
English Stage
Shirley MacLaine. See:
BEATY, SHIRLEY
MACLEAN
Shirley, Penn. See:
CLARKE, SARAH J.
Shirley Ross. See:
GAUNT, BERNICE
Shirra, The. See:
SCOTT, SIR WALTER
SHIRREFFS, GORDON
DONALD (1914-)
[American author]
Gordon Donalds
Stewart Gordon
Shirt Foraker, Bloody. See:

FORAKER, JOSEPH B.
Shoe, The. See:
SHOEMAKER, WILLIAM LEE
Shoeless Joe. See:
JACKSON, JOSEPH
JEFFERSON
Shoemaker, The Learned. See:
SHERMAN, ROGER
SHOEMAKER, WILLIAM LEE
(1931-) [American
jockey]
The Shoe
Willie Shoemaker
SHOLES, CHRISTOPHER
LATHAM (1819-90) [American
inventor of the first prac-
tical typewriter]
The Father of the Typewriter
SHOLL, ANNA McCLURE
(fl. 1903-17) [American
author]
Geoffrey Corson
Shooter, The Ralston Straight.
See: MIX, TOM
SHORE, FRANCES ROSE
(1917-) [American singer
and television personality]
Dinah Shore
Shore, Philippa. See:
HOLBECHE, PHILIPPA
JACK
SHORT, ANNABELLE (1930-)
[English jazz musician
(singer, songwriter)]
Annie Ross
Short Ballot Principle, The
Father of the. See:
CHILDS, RICHARD SPENCER
Short, Bob. See:
POPE, ALEXANDER
SHORT, DEWEY (1898-)
[American politician,
congressman from
Missouri]
Jenny
The Laughing-gas Man
The Preacher
Short, Luke. See:
GLIDDEN, PATRICK DILLEY
Short-nose, Marquis (Marquis
au Court Nez). See:
GUILLAUME D'ORANGE

Short, The. See:
PEPIN (PIPPIN) III
Shortfellow, Tom. See:
UNKNOWN
Shorthand, The Father of.
See: BRIGHT, TIMOTHY
Shorty. See:
BAKER, HAROLD J.
ROGERS, MILTON M.
Shorty Sherock. See:
CHEROCK, CLARENCE
FRANCIS
Shot, Drop. See:
CABLE, GEORGE
WASHINGTON
Shot, Little Sure. See: MOZZEE,
PHOEBE ANNE OAKLEY
Shots, Kid. See:
MADISON, LOUIS
SHOTTER, RALPH CHAMPION
(1907-) [British stage
and motion picture
actor]
Ralph Michael
SHOTTON, BURTON EDWIN
(1884-) [American
professional baseball
manager]
Barney
Burt Shotton
SHOUVALOV, PAUL (1903-)
[Russian motion picture
scenarist]
Paul Sheriff
SHOVLIN, JOSEPH KENNETH
(c.1907-) [American
motion picture actor]
Michael Whalen
Show Music Composers, The
Dean of America's. See:
KERN, JEROME DAVID
Showman Since Barnum, The
Greatest. See:
NORTH, JOHN RINGLING
Showman, The Genial. See:
BROWNE, CHARLES
FARRAR
Showman, The Great American.
See: BARNUM,
PHINEAS TAYLOR
Showmen, Prince of. See:
BARNUM, PHINEAS

TAYLOR
Showmen, The Dean of American
Tent-theater. See:
ECCLES, GEORGE
CLINTON, JR.
Shoy, Lee Ang. See:
SHERIDAN, LIONEL ASTOR
Shu, Eddie. See:
SHULMAN, EDWARD
Shubel Morgan. See:
BROWN, JOHN
Shuberts, The, joint nickname
of JACOB J. SHUBERT
(1880-1964), LEE SHUBERT
(1875-1953) and their
brother SAM S. SHUBERT
(1876-1905) [American
theatrical managers and
producers]
Shufflebottom, Abel. See:
SOUTHEY, ROBERT
SHUFFLEBOTTOM, JEAN
(1928-) [British enter-
tainer and motion picture
actress]
Jeannie Carson
SHUFORD, CECIL EUGENE
(1907-) [American
journalist, educator and
author]
Gene Shuford
Shulberg, Alan. See:
WILKES-HUNTER, RICHARD
SHULMAN, EDWARD
(1918-) [American jazz
musician (saxophone, trumpet,
composer, singer)]
Eddie Shu
SHULMAN, MAX (1919-)
[American author and
humorist]
Cultured Perelman
Master of Undergraduate Humor
SHUMSKY, ZENA FELDMAN
(1926-) [British author]
Jane Collier
Zena Collier
Shura, Mary Francis. See:
CRAIG, MARY FRANCIS
SHURLY. See also:
SHIRLEY
Shirley

SHURLY, ERNEST WILLIAM
(1888-) [English
author]
Martin Hasler
SHUTE, HENRY AUGUSTUS
(1858-1943) [American
humorist and author]
Plupy
Shute, Nevil. See:
NORWAY, NEVIL SHUTE
SHUTER, EDWARD (1728-76)
[English actor]
Ned Shuter
Shy, Timothy. See:
LEWIS, DOMINIC BEVAN
WYNDHAM
Si. See:
BLOOM, SEYMOUR I.
Siamese Twins, The, joint stage
name of ENG BUNKER and
CHANG BUNKER (1811-74)
[Chinese twin boys born con-
genitally united; exhibited
by P.T. BARNUM]
SIBELIUS, JOHANN JULIUS
CHRISTIAN (1865-1957)
[Finnish composer]
Jean Sibelius
SIBLEY, HENRY HASTINGS
(1811-91) [American
statesman; Governor of
Minnesota]
The Father of Minnesota
Tall Pine
Tall Trader
Walker in the Pines
Sibyl, The Singing. See:
VICTOR, MRS. METTA
VICTORIA FULLER
MORSE
Sibylle du Faubourg Saint-
Germain, La. See:
LENORMAND, MARIE
ANNE ADÉLAÏDE
Sicilian Theocritus, The. See:
MELI, GIOVANNI
SICINIUS DENTATUS (died
449 B.C.) [Roman soldier]
The Roman Achilles
The Roman Roland
SICKLES, DANIEL EDGAR
(1825-1914) [American

soldier, diplomat and
congressman from New York]
The Yankee King
Sickly, The. See:
HENRY III
Sid. See:
CAESAR, SIDNEY
Cyd
FLEISCHMAN, ALBERT
SIDNEY
LIPPMAN, SIDNEY
LUCKMAN, SIDNEY
McMATH, SIDNEY SANDERS
SIEGEL, SIDNEY EDWARD
Sid, Big. See:
CATLETT, SIDNEY
SIDDONS. See also:
Sidons
SIDDONS, SARAH KEMBLE
(1755-1831) [English tragic
actress]
Mrs. Siddons
Sidetes. See:
ANTIOCHUS VII
SIDMOUTH, LORD VISCOUNT
(1757-1844) [British
nobleman]
The Doctor
Sidney. See:
OLCOTT, JOHN SIDNEY
SYDNEY
Sidney Allan. See:
HARTMANN, SADAKICHI
Sidney Bedford. See:
MEYNELL, LAURENCE
Sidney, Edward William. See:
TUCKER, NATHANIEL
BEVERLEY
Sidney Franklin. See:
FRUMPKIN, SIDNEY
Sidney, George. See:
GREENFIELD, SAMMY
Sidney Kingsley. See:
KEISCHNER, SIDNEY
Sidney Luska. See:
HARLAND, HENRY
Sidney McCall. See:
FENELLOSA, MARY
McNEIL
Sidney, Margaret. See:
LOTHROP, HARRIET
MULFORD STONE

930

Sidney Sharp. See:
MAPES, VICTOR
SIDNEY (SYDNEY), SIR
PHILIP (1554-86) [English
author and general
officer]
The British Bayard
The English Petrarch
The Flower of Chivalry
The Miracle of Our Age
Sidons. See also:
SIDDONS
Sidons, Charles. See:
POSTL, KARL ANTON
SIDUS, GEORGINA (died 1835)
[English actress and
singer]
Miss George
Mrs. Oldmixon
SIEBER, SAM DIXON (1931-)
[American sociologist,
educator and author]
Norman D. Kerr
SIEGEL, JACOB (1913-)
[American author]
Jack Siegel
SIEGEL, SIDNEY EDWARD
(1927-) [American
composer and conductor]
Sid Siegel
Siena, Laurati da. See:
LORENZETTI, PIETRO
SIERCK, DETLEF (1900-)
[Danish stage and motion
picture director]
Douglas Sirk
Sierras, Robin Hood of the.
See: CARILLO, JOAQUIN
Sierras, The Poet of the.
See: MILLER, CINCIN-
NATUS HEINE (HEINER)
SIEVEKING, LANCELOT DE
GIBERNE (1896-)
[English writer and
dramatist]
Lance Sieveking
Sig Arno. See:
ARON, SIEGFRIED
Sig Ruman. See:
RUMANN, SIEGFRIED
SIGHIBULDI, GUITTONCINO
DEI (c.1270-1337) [Italian

poet and jurist]
Cino da Pistoia
SIGISMUND (1361-1437) [Holy
Roman Emperor]
The Light of the World
Supra Grammaticam (Above
Grammar)
SIGISMUND I (1467-1548)
[King of Poland]
The Great
Sigismund Zápolya (Szapolyai).
See: JOHN II
Sigma. See:
SARGENT, LUCIUS MANLIUS
Sigma Sashun. See:
SASSOON, SIEGFRIED
LORAINE
Sign of the Blue Moon, At the.
See: LEWIS, DOMINIC
BEVAN WYNDHAM
Signe Hasso. See:
LARSSON, SIGNE
Signoret, Simone. See:
KAMINKER, SIMONE-
HENRIETTE-CHARLOTTE
SIGOURNEY, LYDIA HUNTLEY
(1791-1865) [American
poet and author]
The American Hemans
The Mrs. Hemans of America
Sigrid Gurie. See:
HAUKELID, SIGRID GURIE
SIKES, WILLIAM WIRT
(1836-83) [American news-
paperman and novelist]
Burton Saxe
SILAS, MARÍA DE SANTO
(1918-51) [West Indies-
born motion picture
actress]
María Montez
Silas N. Gooch. See:
GLASSCO, JOHN
Silas Water. See:
LOOMIS, NOEL MILLER
Silence Dogood. See:
FRANKLIN, BENJAMIN
Silence Dogood, Mrs. See:
FRANKLIN, BENJAMIN
Silence, The Man of. See:
BONAPARTE, CHARLES
LOUIS NAPOLEON

Silent. See:
SMITH, JAMES HENRY
Silent Cal. See:
BENGE, RAY ADELPHIA
COOLIDGE, JOHN CALVIN
Silent Charley. See:
MURPHY, CHARLES
FRANCIS
Silent Jim. See:
TATUM, JAMES MOORE
Silent Man. See:
GRANT, HIRAM ULYSSES
Silent Senator, The. See:
STURGEON, DANIEL
Silent Serials, The Queen of
the. See:
WHITE, PEARL
Silent, The. See:
WILLIAM I
Silent, Tony the. See:
PIETRUSZKA, ANTHONY
FRANCIS
Silesius, Angelus. See:
SCHEFFLER, JOHANNES
Silingsby, Maurice. See:
URNER, NATHAN DANE
Silk Industry, The Father of
the. See:
RYLE, JOHN
Silk-merchant, The. See:
HARIRI, ABU MOHAMMED
AL KASIM IBN ALI
SILL, EDWARD ROWLAND
(1841-87) [American
poet and essayist]
Andrew Hedbrooke
SILLIMAN, BENJAMIN (1779-
1864) [American scientist
and author]
The Nestor of American
Science
Sillographer, The. See:
TIMON
Sills, Beverly. See:
SILVERMAN, BELLE
Silly Billy. See:
WILLIAM IV
WILLIAM FREDERICK
Silly Duke, The. See:
CHURCHILL, JOHN
Silly, The. See:
CHARLES VI

Silurist, The. See:
VAUGHAN, HENRY
Silvanus, P.W. See:
STRASSER, BERNARD PAUL
Silver Dick. See:
BLAND, RICHARD PARKS
Silver Dollar. See:
TABOR, HORACE AUSTIN
WARNER
Silver Fox of the Northland,
The. See:
BIERMAN, BERNARD
WILLIAM
Silver. Fred. See:
SILVERBERG, FREDERICK
Silver Heels. See:
MARSHALL, JOHN
Silver Leg, Old. See:
STUYVESANT, PETER
Silver Man. See also:
SILVERMAN
Silver Man, The (Shaw-nee-aw-
kee). See:
KINZIE, JOHN
Silver Nails, Old. See:
STUYVESANT, PETER
Silver, Nicholas. See:
FAUST, FREDERICK
SCHILLER
Silver Sage, The. See:
THOMAS, JOHN WILLIAM
ELMER
Silver Spoon Butler. See:
BUTLER, BENJAMIN
FRANKLIN
Silver, The Apostle of Free
Coinage for. See:
ST. JOHN, WILLIAM POPE
Silver, The Father of Free. See:
BLAND, RICHARD PARKS
Silver, The Voice of. See:
PITTMAN, KEY
Silver-tongued and Golden-
hearted, The. See:
WILLARD, FRANCES
ELIZABETH
Silver-tongued Josh. See:
LEE, JOSHUA BRYAN
Silver-tongued Orator of
Lamoille, The. See:
SHAW, HOWARD ELWIN
Silver-tongued Orator of the

South, The. See:
BAKER, ALPHEUS
Silver-tongued Orator, The.
See: BELL, JOSHUA FRY
BRYAN, WILLIAM
JENNINGS
DOUGHERTY, DANIEL
KIRKPATRICK, JOHN
MILTON
ROLLINS, JAMES SIDNEY
Silver-tongued Spellbinder of
the Pacific Coast, The.
See: DELMAS,
DELPHIN MICHAEL
Silver-tongued, The. See:
BATES, WILLIAM
GARRICK, DAVID
HAMMOND, ANTHONY
SYLVESTER, JOSHUA
SILVERBERG, FREDERICK
(1936-) [American
composer and pianist]
Fred Silver
SILVERBERG, ROBERT (fl.
1956-66) [American
author]
Walker Chapman
Walter Drummond
Ivar Jorgenson
Calvin M. Knox
David Osborne
Robert Randall
Lee Sebastian
SILVERIUS (died 537) [Supreme
Pontiff of Roman Catholic
Church]
Pope Silverius
St. Silverius
SILVERMAN, See also:
Silver Man
SILVERMAN, BELLE (1929-)
[American singer]
Beverly Sills
Bubbles Silverman
Silvers, Phil. See:
SILVERSMITH, PHILIP
SILVERSMITH, PHILIP
(1912-) [American
comedian and actor]
Phil Silvers
Silviana. See:
WOLFF-BECKER
ELISABETH

(BETJE)
Silvius, Aeneas. See:
PICCOLOMINI, ENEA
SILVIO DE
Sim, Georges. See:
SIMENON, GEORGES
SIM, KATHARINE THOMASSET
(1913-) [British painter,
journalist and author]
Nuraini
SIMENON, GEORGES (1903-)
[Franco-Belgian mystery
story writer]
Aramis
Bobette
Christian Brulls
Georges Caraman
Germain D'Antibes
Jacques Dersonne
La Deshabilleuse
Georges D'Isly
Jean Dorsage
Luc Dorsan
Jean Dossage
Jean Du Perry
Georges Martin Georges
Gom Gut
Kim
Monsieur Le Coq
Plick et Plock
Poum et Zette
Jean Sandor
Georges Sim
G. Vialio
Gaston Vialis
Gaston Viallis
G. Violis
Simeon. See also:
Cymon
SIMON
Simon
Simeon, St. See:
STYLITES, SIMEON
SIMMONS. See also:
Symmonds
Simmons, Aloysius Harry. See:
SZYMANSKI, ALOYSIUS
HARRY
SIMMONS, THOMAS (died
1808) [English murderer]
The Man of Blood
Simmonseed, Johnny. See:

HATFIELD, BAZIL MUSE
Simms, Hilda. See:
  MOSES, HILDA
SIMMS, WILLIAM GILMORE
  (1806-70) [American author]
  Frank Cooper
  The Cooper of the South
  The Southern Cooper
  W. Gilmore Simms
Simon. See:
  ALLGOOD, MILES
    CLAYTON
  CÁRDENAS, SIMÓN
  Cymon
  PETER
  Simeon
SIMON, ABRAHAM (1897-1957)
  [American jazz
  musician (drums, leader,
  composer)]
  Abe Lyman
Simon, Charlie May. See:
  FLETCHER, CHARLIE
    MAY HOGUE
Simon Dewes. See:
  MURIEL, JOHN
SIMON, FRANÇOIS (1895-)
  [French music-hall and
  motion picture actor]
  Michel Simon
Simon Harvester. See:
  RUMBOLD-GIBBS
    HENRY ST. JOHN
    CLAIR
Simon Jay. See:
  ALEXANDER, COLIN
    JAMES
SIMON MAGUS (fl. c. 37 A.D.)
  [Samarian sorcerer]
  Simon the Magician
  The Supreme Power of God
Simon, Mina Lewiton. See:
  LEWITON, MINA
Simon Nash. See:
  CHAPMAN, RAYMOND
Simon Peter. See:
  PETER
Simon Pure. See:
  SWINNERTON, FRANK
    ARTHUR
Simon Rattray. See:
  TREVOR, ELLESTON

Simon Spunkey. See:
  FESSENDEN, THOMAS
    GREEN
Simon Suggs. See:
  HOOPER, JOHNSON J.
SIMONDS, WILLIAM (1822-59)
  [American editor and
  author]
  Walter Aimwell
Simone, Nina. See:
  WAYMON, EUNICE
    KATHLEEN
Simone Signoret. See:
  KAMINKER, SIMONE-
    HENRIETTE-CHARLOTTE
Simonetta. See:
  CESARIÒ, SIMONETTA
    COLONNA DI
SIMONIDES (556-c. 469 B.C.)
  [Greek poet]
  The Scian Muse
SIMONS, KATHERINE DRAYTON
  MAYRANT (1892-) [Amer-
  ican poet and author]
  Drayton Mayrant
  Kadra Maysi
Simons, Roger. See:
  PUNNETT, IVOR McCAULEY
Simple, The. See:
  CHARLES III
  FREDERICK III
SIMPLICIUS (died 483) [Supreme
  Pontiff of Roman Catholic
  Church]
  Pope Simplicius
  St. Simplicius
SIMPSON, BERTRAM LENOX
  (1877-1930) [English
  journalist]
  Putnam Weale
SIMPSON, EDWARD (fl. 1867)
  [English seller of spurious
  flint arrowheads and other
  articles]
  Flint Jack
SIMPSON, EVAN JOHN (1901-53)
  [English dramatist and
  historical novelist]
  Evan John
SIMPSON, JERRY (1842-1905)
  [American politician]
  Sockless Jerry

The Sockless Sage
Sockless Simpson
Sockless Socrates
The Sockless Statesman
SIMPSON, JOHN NICHOLAS
(fl. 1876) [Texas cattle
rancher]
Hashknife Simpson
SIMPSON, MYRTLE LILLIAS
(1931-) [British
mountaineer, explorer
and author]
M. L. Emslie
SIMPSON, NORMA (1926-)
[British motion picture
actress]
Carol Marsh
SIMPSON, ORENTHAL JAMES
(1947-) [American
football player]
O. J. Simpson
Orange Juice
SIMPSON, STEPHEN (1789-1854)
[American editor,
political writer and
biographer]
Brutus
Simpson Stokes. See:
FAWCETT, FRANK
DUBREZ
SIMPSON, THOMAS (1710-61)
[British mathematician]
The Oracle of Nuneaton
SIMS, GEORGE ROBERT
(1847-1922) [British
poet, playwright and
novelist]
Dagonet
SIMS, JOHN HALEY
(1925-) [American
jazz musician (clarinet,
tenor and alto saxo-
phones)]
Zoot Sims
Sims, Lieut. A. K. See:
WHITSON, JOHN HARVEY
SIMS, PETER (1938-)
[American jazz musician
(drums, composer)]
Pete la Rocca
Sin, The Man of. See:
CROMWELL, OLIVER

Ṣina, Ibn. See:
AVICENNA
SINATRA, FRANCIS ALBERT
(1915-) [American
popular singer and actor]
Chairman of the Board
The Dago
The Leader
The General
The Man
Il Padrone
The Pope
Frank Sinatra
The Voice
Sinclair. See:
LEWIS, HARRY SINCLAIR
Sinclair, Emil. See:
HESSE, HERMANN
Sinclair, Grant. See:
DRAGO, HENRY SINCLAIR
Sinclair, Ian. See:
FOLEY, CEDRIC JOHN
Sinclair, Jo. See:
SEID, RUTH
Sinclair Murray. See:
SULLIVAN, EDWARD
ALAN
SINCLAIR, UPTON BEALL
(1878-1968) [American
author, Socialist and
political reformer]
Clark Fitch
Ensign Clark Fitch, U. S. N.
Frederick Garrison
Lieut. Frederick Garrison
Arthur Stirling
Singe de Racine, Le. See:
CAMPISTRON, JEAN
GALABERT DE
SINGER, ISAAC (1904-)
[Polish writer and trans-
lator of Yiddish literature]
Isaac Bashevis
Isaac Warshofsky
Singer of His Race, The Most
Famous Folk. See:
WHITE, JOSHUA DANIEL
Singer of Michigan, The
Sweet. See:
MOORE, JULIA
Singer of the Air, The Lonesome.
See: MARVIN, JOHN

935

Singer, Psalm. See:
ADAMS, SAMUEL
Singers of the West. See:
Sweet Singers of the
West, The
Singers, The Queen of the
Folk. See:
BAEZ, JOAN
Singing Bishop, The. See:
McCABE, CHARLES
CARDWELL
Singing Chaplain, The. See:
McCABE, CHARLES
CARDWELL
Singing Duse, The. See:
ROQUER, EMMA DE
Singing Secretary, The. See:
McCABE, CHARLES
CARDWELL
Singing Sibyl, The. See:
VICTOR, MRS. METTA
VICTORIA FULLER
MORSE
Singing Story Lady, The. See:
WICKER, IREENE SEATON
Single Speech. See:
HAMILTON, WILLIAM
GERARD
HEMPHILL, JOSEPH
HOUGHTON, RICHARD
MONCTON MILNES
Single Taxer, The. See:
GEORGE, HENRY
Singleton, Arthur. See:
KNIGHT, HENRY
COGSWELL
Singleton, Arthur, Esq. See:
KNIGHT, HENRY
COGSWELL
SINGLETON, ARTHUR JAMES
(1898-) [American jazz
musician (drums)]
Zutty Singleton
Singleton, Penny. See:
McNULTY, DOROTHY
Singular Doctor, The. See:
OCKHAM (OCCAM),
WILLIAM OF
Singular Splendor of the Italian
Race, That. See:
ALIGHIERI, DURANTE
Sinjohn, John. See:

GALSWORTHY, JOHN
Sink or Swim, Old. See:
ADAMS, JOHN
Sinner's Friend, The. See:
MATTHEW, FATHER
THEOBALD
Sinnissippi, The Sage of. See:
LOWDEN, FRANK ORREN
Siegvolk, Paul. See:
MATHEWS. ALBERT
SIOUSSAT, JEAN PIERRE
(1781-18??) [French
official at White House
during administration of
JAMES MADISON]
French John
Sioux Indians, The Apostle to
the. See:
HARE, WILLIAM HOBART
Sir Basil Zaharoff. See:
ZACHARIAS, BASILEIOS
Sir Ben Greet. See:
BARLING, PHILIP
Sir Charles. See:
THOMPSON, CHARLES
PHILIP
Sir George Alexander. See:
SAMSON, GEORGE
ALEXANDER GIBB
Sir Hall Caine. See:
CAINE, THOMAS HENRY
HALL
Sir Harry Lauder. See:
MacLENNAN, HUGH
Sir Henry Irving. See:
BRODRIBB, JOHN HENRY
Sir Henry Morton Stanley. See:
ROWLANDS, JOHN
Sir Henry, Old. See:
VANE, SIR HENRY
Sir Henry, Young. See:
VANE, SIR HENRY
Sir Jack Brag. See:
BURGOYNE, JOHN
Sir Jeffery Hudson. See:
HUDSON, JEFFERY
Sir John Hare. See:
FAIRS, SIR JOHN
Sir John Mandeville. See:
Mandeville, Jehan de
(Sir John)
Sir Norman Angell. See:

LANE, RALPH NORMAN
ANGELL
Sir Peter Lely. See:
VAN DER FAES, PIETER
Sir Roger Charles
Tichborne. See:
ORTON, ARTHUR
Sir Roger de Coverley. See:
ADDISON, JOSEPH
SEWALL, JONATHAN
Sir Veto. See:
JOHNSON, ANDREW
Sir William Courtenay. See:
THOM, JOHN NICHOLS
Sirak Goryan. See:
SAROYAN, WILLIAM
Siren of the Screen, The.
See: WEST, MAE
Siren, The Terrible. See:
WOODHULL, VICTORIA
CLAFLIN
SIRICIUS (died 399) [Supreme
Pontiff of Roman
Catholic Church]
Pope Siricius
St. Siricius
Sirin, V. See:
NABOKOV, VLADIMIR
(VLADIMIROVICH)
Sirk, Douglas. See:
SIERCK, DETLEF
SIROVICH, WILLIAM IRVING
(1882-1939) [American
physician; congressman
from New York]
The Savior of the Arts
Sisines. See:
ARCHELAUS
SISINNIUS (died 708) [Supreme
Pontiff of Roman Catholic
Church]
Pope Sisinnius
SISK, JOHN (1906-) [American
football player]
The Big Train
SISK, MILDRED ELIZABETH
(1900-) [American radio
propagandist for Nazi
government]
Axis Sally
Mildred Elizabeth Gillars
Sister. See:

KENNY, ELIZABETH
Sister Aimee. See:
McPHERSON, AIMEE
SEMPLE
Sister Dora. See:
PATTISON, DOROTHY
WYNDLOW
Sister Mary Dominic. See:
GALLAGHER, SISTER
MARY DOMINIC
Sister of Shakespeare, The.
See: BAILLIE, JOANNA
Sister Rosetta Tharpe. See:
NUBIN, ROSETTA
Sister Teresa Margaret. See:
ROWN, MARGARET KEVIN
Sisters. See:
Fox Sisters, The
Sisters of the West, joint pseud.
of MRS. FRANCES FULLER
BARRITT VICTOR (1826-
1902) and her sister,
MRS. METTA VICTORIA
FULLER MORSE VICTOR
(1831-85) [American poets,
editors and authors]
Sisters of the West. See also:
Two Sisters of the West
VICTOR, MRS. FRANCES
FULLER BARRITT
VICTOR, MRS. METTA
VICTORIA FULLER
MORSE
Sisyphus, The Modern. See:
WEBSTER, DANIEL
Sit-Down Striker, The. See:
HOFFMAN, CLARE E.
Sitting Bull. See:
LAWSON, JOHN DANIEL
MORTON, OLIVER HAZARD
PERRY THROCK
SUMMERALL, CHARLES
PELOT
TATANKA YOTANKA
SITWELL, SIR OSBERT
(1892-) [English author,
poet and satirist]
Miles
Siwáarmill, H.P. See:
SHARP, WILLIAM
SIWARD (died 1055) [Danish
soldier in England; Earl

of Northumberland]
Siward the Strong
Six, Big. See:
  AUKER, ELDEN LEROY
  MATHEWSON,
    CHRISTOPHER
Sixteen-string Jack. See:
  RANN, JOHN
Sixteenth Century, The
  Democritus of the. See:
  CALVIN, JOHN
SIXTUS (died c.125) [Supreme
  Pontiff of Roman
  Catholic Church]
  Pope Sixtus I
  St. Sixtus
  Xystus
SIXTUS (died 258) [Supreme
  Pontiff of Roman
  Catholic Church]
  Pope Sixtus II
  St. Sixtus
SIXTUS (died 440) [Supreme
  Pontiff of Roman
  Catholic Church]
  Pope Sixtus III
  St. Sixtus
Sixtus IV, Pope. See:
  ROVERE, FRANCESCO
    DELLA
Sixtus V, Pope. See:
  PERETTI, FELICE
SJÖKE, EVA (1929-) [Hungarian
  motion picture actress]
  Eva Bartok
Skanderbeg. See:
  CASTRIOTA, GEORGE
SKAVRONSKAYA, MARFA
  (1684?-1727) [Empress of
  Russia]
  Catherine I
  Catherine Alexievna
Skeets. See:
  GALLAGHER, RICHARD
  MORRIS, LEONARD CAR-
    TER
Skeggs, The Honorable
  Wilhelmina Amelia. See:
  THACKERAY, WILLIAM
    MAKEPEACE
SKELTON. See also:
  SHELTON
  Shelton

SKELTON, RICHARD BERNARD
  (1913-) American radio
  motion picture and tele-
  vision comedian]
  Red Skelton
SKELTON, SIR JOHN (1831-97)
  [Scottish essayist and
  biographer]
  Shirley
Skeptic of the Eighteenth Century,
  The Most Thorough-
  going British. See:
  HUME, DAVID
Sketchley, Arthur. See:
  ROSE, GEORGE
Ski-nose. See:
  HOPE, LESLIE TOWNES
Skiagraphos (The Shadow
  Painter). See:
  APOLLODORUS
Skibo Castle, The Laird of. See:
  CARNEGIE, ANDREW
Skibo, The Laird of. See:
  CARNEGIE, ANDREW
SKIKNE, LARUSHKA MISCHA
  (1928-) [Lithuanian-born
  actor]
  Laurence Harvey
Skilled, Unquestionably. See:
  GRANT, HIRAM ULYSSES
Skillful Neily, The (El Neily
  Manoso). See:
  NEILY, HARRY
Skin, The Man Without a. See:
  CUMBERLAND, RICHARD
Skinflint, Obediah. See:
  HARRIS, JOEL CHANDLER
Skinnay. See:
  ENNIS, EDGAR CLYDE, JR.
  Skinny
SKINNER, HUGH (191?-)
  [British ballet dancer]
  Hugh Laing
SKINNER, JUNE O'GRADY
  (1922-) [Canadian
  librarian and author]
  Rohan O'Grady
SKINNER, OTIS (1858-1942)
  [American actor]
  The Dean of the American
    Stage
  The Dean of the American
    Theater

Skinny. See:
    Skinnay
    WAINWRIGHT, JONATHAN
        MAYHEW
Skip. See:
    MARTIN, LLOYD
    REDWINE, WILBUR
Skip Morr. See:
    COOLIDGE, CHARLES
        WILLIAM
Skippack, The Pious School-
    master of. See:
    DOCK, CHRISTOPHER
Skitch. See:
    HENDERSON, LYLE CED-
        RIC
Skitt. See:
    TALIAFERRO, HARDEN E.
SKRYABIN, VYACHESLAV
    MIKHAILOVICH (1890-)
    [Russian statesman]
    Vyacheslav Mikhailovich
        Molotov
Skyagunsta. See:
    PICKENS, ANDREW
Skyscraper, The Father of the.
    See: GILBERT, CASS
Slabsides, The Hermit of. See:
    BURROUGHS, JOHN
SLACK, FREDERICK CHARLES
    (1910-65) [American jazz
    musician (piano, arranger,
    leader, composer)]
    Freddie Slack
Slackwater, Old. See:
    MOORHEAD, JAMES
        KENNEDY
SLADEK, JOHN. See:
    Demijohn, Thom
SLADEN, NORMAN ST. BARBE
    (fl. 1932-58) [British civil
    servant and author]
    Rodney Bullingham
    Dennis Montclair
Slam. See:
    STEWART, LEROY
Slamming Sammy. See:
    SNEAD, SAMUEL
        JACKSON
SLANEY, GEORGE WILSON
    (1884-) [British
    journalist, artist and
    author]

George Woden
Slapsie Maxie. See:
    ROSENBLOOM, MAX
Slapstick, The Mistress of
    Sophisticated. See:
    LILLIE, BEATRICE GLADYS
Slashes, The Mill Boy of the.
    See: CLAY, HENRY
SLATER, ORA E. (1870-1945)
    [American detective]
    Ohio's Ace Investigator
SLATER, SAMUEL (1768-1835)
    [Anglo-American manufac-
    turer]
    The Father of American
        Manufacture
SLATTERY, RAYMOND PAUL
    (1912-) [Australian author]
    Ray Slattery
SLAUGHTER, ELIZABETH
    BLYTHE (1893-) [American
    silent motion picture
    actress]
    Betty Blythe
SLAUGHTER, FRANK GILL
    (1908-) [American
    physician and author]
    C. V. Terry
SLAUGHTER, N. CARTER
    (1885-1956) [British stage
    and motion picture actor]
    Tod Slaughter
Slavenska, Mia. See:
    CORAK, MIA
Slavery, The Napoleon of. See:
    CALHOUN, JOHN
        CALDWELL
Slaves, Attorney General for
    Runaway. See:
    CHASE, SALMON PORTLAND
SLAVITT, DAVID R. (1935-)
    [American teacher, editor,
    book reviewer and author]
    Henry Sutton
Slavs, The Apostle to the. See:
    Apostles to the Slavs
    CONSTANTINE
    METHODIUS
    SCHAUFFLER, HENRY
        ALBERT
Slayer of Bulgarians (Bulgarok-
    tonos). See:
    BASIL II

939

SLEEPER, JOHN SHERBURNE
(1794-1878) [American
mariner, journalist and
author]
Hawser Martingale
Sleep'n Eat. See:
BEST, WILLIE
Sleeps, The Chief Who Never.
See: WAYNE, ANTHONY
Sleepy Phil. See:
KNOX, PHILANDER
CHASE
Sleidanus, Johannes. See:
PHILIPPI, JOHANNES
Slender, Robert, Stocking
Weaver. See:
FRENEAU, PHILIP
MORIN
SLESAR, HENRY (1927-)
[American advertising
executive and author]
O. H. Leslie
Slick. See:
JONES, WILMORE
Slick, Jersey. See:
TICHENOR, ISAAC
Slick, Jonathan. See:
STEPHENS, ANN SOPHIA
WINTERBOTHAM
Slick, Sam. See:
HALLIBURTON, THOMAS
CHANDLER
Slick, Sam, Jr. See:
HAMMETT, SAMUEL
ADAMS
Slide. See:
HAMPTON, LOCKSLEY
WELLINGTON
Slim. See:
GAILLARD, BULEE
SUMMERVILLE,
GEORGE J.
WILLIAMS, CLYDE C.
Slim, Memphis. See:
CHATMAN, PETER
Slim Pickens. See:
LINDLEY, LOUIS BERT
Sling, The Man with the.
See: RANDOLPH, JOHN
Slinging Sammy, See:
BAUGH, SAMUEL ADRIAN
Slingsby, Philip. See:

WILLIS, NATHANIEL
PARKER
Slingshot Charley. See:
TAYLOR, CHARLEY
Slippery Dick. See:
CONNOLLY, RICHARD
Slippery Sam. See:
TILDEN, SAMUEL JONES
SLOAN, JAMES FORMAN
(1874-1933) [American
jockey]
Toad Sloan
Tod Sloan
Todhunter
Slogan. See:
SMYTHE, JOHN HENRY,
JR.
Slogan Man, The. See:
SMYTHE, JOHN HENRY,
JR.
SLOOTS, PATSY (1929-)
[British motion picture
actress]
Susan Shaw
Slop, Doctor. See:
STODDART, SIR JOHN
Slope, The Wild Humorist of
the Pacific. See:
CLEMENS, SAMUEL
LANGHORNE
Sloper, Ally. See:
ROSS, CHARLES HENRY
Sloppy. See:
THURSTON, HOLLIS JOHN
SLOTE, GILBERT MONROE
(1929-) [American
composer]
Gil Slote
Slow Drag. See:
PAVAGEAU, ALCIDE
Slow Trot, Old. See:
THOMAS, GEORGE HENRY
SLOWITZKY, MICHAEL
(1893-1962) [American
violinist and composer]
Michael Edwards
Sluggard, The (Le Fainéant). See:
LOUIS V
Slugger. See:
BURNS, JOHN IRVING
Sly Sweeney, The. See:
SWEENEY, PETER BARR

SLYE, LEONARD (1912-)
[American cowboy singing
star and motion picture
actor]
Roy Rogers
The World's Top Boots-and-
Saddle Star
Smack. See:
HENDERSON, JAMES
FLETCHER
Smek
Small-beer Poet, The. See:
FITZGERALD, WILLIAM
THOMAS
Small-coal Man, The Musical.
See: BRITTON, THOMAS
Small, Ernest. See:
LENT, BLAIR
Small, William. See:
EVERSLEY, DAVID
EDWARD CHARLES
Smectymnuus, composite pseud.
of EDMUND CALAMY (The
Elder) (1600-66), STEPHEN
MARSHALL (c.1594-1655),
MATTHEW NEWCOMEN
(c.1610-69), WILLIAM
SPURSTOWE (c.1605-66)
and THOMAS YOUNG
(Thomas Junius), (1587-
1655), [English churchmen
and pamphleteers]
Smectymnuus. See also:
CALAMY, EDMUND
MARSHALL, STEPHEN
YOUNG, THOMAS
SMEDLEY, FRANCIS
EDWARD (1818-64)
[English novelist]
Frank Smedley
Smek. See:
MAGNUS II
Smack
SMEKALOVA, HANA (c.1915-)
[Franco-Czech motion
picture actress]
Florence Marley
SMETANA, BEDRICH (1824-84)
[Czech musician]
The Father of the Czech
Nationalist School of
Composition

Smiley, Jim. See:
SPEARS, RAYMOND
SMILEY
Smiling Jim. See:
FARLEY, JAMES
ALOYSIUS
Smith. See:
GOW, CAPTAIN JOHN
SMYTHE
Smith, Adam. See:
GOODMAN, GEORGE J.W.
SMITH, ALBERT RICHARD
(1816-60) [English novelist,
humorist and lecturer]
The Monarch of Mont Blanc
SMITH, ALEXANDER (fl.1714-
26) [British biographer]
Captain Smith
SMITH, ALEXANDER (1760?-
1829) [British seaman,
"Bounty" mutineer]
John Adams
SMITH, ALFRED ALOYSIUS
(c.1861-1931) [English
adventurer]
Trader Horn
SMITH, ALFRED EMANUEL
(1873-1944) [American
political leader]
The Happy Warrior
Al Smith
Smith, Augustine. See:
GALLITZIN, DEMETRIUS
AUGUSTINE
SMITH, BARBARA HERRNSTEIN
(1932-) [American educator
and author]
Barbara Herrnstein
SMITH, BERNARD (1630-1708)
[English organ builder]
Father Smith
SMITH, BESSIE (c.1900-37)
[American Negro blues
singer]
The Empress of the Blues
Smith, Carmichael. See:
LINEBARGER, PAUL MYRON
ANTHONY
Smith, Caesar. See:
TREVOR, ELLESTON
SMITH, CHARLES HENRY
(1826-1903) [American

humorist]
Bill Arp
SMITH, CLADYS (1908-)
[American jazz
musician (trumpet,
trombone, singer,
leader)]
Jabbo Smith
SMITH, CLARENCE (1904-29)
[American jazz
musician (piano, singer,
composer)]
Pinetop Smith
SMITH, DODIE (189?-)
[English playwright and
novelist]
C. L. Anthony
Charles Henry Percy
SMITH, DONALD AUMONT
(1922-) [American
musician and composer]
Don Smith
SMITH, DOROTHY JACQUELINE
KEELY (1932-)
[American popular
singer]
Keely Smith
SMITH, DOROTHY STAFFORD
(1905-) [English teacher
and author]
Sarah Stafford Smith
SMITH, DOROTHY WHITEHILL
(1893-) [American
author]
Martha Trent
SMITH, ELIZABETH
OAKES (1806-93) [Amer-
ican lecturer, reformer
and poet]
Ernest Helfenstein
Elizabeth Oaksmith
SMITH, ELLISON DuRANT
(1866-1944) [American
politician; congressman
from South Carolina]
Cotton Ed
SMITH, ERNEST BRAMAH
(1867-1942) [English
humorist and detective
story writer]
Ernest Bramah
Smith, Father. See:

GALITZIN, DIMITRI
AUGUSTINE
SMITH, FLORENCE MARGARET
(1902-) [British poet,
broadcaster and author]
Stevie Smith
SMITH, FRANCES CHRISTINE
(1904-) [American
educator, journalist and
author]
Jean Smith
SMITH, FRANCES OCTAVIA
(1912-) [American
singer, author and
actress]
Dale Evans
The Queen of the Cowgirls
The Queen of the West
SMITH, FRANCIS HENNEY
(1812-80)
[American Confederate
officer; Superintendent
of Virginia Military
Institute]
Old Spex
SMITH, FRANCIS MARION
(1846-1931) [American
borax mine owner]
The Borax King
Borax Smith
SMITH, FRANCES SHUBAEL
(1819-87) [American
publisher; writer of dime
novels]
The Chancellor
Caleb Clootz
Ichabod Crane, Jr.
Daisey
W. A. Devon
Witch Hazel
James A. Maitland
Poningoe
SMITH, FREDERICK ESCREET
(1922-) [British author]
David Farrell
SMITH, GEORGE HENRY
(1873-1931) [American
editor and author]
Farmer Smith
Uncle Henry
SMITH, GEORGE JOSEPH
(1872-1915) [British

murderer]
The Brides in the Bath
Murderer
SMITH, GLADYS MARY (1893-)
[Canadian-American
motion picture actress and
film executive]
America's Sweetheart
America's Sweetheart
Emeritus
Gladys Pickford
Mary Pickford
Queen of the Movies
The World's Sweetheart
SMITH, GOLDWIN (1823-1910)
[British historian and
miscellaneous writer]
A Bystander
SMITH, HARRY ALLEN
(1907-) [American
journalist, humorist
and author]
H. Allen Smith
By Miss Ella Vator
SMITH, HELEN AINSLIE
(fl. 1885-1900) [American
author]
Hazel Shepard
SMITH, HENRY BOYNTON
(1815-77) [American
Presbyterian theologian]
The Hero of Reunion
SMITH, HEZEKIAH LEROY
GORDON (1909-)
[American jazz musician
(composer, leader,
violin, singer)]
Stuff Smith
SMITH, HOLLAND McTYEIRE
(1882-1967) [American
marine general officer]
The Father of Modern
Amphibious Warfare
Howlin' Mad Smith
The Pacific Cyclone
SMITH, HORATIO (1779-1849)
[English poet and
novelist]
Horace Smith
SMITH, HOWARD VAN
(1910-) [American
journalist and author]

David Sommers
SMITH, JAMES ELLISON
(1910-) [American motion
picture actor]
James Ellison
SMITH, JAMES HENRY (18??-
-1907) [American
millionaire]
Silent Smith
SMITH, JAMES, JR. See:
Jim-Jim Crowd, The
SMITH, JAMES MONROE
(1888-1949) [American
educator and embezzler]
Jingle Money Smith
SMITH, JOHN (1570-1612)
[English nonconformist
clergyman]
The Se-baptist
SMITH, JOHN (1580-1631)
[English adventurer and
colonist in America]
Captain John Smith
The Father of Virginia
Thomas Watson
SMITH, JOHN (1618-52)
[British churchman]
John Smith of Cambridge
Smith, John, joint pseud. of
MARVIN THEODORE
HERRICK (1899-1966) and
HOYT HOPEWELL HUDSON
(1893-1944) [American
educators and authors]
SMITH, JOHN (1924-)
[English author]
C. Busby Smith
Smith, John. See also:
VAN ORDEN, ROBERT
SMITH, JOHN THOMAS (1766-
1833) [English engraver,
antiquary and art writer]
Rainy-Day Smith
Smith, Johnston. See:
CRANE, STEPHEN
SMITH, JOSEPH (1805-44)
[American founder of the
Church of Jesus Christ of
Latter Day Saints]
The Father of the Mormons
SMITH, KATHRYN ELIZABETH
(1909-) [American singer

and actress]
Kate Smith
The Moon Over the Mountain
Girl
Radio's Own Statue of
Liberty
The Songbird of the South
Smith, Lafayette. See:
HIGDON, HAL
SMITH, LAURA ROUNTREE
(1876-1924) [American
author]
Caroline Silver June
Smith, Lew. See:
FLOREN, LEE
SMITH, LINELL NASH
(1932-) [American
author and illustrator]
Nell Chenault
SMITH, MARGARET
(1934-) [British
actress]
Maggie Smith
SMITH-MASTERS, MARGARET
(1869-) [British
author]
Félicité le Fevre
Smith, Mr. See:
LOCKWOOD, RALPH
INGERSOLL
LOUIS-PHILIPPE
SMITH, MRS. MARY
PRUDENCE WELLS
(1840-) [American
author]
P. Thorne
SMITH, MONA (1909-)
[Australian-American
motion picture
actress]
Mona Barrie
Smith, Norman Edward Mace.
See: SHERATON, NEIL
SMITH, PHYLLIS (1922?-)
[American classical
singer]
Phyllis Curtin
The Most Intelligent of
American Sopranos
SMITH, RICHARD EMERSON
(1922-) [American
makeup artist]

Dick Smith
SMITH, RICHARD PENN
(1799-1854) [American play-
wright and miscellaneous
writer]
Penn Smith
SMITH, RODNEY (1860-1947)
[English evangelist]
The Gipsy Boy
Gipsy Smith
SMITH, RONALD GREGOR
(1913-) [Scottish
clergyman and author]
Sam Browne
Ronald Maxwell
Smith, S. S. See:
WILLIAMSON, THAMES
ROSS
Smith, Sacheverell. See:
DARLING, WILLIAM
YOUNG
SMITH, SARAH (1832-1911)
[English novelist and
humanitarian]
Hesba Stretton
SMITH, SARAH POGSON
(fl. 1826) [American
author]
A Lady
SMITH, SEBA (1792-1868)
[American author and
political satirist]
Major Jack Downing
Major Jack Downing of
Downingville
SMITH, SOLOMON FRANKLIN
(1801-69) [American actor]
Sol Smith
SMITH, SYDNEY (1778-1845)
[English divine, essayist
and wit]
Peter Plymley
Smith, The Late Ben. See:
MATHEWS, CORNELIUS
SMITH, THOMAS VERNON
(1890-) [American
politician; congressman
from Illinois]
Philosophy Smith
The Political Philosopher
SMITH, WALKER, JR. (1920-)
[American professional

boxer; world's welterweight
and middleweight champion]
Sugar Ray Robinson
SMITH, WALTER BEDELL
(1895-) [American
general officer, author
and statesman]
Beedle
Beetle
Bulldog
The General Manager of
the War
SMITH, WALTER CHALMERS
(1824-1908) [Scottish
poet]
Herman Knott
Orwell
SMITH, WALTER WELLESLEY
(1905-) [American
sports writer]
Red Smith
SMITH, WILLARD LAURENCE
(1927-) [American
management consultant
and author]
Will Laurence
SMITH, WILLIAM (1655-1705)
[Anglo-American
governor of Tangiers,
Africa]
Tangiers Smith
SMITH, WILLIAM (1730-1819)
[British actor]
Gentleman Smith
SMITH, WILLIAM (1769-1839)
[English geologist]
The Father of English
Geology
Fossil Smith
SMITH, WILLIAM (1796-1887)
[American politician,
mail contractor and gover-
nor of Virginia]
Extra Billy
SMITH, WILLIAM (1809-1907)
[American captor of the
pirate GIBBS]
Uncle Billy
SMITH, WILLIAM FARRAR
(1824-1903) [American
Civil War general
officer]

Baldy Smith
SMITH, WILLIAM HENRY
(1825-91) [English
politician; First Lord of the
Admiralty]
Old Morality
SMITH, WILLIAM HENRY
JOSEPH BERTHOL BONA-
PARTE BERTHOLOFF
(1897-) [American jazz
musician (piano, composer)]
Willie the Lion
Smith, William Henry Sedley.
See: SEDLEY, WILLIAM
HENRY
SMITH, WILLIAM RUSSELL
(1815-96) [American
politician]
Little Billy
SMITH, WILLIAM SOOY
(1830-1916) [American
Civil War general officer]
Sookey Smith
SMITH-WOODS, DOROTHY
BERYL (1904-) [English
author]
Beryl Moore
Smith, Z. Z. See:
WESTHEIMER, DAVID
SMITHELLS, ANABEL DOREEN
(fl. mid-20th cent.)
[English author]
Linda Boscawen
SMITHELLS, ROGER WILLIAM
(1905-) [British interior
decorator and author]
Sebastian Cash
SMITHSON, JAMES (1765-1829)
[French-born British
mineralogist and founder
of the Smithsonian
Institution]
James Lewis (Louis) Macie
Smoke, Old. See:
MORRISSEY, JOHN
Smokey. See:
ROBERDS, FRED A.
Smollett of the Stage, The.
See: FARQUHAR, GEORGE
SMOTHERS, RICHARD (1939-)
[American comedian,
singer and bassist]
Dick Smothers

SMOTHERS, THOMAS BOLYN,
JR. (1937-) [American
comedian, singer and
guitarist]
Tom Smothers
Smuggler, The Gentleman. See:
LAFITTE, JEAN
Smugglers, King of the. See:
HANCOCK, JOHN
Smyrnean Poet, The. See:
MIMNERMUS
SMYTHE. See also:
SMITH
Smith
SMYTHE, JOHN HENRY, JR.
(1883-)[American
slogan writer]
The Slogan Man
Slogan Smythe
SMYTHE, MARIA ANNE
(1756-1837) [Roman
Catholic widow, secret
wife of Prince of Wales
who was afterwards
GEORGE V of England]
Mrs. Fitzherbert
Snaeus Flavius. See:
KANTOROWICZ, HERMANN
Snake, The Black. See:
WAYNE, ANTHONY
Snapping Turtle of the Ohio, The.
See: FINK, MIKE
Snapping Turtle, The. See:
GLASS, GEORGE CARTER
SNEAD, SAMUEL JACKSON
(1912-) [American
professional golfer]
Sammy Snead
Slamming Sammy Snead
SNEDDON, ROBERT WILLIAM
(1880-1944) [Scottish-
American author]
Robert Guillaume
SNEIDER (SCHNITTER),
JOHANNES (1494-1566)
[German religious
reformer and follower
of MARTIN LUTHER]
Johannes Agricola
Magister Islebius
SNELL, WILLIAM (1938-)
[American composer,

author and illustrator]
Billy Snel
SNELLEN, JOHN H. (1859-1932)
[Boss canvasman for
Ringling circus]
Happy Jack
SNELLING, OSWALD FREDERICK
(1916-) [British commercial
artist, cartoonist and
author]
Oswald Frederick
SNELLING, WILLIAM JOSEPH
(1804-48) [American
fur trader, miner,
journalist and poet]
Solomon Bell
SNIDER, EDWIN DONALD
(1926-) [American profes-
sional baseball player]
Duke Snider
Snipe. See:
HANSEN, ROY FORD
Snooks, Baby. See:
BORACH, FANNY
Snooky. See:
YOUNG, EUGENE
Snorter. See:
CONNALLY, GEORGE
WALTER
Snow Baby, The. See:
PEARY, MARIE AHNIGHITO
Snow King, The. See:
FREDERICK V
GUSTAVUS II
Snow Queen, The. See:
STUART, ELIZABETH
Snow, Terry. See:
WOOLSEY, MARYHALE
SNOWDEN, ELMER CHESTER
(1900-) [American jazz
musician (banjo, guitar,
leader)]
Pops Snowden
SNOWDEN, JAMES (1860-)
[British author and
journalist]
Keighley Snowden
Snowshoe. See:
THOMPSON, JOHN A.
Snozz. See:
LOMBARDI, ERNEST
NATALI

Snub. See:
  MOSLEY, LAURENCE LEO
Snub Pollard. See:
  FRASER, HAROLD
Snuffy. See:
  STIRNWEISS, GEORGE
  HENRY
SNYDER, CHRISTOPHER
  (c.1755-70) [American
  victim of Revolutionary
  mob action]
  The First Martyr of the
  Revolution
SNYDER, EDWARD (1919-)
  [American composer and
  pianist]
  Eddie Snyder
SNYDER, FRANK J. (1893-1962)
  [American professional
  baseball player]
  Pancho
SNYDER, WILLIAM (1916-)
  [American composer and
  pianist]
  Bill Snyder
Soapy. See:
  WILLIAMS, G. MENNEN
Soapy Sam. See:
  WILBERFORCE, SAMUEL
Sobieski. See:
  JOHN III
Social Historian of the Café
  Society, The. See:
  BEEBE, LUCIUS
Social Settlements, Father
  of. See:
  TOYNBEE, ARNOLD
Socialist, The Boy. See:
  LONDON, JOHN
  GRIFFITH
Societies in America, The
  Father of Historical. See:
  PINTARD, JOHN
Society, The Savior of. See:
  BONAPARTE, CHARLES
  LOUIS NAPOLEON
Society, The Social Historian
  of the Café. See:
  BEEBE, LUCIUS
Sockless. See:
  SIMPSON, JERRY
Sockless Jerry. See:

SIMPSON, JERRY
Sockless Sage, The. See:
  SIMPSON, JERRY
Sockless Socrates. See:
  SIMPSON, JERRY
Sockless Statesman, The. See:
  SIMPSON, JERRY
SOCRATES (c.470-399 B.C.)
  [Greek philosopher]
  The Wisest Man of Greece
Socrates, Sockless. See:
  SIMPSON, JERRY
Socrates, The American. See:
  FRANKLIN, BENJAMIN
Socrates, The British. See:
  BACON, SIR FRANCIS
Socrates, The English. See:
  JOHNSON, DR. SAMUEL
Soda Ash Johnny. See:
  HORAN, JOHN MICHAEL
SODERBERG, PERCY
  MEASDAY (1901-)
  [British educator, broad-
  caster and author]
  George Measday
  G. E. Seebord
  Peter Underhill
Sodoma, Il. See:
  BAZZI, GIOVANNI
  ANTONIO DE'
Sodorna, Il. See:
  BAZZI, GIOVANNI ANTONIO
  DE'
SOHR (SORE), MARTIN
  (1486-1566) [German writer
  on music theory]
  Martin Agricola
Soil, A Son of the. See:
  FLETCHER, JOSEPH
  SMITH
SOKOLOFF, MELVIN (1929-)
  [American jazz musician
  (drums)]
  Mel Lewis
Sol. See:
  SMITH, SOLOMON
  FRANKLIN
Sol Lake. See:
  LACHOFF, SOL
Solange Strong. See:
  HERTZ, NELLIE SOLANGE
  STRONG

Solanito. See:
  SOLANO, RAMÓN
SOLANO, RAMON (1933-)
  [Spanish bullfighter]
  Solanito
SOLARIO, ANTONIO (c. 1382-
  1455) [Neapolitan painter]
  Lo Zingaro
Soldado, El. See:
  CASTRO, LUIS
SOLDANO, ANTHONY (1927-)
  [American composer and
  musician]
  Tony Dano
Soldat, Mon (My Soldier). See:
  HENRY IV
Soldier, My (Mon Soldat). See:
  HENRY IV
Soldier of Democracy, The
  Armed. See:
  BONAPARTE, NAPOLEON
Soldier Parson, The. See:
  CALDWELL, JAMES
Soldier, The Quaker. See:
  BIDDLE, CLEMENT
Soldier, Uniformed. See:
  GRANT, HIRAM ULYSSES
Soldier's Friend, The. See:
  CURTIN, ANDREW GREGG
  WARD, MARCUS
    LAWRENCE
Soleil, Le Roi (The Sun King).
  See: LOUIS XIV
Solemn Doctor, The. See:
  GOETHALS, HENRY
SOLER, ANTONIO RUIZ
  (1921-) [Spanish dancer,
  choreographer and director]
  Antonio
Solid Doctor, The. See:
  BRADWARDINE, THOMAS
Solid Man, The. See:
  MULDOON, WILLIAM
SOLIMAN. See:
  SULAIMAN I or II
Solitaire. See:
  ROBB, JOHN S.
Solitario, El. See:
  ESTÉBANEZ CALDERÓN,
    SERAFÍN
Sologub, Fedor. See:
  TETERNIKOV, FEDOR

  KUZMICH
Solomon. See:
  Bolo, Solomon
  CUTNER, SOLOMON
Solomon Bell. See:
  SNELLING, WILLIAM
    JOSEPH
Solomon Eagle. See:
  SQUIRE, JOHN COLLINGS
Solomon, Elijah (Elias)
  Ben. See:
  WILNA, ELIJAH (ELEAS)
SOLOMON, HERBERT JAY
  (1930-) [American jazz
  musician (flute, composer,
  leader, tenor saxophone)]
  Herbie Mann
Solomon, King. See:
  HOLCOMBE, SOLOMON
Solomon of England, The. See:
  JAMES I
Solomon of France, The. See:
  CHARLES V
  LOUIS IX
Solomon Secondsight. See:
  McHENRY, JAMES
Solomon Secondthoughts. See:
  KENNEDY, JOHN
    PENDLETON
Solomon Shingle. See:
  BELLAW, AMERICUS
    WELLINGTON
Solomon, The British. See:
  JAMES I
Solomon, The English. See:
  JAMES I
Solomon, The Scottish. See:
  JAMES I
Solomon, The Second. See:
  JAMES I
Solomons, Ikey, Esq., Junior.
  See: THACKERAY,
    WILLIAM MAKEPEACE
SOLON. See:
  Seven Sages of Greece,
    The
Solon of French Prose, The.
  See: BALZAC, JEAN
    LOUIS GUEZ DE
Solon of Parnassus, The. See:
  BOILEAU-DESPRÉAUX,
    NICHOLAS

SOLOVIEV, VLADIMIR
(1853-1900) [Russian
philosopher]
The First Russian
Philosopher
SOLTERS, JULIUS JOSEPH
(1908-) [American
professional baseball
player]
Lemons Solters
SOLVAY, ERNEST
(1838-1922) [Belgian
manufacturing chemist]
The Carnegie of Belgium
SOMAN, SHIRLEY (1922-)
[American editor and
author]
Shirley Camper
Sombrerero, El (The Hatmaker).
See: RUIZ, ANTONIO
Somebody Else, The Man Who
Is Always. See:
WEISENFREUND, MUNI
Somebody, M.D.C., 1817.
See: NEAL, JOHN
SOMERBY, FREDERICK
THOMAS (1814-71) [Amer-
ican author]
Cymon
Somers, Paul. See:
WINTERTON, PAUL
Somerset, The Proud Duke of.
See: SEYMOUR,
CHARLES, 6TH DUKE
OF SOMERSET
SOMERSET, WILLIAM (1090?-
1143?) [English churchman
and historian]
William of Malmsbury
SOMERVILLE. See also:
SOMMERVILLE
Sommerville
SOMERVILLE, EDITH ANNA
OENINE. See:
Herring, Geilles
Sommer, Elke. See:
SCHLETZ, ELKE
Sommers, David. See:
SMITH, HOWARD VAN
SOMMERVILLE [Sommerville].
See also:
SOMERVILLE

SOMMERVILLE, ANDREW
(fl. 1861-65) [American
Civil War Union soldier;
active in nursing wounded
soldiers]
Faithful Andy
Handy Andy
Sommerville, Frankfort. See:
STORY, SOMMERVILLE
Son. See:
HOUSE, EDDIE JAMES,
JR.
Son Jimmy. See:
ROOSEVELT, JAMES
Son of His Grandfather, The. See:
HARRISON, BENJAMIN
Son of Texas, The Favorite. See:
GARNER, JOHN NANCE
Son of the Last Man, The. See:
CHARLES II
Son of the Man, The. See:
BONAPARTE, NAPOLEON
FRANÇOIS CHARLES
JOSEPH
Son of the Soil, A. See:
FLETCHER, JOSEPH SMITH
Son of the Star. See:
BAR COCHEBA, SIMON
Son of the Steppe (Stepnyak).
See: KRAVCHINSKY,
SERGIUS MIKHAILOVICH
Son of Thunder (Bonerge). See:
JAMES THE GREATER, ST.
JOHN THE EVANGELIST,
ST.
Son, Seattle's Sensational. See:
ZIONCHECK, MARION A.
Son, The Old Titanic Earth. See:
WEBSTER, DANIEL
Son, York's Tall. See:
PORTER, WILLIAM
TROTTER
Song, Queen of the Gospel. See:
JACKSON, MAHALIA
Song, The Father of. See:
HOMER
Song, The First Lady of. See:
FITZGERALD, ELLA
Song, The Laureate of. See:
LONGFELLOW, HENRY
WADSWORTH
Song, The Morning Star of. See:

949

CHAUCER, GEOFFREY
Song, The Queen of. See:
   CATALANI, ANGELICA
Songbird of the South, The.
   See: SMITH,
      KATHRYN ELIZABETH
Songs, The Father of Modern
   French. See:
   PANARD, CHARLES-
      FRANÇOIS
Songwriter, The G. I. 's Own.
   See: LOESSER, FRANK
      HENRY
Sonia Bleeker. See:
   ZIM, SONIA BLEEKER
Sonia Deane. See:
   SOUTAR, GWENDOLINE
      AMY
Sonia Dresdel. See:
   OBEE, LOIS
Sonnet, The Prince of the. See:
   BELLAY, JOACHIM DU
Sonnie. See also:
   Sonny
   Sunny
Sonnie Hale. See:
   MONRO, ROBERT HALE
Sonny. See:
   BERMAN, SAUL
   BROWN, CLAUDE
   BURKE, J. FRANCIS
   CLARKE, CONRAD
      YEATIS
   COHN, GEORGE THOMAS
   CRISS, WILLIAM
   DUNHAM, ELMER
      LEWIS
   GREER, WILLIAM
      ALEXANDER
   IGOE, OWEN JOSEPH
   LISTON, CHARLES
   PAYNE, PERCIVAL
   ROLLINS, THEODORE
      WALTER
   Sonnie
   STITT, EDWARD
   Sunny
   TUFTS, BOWEN
      CHARLETON
   WHITE, ELLERTON
      OSWALD
Sonny Boy Williamson. See:

MILLER, RICE
Sonny Hendrix. See:
   BARDAN, STANLEY
      HOWARD
Sonny Red. See:
   KYNER, SYLVESTER
Sonny Terry. See:
   TEDDELL, SAUNDERS
Sonrisa, Niño de la Eterna. See:
   TORRES, EMILIO
SONTUP, DANIEL (1922-)
   [American editor and
   author]
   John Clarke
   David Saunders
Soo, Chung Ling. See:
   ROBINSON, WILLIAM
      ELLSWORTH
Sookey. See:
   SMITH, WILLIAM SOOY
SOONG, TSE-VEN (1891-)
   [Chinese financier]
   T. V.
Sophia Loren. See:
   VILLANI (SCICOLONE),
      SOPHIA
Sophie May. See:
   CLARKE, REBECCA
      SOPHIA
Sophie Tucker. See:
   ABUZA, SOPHIE
Sophist, The. See:
   AELIANUS, CLAUDIUS
Sophisticated Slapstick, The
   Mistress of. See:
   LILLIE, BEATRICE
      GLADYS
SOPHOCLES (c. 495-406 B. C.)
   [Greek tragic poet and
   dramatist]
   The Attic Bee
   The Attic Homer
Sopranos, The Most Intelligent
   of American. See:
   SMITH, PHYLLIS
Sordo, El. See:
   MONTES, ANTONIO
SORE. See:
   SOHR (SORE), MARTIN
SOREL, AGNES (1409-50)
   [Mistress of King CHARLES
   VII of France]

La Dame de Beauté
SOROKIN, PITIRIM
   ALEXANDROVITCH
   (1889-) [Russian
   sociologist and author]
Tchaadaieff
SORRELL, VICTOR GARLAND
   (1902-) [American
   professional baseball
   player]
Ace
Baby-doll
Lawyer
The Philosopher
Vic
Sorrow, The Daughter of. See:
   CHARLOTTE, MARIE
   THÉRÈSE
SORYA, FRANÇOISE (1932-)
   [French motion
   picture actress]
Anouk
Anouk Aimee
Sot, The. See:
   SELIM II
SOTER (SOTERUS) (died
   c.175) [Supreme Pontiff
   of Roman Catholic Church]
Pope Soter (Soterus)
St. Soter
St. Soterus
Soter (The Preserver). See:
   ANTIOCHUS I
   ATTALUS I
   DEMETRIUS I
   PTOLEMY I
   PTOLEMY VIII
Sothern. See also:
   SOUTHERN
   Southern
Sothern, Ann. See:
   LAKE, HARRIETTE
SOUBIROUS, MARIE
   BERNARDE (1844-79)
   [French visionary]
St. Bernadette
SOUCHON, EDMOND II, M. D.
   (1897-) [American jazz
   musician (banjo, guitar,
   singer, leader)]
Doc Souchon
Soudley, Henry. See:

WOOD, JAMES PLAY-
   STED
Soul, Having an Immortal
   (Anushirvan). See:
   KHOSRAU I
Soul of Empty Eminence, The.
   See: DODD, JAMES
   WILLIAM
Soul of the Fronde, The. See:
   LONGUEVILLE, ANNE,
   DUCHESSE DE
Soult, Marshall. See:
   KNAPP, SAMUEL
   LORENZO
SOUMAROKOV, ALEXANDRE
   PÉTROVITCH (1718-77)
   [Russian poet]
The Russian Voltaire
Sound Money. See:
   GLASS, GEORGE CARTER
Soup. See:
   SHAUGHNESSY, CLARK
   DANIEL
Soupbone. See:
   HINES, MILTON
Souphouse Charlie. See:
   BONAPARTE, CHARLES
   JOSEPH
Soupy Sales. See:
   HINES, MILTON
SOUSA. See also:
   Souza
SOUSA, JOHN PHILIP (1856-
   1932) [American composer
   and bandmaster]
The March King
SOUTAR, GWENDOLINE AMY
   (1904-) [English author]
Sonia Deane
South America, The Apostle of.
   See: FOWLER, CHARLES
   HENRY
South America, The Washington
   of. See:
   BOLÍVAR, SIMÓN
South Carolina Gamecock, The.
   See: SUMTER, THOMAS
South Carolina, The Eagle
   Orator of. See:
   CALHOUN, JOHN CALD-
   WELL
South Carolina, The Swamp Fox

of. See:
MARION, FRANCIS
South, Clark. See:
SWAIN, DWIGHT
VREELAND
SOUTH, EDWARD OTHA
(1904- 62) [American
jazz musician (violin,
leader)]
The Dark Angel of the
Violin
Eddie South
South, Edwin. See:
CAMPBELL, BARTLEY T.
South, Paul Jones of the. See:
SEMMES, RAPHAEL
South, The Bayard of the. See:
MARION, FRANCIS
South, The Black Knight of
the. See:
McCLUNG, ALEXANDER
South, The Cooper of the.
See: SIMMS, WILLIAM
GILMORE
South, The Doughty of the.
See: RICHARDS,
THOMAS ADDISON
South, The Horace Mann of
the. See: RUFFNER,
WILLIAM HENRY
South, The Laureate of the.
See: HAYNE, PAUL
HAMILTON
South, The Lion of the. See:
HINDMAN, THOMAS
CARMICHAEL
South, The Macaulay of the.
See: JONES, CHARLES
COLCOCK
South, The Nathan Hale of
the. See: DAVIS, SAM
South, The Poet Laureate of the.
See: HAYNE, PAUL
HAMILTON
South, The Riley of the. See:
STANTON, FRANK LEBBY
South, The Silver-tongued
Orator of the. See:
BAKER, ALPHEUS
South, The Songbird of the.
See: SMITH,
KATHRYN ELIZABETH

SOUTHARD, HELEN FAIRBAIRN
(1906-) [American
psychologist and author]
Helen Fairbairn
Southard, J. H. See:
MORRIS, CHARLES
SMITH
Southcote, George. See:
ASHTON, SIR GEORGE
GREY
SOUTHCOTT, JOANNA (c. 1750-
1814) [English religious
fanatic]
The Woman of Rev. XII
SOUTHERN [Southern]. See also:
Sothern
Southern Army, The Florence
Nightingale of the. See:
TRADER, ELLA KING
NEWSOM
Southern Cooper, The. See:
SIMMS, WILLIAM GILMORE
Southern Kentucky, The Daniel
Boone of. See:
LYNN, BENJAMIN
Southern Scott, The. See:
ARIOSTO, LUDOVICO
SOUTHERN, TERRY. See:
Kenton, Maxwell
Southern Tycho, The. See:
HALLEY, EDMUND
SOUTHEY, CAROLINE ANNE
BOWLES (1786-1854)
[British poet and prose
writer]
The Cowper of Our Modern
Poetesses
SOUTHEY, ROBERT (1774-1843)
[English poet and man of
letters]
Bion
Abel Shufflebottom
SOUTHLAND, T. (fl. mid 17th
cent.) [English nobleman
and playwright]
A Person of Honour
SOUTHOUSE-CHEYNEY,
REGINALD EVELYN
PETER (1896-1951)
[English author of detective
stories]
Peter Cheyney

SOUTHWICK, SOLOMON
(1773-1839) [American
editor and poet]
Henry Homespun
SOUTHWOLD, STEPHEN
(1887-1964) [English
novelist and author of
books for juveniles]
Neil Bell
Paul Martens
"Miles"
SOUTHWORTH, WILLIAM H.
(1893-) [American
baseball club manager]
Billy Southworth
Billy the Kid
Souza. See also:
SOUSA
Souza, E. See:
SCOTT, EVELYN
Souza, Madame de. See:
FILLEUL, ADÈLE
MARIE ÉMILIE
Souzay, Gérard. See:
TISSERAND, GÉRARD
MARCEL
Sow, The Great. See:
ISABELLA OF BAVARIA
SOWDEN, SIR WILLIAM JOHN
(1858-) [Australian
author]
Pencil
Scribbler
SOWER. See also:
SAUER
SOWER, CHRISTOPHER
(1721-84) [German-
American pacifist and
humanist]
The Bread-father (Der
Brod-vater)
SOWERBY, ARTHUR LINDSAY
McRAE (1899-) [British
chemist, photography
consultant and author]
Lindsay McRae
SPAATZ, CARL (1891-)
[American general
officer]
Tooey Spaats
Spades Lee, Old. See:
LEE, ROBERT

EDWARD
Spades, Old Ace of. See:
LEE, ROBERT EDWARD
Spades, The Jack of. See:
LOGAN, JOHN ALEXANDER
SPAETH, SIGMUND GOTTFRIED
(1885-1965) [American
musicologist, writer and
lecturer]
The Tune Detective
Spagnoletto, Lo (The Little
Spaniard). See:
RIBERA, JUSEPE DE
Spain, Christina of. See:
MARIA CHRISTINA
Spain, The Livy of. See:
MARIANA, JUAN DE
Spain, The Petrarch of. See:
VEGA, GARCILASSO DE
LA
SPALDING. See also:
SPAULDING
Spaulding
SPALDING, ALBERT (1888-1953)
[American violinist]
America's Own Violinist
SPALDING, GILBERT R.
(1812-80) [American circus
entrepreneur]
Doctor Spalding
Spaniard, The Little (Lo Spagnolet-
to). See:
RIBERA, JUSEPE DE
SPANIER, FRANCIS JOSEPH
(1906-) [American jazz
musician (trumpet, leader)]
Muggsy
Spanish Addison, The. See:
MONTENEGRO, FREY
BENITO FEYJOO Y
Spanish Brutus, The. See:
GUZMÁN, ALPHONSO
PÉREZ DE
Spanish Drama, The Father of
the. See:
CARPIO, LOPE FÉLIX
DE VEGA
ENCINA (ENZINA), JUAN
DEL
Spanish Ennius, The. See:
MENA, JUAN DE
Spanish Horaces, The, name

953

applied to BARTOLOMÉ
LEONARDO DE ARGEN-
SOLA (1562-1631) and his
brother, LUPERCIO DE
ARGENSOLA (1559-1613)
[Spanish poets]
Spanish Jack. See:
GONZÁLES, BLI
Spanish Michelangelo, The. See:
CANO, ALONSO
Spanish Molière, The. See:
MORATÍN, LEANDRO
FERNANDEZ DE
Spanish Petrarch, The. See:
VEGA, GARCILASSO
DE LA
Spanish Poetry, The Prince
of. See:
VEGA, GARCILASSO
DE LA
Spanish Romanticism, The
Spoiled Darling of. See:
MORAL, JOSÉ ZORRILLAY
Spanish Tennyson, The. See:
NÚÑEZ DE ARCE,
GASPAR
Spanish Theater, The
Patriarch of the. See:
ENCINA (ENZINA),
JUAN DEL
SPANNOCHI, MARCELLO
CERVINI DEGLI (1501-55)
[Supreme Pontiff of
Roman Catholic Church]
Pope Marcellus II
Spargo, Tony. See:
SBARBARO, TONY
Sparks, Timothy. See:
DICKENS, CHARLES
JOHN HUFFAM
Sparling, Ned. See:
SENARENS, LUIS
PHILIP
SPAULDING [Spaulding].
See also:
SPALDING
SPAULDING, ELBRIDGE
GERRY (1809-97)
[American politician;
framer of Act providing
for issuance of paper
currency]

The Father of Greenbacks
Spaulding, Leonard. See:
BRADBURY, RAY
DOUGLAS
Speaker, Louisiana's Loud. See:
LONG, HUEY PIERCE
SPEAKER, TRISTRAM E.
(1888-1958) [American
professional baseball
player and manager]
Gray Eagle
Tris Speaker
Speaks Her Mind, The Woman
Who Always. See:
COX-OLIVER, EDNA MAY
Speaks, One Who (Uei Tlatoani).
See: MONTEZUMA II
SPEARS, RAYMOND SMILEY
(1876-) [American
author]
Jim Smiley
Spec, Mr. See:
THACKERAY, WILLIAM
MAKEPEACE
SPECKBACHER, JOSEPH
(1767-1820) [Tirolese
patriot]
Der Mann Vom Rinn
Specs. See:
POWELL, GORDON
Spex
WRIGHT, CHARLES
Specs, The Old Boy in. See:
DAVIS, MATHEW
LIVINGSTON
Speculative Philosopher,
America's Foremost. See:
WEISS, PAUL
Speech Lee, One. See:
LEE, JOSHUA BRYAN
Speech, Single. See:
HAMILTON, WILLIAM
GERARD
HEMPHILL, JOSEPH
HOUGHTON, RICHARD
MONCTON MILNES, 1ST
BARON
Speed. See:
JOHNSON, HAROLD
MELARO, H. J. M.
Speed Magee. See:
JOHNSON, HAROLD

Speed, Nell. See:
    SAMPSON, EMMA SPEED
Speedy. See:
    JONES, RUFUS
Spellbinder of the Pacific
    Coast, The Silver-
    tongued. See:
    DELMAS, DELPHIN
    MICHAEL
SPELLMAN, FRANCIS JOSEPH
    (1889-1967)[American Ro-
    man Catholic Cardinal, edi-
    torial writer and translator]
    Cardinal Spellman
Spence, J.A.D. See:
    ELIOT, THOMAS STEARNS
SPENCE, SIR BASIL UNWIN
    (1907-) [Scottish architect]
    St. Basil
SPENCER [Spencer]. See also:
    SPENSER
    Spenser
Spencer, Cornelia. See:
    YAUKEY, GRACE SYDEN-
    STRICKER
Spencer Davenport. See:
    STRATEMEYER,
    EDWARD L.
Spencer, Dr. Bruce. See:
    ABEL, ALAN IRWIN
SPENCER, ELIHU (1721-84)
    [American clergyman
    and missionary to
    Indians]
    Ready Money Spencer
SPENCER, GABRIEL
    (died 1598) [English
    actor]
    Gabriel
SPENCER, JOHN (fl. 1605)
    [English comedian]
    Hans Stockfisch
Spencer, Norman D. See:
    FACTOR, JOHN
Spencer, Warren. See:
    LENGEL, WILLIAM
    CHARLES
SPENER, PHILIPP JAKOB (1635-
    1705) [German theologian]
    The Father of Pietism
SPENSER [Spenser]. See also:
    SPENCER

Spencer
Spenser, Avis S. See:
    UNKNOWN
SPENSER, EDMUND (c. 1552-99)
    [English poet]
    Colin Clout
    M. Immerito
    The Poet's Poet
    The Prince of Poets
    The Prince of Poets in His
    Time
SPENSER, HENRY (1377-99)
    [British bishop]
    The Fighting Prelate
Spenser of English Prose
    Writers, The. See:
    TAYLOR, JEREMY
Speranza. See:
    WILDE, JANE FRANCISCA
    SPERANZA, LADY
Sperry, J.E. See:
    EISENSTAT, JANE SPERRY
Sperry, Raymond, Jr. See:
    STRATEMEYER,
    EDWARD L.
SPEWACK, BELLA COHEN
    (1899-) [Hungarian-
    American playwright]
    Bella Cohen
SPEWACK, SAMUEL (1898-)
    [Russian-American play-
    wright]
    A.A. Abbott
Spex. See also:
    Specks
Spex, Old. See:
    SMITH, FRANCIS HENNEY
Sphinx of the Rock Island, The.
    See: MOORE, WILLIAM
    HENRY
Sphinx, The. See:
    ROOSEVELT, FRANKLIN
    DELANO
SPICER, BART (1918-) [American
    author]
    Jay Barbette
Spider. See:
    SWEENEY, PETER BARR
Spider, The Universal. See:
    LOUIS XI
Spider Webb. See:
    GOHMAN, FRED JOSEPH

SPIEGEL, CLARA. See:
   Jaynes, Clare
Spiel, Hilde. See:
   DE MENDELSSOHN,
   HILDE MARIA
SPIELMANN, MARION HARRY
   (1858-) [British author,
   art and literary critic]
   M. H. S.
Spike. See:
   HAMILTON, GEORGE
   HUGHES, PATRICK
   JONES, LINDLEY
   ARMSTRONG
   KNOBLAUGH,   GLEN
   GRAY
   MILLIGAN, TERENCE
   ALAN
   WALLACE, J.K.
SPILLANE, FRANK
   MORRISON (1918-)
   [American writer of hard-
   boiled detective
   novels]
   Mickey Spillane
SPILLUS, ELIZABETH JANE
   (1924-) [Canadian
   author]
   Elizabeth Bott
SPILSBURY, SIR BERNARD
   HENRY (1877-1947)
   [British pathologist]
   The Ideal Scientific
   Witness
Spinster, An Elderly. See:
   WILSON, MARGARET
Spiritual Father of Kant, The.
   See: HUME, DAVID
Spiro Igloo. See:
   HOFFMAN, ABBIE
Spit, Sam. See:
   SCHNECK, STEPHEN
SPITELARA, JOSEPH T.
   (1937-) [American
   jazz musician (clarinet,
   saxophone)]
   Pee Wee
Spitfire, The Mexican. See:
   VILLABOS, GUADALOUPE
   VELEZ DE
SPIVERY, WILLIAM (1930-)
   [American composer and

   singer]
   Bill Spivery
Splendid Splinter, The. See:
   WILLIAMS, THEODORE
   SAMUEL
Splendor of God (Baha Ullah).
   See: MIRZA
   HUSEYN ALI
Splendor of the Italian Race,
   That Singular. See:
   ALIGHIERI, DURANTE
Splinter, The Splendid. See:
   WILLIAMS, THEODORE
   SAMUEL
Splitter, The Rail. See:
   LINCOLN, ABRAHAM
SPOCK, BENJAMIN McLANE
   (1903-) [American
   physician, author and
   peace movement leader]
   Dr. Spock
SPOFFORTH, FREDERICK
   ROBERT (1853-1926)
   [Australian cricket player]
   The Demon
Spoiled Darling of Spanish
   Romanticism, The. See:
   MORAL, JOSÉ ZORRILLA Y
Spoilsman, That Candid. See:
   FARLEY, JAMES
   ALOYSIUS
Spoke. See:
   SPEAKER, TRISTRAM E.
Spondee. See:
   TYLER, ROYALL
Spoon. See:
   BUTLER, BENJAMIN
   FRANKLIN
Spoon Butler, Silver. See:
   BUTLER, BENJAMIN
   FRANKLIN
Spoon Stealer. See:
   BUTLER, BENJAMIN
   FRANKLIN
Spoonbill. See:
   REANEY, JAMES CRERAR
Sporting Parson, The. See:
   RUSSELL, JOHN
Sports Writers for Boys, The
   Dean of. See:
   BARBOUR, RALPH HENRY
Sportsman, The Poet. See:

McLELLAN, ISAAC
Sporus. See:
    LORD HERVEY
SPOTSWOOD, ALEXANDER
    (1676-1740) [Governor of
    Virginia Colony and pro-
    prietor of iron foundry]
Tubal Cain
SPRAGUE, ACHSA W.
    (c.1828-62) [American
    trance medium and
    lecturer on spiritualism]
The Preaching Woman
SPRECHER, WILLIAM
    GUNTHER (1924-)
    [German composer, pianist
    and arranger]
William Gunther
SPRECKLES, CLAUS
    (1828-1908) [German-
    American capitalist and
    sugar manufacturer]
The Sugar King
SPRIGG, CHRISTOPHER ST.
    JOHN (1907-1937) [English
    novelist, poet and writer
    on aviation]
Christopher Caudwell
Spring, Philip. See:
    DOBSON, E. PHILIP
SPRINGER, MARILYN HARRIS
    (1931-) [American
    author]
Marilyn Harris
Springfield, The Sage of.
    See: LINCOLN,
    ABRAHAM
SPROAT, EBENEZER
    1805) [American army
    officer and jurist]
The Big Buckeye
Sproston, John. See:
    SCOTT, PETER DALE
SPROUL, WILLIAM CAMERON
    (1870-1928) [American
    manufacturer and politician;
    governor of Pennsylvania]
The Father of Good Roads
Spud. See: DAVIS,
    VIRGIL LAWRENCE
    MURPHY, LYLE
Spunkey, Simon. See:

FESSENDEN, THOMAS
    GREEN
Spurgeon of America, The Black.
    See: WALKER, CHARLES
    THOMAS
Spurious Governor. See:
    LIVINGSTON, WILLIAM
Spurr, Clinton. See:
    ROWLAND, DONALD SYD-
    NEY
Spurs, The Knight of the Golden.
    See: STUART, JAMES
    EWELL BROWN
SPURSTOWE, WILLIAM. See:
    Smectymnuus
Spy. See:
    WARD, SIR LESLIE
Spy of the Cumberland, The.
    See: CUSHMAN, PAULINE
Spy, Pickle the. See:
    MACDONNELL, ALASTAIR
    RUADH
Squab Poet, The. See:
    DRYDEN, JOHN
Squatters, The King of the. See:
    ROBINSON, SOLON
Squeaky. See:
    BLUEGE, OTTO ADAM
Squibob. See:
    DERBY, GEORGE HORATIO
Squibob, John P. See:
    DERBY, GEORGE HORATIO
Squint-Eyed (Guercino). See:
    BARBIERI, GIOVANNI
    FRANCESCO
Squire. See:
    SWEENEY, PETER BARR
SQUIRE, JOHN COLLINGS
    (1884-) [British critic
    and poet]
Solomon Eagle
Squire, Miriam F. See:
    LESLIE, MIRIAM
    FLORENCE FOLLINE
Squire of Hyde Park, The. See:
    ROOSEVELT, FRANKLIN
    DELANO
Squire, Ronald. See:
    SQUIRL, RONALD
Squires, Phil. See:
    BARKER, S. OMAR
SQUIRL, RONALD (1886-1958)

957

[British stage and motion picture actor]
Ronald Squire
St. Items prefixed by this abbreviation will be found indexed as though spelled "Saint"
STABILE, THERESA (190?-)
[American popular singer]
Dolly Dawn
STACEY [Stacey]. See also: Stacy
Stacey, Paul. See:
SAVILL, ROY
STACEY, THOMAS CHARLES GERRARD (1930-) [British author and foreign correspondent]
Tom Stacey
Stachys, Dimitris. See:
CONSTANTELOS, DEMETRIOS J.
Stack. See:
SUTTON, MAURICE LEWIS
STACK, NICOLETE (1896-) [American author]
Kathryn Kenny
Nicolete Meredith
Stacy. See also:
STACEY
Stacey
Stacy, Joel. See:
DODGE, MARY ELIZABETH MAPES
Stadium, The Father of Pitt. See:
HAMILTON, ALFRED REED
STAËL-HOLSTEIN, ANNE LOUISE GERMAINE, BARONNE DE (1766-1817) [French author]
Madame de Staël
Staff, The Disraeli of the Chiefs of. See:
MacARTHUR, DOUGLAS
Stafford, Anne. See:
PEDLER, ANNE I. STAFFORD
Stafford, Muriel. See:
SAUER, MURIEL STAFFORD

Stage, The Dean of the American. See: JEFFERSON, JOSEPH
SKINNER, OTIS
Stage, The Diana of the. See: BRACEGIRDLE, MRS. ANNE
Stage, The Last Minstrel of the English. See: SHIRLEY, JAMES
Stage, The Queen of the English. See: BROWN, ELIZABETH ANN
Stage, The Smollett of the. See: FARQUHAR, GEORGE
Stage, The Whitfield of the. See: GARRICK, DAVID
QUIN, JAMES
Stager, Old. See:
ADAMS, WILLIAM TAYLOR
STAGG, AMOS ALONZO (1862-1965) [American football coach]
Football's "Old Man River"
The Grand Old Man of Football
Lonnie
Stagge, Jonathan. See:
Quentin, Patrick
Stagirite, The. See:
ARISTOTLE
STAHL, LEROY (1908-) [American advertising consultant, television executive and author]
George E. Sheldon
Kirk Wood
Stainville, Comte de. See:
CHOISEUL-AMBOISE, ÉTIENNE FRANÇOIS, DUC DE
Stait, Virginia. See:
RUSSELL, WINIFRED BRENT
Stalin, Joseph. See:
Big Three, The
DJUGASHVILI, YOSIF VISSARIONOVICH
Stalking Library, The. See:
MITCHELL, STEPHEN MIX
Stallings, Mary. See:
EVANS, MARY LORRAINE STALLINGS

958

Stammerer, The. See:
LOUIS II
Stan. See:
HASSELGARD, AKE
KENTON, STANLEY
NEWCOMB
MUSIAL, STANLEY FRANK
Stan Laurel. See:
JEFFERSON, ARTHUR
STANLEY
Stan the Man. See:
MUSIAL, STANLEY
FRANK
Standard Oil King, The. See:
ROCKEFELLER, JOHN
DAVISON
STANDING, DOROTHY
(1909-) [British stage
and motion picture
actress]
Kay Hammond
Standish, Burt L. See:
PATTEN, WILLIAM
GILBERT
WHITSON, JOHN HARVEY
STANDISH, MILES (MYLES)
(c.1584-1656) [Anglo-
American colonist; leader
of activities of Massa-
chusetts Bay Colony]
Captain Miles Standish
The Hero of New England
The Little Indian Fighter
STANFORD, AMASA LELAND.
See: Big Four, The
STANFORD, DONALD EWING
(1913-) [American
educator and author]
Don Stanford
STANFORD, JOHN KEITH
(1892-) [British
soldier and author]
Issachar
STANG, JUDIT (1921-)
[Hungarian artist and
author]
Judy Varga
STANGELAND, KATHARINA
MARIE BECH-BRÖNDUM
(1872-1950) [Danish
novelist and short story
writer]

Karin Michaëlis
STANHOPE, PHILIP DORMER
(1694-1773) [English
statesman and man of
letters; 4th Earl of
Chesterfield]
Geffery Broadbottom
Stanislavsky. See:
ALEXEYEV, KONSTANTIN
SERGEIVITCH
STANKY, EDWARD RAYMOND
(1917-) [American pro-
fessional baseball player]
Eddie Stanky
STANLEY. See:
LORD STANLEY
Stanley, Bennett. See:
HOUGH, STANLEY BENNETT
Stanley Castle. See:
BROWNE, RILMA MARION
Stanley Cortez. See:
KRANZ, STANISLAUS
Stanley Fields. See:
AGNEW, WALTER L.
Stanley Ketchel. See:
KIECHAL, STANISLAUS
Stanley, Kim. See:
REID, PATRICIA
Stanley Laurel. See:
JEFFERSON, ARTHUR
STANLEY
Stanley, Marie. See:
WEST, LILLIE
STANLEY, NORA KATHLEEN
BEGBIE (1886-)
[English author]
Nora K. Strange
Stanley, Phil. See:
IND, ALLISON
Stanley, Scorpion. See:
LORD STANLEY
Stanley, Sir Henry Morton.
See: ROWLANDS, JOHN
Stanley Vestal. See:
CAMPBELL, WALTER
STANLEY
STANNARD, HENRIETTA ELIZA
VAUGHAN (1856-1911)
[British novelist]
Violet Whyte
John Strange Winter
STANNUS, EDRIS (1898-)

959

[British ballerina and choreographer]
Ninette De Valois
STANSFIELD, GRACE (1898-) [British singer, comedienne and motion picture actress]
Gracie Fields
Stanstead, John. See: GROOM, ARTHUR WILLIAM
Stanton. See: FORBES, DELORIS STANTON
Stanton, Coralie. See: HOSKEN, ALICE CECIL SEYMOUR
STANTON, FRANK LEBBY (1857-1927) [American poet and editor]
The Riley of the South
Stanton Page. See: FULLER, HENRY BLAKE
Stanwyck, Barbara. See: STEVENS, RUBY
STAPLETON, VIVIENNE (1921-) [American singer and actress]
Vivian Blaine
Star, Baby. See: WATERS, ETHEL
Star-Man's Padre. See: PATRICK, JOHNSTONE GILLESPIE
Star of Song, The Morning. See: CHAUCER, GEOFFREY
Star of the North, The. See: GUSTAVUS II
Star of the Reformation, The Morning. See: WICKLIFFE, JOHN
Star, Son of the. See: BAR COCHEBA, SIMON
Star, The Lone. See: STARR, FREDERICK
Star, The World's Top Boots-and-Saddle. See: SLYE, LEONARD
STARBIRD, KAYE (1916-) [American author]
C. S. Jennison

Starbuck, Roger. See: COMSTOCK, AUGUSTUS
STARING, ADOLPH (1890-) [Dutch art historian and author]
A. S.
Stark, James. See: GOLDSTON, ROBERT CONROY
STARK, JOHN (1728-1822) [American Revolutionary general officer]
The Leonidas of America
Stark, John. See: GODWIN, JOHN
Stark, Joshua. See: OLSEN, THEODORE VICTOR
STARK, LLOYD CROW (1886-) [American politician; governor of Missouri]
Molly Stark
Stark, Michael. See: LARIAR, LAWRENCE
STARKEY, JAMES SULLIVAN (1879-1958) [Irish poet]
Seumas O'Sullivan
STARKEY, RICHARD (1940-) [English musician (drums); member of The Beatles, singing and instrumental group]
Ringo Starr
STARKEY, RICHARD. See also: Beatles, The
STARKS, KATHRYN (1922-) [American jazz musician (singer)]
Kay Starr
STARR, BELLE (1848-89) [American woman bandit of the Southwest]
The Bandit Queen
The Female Jesse James
STARR, BRYAN BARTLETT (1934-) [American professional football player]
Bart Starr
STARR, FREDERICK (1858-1933) [American anthropologist and educator]
The Lone Star

960

Starr, John A. See:
  GILLESE, JOHN
    PATRICK
Starr, Kay. See:
  STARKS, KATHRYN
STARR, RAYMOND FRANCIS
  (1907-) [American
  professional baseball
  player]
    Ironman
Starr, Ringo. See:
  Beatles, The
    STARKEY, RICHARD
Starret, William. See:
  McCLINTOCK, MARSHALL
Stars, Old. See:
  MITCHELL, ORMSBY
    McKNIGHT
Stars, Old Three. See:
  GRANT, HIRAM ULYSSES
Stars, The Lady of the. See:
  PROCTOR, MARY
Stars, The Maker of. See:
  BONESTEELE, LAURA
    JUSTINE
Starvation. See:
  DUNDAS, HENRY
Starvation, Knight of the
  Most Honorable Order
  of. See:
    LIVINGSTON, WILLIAM
State Boxing Bill, The Father
  of the New York. See:
    WALKER, JAMES JOHN
State of New Jersey, Despot-in-
  Chief in and over the
  Rising. See:
    LIVINGSTON, WILLIAM
State of New Jersey, Extra-
  ordinary Chancellor of the
  Rising. See:
    LIVINGSTON, WILLIAM
State of New York, The Father
  of Presbyterianism in
  the. See:
    McNISH, GEORGE
State of New York, The Father
  of the Bar of the.
  See: VAN VECHEN,
    ABRAHAM
State, The Supreme Military
  Commander of the. See:

CHU TEH
State Universities, The Father
  of. See:
    CUTLER, MANASSEH
States, Columella of the New
  England. See:
    LOWELL, JOHN, JR.
States Grant, United. See:
  GRANT, HIRAM ULYSSES
States' Rights, The Father of.
  See: CALHOUN, JOHN
    CALDWELL
States, United. See:
  GRANT, HIRAM ULYSSES
Statesman, Guano. See:
  BLAINE, JAMES GILLESPIE
Statesman, Magnetic. See:
  BLAINE, JAMES GILLESPIE
Statesman, The Christian. See:
  FRELINGHUYSEN,
    THEODORE
Statesman, The Distressed. See:
  PITT, WILLIAM
Statesman, The Dwarf. See:
  STEPHENS, ALEXANDER
    HAMILTON
Statesman, The Sockless. See:
  SIMPSON, JERRY
Statesman, The Wooden-shoe. See:
  WATSON, JAMES ELI
Staton, Merrill. See:
  OSTRUS, MERRILL
Statue of Liberty, Radio's Own.
  See: SMITH, KATHRYN
    ELIZABETH
Stauffer Clavell. See:
  NAGELE, ANTON
Stauffer, Don. See:
  BERKEBILE, FRED
    DONOVAN
Staunch. See:
  BUCKINGHAM, WILLIAM
    ALFRED
Staunton, Schuyler. See:
  BAUM, LYMAN FRANK
STEAD, JAMES HENRY (-1886)
  [English music-hall per-
  former]
    The Perfect Cure
Steadman, Captain Dick. See:
  HARBAUGH, THOMAS
    CHALMERS

961

STEADMAN, VERA (1900-)
[American motion
picture actress]
The Original Bathing Girl
Stealer, Spoon. See:
BUTLER, BENJAMIN
FRANKLIN
Steamboat Navigation, The
Father of. See:
FULTON, ROBERT
Steamboat, The Father of the.
See: FULTON, ROBERT
Steamer. See:
NASON, LEONARD
HASTINGS
STEARNS, FREDERICK KIM-
BALL (1854-1928)
[American traveler]
Detroit's Greatest Traveler
STEARNS, HAROLD EDMUND
(1891-1943) [American
author, critic and
journalist]
America's Foremost
Expatriate
STEBBINS, GRANT CASE
(1862-1925) [American
oil prospector and
driller]
Dry Hole Stebbins
Stecchetti, Lorenzo. See:
GUERRINI, OLINDO
Stecchetto (The Stick). See:
VILLANI (SCICOLONE),
SOPHIA
STEDMAN, EDMUND CLARENCE
(1833-1908) [American
stockbroker, poet and
editor]
The Banker-Poet
STEEDMAN, JAMES BARRETT
(1818-83) [American Civil
War general officer]
Old Chickamauga
Steel, Kurt. See:
KAGEY, RUDOLF
Steel, Robert. See:
WHITSON, JOHN HARVEY
Steel, The Man of
(Adamantius). See:
ORIGEN (ORIGENES)
Steele. See:

MACKAYE, JAMES
MORRISON STEELE
Steele, Addison. See:
WHITSON, JOHN HARVEY
Steele, Bob. See:
BRADBURY, ROBERT
Steele, Chester K. See:
STRATEMEYER,
EDWARD L.
STEELE, FRANCESCA MARIA
(1848-) [British author]
Darley Dale
STEELE, FRANKLIN (fl. 1838)
[American pioneer in
Minnesota]
The First Citizen of St.
Anthony
STEELE, JAMES (fl. 1873-92)
[American author]
Deane Monahan
STEELE, LOUIS (1911-)
[American composer and
advertising executive]
Ted Steele
STEELE, MARY QUINTARD
GOVAN (1922-)
[American author]
Wilson Gage
STEELE, SIR RICHARD (1672-
1729) [English essayist and
dramatist]
A Gentleman of the Army
Isaac Bickerstaff
Impartial Hand
Francis Hicks
Nestor Ironside
Humphrey Philroye
Captain Steele
Steele, Tommy. See:
HICKS, TOMMY
STEELY, ANN (1925-)
[American stage and
motion picture actress]
Cathy O'Donnell
STEENDAM, JACOB (1616?-72)
[Dutch-American poet]
The First American Poet
Noch Vaster (Even Firmer]
Steenie. See:
BUCKINGHAM, GEORGE
VILLIERS, 1ST DUKE OF
Steer, Charlotte. See:

HUNTER, MAUD LILY
STEEVENS. See also:
  STEFFENS
  STEPHENS
  STEVENS
STEEVENS, GEORGE
  (1736-1800) [English
  Shakespearian
  commentator]
  The Puck of Commentators
Stefan. See:
  BAUMRIN, BERNARD
    HERBERT
  STEFFAN
  STEPHEN
  Stephen
Stefan Bernard. See:
  BAUMRIN, BERNARD
    HERBERT
STEFAN, KARL (1884-)
  [American radio
  announcer and politician,
  congressman from
  Nebraska]
  The Voice of the Radio
STEFFAN. See also:
  STEFAN
  Stefan
  STEPHEN
  Stephen
STEFFAN, ALICE KENNEDY
  (1907-) [American
  author]
  Jack Steffan
STEFFENS. See also:
  STEEVENS
  STEPHENS
  STEVENS
STEFFENS, JOSEPH LINCOLN
  (1866-1936) [American
  muckraker and author]
  Lincoln Steffans
STEIGER, RODNEY STEPHEN
  (1925-) [American
  actor]
  Rod Steiger
STEIN, AARON, MARC (1906-)
  [American reporter,
  critic, columnist and
  author]
  George Bagby
  Hampton Stone

STEIN, GEORGE (1903-)
  [Polish motion picture and
  television actor]
  George E. Stone
STEINDLER, ROBERT A.
  (1920-) [American editor
  and author]
  Bob Tremaine
STEINER, MAXIMILIAN
  RAOUL (1888?-)
  [Viennese composer and
  conductor]
  Max Steiner
STEINHAEUSER, WALTER
  PHILIP (1878-)
  [American educator and
  author]
  S. P. Retlaw
Steinmetz, Eulalie. See:
  ROSS, EULALIE STEIN-
    METZ
STEINMETZ, KARL AUGUST
  RUDOLF
  (1865-1923) [German-
  American electrical
  engineer and inventor]
  The Electrical Wizard
  Proteus
  Charles Proteus Steinmetz
Stella. See:
  JOHNSON, ESTHER
  LEWIS, ESTELLE ANNA
    BLANCHE ROBINSON
  RICH, PENELOPE
    DEVEREUX
Stella March. See:
  MARSHALL, MARJORIE
    BELL
Sten, Anna. See:
  SUJAKEVITCH, ANJUSCHLA
    STENSKI
Stendahl. See:
  BEYLE, MARIE HENRI
Stendahl, de. See:
  BEYLE, MARIE HENRI
STENGEL, CHARLES
  DILLON (1891-)
  [American professional
  baseball manager]
  Casey Stengel
STENSLAND, INGER
  (1935-70)

963

[Swedish motion picture
actress]
Inger Stevens
Stenus. See:
    HUXLEY, HERBERT
    HENRY
STENVALL, ALEKSIS
    (1834-72) [Finnish
    writer]
    Aleksis Kivi
Stepfather of His Country, The.
    See: WASHINGTON,
    GEORGE
Stephanie Lloyd. See:
    GOLDING, MORTON JAY
Stephen. See:
    GRELLET, ÉTIENNE DE
    McNALLY, HORACE
    STEFAN
    Stefan
    STEFFAN
STEPHEN (died 257)
    [Supreme Pontiff of
    Roman Catholic Church]
    Pope Stephen I
    St. Stephen
STEPHEN (died 752) [Supreme
    Pontiff of Roman
    Catholic Church]
    Pope Stephen II
STEPHEN (died 757) [Supreme
    Pontiff of Roman
    Catholic Church]
    Pope Stephen III
    St. Stephen
STEPHEN (died 772) [Supreme
    Pontiff of Roman
    Catholic Church]
    Pope Stephen IV
STEPHEN (died 817)
    [Supreme Pontiff of
    Roman Catholic Church]
    Pope Stephen V
STEPHEN (died 891) [Supreme
    Pontiff of Roman
    Catholic Church]
    Pope Stephen VI
STEPHEN (died 897) [Supreme
    Pontiff of Roman
    Catholic Church]
    Pope Stephen VII
STEPHEN (died 931) [Supreme

Pontiff of Roman Catholic
    Church]
    Pope Stephen VIII
STEPHEN (died 942) [Supreme
    Pontiff of Roman Catholic
    Church]
    Pope Stephen IX
STEPHEN I (975?-1038) [King
    of Hungary]
    St. Stephen
STEPHEN II (c. 1114-31) [King
    of Hungary]
    The Thunderer
Stephen X, Pope. See:
    FREDERICK OF LORRAINE
Stephen Acre. See:
    GRUBER, FRANK
Stephen Boyd. See:
    MILLAR (MILLER),
    WILLIAM
Stephen Cole. See:
    WEBBE, GALE DUDLEY
Stephen Cuyler. See:
    BATES, BARBARA
    SNEDEKER
Stephen Edwards. See:
    PALESTRANT, SIMON S.
Stephen Grendon. See:
    DERLETH, AUGUST
    WILLIAM
Stephen Holt. See:
    THOMPSON, HARLAN H.
Stephen Hudson. See:
    SCHIFF, SYDNEY
STEPHEN, SIR LESLIE
    (1832-1904) [English critic
    and editor]
    Don
Stephen, The British St. See:
    ALBAN, ST.
Stephen Vizard. See:
    JAMES, DAVID BURNETT
    STEPHEN
Stephen Yorke. See:
    LINSKILL, MARY
STEPHENS. See also:
    STEEVENS
    STEFFENS
    STEVENS
STEPHENS, ALEXANDER
    HAMILTON (1812-83)
    [American vice president

964

of the Confederacy]
The Dwarf Statesman
Little Aleck
STEPHENS, ALEXANDER
    HAMILTON. See also:
    Castor and Pollux of
    Georgia, The
STEPHENS, ANN SOPHIA
    WINTERBOTHAM
    (1813-86) [American
    editor and novelist]
Jonathan Slick
STEPHENSON [Stephenson].
    See also:
    STEVENSON
Stephenson, Henry. See:
    GARROWAY, HENRY
    STEPHENSON
STEPHENSON, JACKSON RIGGS
    (1809-   [American pro-
    fessional baseball
    player]
Old Hoss
Stevie
STEPHENSON, JOHN (1809-
    93) [Irish-American
    businessman]
Honest John
Stepin Fetchit. See:
    PERRY, LINCOLN
Stepnyak (Son of the Steppe).
    See: KRAVCHINSKY,
    SERGIUS MIKHAILOVICH
Steppe, Son of the (Stepnyak).
    See: KRAVCHINSKY,
    SERGIUS MIKHAILO-
    VICH
Steptoe, Lydia. See:
    BARNES, DJUNA
Sterling. See also:
    STIRLING
    Stirling
Sterling, Anthony. See:
    CAESAR, EUGENE LEE
Sterling, Ford. See:
    STITCH, GEORGE FORD
Sterling, Jan. See:
    ADRIANCE, JAN
    STERLING
Sterling, Jean. See:
    TAYLOR, MARY VIRGINIA
Sterling, Robert. See:

HART, WILLIAM STERLING
Stern, Daniel. See:
    AGOULT, COMTESSE D',
    MARIE CATHERINE
    SOPHIE DE FLAVIGNY
STERN, DAVID (1909-)
    [American novelist]
Peter Stirling
STERN, ELIZABETH GERTRUDE
    (1890-) [Polish-American
    novelist]
Leah Morton
Stern, G.B. See:
    HOLDSWORTH, GLADYS
    BRONWYN
Stern in Council (Hardrata).
    See: HAROLD III
STERN, JOE (1894-)
    [Austrian motion picture
    director]
Joseph Von Sternberg
STERN, PHILIP VAN DOREN
    (1900-) [American
    journalist, editor and
    author]
Peter Storme
STERNE, EMMA GELDERS
    (1894-) [American editor
    and author]
Emily Brown
STERNE, EMMA GELDERS.
    See also:
    James, Josephine
Sterne, Hedda. See:
    LINDENBERG, HEDDA
STERNE, LAURENCE (1713-68)
    [English clergyman and
    novelist]
Mr. Yorick
The English Rabelais
Sterne, Stuart. See:
    BLOEDE, GERTRUDE
Steve. See:
    ALLEN, STEPHEN
    VALENTINE PATRICK
    WILLIAM
    DONOGHUE, STEVEN
    HANNAGAN, STEPHEN
    JEROME
    KAHN, STEPHEN
    McQUEEN, TERENCE
    STEPHEN

OWEN, STEPHEN
JOSEPH
REEVES, STEPHEN
Steve, Big. See:
OWEN, STEPHEN
JOSEPH
Steve Brodie. See:
STEVENS, JOHN
Steve Cartier. See:
CAMERON, LOU
Steve Dodge. See:
BECKER, STEPHEN
DAVID
Steve Forrest. See:
ANDREWS, WILLIAM
FORREST
Steve Geray. See:
GYERGYAY, STEFAN
Steve Lacy. See:
LACKRITZ, STEVEN
Steve Lawrence. See:
LIEBOWITZ, SIDNEY
Steve Lomas. See:
BRENNAN, JOSEPH
LOMAS
Steve Mees. See:
FLEXNER, STUART
BERG
Steve Michaels. See:
AVALLONE, MICHAEL
ANGELO, JR.
Steve Phillips. See:
WHITTINGTON, HARRY
Steve Sekely. See:
SZEKELY, ISTVAN
Steve Wilson. See:
GOLDENBERG, EMANUEL
Steve Wyandotte. See:
THOMAS, STANLEY
STEVENS. See also:
STEEVENS
STEFFENS
STEPHENS
STEVENS, ALFRED PECK
(1839-88) [English music-
hall singer and comedian]
Vance the Great
STEVENS, CASANDRA MAYO
(-1966) [American com-
poser and dancer]
Cass Mayo
Stevens, Clysle. See:
WADE, JOHN STEVENS

Stevens, Connie. See:
INGOLIA, CONCETTA
STEVENS, CONSTANCE (1916-)
[British stage and motion
picture actress]
Sally Gray
Stevens, Craig. See:
SHEKLES, GAIL
Stevens, Dan J. See:
OVERHOLSER, WAYNE D.
Stevens, E. S. See:
DROWER, ETHEL
STEFANA MAY
STEVENS, FRANCES ISTED
(1907-) [Australian
teacher, nurse and author]
Fae Hewston Stevens
Stevens, George (Kingfish). See:
GOSDEN, FREEMAN F.
STEVENS, HAROLD (1909-71)
[American singer]
Elliot Stevens
Stevens, Inger. See:
STENSLAND, INGER
Stevens, J. D. See:
ROWLAND, DONALD
SYDNEY
STEVENS, JOHN (1919-)
[American motion picture
actor]
Steve Brodie
STEVENS, JOHN H. (1820-1900)
[Canadian pioneer in
Minnesota]
The Father of Minneapolis
Stevens, K. T. See:
WOOD, GLORIA
Stevens, Margaret Dean. See:
ALDRICH, BESS STREETER
Stevens, Maurice. See:
WHITSON, JOHN HARVEY
Stevens, Onslow. See:
STEVENSON, ONSLOW
FORD
Stevens, Peter, joint pseud. of
DARLENE STERN GEIS
(fl. 1947-64) and her
husband BERNARD GEIS
(fl. 1947-64) [American
authors]
Stevens, Peter. See also:
GEIS, DARLENE STERN
STEVENS, RUBY (1907-)

[American motion picture and television actress]
Barbara Stanwyck
Stevens, S. P. See:
PALESTRANT, SIMON S.
STEVENS, THADDEUS (1792-1868) [American statesman and abolitionist]
The American Pitt
The Arch-Priest of Anti-Masonry
The Chief Old Woman
The Great American Commoner
The Great Commoner
The Old Commoner
Thad Stevens
STEVENSON. See also:
STEPHENSON
Stephenson
STEVENSON, ONSLOW FORD (1902-) [American stage and motion picture actor]
Onslow Stevens
STEVENSON, ROBERT LOUIS BALFOUR (1850-94) [Scottish novelist, poet and essayist]
R. L. S.
Teller of Tales (Tusitala)
STEVENSON, WILLIAM (1925-) [British correspondent and author]
Chen Hwei
Steverino. See:
ALLEN, STEPHEN VALENTINE PATRICK WILLIAM
Stevie. See:
SMITH, FLORENCE MARGARET
STEPHENSON, JACKSON RIGGS
Steward. See also:
STEWART
Stewart
STUART
Stuart
Steward, Reverend James. See:
TRUMBULL, HENRY
Steward, The. See:
ROBERT II

STEWART [Stewart]. See also:
Steward
STUART
Stuart
STEWART, ALEXANDER PETER (1821-1908)
[American Civil War general officer and educator]
Old Straight
STEWART, ALFRED WALTER (1880-1947) [Scottish scientist and author of detective stories]
John Jervis Connington
J. J. Connington
Stewart Cross. See:
DRAGO, HENRY SINCLAIR
Stewart, David. See:
POLITELLA, DARIO
Stewart, Eleanor. See:
PORTER, MRS. ELEANOR HODGMAN
Stewart, Elizabeth Grey. See:
REED, ELIZABETH STEWART
Stewart, Eve. See:
NAPIER, PRISCILLA
Stewart, Gordon. See:
RATHBONE, ST. GEORGE HENRY
Stewart Gordon. See:
SHIRREFFS, GORDON DONALD
STEWART, JAMES (1913-)
[British stage and motion picture actor]
Stewart Granger
STEWART, JAMES MAITLAND (1908-) [American actor, aviator and general officer]
Jimmy Stewart
Stewart, Jay. See:
PALMER, STUART
STEWART, JOHN (1749-1822)
[English traveler and pedestrian]
Walking Stewart
STEWART, JOHN INNES MACKINTOSH (1906-)
[British detective story writer]
Michael Innes

967

STEWART, LEROY (1914-)
[American jazz musician
(bass)]
Slam Stewart
Stewart London. See:
WILSON, ROGER C.
STEWART, NEIL. See:
Lombard, Nap
STEWART, ROBERT
ARMISTEAD (1877-1950)
[American educator, author
and poet]
Gordon Stuart
Stewart Rome. See:
RYOTT, SEPTIMUS
WILLIAM
STEWART, SIR ALEXANDER
(1343?-1405?) [Scottish
nobleman]
The Wolf of Badenoch
Stewart, Will. See:
WILLIAMSON, JOHN
STEWART
Stick, The (Stecchetto). See:
VILLANI (SCICOLONE),
SOPHIA
Sticks. See:
HOOPER, NESBERT
Stix
Sticks, The Devil on Two. See:
MORTON, OLIVER HAZ-
ARD PERRY THROCK
Stijn Streuvels. See:
LATEUR, FRANK
STILES, EZRA CLARKE
(1727-95) [American
educator and historian]
Keal Setis
Stilling, Jung. See:
JUNG, JOHANN
HEINRICH
STILLMAN, WILLIAM JAMES
(1828-1901) [American
painter and journalist]
The American Pre-
Raphaelite
Stilt, Wilt the. See:
CHAMBERLAIN, WILTON
NORMAN
STILWELL, JOSEPH WARREN
(1883-1946) [American
general officer]

Old Tu'key Neck
Uncle Joe
Vinegar Joe
STILWELL, SILAS MOORE
(1800-81) [American lawyer
and politician]
King Caucus
STIMSON, FREDERIC JESUP
(1855-1943) [American
lawyer and author]
J.S. of Dale
STIMSON, HENRY LEWIS
(1867-1950) [American
politician; Secretary of
State and Secretary of War]
Stimy
Stimy. See:
STIMSON, HENRY LEWIS
Stinky. See:
DAVIS, HARRY ALBERT
STIRLING [Stirling]. See also:
Sterling
STIRLING, ANNA MARIA
DIANA WILHELMINA
PICKERING (1865-)
[British author]
Percival Pickering
Stirling, Arthur. See:
SINCLAIR, UPTON BEALL
Stirling, Edward. See:
LAMBERT, EDWARD
Stirling, Fanny. See:
KEHL, MARY ANNE
Stirling, Lord. See:
ALEXANDER, WILLIAM
Stirling, Peter. See:
STERN, DAVID
Stirner, Max. See:
SCHMIDT, KASPAR
STIRNWEISS, GEORGE HENRY
(1919-) [American pro-
fessional baseball player
and athletic coach]
Snuffy Stirnweiss
STITCH, GEORGE FORD (1883-
1939) [American motion
picture actor and comedian]
Ford Sterling
STITT, EDWARD (1924-)
[American jazz musician
(saxophones)]
Sonny Stitt

STITZEL, MELVILLE J.
(1902-52) [American
composer and pianist]
Mel Stitzel
Stix. See:
HOOPER, NESBERT
Sticks
STOBART, THOMAS RALPH
(1914-) [English author]
Tom Stobart
STOCKARD, JAMES WRIGHT,
JR. (1935-) [American
educator and author]
Jimmy Stockard
Stockfisch, Hans. See:
SPENCER, JOHN
Stocking-foot Orator, The. See:
McKINLEY, WILLIAM
Stocking Weaver, Robert
Slender. See:
FRENEAU, PHILIP MORIN
STOCKTON, FRANCIS
RICHARD (1834-1902)
[American author]
Paul Fort
Frank Richard Stockton
STOCKTON, RICHARD
(1764-1828) [American
politician; congressman
from New Jersey]
The Duke
STODDARD, CHARLES WARREN
(1843-1909) [American
poet and travel writer]
Pip Pepperpod
STODDARD, CHARLES WARREN
See also:
Golden Gate Trinity, The
Stoddard, Major Henry B. See:
INGRAHAM, COLONEL
PRENTISS
STODDART, SIR JOHN
(1773-1856) [English
physician and nobleman]
Doctor Slop
STODDARD, WILLIAM
OSBORNE (1835-1925) [Am-
erican inventor and author]
Col. Chris Forrest
STOKELY, WILMA DYKEMAN
(1920-) [American
lecturer and author]

Wilma Dykeman
STOKER, ABRAHAM (1847-1912)
[British novelist and
miscellaneous writer]
Bram Stoker
Stokes, Simpson. See:
FAWCETT, FRANK
DUBREZ
STOKES, WILLIAM BRICKLY
(1814-97) [American
soldier and lawyer;
congressman from Ten-
nessee]
The Eagle Orator
Stokowski, Leopold. See:
ANTONI, BOLESLAWOWICZ
STANISLAW
STOLL, DENNIS GRAY
(1912-) [British composer
and writer on music]
Denys Craig
Stolterforth, George. See:
BONUS, ARTHUR
STOLZ, LOIS MEEK (1891-)
[American educator and
author]
Lois Hayden Meek
Stone, Alan. See:
STRATEMEYER,
EDWARD L.
Stone, Arthur. See:
GLADSTONE, ARTHUR
STONE, EUGENIA (1879-)
[American poet and author]
Gene Stone
Stone Face, The Great. See:
WEBSTER, DANIEL
STONE, FREDERICK MATHER
(1861-1932) [American
lawyer and politician]
Rocks
Stone, George E. See:
STEIN, GEORGE
Stone Hammer, Old. See:
METCALFE, THOMAS
Stone, Hampton. See:
STEIN, AARON MARC
Stone, Irving. See:
TANNENBAUM, IRVING
STONE, JOHN THOMAS
(1906-) [American
professional baseball player]

Rocky Stone
Stone, Lucy. See:
    BLACKWELL, MRS.
    HENRY BROWN
STONE, MRS. GRACE
    ZARING (1896-)
    [American novelist]
Ethel Vance
STONE, NICHOLAS (1586-
    1647)[English mason
    and architect]
The Elder
STONE, PATTI (1926-)
    [American script
    writer and author]
Leal Patrick
Stone, Raymond. See:
    STRATEMEYER,
    EDWARD L.
Stone, Richard A. See:
    STRATEMEYER,
    EDWARD L.
STONEHOUSE, ALPHEUS
    GEORGE BARNES
    (1862-1931) [Canadian
    circus entrepreneur]
Al G. Barnes
Stonewall. See:
    JACKSON, THOMAS
    JONATHAN
Stonewall of the West, The.
    See: CLEBURNE,
    PATRICK RONAYE
Stonewall, The Invincible. See:
    JACKSON, THOMAS
    JONATHAN
STONG, PHILIP DUFFIELD
    (1899-1957) [American
    author]
Phil Stong
STONOR, OLIVER (1903-)
    [British critic, journalist
    and author]
E. Morchard Bishop
Evelyn Morchard Bishop
Morchard Bishop
Stony Point, The Hero of. See:
    WAYNE, ANTHONY
Stooges, The Three, stage name
    of LARRY FINE (-),
    JEROME HOWARD (Curly)
    (1905-52), MOE HOWARD

(-); later SHEMP
    HOWARD (1895-1955) and
    JOE DE RITA [American
    motion picture comedians]
Stookey, Aaron W. See:
    BEATTY, JEROME, JR.
Stoopnagle, Colonel. See:
    TAYLOR, FREDERICK
    CHASE
Stoopnagle, Lemuel Q. See:
    TAYLOR, FREDERICK
    CHASE
Stopelman, Francis. See:
    STOPPELMAN, FRANS
STOPES, MRS. MARIE CHAR-
    LOTTE CARMICHAEL
    (1880-1958) [English
    paleobotanist, birth-control
    advocate and author]
Marie Carmichael
Erica Fay
STOPPELMAN, FRANS (1921-)
    [Dutch correspondent,
    photographer and author]
Francis Stopelman
Francis Stoppelman
Stories, The Godmother of
    Detective. See:
    GREEN, ANNA KATHARINE
Stories, The Mother of
    Detective. See:
    GREEN, ANNA KATHARINE
Storm. See:
    JAMESON, MARGARET
    STORM
Storm, Christopher. See:
    OLSEN, THEODORE
    VICTOR
Storm, Gale. See:
    COTTLE, JOSEPHINE
Storm King, The. See:
    ESPEY, JAMES POLLARD
Storm, The Pilot that Weathered
    the. See:
    PITT, WILLIAM
Storm, Virginia. See:
    TEMPEST, JAN
Storme, Peter. See:
    STERN, PHILIP VAN
    DOREN
Stormer of Cities (Sforza). See:
    ATTENDOLO, MUZIO

Stormy Petrel. See:
CHANDLER, WILLIAM
EATON
STORR, CATHERINE COLE
(1913-   ) [British
psychiatrist and author]
Irene Adler
Helen Lourie
STORY, ISAAC (1774-1803)
[American essayist and
poet]
From the Desk of Beri
Headin
Peter Quince
The Traveler
Story, Josephine. See:
LORING, EMILIE BAKER
Story Lady, The. See:
FAULKNER, GEORGENE
Story Lady, The Singing. See:
WICKER, IREENE SEATON
STORY, SOMMERVILLE
(fl. early 20th cent.)
[German editor and
journalist]
Frankfort Sommerville
Story, Sydney A., Jr. See:
PIKE, MARY HAYDEN
GREEN
Story-tellers, The Prince of.
See: BOCCACCIO,
GIOVANNI
STOUT, ALLYN McCLELLAND
(1904-   ) [American
professional baseball
player]
Fish Hooks
STOUT, HERBERT E. (1905-)
[American composer and
businessman]
Bert Stout
STOUT, REX TODHUNTER
(1886-   ) [American
author of detective
stories]
The Doyen of Mystery
Writers in English and
Probably in any Language
STOUTENBURG, ADRIEN
PEARL (1916-) [American
librarian, editor and author]

Barbie Arden
Lace Kendall
Nelson Minier
Stove, The Father of the. See:
FRANKLIN, BENJAMIN
STOVENOUR, JUNE (1926-)
[American motion picture
actress]
June Haver
STOWE, HARRIET BEECHER
(1811-96) [American author]
Christopher Crowfield
Strabo, The British. See:
CAMDEN, WILLIAM
STRACHAN, MARGARET PIT-
CAIRN (1908-) [American
reporter, publicity director
and author]
Caroline More
STRACHEY, GILES LYTTON
(1880-1932) [English
biographer]
Lytton Strachey
STRADER, JOHN GARY (1932-)
[American singer]
John Gary
STRAIGHT, CHARLES (1891-1940)
[American jazz musician
(composer, leader)]
Charley Straight
Straight Jake, Four. See:
RUPPERT, JACOB, SR.
Straight, Old. See:
STEWART, ALEXANDER
PETER
Straight-shooter, The Ralston.
See: MIX, TOM
Straight Tongue. See:
WHIPPLE, HENRY
BENJAMIN
STRANAHAN, JAMES SAMUEL
THOMAS (1808-98)
[American philanthropist,
active in Brooklyn, N.Y.)
The First Citizen of Brooklyn
Strand, Paul E. See:
PALESTRANT, SIMON S.
Strand, The Blind Bard of the
Chian. See:
HOMER
STRANG, JAMES JESSE (1813-

971

56) [American religious
fanatic and author]
St. James
Strange, Joseph. See:
CRAWFURD, OSWALD
Strange, Michael. See:
OELRICHS, BLANCHE
MARIE LOUISE
Strange, Nora K. See:
STANLEY, NORA
KATHLEEN BEGBIE
Stranger Murderer, The
Ragged. See:
WANDERER, CARL
Stranger, The Ragged. See:
RYAN, EDWARD JOSEPH
Strangler, The Boston. See:
DE SALVO, ALBERT H.
STRASSER, BERNARD PAUL
(1895-) [German
Roman Catholic priest
and author]
P.W. Silvanus
Strategist, Unprecedented. See:
GRANT, HIRAM
ULYSSES
STRATEMEYER, EDWARD L.
(1862-1930) [American
author of books for
juveniles]
Manager Henry Abbott
Harrison Adams
Captain Ralph Bonehill
Jim Bowie
Franklin Calkins
Allen Chapman
Louis Charles
James R. Cooper
Jim Daly
Spencer Davenport
Julie Edwards
Albert Lee Ford
Robert W. Hamilton
Hal Harkaway
Harvey Hicks
Dr. Willard Mackenzie
Ned St. Myer
Chester K. Steele
E. Ward Strayer
Arthur M. Winfield
Edna Winfield
Nat Woods

Stratemeyer Syndicate pseudonyms:
Victor Appleton
Victor Appleton II
Richard Barnum
Philip A. Bartlett
May Hollis Barton
Charles Amory Beach
Captain James Carson
Lester Chadwick
Allen Chapman
John R. Cooper
Elmer A. Dawson
Franklin W. Dixon
Julia K. Duncan
Alice B. Emerson
James Cody Ferris
Graham B. Forbes
Frederick Gordon
Alice Dale Hardy
Mabel C. Hawley
Brooks Henderley
Grace Brooks Hill
Laura Lee Hope
Francis Hunt
Frances K. Judd
Carolyn Keene
Clinton W. Locke
Helen Beecher Long
Amy Bell Marlowe
Eugene Martin
Fenworth Moore
Gert W. Morrison
Margaret Penrose
Nat Ridley, Jr.
Roy Rockwood
Henry Mason Roe
Dan Scott
Ann Sheldon
Raymond Sperry, Jr.
Alan Stone
Raymond Stone
Richard A. Stone
Helen Louise Thorndyke
Frank A. Warner
Frank V. Webster
Jerry West
Janet D. Wheeler
Ramy Allison White
Clarence Young
Stratford Davis. See:
BOLTON, MAISIE SHARMAN
Strathearn, The Flower of. See:

NAIRNE, CAROLINA
OLIPHANT
Stratten. See also:
STRATTON
Stratton
Stretton
Stratten, John. See:
ALLDRIDGE, JOHN
STRATTEN
STRATTON [Stratton]. See
also: Stratten
Stretton
STRATTON, CHARLES
SHERWOOD (1838-83)
[American dwarf; ex-
hibited by P. T. BARNUM]
The Pet of the Palace
General Tom Thumb
Tom Thumb
Stratton, Henry. See:
NELSON, MICHAEL
HARRINGTON
Stratton, Thomas, joint
pseud. of ROBERT S.
COULSON (1928-) and
GENE DeWEESE (-)
[American authors]
STRAUSS, JOHANN (1804-49)
[Viennese composer
and conductor]
The Elder
STRAUSS, JOHANN (1825-99)
[Viennese composer and
conductor]
The Younger
STRAUSS, MARY LUCILLE
JACKSON (1908-)
[American librarian and
author]
Lucille Jackson
Strauss, The American Suc-
cessor to Johann. See:
ROMBERG, SIGMUND
Straw Hat, The Man in the.
See: CHEVALIER,
MAURICE AUGUSTE
Strawberry. See:
TOWNSEND, JOHN G.,
JR.
Strayer, E. Ward. See:
STRATEMEYER,
EDWARD L.

STRAYHORN, WILLIAM (1915-)
[American jazz musician
(composer, piano)]
Billy Strayhorn
Swee' Pea
Stream of Gold (Chrysorrhoas).
See: JOHN OF DAMAS-
CUS (JOHANNES
DAMASCENUS)
STREET, CECIL JOHN CHARLES
(1884-) [English detective
story writer]
Miles Burton
F. O. O.
John Rhode
X. X.
STREET, CHARLES EVARD
(1882-) [American pro-
fessional baseball player
and manager]
Gabby Street
Street, Lee. See:
HAMPTON, KATHLEEN
Street, Robert. See:
THOMAS, GORDON
Street, The Antiquarian of
Nassau. See:
GOWANS, WILLIAM
STREIDLER, BETTY (1930-)
[American stage and
motion picture actress]
Betta St. John
Stretton. See also:
Stratten
STRATTON
Stratton
Stretton, Charles. See:
DYER, CHARLES
Stretton, Hesba. See:
SMITH, SARAH
Stretton, Renshaw. See:
DYER, CHARLES
Streuvels, Stijn. See:
LATEUR, FRANK
STRIBLING, THOMAS
SIGISMUND (1881-1965)
[American author]
T. S. Stribling
Striker, The Sit-down. See:
HOFFMAN, CLARE E.
STRINDBERG, JOHAN AUGUST
(1849-1912) [Swedish

dramatist and fiction writer]
August Strindberg
Stringbean, Sweet Mama. See:
WATERS, ETHEL
Strip Tease, The Mother of the.
See: DENNIS, RUTH
STRIPP, JOSEPH VALENTINE
(1903-) [American pro-
fessional baseball player]
Jersey Joe
STRODE, WILLIAM. See:
Five Members, The
STRODE, WOODROW (c. 1923-)
[American Negro motion
picture actor]
Woody Strode
Strong Boy of Boston, The.
See: SULLIVAN,
JOHN LAWRENCE
Strong Boy, The Boston. See:
SULLIVAN, JOHN
LAWRENCE
Strong, Charles. See:
EPSTEIN, SAMUEL
STRONG, CHARLES STANLEY
(1906-) [American author]
Nancy Bartlett
Kelvin McKay
William McClelland
Carl Sturdy
Strong, Harrington. See:
McCULLEY, JOHNSTON
Strong, Hero. See:
TRASK, CLARA AUGUSTA
JONES
STRONG, JOHN (1732-98)
[English mechanical
genius, blind from birth]
The Blind Mechanician
STRONG, LEONARD ALFRED
GEORGE (1896-) [English
author]
L. A. G. Strong
STRONG, REV. GEORGE A.
(1832-1912)[American writer]
Marc Antony Henderson
Strong, Solange. See:
HERTZ, NELLIE SOLANGE
STRONG
Strong, The. See:
AUGUSTUS II
SANCHO II
SIWARD

Strongbow. See:
DE CLARE, RICHARD
FITZHERBERT, RICHARD,
2ND EARL OF PEMBROKE
STROOCK, GERALDINE
(1925-) [American
motion picture actress]
Geraldine Brooks
STROSS, MRS. RAYMOND
(c. 1933-) [British
motion picture actress]
Anne Heywood
Violet Pretty
STROTHER, DAVID HUNTER
(1816-88) [American soldier,
illustrator and author]
Porte Crayon
STROVER, DOROTHEA (fl. 1946-
57) [British artist,
horticulturist and author]
Dorothea Tinne
E. D. Tinne
STROZZI, FILIPPO (1428-91)
[Prominent citizen of
Florence]
The Elder
STROZZI, FILIPPO (1489-1538)
[Prominent citizen of
Florence]
The Younger
STRUBE, HERMANN (1879-)
[German artist and poet]
Hermann Burte
Struble, Virginia. See:
BURLINGAME, VIRGINIA
STRUBLE
Strudwick, Shepperd. See:
SHEPPERD, JOHN
Struther, Jan. See:
MAXTONE GRAHAM, MRS.
JOYCE ANSTRUTHER
Strutt, Lord. See:
CHARLES II
STRYPE, JOHN (1643-1737)
[British ecclesiastical
historian and biographer]
Appendixmonger
Dryasdust
STUART [Stuart]. See also:
Steward
STEWART
Stewart
Stuart Brock. See:

TRIMBLE, LOUIS P.
Stuart, Charles. See:
MACKINNON, CHARLES
ROY
STUART, CHARLES EDWARD
LOUIS PHILIP CASIMIR
(1720-88) [English prince;
claimant to the British
throne]
Father Bonaventura
Bonny Prince Charlie
Betty Burke
Charles Edward Stuart
Count of Albany
The Highland Laddie
The Young Adventurer
The Young Chevalier
The Young Pretender
Stuart, Clay. See:
WHITTINGTON, HARRY
Stuart Cloete. See:
CLOETE, EDWARD FAIR-
LIE STUART GRAHAM
Stuart, Don A. See:
CAMPBELL, JOHN WOOD
Stuart, Dorothy Margaret. See:
BROWNE, DOROTHY
MARGARET STUART
Stuart, Eleanor. See:
CHILDS, ELEANOR
STUART
STUART, ELIZABETH
(1596-1662) [Queen of
Bohemia]
Goody Palsgrave
The Queen of Hearts
The Snow Queen
The Winter Queen
STUART, GILBERT (1755-
1828) [American portrait
painter]
The Painter of Presidents
The Portrait Painter of
Presidents
Stuart, Gordon. See:
SAYLER, HARRY
LINCOLN
STEWART, ROBERT
ARMISTEAD
Stuart, Harriet. See:
LENNOX, CHARLOTTE
RAMSAY

STUART, HENRY ROBSON
(1836-1903) [American
comedian]
Stuart Robson
STUART, ISAAC WILLIAM
(1809-61) [American histori-
an, orator and author]
Scaeva
STUART, JAMES (1533-70) [Earl
of Murray (Moray); Regent
of Scotland]
The Good Regent
STUART, JAMES (1713-88)
[British painter and
architect]
The Athenian Stuart
STUART, JAMES (18??-51)
[Australian convict, outlaw
in San Francisco]
English Jim
STUART, JAMES EWELL BROWN
(1833-64) [American Con-
federate general officer]
Beauty Stuart
The Bible-Class Man
Jeb Stuart
The Knight of the Golden
Spurs
Old Jeb
The Plumed Knight of the
Confederacy
The Prince Rupert of the
Confederacy
STUART, JAMES FRANCIS
EDWARD (1688-1766)
[English Prince of Wales;
claimant to the British
throne]
James Edward
James III
The Old Pretender
The Chevalier de St. George
STUART, JOHN (1713-92)
[English statesman]
One Behind the Throne Greater
than the Throne Itself
Stuart, John. See:
CROALL, JOHN
STUART, JOHN SOBIESKI
STOLBERG (1795-1872)
[English son of LT. THOMAS
ALLEN, R.N. who claimed

975

to be the son of PRINCE
CHARLES EDWARD
STUART (STEWART)
Count of Albany
Stuart, Kirk. See:
KINCHELOE, CHARLES
Stuart, Leslie. See:
MARLOWE, KENNETH
Stuart McHugh. See:
ROWLAND, DONALD
SYDNEY
Stuart, Mary. See:
MARY
STUART, MOSES (1780-1852)
[American Biblical
scholar and theologian]
The Father of Biblical
Learning in America
Stuart of Italy, The Mary.
See: JANE I
Stuart Pennington. See:
GALBRAITH, GEORGIE
STARBUCK
STUART, ROBERT (1785-1848)
[Scottish-American
Indian commissioner in
Northwest Territory]
Friend of the Indian
Stuart, Sheila. See:
BAKER, MARY GLADYS
Stuart Sterne. See:
BLOEDE, GERTRUDE
Stuart, The Athenian. See:
STUART, JAMES
STUART, VIVIAN FINLAY
(1914-) [British
romance novelist]
Barbara Allen
Finona Finlay
Alex Stuart
STUBBS, HARRY CLEMENT
(1922-) [American
educator and author]
Hal Clement
STUBBS, MORTON (1860-1940)
[British stage and
motion picture actor]
Morton Selten
STUBER, STANLEY IRVING
(1903-) [American
Baptist minister and
author]

M. Nott Erasmus
Student in Physick and
Astronomy. See:
AMES, NATHANIEL
Student Nurse of Danville, The.
See:
BURCHARD, SAMUEL
DICKINSON
Stuff. See:
SMITH, HEZEKIAH LEROY
GORDON
Stuffed Prophet, The. See:
CLEVELAND, STEPHEN
GROVER
STUKELEY, WILLIAM (1687-
1765) [English antiquarian]
The Archdruid
Stump, The Napoleon of the. See:
POLK, JAMES KNOX
Stupid. See:
BRUTUS, LUCIUS JUNIUS
Sturdy, Carl. See:
STRONG, CHARLES
STANLEY
STURE, STEN (1440?-1503)
[Swedish regent]
The Elder
STURE, STEN (1393-1520)
[Swedish regent]
The Younger
STURE-VASA, MARY O'HARA
ALSOP (1885-)
[American author and
composer]
Mary O'Hara
STURGEON, DANIEL (1789-
1878) [American politician;
senator from Pennsylvania]
The Silent Senator
Sturges, Preston. See:
BIDEN, EDMOND P.
STURLESON, SNORRE
(1179-1241) [Icelandic
historian]
The Northern Herodotus
Sturton, Hugh. See:
JOHNSON, HUGH ANTHONY
STEPHEN
STURTZEL, HOWARD ALLISON
(1894-) [American author]
Paul Annixter
STURTZEL, JANE LEVINGTON

(1903-) [American author]
Jane Annixter
Jane Levington Comfort
STUYVESANT, PETER
(1602-82) [last Dutch governor of New Amsterdam]
Hard-headed Pete
Headstrong Peter
Old Silver Leg
Old Silver Nails
The One-legged Governor
Wooden Leg
STYLES, FRANK SHOWELL
(1908-) [British geographer and author]
Glyn Carr
S. Howell
STYLITES, SIMEON
(c. 390-459) [Christian monk]
The Father of the Pillar Saints
St. Simeon
SUAREZ, FRANCISCO
(1548-1617) [Spanish Jesuit theologian and scholastic philosopher]
The Last of the Schoolmen
Sub, Junior. See:
BEITH, JOHN HAY
SUBARRA, CORRADO DELLA
(died 1154) [Supreme Pontiff of Roman Catholic Church]
Pope Anastasius IV
Subhadra-Nandan. See: DAS, PRAFULLA CHANDRA
Sublime Dandy, The. See:
LEWIS, MERIWETHER
Subsidy. See:
POMEROY, SAMUEL CLARKE
Subtilis, Doctor (The Cunning Teacher). See:
DUNS SCOTUS, JOHN
Succat. See:
PATRICK, ST.
Successor of Houdini, The Legal. See: WEISS, THEO
Successor to Johann Strauss,

The American. See:
ROMBERG, SIGMUND
Sue Kaufman. See:
BARONDESS, SUE KAUFMAN
Sue McVeigh. See:
NEARING, ELIZABETH CUSTER
SUE, MARIE JOSEPH EUGÈNE
(1804-59) [French novelist]
Eugène Sue
Sue Mundy. See:
CLARK, M. JEROME
Sue Raney. See:
CLAUSSEN, RAELENE SUE
Sue Wood. See:
TAYLOR, MARY VIRGINIA
SUETT, RICHARD (1755-1805)
[English comedian]
Dicky Suett
SUFANA, EUGENE (1928-)
[American jazz musician (saxophones)]
Gene Allen
Sugar. See:
CAIN, MERRITT PATRICK
Sugar Beets. See:
CUMMINGS, FRED
Sugar Cain. See:
CAIN, MERRITT PATRICK
Sugar King, The. See:
SPRECKLES, CLAUS
Sugar Ray Robinson. See:
SMITH, WALKER, JR.
Sugartail. See:
HARRIS, GEORGE WASHINGTON
Suggs, Simon. See:
HOOPER, JOHNSON J.
Suitcase. See:
SEEDS, ROBERT I.
SUITER, ARLENDO D. (1919-)
[American composer]
Don Suiter
SUITGER, COUNT OF MORSLEBEN (died 1047) [Supreme Pontiff of Roman Catholic Church]
Pope Clement II
SUJAKEVITCH, ANJUSCHLA STENSKI (1908-) [Russian motion picture actress]
Anna Sten

SULAIMAN I or II (1494-
1566) [Sultan of
Turkey]
Kanuni (The Lawgiver)
The Lord of the Age
The Magnificent
SULLA, LUCIUS CORNELIUS
(138-78 B.C.) [Roman
general officer and
statesman]
Felix
SULLIVAN [Sullivan]. See also:
O'SULLIVAN
O'Sullivan
SULLIVAN, BONAR (1924-59)
[American motion picture
actor]
Bonar Colleano
SULLIVAN, EDWARD ALAN
(1868-) [Canadian
author]
Sinclair Murray
SULLIVAN, EDWARD VINCENT
(1902-) [American news-
paper columnist and
television personality]
Ed Sullivan
Sullivan, Frank. See:
DILLINGER, JOHN
HERBERT
SULLIVAN, HARRY
JOSEPH (1919-)
[American concert
singer]
Brian Sullivan
Sullivan, Joe. See:
O'SULLIVAN, DENIS
PATRICK TERENCE
JOSEPH
SULLIVAN, JOHN
FLORENCE (1894-1956)
[American stage, screen,
radio and television
comedian]
Fred Allen
SULLIVAN, JOHN LAW-
RENCE (1858-1918)
[American professional
boxer; world's heavy-
weight champion]
The Boston Strong Boy

The Great John L.
John L.
The Strong Boy of Boston
SULLIVAN, LOUIS HENRI
(1856-1924) [American
architect]
The Father of Modernism
SULLIVAN, TIMOTHY DANIEL
(1862-1913) [American
politician; congressman from
New York]
The Big Feller
Big Tim
SULLIVAN, TIMOTHY P.
(18??-1909) [American
Tammany Hall politician
and alderman]
Boston Tim
The Little Feller
Little Tim
Sullivan, Yankee. See:
AMBROSE, JAMES
Sulphur King, The. See:
FRASCH, HERMAN
Sultan of Swat, The. See:
RUTH, GEORGE HERMAN
Sumac, Yma. See:
CHAVARRI, EMPERATRIZ
SUMMERALL, CHARLES PELOT
(1867-1955) [American
general officer]
Sitting Bull
Summerfield, Charles. See:
ARRINGTON, ALFRED W.
SUMMERFIELD, JOAN (1921-)
[British dancer and
motion picture actress]
Jean Kent
Summerforest, Ivy B. See:
KIRKUP, JAMES
Summerley, Felix. See:
COLE, SIR HENRY
SUMMERS, COLLEEN (1924-)
[American jazz musician
(singer, guitar)]
Mary Ford
Summers, Gordon. See:
HORNBY, JOHN
SUMMERS, HOLLIS SPURGEON,
JR. (1916-) [American
educator and author
Jim Hollis

978

Summers, John A. See:
LAWSON, HORACE LOWE
Summersetts, The Duke of. See:
HOLMES, JOHN
SUMMERVILLE, GEORGE J.
(1892-1946) [American
motion picture actor]
Slim Summerville
Summoned, The (El Emplazado).
See: FERDINAND IV
SUMNER, CHARLES (1811-74)
[American politician;
senator from Massachu-
setts]
The Bull of the Woods
Sumner, Charles. See:
HALL, HOWARD
Sumner County, The War Horse
of. See:
TROUSDALE, WILLIAM
Sumter, The Hero of Fort. See:
BEAUREGARD, PIERRE
GUSTAVE TOUTANT
SUMTER, THOMAS (1734-1832)
[American Revolutionary
War general officer]
The Carolinian Gamecock
The Gamecock
The South Carolina Gamecock
Sun King, The (Le Roi Soleil).
See: LOUIS XIV
Sun, The Lady of the. See:
PETERS (PERRERS)
(PIERCE) (PERREN),
ALICE
SUN YAT-SEN (1866-1925)
[Chinese revolutionary]
The Father of the Chinese
Republic
Sun Wen
Sunday Gentleman, The. See:
FOE, DANIEL
Sunday of Japan, The Billy. See:
KIMURA, HENRY
SEIMATSU
Sunday, The Black Billy.
See: WILLBANKS,
ALEXANDER
SUNDAY, WILLIAM ASHLEY
(1863-1935) [American
professional baseball
player and evangelist]

Billy Sunday
Sungel, Anak. See:
BROOKE, GILBERT
EDWARD
SUNNERS, WILLIAM (1903-)
[American teacher, con-
sultant and author]
Weston Satterly
Sunny. See:
CLAPP, CHARLES
MURRAY, JAMES ARTHUR
Sonnie
Sonny
Sunny Jim. See:
WATSON, JAMES ELI
Sunrise Poet, The. See:
LANIER, SIDNEY
Sunset. See:
COX, SAMUEL SULLIVAN
Sunshine. See:
HOOD, DOROTHY BROWN-
ING
Sunshine, Marion. See:
IJAMES, MARY TUNSTALL
Sunshine, The Apostle of. See:
TAYLOR, ROBERT LOVE
Superb, The. See:
HANCOCK, WINFIELD
SCOTT
Supper Clubs, The First Lady of.
See: SELL, HILDEGARDE
LORETTA
Supra Grammaticam (Above
Grammar). See:
SIGISMUND
Supreme Colorists of the World,
One of the. See:
TURNER, JOSEPH
MALLORD WILLIAM
Supreme Military Commander of
the State, The. See:
CHU TEH
Supreme Power of God, The.
See: SIMON MAGUS
Sure Shot, Little. See:
MOZZEE, PHOEBE ANNE
OAKLEY
SURFACE, WILLIAM E.
(1935-) [American sports
writer, columnist and author]
Bill Surface
Surfaceman. See:

ANDERSON, ALEXANDER
Surgeon of the Revolution, The
Fighting. See:
DOWNER, ELIPHALET
Surgeon Scout, The. See:
POWELL, DAVID FRANK
Surgery, The Father of
American. See:
PHYSICK, PHILIP SYNG
Surgery, The Father of Anti-
septic. See:
LISTER, JOSEPH
Surgery, The Father of English.
See: WISEMAN, RICHARD
Surgery, The Father of French.
See: PARÉ, AMBROISE
Surrender, Unconditional. See:
GRANT, HIRAM
ULYSSES
Surrey, Earl of. See:
HOWARD, HENRY
Surrey, Richard. See:
BROOKER, BERTRAM
Surry, Colonel. See:
COOKE, JOHN ESTEN
SURTEES, ROBERT SMITH
(1805-64) [English
novelist]
John Jorrocks
Surveyor President, The.
See: WASHINGTON,
GEORGE
Survilliers, Comte de. See:
BONAPARTE, JOSEPH
Susan. See:
GRAHAM, MAUDE
FITZGERALD SUSAN
Susan Ash. See:
BEST, CAROL ANN
Susan Coolidge. See:
WOOLSEY, SARAH
CHAUNCEY
Susan Ertz. See:
McCRINDLE, MRS.
RONALD
Susan Hayward. See:
MARRINER, EDYTHE
Susan Peters. See:
CARNAHAN, SUZANNE
Susan Pleydell. See:
SENIOR, ISABEL JANET
COUPER

Susan Schlacter. See:
THALER, SUSAN
Susan Shaw. See:
SLOOTS, PATSY
Susanna Foster. See:
LARSEN, SUZAN
Suspense, The Cherubic Master
of. See:
HITCHCOCK, ALFRED
JOSEPH
SUSSMAN, CORNELIA SILVER
(1914-) [American author]
Cornelia Jessey
Sut Lovingood. See:
HARRIS, GEORGE
WASHINGTON
SUTHERLAND, DR. EDWIN H.
(1883-1950) [American
author, educator and
criminologist]
The Dean of American
Criminologists
SUTHERLAND, DR. JOHN BAIN
(1889-) [Scottish-
American football coach]
Jock Sutherland
Sutherland Ross. See:
CALLARD, MAURICE
FREDERICK THOMAS
SUTHPIN, WILLIAM HALSTEAD
(1887-) [American
politician; congressman
from New Jersey]
Barnacle Bill
SUTTER, JOHN AUGUSTUS
(1803-80) [Swiss pioneer in
the settlement of California]
Captain Sutter
SUTTLES, SHIRLEY SMITH
(1922-) [American author]
Lesley Conger
Sutton, Dick. See:
SCHWARTZ, RICHARD
Sutton, Henry. See:
SLAVITT, DAVID R.
SUTTON, JEFFERSON H.
(1913-) [American news
photographer, reporter,
engineer and author]
Jeff Sutton
SUTTON, MAURICE LEWIS
(1927-) [American

educator and author]
Stack Sutton
SUTTON, RACHEL IRENE
BEEBE (1903-) [American
author]
Irene Ray
Margaret Beebe Sutton
SUTTON, WILLIAM (1901-)
[American bank
robber]
The Actor
Willy Sutton
Suzanne Farrell. See:
FICKER, ROBERTA SUE
SUZUKI, CHIYOKO (1930?-)
[Japanese-American
actress and singer]
Pat Suzuki
Suzy. See:
PARKER, CECELIA
Suzy Yorke. See:
BURTON, JOAN EILEEN
VERONICA
SVEDBERG, THEODOR (1884-)
[Swedish chemist]
The
SVENSON, ANDREW E. (1910-)
[American journalist,
teacher and author]
Jerry West
SVENSON, MRS. SVEN
GUSTAV (1927-) [English
ballerina]
Beryl Grey
Svevo, Italo. See:
SCHMITZ, ETTORE
SVOBODA, MADELEINE
(1916-) [French stage
and motion picture
actress]
Madeleine Robinson
SWABIA. See:
JOHN (JOHANNES)
OF SWABIA
Swabia, Philip of. See:
PHILIP
SWAIN, CHARLES (1801-74)
[English poet]
The Manchester Poet
SWAIN, DWIGHT VREELAND
(1915-) [American
journalist and author]

Clark South
SWAIN, FREDERICK DWIGHT
(1909-) [American jazz
musician (leader, drums,
string bass)]
Teeny Swain
SWALLOW, NORMAN (1921-)
[British television execu-
tive and author]
George Leather
SWALLOW, SILAS COMFORT
(1839-1930) [American
clergyman, reformer and
politician]
The Fighting Parson
Swamp Fox of Mississippi, The.
See: FORREST, NATHAN
BEDFORD
Swamp Fox of South Carolina, The.
See: MARION, FRANCIS
Swamp Fox of the Tennessee
Valley, The. See:
RODDEY, PHILIP DALE
Swamp Fox, The. See:
MARION, FRANCIS
Swamp Fox, The Old. See:
MARION, FRANCES
Swamps, Master of the. See:
HATFIELD, BAZIL MUSE
Swan, Don. See:
SCHWANDT, WILBUR
Swan, Marie. See:
BARTLETT, MARIE SWAN
Swan of Avon, Sweet. See:
SHAKESPEARE, WILLIAM
Swan of Lichfield, The. See:
SEWARD, ANNA
Swan of Mantua, The. See:
MARO, PUBLIUS
VERGILIUS
Swan of Padua, The. See:
ALGAROTTI, COUNT
FRANCESCO
Swan of Pesaro, The. See:
ROSSINI, GIOACHINO
ANTONIO
Swan of the Meander, The. See:
HOMER
Swan of the Thames, The. See:
TAYLOR, JOHN
Swan, The Black. See:
GREENFIELD, ELIZABETH

TAYLOR

Swan, The Dircaean. See:
PINDAR
Swan, The Maeonian. See:
HOMER
Swan, The Mantuan. See:
MARO, PUBLIUS
VERGILIUS
Swan, The Theban Garden.
See: PINDAR
SWANN, DONALD IBRAHIM
(1923-) [English song-
writer, musician, enter-
tainer and author]
Hilda Tablet
SWANSON, CLAUDE AUGUSTUS
(1862-1939) [American poli-
tician; Secretary of the Navy]
Big-Navy Claude
Swanson, Gloria. See:
SWENSON, JOSEPHINE
MAY
SWANSON, HAROLD NORLING
(1899-) [American editor
and author]
Kerry Scott
SWARTHOUT, GLADYS (1904-
69) [American singer]
The Prettiest Carmen on
Record
Swastika, The Scourge of the.
See: HIMMLER, HEINRICH
Swat, The Sultan of. See:
RUTH, GEORGE HERMAN
SWATRIDGE, CHARLES. See:
Charles, Theresa
SWATRIDGE, IRENE. See:
Charles, Theresa
Swayne, Geoffrey. See:
CAMPION, SIDNEY
RONALD
Swearing Jack Waller. See:
WALLER, JOHN
Sweater Girl, The. See:
TURNER, JULIA JEAN
MILDRED FRANCES
Sweatshirt Kid, The. See:
FISCHER, ROBERT JAMES
Sweden, King of (Charles XIV).
See: BERNADOTTE, JEAN
BAPTISTE JULES
Sweden, The Lion of. See:
BANÉR, JOHAN

Sweden, The Luther of. See:
PETRI, OLAUS (OLAF)
Swedish Maccabaeus, The. See:
GUSTAVUS II
Swedish Nightingale, The. See:
LIND, JOHANNA MARIA
Swee'. See also:
Sweet
Sweets
Swee' Pea. See:
STRAYHORN, WILLIAM
SWEENEY, CHARLES (1922-)
[English entomologist and
author]
R. C. H. Sweeney
SWEENEY, PETER BARR
(1825-1911) [American
politician; member of the
Tweed Ring]
Brains
The Great Democratic Warwick
The Nephew of My Uncle
Peter the Paragon
The Sly Sweeney
Spider Sweeney
Squire
Sweet. See also:
Swee'
Sweets
Sweet Emma the Bell Gal. See:
BARRETT, EMMA
Sweet Mama Stringbean. See:
WATERS, ETHEL
Sweet-potato Man, The. See:
CARVER, DR. GEORGE
WASHINGTON
Sweet Singer of Michigan, The.
See: MOORE, JULIA
Sweet Singers of the West, The,
name applied to ALICE
CAREY (1820-71) and her
sister PHOEBE CAREY
(1824-71) [American poets,
authors and hymn writers]
Sweet singers of the West, The.
See also:
CAREY, ALICE
Sweet-spirited Advocate of Jus-
tice, Love and Humanity,
The. See:
MOTT, LUCRETIA
Sweet Swan of Avon. See:

SHAKESPEARE,
WILLIAM
Sweetheart, America's. See:
SMITH, GLADYS MARY
Sweetheart Emeritus,
America's. See:
SMITH, GLADYS MARY
Sweetheart of the Foxholes,
The. See:
KAUMEYER, DOROTHY
Sweetheart of the Treasury,
The. See:
O'REILLY, MARY M.
Sweetheart, The World's. See:
SMITH, GLADYS MARY
Sweethearts of the Air, joint
stage name of MAY
SINGHI BREEN (190?-)
[American composer, uku-
lele player and radio
entertainer, and her husband
PETER DE ROSE
(1900-53) [American com-
poser, pianist and radio
entertainer]
Sweets. See:
EDISON, HARRY
Swee'
Sweet
SWENSON, JOSEPHINE MAY
(189?-) [American
motion picture actress]
Gloria Swanson
SWERLING, JOSEPH (1894-)
[Russian-American motion
picture writer]
Jo Swerling
SWEYN I (died 1014) [King of
Denmark]
Sweyn Forkbeard
SWEYN II (died 1075) [King of
Denmark]
Sweyn Estrithson
Swift, Benjamin. See:
PATERSON, WILLIAM
ROMAINE
Swift Bird. See:
HARE, WILLIAM HOBART
SWIFT, JONATHAN (1667-1745)
[English churchman and
satirist]
Isaac Bickerstaff

The Dean of St. Patrick's
A Dissenter
M. B. Drapier
The English Rabelais
The Gloomy Dean
Lemuel Gulliver
A Person of Honour
A Person of Quality
T. R. D. J. S. D. O. P. I. I.
Swift, Lewis J. See:
GARDNER, LEWIS J.
Swim, Old Sink or. See:
ADAMS, JOHN
SWINBURNE, ALGERNON
CHARLES (1837-1909)
[English poet, playwright
and critic]
Mad Swinburne
SWINBURNE, SIR JAMES, 9TH
BARONET (1858-1958)
[British scientist and in-
dustrialist]
The Father of British Plastics
SWINFORD, BETTY JUNE
WELLS (1927-) [American
author]
Linda Haynes
Kathryn Porter
Bob Swinford
June Wells
SWING, JOSEPH MAY (1894-)
[American general officer]
Uncle Joe
Swing, The King of. See:
GOODMAN, BENJAMIN
DAVID
Swing, The Sentimental Gentle-
man of. See:
DORSEY, THOMAS
SWINGS, POLIDORE F. F.
(1906-) [Belgian astro-
physicist and university
professor]
Paul Swings
Pol Swings
SWINNERTON, FRANK ARTHUR
(1884-) [English author]
Simon Pure
SWINTON, SIR ERNEST DUNLOP
(1868-1951) [British
soldier, writer and inventor]
Ole Luke-oie

Swiss History, The Father of.
See: TSCHUDI,
AEGIDIUS (GILG)
SWITZER, CARL (1926-59)
[American motion
picture actor]
Alfalfa
Switzerland, The Tintoretto of.
See: HUBER, JOHANN
RUDOLPHE
Switzerland, The Wallace of.
See: HOFER, ANDREAS
Sword, Long. See:
WILLIAM
Sword of God, The. See:
KHALID (KALED)
Sword of Rome, The. See:
MARCELLUS (MARCUS
CLAUDIUS)
Sword of the Confederacy, The.
See: JACKSON, THOMAS
JONATHAN
Sword of the Revllution, The.
See: WASHINGTON,
GEORGE
Sword, The Apostle of the.
See: MOHAMMED
Swordsman, Handsome
(Beau Sabreur). See:
MURAT, JOACHIM
SWOYER, ANNA MYRTLE
(1922-) [American actress
and comedienne]
Nancy Walker
Sy. See:
MILLER, SEYMOUR
OLIVER, MELVIN JAMES
TAYLOR, SEYMOUR
Sybil Forrest. See:
MARKUN, PATRICIA
MALONEY
Sybil Norton. See:
COURNOS, HELEN SYBIL
NORTON
Sycamore of the Wabash, The.
Tall. See:
VOORHEES, DANIEL
WOLSEY
SYDENHAM, THOMAS (1624-89)
[English physician]
The English Hippocrates
SYDNEY. See:

SIDNEY
Sidney
SIDNEY (SYDNEY), SIR
PHILIP
Sydney A. Story, Jr. See:
PIKE, MARY HAYDEN
GREEN
Sydney, C. See:
TRALINS, S. ROBERT
Sydney Fairbrother. See:
TAPPING, SYDNEY
Sydney W. Carroll. See:
WHITEMAN, GEORGE
FREDERICK
Sydney Yendys. See:
DOBELL, SYDNEY
THOMPSON
SYKES, ARTHUR ALKIN (1861-)
[British author]
Z. Y. Z.
Zigzag
Sykes, Roosevelt. See:
BEY, ROOSEVELT SYKES
Syllable-accenting American,
The. See:
WEISS, EHRICH
(ERIK WEISZ)
Sylva, Carmen. See:
ELISABETH
Sylvander. See:
BURNS, ROBERT
Sylvanus Urban. See:
CAVE, EDWARD
SYLVESTER (died 335) [Supreme
Pontiff of Roman Catholic
Church]
Pope Sylvester I
St. Sylvester
SYLVESTER (died 1003) [Supreme
Pontiff of Roman Catholic
Church]
Pope Sylvester II
SYLVESTER (died 1045) [Supreme
Pontiff of Roman Catholic
Church]
Pope Sylvester III
Sylvester, Arthur. See:
TUBBS, ARTHUR LEWIS
SYLVESTER, JOSHUA (1563-
1618) [English poet and
translator]
The Silver-tongued

Sylvia Dee. See:
PROFFITT, JOSEPHINE
MOORE
Sylvia E. Kamerman. See:
BURACK, SYLVIA
Sylvia Paul Jerman. See:
COOPER, SYLVIA
Sylvia Thorpe. See:
THIMBLETHORPE, JUNE
SYLVIA
Sylvin, Francis, joint pseud.
of FRANCES SCHWARTZ
(fl. 1943-68) and
SYLVIA S. SEAMAN
(fl. 1943-68) [American
authors]
SYMACCHUS (died 514) [Supreme
Pontiff of Roman Catholic
Church]
Pope Symacchus
St. Symacchus
Symmonds. See also:
SIMMONS
Symmonds, John. See:
GONZALES, BLI
SYMNES, FRANCIS EDWARD
(1851-1927) [Canadian
Congregational minister;
founder of Christian
Endeavor]
Francis Edward Clark
Symphony, The Father of. See:
HAYDN, FRANZ JOSEPH
Symus, The Pilgrim. See:
COBB, SYLVANUS, JR.
Syncerus, Actius. See:
SANNAZARO, JACOPO
Syntax, John. See:
DENNETT, HERBERT
VICTOR
Syrian, The. See:
EPHRAIM (EPHRAEM)
Syrians, The Prophet of the.
See: SYRUS, EPHRAEM
SYRUS. See also:
CYRUS
Cyrus
SYRUS, EPHRAEM (c. 308-
c. 373) [Syrian theologian
and sacred poet]
The Prophet of the Syrians
System in New Jersey, The

Father of the Free School.
See: CUTLER, AUGUSTUS
WILLIAM
System in Ohio, The Father of
the Public School. See:
RICE, HARVEY
System of Common-School
Education, The Father of
the. See:
TREADWELL, JOHN
System of Pennsylvania, The
Father of the Public
School. See:
WOLF, GEORGE
System, The Father of the
English Public School.
See: WYKEHAM (WICK-
HAM), WILLIAM OF
System, The Father of the
Federal Reserve. See:
GLASS, GEORGE CARTER
System, The Father of the Free
School. See:
ENGLISH, JAMES
EDWARD
SYYED SHAYKH ACHMED AB-
DULLAH NADIR KHAN EL-
IDRISSVIEH EL-DURANI
(1881-1945) [Indian novelist
and playwright]
Achmed Abdullah
SZAKALL, EUGENE GERO
(1884-1955) [Hungarian
vaudeville, stage and
motion picture actor]
S. Z. Sakall
Szapolyai (Sigismund Zápolya).
See: JOHN II
Szapolyai (Zápolya). See:
JOHN I
SZEKELY, ISTVAN (1899-)
[Hungarian motion picture
director]
Steve Sekely
SZYMANSKI, ALOYSIUS HARRY
(1903-56) [American pro-
fessional baseball player]
Bucketfoot
Aloysius Harry Simmons

T

T. See:
TATLOW, TISSINGTON
T. B. See:
THORPE, THOMAS BANGS
T. B. Bostwick, Colonel. See:
HARBAUGH, THOMAS
CHALMERS
T. B. Dowd. See:
PORTER, WILLIAM
SYDNEY
T, Big. See:
TEAGARDEN, WELDON
JOHN
T-Bone. See:
WALKER, AARON
T. C. H. Jacobs. See:
PENDOWER, JACQUES
T. Carmi. See:
CHARNEY, CARMI
T. Caspipina. See:
DUCHÉ, JACOB
T. Clark. See:
GALT, JOHN
T. D. See:
DORSEY, THOMAS
T. E. Shaw, Private. See:
LAWRENCE, THOMAS
EDWARD
T. F. See:
POWYS, THEODORE
FRANCIS
T. F. James. See:
FLEMING, THOMAS
JAMES
T in Punch. See:
THORP, JOSEPH
PETER
T. N. T. See:
THOMAS, CORNELIUS
DICKINSON
T. R. D. J. S. D. O. P. I. I. See:
SWIFT, JONATHAN
T. S. See:
ELIOT, THOMAS STEARNS
STRIBLING, THOMAS
SIGISMUND
T. Talker. See:
RANDS, WILLIAM
BRIGHTY
T. Taylor. See:

FOE, DANIEL
T. V. See:
SOONG, TSE-VEN
T. V. A. See:
RANKIN, JOHN ELLIOTT
T. W. King. See:
INGRAHAM, COLONEL
PRENTISS
T. W. R. See:
RIDDLE, THOMAS
WILKINSON
Ta-shun, Pai. See:
PETERSON, FREDERICK
TAAFE, ALICE (1899-)
[American silent motion
picture actress]
Alice Terry
Taaffe, Michael. See:
MAGUIRE, ROBERT
AUGUSTINE JOSEPH
Tab Hunter. See:
GELIEN, ART
Tabard, Toom (Empty Jacket).
See: JOHN DE BALIOL
Tabarin. See:
GIRARD, ANTOINE
TABB, JOHN BANISTER (1845-
1909) [American poet,
churchman and teacher]
Father Tabb
Table, The Knight of Our Round.
See: AEGIDUS OF
ASSISI
Tablet, Hilda. See:
SWANN, DONALD
IBRAHIM
Tablet Triturate, The Father of
the. See:
FULLER, ROBERT MASON
TABOR, HORACE AUSTIN
WARNER (1830-99) [Amer-
ican miner and capitalist]
Haw Tabor
Silver Dollar Tabor
Tabor, Paul. See:
TABORI, PAUL
TABORI, PAUL (1908-)
[Hungarian journalist,
political scientist and
author]
Paul Tabor
Taciturn, Hellmuth the. See:

VON MOLTKE, HELL-
MUTH KARL BERNHARD
Tacoma, The Father of. See:
WRIGHT, CHARLES
BARSTOW
Tacubaya, The Tiger of. See:
MARQUEZ, LEONARDO
Tad. See:
DORGAN, THOMAS
ALOYSIUS
MOSEL, GEORGE
AULT, JR.
Tadd. See:
DAMERON, TADLEY
EWING
Tadrack, Moss. See:
CARYL, WARREN
Tae-yong, Rò. See:
RUTT, RICHARD
Taffrail. See:
DORLING, HENRY
TAPRELL
Taft. See:
JORDAN, JAMES TAFT
TAFT, ROBERT ALPHONSO
(1889-1953) [American
politician; congressman
from Ohio]
Mr. Republican
TAH-GAH-JUTE (c.1725-80)
[Mingo Indian chief and
orator]
Logan
Tahan. See:
GRIFFIS, JOSEPH K.
Tailor, The Arabian. See:
WILD, HENRY
Tailor, The Learned. See:
WILD, HENRY
Tailor, The Literary. See:
BROWN, THEOPHILUS
Tailor, The Tennessee. See:
JOHNSON, ANDREW
TAINE, HIPPOLYTE ADOLPHE
(1828-93) [French
critic]
Henri Taine
Taine, John. See:
BELL, ERIC TEMPLE
Takkie Caution. See:
HATFIELD, CLARENCE
E.

Tal. See:
FARLOW, TALMADGE
HOLT
TALBERT, WILLIAM FRANK-
LIN III (1918-) [American
tennis player and sales
executive]
Billy Talbert
TALBOT, CHARLES REMING-
TON (1851-91) [American
Episcopal clergyman and
author of children's books]
John Brown John
Magnus Merriweather
TALBOT, JOHN (c.1373-1453)
[1st Earl of Shrewsbury]
The English Achilles
Talbot, Kay. See:
ROWLAND, DONALD
SYDNEY
Talbot, Lyle. See:
HENDERSON, LISLE
TALBOT, MARY ANNE (1778-
1808) [British "drummer
boy" and "cabin boy"]
The British Amazon
TALBOT, RICHARD (1630-91)
[Duke of Tyrconnel; Lord
Lieutenant of Ireland]
Lying Dick Talbot
TALBOT, WILLIAM HENRY
FOX (1800-77) [English
photographer, philologist
and archaeologist]
The Father of Photography
TALCOTT, JOHN (c.1630-88)
[Anglo-American soldier
and public official]
The Indian Fighter
TALENT, LEO (1906-)
[American composer,
violinist and publisher]
Jack Winters
Talented Young Composer in
America, The Most. See:
GOULD, MORTON
Tales, Teller of (Tusitala).
See: STEVENSON,
ROBERT LOUIS BAL-
FOUR
TALFOURD, SIR THOMAS NOON
(1795-1854) [British

dramatist]
Sarjeant Talfourd
TALIAFERRO, HARDEN E.
(c. 1818-75) [American
author]
Skitt
Talisman, Our. See:
LIPPARD, GEORGE
Talkative Tom. See:
BLANTON, THOMAS
LINDSAY
Talker, T. See:
RANDS, WILLIAM
BRIGHTY
Tall Pine. See:
SIBLEY, HENRY
HASTINGS
Tall Son, York's. See:
PORTER, WILLIAM
TROTTER
Tall Sycamore of the Wabash,
The. See:
VOORHEES, DANIEL
WOLSEY
Tall, The. See:
ALBERT
PHILIP V
Tall Trader. See:
SIBLEY, HENRY
HASTINGS
TALLEYRAND-PÉRIGORD,
CHARLES MAURICE DE
(1754-1838) [French
statesman and diplomat]
The Prince of Diplomatists
Talleyrand, The American.
See: VAN BUREN,
MARTIN
TALLIS, THOMAS (c. 1510-85)
[English musician]
The Father of English
Cathedral Music
Tallu. See:
BANKHEAD, TALLULAH
Tallulah's Papa. See:
BANKHEAD, WILLIAM
BROCKMAN
Tally Mason. See:
DERLETH, AUGUST
WILLIAM
TALMA, FRANÇOIS JOSEPH
(1763-1826) [French tragic

actor]
The French Roscius
Talvi. See:
ROBINSON, MRS. THÉRÈSE
ALBERTINE
Tama Jim. See:
WILSON, JAMES
Tamate. See:
CHALMERS, JAMES
Tamburlaine. See:
TIMUR LENK
Tamer of the Lightning, The.
See: FRANKLIN,
BENJAMIN
Tamerlane. See:
TIMUR LENK
Tammany Hall, The Sachem of.
See: KELLY, JOHN
TWEED, WILLIAM
MARCY
Tan Yun. See:
LIN, ADET JUSU
TANEY, ROGER BROOKE
(1777-1864) [American
jurist; Chief Justice of
the U.S. Supreme Court]
King Coody
Tangiers. See:
SMITH, WILLIAM
TANNENBAUM, IRVING (1903-)
[American educator,
biographer and author]
Irving Stone
Tanner, John. See:
MATCHA, JACK
Tanner President, The. See:
GRANT, HIRAM ULYSSES
Tanner, The Galena. See:
GRANT, HIRAM ULYSSES
Tante, Dilly. See:
KUNITZ, STANLEY
JASSPON
Tapissier de Notre Dame, Le.
See: MONTMORENCY-
BOUTEVILLE, HENRI
DE
TAPPING, SYDNEY (1873-1941)
[British motion picture
actress]
Sydney Fairbrother
Tar Baby, The Boston. See:
LANGFORD, SAM

TARBELL, IDA MINERVA
(1875-1944) [American
author and biographer]
The Dean of Woman
Authors of America
Tardy George. See:
McCLELLAN, GEORGE
BRINTON
TARDY, MARY T. (fl. 1870)
[American author]
Ida Raymond
TARENTAISE, PETER OF
(c.1225-76) [Supreme
Pontiff of Roman
Catholic Church]
Pope Innocent V
Tariff, The Father of the. See:
HAMILTON, ALEXANDER
TARKENTON, FRANCIS
ASBURY (1940-)
[American professional
football player]
Fran Tarkenton
TARKINGTON, NEWTON BOOTH
(1869-1946) [American
novelist and playwright]
Booth Tarkington
TARLTON, RICHARD (died
1588) [English
comedian]
The Man of Happy Unhappy
Answers
Tarquin the Proud. See:
TARQUINIUS SUPERBUS,
LUCIUS
TARQUINIUS SUPERBUS,
LUCIUS (reigned 534-510
B.C.) [Seventh and
last legendary King of
Rome]
Tarquin the Proud
Tarsus, Saul of. See:
SAUL
Tartarin. See:
DAUDET, ALPHONSE
Tartuffe of the Revolution,
The. See:
NICOLAS, JEAN
TASSO, TORQUATO. See:
Immortal Four of Italy,
The
TATANKA YOTANKA (1837-90)

[Sioux Indian Chief]
Sitting Bull
Tate, Ellalice. See:
HIBBERT, ELEANOR
BURFORD
TATE, GEORGE HOLMES
(1915-) [American jazz
musician (tenor saxophone,
leader)]
Buddy Tate
Tate, Hal. See:
TEITELMAN, ALEX
TATE, JOHN ORLEY ALLEN
(1899-) [American poet,
literary critic and
biographer]
Allen Tate
TATE, MARGARET (1889-)
[English concert singer]
Maggie Teyte
Tate, Mary Anne. See:
HALE, ARLENE
TATE, VELMA (1913-)
[American advertising
executive and author]
Francine Davenport
Valerie Taylor
Nacella Young
Tatham, Campbell. See:
ELTING, MARY
TATHAM, LAURA ESTHER
(1919-) [British editor,
journalist and author]
John Martin
Margaret Phipps
Tati. See also:
TATTI
Tati, Jacques. See:
TATISCHEFF, JACQUES
TATIAN (fl. 2nd cent. A.D.)
[Assyrian Christian
convert and churchman]
The Apologist
TATISCHEFF, JACQUES
(1908-) [French panto-
mimist and actor]
Jacques Tati
TATLOW, TISSINGTON (1876-)
[British clergyman and
author]
T
Tato, El (Baby Brother). See:

SÁNCHEZ, ANTONIO
Tatray, Istvan. See:
RUPERT, RAPHAEL
RUDOLPH
TATTERSALL, MURIEL JOYCE
(1931-) [British
educator and author]
Elizabeth Waud
TATTI. See also:
Tati
TATTI, JACOPO (1479-1570)
[Italian sculptor and
architect]
Sansovino
Tattooed Knight. See:
BLAINE, JAMES
GILLESPIE
Tattooed Man. See:
BLAINE, JAMES
GILLESPIE
TATUM, JAMES MOORE
(1913-) [American
football coach]
Jim Tatum
Silent Jim
TAULER, JOHANN (c. 1300-61)
[German mystic and
preacher]
Doctor Illuminatus
TAUSEN, HANS (1494-1561)
[Danish religious
reformer]
The Danish Luther
TAVES, ISABELLA (1915-)
[American author]
Christy Munro
Tavo, Gus, pseud. of
MARTHA MILLER PFAFF
IVAN (1909-) and some-
times with her husband
GUSTAVE E. IVAN
(-) [American authors]
Tavo, Gus. See also:
IVAN, MARTHA
MILLER PFAFF
Tax Harry, High. See:
TRUMAN, HARRY S
Taxer, The Single. See:
GEORGE, HENRY
Tay Pay. See:
O'CONNOR, THOMAS
POWER

TAYLOR, ALFRED ALEXANDER
(1848-1931) [American poli-
tician; governor of and con-
gressman from Tennessee]
The Knight of the Red Rose
The Sage of Happy Valley
Uncle Alf
TAYLOR, BENJAMIN FRANKLIN
(1819-87) [American poet]
The Oliver Goldsmith of
America
TAYLOR, BERT LESTON
(1866-1921) [American
poet and columnist]
B. L. T.
Taylor, Captain Alfred B. See:
INGRAHAM, COLONEL
PRENTISS
TAYLOR, CATHERINE (1944-)
[Canadian composer, singer,
actress and guitarist]
Cathie Taylor
TAYLOR, CHARLES A. (1864-
1942) [American playwright]
The King of the Mellers
TAYLOR, CHARLES R. S.
(1915-) [American
musician and composer]
Russ Taylor
TAYLOR, CHARLEY (1894-)
[American hunting guide
and champion slingsman]
Slingshot Charley
TAYLOR, FREDERICK CHASE
(1897-1950) [American
author and radio comedian]
Colonel Stoopnagle
Lemuel Q. Stoopnagle
TAYLOR, H. BALDWIN. See:
WAUGH, HILLARY
BALDWIN
Taylor Hemingway. See:
RYWELL, MARTIN
TAYLOR, ISAAC (1759-1829)
[British juvenile writer;
head of the writing family
"The Taylors of Ongar"]
The Elder
TAYLOR, ISAAC (1787-1865)
[British religious writer]
The Younger
TAYLOR, JAMES BAYARD (1827-
78) [American poet, novelist

and traveler]
Bayard Taylor
TAYLOR, JAMES WREN
(1898-) [American
professional baseball
player]
Zack Taylor
TAYLOR, JEREMY
(1613-67) [English
bishop and theological
writer]
The Shakespeare of Divines
The Spenser of English
Prose Writers
TAYLOR, JOHN (1580-1653)
[English poet]
The Swan of the Thames
The Water Poet
TAYLOR, JOHN (1753-1824)
[American soldier,
lawyer and statesman]
John Taylor of Caroline
TAYLOR, JOSEPH DEEMS
(1885-1966) [American
composer and music
critic]
Deems Taylor
Taylor, Judson R. See:
HALSEY, HARLAN P.
Taylor, Kent. See:
WEISS, LOUIS
Taylor, Laurette. See:
COONEY, HELEN LAU-
RETTE MAGDALENE
TAYLOR, LIONEL (1916-)
[American composer and
musician]
Les Taylor
Taylor, Margaret. See:
BURROUGHS, MARGARET
TAYLOR
TAYLOR, MARION SAYLE
(1889-) [American radio
lecturer and author]
The Voice of Experience
TAYLOR, MARY VIRGINIA
(1912-) [American
author and educator]
Jean Sterling
Sue Wood
Taylor of Norwich. See:
BORROW, GEORGE HENRY

TAYLOR, PHOEBE ATWOOD
(1909-) [American detective
story writer]
Alice Tilton
TAYLOR, RICHARD (1919-)
[American educator, editor
and author]
Diodorus Cronus
Taylor, Robert. See:
BRUGH, SPANGLER
ARLINGTON
TAYLOR, ROBERT LOVE (1850-
1912) [American politician;
Governor of Tennessee]
The Apostle of Sunshine
Fiddling Bob
The Knight of the White Rose
Our Bob
TAYLOR, SEYMOUR (1912-)
[American musician]
Sy Taylor
Taylor, T. See:
FOE, DANIEL
TAYLOR, THOMAS (1743-1833)
[American army officer and
pioneer in Columbia, South
Carolina]
The Patriarch of Columbia
TAYLOR, THOMAS (1758-1835)
[British scholar and
translator]
The Platonist
Taylor, Valerie. See:
TATE, VELMA
TAYLOR, WILLIAM (1921-)
[American musician and
composer]
Billy Taylor
TAYLOR, ZACHARY (1784-1850)
[American general officer
and twelfth President of
the United States]
Old Buena Vista
Old Rough and Ready
Old Zach
Zach
Taylors of Ongar, The. See:
TAYLOR, ISAAC
Taystee Loafers, The. See:
Happiness Boys, The
Tchaadaieff. See:
SOROKIN, PITRIM

ALEXANDROVITCH
TEACH (THATCH), EDWARD
(16??-1718) [Anglo-
American pirate]
Blackbeard
Blackbeard the Buccaneer
Teacher of Germany, The. See:
SCHWARZERT, PHILIPP
Teacher President, The. See:
GARFIELD, JAMES
ABRAM
Teacher, The Cunning (Doctor
Subtilis). See:
DUNS SCOTUS, JOHN
Teacher, The Honeyed. See:
BERNARD OF CLAIRVAUX
TEAGARDEN, CHARLES
(1913-) [American jazz
musician (trumpet)]
Charlie Teagarden
TEAGARDEN, CLOIS LEE
(1915-) [American jazz
musician (drums)]
Cub Teagarden
TEAGARDEN, WELDON JOHN
(1905-64) [American jazz
musician (trombone,
singer, leader)]
Jack Teagarden
Big T
Tear 'em. See:
ROEBUCK, JOHN ARTHUR
Tearle, Conway. See:
LEVY, FREDERICK
Tears, The Queen of. See:
MARY OF MODENA
Tease, The Mother of the
Strip. See:
DENNIS, RUTH
Technicolor, The Queen of.
See: BROWN, MAUREEN
FITZSIMONS
Tecumseh, Old. See:
SHERMAN, WILLIAM
TECUMSEH
Ted. See:
CARROLL, THOMAS
THEODORE, JR.
COOK, PROCTOR FYFFE
DEALEY, EDWARD
MUSGROVE
HEATH, EDWARD

HUSING, EDWARD BRITT
KENNEDY, EDWARD
MOORE
KEY, THEODORE
KLAGES, THEODORE
ROBINSON, EDWIN MEADE
SHAWN, EDWIN MYERS
STEELE, LOUIS
THORNE, BLISS KIRBY
WEAR, THEODORE GRAHAM
WEEMS, WILFRED
THEODORE
WHITE, THEODORE EDWIN
WILLIAMS, THEODORE
SAMUEL
Ted Addy. See:
WINTERBOTHAM, RUSSELL
ROBERT
Ted Borch. See:
LUND, A. MORTEN
Ted Johnstone. See:
McDANIEL, DAVID EDWARD
Ted Lawson. See:
LEHRMAN, THEODORE H.
Ted Lewis. See:
FRIEDMAN, THEODORE
LEOPOLD
Ted Mack. See:
MAGUINESS, WILLIAM
EDWARD
Ted Murry. See:
MENCHER, MURRAY
Ted Ray. See:
OLDEN, CHARLES
TEDDELL, SAUNDERS
(1911-) [American jazz
musician (harmonica,
singer)]
Sonny Terry
TEDDER, ARTHUR WILLIAM
(1890-1967) [Scottish
soldier, statesman and
author]
Lord Tedder
Teddy. See:
KENNEDY, EDWARD MOORE
ROOSEVELT, THEODORE
WILSON, THEODORE
Teddy Charles. See:
COHEN, THEODORE
CHARLES
Teddy, Telescope. See:

ROOSEVELT, THEODORE
Teeny. See:
SWAIN, FREDERICK
DWIGHT
TEGNER, HENRY STUART
(1901-) [British
business executive and
author]
The Northumbrian
Gentleman
The Ruffle
Teh, Kang. See:
HSUAN T'UNG
TEICHMAN, ARTHUR
MURRAY (1895-) [Amer-
ican dancing teacher]
Arthur Murray
TEILHET, DARWIN (1904-)
[American novelist]
Cyrus Fisher
TEITELMAN, ALEX (1912-)
[American author]
Hal Tate
Tek-cheung, Cheng. See:
CHENG, CHU-TUAN
Telegraph, The Father of
the. See:
MORSE, SAMUEL
FINLEY BREESE
Telephone, The Father of the.
See: BELL,
ALEXANDER GRAHAM
Telescope Teddy. See:
ROOSEVELT, THEODORE
TELESPHORUS (died c.136)
[Supreme Pontiff of
Roman Catholic Church]
Pope Telesphorus
St. Telesphorus
Television Comedian,
America's Favorite. See:
JACOBS, AMOS
Television, Mr. See:
BERLINGER, MILTON
Television, The Father of. See:
FARNSWORTH, PHILO
TAYLOR
Television, The First Lady
of. See:
BALL, LUCILLE
Telfair, Nancy. See:
DuBOSE, LOUISE JONES

Teller of Tales (Tusitala). See:
STEVENSON, ROBERT
LOUIS BALFOUR
TÉLLEZ, GABRIEL (c.1571-1648)
[Spanish dramatist and
ecclesiastic]
Tirso de Molina
Temperance Reformation, The
Luther of the Early. See:
HEWIT, NATHANIEL
Temperance, The Apostle of. See:
MATTHEW, FATHER
THEOBALD
MURPHY, FRANCIS
TEMPEST, JAN (fl. early 20th
cent.) [English author of
detective stories]
Fay Chandos
Virginia Storm
Tempest, Marie. See:
ETHERINGTON, MARY
SUSAN
Tempest, The. See:
JUNOT, ANDOCHE
Tempest, Theresa. See:
KENT, LOUISE ANDREWS
Tempest, Victor. See:
PHILIPP, ELLIOT ELIAS
Templar, Maurice. See:
GROOM, ARTHUR WILLIAM
Temple. See:
BAILEY, IRENE TEMPLE
Temple, Dan. See:
NEWTON, DWIGHT
BENNETT
Temple, The Anacreon of the.
See: AMFRYE,
GUILLAUME
Temple, The Idol of the. See:
MARIE CHARLOTTE
Temple, The Orphan of the. See:
CHARLOTTE, MARIE
THÉRÈSE
Templeton, Laurence. See:
SCOTT, SIR WALTER
TEMUJIN (1162?-1227) [Mongol
conqueror]
Chinghiz Khan (Precious
Warrior)
Genghis Khan (Precious
Warrior)
Genghis Khan (Very Mighty

Ruler)
Jenghiz Khan (Precious
Warrior)
Ten. See:
Hollywood Ten, The
Ten-cent Jimmy. See:
BUCHANAN, JAMES
Ten Thousand Dollar Beauty,
The. See:
KELLY, MICHAEL J.
Tenella. See:
CLARKE, MARY
BAYARD DEVEREUX
TENER, MARTIN J.
(1935-) [American
composer and teacher]
Jay Martins
TENIERS, DAVID (1582-1649)
[Flemish genre painter]
The Elder
TENIERS, DAVID (1610-90)
[Flemish genre painter]
The Younger
Teniers of Comedy, The. See:
DANCOURT, FLORENT
CARTON
Teniers, The English. See:
MORLAND, GEORGE
Teniers, The Scottish. See:
WILKIE, SIR DAVID
Tennant, Kylie. See:
RODD, KYLIE TENNANT
TENNANT, NORA JACKSON
(1915-) [British educator
and author]
Nora Jackson
Tenneshaw, S. M. See:
BEAUMONT, CHARLES
Tennessee. See:
WILLIAMS, THOMAS
LANIER
Tennessee Ernie Ford. See:
FORD, ERNEST JENNINGS
Tennessee Plowboy, The. See:
ARNOLD, RICHARD
EDWARD
Tennessee Tailor, The.
See: JOHNSON, ANDREW
Tennessee, That Father of
Equity in. See:
GREEN, NATHAN
Tennessee, The Democratic

War Horse of. See:
McMILLIN, BENTON
Tennessee, The Eagle Orator of.
See: HENRY, GUSTAVUS
ADOLPHUS
Tennessee, The Father of Middle.
See: ROBERTSON, JAMES
Tennessee, The Hardwicke of.
See: GREEN, NATHAN
Tennessee Valley, The Swamp
Fox of the. See:
RODDEY, PHILIP DALE
TENNYSON, ALFRED, 1ST
BARON TENNYSON (1809-
92) [English poet laureate]
Alcibiades
Alfred, Lord Tennyson
Lord Tennyson
Merlin
TENNYSON, CHARLES (1808-79)
[English poet]
Charles Tennyson Turner
Tennyson J. Daft. See:
MORGAN, THOMAS P.
Tennyson, The Spanish. See:
NÚÑEZ DE ARCE,
GASPAR
Tenor Man, The World's Wildest.
See: COBB, ARNETT
CLEOPHUS
Tenor, The Whispering. See:
AUSTIN, GENE
Tensas, Madison, M. D. See:
LEWIS, HENRY CLAY
Tent, Ned. See:
DENNETT, HERBERT
VICTOR
Tent-theater Showmen, The Dean
of American. See:
ECCLES, GEORGE CLINTON,
JR.
Tenth Muse, The. See:
BRADSTREET, ANNE
DUDLEY
CRUZ, JUANA INÉS DE LA
DESHOULIÈRES, ANTOIN-
ETTE DU LIGIER DE
LA GARDE
SCUDÉRI, MADELEINE DE
UNKNOWN
Tentmaker, The. See:
OMAR KHAYYAM

TERADA, TORAHIKO (1878-)
[Japanese physicist and
author]
Huyukiko Yosimura
Tere Rios. See:
VERSACE, MARIE
TERESA RIOS
Terence Clyne. See:
BLATTY, WILLIAM
PETER
Terence McGrant. See:
PECK, GEORGE WILBUR
Terence of England, The. See:
CUMBERLAND, RICHARD
Terence O'Toole. See:
OTWAY, CAESAR
Terence, The English. See:
CUMBERLAND,
RICHARD
Terentius Phlogobombos. See:
JUDAH, SAMUEL
BENJAMIN HELBERT
TERESA [Teresa]. See also:
Theresa
Therese
Teresa Margaret, Sister. See:
ROWE, MARGARET
KEVIN
TERESA OF ÁVILA (1515-82)
[Spanish Catholic nun;
founder of Discalced
Carmelite convents for
nuns]
Theresa de Jesus
St. Teresa
TERESA OF LISIEUX, ST.
(1873-97) [French
Carmelite nun]
Little Flower of Jesus
TERHUNE, MARY VIRGINIA
HAWES (1830-1922)
[American novelist and
writer on household
management]
Marion Harland
TERNI, FAUSTA CIALENTE
(1900-) [Italian author]
Fausta Cialente
TERPANDER (fl. 7th cent.
B.C.) [Greek musician
and lyric poet]
The Father of Greek Music

TERR, MISCHA R. (1899-)
[Russian composer and
conductor]
Michael Terr
Terrave Bernarn. See:
BURNETT, DAVID
Terrell, St. John. See:
ECCLES, GEORGE CLINTON,
JR.
Terrence, Frederick J. See:
HAYES, JOHN F.
Terrible. See:
TOUHY, ROGER
Terrible, Ivan The. See:
IVAN IV VASILIEVICH
Terrible Siren, The. See:
WOODHULL, VICTORIA
CLAFLIN
Terrible Terry. See:
ALLEN, TERRY DE LA
MESA
Terrible Turk, The. See:
REED, THOMAS BRACKETT
Terriss, Dorothy. See:
MORSE, THEODORA
Terriss, No. 1 Adelphi. See:
LEWIN, WILLIAM
CHARLES JAMES
Terriss, William. See:
LEWIN, WILLIAM CHARLES
JAMES
Territory, Liberator of the. See:
THIERS, LOUIS ADOLPHE
Terror of France, The. See:
JOHN
Terror of the Gulf, The. See:
LAFITTE, JEAN
Terror of the House, The. See:
HARDIN, BENJAMIN
Terror of the Tories, The. See:
CLINCH, JOSEPH
Terror of the World, The. See:
ATTILA (ETZEL)
(ETHELE)
Terror, The Michigan. See:
HESTON, WILLIAM M.
Terror, The Witling of. See:
VIEUZAC, BERTRAND
BARÈRE DE
Terry. See:
CAULEY, TROY JESSE
KAY, TERENCE

Terry, Alice. See:
   TAAFE, ALICE
Terry, C. V. See:
   SLAUGHTER, FRANK GILL
TERRY, DAME ELLEN
   ALICE (1848-1928)
   [English actress]
   Ellen Terry
Terry, Dan. See:
   KOSTRABA, DANIEL
TERRY, DENNIS (1895-1932)
   [British actor]
   Derrick Dennis
TERRY, FLORENCE (1854-96)
   [English actress]
   Floss
Terry Gibbs. See:
   GUBENKO, JULIUS
Terry Moore. See:
   KOFORD, HELEN
Terry, Ron. See:
   PRITKIN, RON
TERRY, SARAH BALLARD
   (1819-92) [English
   actress]
   Miss Yerrit
Terry Shannon. See:
   MERCER, JESSIE
Terry Snow. See:
   WOOLSEY, MARYHALE
Terry, Sonny. See:
   TEDDELL, SAUNDERS
Terry, Terrible. See:
   ALLEN, TERRY DE LA
   MESA
Terry-Thomas. See:
   HOAR-STEVENS,
   THOMAS TERRY
TERRY, WILLIAM HAROLD
   (1898-) [American
   professional baseball
   player and manager]
   Bill Terry
   Memphis Bill
TERWAGNE, ANNE JOSEPH
   (1762-1817) [Heroine of
   the French Revolution]
   The Amazon of the Revolution
   La Belle Liégeoise
   The Fury of the Gironde
TESONE, WILLIAM N. (1927-)
   [American composer,

author and singer]
   Billy Duke
Teswood. See:
   DOWSETT, JOSEPH
   MOREWOOD
TETERNIKOV, FEDOR
   KUZMICH (1863-1927)
   [Russian novelist]
   Fedor Sologub
TETZNER, MARTHA HELENE
   (1872-) [German author]
   R. Von Einseidel
Teufelsdröch, See:
   CARLYLE, THOMAS
Teutonic James Dean, The. See:
   BUCHHOLZ, HORST
   WERNER
Tex. See:
   BENEKE, GORDON
   CARLETON, JAMES O.
   GARMS, DEBS G.
   IRVIN, CECIL P.
   MAULE, HAMILTON BEE
   RICKARD, GEORGE LEWIS
   RITTER, WOODWARD
   SATTERWHITE, COLLEEN
   GRAY
Tex Burns. See:
   L'AMOUR, LOUIS DEARBORN
Tex Holt. See:
   JOSCELYN, ARCHIE L.
Tex Riley. See:
   CREASEY, JOHN
Texas. See:
   GRANT, HIRAM ULYSSES
   GUINAN, MARY LOUISE
   CECELIA
Texas Doll Lady, The. See:
   WEAVER, GUSTINE
   NANCY COURSON
Texas Jack. See:
   OMOHUNDRO, JOHN B.
Texas Jim. See:
   ROBERTSON, JAMES B.
Texas, The Demosthenes of.
   See: HUBBARD,
   RICHARD BENNETT
Texas, The Father of. See:
   AUSTIN, STEPHEN FULLER
   HOUSTON, SAMUEL
Texas, The Favorite Son of. See:
   GARNER, JOHN NANCE

Texas Tom. See:
  CONNALLY, THOMAS
    TERRY
Texas Wildcatters, The King
  of the. See:
  CULLEN, HUGH TROY
Tey, Josephine. See:
  MACKINTOSH, ELIZABETH
Teyte, Maggie. See:
  TATE, MARGARET
THACKERAY, WILLIAM
  MAKEPEACE (1811-63)
  [English novelist]
  Mr. Brown
  The Fat Contributor
  George Fitz-Boodle
  Major Goliah Gahagan
  Arthur Pendennis
  Peter Perseus
  Jeames de la Pluche
  Dorothea Julia Ramsbottom
  The Honorable Wilhelmina
    Amelia Skeggs
  Ikey Solomons, Esq., Junior
  Mr. Spec
  Miss Tickletoby
  M. A. Titmarsh
  Michael Angelo Titmarsh
  Lancelot Wagstaff
  Théophile Wagstaff
  Charles Yellowplush, Esq.
Thad. See:
  STEVENS, THADDEUS
Thaddeus O'Finn. See:
  McGLOIN, JOSEPH
    THADDEUS
THALBERG, IRVING GRANT
  (1899-1936) [American
  motion picture producer]
  The Boy Producer
THALER, SUSAN (1939-)
  [American editor and
  author]
  Susan Schlacter
THALES. See:
  Seven Sages of Greece, The
Thalia Mara. See:
  MAHONEY, ELIZABETH
Thames, C. H. See:
  MARLOWE, STEPHEN
Thames, The Swan of the. See:
  TAYLOR, JOHN

Thanet, Octave. See:
  FRENCH, ALICE
Thanksgiving, The Mother of.
  See: HALE, SARAH
    JOSEPHA
Tharpe, Sister Rosetta. See:
  NUBIN, ROSETTA
That Ace Drummer Man. See:
  KRUPA, EUGENE BERTRAM
That Candid Spoilsman. See:
  FARLEY, JAMES
    ALOYSIUS
That Singular Splendor of the
  Italian Race. See:
  ALIGHIERI, DURANTE
That Man in the White House. See:
  ROOSEVELT, FRANKLIN
    DELANO
THATCH. See:
  TEACH (THATCH),
    EDWARD
THATCHER, JOHN WELLS
  (1858-) [British barrister
  and author]
  Pauper et Ignotus
  Rambler
THATCHER, MOSES (1842-1909)
  [American frontiersman]
  Little Chief
THAUMATURGUS. See:
  GREGORY THAUMATURGUS
THAYENDANEGEA (1742-1807)
  [Mohawk Indian chief]
  Joseph Brant
THAYER, EMMA REDINGTON
  LEE (1874-) [American
  artist and author]
  Lee Thayer
Thayer, Jane. See:
  WOOLLEY, CATHERINE
THAYER, JOHN (1758-1815)
  [American Roman
  Catholic missionary;
  former Congregationalist
  minister]
  John Turncoat
THAYER, SIMEON (1737-1800)
  [American army officer]
  The Hero of Fort Mifflin
THAYER, SYLVANUS (1785-
  1872) [American general
  officer; superintendent of

997

the U.S. Military Academy
at West Point]
The Father of the United
States Military Academy
The. See:
SVEDBERG, THEODOR
Thearcher. See:
HODGSON, WILLIAM
ARCHER
Theater, The Dean of the
American. See:
SKINNER, OTIS
Theater, The First Lady of
the American. See:
BROWN, HELEN HAYES
Theater, The Patriarch of the
Spanish. See:
ENCINA (ENZINA),
JUAN DEL
Theater, The Present
Champion of the English.
See: OLIVIER, SIR
LAURENCE
Theatrical King, The. See:
MURAT, JOACHIM
Theban Bard, The. See:
PINDAR
Theban Eagle, The. See:
PINDAR
Theban Garden Swan, The.
See: PINDAR
Theban Lyre, The. See:
PINDAR
Thebes, Antony of. See:
ANTONY (ANTHONY),
ST.
Theda Bara. See:
GOODMAN, THEODOSIA
Them All, The Noblest
Roman of. See:
McMILLIN, BENTON
THURMAN, ALLAN
GRANBERRY
Theo Callas. See:
McCARTHY, SHAUN
Theo LeSieg. See:
GEISEL, THEODOR SEUSS
Theobald, Alfred Herbert. See:
TUBBY, ALFRED
HERBERT
Theocritus, The Portuguese.
See: MIRANDA,

FRANCISCO DA SÁ DE
Theocritus, The Scottish. See:
RAMSAY, ALLAN
Theocritus, The Sicilian. See:
MELI, GIOVANNI
Theodate Geoffrey. See:
WAYMAN, DOROTHY
THEODORA (508-48) [Byzantine
empress]
The Empress Theodora
Theodore. See:
Chamberlain, Theodore
KOMISARJEVSKY, FEDOR
THOMAS, CHRISTIAN
FRIEDRICH THEODORE
THEODORE (died 649) [Supreme
Pontiff of Roman Catholic
Church]
Pope Theodore I
THEODORE (died 897) [Supreme
Pontiff of Roman Catholic
Church]
Pope Theodore II
THEODORE II (1818-68) [King
of Abyssinia]
Negus
Theodore de la Guard. See:
WARD, NATHANIEL
Theodore, King of Corsica. See:
VAN NEUHOFF, BARON
Theodore the Meddler. See:
ROOSEVELT, THEODORE
THEODORIC (c. 455-526) [King
of the Ostrogoths and of
Italy]
The Great
Patricius and Magister Mili-
tum
Dietrich von Bern
Theodosia Garrison. See:
FAULKS, MRS. FREDERIC
J.
THEODOSIUS (died 376) [Roman
general officer],
The Elder
THEODOSIUS I (c. 346-95) [Roman
emperor and general officer]
The Great
THEODOSIUS II (401-50)
[Emperor of Eastern Roman
Empire]
The Calligrapher

Theologian, The. See:
GREGORY OF
NAZIANZUS, ST.
Theologians, The Monarch of.
See: ALEXANDER OF
HALES
Theologus. See:
GREGORY OF NAZIANZUS,
ST.
Theology, The Bacon of. See:
BUTLER, BISHOP
JOSEPH
Theology, The Franklin of.
See: FULLER, ANDREW
Théophile. See:
VIAU, THÉOPHILE DE
Théophile Delaporte. See:
GREEN, JULIEN
HARTRIDGE
Théophile Wagstaff. See:
THACKERAY, WILLIAM
MAKEPEACE
Theophoros (God-bearer). See:
IGNATIUS OF ANTIOCH,
ST.
Theophrastus. See:
CREECH, WILLIAM
Theophrastus of France, The.
See: BRUYÈRE, JEAN
DE LA
THEORELL, AXEL HUGO
(1903-) [Swedish
biochemist]
Hugo Theorell
Theoretical Physicist of the
Nineteenth Century, The
Greatest. See:
MAXWELL, JAMES
CLERK
Theory, The Father of Modern.
See: FERMAT,
PIERRE DE
Theos (God). See:
ANTIOCHUS II
THEOTOKOPOULOS, KYRIAKOS
(1541-1614) [Spanish
painter, born near
Crete]
Domenico
El Greco (The Greek)
Theresa. See:
Charles, Theresa
TERESA

Teresa
Therese
Theresa de Jesus. See:
TERESA OF ÁVILA
Theresa Tempest. See:
KENT, LOUISE ANDREWS
Therese. See also:
TERESA
Teresa
Terese
Therese Benson. See:
KNIPE, EMILIE BENSON
THESPIS (fl. 6th cent. B.C.)
[Athenian poet]
The Father of Greek Tragedy
Thévenin, Denis. See:
DUHAMEL, GEORGES
THIARD, PONTIUS DE
(c. 1521-1605) [French
poet]
The French Anacreon
THIBAULT, JACQUES ANATOLE
FRANÇOIS (1844-1924)
[French author]
Anatole France
THIBAULT, MARALEE G.
(1924-) [American
broadcaster, journalist
and author]
Maralee G. Davis
Thief, The Professional. See:
UNKNOWN
THIELEMANS, JEAN (1922-)
[Belgian jazz musician
(guitar, harmonica)]
Jon
Toots
THIERS, LOUIS ADOLPHE
(1797-1877) [French his-
torian and politician]
Liberator of the Territory
Thieves, The King of. See:
SCOTT, ADAM, OF
TUSHIELAW
Thieves, The Prince of. See:
MANOLESCO, GEORGE
THIMBLETHORPE, JUNE
SYLVIA (1926-) [English
author]
Sylvia Thorpe
Third Founder of Rome, The. See:
CAIUS MARIUS
Thirlmere, Rowland. See:

WALKER, JOHN
Thirsty. See:
  Thursty
Thirteenth Apostle, The. See:
  CHRYSOSTOM, ST. JOHN
Thistle, Donald. See:
  BROWN, H. CLARK
Thom. See:
  Demijohn, Thom
  Tom
  Toom
THOM, JOHN NICHOLS
  (c. 1796-1838) [Demented
  Cornishman, claimed to be
  a Knight of Malta]
  Sir William Courtenay
THOM, WILLIAM (1799-1850)
  [Scottish poet]
  The Weaver-Poet of Inverurie
Thomas, See:
  BECKET, THOMAS À
  LUCHESE, GAETANO
  Stratton, Thomas
Thomas à Becket, St. See:
  BECKET, THOMAS À
Thomas à Kempis. See:
  KEMPEN, THOMAS
  HAMERKEN VAN
Thomas Ahrens. See:
  WILSON, ROGER C.
THOMAS, ALFRED (1870-)
  [British clergyman,
  journalist and author]
  Alfred Gwalia
Thomas, Andrea. See:
  HILL, MARGARET OHLER
Thomas Brown the Younger. See:
  MOORE, THOMAS
Thomas Burton. See:
  LONGSTREET, STEPHEN
Thomas, Carl H. See:
  DOERFFLER, ALFRED
Thomas, Caroline. See:
  DORR, JULIA CAROLINE
  RIPLEY
Thomas Castro. See:
  ORTON, ARTHUR
THOMAS, CHARLES LOUIS
  AMBROISE (1811-96)
  [French composer]
  Ambroise Thomas
THOMAS, CHRISTIAN FRIEDRICH

THEODORE (1831-1905) [Ger-
  man-American orchestral
  conductor]
  Theodore Thomas
THOMAS, CORNELIUS
  DICKINSON (1920-)
  [American artist, educator
  and author]
  T. N. T.
  Neal Thomas
Thomas Curtis Hicks Jacobs. See:
  PENDOWER, JACQUES
Thomas, Danny. See:
  JACOBS, AMOS
THOMAS, DAVID (1794-1882)
  [Anglo-American iron
  master]
  The Father of the American
  Anthracite Iron Industry
Thomas, Egbert S. See:
  ELLIS, EDWARD
  SYLVESTER
THOMAS, EUGENE (1893-)
  [American author]
  Donald Grey
THOMAS, FRANK WILLIAM
  (1898-) [American
  football coach]
  Rat
THOMAS, FREDERICK. See:
  Laklan, Carli
Thomas, G. K. See:
  DAVIES, LESLIE PURNELL
THOMAS, GEORGE HENRY
  (1816-70) [American Civil
  War general officer]
  Lion Hearted Thomas
  Old Pap Safety
  Old Reliable
  Old Slow Trot
  Pap Thomas
  The Rock of Chickamauga
  Uncle George
  George Washington
THOMAS, GORDON (1933-)
  [British journalist and
  author]
  Tom Gordon
  Brian James
  Robert Street
Thomas, H. C. See:
  KEATING, LAWRENCE A.

Thomas Hämmerlein. See:
    KEMPEN, THOMAS
        HAMERKEN VAN
Thomas, Henry. See:
    SCHNITTKIND, HENRY
        THOMAS
Thomas Howard, Mr. See:
    JAMES, JESSE WOODSON
Thomas Ingoldsby, Esq. See:
    BARHAM, RICHARD
        HARRIS
THOMAS, ISAIAH (1749-1831)
    [American printer,
    author and publisher]
    The Baskerville of America
Thomas, J. F. See:
    FLEMING, THOMAS
        JAMES
THOMAS, JEANETTE BELL
    (1881-) [American
    folklorist]
    The Traipsin' Woman
Thomas Jefferson of Folk
    Music, The. See:
    SEEGER, PETER
Thomas, Joan Gale. See:
    ROBINSON, JOAN MARY
        GALE THOMAS
THOMAS, JOHN PARNELL
    (1895-) [American
    politician; congressman
    from New Jersey]
    Impeachment Thomas
THOMAS, JOHN WILLIAM
    ELMER (1876-)
    [American lawyer and
    politician; Congressman
    from Oklahoma]
    The Silver Sage
    Elmer Thomas
Thomas Junius. See:
    Smectymnuus
    YOUNG, THOMAS
Thomas, K. H. See:
    KIRK, THOMAS HOBSON
Thomas, Kid. See:
    VALENTINE, THOMAS
Thomas Kyd. See:
    HARBAGE, ALFRED
        BENNETT
Thomas, Lee. See:
    FLOREN, LEE

Thomas Little. See:
    MOORE, THOMAS
Thomas Matthew. See:
    ROGERS, JOHN
THOMAS, MAURICE (1876-1961)
    [French motion picture
    director]
    Maurice Tourneur
Thomas, Mervyn. See:
    CURRAN, MONA ELISA
Thomas Morton of Clifford's
    Inn, Gent. See:
    MORTON, THOMAS
Thomas of Aquino. See:
    AQUINAS, ST. THOMAS
Thomas of London, St. See:
    BECKET, THOMAS À
Thomas, Paul. See:
    MANN, THOMAS
Thomas Phillips. See:
    DAVIES, LESLIE
        PURNELL
Thomas Picton. See:
    MILNER, THOMAS PICTON
Thomas Rainham. See:
    BARREN, CHARLES
Thomas Rhymour of Ercildoune.
    See: KEARMOUNT,
        THOMAS, OF ERCIL-
        DOUNE
THOMAS, ROBERT MURRAY
    (1921-) [American
    educator and author]
    Tom Roberts
Thomas Rowley. See:
    CHATTERTON, THOMAS
THOMAS, STANLEY (1933-)
    [British author]
    Steven Wyandotte
THOMAS, STANLEY POWERS
    ROWLAND (1879-)
    [American author]
    Rowland Thomas
Thomas Stewart Currie. See:
    RICHARDSON, ANTHONY
Thomas, Terry. See:
    HOAR-STEVENS, THOMAS
        TERRY
Thomas the Bastard. See:
    FAUCONBERG, THOMAS
Thomas the Rhymer. See:
    LEARMOUNT, THOMAS, OF

ERCILDOUNE
Thomas, True. See:
  LEARMOUNT, THOMAS,
    OF ENCILDOUNE
THOMAS, WALTER PURL
    (1907-) [American
    jazz musician (tenor,
    saxophone, flute,
    arranger)]
  Foots Thomas
Thomas Watson. See:
  SMITH, JOHN
Thomas Wills. See:
  ARD, WILLIAM
    THOMAS
THOMPSON, ALEXANDER
    MATTOCK (1861-)
    [English author and
    playwright]
  Dangle
THOMPSON, CHARLES
    PHILIP (1918-)
    [American musician
    (piano, arranger)]
  Sir Charles
THOMPSON, CHARLIE
    (1729-1824) [Irish-
    American Secretary of the
    Continental Congress]
  The Hand and Pen of the
    Congress
  The Perpetual Secretary
Thompson, Dorothy. See:
  LEWIS, MRS. SINCLAIR
Thompson, Eileen. See:
  PANOWSKI, EILEEN
    THOMPSON
THOMPSON, ELI (1924-)
    [American jazz musician
    (saxophones, composer)]
  Lucky Thompson
THOMPSON, ERNEST SETON
    (1860-1946) [Anglo-
    American author and
    illustrator]
  Ernest Thompson Seton
  Wolf
THOMPSON, ESTELLE
    O'BRIEN MERLE
    (1911-) [British
    dancer and motion picture
    actress]
  Merle Oberon

THOMPSON, FREDERICK B.
    (1836-99) [Giver of
    financial assistance to
    Vassar College]
  Uncle Fred
THOMPSON, GEORGE (fl. 1840-85)
    [American author]
  Greenhorn
THOMPSON, GEORGE SELDEN
    (1929-) [American author]
  George Selden
THOMPSON, HARLAN H. (1894-)
    [American author]
  Stephen Holt
THOMPSON, HUNTER STOCKTON
    (1939-) [American cor-
    respondent and author]
  Sebastian Owl
Thompson, James H. See:
  FREEMAN, GRAYDON LA
    VERNE
THOMPSON, JAMES MAURICE
    (1844-1901) [American
    miscellaneous writer and
    editor]
  Maurice Thompson
THOMPSON, JENNINGS L., JR.
    (1927-) [American
    composer and musician]
  Jay Thompson
THOMPSON, JOHN A. (1827-76)
    [Norwegian-American mail
    carrier]
  Snowshoe Thompson
THOMPSON, JOHN JENNER
    (1918-) [American motion
    picture actor]
  John Dall
THOMPSON, PHILIP BURTON,
    JR. (1845-1909) [American
    politician; congressman
    from Kentucky]
  Little Phil
THOMPSON, PHILIP BURTON,
    SR. (1821-) [American
    criminal lawyer and
    Kentucky politician]
  Old Phil
Thompson, William C.L. See:
  EDWARDS, WILLIAM
    BENNETT
THOMPSON, WILLIAM HALE
    (1869-1944) [American

politician; Mayor of
Chicago]
Big Bill Thompson
THOMPSON, WILLIAM HENRY
(1881-1947) [English
music-hall singer and
performer]
Billy Merson
THOMPSON, WILLIAM
TAPPAN (1812-82)
[American editor and
humorist]
Major Jones
THOMSON, GEORGE MALCOLM
(1899-) [Scottish
journalist, civil servant
and author]
Aeneas MacDonald
THOMSON, JAMES (1834-82)
[Scottish poet]
B.V.
The Poet of Despair
Bysshe Vanolis
THOMSON, MARY AGNES
(1885-1960) [HELEN
KELLER'S teacher]
Polly
THOMSON, MORTIMER NEAL
(1831-75) [American
journalist and humorist]
Q.K. Philander Doesticks,
P.B.
Thor, A Political. See:
FARLEY, JAMES
ALOYSIUS
Thor, The Hammer of. See:
TOWNSEND, FRANCIS
EVERETT
THORBURN, GRANT
(1773-1863) [Scottish-
American merchant and
author]
Laurie Todd
THOREAU, HENRY DAVID
(1817-62) [American
naturalist and essayist]
The Hermit of Walden
The Poet Naturalist
The Sage of Walden Pond
Thorn. See also:
THORNE
Thorne
Thorn, Kate. See:

TRASK, CLARA AUGUSTA
JONES
Thorn, Ronald Scott. See:
WILKINSON, RONALD
THORNBURG, BETTY JANE
(1921-) [American
singer, entertainer and
motion picture actress]
Betty Hutton
THORNBURG, MARION
(1920-) [American
popular singer and motion
picture actress]
Marion Hutton
Thorndyke, Helen Louise. See:
STRATEMEYER, EDWARD
L.
THORNE [Thorne]. See also:
Thorn
THORNE, BLISS KIRBY
(1916-) [American
journalist, columnist and
author]
B.K. Ted Thorne
B. Kirby Thorne
Kirby Thorne
Ted Thorne
Cameron Vandal
Thorne, Dora. See:
BRAME, CHARLOTTE
MARY
Thorne, Harley. See:
BRAYMAN, JAMES O.
Thorne, Hart. See:
CARHART, ARTHUR
HAWTHORNE
Thorne, Lieut. Alfred B. See:
AIKEN, ALBERT W.
Thorne, Marion. See:
THURSTON, IDA
TREADWELL
Thorne, P. See:
SMITH, MRS. MARY
PRUDENCE WELLS
Thorne, Victor. See:
JACKSON, FREDERICK
THORNTON, ARGONNE DENSE
(1922-) [American jazz
musician (piano)]
Sadik Hakim
THORNTON, DANIEL I.J.
(1911-) [American
cattleman and politician;

Governor of Colorado]
Dan Thornton
Thornton, Maimee. See:
JEFFREY-SMITH, MAY
THORNTON
Thoroughgoing British Skeptic
of the Eighteenth Century,
The Most. See:
HUME, DAVID
THORP, JOSEPH PETER
(1873-) [British
journalist]
T in Punch
Thorpe, Dobbin. See:
DISCH, THOMAS M.
THORPE, JAMES FRANCIS
(1888-1953) [American
Indian athlete]
Jim Thorpe
Wa-Tho-Huck (Bright Path)
Thorpe, Kamba. See:
BELLAMY, ELIZABETH
WHITFIELD CROOM
THORPE, ROLLO SMOLT
(1896-) [American
motion picture director]
Richard Thorpe
Thorpe, Sylvia. See:
THIMBLETHORPE, JUNE
SYLVIA
THORPE, THOMAS BANGS
(1815-78) [American
humorist]
T.B. Thorpe
Thorstein, Eric. See:
GROSSMAN, JOSEPHINE
JUDITH
Thought, The Columbus of
Modern. See:
EMERSON, RALPH
WALDO
Thought, The Father of. See:
CATINAT, NICOLAS
Thousand Daughters, The
Mother of a. See:
AGNEW, ELIZA
Thousand Dollar Beauty, The
Ten. See:
KELLY, MICHAEL J.
Thousand Faces, The Man of a.
See: CHANEY, LON
Thracian, The. See:

LEO I
Thrale, Mrs. See:
PIOZZI, HESTER LYNCH
SALUSBURY
Three. See:
Big Three, The
Stooges, The Three
Wondrous Three, The
Three-Finger Brown. See:
BROWN, MORDECAI PETER
CENTENNIAL
LUCHESE, GAETANO
Three Fingered Jack. See:
GARCÍA, MANUEL
Three Fingers. See:
FITZPATRICK, THOMAS
Three-minute. See:
BRUMM, GEORGE
FRANKLIN
Three Musketeers, The, joint
nickname of MANUEL
CAPETILLO (1926-)
JESÚS CORDOBA (1927-)
and RAFAEL RODRÍGUEZ
(1929-) [Mexican bull-
fighters]
Three Stars, Old. See:
GRANT, HIRAM ULYSSES
Three Stooges, The. See:
Stooges, The Three
Three, The Overland. See:
Golden Gate Trinity, The
Three Wise Men, joint nickname
of LOUIS ARMAND (-),
[French chemist], FRANK
ETZEL (-) [West Ger-
man chemist] and
GIORDANI FRANCESCO
(1896-1961) [Italian chemist,
all of whom helped lay
groundwork for European
Atomic Energy Commission]
Thrice-Accursed Judas, A. See:
BERIA, LAVRENTI
PAVLOVICH
Thrice, Luke. See:
RUSSELL, JOHN
Thrillers, The World's Most
Prolific and Popular Writer
of. See:
OPPENHEIM, EDWARD
PHILLIPS

1004

Throne Itself, One Behind
the Throne Greater than
the. See:
STUART, JOHN
Throne, Ornament of the
(Aurangzeb). See:
MOHAMMED
Throne, Ornament of the
(Aurungzeb). See:
MOHAMMED
THROSSELL, KATHARINE
SUSANNAH PRICHARD
(1884-) [Australian
author, verse writer and
playwright]
Katharine Susannah Prichard
Thrush, The Irish. See:
DOWNEY, MORTON
Thumb, General Tom. See:
STRATTON, CHARLES
SHERWOOD
Thumb, Tom. See:
STRATTON, CHARLES
SHERWOOD
THUNA, LEONORA (1929-)
[American playwright]
Lee Thuna
Thunder and Lightning. See:
WILLIAMS, DAVID
ROGERSON
Thunder, Big. See:
WAYNE, ANTHONY
Thunder, Son of (Bonerge). See:
JAMES THE GREATER, ST.
JOHN THE EVANGELIST,
ST.
Thunderbolt of Italy, The. See:
FOIX, GASTON DE
Thunderbolt of Painting, The.
See: ROBUSTI, JACOPO
Thunderbolt, The. See:
BAJAZET I
HÄNDEL, GEORG
FRIEDRICH
PTOLEMY KERAUNOS
Thunderbolt, Young. See:
LEA, LUKE
Thunderer, The. See:
STEPHEN II
Thunderer, The Massachusetts.
See: WEBSTER, DANIEL
Thundering Jimmy. See:

JENKINS, JAMES
Thundering Rooster, The Great.
See: JOHNSON, HUGH
SAMUEL
THURMAN, ALLAN GRANBERRY
(1813-95) [American jurist;
senator from Ohio]
The Noblest Roman of Them All
Old Bandanna
The Old Roman
Right-angled, Tri-angled
Thurman
THURSTON, CHARLES MYNN
(1738-1812) [American
Episcopal clergyman, army
officer and jurist]
The Warrior Parson
THURSTON, HOLLIS JOHN (1899-
) [American professional
baseball player]
Sloppy Thurston
THURSTON, IDA TREADWELL
(1848-1918) [American
author]
Marion Thorne
Thurston, Oliver. See:
FLANDERS, HENRY
Thursty McQuill. See:
BRUCE, WALLACE
Tibber, Robert. See:
FRIEDMAN, EVE ROSEMARY
TIBBER
Tibbetts, William. See:
BRANNON, WILLIAM T.
TIBBLES, PERCY THOMAS
(1879-1938) [British
illusionist and magician]
P. T. Selbit
Tibbs. See:
DICKENS, CHARLES JOHN
HUFFAM
Tibullus of His Age, The. See:
SEDLEY, SIR CHARLES
Tibullus, The French. See:
DEFORGE, EVARISTE
DÉSIRÉ
Tich, Little. See:
RELPH, HARRY
Tichborne, Sir Roger Charles.
See: ORTON, ARTHUR
TICHENOR, ISAAC (1754-1838)
[American politician;

Governor of Vermont]
Jersey Slick
TICKER, REUBEN (1913-)
  [American opera singer]
  Richard Tucker
Tickletoby, Miss. See:
  THACKERAY, WILLIAM
  MAKEPEACE
Tiddy-Doll. See:
  GRENVILLE, RICHARD
  TEMPLE
TIERNAN, FRANCES CHRISTINE
  FISHER (1846-1920)
  [American novelist]
  Christian Reid
TIERNEY, GERALD (1924-)
  [American motion picture
  actor]
  Scott Brady
TIERNEY, JOHN LAWRENCE
  (1892-) [Australian
  teacher and author]
  Brian James
Tige, Old. See:
  ANDERSON, GEORGE
  THOMAS
Tiger (Baber) (Babur). See:
  MUHAMMAD, ZAHIR
  UD-DIN
Tiger, Bengal. See:
  TWIGGS, DAVID EMANUEL
Tiger Lily. See:
  BLAKE, LILLIE
  DEVEREUX
Tiger of Central America, The.
  See:
  GUARDIOLA, SANTOS
Tiger of Malaya, The. See:
  YAMASHITA, TOMOYUKI
Tiger of Tacubaya, The. See:
  MARQUEZ, LEONARDO
Tiger, The. See:
  CLEMENCEAU, GEORGES
TIGLATH-PILESER III (745-
  727 B.C.) [King of
  Assyria]
  Pulu
TIGRANES I (died after 56 B.C.)
  [King of Armenia]
  The Great
TIKEKAR, SHRIPAD RAM-
  CHANDRA (1901-)

[Indian author]
Kartikeya Skylar Mushafir
TILDEN, SAMUEL JONES
  (1814-86) [American lawyer
  and statesman]
  Old Usufruct
  The Sage of Gramercy Park
  The Sage of Greystone
  Slippery Sam
TILDEN, WILLIAM TATEM, JR.
  [1893-1953) [American
  tennis player]
  Big Bill Tilden
  Bill Tilden
Tilley. See also:
  Tilly
Tilley, Vesta. See:
  POWLES, MATILDA ALICE
TILLMAN, BENJAMIN RYAN
  (1847-1918) [American
  politician; congressman
  from South Carolina]
  The Agricultural Moses
  Pitchfork Ben
  Pitchfork Tillman
Tilly. See:
  LOSCH, OTTILIE ETHEL
  Tilley
TILTMAN, RONALD FRANK
  (1901-) [British civil
  servant, journalist and
  author]
  Ronald Fraser
Tilton, Alice. See:
  TAYLOR, PHOEBE
  ATWOOD
Tim. See:
  CAREW, JOHN MOHUN
Tim, Big. See:
  SULLIVAN, TIMOTHY
  DANIEL
Tim Bobbin. See:
  COLLIER, JOHN
Tim, Boston. See:
  SULLIVAN, TIMOTHY P.
Tim Brennan. See:
  CONROY, JOHN WESLEY
Tim, Little. See:
  SULLIVAN, TIMOTHY P.
Tim, Tiny. See:
  KHAURY, HERBERT
  BUCKINGHAM

Time, The Bard of All. See:
SHAKESPEARE, WILLIAM
Time, The Foremost Greek
Scholar of Our. See:
MURRAY, GEORGE
GILBERT AIMÉ
Time, The Prince of Poets in
His. See:
SPENSER, EDMUND
Timer, Old. See:
MERRILL, JAMES MILFORD
Timmie. See:
ROGERS, TIMOTHY
LOUIS AIVERUM
TIMON (fl. 5th cent. B.C.)
[Athenian nobleman]
The Misanthrope of Athens
TIMON (c. 320-c. 230 B.C.)
[Greek poet and philosopher]
The Sillographer
Timon, John. See:
MITCHELL, DONALD
GRANT
Timothy Brace. See:
PRATT, THEODORE
Timothy Crabshaw. See:
LONGSTREET, AUGUSTUS
BALDWIN
Timothy Dexter, Lord. See:
DEXTER, TIMOTHY
Timothy Shy. See:
LEWIS, DOMINIC BEVAN
WYNDHAM
Timothy Sparks. See:
DICKENS, CHARLES
JOHN HUFFAM
Timothy Titcomb. See:
HOLLAND, JOSIAH
GILBERT
Timour. See:
TIMUR LENK
TIMROD, HENRY (1828-67)
[American poet]
Aglaius
The Poet Laureate of the
Confederacy
Timsol, Robert. See:
BIRD, FREDERIC
MAYER
TIMUR LENK (1333?-1405)
[Mongol conqueror; ruler
of Samarkand]

The Firebrand of the
Universe
The Prince of Destruction
Tamburlaine
Tamerlane
Timour
Timur
Timur the Lame
Tina Leser. See:
SHILLARD-SMITH,
CHRISTINE WETHERILL
TINDALE. See:
TYNDALE (TINDALE),
WILLIAM
TINDALL, WILLIAM YORK
(1903-) [American
educator and author]
A. P. Yorick
TINKER, JOSEPH BERT
(1880-1948) [American
professional baseball
player and manager]
Joe Tinker
Tinker, The Immortal. See:
BUNYAN, JOHN
TINKHAM, GEORGE HOLDEN
(1870-) [American
politician; Congressman
from Massachusetts]
The Big Game Hunter
The Lion Hunter
Wiskers
Tinne, Dorothea. See:
STROVER, DOROTHEA
Tinne, E. D. See:
STROVER, DOROTHEA
TINNEY, CALVIN LAWRENCE
(1908-) [American radio
commentator]
Cal Tinney
Tino, See:
COMINI, RAILBERTO
Tino, El. See:
BLAU, VICENTE
TINSLEY, JAMES ROBERT
(1921-) [American
singer, guitarist, actor
and author]
Jim Bob Tinsley
Tinto, Dick. See:
GOODRICH, FRANK
BOOTT

Tintoret. See:
ROBUSTI, JACOPO
Tintoretto. See:
ROBUSTI, JACOPO
Tintoretto of Switzerland, The.
See:
HUBER, JOHANN
RUDOLPHE
Tintoretto, The English. See:
DOBSON, WILLIAM
Tiny. See:
GRIMES, LLOYD
KAHN, NORMAN
Tiny, Big. See:
LITTLE, DUDLEY
Tiny Tim. See:
KHAURY, HERBERT
BUCKINGHAM
Tip, Old. See:
HARRISON, WILLIAM
HENRY
Tippecanoe. See:
HARRISON, WILLIAM
HENRY
Tippecanoe, Old. See:
HARRISON, WILLIAM
HENRY
Tippecanoe, The Hero of.
See: HARRISON,
WILLIAM HENRY
TIPTOFT, JOHN (1427?-70)
[Earl of Worcester]
The Butcher of England
Tipuca. See:
WILSON, T. P. CAMERON
Tirso de Molina. See:
TÉLLEZ, GABRIEL
Tishomingo, The Sage of. See:
MURRAY, WILLIAM
HENRY
TISI, BENVENUTO (1481-1559)
[Italian painter]
Garofalo
TISSERAND, GÉRARD MARCEL
(1920-) [French singer]
Gérard Souzay
Titanic Earth-son, The Old.
See: WEBSTER, DANIEL
Titcomb, Timothy. See:
HOLLAND, JOSIAH
GILBERT
Titi, Prince. See:

FREDERICK LOUIS
Titian. See:
VECELLI (VECELLIO),
TIZIANO
Titian, The American. See:
ALLSTON, WASHINGTON
Titian, The French. See:
BLANCHARD, JACQUES
Titian, The Portuguese. See:
COELLO, ALONSO
SÁNCHEZ
Titmarsh, M.A. See:
THACKERAY, WILLIAM
MAKEPEACE
Titmarsh, Michael Angelo. See:
THACKERAY, WILLIAM
MAKEPEACE
Tito. See:
PUENTE, ERNEST, JR.
Tito, Marshal. See:
BROZ, JOSIP
TITTLE, YELBERTON ABRA-
HAM (1926-) [American
football player]
Y.A.
Titus. See:
VESPASIANUS, TITUS
FLAVIUS SALINUS
TITUS LIVIUS (59 B.C.-17 A.D.)
[Roman historian]
Livy
Tityrus. See:
CHAUCER, GEOFFREY
Tjalmar Breda. See:
DeJONG, DAVID CORNEL
Tlatoani, Uei (One Who Speaks).
See: MONTEZUMA II
Toad. See:
SLOAN, JAMES FORMAN
Tobias Guarnerius, Jr. See:
DIMITRY, CHARLES PAT-
TON
TOBIN, JAMES EDWARD
(1905-) [American
journalist, educator and
author]
Alan Rayne
Toby. See:
HARDWICKE, OTTO
Toby, Liz. See:
MINSKY, BETTY JANE
TOEBE

Toby, M. P. See:
    LUCY, SIR HENRY
    WILLIAM
Toby, Uncle. See:
    CROSS, WILBUR
    LUCIUS
Tod. See:
    SLAUGHTER, N. CARTER
    SLOAN, JAMES
    FORMAN
Tod Conrad. See:
    WILKES-HUNTER,
    RICHARD
TOD, OSMA GALLINGER
    (1898-) [American
    businesswoman, writer
    and lecturer]
    Osma Couch Gallinger
Todd, Ann. See:
    MAYFIELD, ANN TODD
Todd, Anne Ophelia. See:
    DOWDEN, ANNE
    OPHELIA TODD
TODD, ARTHUR W. (1920-)
    [American composer,
    singer and guitarist]
    Art Todd
TODD, CHAPMAN C. (fl. 1898)
    [American naval officer]
    The Dewey of Manzanillo
TODD, JOHN PAYNE
    (1792-) [Step-son of
    JAMES MADISON,
    fourth President of the
    United States]
    The Prince of America
Todd, Laurie. See:
    THORBURN, GRANT
Todd, Mike. See:
    GOLDBOGEN, AVROM
    HIRSCH
Todd, Richard. See:
    PALENTHORPE-TODD,
    RICHARD ANDREW
TODD, THELMA (c.1908-35)
    [American motion picture
    actress]
    Hot Toddy
Toddy. See also:
    Tody
Toddy, Hot. See:
    TODD, THELMA

Todhunter. See:
    SLOAN, JAMES FORMAN
Tody. See:
    Toddy
    HAMILTON, RICHARD F.
Token West. See:
    HUMPHRIES, ADELAIDE M.
Tokyo Rose. See:
    D'AQUINO, IVA IKUKO
    TOGURI
Tolby, Arthur. See:
    INFIELD, GLENN BERTON
Toleration, The Apostle of.
    See:
    WILLIAMS, ROGER
Tolmage, Gerald. See:
    GARDNER, MAURICE
TOLSTOI, COUNT LEV
    NIKOLAEVICH (1828-1910)
    [Russian novelist, moral
    philosopher and social
    reformer]
    Leo Tolstoi
Tom. See:
    ADAIR, THOMAS M.
    BROWN, THOMAS
    CONNALLY, THOMAS
    TERRY
    COURTENAY, THOMAS
    DANIEL
    CUSHING, CHARLES
    CYPRIAN STRONG
    DEWEY, THOMAS EDMUND
    D'URFEY, THOMAS
    GALT, THOMAS FRANKLIN,
    JR.
    GARRETT, THOMAS
    SAMUEL
    GIRTIN, THOMAS
    KINES, THOMAS ALVIN
    McGOWEN, THOMAS
    MAHONEY, JOHN THOMAS
    MOONEY, THOMAS J.
    MORGAN, THOMAS P.
    MURRAY, THOMAS
    JEFFERSON
    PAXTON, THOMAS R.
    POSTON, THOMAS
    PURDOM, THOMAS E.
    ROBERTS, THOMAS
    WILLIAM
    RONAN, THOMAS MATTHEW

SCOTT, THOMAS
    JEFFERSON
SEAVER, GEORGE THOMAS
SMOTHERS, THOMAS
    BOLYN JR.
STACEY, THOMAS CHARLES
    GERRARD
STOBART, THOMAS
    RALPH
THOM
    Thom
    Toom
WISWELL, THOMAS
    GEORGE
WOLFE, THOMAS
    KENNERLY, JR.
Tom, Black. See:
    CORWIN, THOMAS
Tom, Blind. See:
    BETHUNE, THOMAS
    GREEN
Tom Brandt. See:
    DEWEY, THOMAS
    BLANCHARD
Tom Brown. See:
    BROWN, THOMAS
    HUGHES, THOMAS
Tom Cobleigh. See:
    RAYMOND, WALTER
Tom Collins. See:
    FURPHY, JOSEPH
Tom Conway. See:
    SANDERS, THOMAS
Tom Crib. See:
    MOORE, THOMAS
Tom Curtis. See:
    PENDOWER, JACQUES
Tom Dewey, Missouri's. See:
    MILLIGAN, MAURICE
    MORTON
Tom Dewey, The New Deal's.
    See: MURPHY, FRANK
Tom Drake. See:
    ALDERDICE, ALFRED
Tom Ewell. See:
    TOMKINS, S. YEWELL
Tom, Father. See:
    BEECHER, THOMAS
    KINNICUT
Tom, Fighting. See:
    HOYNE, THOMAS
Tom Folio. See:
    RAWLINSON, THOMAS

Tom Form. See:
    O'KEEFE, LESTER
Tom Gordon. See:
    THOMAS, GORDON
Tom Graham. See:
    LEWIS, HARRY
    SINCLAIR
Tom Hardin. See:
    BAUER, ERWIN A.
Tom Jackson, Fool. See:
    JACKSON, THOMAS
    JONATHAN
Tom Jackson, Old. See:
    JACKSON, THOMAS
    JONATHAN
Tom Jones. See:
    WOODWARD, THOMAS
    JONES
Tom, Long. See:
    JEFFERSON, THOMAS
    PERKINS, THOMAS
    HANDASYD
Tom, Mad. See:
    SHERMAN, WILLIAM
    TECUMSEH
Tom Parsons. See:
    MACPHERSON, THOMAS
    GEORGE
Tom Perkins, Long. See:
    PERKINS, THOMAS
    HANDASYD
Tom Roberts. See:
    THOMAS, ROBERT
    MURRAY
Tom, Shepherd. See:
    HAZARD, THOMAS
    ROBINSON
Tom Shortfellow. See:
    UNKNOWN
Tom, Talkative. See:
    BLANTON, THOMAS
    LINDSAY
Tom, Texas. See:
    CONNALLY, THOMAS
    TERRY
Tom Thumb. See:
    STRATTON, CHARLES
    SHERWOOD
Tom Thumb, General. See:
    STRATTON, CHARLES
    SHERWOOD
Tom Tyler. See:
    BURNS, WILLIAM

Tom W. Hall, Midshipman.
See: INGRAHAM,
COLONEL PRENTISS
TOMACELLI, PIETRO (c.1355-
1404) [Supreme Pontiff
of Roman Catholic Church]
Pope Boniface IX
Tomares, Niño de. See:
TORRES, EMILIO
Tomasito, Don. See:
ROBERTSON, THOMAS
ANTHONY
Tomassee, The Wizard of. See:
PICKENS, ANDREW
Tomboy With the Voice, The.
See: VON KAPPELHOFF,
DORIS
Tomcat of the Keys, The Old.
See: ZURKE, ROBERT
Tome Burguillos. See:
CAPIO, LOPE FÉLIZ
DE VEGA
Tomfool. See:
FARJEON, ELEANOR
Tomislav Vitezovic. See:
KUEHNELT-LEDDIHN,
ERIK RITTER VON
TOMKINS, See also:
TOMPKINS
TOMKINS, S. YEWELL
(1909-) [American stage
and motion picture actor]
Tom Ewell
Tomkinson, Constance. See:
WEEKS, CONSTANCE
TOMKINSON
TOMLIN, TRUMAN (1908-)
[American jazz musician
(singer, guitar, com-
poser, leader)]
Pinky Tomlin
TOMLINSON, HENRY MAJOR
(1873-1958) [English
author]
H. M. Tomlinson
Tommy. See:
DORSEY, THOMAS
HITCHCOCK, THOMAS
SANDS, THOMAS
ADRIAN
WOLF, THOMAS J., JR.
Tommy Brown. See:

LUCHESE, GAETANO
Tommy Scott. See:
WOODWARD, THOMAS
JONES
Tommy Steele. See:
HICKS, TOMMY
Tommy the Cork. See:
CORCORAN, THOMAS
GARDINER
Tommy, White House. See:
CORCORAN, THOMAS
GARDINER
Tomorrow, Old. See:
MACDONALD, SIR JOHN
ALEXANDER
TOMPKINS. See also:
TOMKINS
TOMPKINS, HERBERT WINCK-
WORTH (1867-) [British
journalist and author]
Pepys in Essex
Ton, Two. See:
BAKER, RICHARD E.
Tonashi. See:
HARRINGTON, MARK
RAYMOND
TONEY. See also:
Tony
TONEY, LEMUEL GORDON
(1875-1941) [American
composer, singer and
actor]
Eddie Leonard
Tongue, Straight. See:
WHIPPLE, HENRY
BENJAMIN
Tonguepoint. See:
MOTT, JAMES WHEATON
TONNIES, FERDINAND JULIUS
(1855-) [German educator
and author]
Normannus
Tonsil, The Golden. See:
VON KAPPELHOFF,
DORIS
TONSON, JACOB (c.1656-1736)
[English bookseller and
publisher]
The Prince of Publishers
Tonson, Jacob. See:
BENNETT, ENOCH
ARNOLD

Tony. See:
BOYLE, WILLIAM
ANTHONY
CONNOR, JOHN ANTHONY
FOYT, ANTHONY JOSEPH,
JR.
HULMAN, ANTON, JR.
JACKSON, ANTHONY
LAZZERI, ANTHONY
MICHAEL
MOTTOLA, ANTHONY
CHARLES
ORTEGA, ANTHONY
ROBERT
PASTOR, ANTONIO
RANDALL, ANTHONY
SARG, ANTHONY
FREDERICK
TONEY
TRABERT, MARION
ANTHONY
Tony Bennett. See:
BENEDETTO, ANTHONY
DOMINICK
Tony Curtis. See:
SCHWARTZ, BERNARD
Tony Dano. See:
SOLDANO, ANTHONY
Tony Granite. See:
POLITELLA, DARIO
Tony Gray. See:
GRAY, GEORGE HUGH
Tony Hart. See:
CANNON, ANTHONY
Tony Martin. See:
MORRIS, ALVIN
Tony Pastor. See:
PASTOR, ANTONIO
PASTRITTI, ANTONIO
Tony Piet. See:
PIETRUSZKA, ANTHONY
FRANCIS
Tony Scott. See:
SCIACCA, ANTHONY
Tony Spargo. See:
SBARBARO, TONY
Tony the Silent. See:
PIETRUSZKA, ANTHONY
FRANCIS
Tony Zale. See:
ZALESKI, ANTHONY
FLORIAN

Tooey. See:
SPAATZ, CARL
TOUHY
TUOHY
Tooke. See:
HORNE, JOHN
Toole, Rex. See:
TRALINS, S. ROBERT
Tooley, Nicholas. See:
WILKINSON, NICHOLAS
TOOLEY, SARAH ANNE
(fl. late 19th, early 20th
cent.) [British author]
Marion Leslie
Toom. See also:
THOM
Thom
Tom
Toom Tabard (Empty Jacket).
See: JOHN DE BALIOL
TOOMBS, ROBERT (1810-85)
[American politician, active
in Georgia politics]
The Georgia Fire-eater
TOOMBS, ROBERT. See also:
Castor and Pollux of
Georgia, The
Toonder, Martin. See:
GROOM, ARTHUR WILLIAM
Tooth, Iron. See:
FREDERICK II
Tootie. See:
HEATH, ALBERT
Toots. See:
MONDELLO, NUNCIO
THIELEMANS, JEAN
Top Boots-and-Saddle Star, The
World's. See:
SLYE, LEONARD
Top Football Coach in America,
The. See:
PARKER, RAYMOND KLEIN
Top, The Hero of Little Round.
See: CHAMBERLAIN,
JOSHUA LAWRENCE
TOPHAM, THOMAS (1710-52)
[English strong man]
The British Samson
The English Milo
Toran Beg. See:
McKILLOP, NORMAN
TORBETT, HARVEY DOUGLAS

LOUIS (1921-) [British
librarian, educator and
author]
Henry Dee
Isis
Torchy. See:
HAMILTON, JOHN
DANIEL MILLER
Tories, The Terror of the. See:
CLINCH, JOSEPH
TORMÉ, MELVIN HOWARD
(1925-) [American popular
singer]
Mel Tormé
The Velvet Fog
TORN, ELMORE (1931-)
[American stage,
television and motion
picture actor]
Rip Torn
Tornado, The. See:
WAYNE, ANTHONY
Torquemada. See:
MATHERS, EDWARD
POWYS
Torquemada, Young. See:
MITCHEL, JOHN
PURROY
Torr, Iain. See:
MACKINNON, CHARLES
ROY
Torre-Bueno, Lillian de la. See:
See: McCUE, LILLIAN
BUENO
Torre, Lillian de la. See:
McCUE, LILLIAN BUENO
TORRENCE, FREDERIC
RIDGELY (1875-1950)
[American poet]
Ridgely Torrence
TORRES, EMILIO (1874-)
[Spanish bullfighter]
Bombita
Niño de la Eterna Sonrisa
Niño de Tomares
TORRES, RICARDO (1879-1936)
[Spanish bullfighter]
Bombita
Torrey, Marjorie. See:
CHANSLOR, MARJORIE
TORREY HOOD
Torrie. See:

ZITO, SALVATORE
TORSVAN, TRAVEN (1890-1969)
[Scandinavian author]
B. Traven
Tory Traitor, The. See:
HONEYMAN, JOHN
TOTAH, NABIL MARSHALL
(1930-) [American jazz
musician (bass)]
Knobby
Toto. See:
CURTIS-GAGLIARDI,
ANTONIO FURST DE
Touch Doctor, The. See:
GREATRAKES
(GREATOREX),
VALENTINE
TOUHY. See also:
Tooey
TUOHY
TOUHY, ROGER (1898-1959)
[American bootlegger and
kidnapper]
Black Roger
Rog Touhy
Terrible Touhy
Toulouse-Lautrec. See:
MONFA, HENRI MARIE
RAYMOND DE
TOULOUSE-LAUTREC
Toulouse, The Sappho of. See:
ISAURE, CLÉMENCE
TOURGÉE, ALBION WINEGAR
(1838-1905)
[American novelist]
Henry Churton
Tourneur, Maurice. See:
THOMAS, MAURICE
Tours, St. Gregory of. See:
FLORENTIUS, GEORGIUS
TOUSEZ, FRANÇOIS JOSEPH
PIERRE (1807-85) [French
actor]
Réginer
Towel, Bathing. See:
BADEN-POWELL, ROBERT
STEPHENSON SMYTHE,
1ST BARON BADEN-
POWELL
Tower, Joan of the. See:
JOAN
Town Crier, The. See:

1013

WOOLLCOTT, ALEXANDER
HUMPHREYS
Town Meeting, Man of the.
See: ADAMS, SAMUEL
Townley, Arthur. See:
DUGANNE, AUGUSTINE
JOSEPH HICKEY
TOWNSEND, FRANCIS
EVERETT (1867-1960)
[American physician and
humanist]
The Father of the Townsend
Plan
The Hammer of Thor
Dr. Townsend
TOWNSEND, GEORGE ALFRED
(1841-1914) [American
journalist and novelist]
Garth
TOWNSEND, HAWORTH NOT-
TINGHAM (1864-1927)
[Anglo-American
authority on marine
insurance]
The King of the Marine
Insurance Business
TOWNSEND JOHN G., JR.
(1871-) [American
politician; senator from
Delaware]
Strawberry Townsend
TOWNSEND, MARY ASHLEY
VAN VOORHIS (1832-
1901) [American poet
and essayist]
Mary Ashley
Xariffa
Townsend of Florida, Doc.
See: HENDRICKS,
JOSEPH EDWARD
TOWNSHEND, CHARLES
(1725-67) [English
politician]
The Weathercock
Toxicology, The Father of.
See: ORFILA, MATHIEU
JOSEPH BONAVENTURE
TOYNBEE ARNOLD (1852-83)
[British economic his-
torian and social reformer]
Father of Social Settlements
TOYNE, CLARICE JOY (1906-)

[English author]
Armido
TOZER, BASIL JOHN JOSEPH
(fl. late 19th-early 20th
cent.) [British journalist
and author]
Villain Regardant
TRABERT, MARION ANTHONY
(1930-) [American tennis
player]
Tony Trabert
TRACHSEL, MYRTLE JAMISON
(fl. 1927-39) [American
author]
Jane Jamison
TRACY, DONALD FISKE
(1905-) [American
journalist and author]
Roger Fuller
Tracy, Powers. See:
WARD, DONALD G.
Trade, The Apostle of Free. See:
BRIGHT, JOHN
COBDEN, RICHARD
TRADER, ELLA KING NEWSOM
(fl. 1861-65) [American
Civil War Confederate
nurse]
The Florence Nightingale of
the Southern Army
Trader Horn. See:
SMITH, ALFRED ALOYSIUS
Trader, Tall. See:
SIBLEY, HENRY
HASTINGS
Trafford, F.G. See:
RIDDELL, CHARLOTTE
ELIZA LAWSON
Tragedian of Jazz, The High-
hatted. See:
FRIEDMAN, THEODORE
LEOPOLD
Tragedy, The Father of French.
See: CORNEILLE, PIERRE
GARNIER, ROBERT
Tragedy, The Father of Greek.
See: AESCHYLUS
THESPIS
Traherne, Michael. See:
WATKINS-PITCHFORD,
DENYS JAMES
Train, The Big. See:

JOHNSON, WALTER
PERRY
SISK, JOHN
Traipsin' Woman, The. See:
THOMAS, JEANETTE
BELL
Traitor, The Tory. See:
HONEYMAN, JOHN
Traitorous Hero, The. See:
ARNOLD, BENEDICT
Tralee, The Duke of. See:
BRESNAHAN, ROGER
PATRICK
TRALINS, S. ROBERT
(1926-) [American
author]
Ray Z. Bixby
Norman A. King
Sean O'Shea
Rex O'Toole
C. Sydney
Rex Toole
Bob Tralins
Robert S. Tralins
Ruy Traube
Tram. See:
TRUMBAUER, FRANK
Tramp Poet, The. See:
KEMP, HIBBARD
Tramp, The Little. See:
CHAPLIN, CHARLES
SPENCER
Tramp, The Millionaire.
See: HOW, JAMES
EADS
Translator-General in His
Age, The. See:
HOLLAND, PHILEMON
Translator General, The. See:
HOLLAND, PHILEMON
TRANTER, NIGEL (1909-)
[Scottish broadcaster
and author]
Nye Tredgold
TRAPASSI, PIETRO ANTONIO
DOMENICO BONAVENTURA
(1698-1782) [Italian poet
and dramatist]
Metastasio
The Racine of Italy
TRAPPIER, ARTHUR
BENJAMIN (1910-)

[American jazz musician
(drums)]
Traps Trappier
Traprock, Walter. See:
CHAPPELL, GEORGE
SHEPARD
Traprock, Walter E. See:
CHAPPELL, GEORGE
SHEPARD
Traps. See:
TRAPPIER, ARTHUR
BENJAMIN
Traps, Baby. See:
RICH, BERNARD
TRASK, CLARA AUGUSTA
JONES (1839-1905)
[American author]
Clara Augusta
Hero Strong
Kate Thorn
TRASK, KATE NICHOLS
(1853-1922) [American
poet and novelist]
Katrina Trask
Trausti, Jón. See:
MAGNUSSON, GUND-
MUNDUR
TRAVASCIO, NICHOLAS
ANTHONY (1925-64)
[American jazz musician
(trumpet)]
Nick Travis
Traveler, Detroit's Greatest.
See: STEARNS, FREDERICK
KIMBALL
Traveler, The. See:
STORY, ISAAC
Traveler, The Blind. See:
HOLMAN, JAMES
Traveler, The Great American.
See: PRATT, DANIEL
Traveling Bachelor, A. See:
COOPER, JAMES
FENIMORE
Traveller. See:
DOWSETT, JOSEPH
MOREWOOD
Traven, B. See:
TORSVAN, TRAVEN
Traver, Robert. See:
VOELKER, JOHN
DONALDSON

Travers, Henry. See:
 HEAGERTY, TRAVERS
Travers, Linden. See:
 LINDON-TRAVERS,
 FLORENCE
Travers, Will. See:
 ROWLAND, DONALD
 SYDNEY
Travis, Gerry. See:
 TRIMBLE, LOUIS P.
Travis MacRae. See:
 FEAGLES, ANITA
 MACRAE
Travis, Nick. See:
 TRAVASCIO, NICHOLAS
 ANTHONY
TRAYNOR, HAROLD JOSEPH
 (1899-1922)[American
 professional baseball
 player]
 Pie Traynor
TREADWELL, JOHN (1745-1823)
 [American politician;
 Governor of Connecticut]
 The Father of the System of
 Common-School Education
Treasurer, Bobby The. See:
 MORRIS, ROBERT
Treasury, The Cerebus of the.
 See: ELLSWORTH,
 OLIVER
Treasury, The Sweetheart of
 the. See:
 O'REILLY, MARY M.
Treasury, The Watchdog of the.
 See: BLANTON,
 THOMAS LINDSAY
 BYRD, HARRY FLOOD
 CANNON, JOSEPH
 GURNEY
 GALLATIN, ABRAHAM
 ALPHONSE ALBERT
 HAGNER, PETER
 HOLMAN, WILLIAM
 STEELE
 McCARL, JOHN RAYMOND
 WASHBURNE, ELIHU
 BENJAMIN
TREDEZ, DENISE (1930-)
 [French editor and
 author]
 Denise Trez
Tredgold, Nye. See:

TRANTER, NIGEL
Trees Nemesis, The Cherry. See:
 JENCKES, VIRGINIA ELLIS
Trefor, Eirlys. See:
 WILLIAMS, EIRLYS
 OLWEN
Tremaine, Bob. See:
 STEINDLER, ROBERT A.
Tremaine, Linda. See:
 MORGAN, DIANA
TREMBLAY, FRANÇOIS LE
 CLERC DU (1577-1638)
 [French monk and diplomat;
 alter ego of CARDINAL
 RICHELIEU]
 Éminence Grise (Gray
 Eminence)
 Father Joseph (Père Joseph)
Trent, Martha. See:
 SMITH, DOROTHY
 WHITEHILL
Treorky, Member for. See:
 BOWEN-ROWLANDS,
 ERNEST BOWEN BROWN
Tressidy, Jim. See:
 NORWOOD, VICTOR GEORGE
 CHARLES
Trevelyan, Hilda. See:
 TUCKER, HILDA
Trevena, John. See:
 HENHAM, ERNEST
 GEORGE
Treves, Kathleen. See:
 WALKER, EMILY
 KATHLEEN
TREVETHICK, RICHARD
 (1771-1833) [English mining
 engineer and inventor]
 The Father of the
 Locomotive
Trevor, Austin. See:
 SCHILSKY, AUSTIN
Trevor, Claire. See:
 WEMLINGER, CLAIRE
TREVOR, ELLESTON (1920-)
 [British author]
 Mansell Black
 Trevor Burgess
 Adam Hall
 Simon Rattray
 Warwick Scott
 Caesar Smith
Trevor, Ernest. See:

POWELL, THOMAS
Trevor, Glen. See:
    HILTON, JAMES
Trez, Denise. See:
    TREDEZ, DENISE
Tri-angled Thurman, Right-
    angled. See:
    THURMAN, ALLAN
        GRANBERRY
Tri-borough Bridge, The Father
    of the. See:
    FRANKLIN, BENJAMIN
Triana, Gitanillo de. See:
    REYES, FRANCISCO
        VEGA DE LOS
Triana II, Gitanillo de.
    See: REYES, RAFAEL
        VEGA DE LOS
Trianero. See:
    JIMÉNEZ, JUAN
Tribune. See:
    ARMSTRONG, DOUGLAS
        ALBERT
Tribune of the People, The.
    See:
    ADAMS, SAMUEL
    BRIGHT, JOHN
Tribunes, The Last of the.
    See: RIENZI, COLA DI
Tribute, Brian of the (Brian
    Boru). See:
    See: BRIAN
Trice, Borough. See:
    ALLEN, ARTHUR
        BRUCE
TRICE, MARGUERITE GWYNNE
    (1918-) [American
    model and motion picture
    actress]
    Anne Gwynne
Tricky. See:
    LOFTON, LAWRENCE
Tricky Dick. See:
    NIXON, RICHARD
        MILHOUS
Tricky Sam. See:
    NANTON, JOSEPH
Trigger. See:
    ALPERT, HERMAN
TRIMBLE, JACQUELYN
    WHITNEY (1927-) [Amer-
    ican librarian and author]

J.L.H. Whitney
TRIMBLE, LOUIS P. (1917-)
    [American educator and
    author]
    Stuart Brock
    Gerry Travis
TRIMMER, ERIC J. (1923-)
    [British physician and
    author]
    Eric Jameson
Trinculo. See:
    WHEELER, ANDREW
        CARPENTER
Trini. See:
    LOPEZ, TRINIDAD
Trinity. See:
    Golden Gate Trinity, The
    JONES, WILLIAM
Trinity, Admiral of the. See:
    HATFIELD, BAZIL MUSE
Trio, The Immortal. See:
    Great Triumvirate, The
Trio, The Last of the Unholy.
    See: SHEIL, LILY
Tripp, C.E. See:
    MORRIS, CHARLES
        SMITH
TRIPP, MILES (1923-) [English
    writer]
    Michael Brett
Tris. See:
    SPEAKER, TRISTRAM E.
Trismegistus, The German. See:
    RUDOLF (RUDOLPH) II
Tristan. See:
    BERNARD, PAUL
Tristan Derème. See:
    HUC, PHILIPPE
Tristram Langstaff. See:
    LORD, WILLIAM
        WILBERFORCE
TRITHEIM, JOHANNES
    (1462-1516) [German abbot
    and bibliographer]
    The Father of Bibliography
Triturate, The Father of the
    Tablet. See:
    FULLER, ROBERT
        MASON
Triumvirate. See:
    Great Triumvirate, The
    Great Triumvirate of Italian

1017

Literature, The
Saulsbury Triumvirate, The
Trojan, The. See:
    EVERS, JOHN JOSEPH
Troll, Gustav. See:
    BRESTOWSKI, CARL
    AUGUST
Trot, Old Slow. See:
    THOMAS, GEORGE
    HENRY
Trotsky, Leon. See:
    BRONSTEIN, LEV
    DAVIDOVICH
TROTTER, CANON JOHN
    CRAWFORD (1848-) [Irish
    clergyman and author]
    Fergus O'Dhu
TROTTER, GRACE VIOLET
    (fl. 1950) [American
    speaker and author]
    Nancy Paschal
Trotwood. See:
    MOORE, JOHN TROTWOOD
Trotzendorf. See:
    FRIEDLAND, VALENTIN
Troubadour, The American.
    See: SCOTT,
    THOMAS JEFFERSON
Troubadour, The Crooning.
    See: LUCANESE, NICK
Troubadour, The Reincarnated.
    See: SEEGER, PETER
Troubadours, The Last of
    the. See:
    BOÉ, JACQUES
TROUBETZKOY, PRINCESS
    AMÉLIE RIVES (1863-
    1945) [American
    novelist, poet and
    playwright]
    Amélie Rives
TROUP, ROBERT WILLIAM
    (1918-) [American
    composer and musician]
    Bobby Troup
Trouper, The Old. See:
    KOERBER, LEILA
TROUSDALE, WILLIAM
    (1790-1872) [American
    soldier in Seminole
    and Mexican Wars]
    The War Horse of Sumner
    County

TROWBRIDGE, JOHN TOWNSEND
    (1827-1916) [American
    author, poet and editor]
    Paul Creyton
    J. T. Trowbridge
Troy Donohue. See:
    JOHNSON, MERLE
Troy Nesbit. See:
    FOLSOM, FRANKLIN
    BREWSTER
Trube, Ruy. See:
    TRALINS, S. ROBERT
Truck. See:
    PARHAM, CHARLES
    VALDEZ
True Thomas. See:
    LEARMOUNT, THOMAS,
    OF ERCILDOUNE
Truman Capote. See:
    PERSONS, TRUMAN
    STRECKFUS
Truman Garrett. See:
    JUDD, MARGARET HAD-
    DICAN
TRUMAN, HARRY S (1884-)
    [Thirty-third President of
    the United States]
    Give 'em Hell Harry
    H. S. T.
    High Tax Harry
    The Man from Missouri
    The Man of Independence
TRUMBAUER, FRANK (1901-56)
    [American jazz musician
    (C melody saxophone,
    leader)]
    Tram
TRUMBO, DALTON (1905-)
    [American editor, cor-
    respondent and author]
    Sam Jackson
    Robert Rich
TRUMBO, DALTON. See also:
    Hollywood Ten, The
TRUMBULL, HENRY (fl. 1810)
    [American author]
    Reverend James Steward
TRUMBULL, JOHN (1750-1831)
    [American poet, essayist
    and judge]
    The Celebrated Author of
    "M'Fingal"
    The Meddler

The Schemer, an Ally of
the Meddler J.
Hammond Trumbull
TRUMBULL, JOHN See also:
Hartford Wits, The
TRUMBULL, JONATHAN
(1710-85) [American
Revolutionary patriot;
Governor of Connecticut]
Brother Jonathan
The Rebel Governor
Trummy. See:
YOUNG, JAMES OSBORNE
TRUMPER, HUBERT BAGSTER
(1902-) [British physician
and author]
Hubert Bagster
Trumpeting Behemoth. See:
HIRT, ALOIS MAXWELL
Trundlett, Helen B. See:
ELIOT, THOMAS
STEARNS
TRUSCOTT-JONES, REGINALD
(1905-) [Welsh-born
motion picture actor]
Ray Milland
Truss, Seldon. See:
SELDON-TRUSS, LESLIE
Trust-buster, The. See:
ROOSEVELT, THEODORE
Trust-busting President, The.
See:
ROOSEVELT, THEODORE
Trust Company, The One-man.
See: WILSON, CHARLES
MOSEMAN
Trust, The Barrymore of the
Brain. See:
TUGWELL, REXFORD
GUY
Trusta, H. See:
PHELPS, ELIZABETH
STUART
Tryggvesson, Olaf. See:
OLAF I
TRYON, WILLIAM (1725-88)
[Irish Indian trader in
New England]
The Great Wolf
TSCHIRKY, OSCAR MICHEL
(1866-1950) [Maitre d'hotel
at Waldorf-Astoria Hotel,
New York City]

Oscar of the Waldorf
TSCHUDI, AEGIDIUS (GILG)
(1505-72) [Swiss historian
and Roman Catholic
theologian]
The Father of Swiss History
Tseng Yu-ho. See:
ECKE, BETTY TSENG
YU-HO
TSEU, YIH-ZAN (1886-)
[Chinese educator and
author]
A. N. Tyz
TSU, ANDREW YU-YUE (1887-)
[Chinese clergyman and
author]
Y. Y. Tsu
Tsu-chien Liu. See:
LIU, JAMES TZU CHIEN
TSUNE-CHI, YU (1899-)
[Chinese diplomat and
author]
James T. C. Yu
Tubal Cain. See:
SPOTSWOOD, ALEXANDER
TUBBS, ALICE (1853-1930)
[Anglo-American frontier
gambler]
Poker Alice Tubbs
TUBBS, ARTHUR LEWIS (1867-)
[American playwright, drama
and music critic]
Arthur Sylvester
Tubby. See:
HALL, ALFRED
HAYES, EDWARD BRIAN
TUBBY, ALFRED HERBERT
(1862-) [British consulting
surgeon and author]
Alfred Herbert Theobald
TUBMAN, HARRIET (c. 1821-
1913) [American abolition-
ist, nurse and spy]
Moses
The Negro Moses
TUCK, PORTER (1932-)
[American bullfighter]
El Rubio de Bostón
TUCKER, ABRAHAM (1705-74)
[English moral philosopher
and author]
Edward Search
Tucker, Caroline. See:

NOLAN, JEANNETTE
COVERT
TUCKER, CHARLOTTE MARIA
(1821-93) [English
juvenile writer]
A. L. O. E. (A Lady of
England)
TUCKER, GEORGE (1775-1861)
[American public official,
economist, teacher and
writer]
Joseph Atterley
TUCKER, HILDA (1880-1959)
[English actress]
Hilda Trevelyan
TUCKER, JAMES (1929-)
[British journalist and
author]
David Craig
TUCKER, JOHN RANDOLPH
(1812-83) [American
naval officer]
Handsome Jack
Tucker, Lael. See:
WERTENBAKER, LAEL
TUCKER
TUCKER, MRS. THOMAS. See:
BLAND, MRS. HUBERT
TUCKER, NATHANIEL BEVER-
LEY (1784-1851) [Ameri-
can educator and novelist]
Edward William Sidney
Beverley Tucker
Tucker, Richard. See:
TICKER, REUBEN
TUCKER, SAINT GEORGE
(1752-1827) [American
lawyer and educator]
The American Blackstone
Tucker, Sophie. See:
ABUZA, SOPHIE
TUDE, CLAIRE JOSEPHE
HIPPLOYTE LEYRIS
DE LA (1723-1803) [French
tragic actress]
Clairon
TUDOR, FREDERIC (1783-1864)
[American merchant;
dealer in ice]
The Ice King
Tudor, Henry. See:
HENRY VII

HENRY VIII
Tudor, Mary. See:
MARY I
TUEL, JOHN E. (fl. 1849-78)
[American author]
J. E. T.
Jet
Tuffy. See:
LEEMANS, ALPHONSE
TUFTS, BOWEN CHARLETON
(c. 1918-70) [American
motion picture actor]
Sonny Tufts
TUGWELL, REXFORD GUY
(1891-) [American
economist and government
official; Undersecretary of
Agriculture]
The Barrymore of the Brain
Trust
Mr. American
Tu'key Neck, Old. See:
STILWELL, JOSEPH
WARREN
Tuli. See:
KUPFERBERG, NAPHTALI
Tully. See:
CICERO, MARCUS TULLIUS
TULLY, JAMES (1891-1947)
[American author]
Jim Tully
Tully Marshall. See:
PHILLIPS, TULLY
MARSHALL
Tun, Mao. See:
SHEN YEN-PING
Tune Detective, The. See:
SPAETH, SIGMUND
GOTTFRIED
Tuning Fork, America's. See:
SEEGER, PETER
TUNNEY, JAMES JOSEPH
(1897-) [American
professional boxer; world's
heavyweight champion]
The Fighting Marine
Gene Tunney
TUNSTALL, ALFRED MOORE
(1863-1935) [American
statesman; active in
Alabama politics]
The Dean of the Alabama

Legislature
The Gentleman from Hale
Uncle Alf
TUNSTALL-BETHRENS, MARTIN
HILARY (1927-) [English
author]
Hilary Tunstall-Bethrens
TUOHY. See also:
Tooey
TUOHY
TUOHY, FRANK (1925-)
[English educator and
author]
John Francis Tuohy
TUPPER, MARTIN FARQUHAR
(1810-89) [English
author]
Peter Query
Tupper, The American. See:
HOLLAND, JOSIAH
GILBERT
Turenne, The Father of. See:
BOUILLON, HENRI DE
LA TOUR D'AUVERGNE,
DUKE DE
Turf, The Father of the. See:
FRAMPTON, TREGONWELL
VERNON, RICHARD
Turf, The Father of the New
York. See:
DE LANCEY, JAMES
Turf, The Napoleon of the. See:
JOHNSON, WILLIAM
RANSOM
Turhan. See:
BEY, TURHAN SELAHAT-
TIN SAHULTAVY
Turia, El. See:
BARRIOS, FRANCISCO
Turk. See:
MURPHY, MELVIN E.
Turk, The Terrible. See:
REED, THOMAS BRACKETT
Turk Van Lake. See:
HOUSEPIAN, VANIG
Turkey. See:
Tu'key
Turlupin. See:
LEGRAND, HENRI
Turncoat, John. See:
THAYER, JOHN
Turner, Alex Frecke. See:

CRAWFURD, OSWALD
TURNER, ALFRED L. (1911-)
[American professional
football player]
Warhorse
Turner, Charles Tennyson. See:
TENNYSON, CHARLES
TURNER, DR. WILLIAM MASON
(1835-77) [American
physician and author]
Lennox Wylder
TURNER, EILEEN ARBUTHNOT
ROBERTSON (1903-)
[English novelist]
E. Arnot Robertson
Turner Hodges. See:
MOREHEAD, ALBERT
HODGES
TURNER, JOHN C. (1896-1949)
[American composer, pianist
and singer]
Happy Turner
TURNER, JOSEPH (1911-)
[American jazz
musician (singer)]
Big Joe Turner
TURNER, JOSEPH MALLORD
WILLIAM (1775-1851)
[British landscape painter
and illustrator]
One of the Supreme Colorists
of the World
TURNER, JULIA JEAN MILDRED
FRANCES (1920-)
[American motion picture
actress]
The Sweater Girl
Judy Turner
Lana Turner
Turner, Len. See:
FLOREN, LEE
TURNER, LIDA LARRIMORE
(1897-) [American author]
Lida Larrimore
Turner, Peter Paul. See:
JEFFERY, GRANT
TURNER, WILLIAM PRICE
(1927-) [English artist,
educator and author]
Bill Turner
Turnip-hoer, The. See:
GEORGE I

Turnvater (Father of Gym-
 nastics). See:
  JAHN, FRIEDRICH
   LUDWIG
TURPIN, C. MURRAY
 (1878-) [American
 politician; Congress-
 man from
 Pennsylvania]
 Ben Turpin
Turpin of France, The Dick. See:
 BOURGUIGNON, LOUIS-
  DOMINIQUE
TURPIN, RANDOLPH (1928-)
 [English professional
 boxer]
 Randy Turpin
TURPIN, RICHARD (1706-39)
 [English highwayman]
 Dick Turpin
Turtle of the Ohio, The
 Snapping. See:
  FINK, MIKE
Turtle, The Snapping. See:
 GLASS, GEORGE
  CARTER
Tuscan Poet, The. See:
 ARIOSTO, LUDOVICO
Tuscarora John. See:
 BARNWELL, JOHN
TUSCULUM. See:
 JOHN, COUNT OF
  TUSCULUM
Tush, Old. See:
 DAVIES, CHARLES
TUSHIELAW. See:
 SCOTT, ADAM, OF
  TUSHIELAW
Tusitala (Teller of Tales). See:
 STEVENSON, ROBERT
  LOUIS BALFOUR
TUSSAUD, MARIE GROSHOLTZ
 (1760-1850) [Swiss
 modeler in wax; proprietor
 of wax museum in London]
 Madame Tussaud
TUSSER, THOMAS (c.1527-80)
 [English poet]
 The British Varro
Tut, King. See:
 KING TUTANKHAMEN
TUTANKHAMEN. See:

KING TUTANKHAMEN
Tutbury, The Fasting Woman of.
 See: MOORE, ANNE PEGG
TUTWILER, JULIA STRUDWICK
 (18??-1916) [American
 prison reformer]
 The Angel of the Prisons
TUVIM, JUDITH (1923-65)
 [American stage and motion
 picture actress]
 Judy Holliday
Twain, Mark. See:
 CLEMENS, SAMUEL
  LANGHORNE
 SELLERS, ISAIAH
Twain of Cartoonists, The Mark.
 See: WEBSTER, HAROLD
  TUCKER
TWEED,WILLIAM MARCY
 (1823-78) [American
 politician and grafter;
 head of Tweed Ring]
 Boss Tweed
 The Sachem of Tammany Hall
Tweedale, J. See:
 BICKLE, JUDITH
  BRUNDRETT
TWEEDSMUIR, BARON JOHN
 BUCHAN (1875-1940)
 [English author]
 John Buchan
Twelvetrees, Helen. See:
 JURGENS, HELEN
Twentieth Amendment to the
 Constitution, The Father
 of the. See:
  NORRIS, GEORGE
   WILLIAM
Twentieth Century Gabriel, The.
 See: HAWKINS, ERSKINE
Twentieth Century Moses. See:
 CHAPLIN, CHARLES
  SPENCER
Twickenham, The Bard of. See:
 POPE, ALEXANDER
TWIGGS, DAVID EMANUEL
 (1790-1862) [American
 army officer; military
 governor of Vera Cruz]
 Bengal Tiger
 The Horse
 Old Davy

Twiggy. See:
HORNBY, LESLIE
Twin of Heavenlier Birth, The.
See: BEAUMONT,
FRANCIS
Twins. See:
Nurk Twins, The
Poison Twins, The
Siamese Twins, The
Twist, Ananias. See:
NUNN, WILLIAM
CURTIS
Twitcher, Harry. See:
BROUGHAM, HENRY
PETER
Twitcher, Jemmy. See:
MONTAGU, JOHN
Two Black Crows
Moran and Mack, joint
stage names of CHARLES
MACK (1887-1934) and
GEORGE SEARCY (George
Moran) (1882-1949)
[American blackface
entertainers]
Two-edged Knife, The. See:
BILBO, THEODORE
GILMORE
Two-gun Girl, The. See:
GUINAN, MARY LOUISE
CECELIA
Two Sisters of the West, joint
pseud. of MRS.
CATHERINE ANN WARE
WARFIELD (1816-77) and
her sister ELEANOR
WARE (1820-) [American
authors and poets]
Two Sisters of the West. See
also: Sisters of the West
Two Sticks, The Devil on. See:
MORTON, OLIVER
HAZARD PERRY
THROCK
Two Ton. See:
BAKER, RICHARD E.
Ty. See:
COBB, TYRUS RAYMOND
Tycho, The Southern. See:
HALLEY, EDMUND
Tycoon, The. See:
LINCOLN, ABRAHAM

Tycoon, The Old. See:
PRICE, STERLING G.
Tyler. See:
MASON, MADELINE
TYLER, JOHN (1790-1862)
[Tenth President of the
United States]
The Accidental President
His Accidency
Young Hickory
TYLER, ROYALL (1757-1826)
[American jurist, poet,
novelist and playwright]
Spondee
Tyler, Tom. See:
BURNS, WILLIAM
TYLER-WHITTLE, MICHAEL
SIDNEY (1927-) [British
broadcaster, painter and
author]
Mark Oliver
Tyler Whittle
Tyman Currio. See:
CORYELL, JOHN RUSSELL
Tynan, Katharine. See:
HINKSON, MRS.
KATHARINE TYNAN
TYNDALE (TINDALE), WILLIAM
[1492?-1536) [English
translator of the Bible]
William Hutchins
Tyneman, The (Loser). See:
DOUGLAS, ARCHIBALD
Typewriter, The Father of the.
See: SHOLES, CHRISTOPHER
LATHAM
Typhoid Mary. See:
MALLON, MARY
Typical American, The. See:
ROOSEVELT, THEODORE
Tyrant, The. See:
LINCOLN, ABRAHAM
Tyree. See:
GLENN, EVANS TYREE
Tyrol, Horatius Cocles of the.
See: DUMAS, ALEXANDRE
DAVY DE LA PAILLE-
TERIE
TYRONE, HUGH O'NEIL, EARL
OF (1540-1616) [Irish
revolutionist]
The O'Neil

Tyrwhitt, Gerald. See:
　　BERNERS, GERALD HUGH
　　TYRWHITT-WILSON,
　　14TH BARON
TYTLER, JAMES (1747-1805)
　　[Scottish literary hack,
　　balloonist and scientific
　　dabbler]
　　Balloon Tytler
Tyz, A.N. See:
　　TSEU, YIH-ZAN

U

U.S. Detective, A, E.S. St.
　　Mox. See:
　　ELLIS, EDWARD
　　SYLVESTER
UALE, FRANCESCO (-1928)
　　[American gangster and
　　racketeer]
　　The Beau Brummel of the
　　Brooklyn Underworld
　　Frankie Yale
Uccello, Paolo. See:
　　DONO, PAOLO DE
Udall, Lyn. See:
　　KEATING, JOHN HENRY
Uei Tlatoani (One Who Speaks).
　　See: MONTEZUMA II
Ugliest Man in Canada, The.
　　See: CHAPELSKI,
　　ALEX SAMUEL
UGOLINO, COUNT OF SEGNI
　　(c. 1145-1241) [Supreme
　　Pontiff of Roman Catholic
　　Church]
　　Pope Gregory IX
Uhl, Ruth. See:
　　FRANK, RUTH VERD
Ukulele Ace, The. See:
　　MARVIN, JOHN
Ukulele Ike. See:
　　EDWARDS, CLIFF
Ukulele Lady, The. See:
　　BREEN, MAY SINGHI
ULENSPIEGEL. See:
　　EULENSPIEGEL
　　(ULENSPIEGEL), TILL
Ullah, Baha (Splendor of God).
　　See: MIRZA HUSEYN ALI

ULLAH, SALAMAT (1913-)
　　[Indian educator and author]
　　Salamatullah
ULLMAN, JULIUS (1883-1939)
　　[American motion picture
　　actor]
　　Doug Fairbanks
　　Douglas Fairbanks
　　The Fourth Musketeer
Ulmar, Genevieve. See:
　　COBB, WELDON J.
ULYANOV, VLADIMIR ILYICH
　　(1870-1924) [Russian
　　Marxist revolutionary;
　　founder of bolshevik com-
　　munism]
　　The Father of the Russian
　　Revolution
　　Nikolai Lenin
　　Vladimir Ilyich Lenin
Ulysses of Germany, The. See:
　　ALBERT III
Ulysses of the Highlands, The.
　　See: CAMERON, SIR EVAN
Ulysses Simpson Grant. See:
　　GRANT, HIRAM ULYSSES
'un. See also:
　　One
'un. See:
　　Old 'un
'un, The Long. See:
　　LINCOLN, ABRAHAM
'un, Young. See:
　　Old 'un
Uncle Abe. See:
　　LINCOLN, ABRAHAM
Uncle Alf. See:
　　TAYLOR, ALFRED
　　ALEXANDER
　　TUNSTALL, ALFRED
　　MOORE
Uncle Bill. See:
　　WOLSEY, WILLIAM
　　FRANKLYN
Uncle Billy. See:
　　SHERMAN, WILLIAM
　　TECUMSEH
　　SMITH, WILLIAM
　　WORKMAN, WILLIAM
　　HENRY
Uncle Dan. See:
　　BEARD, DANIEL CARTER

Uncle Dan'l. See:
DREW, DANIEL
Uncle Dick. See:
OGLESBY, RICHARD
JAMES
Uncle Esek. See:
SHAW, HENRY
WHEELER
Uncle Feininger, Your. See:
FEININGER, LYONEL
Uncle Fred. See:
THOMPSON, FREDERICK
B.
Uncle George. See:
PERKINS, GEORGE
DOUGLAS
THOMAS, GEORGE
HENRY
Uncle Gordon. See:
ROE, FREDERIC GORDON
Uncle Gus. See:
REY, HANS AUGUSTO
Uncle Henry. See:
SMITH, GEORGE HENRY
Uncle Jerry. See:
RUSK, JEREMIAH
Mc LAIN
Uncle Jimmie. See:
DOUGHTY, JAMES P.
Uncle Joe. See:
CANNON, JOSEPH
GURNEY
STILWELL, JOSEPH
WARREN
SWING, JOSEPH MAY
Uncle John. See:
SEDGWICK, JOHN
Uncle Jumbo. See:
CLEVELAND, STEPHEN
GROVER
Uncle Leopold. See:
LEOPOLD I
Uncle Milty. See:
BERLINGER, MILTON
Uncle Noah. See:
BROOKS, NOAH
Uncle Ralph. See:
SHAW, RALPH ROBERT
Uncle Ray. See:
COFFMAN, RAMON
PEYTON
Uncle Remus. See:

HARRIS, JOEL CHANDLER
Uncle Robert. See:
LEE, ROBERT EDWARD
Uncle Sam. See:
GRANT, HIRAM ULYSSES
WILSON, SAMUEL
Uncle Sam's Favorite Niece. See:
KAUMEYER, DOROTHY
Uncle, The Nephew of My. See:
SWEENEY, PETER BARR
Uncle Toby. See:
CROSS, WILBUR LUCIUS
Unconditional Surrender. See:
GRANT, HIRAM ULYSSES
Uncrowned King. See:
BLAINE, JAMES
GILLESPIE
Uncrowned King of Ireland, The.
See: PARNELL, CHARLES
STEWART
Uncrowned King of Scotland, The.
See: DUNDAS, HENRY
Undergraduate Humor, Master of.
See: SHULMAN, MAX
Underhill, Peter. See:
SODERBERG, PERCY
MEASDAY
Underwood, Lewis Graham. See:
WAGNER, CHARLES
PETER
UNDERWOOD, MARVIS EILEEN
(1916-) [English author]
Sarah Kilpatrick
Underwood, Michael. See:
EVELYN, JOHN MICHAEL
Underwood, Miles. See:
GLASSCO, JOHN
Underworld, The Beau Brummel
of the Brooklyn. See:
UALE, FRANCESCO
Underworld, The Lone Wolf of
the. See:
MILLMAN, HARRY
Undisputed King of Handcuffs.
See: WEISS, EHRICH
(ERIK WEISZ)
UNETT, JOHN (fl. 1930-64)
[British author]
James Preston
Unfair Preacher, The. See:
BARROW, ISAAC
UNGER, MAURICE ALBERT

(1917-) [American
attorney, educator and
author]
Al Munger
Ungodly, The. See:
AËTIUS
Unhappy Answers, The Man of
Happy. See:
TARLTON, RICHARD
Unholy Trio, The Last of the.
See: SHEIL, LILY
Uniformed Soldier. See:
GRANT, HIRAM ULYSSES
Unintentional Defaulter, The.
See: WEBSTER,
DANIEL
Union Army, The Murat of the.
See: LOGAN, JOHN
ALEXANDER
Union Party of California, The
Father of the. See:
VAN DYKE, WALTER
Union Safeguard. See:
GRANT, HIRAM ULYSSES
Union, The Belle of the. See:
LE VERT, OCTAVIA
WALTON
Union, The Defender of the.
See: WEBSTER, DANIEL
Union's Grand Old Man, The.
See: SAVAGE, GEORGE
MARTIN
Unitarianism, The Apostle of.
See: CHANNING, WILLIAM
ELLERY
Unitarianism, The Father of
English. See:
BIDDLE, JOHN
UNITAS, JOHN (1933-)
[American football player]
Johnny Unitas
United States. See:
GRANT, HIRAM ULYSSES
United States, A Lay Preacher
to the Largest Congregation
in the. See:
BOK, EDWARD WILLIAM
United States Grant. See:
GRANT, HIRAM ULYSSES
United States Military Academy,
The Father of the. See:
THAYER, SYLVANUS

United States Sculptors, The Dean
of. See:
DAVIDSON, JO
United States, The Father of
Prison Reform in. See:
OSBORNE GEORGE O.
United States, The Greatest
Citizen in the. See:
ELIOT, CHARLES WILLIAM
United States, The Mother of
Methodism in the. See:
HECK, BARBARA RUCKLE
United States, The Picturesque
Explorer of the. See:
LANMAN, CHARLES
Universal Bibliography, The
Father of. See:
GESSNER, KONRAD VON
Universal Doctor, The. See:
ALAIN DE LILLE
(ALANUS DE INSULIS)
Universal Genius, The. See:
PETTY, WILLIAM
Universal Man, The (Homo
Universale). See:
VINCI, LEONARDO DA
Universal Spider, The. See:
LOUIS XI
Universale, Homo (The Universal
Man). See:
VINCI, LEONARDO DA
Universalis, Doctor. See:
ALBERTUS MAGNUS,
SAINT, COUNT OF BOLL-
STÄDT
AQUINAS, ST. THOMAS
Universalism in America, The
Father of. See:
MURRAY, JOHN
Universalism, The Father of
American. See:
BALLOU, HOSEA
MURRAY, JOHN
Universe, Mr. See:
REEVES, STEPHEN
Universe, The Firebrand of the.
See: TIMUR LENK
Universities, The Father of
State. See:
CUTLER, MANASSEH
University of Minnesota, The
Father of the. See:

PILLSBURY, JOHN
SARGENT
University of Missouri, The
Father of the. See:
ROLLINS, JAMES
SIDNEY
University of North Carolina,
The Father of the. See:
DAVIE, WILLIAM
RICHARDSON
University of Virginia,
The Father of the.
See:
JEFFERSON, THOMAS
University, The Father of Ohio.
See: CUTLER, MANAS-
SEH
University, The Father
of Organized
Alumni Work at
Fisk. See:
PROCTOR, HENRY HUGH
UNKNOWN (fl. 600 B.C.)
[Lesbian poetess]
Psappho
Sappho
The Tenth Muse
UNKNOWN (c. 1100-c. 1175) [Nor-
man-French poet and
historian]
Canon Wace
Robert
Wace
UNKNOWN (fl. mid 13th cent.)
[Dutch mystic and poet]
Hadewijch
UNKNOWN (fl. mid 17th cent.)
[English poet]
Ephelia
UNKNOWN (fl. mid-17th cent.)
[English playwright]
L.W.
UNKNOWN (died 1703) [French
political prisoner]
The Man in the Iron Mask
Marchiali
UNKNOWN (1697?-1763) [French
or Swiss literary impostor
and adventurer]
The Formosan
George Psalmanazar
UNKNOWN (1826?-73) [Anglo-

American actress and theater
manager]
Laura Keene
UNKNOWN (fl. 1845-46) [American
novelist]
Tom Shortfellow
UNKNOWN (fl. 1845-50) [English
criminal in San Francisco]
Bristol Bill
UNKNOWN (fl. 1846-58) [American
novelist]
Emma Carra
Avis S. Spenser
UNKNOWN (fl. 1847-48) [American
novelist]
Harry Halyard
UNKNOWN (fl. mid 19th cent.)
[British author, imitator of
CHARLES JOHN HUFFAM
DICKENS]
Bos
UNKNOWN (fl. 1860-70) [American
novelist]
Wesley Bradshaw
UNKNOWN (fl. 1888) [Unidentified
English murderer of six
prostitutes]
Jack The Ripper
UNKNOWN (1926-) [British author]
Jeffrey Ashford
UNKNOWN (fl. 3rd decade of 20th
century) [Radio news
commentator]
Q. E. D.
UNKNOWN (-1933) [Professional
thief and author]
Chic Conwell
The Professional Thief
UNKNOWN. See also:
Ashdown, Clifford
Unknown Philosopher, The. See:
ST. MARTIN, LOUIS-CLAUDE
DE
Unknown, The Great. See:
SCOTT, SIR WALTER
Unmelancholy Dane, The. See:
ROSENBAUM, BORGE
Unprecedented Strategist. See:
GRANT, HIRAM ULYSSES
Unquestionably Skilled. See:
GRANT, HIRAM ULYSSES
Unready Mac, The. See:

McCLELLAN, GEORGE
BRINTON
Unready, The. See:
  ETHELRED (AETHELRED)
  II
Unreconstructed Rebel. See:
  GLASS, GEORGE CARTER
Unser Fritz (Our Fritz). See:
  FREDERICK WILLIAM
Unsought Fields, Little
  Corporal of. See:
  McCLELLAN, GEORGE
  BRINTON
Untamed Heifer, The. See:
  ELIZABETH I
UNWIN, DAVID STORR (1918-)
  [British journalist, art
  editor, publisher's reader
  and author]
David Severn
Updyke, James. See:
  BURNETT, WILLIAM
  RILEY
Upholder of the Constitution,
  The. See:
  WEBSTER, DANIEL
Upright, Aaron the. See:
  HARUN AL-RASHID
Upright, The. See:
  FREDERICK IV
UPSON, DOROTHY BARBARA
  (1904-) [English author]
Barbara Fawcett
Elizabeth Furness
Upton Close. See:
  HALL, JOSEF
  WASHINGTON
UPTON, GEORGE PUTNAM
  (1834-1919) [American
  journalist, music critic
  and author]
Peregrine Pickle
UPWARD, EDWARD FALASIE
  (1903-) [English author]
Allen Chalmers
Uqsor, El. See:
  BORGMANN, DMITRI
  ALFRED
URBAN (died 230) [Supreme
  Pontiff of Roman
  Catholic Church]
Pope Urban I

St. Urban
Urban II, Pope. See:
  ODA OF LAGERY
Urban III, Pope. See:
  CRIVELLI, UBERTO
Urban IV, Pope. See:
  PANTALÉON, JACQUES
Urban V, Pope. See:
  GRIMORD, GUILLAUME DE
Urban VI, Pope. See:
  PRIGNANO, BARTOLOMMEO
Urban VII, Pope. See: CASTAGNA,
  GIAMBATTISTA
Urban VIII, Pope. See:
  BARBERINI, MAFFEO
Urban, Septimus R. See:
  RYMER, JAMES MALCOLM
  URNER, NATHAN DANE
Urban, Sylvanus. See:
  CAVE, EDWARD
Urbie. See:
  GREEN, URBAN CLIFFORD
URIS, AUREN (1913-)
  [American editor, wood
  sculptor and author of
  books for businessmen]
Auren Paul
URNER, NATHAN DANE (1839-93)
  [American journalist and
  author]
Bryant Bainbridge
Burke Brentford
Bartley Campbell
Clarence Clancool
Carl Courteney
Professor Gildersleeve
Mentor
Edward Minturn
Ingoldsby North
Maurice Silingsby
Septimus R. Urban
Ursa Major. See:
  JOHNSON, DR. SAMUEL
Ursula Jeans. See:
  McMINN, URSULA
Useless. See:
  GRANT, HIRAM ULYSSES
USHER, FRANK (1909-)
  [British journalist and
  author]
Charles Franklin
Frank Lester
Usufruct, Old. See:

TILDEN, SAMUEL
JONES
Usikota. See:
BRINITZER, CARL
Usurpers, The Sagest of the.
See: CROMWELL,
OLIVER
Uticensis. See:
CATO, MARCUS PORCIUS
Utilitarian School of Philosophy,
Founder of the. See:
CUMBERLAND, RICHARD
Utility Regulation, The Father
of Public. See:
NORRIS, GEORGE
WILLIAM
UTLEY, ULDINE (1912-)
[Methodist Episcopal
minister and revivalist]
The Joan of Arc of the
Modern Religious World
Uvalde Jack. See:
GARNER, JOHN NANCE
Uvalde, The Sage of. See:
GARNER, JOHN NANCE

V

V.A. Van Sickle. See:
CARHART, ARTHUR
HAWTHORNE
V. Helen Fox. See:
COUCH, HELEN FOX
V.S. Warren. See:
MANNING, WILLIAM
HENRY
V. Sirin. See:
NABOKOV, VLADIMIR
(VLADIMIROVICH)
Vachel. See:
LINDSAY, NICHOLAS
VACHEL
Vechel
VACZEK, LOUIS (1913-)
[Hungarian teacher,
editor and author]
Peter Hardin
Vadim, Roger. See:
PLEMIANNIKOW,
ROGER VADIM
Vagabond Lover, The. See:

VALLEE, HUBERT PRIOR
VAGG, SAMUEL (1826-65)
[English music-hall
comedian]
Sam Collins
VAGRAMIAN, ARAM (1921-)
[American composer,
pianist and conductor]
Al Vega
Vague, Vera. See:
ALLEN, BARBARA JO
VAJIRAVUDH (1881-1925)
[King of Thailand (Siam)]
Rama VI
Val Valentine. See:
GERICH, VALENTINE
Val Versatile. See:
ENTON, DR. HARRY
VALDÉS, JUAN MELENDEZ
(1754-1817) [Spanish poet]
The Restorer of Parnassus
VALDÉZ, CARLOS (1913-)
[American jazz musician
(guitar)]
Potato Valdéz
VALE, HENRY EDMUND
THEODORIC (1888-)
[British author]
John Bledlow
Vale, Lady of the. See:
BUTLER, LADY ELEANOR
PONSONBY, MISS SARAH
Valencia II. See:
ROGER, VICTORIANO
Valencia, Morenito de. See:
PUCHOL, AURELIO
Valentina. See:
SCHLEE, VALENTINA
NICHOLAEVNA SANINA
Valentine. See:
PECHEY, ARCHIBALD
THOMAS
VALLENTINE
WILLIAMS, GEORGE
VALENTINE
VALENTINE (died 827) [Supreme
Pontiff of Roman Catholic
Church]
Pope Valentine
Valentine, David. See:
LUDOVICI, ANTHONY MARIO
Valentine, Douglas. See:

WILLIAMS, GEORGE
VALENTINE
Valentine, Jimmy. See:
LYTELL, BERT
Valentine, Jo. See:
ARMSTRONG, CHARLOTTE
Valentine, Roger. See:
DUKE, DONALD NORMAN
VALENTINE, SISTER MARY
HESTER (1909-)
[American Roman Catholic
nun and author]
Helen Valentine
VALENTINE, THOMAS
(1896-) [American
jazz musician (trumpet)]
Kid Thomas
Valentine, Val. See:
GERICH, VALENTINE
Valentino, Rudolph. See:
D'ANTONGUOLLA
RODOLPHO ALFONZO
RAFAELO PIERRE
FILIBERT GUGLIELMO
DI VALENTIN
Valerie Baxter. See:
MEYNELL, LAURENCE
Valerie Rift. See:
BARTLETT, MARIE
SWAN
Valerie Taylor. See:
TATE, VELMA
Valerie Watkinson. See:
ELLISTON, VALERIE
MAE WATKINSON
Valiant, The. See:
ALFONSO VI
JOHN V
Valjean, Jean, Philadelphia's.
See: BURKE, WILLIAM
VALLEE, HUBERT PRIOR
(1901-) [American jazz
musician (saxophone);
conductor of the "Con-
necticut Yankees"
orchestra]
The Crooner
Rudy Vallee
The Vagabond Lover
Vallee, The Modern Generation's
Rudy. See:
MONROE, VAUGHN

WILTON
VALLENTINE. See also:
VALENTINE
Valentine
VALLENTINE, BENJAMIN BEN-
NATON (1843-1926)
[British journalist and
playwright]
Fitznoodle
Valley, The Patriot Mother of
the Mohawk. See:
VAN ALSTINE, MRS.
MARTIN J.
Valley, The Poet of the
Shenandoah. See:
LUCAS, DANIEL BEDINGER
Valley, The Sage of Happy. See:
TAYLOR, ALFRED
ALEXANDER
Valley, The Savior of the. See:
ROSSER, THOMAS
LAFAYETTE
Valley, The Swamp Fox of the
Tennessee. See:
RODDEY, PHILIP DALE
Valli, Alida. See:
ALTENBURGER, ALIDA
MARIA
VALLI, VIRGINIA (1899-)
[American motion picture
actress]
The Outdoor Girl of the
Films
VALOIS. See:
ISABELLA OF VALOIS
MARGARET OF VALOIS
Valois, Ninette De. See:
STANNUS, EDRIS
Valtin, Jan. See:
KREBS, RICHARD
JULIUS HERMAN
Valuable Friend, Wesley's
Most. See:
FLETCHER, JOHN WILLIAM
Vamp, The Baby. See:
WEST, MAE
Vampires, The Queen of The.
See: GOODMAN,
THEODOSIA
VAN [Van]. Those names so pre-
fixed and not listed below
may be found indexed under

1030

that part of the name
following "VAN" or "Van"
Van. See:
  HEFLIN, EMMET EVAN,
    JR.
VAN AEKEN, HIERONYMUS
  (c.1450-1516) [Dutch
  painter]
Hieronymus Bosch (Bos)
VAN ALSTINE, MRS. MARTIN
  J. (fl. 18th cent.)
  [American heroine and
  missionary to Mohawk
  Indians]
The Patriot Mother of the
  Mohawk Valley
VAN ALSTYNE, MRS. FRANCES
  JANE CROSBY (1820-1915)
  [American hymn writer]
Fanny Crosby
VAN ANROOY, FRANCINE
  (1924-) [Dutch author]
Frans van Anrooy
VAN ARTEVELDE, JACOB
  (1290-1345) [Flemish
  statesman and political
  leader]
The Brewer of Ghent
VAN ATTA, WINFRED
  LOWELL (1910-)
  [American editor and
  author]
Lowell Ryerson
VAN BRIGGLE, MARGARET
  FRANCES JESSUP (1917-)
  [American administrator
  and author]
Frances Jessup
VAN BROCKLIN, NORMAN
  (1926-) [American
  football player]
Norm
Van Buren, Abigail. See:
  PHILLIPS, PAULINE
    ESTHER FRIEDMAN
VAN BUREN, JOHN (1810-66)
  [Son of President
  MARTIN VAN BUREN]
Prince John
VAN BUREN, MARTIN (1782-
  1862) [Eighth President
  of the United States]

The American Talleyrand
The Enchanter
The Fox
The Kinderhook Fox
King Martin the First
The Little Magician
Little Van
The Machiavellian Belshazzar
Matey
The Mistletoe Politician
The Petticoat Pet
The Red Fox of Kinderhook
The Sage of Kinderhook
The Sage of Lindenwald
Whiskey Van
The Wizard of Kinderhook
The Wizard of the Albany
  Regency
VAN COEVERING, JAN ADRIAN
  (1900-) [Dutch-American
  journalist and author]
Jack Van Coevering
VAN CORTLANDT, PHILIP
  (1749-1831) [American
  soldier and legislator]
The Great White Devil
VAN DAMME, ARTHUR
  (1920-) [American
  accordionist]
Art Van Damme
VAN DE VELDE, WILLEM
  (c.1611-93) [Dutch
  marine painter]
The Elder
VAN DE VELDE, WILLEM
  (1633-1707) [Dutch marine
  painter]
The Younger
VAN DER FAES, PIETER
  (1618-80) [Dutch painter]
Sir Peter Lely
Van Der Meer Van Delft, Jan.
  See: VERMEER, JAN
VAN DER SMISSEN,
  MARGARET ELISABETH
  (1927-) [American educator
  and author]
Betty van der Smissen
Van Dine. See also:
  Van Dyne
Van Dine, S.S. See:
  WRIGHT, WILLARD

1031

HUNTINGTON
Van Doren, Dirck. See:
  DEY, FREDERIC VAN
    RENSSELAER
Van Doren, Mamie. See:
  OLANDER, JOAN
    LUCILLE
VAN DUNGEN, FRITZ
  (1905-) [Dutch stage
  and motion picture
  actor]
  Philip Dorn
Van Dyck in Little. See:
  COOPER, SAMUEL
Van Dyck of Sculpture, The.
  See: COYSEVOX,
    ANTOINE
Van Dyck, The English. See:
  DOBSON, WILLIAM
Van Dyck, The French. See:
  RIGAUD, HYACINTHE
VAN DYKE, WALTER(1823-
  1905) [American
  politician in California]
  The Father of the Union
  Party of California
Van Dyne. See also:
  Van Dine
Van Dyne, Edith. See:
  BAUM, LYMAN
    FRANK
VAN EPS, WORSTER (1912-)
  [American stage and
  motion picture actor]
  Willard Parker
van Haarlem, Jan Vermeer.
  See: MEER, JAN VAN
    DER
VAN HEEMSTRA, EDDA
  HEPBURN (1929-) [Irish-
  Dutch motion picture
  actress]
  Audrey Hepburn
Van Heusen, James. See:
  BABCOCK, EDWARD
    CHESTER
VAN HORNE, HARRY
  RANDALL (1924-)
  [American composer
  and conductor]
  Randy Van Horne
Van Kampen, Karl. See:

CAMPBELL, JOHN
  WOOD
Van Lake, Turk. See:
  HOUSEPIAN, VANIG
Van Leyden, Lucas. See:
  HUGENSZ, LUCAS
VAN LIERDE, JOHN (1907-)
  [Dutch theologian,
  musician, linguist and
  author]
  Peter Canisius Van Lierde
Van, Little. See:
  VAN BUREN, MARTIN
VAN MAERLANT, JAKOB DE
  COSTER (died after 1291)
  [Belgian poet]
  The Father of Dutch Poetry
  The Father of Dutch Poets
  The Father of Flemish
    Poets
VAN MATTIMORE, RICHARD
  (1899-) [American
  motion picture actor]
  Richard Arlen
VAN METER, HOMER (190?-34)
  [American outlaw]
  Wayne Van Meter
VAN NEUHOFF, BARON
  (1681-1756) [German
  adventurer]
  Theodore, King of Corsica
VAN ORDEN, ROBERT (1931-)
  [American motion picture
  actor]
  John Smith
van Porter, Henry. See:
  CORRELL, CHARLES J.
VAN PRAAGH, MARGARET
  (1910-) [British ballerina
  and author]
  Peggy Van Praagh
VAN RIJN (RYN), REMBRANDT
  HARMESZ (HARMENZOON)
  (1606-69) [Dutch painter
  and etcher]
  Rembrandt
VAN SANTVOORD, ALFRED
  (1819-1901) [American
  shipping magnate]
  Commodore Van Santvoord
Van Sickle, V.A. See:
  CARHART, ARTHUR

1032

HAWTHORNE
van Someren, Leisje. See:
    LICHTENBERG,
    ELISABETH JACOBA
VAN VECHEN, ABRAHAM
    (1762-1837) [American
    jurist]
    The Father of the Bar of
    the State of New York
Van, Whisky. See:
    VAN BUREN, MARTIN
VAN WINKLE, HAROLD E.
    (1939-) [American
    composer]
    Rip Van Winkle
VAN WORMER, JOSEPH
    EDWARD (1913-)
    [American accountant,
    photographer and writer]
    Joe Van Wormer
Van Wyck. See:
    MASON, FRANCIS VAN
    WYCK
VAN WYNKYN, JAN(14??-
    c.1534/5) [English
    stationer and printer]
    Wynkyn de Worde
VAN ZANT, JAMES E.
    (1898-) [American
    politician; congressman
    from Pennsylvania]
    The Father of the Bonus
VAN ZELLER, HUBERT
    (1905-) [British
    Benedectine monk and
    author]
    Brother Choleric
    Claud Van Zeller
    Hugh Venning
Vance, Clara. See:
    DENISON, MARY
    ANDREWS
VANCE, CLARENCE ARTHUR
    (1893-1961) [American
    professional baseball
    player]
    Dazzy Vance
Vance, Edgar. See:
    AMBROSE, ERIC
Vance, Ethel. See:
    STONE, MRS. GRACE
    ZARING

VANCE, JOSEPH ALBERT
    (1905-) [American
    professional baseball
    player]
    Sandy Vance
Vance the Great. See:
    STEVENS, ALFRED PECK
Vancouver, The Archbishop
    John I of. See:
    WOLSEY, WILLIAM
    FRANKLYN
Vandal, Cameron. See:
    THORNE, BLISS KIRBY
Vandegrift, Margaret. See:
    JANVIER, MARGARET
    THOMPSON
VANDERBILT, CORNELIUS
    (1794-1877) [American
    financier and capitalist]
    Commodore Vanderbilt
VANDERBILT, GLORIA (1924-)
    [American heiress]
    The Poor Little Rich Girl
Vane, Michael. See:
    HUMPHRIES, SIDNEY
    VERNON
Vane, Roland. See:
    McKEAG, ERNEST LIONEL
VANE, SIR HENRY (1589-1654)
    [British statesman]
    Old Sir Henry
VANE, SIR HENRY (1613-62)
    [British statesman]
    Young Sir Henry
Vanessa. See:
    VANHOMRIGH, ESTHER
Vanessa Brown. See:
    BRIND, SMYLLA
VANHOMRIGH, ESTHER
    (1690-1723) [Pupil and
    friend of JONATHAN SWIFT]
    Vanessa
VANNUCCHI, ANDREA
    DOMENICO D'AGNOLO DI
    FRANCESCO DI LUCA
    (1486-1531) [Florentine
    painter of the High Renais-
    sance]
    Andrea del Sarto
    The Faultless Painter
VANNUCCI, PIETRO (c.1450-1523)
    [Italian painter]

Perugion (The Perugian)
Vanolis, Bysshe. See:
    THOMSON, JAMES
Vansittart, Jane. See:
    MOORHOUSE, HILDA
    VANSITTART
VARAHAGIRI, VENKATA
    GIRI (1894-) [Indian
    barrister and author]
Giri
Varconi, Victor. See:
    VARKONYI, MIHALY
Vardre, Leslie. See:
    DAVIES, LESLIE
    PURNELL
Varelito. See:
    GARCÍA, MANUEL VARÉ
Varga, Judy. See:
    STANG, JUDIT
VARGAS, ENRIQUE (1869-1930)
    [Spanish bullfighter]
Minuto
VARICK, ALFRED (1881-1949)
    [British stage and
    motion picture actor]
Alfred Drayton
Varick Venardy. See:
    DEY, FREDERICK VAN
    RENSSELAER
Variety, The Father of. See:
    PARNELL, THOMAS
    FREDERICK
Varina. See:
    WARING, JANE
VARKONYI, MIHALY (1896-)
    [Hungarian motion
    picture actor]
Victor Varconi
VARNADOW, PEGGY (1928-)
    [American motion
    picture actress]
Peggy Dow
VARRO, MARCUS TERENTIUS
    (c.116-c.27 B.C.)
    [Roman scholar and
    author]
    The Most Learned of the
    Romans
Varro, The British. See:
    TUSSER, THOMAS
VARRO, WILLIAM (fl. last half
    of 13th cent.) [English Minor-
    ite and scholastic philosopher]

Doctor Fundatus
Vasa, Gustavus. See:
    GUSTAVUS I
Vaster, Noch (Even Firmer). See:
    STEENDAM, JACOB
Vasu, Nirmala-Kumara. See:
    BOSE, NIRMAL KUMAR
Vatatzes. See:
    JOHN III
Vatican, The Prisoner of the.
    See: FERRETTI, GIOVAN-
    NI MARIA MASTAI
Vator, By Miss Ella. See:
    SMITH, HARRY ALLEN
Vaudeville, The Joyous Father
    of the. See:
    BASSELIN, OLIVER
Vaudeville's Youngest Headliner.
    See: WEST, MAE
VAUGHAN, FLOYD E. (1912-)
    [American professional
    baseball player]
Arkie
VAUGHAN, HENRY (1622-95)
    [British mystic poet]
The Silurist
Vaughan, Hilda. See: MORGAN,
    HILDA CAMPBELL
Vaughan, Kate. See:
    CANDELON, CATHERINE
Vaughan, Leo. See:
    LENDON, KENNETH HARRY
Vaughan, Miss. See:
    PRITCHARD, HANNAH
VAUGHAN, WILLIAM EDWARD
    (1915-) [American journalist,
    columnist and author]
Bill Vaughan
VAYSSE, CHARLES (1910-)
    [French author]
Connie Fennell
VECCHI, AUGUSTUS VICTOR
    (1842-) [Italian author]
Jack La Bolina
Vecchio, Il (The Elder) See:
    PAUMA, JACOPO
Vecchio, Palma (Old Palma).
    See: PALMA, JACOPO
VECELLI (VECELLIO),
    TIZIANO (1477-1576)
    [Venetian painter of the
    High Renaissance]
Da Cadore

Il Divino
Titian
Vechel. See also:
Vachel
Vechel Howard. See:
RIGSBY, HOWARD
Vedder, John K. See:
GRUBER, FRANK
Vedette. See:
WILLIAMS, GEORGE
VALENTINE
VEECK, WILLIAM LOUIS, JR.
(1914-) [American
baseball team president]
A Midwestern Larry
McPhail
Bill Veeck
Veep, The. See:
BARKLEY, ALBEN
WILLIAM
VEGA. See:
GARCILASO DE LA VEGA
REYES, FRANCISCO
VEGA DE LOS
REYES, RAFAEL VEGA
DE LOS
Vega, Al. See:
VAGRAMIAN, ARAM
VEGA, GARCILASSO DE LA
(1503-36) [Spanish poet]
The Petrarch of Spain
The Prince of Spanish
Poetry
The Spanish Petrarch
Vega, Lope de. See:
CARPIO, LOPE FÉLIX
DE VEGA
Veiled, The (Al Mokanna). See:
DEN ATTA, HAKIM
VELDE, WILLEM VAN DE
(c. 1611-93) [Dutch
marine painter]
Willem the Elder
VELDE, WILLEM VAN DE
(1633-1707) [Dutch
marine painter]
Willem the Younger
Velez, Lupe. See:
VILLABOS, GUADALOUPE
VELEZ DE
Velvet. See:
BRUEGHEL (BREUGHEL),
JAN

Velvet Fog, The. See:
TORMÉ, MELVIN HOWARD
VENABLE, CLARKE (1892-)
[American author]
Covington Clarke
Venardy, Varick. See:
DEY, FREDERICK VAN
RENSSELAER
Venerabilis, Doctor (Venerable
Doctor). See:
CHAMPEAUX, GUILLAUME
DE
Venerabilis Inceptor. See:
OCKHAM (OCCAM),
WILLIAM OF
Venerable Bede, The. See:
BEDE (BEDA) (BAEDA), ST.
EUSEBIUS OF CAESAREA
Venerable Doctor (Doctor
Venerabilis). See:
CHAMPEAUX, GUILLAUME
DE
Venerable Initiator, The. See:
OCKHAM (OCCAM),
WILLIAM OF
Venetian, The. See:
Andrew III
Veneziano, Bonifazio. See:
PITATI, BONIFAZIO
Venice, Peter of. See:
GUARNIERI, PIETRO
Venison, Alfred. See:
POUND, EZRA LOOMIS
Venning, Hugh. See:
VAN ZELLER, HUBERT
Ventura, Charlie. See:
VENTURO, CHARLES
VENTURI, KENNETH (1931-)
[American professional
golfer]
Ken Venturi
VENTURO, BETTY LOU BAKER
(1928-) [American author]
Betty Baker
VENTURO, CHARLES (1918-)
[American jazz musician
(tenor saxophone, leader)]
Charlie Ventura
VENUTI, GUISEPPE (1904-)
[American jazz musician
(violin, leader)]
Joe Venuti
VER PLANCK, JOHN (1930-)

1035

[American trombonist
and composer]
Billy Ver Planck
VERA, CARLOS (1920-)
[Mexican bullfighter]
Cañitas
Vera-Ellen. See:
ROHE, VERA-ELLEN
WESTMEYR
Vera Miles. See:
RALSTON, VERA
Vera Vague. See:
ALLEN, BARBARA JO
Vera Zorina. See:
HARTWIG, EVA BRIGITTA
Vercors. See:
CONNOLLY, CYRIL
VERNON
VERDON, GWYNETH EVELYN
(1925-) [American
dancer and actress]
Gwen Verdon
Verdu, Matilde. See:
CELA, CAMILO JOSÉ
Verduga Hills, The Sage of
the. See:
McGROARTY, JOHN
STEVEN
Verdy, Violette. See:
GUILLERM, NELLY
Vergil. See:
MARO, PUBLIUS
VERGILIUS
Virgil
VERGIL, POLYDORE (c.1475-
1555) [Italian-English
historian and
ecclesiastic]
De Castello
VERHAGEN, JEAN (c.1925-)
[American stage and
motion picture actress]
Jean Hagen
VERMEER, JAN (1632-75)
[Dutch genre, landscape
and portrait painter
and colorist]
Jan Van Der Meer
Van Delft
Vermeer van Haarlem, Jan.
See: MEER, JAN VAN
DER

VERMIGLI, PIETRO MARTIRE
(1500-62) [Italian
religious reformer]
Peter Martyr
Vermont, The Founder of. See:
ALLEN, IRA
Verne, Hibbert. See:
FRAZER-HURST, REV.
DOUGLAS
VERNE, JULES (1828-1905)
[French novelist]
The Father of Science
Fiction
Verne, Karen. See:
KLINCKERFUSS, INGABOR
KATRINE
VERNET, ANTOINE CHARLES
HORACE (1758-1835)
[French painter]
Carle
VERNET, ÉMILE JEAN
HORACE (1789-1863)
[French painter]
Horace
Verney, Sarah. See:
HOLLOWAY, BRENDA
WILMAR
Vernon, Anne. See:
VIGNAUD, EDITH
Vernon Castle. See:
BLYTHE, VERNON
Vernon Duke. See:
DUKELSKY, VLADIMIR
VERNON, EDWARD (1684-1757)
[English admiral]
Old Grog
Vernon L. Kingsbury. See:
LUKENS, HENRY CLAY
Vernon Lee. See:
PAGET, VIOLET
Vernon, Max. See:
KELLOGG, VERNON
LYMAN
Vernon, Olivia. See:
BRONTË, ANNE
Vernon, Peter. See:
HUDDLESTON, SISLEY
VERNON, RICHARD (1726-1800)
[English sportsman]
The Father of the Turf
Vernon, The Sage of Mount.
See: WASHINGTON, GEORGE

Vernon Warren. See:
  CHAPMAN, GEORGE
    WARREN VERNON
Vernor, D. See:
  CASEWIT, CURTIS
VÉRON, LOUIS DÉSIRÉ
  (1798-1867) [French
  journalist]
  Docteur Véron
Veronese, Bonifazio. See:
  PITATI, BONIFAZIO
Veronese, Paolo. See:
  CAGLIARI (CALIARI),
    PAOLO
Veronica Heath. See:
  BLACKETT, VERONICA
    HEATH STUART
Veronica Lake. See:
  KEANE, CONSTANCE
VERRAL, CHARLES SPAIN
  (fl. 1927-62) [Canadian
  commercial artist and
  author]
  George L. Eaton
Verrocchio, Andrea del. See:
  CIONE, ANDREA DI
    MICHELE DI
    FRANCESCO
VERROCOSUS, QUINTUS
  FABIUS MAXIMUS (died
  203 B.C.) [Roman
  general officer]
  Cunctator (The Delayer)
  The Shield of Rome
VERSACE, MARIE TERESA
  RIOS (1917-) [Puerto
  Rican-American author]
  Tere Rios
Versatile, Val. See:
  ENTON, DR. HARRY
Versatile Woman, Hollywood's
  Busiest and Most. See:
  HOPPER, ELDA FURRY
VERSCHOYLE, WINIFRED
  MABEL LETTS (1882-)
  [British poet and author]
  W. M. Letts
Verse, The Father of Iambic.
  See: ARCHILOCHUS
Versois, Odile. See:
  POLIAKOFF-BAIDAROV,
    MARINA DE

VERUS, MARCUS ANNIUS
  (121-80 A.D.) [Roman
  emperor and Stoic
  philosopher]
  Antonius
  Marcus Aurelius
Very Mighty Ruler (Genghis Khan).
  See: TEMUJIN
Vesey Norman. See:
  NORMAN, ALEXANDER
    VESEY BETHUNE
VESPASIANUS, TITUS FLAVIUS
  SALINUS (c. 40-81) [Roman
  emperor]
  Delight of Mankind
  Titus
Vesta Tilley. See:
  POWLES, MATILDA ALICE
Vestal, Stanley. See:
  CAMPBELL, WALTER
    STANLEY
VESTRIS, GAETANO APOLLINO
  (1729-1808) [Italian
  dancer]
  The God of Dancing
Vestris, Madame. See:
  BARTOLOZZI, LUCIA
    ELIZABETH
Vesuvius Nasby, Rev.
  Petroleum. See:
  LOCKE, DAVID ROSS
Veteran Observer. See:
  MANSFIELD, EDWARD
    DEERING
Veto Governor, The. See:
  CLEVELAND, STEPHEN
    GROVER
  WINSTON, JOHN ANTHONY
Veto Mayor, The. See:
  CLEVELAND, STEPHEN
    GROVER
Veto, Old. See:
  CLEVELAND, STEPHEN
    GROVER
  HUMPHREYS, BENJAMIN
    GRUBB
  JOHNSON, ANDREW
Veto President, The. See:
  CLEVELAND, STEPHEN
    GROVER
  JOHNSON, ANDREW
Veto, Sir. See:

JOHNSON, ANDREW
VEUSTER, JOSEPH DAMIEN
DE (1840-89) [Belgian
Roman Catholic mis-
sionary to Hawaiian
Islands]
Father Damien
Vexillum. See:
BANNER, HERBERT
STEWART
Vi Redd. See:
GOLDBERG, ELVIRA
REOD
Via Hartford. See:
DONSON, CYRIL
Vialio, G. See:
SIMENON, GEORGES
Vialis, Gaston. See:
SIMENON, GEORGES
Viallis, Gaston. See:
SIMENON, GEORGES
VIAN, SIR PHILIP LOUIS
(1894-1968) [Admiral
of the British navy]
Vian of the Cossack
Viana, Prince of. See:
CHARLES IV
Viator, Scotus. See:
SETON-WATSON,
ROBERT WILLIAM
VIAU, THÉOPHILE DE
(1590-1626) [French poet
and dramatist]
Théophile
VIAUD, LOUIS MARIE
JULIEN (1850-1923)
[French novelist and
naval officer]
Pierre Loti
Vic. See:
DICKENSON, ALBERT
VICTOR
SORRELL, VICTOR
GARLAND
Vic Baron. See:
BARONI, VASCO
Vic Damone. See:
FARINOLA, VITO
Vic Oliver. See:
VON SAMEK, VICTOR
Vicary, Dorothy. See:
RICE, DOROTHY MARY

VICELLIO. See:
VECELLI (VICELLIO)
VICENTE, GIL (c. 1470-1537)
[Portuguese silversmith
and playwright]
The Father of Portuguese
Drama
Viceroy of India. See:
CORNWALLIS, CHARLES
CORNWALLIS, 1ST
MARQUIS
Viceroy, The King of England's.
See: LOUIS XVIII
Vicker, Angus. See:
FELSEN, HENRY GREGOR
Vickers, Martha. See:
MacVICAR, MARTHA
Vickie MacLean Hunter. See:
HUNTER, VICTORIA
ALBERTA
Vicomte de Mirabeau. See:
REQUETI, ANDRÉ
BONIFACE LOUIS
Victim in England, The First.
See: SAWTREY, WILLIAM
VICTOR [Victor]. See also:
Viktor
VICTOR (died 199) [Supreme
Pontiff of Roman Catholic
Church]
Pope Victor I
St. Victor
Victor II, Pope. See:
GEBHARD, COUNT OF
HIRSCHBERG
Victor III, Pope. See:
DESIDERIUS, PRINCE OF
BENEVENTO
Victor Appleton. See:
STRATEMEYER,
EDWARD L.
Victor Appleton, Jr. See:
STRATEMEYER,
EDWARD L.
Victor Bonnette. See:
ROY, EWELL PAUL
Victor Borge. See:
ROSENBAUM, BORGE
VICTOR EMMANUEL II (1820-78)
[King of Sardinia and
Italy (as VICTOR
EMMANUEL I)

The Honest King
Victor France. See:
    JORDAN, PHILIP
    FURNEAUX
Victor Lamont. See:
    MAIORANA, VICTOR E.
VICTOR, MRS. FRANCES
    FULLER BARRITT
    (1826-1902) [American
    author, editor and poet]
    Florence Fane
VICTOR, MRS. FRANCES
    FULLER BARRITT.
    See also:
    Sisters of the West
VICTOR, MRS. METTA
    VICTORIA FULLER
    MORSE (1831-85) [American
    author, poet and editor]
    Eleanor Lee Edwards
    Walter T. Gray
    Rose Kennedy
    Mrs. Mark Peabody
    Seeley Regester
    The Singing Sibyl
VICTOR, MRS. METTA
    VICTORIA FULLER
    MORSE. See also:
    Sisters of the West
VICTOR, ORVILLE J.
    (1827-1910) [American
    editor and author]
    Louis Legrand, M.D.
Victor, Richard of St. See:
    RICHARD
Victor St. Clair. See:
    BROWNE, GEORGE
    WALDO
Victor Tempest. See:
    PHILIPP, ELLIOT ELIAS
Victor Thorne. See:
    JACKSON, FREDERICK
Victor Varconi. See:
    VARKONYI, MIHALY
Victoria. See also:
    Viktoria
Victoria de Los Angeles. See:
    CIMA, VICTORIA
    GAMEZ
Victoria Holt. See:
    HIBBERT, ELEANOR
    BURFORD

Victoria Lucas. See:
    PLATH, SYLVIA
Victoria Shaw. See:
    ELPHICK, JEANETTE
Victoria, The Founder of. See:
    BATMAN, JOHN
Victorians, The International
    Bad Girl of the Mid. See:
    GILBERT, MARIE DOLORES
    ELIZA ROSANNA
Victorious, The. See:
    CALIPH ABU-JAFAR
    CHARLES VII
    FREDERICK I
    OSMAN (OTHMAN) I
    WALDEMAR II
Victorious, The (Parvez). See:
    KHOSRAU II
Victory, The Organizer of.
    See: CARNOT, LAZARE-
    NICHOLAS MARGUERITE
Victory's Darling Child. See:
    MASSÉNA, ANDRÉ
VIDA, MARCO GIROLAMO
    (c.1480-1566) [Italian Latin
    poet]
    The Christian Virgil
    The Parthenope of Naples
VIDACOVICH, I.J. (1894-)
    [American musician and
    composer]
    Pinky Vidacovich
VIDAL, GORE (1925-)
    [American author]
    Edgar Box
VIDOCQ, EUGÈNE FRANÇOIS
    (1775-1857) [French
    criminal; later law en-
    forcement spy]
    The Detective
Viejo, El (The Elder). See:
    HERRERA, FRANCISCO
VIÉLÉ, EGBERT LUDOVICUS
    (1863-1937) [American
    poet]
    Francis Viélé-Griffin
VIESPI, ALEXANDER (c.1938-)
    [American stage, television
    and motion picture actor]
    Alex Cord
VIEUZAC, BERTRAND BARÈRE
    DE (1755-1841) [French

lawyer and politician]
The Anacreon of the
  Guillotine
The Witling of Terror
VIGARA, RAFAEL MARTÍN
  (1931-58) [Spanish
  bullfighter]
El Zorro
VIGILIUS (died 555) [Supreme
  Pontiff of Roman
  Catholic Church]
Pope Vigilius
VIGNAUD, EDITH (1925-)
  [French motion picture
  actress]
Anne Vernon
Vigo, Jean. See:
  ALMEREYDA, JEAN
VIGUERS, RUTH HILL
  (1903-) [American
  librarian and author]
Ruth A. Hill
Viking, The Old. See:
  FURUSETH, ANDREW
Viktor. See also:
  VICTOR
  Victor
Viktor Flambeau. See:
  BRIGHAM, GERTRUDE
  RICHARDSON
Viktoria. See also:
  Victoria
Viktoria Rehn. See:
  KOHN-BEHRENS,
  CHARLOTTE
Villa, Francisco. See:
  ARANGO, DOROTEO
Villa, Pancho. See:
  ARANGO, DOROTEO
VILLABOS, GUADALOUPE
  VELEZ DE (1910-44)
  [Mexican motion picture]
  actress]
The Mexican Spitfire
Lupe Velez
VILLAIN-MARAIS, JEAN
  (1913-) [French actor]
Jean Marais
Villain Regardant. See:
  TOZER, BASIL JOHN
  JOSEPH
VILLANI (SCICOLONE), SOPHIA

(1934-) [Italian actress]
Sophia Loren
Stecchetto (The Stick)
Villard, Frank. See:
  DROUINEAU, FRANÇOIS
VILLE, BERNARD GERMAIN
  ÉTIENNE DE LA
  (1756-1825) [Count
  Lacépède; French natural
  history researcher]
The King of Reptiles
VILLEHARDOUIN, GEOFFROI DE
  (c. 1160-1213) [French
  historian]
The First of the French
  Historians
VILLENEUVA, ARNAUD DE
  (1238-1314) [French
  chemist, astrologer and
  theologian]
The Father of Chemistry
VILLIERS, CHARLES PELHAM
  (1802-98) [British
  statesman]
The Father of the House of
  Commons
VILLIERS, GEORGE, 2ND DUKE
  OF BUCKINGHAM. See:
  BUCKINGHAM, GEORGE
  VILLIERS, 2ND DUKE OF
  Cabal, The
Villon, François. See:
  MONTCORBIER,
  FRANÇOIS DE
Villon, Jacques. See:
  DUCHAMP, GASTON ÉMILE
Vinard, F.N. See:
  VINCENT, NATHANIEL
  HAWTHORNE
Vince. See:
  LOMBARDI, VINCENT
  THOMAS
Vince Black. See:
  CERNEY, JAMES VINCENT
Vince Destry. See:
  NORWOOD, VICTOR
  GEORGE CHARLES
Vincennes, The Hero of. See:
  CLARK, GEORGE ROGERS
Vincent, Cecil. See:
  BURTON, JOAN EILEEN
  VERONICA

VINCENT DE PAUL (c.1580-
1660) [French Catholic
priest and humanitarian]
The Apostle of Organized
Charity
St. Vincent de Paul
Vincent, E.L. See:
MORRIS, CHARLES
SMITH
Vincent Edwards. See:
ZOINO, VINCENT
EDWARD
Vincent, Mary Keith. See:
ST. JOHN, WYLLY FOLK
VINCENT, NATHANIEL
HAWTHORNE (1889-)
[American composer and
singer]
Jaan Kenbrovin
F.N. Vinard
Vincent Percival. See:
BONNER, CAREY
VINCI, LEONARDO DA
(1452-1519) [Florentine
painter, sculptor,
architect, engineer and
scientist]
Homo Universale (The
Universal Man)
Vinegar, Captain Hercules
See: FIELDING, HENRY
Vinegar Joe. See:
STILWELL, JOSEPH
WARREN
VINICOMBE, WALTER
(1888-) [British stage
and motion picture actor]
Wally Patch
VINING, ELIZABETH GRAY
(1902-) [American
educator and author]
Elizabeth Janet Gray
Vinnie. See:
RICHARDS, VINCENT
Vinnie Burke. See:
BUCCI, VINCENT
Vinokur, Grigory. See:
WEINRAUCH, HERSCHEL
VINSON, FREDERICK MOORE
(1890-1953) [American
jurist; Chief Justice of
the U.S. Supreme Court]

Fred Vinson
Vinson, Helen. See:
RULFS, HELEN
VINTON, STANLEY ROBERT
(1935-) [American
composer and musician]
Bobby Vinton
Viola Lyel. See:
WATSON, VIOLET
Violence, The Poet of. See:
CHANDLER, RAYMOND
Violet Fane. See:
CURRIE, LADY MARY
MONTGOMERY LAMB
Violet Pretty. See:
STROSS, MRS. RAYMOND
Violet Rosa Markham. See:
CARRUTHERS, MRS.
JAMES
Violet Whyte. See:
STANNARD, HENRIETTA
ELIZA VAUGHAN
Violette Verdy. See:
GUILLERM, NELLY
Violin, The Dark Angel of the.
See: SOUTH, EDWARD
OTHA
Violinist, America's Own. See:
SPALDING, ALBERT
Violinsky. See:
GINSBERG, SOL
Violis, G. See:
SIMENON, GEORGES
Vip. See:
PARTCH, VIRGIL FRANK-
LIN
VIRCHOW, HANS JAKOB PAUL
(1852-) [German
anatomist and author]
Hans
Virgil. See:
MARO, PUBLIUS VERGILIUS
Vergil
Virgil of the French Drama, The.
See: RACINE, JEAN
BAPTISTE
Virgil, The Christian. See:
SANNAZARO, JACOPO
VIDA, MARCO GIROLAMO
Virgin Mary, The Blessed. See:
MARY, ST.
Virgin Modesty. See:

1041

WILMOT, JOHN
Virgin Queen, The. See:
  ELIZABETH I
Virgin, The Champion of the.
  See: CYRIL OF
  ALEXANDRIA, ST.
Virginia. See:
  FIELD, MARGARET
  CYNTHIA
  WOOLF, ADELINE
  VIRGINIA
Virginia, By a Gentleman of.
  See: DAWSON,
  WILLIAM
Virginia, Cousin. See:
  JOHNSON, VIRGINIA
  WALES
Virginia Curzon. See:
  HAWTON, HECTOR
Virginia Graham. See:
  KOMISS, VIRGINIA
Virginia Judge, The. See:
  KELLY, WALTER C.
Virginia, Julia. See:
  LAENGSDORFF, JULIA
  VIRGINIA
Virginia Kirkus. See:
  GLICK, VIRGINIA
  KIRKUS
Virginia Mayo. See:
  JONES, VIRGINIA
Virginia Nielsen. See:
  McCALL, VIRGINIA
  NIELSEN
Virginia Rebel, The. See:
  BACON, NATHANIEL
Virginia Roberts. See:
  DEAN, NELL MARR
Virginia Stait. See:
  RUSSELL, WINIFRED
  BRENT
Virginia Storm. See:
  TEMPEST, JAN
Virginia Struble. See:
  BURLINGAME, VIRGINIA
  STRUBLE
Virginia, The Dry Bishop from.
  See: CANNON, BISHOP
  JAMES, JR.
Virginia, The Father of. See:
  SMITH, JOHN
Virginia, The Father of

Presbyterianism in. See:
  MORRIS, SAMUEL
Virginia, The Father of the Uni-
  versity of. See:
  JEFFERSON, THOMAS
Virginia, The Good Governor of.
  See: BOTETOURT, LORD
  NORBORNE BERKELEY
Virginia, The Political Savior of.
  See: WALKER, GILBERT
  CARLTON
Virginius. See:
  CONNETT, EUGENE
  VIRGINIUS III
Virna Lisi. See:
  PIERALISI, VIRNA
VISCHER, HERMANN (died 1488)
  [German sculptor and bronze
  founder]
  The Elder
VISCHER, HERMANN (1486?-1517)
  [German sculptor and bronze
  founder]
  The Younger
VISCHER, PETER (1460?-1529)
  [German sculptor and
  bronze founder]
  The Elder
VISCHER, PETER (1487-1528)
  [German sculptor and
  bronze founder]
  The Younger
VISCONTI, MATTEO (1250-1323)
  [Lord of Milan]
  The Great
VISCONTI, TEOBALDO (1210-76)
  [Supreme Pontiff of Roman
  Catholic Church]
  Pope Gregory X
Viscount Bolingbroke. See:
  ST. JOHN, HENRY
VITALIAN (died 672) [Supreme
  Pontiff of Roman Catholic
  Church]
  Pope Vitalian
  St. Vitalian
Vitesse, Grande. See:
  WALKERLEY, RODNEY
  LEWIS
Vitezovic, Tomislav. See:
  KUEHNELT-LEDDIHN, ERIK
  RITTER VON

VIVALDI, ANTONIO (1678-1741)
[Venetian violinist, com-
poser and churchman]
The Red Priest
Vivante, l'Anatomie (The
Living Anatomy). See:
AROUET, FRANÇOIS
MARIE
VIVAR, RODRIGO DÍAZ DE
(1043?-1099?)[Spanish
nobleman and soldier]
El Cid
The Cid
El Cid Campeador
VIVES, JUAN LUIS (1492-1540)
[Spanish philosopher and
humanist]
Ludovicus Vives
Vivian Blaine. See:
STAPLETON, VIVIENNE
Vivian Breck. See:
BRECKENFELD, VIVIAN
GURNEY
Vivian Donald. See:
MACKINNON, CHARLES
ROY
Vivian, Francis. See:
ASHLEY, ARTHUR
ERNEST
Vivian Mort. See:
CROMIE, ALICE
HAMILTON
Vivian Oakland. See:
ANDERSON, VIVIAN
Vivian Poole. See:
JAFFE, GABRIEL VIVIAN
Vivian Shaw. See:
SELDES, GILBERT
VIVIAN
Vivien Leigh. See:
HARTLEY, VIVIAN MARY
Vizard, Stephen. See:
JAMES, DAVID BURNETT
STEPHEN
VIZETELLY, ERNEST ALFRED
(1853-1922) [English
journalist and editor]
Le Petit Homme Rouge
VLADIMIR I (c. 956-1015)
[Russian ruler]
The Great
St. Vladimir

VLADIMIR II (1053-1125)
[Russian ruler]
Monomachus
Vladimir Ilyich Lenin. See:
ULANYOV, VLADIMIR
ILYICH
Vladimirov, Leonid. See:
FINKELSTEIN, LEONID
VLADIMIROVITCH
Vlady, Marina. See:
POLIAKOFF-BAIDAROV,
MARINA DE
VLASEK, JUNE (1917-)
[American dancer and motion
picture actress]
June Lang
VOELKER, JOHN DONALDSON
(1903-) [American
attorney and author]
Robert Traver
VOGAU, BORIS ANDREYEVICH
(1894-1937?) [Russian
author]
Boris Pilnyak
Vogel, Dr. Johannes. See:
HOFPREDIGER, JOHANNES
MARTIN VOGEL
VOGEL, HARRY BENJAMIN
(1868-) [New Zealand
novelist]
Richard Kinver
VOGLER, GEORG JOSEPH
(1749-1814) [German
organist, composer and
writer on music]
Abt (Abbé) Vogler
VOGT, CARL (1895-1956)
[American stage and motion
picture actor]
Louis Calhern
Voice of Experience, The. See:
TAYLOR, MARION SAYLE
Voice of New England, The.
See: FROST, ROBERT LEE
Voice of Radio, The Golden. See:
MUNN, FRANK
Voice of Silver, The. See:
PITTMAN, KEY
Voice of the Hangover Generation,
The. See:
O'HARA, JOHN HENRY
Voice of the Radio, The. See:

STEFAN, KARL
Voice of the Revolution, The.
    See: HENRY, PATRICK
Voice, The. See:
    SINATRA, FRANCIS
    ALBERT
Voice, The Tomboy with the.
    See: VON KAPPELHOFF,
    DORIS
Voisine, La. See:
    MONVOISON, CATHERINE
Voltaire. See:
    AROUET, FRANÇOIS
    MARIE
Voltaire of Germany, The.
    See: BAUER, BRUNO
    WIELAND, CHRISTOPHER
    MARTIN
Voltaire of Grecian Literature,
    The. See:
    LUCIAN OF SAMOSATA
Voltaire, The Russian. See:
    SOUMAROKOV, ALEX-
    ANDRE PÉTROVITCH
Vom Rinn, Der Mann. See:
    SPECKBACHER, JOSEPH
VON [Von]. Those names so
    prefixed and not listed
    below may be found in-
    dexed under that part of
    the name following "VON"
    or "Von"
von Almedingen, Martha Edith.
    See: ALMEDINGEN,
    EDITH MARTHA
VON BERLICHINGEN, GÖTZ
    (GOTTFRIED) (1480-1562)
    [German feudal knight]
    Götz with the Iron Hand
von Bern, Dietrich. See:
    THEODORIC
VON BERNBRUNN, KARL
    ANDREAS (1789-1854)
    [American actor and
    impresario]
    Karl Carl
VON BERNSTORFF, COUNT
    JOHANN HARTWIG
    ERNST (1712-72) [Danish
    statesman]
    The Oracle of Denmark
VON BISMARCK, PRINCE
    OTTO EDUARD LEOPOLD

(1815-98) [Prusso-German
    statesman]
    The Iron Chancellor
    The Man of Blood and Iron
Von der Cláña, Henrich. See:
    WEISS, ALBERT MARIA
Von Einseidel, R. See:
    TETZNER, MARTHA
    HELENE
von Fallersleben, Hoffmann. See:
    HOFFMANN, AUGUST
    HEINRICH
VON GERBER, FRANCESCA
    MITZI MARLENE DE
    CHARNEY (1930-)
    [Hungarian-American motion
    picture actress]
    Mitzi Gaynor
VON GOETHE, JOHANN WOLF-
    GANG (1749-1832) [German
    poet, playwright and
    prose writer]
    The Master (Der Meister)
VON GRIMMELSHAUSEN, JOHANN
    HANS JAKOB CHRISTOFFEL
    (c.1622-76) [German
    novelist]
    J.J.C. Von Grimmelshausen
VON HALLER, ALBRECHT
    (1708-77) [Swiss psycholo-
    gist, anatomist, biologist
    and poet]
    The Father of Philosophy
    The Father of Physiology
VON HEEMSKERK (HEMSKERK),
    MARTIN (1498-1574) [Dutch
    historical painter]
    The Raphael of Holland
VON HERNREID, PAUL (1907-)
    [Austrian stage and motion
    picture actor]
    Paul Henreid
VON HILDEBRAND, DIETRICH
    (1889-) [German-American
    educator and author]
    Peter Ott
VON HOFMANNSTHAL, HUGO
    (1874-1929) [Australian
    poet and dramatist]
    Loris
VON HOHENHEIM, THEOPHRAS-
    TUS BOMBASTUS (1493?-
    1541) [Swiss alchemist and

physician]
Philippus Aureolus Paracelsus
Von Homberg, Otto. See:
GEISE, DR. OTTO
VON HUTTEN, ZUM STOLZEN-
BERG, BETSY RIDDLE,
FREIFRAU (1874-)
[American author]
Bettina von Hutten
VON KAPPELHOFF, DORIS
(1924-) [American
singer and actress]
Doris Day
The Girl We Would Like
to Take a Slow Boat Back
to the States With
The Golden Tonsil
The Prettiest Three-million-
dollar Corporation with
Freckles in America
The Tomboy With the Voice
VON KOTZEBUE, AUGUST
FREDERICK FERDINAND
(1761-1819) [German
dramatist]
The Shakespeare of
Germany
VON LAUCHEN, GEORG
JOACHIM (1514-76)
[German astronomer and
mathematician]
Rheticus
Von Linden, E. See:
MAY, KARL
FRIEDRICH
VON LINNÉ, CARL (1707-78)
[Swedish botanist; founder
of the modern system of
classification of organisms]
Carolus Linnaeus
VON LOSCH, MARIA MAG-
DALENE (1902-)
[German-American motion
picture actress]
Marlene Dietrich
VON LUCKNER, COUNT FELIX
(1881-1966) [German
naval officer; commander
of the raider "Seeadler"
in World War I]
The Sea Devil
VON MOLTKE, HELLMUTH
KARL BERNHARD

(1800-91) [Prussian field
marshal]
Hellmuth the Taciturn
VON NORDENWALL, HANS
EHRICH MARIA STROHEIM
(1885-1957) [Austrian
motion picture actor and
director]
Ehrich von Stroheim
Von O'Hall, Mayor, See:
HALL, ABRAHAM OAKEY
VON OST, HENRY LERNER, JR.
(1915-) [American radio
and television comedian]
Henry Morgan
VON REGENSBURG, BERTHOLD
(1210-72) [German
Franciscan preacher]
The Chrysostom of the
Middle Ages
VON RICHTHOFEN, BARON
MANFRED (1892-1918)
[German military aviator]
The Bloody Red Baron
The Red Baron
The Red Knight of Germany
VON SAMEK, VICTOR (1898-
1964) [Austrian-born
comedian, musician, con-
ductor and motion picture
actor]
Vic Oliver
von Schwarzenfeld, Gertrude. See:
COCHRANE DE ALENCAR,
GERTRUDE E.L.
Von Sternberg, Joseph. See:
STERN, JOE
VON STREHLENAU, NIKOLAUS
NIEMBSCH (1802-50)
[Austrian poet]
Nikolaus Lenau
von Stroheim, Ehrich. See:
VON NORDENWALL, HANS
EHRICH MARIA
STROHEIM
von Szlatna. See:
HUBAY, JENÓ
VON ZELL, HARRY (1906-)
[American radio announcer
and actor]
Giggles
VOORHEES, DANIEL WOLSEY
(1827-97) [American

politician; congressman
from Indiana]
The Tall Sycamore of the
Wabash
VOORHEES, DONALD (1903-)
[American conductor and
music director]
Don Voorhees
Voyle, Mary. See:
MANNING, ROSEMARY
JOY
Vradinos, Zeffros. See:
HATZIDAKIS, NICHOLAS
Vrchlický, Jaroslav. See:
FRÍDA, EMIL
VUJOVIC, VLADIMIR (1922-)
[French motion picture ac-
tor]
Michel Auclair
Vyacheslav Mikhailovich
Molotov. See:
SKRYABIN, VYACHESLAV
MIKHAILOVICH

W

W.A. Devon. See:
SMITH, FRANCIS
SHUABEL
W.B.K. See:
KEMPLING, WILLIAM
BAILEY
W.B. Lawson. See: COOK,
WILLIAM WALLACE
INGRAHAM, COLONEL
PRENTISS
JENKS, GEORGE CHARLES
RATHBONE, ST. GEORGE
HENRY
W. Bolingbroke Johnson. See:
BISHOP, MORRIS
W.C. Fields. See:
DUKINFIELD, WILLIAM
CLAUDE
W. Clark Russell. See:
RUSSELL, WILLIAM
CLARK
W. Dane Bank. See:
WILLIAMSON, WILLIAM
HENRY
W.H. See:

AUDEN, WYSTAN HUGH
HUDSON, WILLIAM HENRY
W.H., Mr. See:
HERBERT, WILLIAM
W.J. Earle. Sec:
SENARENS, LUIS PHILIP
W.J. Hamilton. See:
CLARK, CHARLES
DUNNING
W.J. Rimmer. See:
ROWLAND, DONALD
SYDNEY
W. Kinsayder. See:
MARSTON, JOHN
W.L. See:
GEORGE, WALTER LIONEL
W.M. Hoyt. See: MANNING,
WILLIAM HENRY
W.M. Knight-Patterson. See:
KULSKI, WLADYSLAW
WSZEBOR
W.M.L. Jay. See:
WOODRUFF, JULIA
LOUISA MATILDA
W.M. Letts. See:
VERSCHOYLE, WINIFRED
MABEL LETTS
W.N.P. Barbellion. See:
CUMMINGS, BRUCE
FREDERICK
W.R. See:
BURNETT, WILLIAM RILEY
W.R. Marvin. See:
CAMERON, LOU
W. Rye Leigh. See:
RILEY, WILLIE
W. Shaw Heath. See:
WILLIAMSON, WILLIAM
HENRY
W. Somerset Maugham. See:
MAUGHAM, WILLIAM
SOMERSET
W. Storrs Lee. See:
LEE, WILLIAM STORRS
W.T. See: BALLARD,
WILLIS TODHUNTER
W.W. See:
JACOBS, WILLIAM WYMARK
W.W. Coole. See:
KULSKI, WLADYSLAW
WSZEBOR
Wa-Tho-Huck (Bright Path). See:
THORPE, JAMES FRANCIS

Wabash, The Tall Sycamore of
the. See:
VOORHEES, DANIEL
WOLSEY
Wace. See:
UNKNOWN
Wace, Canon. See:
UNKNOWN
WACHSMANN, FRANZ
(1906-67) [German
composer]
Franz Waxman
WADDELL, GEORGE
EDWARD (1876-1914)
[American professional
baseball player]
Rube Waddell
WADDELL, JAMES (1730-1805)
[Irish-American clergy-
man and pulpit orator]
The Blind Preacher
WADDINGTON, MIRIAM
(1917-) [Canadian poet,
script writer and author]
E.B. Merritt
Wade. See:
Miller, Wade
Waud
WADE, BENJAMIN FRANKLIN
(1800-78) [American
abolitionist and politician;
senator from Ohio]
Bluff Ben Wade
Old Ben Wade
WADE, BOB. See:
Miller, Wade
Wade Everett. See:
COOK, WILLIAM EVERETT
Wade Fisher. See:
NORWOOD, VICTOR
GEORGE CHARLES
WADE, GEORGE EDWARD
(1869-1954) [British music-
hall comedian and motion
picture actor]
The Prime Minister of Mirth
George Robey
Wade Hamilton. See:
FLOREN, LEE
Wade, Henry. See:
AUBREY-FLETCHER,
HENRY LANCELOT

Wade, Herbert. See:
WALES, HUGH GREGORY
Wade, Joanna. See:
BERCKMAN, EVELYN
DOMENICA
WADE, JOHN STEVENS (1927-)
[American poet, editor and
lecturer]
Clysle Stevens
Wade Rogers. See:
MADLEE, DOROTHY
HAYNES
WADE, ROSALIND HERSCHEL
(1909-) [British teacher
and author]
Catherine Carr
WADE (WARDE), ARTHUR
SARSFIELD (1883-1959)
[English fiction writer]
Sax Rohmer
WAGNER. See also:
Wegner
WAGNER, CHARLES PETER
(1930-) [American Baptist
clergyman, missionary
and author]
Epafrodito
Lewis Graham Underwood
WAGNER, HANS (1872-)
[German musician and
author]
Hans Wagner-Schonkirch
WAGNER, JOHN PETER
(1874-1955) [American
professional baseball
player]
The Flying Dutchman
Hans Wagner
Honus Wagner
WAGNER, MARGARET D.
(1949-) [American author]
Peggy Wagner
Wagner, The Modern. See:
HUMPERDINCK, ENGEL-
BERT
WAGNER, WILHELM RICHARD
(1813-83) [German opera
composer and musical
theorist]
Richard Wagner
Wagon Boy, The. See:
CORWIN, THOMAS

Wagonmaster, Bill Cody the.
See: CODY, WILLIAM
FREDERICK
Wagstaff, Lancelot. See:
THACKERAY, WILLIAM
MAKEPEACE
Wagstaff, Théophile. See:
THACKERAY, WILLIAM
MAKEPEACE
Wah-Kat-Yu-Ten (Beautiful
Rainbow). See:
BEAUCHAMP, WILLIAM
MARTIN
WAHL, CAEDMON THOMAS
(1931-) [American Roman
Catholic priest and
author]
Father Caedmon
Wahoo Sam. See:
CRAWFORD, SAMUEL
EARL
Wainer, Cord. See:
DEWEY, THOMAS
BLANCHARD
WAINEWRIGHT, THOMAS
GRIFFITHS (1794-1847)
[English art critic,
painter, forger, writer
and possibly poisoner]
Janus Weathercock
WAINRIGHT, JONATHAN MAY-
HEW (1883-1953) [Amer-
ican general officer]
Skinny Wainright
WAINWRIGHT, VIRGINIA
(1891-) [American poet]
The Daisy Ashford of
America
WAITE, DAVID HANSON
(1825-1901) [American
politician; Governor of
Colorado]
Bloody Bridles Waite
Wake, The. See:
HEREWARD
WAKOSKI, DIANE (1937-)
[American educator,
editor and poet]
Diane Wakoski-Sherbell
WALBERG, GEORGE (1900-)
[American professional
baseball player]
Rube Walberg

Walbrook, Anton. See:
WOHLBRUCK, ADOLF
Walcott. See also:
WOLCOT
WOLCOTT
WOOLLCOTT
Walcott, Jersey Joe. See:
CREAM, ARNOLA RAY-
MOND
WALD, JEROME IRVING
(1911-) [American
motion picture producer]
Jerry Wald
WALDEMAR (1281?-1319)
[Margrave of Brandenburg]
The Great
WALDEMAR I (1131-82) [King
of Denmark]
The Great
WALDEMAR II (1170-1241)
[King of Denmark]
The Victorious
WALDEMAR IV (1320?-75)
[King of Denmark]
Atterdag
Walden Pond, The Sage of. See:
THOREAU, HENRY DAVID
Walden, The Hermit of. See:
THOREAU, HENRY DAVID
Waldo, Dave. See:
CLARKE, DAVID WALDO
WALDO, HIRAM H. (18??-1912)
[American baseball
promoter in the Middle West]
The Father of Baseball in the
West
Waldorf, Oscar of the. See:
TSCHIRKY, OSCAR MICHEL
WALDRON-SHAH, DIANE LYNN
(1936-) [American cor-
respondent, artist and
author]
D'Lynn Waldron
WALDROP, GIDEON (1919-)
[American composer and
conductor]
Gid Waldrop
WALE, HENRY (1891-) [British
stage and motion picture
actor]
Henry Oscar
WALES. See: EDWARD
PRINCE OF WALES

WALES, HUGH GREGORY
(1910-) [American
educator and author]
Herbert Wade
Wales, Windy. See:
KNOTTS, DON
WALKER, AARON (1913-)
[American jazz musician
(singer, guitar)]
T-Bone Walker
Walker Chapman. See:
SILVERBERG, ROBERT
WALKER, CHARLES THOMAS
(1858-) [American
Negro Baptist clergyman]
The Black Spurgeon of
America
WALKER, DONALD JOHN
(1907-) [American
composer and arranger]
Don Walker
Walker E. Blake. See:
BUTTERWORTH, WIL-
LIAM EDMUND III
WALKER, EDMUND (1934-)
[British television and
motion picture actor]
Jeremy Kemp
WALKER, EMILY KATHLEEN
(1913-) [English author]
Kathleen Treves
WALKER, FRED (1910-)
[American professional
baseball player]
Dixie Walker
WALKER, GILBERT CARLTON
(1833-85) [American
politician; Governor of
Virginia]
The Political Savior of
Virginia
Walker, Harry. See:
WAUGH, HILLARY
BALDWIN
Walker in the Pines. See:
SIBLEY, HENRY
HASTINGS
WALKER, IRMA RUTH
RODEN (1921-)
[American author]
Ira Walker
WALKER, JAMES JOHN (1881-
1946) [American politician;

Mayor of New York City]
Beau James
The Father of the New York
State Boxing Bill
Jimmy Walker
The Playboy of New York
The Wisecracker
WALKER, JOHN (1732-1807)
[English orthoëpist,
lexicographer and teacher
of elocution]
Elocution Walker
WALKER, JOHN (1861-)
[British author]
Rowland Thirlmere
Walker, Joseph. See:
McSPADDEN, JOSEPH
WALKER
WALKER, KENNETH MAC-
FARLANE (1882-) [British
physician and author]
Kenneth MacFarlane
Walker, Mildred. See:
SCHEMM, MILDRED
WALKER
Walker, Nancy. See:
SWOYER, ANNA MYRTLE
WALKER, WILLIAM (1824-60)
[American adventurer and
filibuster]
Filibuster
The Green-eyed Man of Destiny
The Grey-eyed Man of Destiny
Honey
Missy
WALKERLEY, RODNEY LEWIS
(1905-) [British journalist
and author]
Athos
Grande Vitesse
Walking. See:
STEWART, JOHN
Walking Library, The. See:
CAMERON, JOHN
HALES, JOHN
Walking Polyglot, The. See:
MEZZOFANTI, CARDINAL
GIUSEPPE
WALL, ARTHUR JONATHAN,
JR. (1923-) [American
professional golfer]
Art Wall, Jr.
Wall Street, The Witch of. See:

1049

GREEN, HENRIETTA
HOWLAND
WALLACE [Wallace]. See also:
WALLIS
Wallace Blue. See:
KRAENZEL, MARGARET
POWELL
Wallace, Doreen. See:
RASH, DORA EILEEN
AGNEW WALLACE
Wallace Ford. See:
GRUNDY, SAM
WALLACE, HENRY AGARD
(1888-1965) [American
editor and statesman;
Vice President of the
United States]
Plow 'em Under Wallace
WALLACE, J.K. (1891-1950)
[American musicians'
union executive, trom-
bonist and manufacturer
of trombones]
Spike Wallace
Wallace, Jean. See:
WALLASEK, JEAN
WALLACE, LEWIS (1827-
1905) [American general
officer, lawyer, states-
man and novelist]
General Lew Wallace
Lew Wallace
Louisa
WALLACE, MYRON LEON
(1918-) [American
television interviewer]
Mike Wallace
Wallace of Switzerland, The.
See: HOFER, ANDREAS
Wallace, Richard. See:
IND, ALLISON
WALLACE, RICHARD HORATIO
EDGAR (1875-1932) [English
journalist and author of
detective stories]
Edgar Wallace
WALLACE, SIR WILLIAM
(c. 1274-1305) [Scottish
national hero and patriot]
The Hammer and Scourge of
England
WALLACE, WILLIAM

ALEXANDER ANDERSON
(1817-99) [Texas frontiers-
man]
Bigfoot Wallace
WALLACE, WILLIAM N. (1924-)
[American journalist and
author]
Bill Wallace
Wallach, Meyer. See:
FINKELSTEIN, MEYER
Wallachia, The White Devil of.
See: CASTRIOTA, GEORGE
WALLASEK, JEAN (c.1927-)
[American motion picture
actress]
Jean Wallace
WALLER, FREDERIC (1886-)
[American inventor, motion
picture producer and manu-
facturer]
Fred Waller
WALLER, JOHN (1741-1802)
[American anti-Baptist;
later became Baptist
preacher]
The Devil's Adjutant
Swearing Jack Waller
Waller, Lewis. See:
LEWIS, WILLIAM WALLER
WALLER, THOMAS WRIGHT
(1904-43) [American jazz
musician (piano, organ,
singer, leader, composer)]
The Black Horowitz
Fats Waller
WALLGREN, MONRAD CHARLES
(1891-) [American
politician; Governor of
Washington State]
Mon C. Wallgren
WALLIN, JOHAN OLOF (1779-
1839) [Swedish poet,
orator, archbishop and hymn
writer]
David's Harp of the North
Wallington, George. See:
FIGLIA, GIORGIO
WALLIS. See also:
WALLACE
Wallace
WALLIS, FRANK EDWIN (1862-
1929) [American authority

on Colonial (Georgian)
architecture]
Colonial Wallis
WALLOP, LUCILLE FLETCHER
(1912-) [American
author]
Lucille Fletcher
Wallop, Willie the. See:
MAYS, WILLIE
HOWARD
WALLS, IAN GASCOIGNE
(1922-) [Scottish author]
Mr. Greenfingers
David Lindsay
Wally. See:
BUTTS, JAMES
WALLACE, JR.
COX, WALLACE
MAYNARD
ROSE, WALTER
Wally Patch. See:
VINICOMBE, WALTER
WALN, ROBERT (1794-1825)
[American author and
poet]
Peter Atall
Peter Atall, Esq.
WALPOLE, HORATIO
(1717-97) [English author
and wit]
William Marshal, Gent.
Horace Walpole
WALPOLE, SIR ROBERT
(1676-1745) [English
statesman]
Robin Bluestring
The Grand Corrupter
Walpole, The Sage of. See:
BIRD, FRANCIS
WILLIAM
Walraven, E.G. See:
JONES, EMMA
GARRISON
Walrus, The. See:
MACKIE, ALBERT DAVID
WALSH, EDWARD AUGUSTIN
(1881-1959) [American
professional baseball
player]
Big Moose
Ed Walsh
WALSH, MARY (1912-)

[American author]
Mary Lavin
WALSH, WILLIAM SHEPARD
(1854-1919) [American
editor, critic and author]
William Shepard
Walt. See:
DISNEY, WALTER ELIAS
KELLY, WALTER
CRAWFORD
WHITMAN, WALTER
Walt Cody. See:
NORWOOD, VICTOR
GEORGE CHARLES
Walt Wilmot, Major. See:
HARBAUGH, THOMAS
CHALMERS
Walt Winton, Captain. See:
HARBAUGH, THOMAS
CHALMERS
Walter Aimwell. See:
SIMONDS, WILLIAM
Walter Barrett. See:
SCOVILLE, JOSEPH
ALFRED
Walter Brisbane, Major. See:
HARBAUGH, THOMAS
CHALMERS
Walter, Bruno. See:
SCHLESINGER, BRUNO
Walter Chiari. See:
ANNICHIARICO, WALTER
WALTER, DOROTHY BLAKE
(1908-) [American
teacher and author]
Katherine Blake
Kay Blake
Katherine Ross
Walter Drummond. See:
SILVERBERG, ROBERT
Walter E. Traprock. See:
CHAPPELL, GEORGE
SHEPARD
Walter Ericson. See:
FAST, HOWARD MELVIN
Walter Fitzgerald. See:
BOND, WALTER
Walter Hampden. See:
DOUGHERTY, WALTER
HAMPDEN
Walter Leslie. See:
LIVINSKY, WALTER

Walter P. Dunlap, Colonel. See:
COBB, SYLVANUS, JR.
Walter Price. See:
WILSON, ROGER C.
Walter Ramel. See:
DE LA MARE, WALTER
JOHN
Walter Rault. See:
GORHAM, MAURICE
ANTHONY CONEYS
Walter Scott of Belgium, The.
See: CONSCIENCE,
HENDRICK
Walter Scott of the Middle
Ages. The. See:
FROISSART, JEAN
Walter T. Gray. See:
VICTOR, MRS. METTA
VICTORIA FULLER
MORSE
Walter Traprock. See:
CHAPPELL, GEORGE
SHEPARD
Walter Winchell. See:
WINCHEL, WALTER
Walters, Hugh. See:
HUGHES, WALTER
LLEWELLYN
Walters, Rick. See:
ROWLAND, DONALD
SYDNEY
Walters, Warren. See:
MANNING, WILLIAM
HENRY
WALTHALL, HENRY B.
(1878-1936) [American
stage and motion picture
actor]
The Mansfield of the Screen
WALTMAN, WILLIAM JOHN
(1905-) [Dutch author]
Iain Waltmore
Waltmore, Iain. See:
WALTMAN, WILLIAM
JOHN
WALTON, IZAAK (1593-1683)
[British author,
biographer, poet and
fisherman]
The Compleat Angler
The Father of Angling
The First Professional

English Biographer
WALTON, JULIA ELIZABETH
WELLS (1935-) [English
actress and singer]
Julie Andrews
WALTZ, J. JACQUES (1873-)
[French author]
Hansi
Waltz King, The. See:
KING, WAYNE HAROLD
WALWORTH, JEANETTE
RITCHIE HADERMAN
(1837-1918) [American
author]
Ann Atom
Janet H. Haderman
Wampum, King. See:
PEMBERTON, ISRAEL
WANAMAKER, JOHN (1839-1922)
[American merchant
prince]
Pious John
WANDERER, CARL (-1921)
[American murderer of his
wife RUTH and of EDWARD
JOSEPH RYAN]
The Butcher Boy
The Hero Husband
The Ragged Stranger
Murderer
WANDERER, CARL. See also:
RYAN, EDWARD JOSEPH
WANER, LLOYD JAMES
(1906-) [American
professional baseball
player]
Little Poison
Muscles
WANER, LLOYD JAMES. See
also: Poison Twins, The
WANER, PAUL GLEE (1903-)
[American professional
baseball player]
Big Poison
WANER, PAUL GLEE. See also:
Poison Twins, The
WANNAN, WILLIAM FIELDING
(1915-) [Australian
anthologist and author]
Bill Wannan
Wanstall, Ken. See: GREEN-
WANSTALL, KENNETH

WANTON, JOHN (1672-1740)
[American politician and
militaristic Quaker]
The Fighting Quaker
War Croesus, The World. See:
McADOO, WILLIAM GIBBS
War Governor, The. See:
MORTON, OLIVER HAZ-
ARD PERRY THROCK
War Governor, The Great. See:
CURTIN, ANDREW
GREGG
War Horse, Lee's Old. See:
LONGSTREET, JAMES
War Horse of Reform, The Old.
See: BLANKENBURG,
RUDOLPH
War Horse of Sumner County,
The. See:
TROUSDALE, WILLIAM
War Horse of Tennessee, The
Democratic. See:
McMILLIN, BENTON
War Horse of the Confederacy,
The. See:
LONGSTREET, JAMES
War Horse, The Democratic.
See: McMILLIN,
BENTON
War Horse, The Old. See:
COOK, PHILIP
DEVIN, THOMAS
CASIMIR
War, The General Manager
of the. See:
SMITH, WALTER BEDELL
War, The Mary Pickford of
This. See:
KAUMEYER, DOROTHY
Warbling Banjoist, Red
Godfrey the. See:
GODFREY, ARTHUR
MICHAEL
Warborough, Martin Leach.
See: ALLEN, CHARLES
GRANT BLAIRFINDIE
WARBURG, JAMES PAUL
(1896-1969) [German-
American banker, econo-
mist and author]
Paul James
WARBURTON, ELLIOT GEORGE

(1810-52) [English
historian]
Eliot Warburton
Ward, Artemus. See:
BROWNE, CHARLES
FARRAR
Ward, Diane. See:
BUNCE, CORAJANE
DIANE
WARD, DONALD G. (1911-)
[American educator,
editor and author]
Powers Tracy
WARD, EDWARD (1667-1731)
[English "Grubstreet"
writer, satirist and tavern
keeper]
Ned Ward
Ward Edwards. See:
RATHBONE, ST. GEORGE
HENRY
WARD, ELIZABETH HONOR
SHEDDEN (1926-)
[British educator and
author]
Ward S. Leslie
WARD, ELIZABETH REBECCA
(1881-) [English author]
Fay Inchfawn
WARD, JAMES WARNER
(1816-97) [American
librarian and author]
Yorick
Ward, Janice. See:
HARTMAN, RACHEL
FRIEDA
Ward, Jonas. See:
ARD, WILLIAM THOMAS
WARD, MARCUS LAWRENCE
(1812-84) [American
humanist]
The Soldier's Friend
WARD, MARION INEZ DOUGLAS
(1885-) [British author]
Marion Fox
Ward, Mrs. H.O. See:
MOORE, CLARA SOPHIA
JESSUP
Ward, Mrs. Humphry. See:
ARNOLD, MARY AUGUSTA
WARD, NATHANIEL (c.1578-
1652) [British Congrega-

tional clergyman and
author]
Theodore de la Guard
Ward, Polly. See:
POLUSKI, BYNO
Ward, R. Patrick. See:
HOLZAPFEL, RUDOLF
PATRICK
WARD, SAMUEL (1814-84)
[American author and
diplomat]
The King of the Lobby
WARD, SIR LESLIE
(1851-1922) [English
caricaturist]
Spy
WARD, THOMAS (1807-73)
[American poet, musician
and playwright]
Flaccus
WARD-THOMAS, EVELYN
BRIDGET PATRICIA
STEPHENS (1928-)
[British author]
Evelyn Anthony
Anthony Evelyn
Ward Weaver. See:
MASON, FRANCIS VAN
WYCK
Ward West. See:
BORLAND, HAROLD GLEN
WARDE. See:
WADE (WARDE), ARTHUR
SARSFIELD
Warde, Margaret. See:
DUNTON, EDITH
KELLOGG
WARE, ELEANOR. See:
Two Sisters of the West
WARE, EUGENE FITCH
(1841-1911) [American
poet and historian]
Ironquill
WARES, CLYDE (1886-)
[American professional
baseball player]
Buzzy Wares
Warfare, The Father of
Modern Amphibious. See:
SMITH, HOLLAND
McTYEIRE
WARFIELD, MRS. CATHERINE

ANN WARE. See:
Two Sisters of the West
Warhawk. See:
CALHOUN, JOHN
CALDWELL
CLAY, HENRY
Warhorse. See:
TURNER, ALFRED L.
WARING, JANE (fl. late 17th-
early 18th cents.) [Irish
friend of JONATHAN
SWIFT]
Varina
Waring, Marcus H. See:
MANNING, WILLIAM
HENRY
Warlike, The. See:
FREDERICK I
Warlock, Peter. See:
HESELTINE, PHILIP
ARNOLD
Warne Miller. See:
RATHBONE, ST. GEORGE
HENRY
WARNECKE, LONNIE (1909-)
[American professional
baseball player and
umpire]
The Arkansas Humming Bird
Country
Dixie
Ol' Arkansas
WARNER, ANNA BARTLETT
(1827-1915) [American
novelist and author of
children's books]
Amy Lothrop
WARNER, ANNA BARTLETT.
See also:
Warner Girls, The
Warner Brown. See:
BOROSON, WARREN
Warner Fabian. See:
ADAMS, SAMUEL HOPKINS
Warner, Frank A. See:
STRATEMEYER,
EDWARD L.
WARNER, GEORGE GEOFFREY
JOHN (1923-) [British
author]
Geoffrey Johns
Warner Girls, The, joint nickname

1054

of ANNA BARTLETT
WARNER (1827-1915) and her
sister SUSAN BOGERT
WARNER (1819-85) [American novelists]
Warner Girls, The. See also:
WARNER, ANNA
BARTLETT
WARNER, SUSAN BOGERT
WARNER, GLENN SCOBEY
(1871-1954) [American
football coach]
Pop Warner
Warner, Hannah. See:
JEWETT, JOHN
HOWARD
Warner, Hans. See:
BLAZE, ANGE HENRI
Warner, Jack. See:
WATERS, JACK
WARNER, KENNETH LEWIS
(1915-) [British
educator, editor and
author]
Dighton Morel
WARNER, SIR PELHAM
(1873-) [English
cricketer]
Plum
WARNER, SUSAN BOGERT
(1819-85) [American
author and hymnologist]
Elizabeth Wetherell
WARNER, SUSAN BOGERT.
See also:
Warner Girls, The
WARNOW, HARRY (1910-)
[American jazz musician
(leader, arranger, piano,
composer)]
Raymond Scott
Warren. See:
ST. JOHN, PERCY
BOLLINGBROKE
Warren Beatty. See:
BEATY, WARREN
Warren, Dave. See:
WIERSBE, WARREN
WENDELL
WARREN, EDWARD (1939-)
[American jazz musician
(bass, composer)]

Butch Warren
Warren Edwards. See:
MANNING, WILLIAM
HENRY
WARREN, ELIZABETH
AVERY (1916-) [American
music teacher, author and
illustrator]
Betsy Warren
Warren F. Kent. See:
MANNING, WILLIAM
HENRY
Warren Howard. See:
GIFFORD, JAMES NOBLE
Warren, Hugh. See:
MANNING, WILLIAM
HENRY
Warren, J.T. See:
MANNING, WILLIAM
HENRY
WARREN, JOHN BYRNE
LEICESTER (1835-95)
[English poet and dramatist;
3rd Baron de Tabley]
William Lancaster
George F. Preston
WARREN, JOSIAH (1798?-1874)
[American social reformer
and author]
The Father of Anarchy
Warren, Lavinia. See:
BUMP, MERCY LAVINIA
WARREN
WARREN, LINDSAY CARTER
(1889-) [American
politician; congressman
from North Carolina]
Accounts Warren
Warren Madden. See:
CAMERON, KENNETH
NEILL
WARREN, MERCY OTIS
(1728-1814) [American
author, poet and playwright]
Marcia
Warren, Ned. See:
MANNING, WILLIAM
HENRY
Warren Spencer. See:
LENGEL, WILLIAM
CHARLES
Warren T. Ashton. See: ADAMS,

WILLIAM TAYLOR
Warren, V.S. See:
MANNING, WILLIAM
HENRY
Warren, Vernon. See:
CHAPMAN, GEORGE
WARREN VERNON
Warren Walters. See:
MANNING, WILLIAM
HENRY
Warren William. See:
KRECH, WARREN
WARREN, WILLIAM STEPHEN
(1882-1968) [American
illustrator and author]
Billy Warren
WARRICK, MARIE DIONNE
(1940-) [American
Negro singer]
Dionne Warwick
Warrington. See:
ROBINSON, WILLIAM
STEVENS
Warrior in Righteous Causes,
The Invincible. See:
MOTT, LUCRETIA
Warrior Parson, The. See:
THURSTON, CHARLES
MYNN
Warrior, Precious (Chinghiz
Khan). See:
TEMUJIN
Warrior, Precious (Genghis
Khan). See:
TEMUJIN
Warrior, Precious (Jenghiz
Khan). See:
TEMUJIN
Warrior, The. See:
MICHAEL VI
Warrior, The Happy. See:
ROOSEVELT, THEODORE
SHEETS, FREDERICK
HILL
SMITH, ALFRED EMANUEL
Warshovsky, Isaac. See:
SINGER, ISAAC
WARTON. See also:
Wharton
WARTON, THOMAS (1688?-
1745) [British poet]
The Elder

WARTON, THOMAS (1728-90)
[British poet, critic and
poet laureate]
The Younger
Warville, De. See:
BRISSOT, JACQUES
PIERRE
Warwick. See:
DEEPING, GEORGE
WARWICK
Warwick, Dionne. See:
WARRICK, MARIE DIONNE
Warwick, Dolores. See:
FRESE, DOLORES
WARWICK
Warwick, George. See:
DEEPING, GEORGE
WARWICK
Warwick, John. See:
BEATTIE, JOHN
McINTOSH
Warwick Mannon. See:
HOPKINS, KENNETH
Warwick, Robert. See:
BIEN, ROBERT TAYLOR
Warwick Scott. See:
TREVOR, ELLESTON
Warwick, The Great Democratic.
See: SWEENEY, PETER
BARR
Wash, Redbarn. See:
SHAW, GEORGE BERNARD
WASHBURNE, ELIHU BENJAMIN
(1816-67) [American
politician; Congressman
from Illinois]
The Watchdog of the Treasury
WASHBURNE, JOSEPH (1904-)
[American jazz musician
(bass, composer, singer,
leader)]
Country Washburne
Washington Bloom, George. See:
BLOOM, SOL
Washington, Dinah. See:
JONES, RUTH
WASHINGTON, FORD LEE
(1903-55) [American jazz
musician (piano, singer,
dancer, trumpet,
comedian)]
Buck Washington

WASHINGTON, GEORGE
(1732-99) [American
general officer; first
President of the United
States]
The American Fabius
The Atlas of America
The Cincinnatus of the
Americans
The Cincinnatus of the
West
The Deliverer of America
The Farmer-President
The Father of America
The Father of His Country
The Father of Pittsburgh
The Old Fox
The Sage of Mount Vernon
The Savior of His Country
The Stepfather of His
Country
The Surveyor President
The Sword of the Revolution
Washington, George. See:
BLOOM, SOL
THOMAS, GEORGE HENRY
WASHINGTON, MARGUERITE
BEAUCHAMP (1900-)
[British home economist
and author]
Anne Beaton
Pat Beauchamp
Pat Beauchamp Washington
Washington of Colombia, The.
See: BOLÍVAR, SIMÓN
Washington of South America,
The. See:
BOLIVAR, SIMON
Washington of the West, The.
See:
CLARK, GEORGE
ROGERS
HARRISON, WILLIAM
HENRY
Washington, The Second. See:
CLAY, HENRY
Washington Whitehorn. See:
BELLAW, AMERICUS
WELLINGTON
Washington's First Mayoress.
See: NORTON, MARY
TERESA

WASON, ELIZABETH
(1912-) [American
foreign correspondent
and author]
Betty Wason
WASSERSUG, JOSEPH D.
(1912-) [American
physician and author]
Adam Bradford, M.D.
Wast. See also:
WEST
West
Wast, Hugo. See:
MARTÍNEZ, ZUVIRÍA
GUSTAVO ADOLFO
Watanna, Onoto. See:
BABCOCK, WINNIFRED
EATON
Watchdog of Central Park, The.
See: OCHS, ADOLPH
SIMON
Watchdog of the Treasury, The.
See:
BLANTON, THOMAS
LINDSAY
BYRD, HARRY FLOOD
CANNON, JOSEPH GURNEY
GALLATIN, ABRAHAM
ALPHONSE ALBERT
HAGNER, PETER
HOLMAN, WILLIAM STEELE
McCARL, JOHN RAYMOND
WASHBURNE, ELIHU
BENJAMIN
Watchdog, The Lady of the Iron.
See: INGALLS, MARILLA
BAKER
Watchmaking, The Father of
American. See:
DENNISON, AARON
LUFKIN
Water, Boiling. See:
LEE, CHARLES
Water Poet, The. See:
TAYLOR, JOHN
Water, Silas. See:
LOOMIS, NOEL MILLER
WATERFIELD, ROBERT (1920-)
[American football
player]
Bob Waterfield
Waterford, Roberts of Kandagar,

Pretoria and. See:
ROBERTS, FREDERICK
SLEIGH
WATERHOUSE, KEITH. See:
Froy, Herald
Waterloo Hero, The. See:
HILL, ROWLAND
WATERMAN, NIXON (1859-)
[American author]
Peter Martin
WATERS, CLARA ERSKINE
CLEMENT (1834-1916)
[American author]
Clara Erskine Clement
WATERS, ETHEL
(1900-) [American jazz
musician (singer)]
Baby Star
Sweet Mama Stringbean
WATERS, JACK (1894-)
[British music-hall
comedian and motion
picture actor]
Jack Warner
Waters, Muddy. See:
MORGANFIELD,
McKINLEY
WATKINS, ARTHUR THOMAS
LEVI (1907-) [English
author]
Arthur Watkyn
WATKINS-PITCHFORD,
DENYS JAMES (1905-)
[British educator and
author]
BB
Michael Traherne
WATKINS, TOBIAS (1780-1855)
[American physician,
editor and author]
Pertinax Particular
Watkinson, Valerie. See:
ELLISTON, VALERIE
MAE WATKINSON
Watkyn, Arthur. See:
WATKINS, ARTHUR
THOMAS LEVI
WATNEY, JOHN BASIL (1915-)
[British journalist,
columnist and author]
Anthony Roberts
WATROUS, HARRY WILSON

(1857-1940) [American
painter]
The American Meissonier
Watson, Betty. See: HALL,
ELIZABETH WATSON
WATSON, EDMUND HENRY LA-
CON (1865-) [British author]
Lacon
Watson, Frank. See:
AMES, FRANCIS H.
WATSON, JAMES ELI (1864-1948)
[American politician; con-
gressman from Indiana]
Sunny Jim
The Wooden-shoe Statesman
WATSON, JANE WERNER
(1915-) [American editor
and author]
Annie North Bedford
Monica Hill
Elsa Ruth Nast
WATSON, JOHN (1850-1907)
[Scotch-English novelist
and clergyman]
Ian Maclaren
WATSON, MILTON (1894-)
[American professional
baseball player]
Mule Watson
WATSON, REATHA (1896-1926)
[American silent motion
picture actress]
Barbara La Marr
Watson, Thomas. See:
SMITH, JOHN
WATSON, THOMAS EDWARD
(1856-1922) [American
politician; senator from
Georgia]
The Sage of Hickory Hill
The Sage of McDuffie
WATSON, VIOLET (1900-)
[British stage and motion
picture actress]
Viola Lyel
Watson, Will. See:
FLOREN, LEE
WATSON, WILLIAM ALEXANDER
JARDINE (1933-) [Scottish
writer and lecturer on law]
Alan Watson
Watson, Wylie. See:

ROBERTSON, JOHN
WYLIE
Watt of America, The. See:
EVANS, OLIVER
WATTERS, HENRY EUGENE
(1876-1938) [American
educator]
H. E. Watters
WATTERSON, HENRY (1840-
1921) [American
journalist, author and
politician]
Henry of Navarre
Light Horse Harry
Marse Henry
WATTS, MABEL PIZZEY
(1906-) [British author]
Patricia Lynn
Waud. See also:
WADE
Wade
Waud, Elizabeth. See:
TATTERSALL,
MURIEL JOYCE
WAUGH, ALEXANDER RABAN
(1898-) [British author]
Alec Waugh
WAUGH, EDWIN (1817-90)
[English dialect poet]
The Lancashire Burns
The Lancashire Poet
WAUGH, HILLARY BALDWIN
(1920-) [American author]
H. Baldwin Taylor
Harry Walker
"Waverley," By the Author
of. See:
SCOTT, SIR WALTER
Waxman, Franz. See:
WACHSMANN, FRANZ
Way, Wayne. See:
HUMPHRIES, ADELAIDE
M.
Waylan, Mildred. See:
HARRELL, IRENE BURK
WAYMAN, DOROTHY (1893-)
[American author]
Theodate Geoffrey
WAYMON, EUNICE KATHLEEN
(1935-) [American
Negro singer, composer
and pianist]
Nina Simone

Wayne. See:
MORRIS, BERTDE WAYNE
VAN METER, HOMER
WEBB, FRANCIS WAYNE
Wayne, Anderson. See:
DRESSER, DAVIS
WAYNE, ANTHONY (1745-96)
[American Revolutionary
War general officer]
Big Thunder
The Black Snake
The Chief Who Never Sleeps
Dandy Wayne
Drover Wayne
The Hero of Stony Point
Mad Anthony Wayne
The Tornado
The Wind
WAYNE, CHARLES STOKES
(1858-) [American
author]
Horace Hazeltine
Wayne, Chuck. See:
JAGELKA, CHARLES
Wayne, David. See:
McMEEKAN, DAVID
Wayne, Dorothy. See:
SAINSBURY, NOEL
EVERINGHAM
Wayne, Frances. See:
BERTOCCI, CHIARINA
FRANCESCA
WEDGE, FLORENCE
Wayne, John. See:
MORRISON, MARION
MICHAEL
Wayne, Joseph. See:
OVERHOLSER, WAYNE D.
Wayne, Richard. See:
DECKER, DUANE
Wayne Roberts. See:
OVERHOLSER, WAYNE D.
Wayne Way. See: HUMPHRIES,
ADELAIDE M.
WEALE, ANNE (1929-) [English
author]
Andrea Blake
Weale, Putnam. See:
SIMPSON, BERTRAM
LENOX
WEAR, THEODORE GRAHAM
(fl. 1925-62) [American
journalist and author]

1059

Ted Wear
WEARIN, OTHA DONNER
(1903-) [American
farmer and politician;
congressman from Iowa]
Red Necktie
Weary, Ogdred. See:
GOREY, EDWARD ST.
JOHN
Weasel Words, Coiner of.
See: WILSON,
THOMAS WOODROW
Weathercock, Janus. See:
WAINEWRIGHT, THOMAS
GRIFFITHS
Weathercock, The. See:
ROMAINE, LAWRENCE B.
TOWNSHEND, CHARLES
Weathered the Storm, The
Pilot That. See:
PITT, WILLIAM
WEAVER, BERTRAND (1908-)
[American Roman
Catholic priest and
author]
Paul Hunter
Weaver, Charley. See:
ARQUETTE, CLIFFORD
WEAVER, GUSTINE NANCY
COURSON (1873-)
[American author]
The Texas Doll Lady
WEAVER, MONTE MORTON
(1908-) [American
professional baseball
player]
Prof Weaver
Weaver-Poet of Inverurie, The.
See: THOM,
WILLIAM
Weaver, Polly the. See:
JOHNSON, MARY
McDONOUGH
Weaver, Ward. See:
MASON, FRANCIS VAN
WYCK
WEAVER, ZEBULON (1872-
1948) [American lawyer
and politician; congress-
man from North Carolina]
Old Zeb
Webb, Anthony. See:

WILSON, NORMAN
SCARLYN
Webb Beech. See:
BUTTERWORTH, WILLIAM
EDMUND III
WEBB, CHARLES HENRY
(1834-1905) [American
humorist and playwright]
John Paul
Webb, Clifton. See:
HOLLENBECK, WEBB
PARMELEE
WEBB, FRANCIS WAYNE
(1907-) [American jazz
musician (trombone,
leader)]
Wayne Webb
WEBB, HAROLD (1940-)
[British singer and motion
picture actor]
Cliff Richards
WEBB, JEAN FRANCIS
(1910-) [American author]
Ethel Hamill
Webb Jones. See:
HENLEY, ARTHUR
Webb, Neil. See:
ROWLAND, DONALD
SYDNEY
WEBB, RICHARD WILSON
(191?-) [American
author of detective stories]
Q. Patrick
WEBB, RICHARD WILSON.
See also:
Patrick, Q.
Quentin, Patrick
WEBB, RUTH ENID BORLASE
MORRIS (1926-)
[Australian teacher and
author]
Ruth Morris
Webb, Spider. See:
GOHMAN, FRED JOSEPH
WEBB, WILLIAM (1907-39)
[American jazz musician
(drums, leader)]
Chick Webb
WEBBE, GALE DUDLEY (1909-)
[American Episcopal clergy-
man and author]
Stephen Cole

WEBBER, CHARLES WILKINS
(1819-56) [American
explorer, journalist,
naturalist and author]
Charles Winterfield
Webber, Frank. See:
BUSHNELL, WILLIAM H.
Webby. See:
WEBSTER, HAROLD
TUCKER
WEBER, JOSEPH M. (1867-1942)
[American comedian]
Joe Weber
WEBER, RICHARD ANTHONY
(1929-) [American
professional bowler and
organization official]
Dick Weber
WEBSTER, ALICE JANE
CHANDLER (1876-1916)
[American novelist]
Jean Webster
WEBSTER, BENJAMIN
FRANCIS (1909-) [Amer-
ican jazz musician
(saxophone, composer)]
Ben Webster
WEBSTER, DANIEL (1782-1852)
[American statesman,
orator and lawyer]
All Eyes
Black Dan
The Black Giant
The Defender of the
Constitution
The Defender of the Union
The Eagle of the East
The Expounder of the
Constitution
The God-like Daniel
The Great Interpreter
The Great Stone Face
The Illustrious Defender
Immortal Webster
Indian Dan
Little Black Dan
The Massachusetts Giant
The Massachusetts Thunderer
The Modern Sisyphus
The New England Cicero
The New Hampshire
Demosthenes

The Old Titanic Earth-son
The Pillar of the Constitution
The Unintentional Defaulter
The Upholder of the Constitu-
tion
The Whig Gulliver
WEBSTER, DANIEL. See also:
Golden Calves of the
People, The
Great Triumvirate, The
Webster, Frank V. See:
STRATEMEYER,
EDWARD L.
Webster, Gary. See:
GARRISON, WEBB BLACK
WEBSTER, HAROLD TUCKER
(1885-1952) [American car-
toonist and satirist]
The Mark Twain of Cartoonists
Webby
Webster, Jesse. See:
CASSILL, RONALD VERLIN
WEBSTER, JULIA AUGUSTA
(1837-94) [English poet and
dramatist]
Cecil Home
WEBSTER, NOAH (1758-1843)
[American lexicographer]
The Schoolmaster of the Repub-
lic
The Schoolmaster to America
Weda, Richard. See:
DALLWITZ-WEGNER,
RICHARD VON
Wedded Poets, The, joint
nickname of JOHN JAMES
PLATT (1835-1917) and his
wife SARAH MORGAN
RYAN PIATT (1836-1919)
[American poets]
Wedecee. See:
CAROE, WILLIAM DOUGLAS
WEDELL, H.C. (1712-82)
[Prussian general officer]
Leonidas Wedell
WEDGE, FLORENCE (1919-)
[Canadian journalist and
author]
Frances Wayne
WEDGEWOOD, JOSIAH (1730-95)
[English potter]
The Father of the Potteries

WEDGWOOD, EDGAR A.
(1856-1920) [American
sheriff of Hall County,
Nebraska]
The Kid Sheriff of Nebraska
Wee Willie. See:
KEELER, WILLIAM
HENRY
Weeb. See:
EWBANK, WILBUR
CHARLES
WEED, HAROLD (1918-)
[American jazz musician
(piano, leader)]
Buddy Weed
WEEDEN, CHARLES FOSTER
(1856-1928) [American
Congregational clergyman]
Bishop of Congregational
Churches
WEEKS, AGNES RUSSELL (1880-)
[English novelist]
Anthony Pryde
WEEKS, ANSON (1898-1969)
[American jazz musician
(piano, composer,
arranger, leader)]
Ans
WEEKS, CONSTANCE TOMKINSON
(1915-) [Canadian dancer,
actress and author]
Constance Tomkinson
WEEMS, JOHN EDWARD (1924-)
[American journalist, edu-
cator and author]
J. Eddie Weems, Jr.
WEEMS, MASON LOCKE
(1759-1825) [American
preacher and writer;
biographer of GEORGE
WASHINGTON]
Parson Weems
WEEMS, WILFRED
THEODORE (1901-63)
[American jazz
musician (leader)]
Ted Weems
Weeping Philosopher, The. See:
HERACLITUS
Weeping Prophet, The. See:
SEWALL, JOSEPH
Weeping Willie. See:
WINTER, WILLIAM

WEGIER BELLA (1928-)
[Polish-French motion
picture actress]
Bella Darvi
Wegner. See also:
WAGNER
Wagner
Wegner, Richard. See:
DALLWITZ-WEGNER,
RICHARD VON
Wehrzy, Zehrzy. See:
SHARP, MARJORIE BARN-
HILL ZEHR
WEIMAR, MARGUERITE
JOSÉPHINE (1787-1867)
[French tragic actress]
Mademoiselle George
WEINBERG, CHARLES
(1889-1955) [American
composer and conductor]
Charles Wynn
WEINBERGER, MOSES (fl. last
half 19th cent.)
[Hungarian-born Oklahoma
pioneer and saloon keeper]
The Same Old Mose
The Same Young Mose
WEINGARTEN, DAVID (1902-)
[South African-American
composer and businessman]
Dave Gardner
WEINRAUCH, HERSCHEL (1905-)
[Russian-American editor,
broadcaster and author]
Grigory Vinokur
WEINSTEIN, NATHAN (1903-40)
[American author]
Nathanael West
WEINSTEIN, SOL (1928-)
[American journalist,
television script writer
and author]
Pumpernickel
Weir, John. See:
CROSS, COLIN JOHN
WEISENFREUND, MUNI
(1895-) [Polish-American
stage and screen actor]
The Man of Many Faces
The Man Who Is Always
Somebody Else
Paul Muni
WEISS, ALBERT MARIA

(1844-1925) [Roman
Catholic Dominican
theologian and writer]
Henrich von der Cláña
WEISS, EHRICH (ERIK WEISZ)
(1874-1926) [American
magician, illusionist, actor
and escape artist]
Champion Jail Breaker
The Handcuff King
Harry Houdini
Houdini The Great
The King of Escapologists
The King of Handcuffs
The Monarch of Leg Shackles
Herr N. Osey
The Prince of the Air
The Syllable-accenting
American
Undisputed King of Handcuffs
WEISS, IRVING J. (1921-)
[American educator and
author]
Robert Forio
WEISS, LOUIS (1907-)
[American motion picture
actor]
Kent Taylor
Weiss, Miriam. See:
SCHLEIN, MIRIAM
WEISS, PAUL (1901-)
[American philosopher
and university professor]
America's Foremost
Speculative Philosopher
WEISS, THEO (1876-)
[American magician and
escape artist; brother of
EHRICH WEISS (Harry
Houdini)]
Dash
Harden
Hardeen
The Legal Successor of
Houdini
WEISSMAN, JACK (1921-)
[American journalist,
editor and author]
George Anderson
WEISZ, EHRICH. See:
WEISS, EHRICH (ERIK
WEISZ)
WEITENKAMPF, FRANK

(1866-) [American
librarian and author]
Frank Linstow White
WELBY, AMELIA
BALL COPPUCK
(1819-52) [American
author]
Amelia
WELCH [Welch]. See also:
Welsh
WELSCH
WELCH, GEORGE PATRICK
(1901-) [American
investment banker and
author]
Patrick Welch
WELCH, MARILYN (1933-)
[American composer and
entertainer]
Mitzie Welch
WELCH, NORMAN A. (1933-)
[American composer]
Norm Welch
Welch, Pauline. See:
BODENHEIM, HILDA
MORRIS
Welch, Ronald. See:
FELTON, RONALD
OLIVER
Welch, Rowland. See:
DAVIES, LESLIE
PURNELL
WELCH, RUFUS (1801-56)
[American circus
entrepreneur]
General Welch
Welcome, John. See:
BRENNAN, JOHN NEED-
HAM HUGGARD
WELD, HORATIO HASTINGS
(1811-88) [American
Episcopal clergyman and
author]
Ezekiel Jones
WELK, LAWRENCE (1903-)
[American television
personality and jazz
musician (accordion, organ,
leader)]
The King of Musical Corn
The Liberace of the Accordion
Mr. Music Maker
Well-Beloved, The. See:

CHARLES VI
Well-Beloved, The (Le
Bien-Aimé). See:
LOUIS XV
Well-digger, The. See:
MATTHEWS, JOSEPH W.
Well-languaged Daniel, The.
See: DANIEL, SAMUEL
WELLER, BERNARD WILLIAM
(1870-) [British author,
critic and journalist]
B.W.
WELLES. See also:
WELLS
Wells
WILLS
Wills
WELLES, GEORGE ORSON
(1915-) [American actor,
playwright, director and
producer]
Orson Welles
Your Obedient Servant
WELLES, GIDEON (1802-78)
[American politician,
author, editor and Secre-
tary of the Navy under
President ABRAHAM
LINCOLN]
Father Noah
Wellesley Hills, The Seer of.
See: BABSON, ROGER
WARD
Wellesley, Lord Charles. See:
BRONTË, CHARLOTTE
WELLHOUSE, FREDERICK
(1828-1911) [American
apple orchardist and
horticulturist]
The Apple King
WELLINGTON, ARTHUR
WELLESLEY, 1ST DUKE
OF (1769-1852) [English
general officer and
statesman]
The English Achilles
Europe's Liberator
The Great Duke
The Hero of a Hundred
Fights
The Iron Duke
Nosey

Old Douro
The Savior of the Nations
WELLS [Wells]. See also:
WELLES
WILLS
Wills
WELLS, AMOS, JR. (1934-)
[American jazz musician
(singer)]
Junior Wells
WELLS, CAROLYN (1869-1942)
[American anthologist and
detective story writer]
Rowland Wright
WELLS, CATHERINE BOOTH
GARNETT (1838-1911)
[British novelist]
Kate Garnett Wells
WELLS, CHARLES JEREMIAH
(c.1799-1879) [English
poet and lawyer]
H.L. Howard
WELLS, HERBERT GEORGE
(1866-1946) [English
novelist and social
philosopher]
Reginald Bliss
H.G. Wells
Wells, Hondo. See:
WHITTINGTON, HARRY
Wells, J. Wellington. See:
DE CAMP, LYON SPRAGUE
Wells, June. See:
SWINFORD, BETTY JUNE
WELLS
Wells, Michael. See:
MULLINS, RICHARD
WELLS, ROBERT (1922-)
[American composer]
Bob Levinson
Wells, Robert. See:
WELSCH, ROGER LEE
Wells, Roy. See:
DOWNEY, RAYMOND
JOSEPH
WELLS, WILLIAM (1910-)
[American jazz musician
(trombone)]
Dicky Wells
WELSCH. See also:
WELCH
Welch

Welsh
WELSCH, ROGER LEE
(1936-) [American
folklorist, educator and
author]
Robert Wells
Welsh. See also:
WELCH
Welch
WELSCH
Welsh Parson, The. See:
DAVIS, JAMES JOHN
Welsh Shakespeare, The. See:
WILLIAMS, EDWARD
Welsh Wonder, The. See:
WILDE, JIMMY
WELTER, BLANCA ROSA
(1923-) [Motion picture
actress of mixed
nationalities]
Linda Christian
WELTY, SUSAN F. (1905-)
[American educator and
author]
S. F. Welty
WEMLINGER, CLAIRE (1909-)
[American stage and
motion picture actress]
Claire Trevor
Wen Ching. See:
LIM, BOON KENG
Wen, Sun. See:
SUN YAT-SEN
WENCESLAUS (c.903-935)
[Duke and patron of
Bohemia]
Good King Wenceslaus
St. Wenceslaus
WENCESLAUS IV (1359-1419)
[King of Bohemia and
Emperor of Germany]
The Drunkard
The Nero of Germany
The Sardanapalus of Germany
Wendal Parrish. See:
MERRILL, JAMES
MILFORD
Wendelstein. See:
COCHLAEUS (DOBNECK),
JOHANN
Wendy Barrie. See:
JENKINS, WENDY

WENE, ELMER H. (1892-)
[American poultryman and
politician; congressman from
New Jersey]
The Day-old Chick
Wenona Gilman. See:
ENTON, DR. HARRY
Wentworth, Barbara. See:
PITCHER, GLADYS
WENTWORTH, JOHN (1815-88)
[American journalist and
politician; Mayor of
Chicago]
Long John
WENZLAFF, GEORGE (1946-)
[American motion picture
actor]
Foghorn
George Winslow
Werner, K. See:
CASEWIT, CURTIS
Werner, Oskar. See:
BSCHLIESSMAYER, OSKAR
JOSEPH
WERSCHKUL, GORDON M.
(1927-) [American physical
culturist and motion picture
actor]
Gordon Scott
WERTENBAKER, LAEL TUCKER
(1909-) [American
theatrical executive,
journalist and author]
Lael Tucker
Wes. See:
MONTGOMERY, JOHN
LESLIE
Wes Corteen. See:
NORWOOD, VICTOR GEORGE
CHARLES
Wes Hardin. See:
KEEVIL, HENRY JOHN
Wesley Bradshaw. See:
UNKNOWN
WESLEY, CHARLES (1708-88)
[English churchman and
hymnologist]
The Hymnist of the English
Revival
Wesley Craille. See:
ROWLAND, DONALD
SYDNEY

Wesley, Elizabeth. See:
  McELFRESH,
    ELIZABETH ADELINE
Wesley Ray. See:
  GAULDEN, RAY
Wesley's Most Valuable
  Friend. See:
  FLETCHER, JOHN
    WILLIAM
WESSEL, JOHANN (1419-89)
  [Dutch divine and
  philosopher]
  The Wise Doctor
West. See:
  Sweet Singers of the
    West, The
  Two Sisters of the West
    Wast
West, Avalon. See:
  CHAMBERS, BERTRAM
    MORDAUNT
WEST, BENJAMIN (1730-1813)
  [American mathematician,
  astronomer and almanac
  maker]
  Isaac Bickerstaff
WEST, BETTY (1921-)
  [American author]
  Betty Morgan Bowen
West, Elizabeth. See:
  WILSON, MARGARET
WEST, HAROLD (1915-51)
  [American jazz musician
  (drums)]
  Doc West
West, Harold. See:
  WILSON, ROGER C.
West, Harry of the. See:
  CLAY, HENRY
West, Harvard's Gift to the.
  See: CUTTING, BRONSON
West, Jerry. See:
  STRATEMEYER,
    EDWARD L.
  SVENSON, ANDREW E.
West, Kenyon. See:
  HOWLAND, FRANCES
    LOUISE MORSE
West, Kirkpatrick. See:
  HARRIS, FRANK
    BRAYTON
WEST, LILLIE (1860-1939)

[American actress, drama
  critic and author]
  Amy Leslie
  Marie Stanley
WEST, MAE (1892-) [American
  stage and screen actress,
  playwright and sex symbol]
  The Baby Vamp
  Diamond Lil
  Jane Mast
  The Screen's Bad Girl
  The Siren of the Screen
  Vaudeville's Youngest
    Headliner
West, Mark. See:
  RUNYON, CHARLES W.
WEST, MORRIS LANGLO
  (1916-) [Australian
  educator and author]
  Michael East
West, Nancy Richard. See:
  WESTPHAL, WILMA ROSS
West, Nathanael. See:
  WEINSTEIN, NATHAN
West of the Pecos, The Law.
  See: BEAN, ROY
West, Rebecca. See:
  FAIRFIELD, CECILY
    ISABEL
West, Sisters of the. See:
  Sisters of the West
  Sisters of the West, Two
  VICTOR, MRS. FRANCES
    FULLER BARRITT
  VICTOR, MRS. METTA
    VICTORIA FULLER
    MORSE
West, The Athanasius of the.
  See: HILARY OF POITIERS
West, The Cincinnatus of the.
  See: WASHINGTON, GEORGE
West, The Coolidge of the. See:
  LANDON, ALFRED MOSS-
    MAN
West, The Emperor of the. See:
  MACKENZIE, KENNETH
  MURRAY, JOHN
West, The Father of Baseball
  in the. See:
  WALDO, HIRAM H.
West, The Franklin of the. See:
  BRADFORD, JOHN

West, The Homer of the Middle. See: MASON, WALT
West, The Light of the. See: MAIMONIDES
West, The Münchausen of the. See: CROCKETT, DAVID
West, The Queen of the. See: SMITH, FRANCES OCTAVIA
West, The Stonewall of the. See: CLEBURNE, PATRICK RONAYE
West, The Washington of the. See: CLARK, GEORGE ROGERS HARRISON, WILLIAM HENRY
West, Token. See: HUMPHRIES, ADELAIDE M.
West, Ward. See: BORLAND, HAROLD GLEN
WEST, WILLIAM HENRY (1824-1911) [Blind American orator]
Blind Man Eloquent
Westbrook. See: PEGLER, JAMES WESTBROOK
Westchester, The Bald Eagle of. See: HUSTED, JAMES WILLIAM
Westcott, Helen. See: HICKMAN, MYRTHAS HELEN
Western Churches, The Light of the. See: HOOKER, THOMAS
Western Monasticism, Founder of. See: BENEDICT OF NURSIA, ST.
Western Mysticism, The Father of. See: BERNARD OF CLAIRVAUX
WESTHEIMER, DAVID (1917-) [American journalist and author]
Z. Z. Smith
Westland, Lynn. See: JOSCELYN, ARCHIE L.
Westley, George Hembert. See: HIPPISLEY, GEORGE

WESTMACOTT, CHARLES MALLOY (1787-1868) [British journalist]
Bernard Blackmantle
Westmacott, Mary. See: MILLER, AGATHA MARY CLARISSA
WESTMORELAND, WILLIAM CHILDS (1914-) [American general officer]
Westy
WESTON, AGNES (1840-1918) [English missionary]
The Sailors' Friend
Weston, Ann. See: PITCHER, GLADYS
Weston, Philip. See: DE FILIPPI, AMEDEO
WESTON, RANDOLPH E. (1926-) [American composer, pianist and conductor]
Randy Weston
Weston Satterly. See: SUNNERS, WILLIAM
WESTPHAL, WILMA ROSS (1907-) [American missionary, designer and author]
Nancy Richard West
WESTWATER, SISTER AGNES MARTHA (1929-) [American Roman Catholic nun and author]
Martha Earley
Westy. See: WESTMORELAND, WILLIAM CHILDS
Wetherell, Elizabeth. See: WARNER, SUSAN BOGERT
WETHERELL-PEPPER, JOAN ALEXANDER (1920-) [British author]
Joan Pepper
WETTACH, ADRIAN (ARNOLD) (1880-1959) [Swiss circus clown]
Grock
Wetzel, Bonnie. See: ADDLEMAN, BONNIE JEAN
WEYDEN, ROGIER VAN DER (1399?-1464) [Flemish painter]

1067

Rogelet de la Pasture
Roger de la Pasture
WEYLER Y NICOLAU,
VALERIANO (1830-1930)
[Spanish general officer;
governor and military
commander of Cuba]
Butcher Weyler
WEYMEN, STANLEY JOHN
See: Merriman, Henry
Seton
WEYMER. See:
WEIMAR
WHALEN, GROVER ALOYSIUS
(1886-1962) [American
businessman and politician]
New York City's Official
Greeter of Famous People
Whalen, Michael. See:
SHOVLIN, JOSEPH
KENNETH
WHALLEY, DOROTHY (1911-)
[British author]
Dorothy Cowlin
Wharton. See also:
WARTON
Wharton, Anthony. See:
McALLISTER, ALISTER
WHATELY, RICHARD
(1787-1863) [Archbishop
of Dublin and author]
John Search
WHEAT, CHATHAM ROBER-
DEAU (1826-62) [American
army officer]
The Murat of America
Wheatland, The Sage of. See:
BUCHANAN, JAMES
WHEATLEY, PHILLIS (1753-84)
[Afro-American poet]
The Negro Sappho
Wheaton, Iceman, The. See:
GRANGE, HAROLD
EDWARD
Wheel Horse of Democracy, Old.
See: MEDARY, SAMUEL
Wheel Horse of the Senate, The.
See: RUGGLES,
BENJAMIN
WHEELER, ANDREW CARPEN-
TER (1835-1903) [Amer-
ican journalist, critic and

author]
Nym Crinkle
J. P. M.
J. P. Mowbray
Trinculo
WHEELER, BURTON KENDALL
(1882-) [American
politician; senator from
Montana]
The Great Liberal
Wheeler, Captain. See:
ELLIS, EDWARD SYLVESTER
WHEELER, EDWARD LYTTON
(c.1854-85) [American
author of dime novels]
Edward Lytton
WHEELER, HUGH CALLINGHAM.
See: Quentin, Patrick
Wheeler, Janet D. See:
STRATEMEYER,
EDWARD L.
WHEELER, JOSEPH (1836-1906)
[American politician and
Civil War Confederate
general officer]
Fighting Joe
The Little Hero
Little Joe
Wheelhouse. See:
SEMPLE, DUGALD
WHELPTON, GEORGE ERIC
(1894-) [British editor,
educator, broadcaster and
author]
Richard Lyte
John Parry
Whig Gulliver, The. See:
WEBSTER, DANIEL
Whig, Old Line. See:
WILLIAMS, JAMES
Whig, The. See:
JOHNSON, SAMUEL
Whig, The First. See:
SACHEVERELL, WILLIAM
Whig, The Little. See:
ANNE
WHIGHAM, HAYDN (1943-)
[American jazz musician
(trombone)]
Jiggs
Whip McCord. See:
NORWOOD, VICTOR

GEORGE CHARLES
WHIPPLE, HENRY BENJAMIN
(1822-1901) [Episcopalian
Church Bishop and Indian
missionary in Minnesota]
Straight Tongue
WHIPPLE, SQUIRE (1804-88)
[American civil engineer
and bridge builder]
The Father of American
Bridge Building
Whiskers. See also:
Wiskers
Whiskers, Old. See:
WILES, GREENBURY F.
Whiskers, Pink. See:
LEWIS, JAMES HAMILTON
Whisky Van. See:
VAN BUREN, MARTIN
Whispering Tenor, The. See:
AUSTIN, GENE
Whist, The Father of. See:
HOYLE, EDMOND
Whist, The Father of the Game
of. See:
HOYLE, EDMOND
Whistlecraft, William and
Robert. See:
FRERE, JOHN HOOKHAM
WHISTLER, GEORGE WASHING-
TON (1800-49) [American
construction engineer; son
of JAMES ABBOTT
McNEILL WHISTLER]
Pipes
Whit Harrison. See:
WHITTINGTON, HARRY
Whit Masterson. See:
Miller, Wade
WHITCHER, FRANCES MIRIAM
BERRY (1814-52)
[American humorist]
Frank
The Widow Bedott
WHITCOMB, KENNETH G.
(1926-) [American
composer, conductor
and arranger]
George Kenny
WHITE [White]. See also:
WHYTE
Whyte

White, Babington. See:
MAXWELL, MARY
ELIZABETH BRADDON
White Beaver, The. See:
POWELL, DAVID FRANK
White, Bob. See:
HOLLAND, RAY P.
White, Charles Erskine, D.D.
See: OSBORN, LAUGHTON
WHITE, CHARLES WILLIAM
(1906-) [American
novelist]
Max White
White Chief, Great. See:
ROOSEVELT, THEODORE
White Chief of the Pawnees, The.
See: LILLIE, MAJOR
GORDON W.
WHITE, CONSTANCE M.
(1903-) [English author]
Constance Howard
White, Dale. See:
PLACE, MARIAN
TEMPLETON
White Devil of Wallachia,
The. See:
CASTRIOTA, GEORGE
White Devil, The Blind. See:
BUCKLEY, CHRISTOPHER
A.
White Devil, The Great. See:
VAN CORTLANDT, PHILIP
WHITE, ELLERTON OSWALD
(1917-) [Panamanian
jazz musician (piano)]
Sonny White
WHITE, ELWYN BROOKS
(1899-) [American author]
E.B. White
White, Frank Linstow. See:
WEITENKAMPF, FRANK
White, Harry. See:
WHITTINGTON, HARRY
White Hat, Old. See:
GREELEY, HORACE
WHITE, HENRY KIRKE
(1785-1806) [British poet]
The Boy Poet of Nottingham
White House, Chief Incendiary of
the. See:
ADAMS, SAMUEL
White House Pet, The. See:

O'DAY, CAROLINE
GOODWIN
White House, That Man in the.
See: ROOSEVELT,
FRANKLIN DELANO
White House, The Houdini in
the. See:
ROOSEVELT, FRANKLIN
DELANO
White House Tommy. See:
CORCORAN, THOMAS
GARDINER
WHITE, HUGH LAWSON
(1773-1840) [American
statesman; senator from
Tennessee]
The Cato of America
The Cato of the Senate
WHITE, HUGH LAWSON. See also:
Golden Calves of the
People, The
WHITE, JAMES (-1876)
[American frontiersman
and scout]
Buffalo Chips
Charles White
Jonathan White
WHITE, JAMES (1840-85)
[Scottish founder of the
Jezreelites]
James Jershom Jezreel
WHITE, JAMES DILLON
(1913-) [British insurance
executive and author]
Felix Krull
Peto
James Peto
WHITE, JOHN (1590-1645)
[English theologian]
Century White
WHITE, JOSEPH BLANCO
(1775-1841) [British
author, born in Spain]
Giuseppe Blanco
WHITE, JOSHUA DANIEL
(1908-69) [American
Negro ballad singer]
Josh White
The Most Famous Folk
Singer of his Race
WHITE, JOYNER (1909-)
[American professional

baseball player]
Jo-Jo
WHITE, KATHLEEN
ELIZABETH (1916-)
[American motion picture
actress]
Marie Wilson
White King, The. See:
CHARLES I
White Line, The Father of the.
See: HINES, EDWARD
NORRIS
White Mountain Giant, The. See:
CRAWFORD, ETHAN ALLEN
WHITE, PATRICIA LORRAIN-
ANN (1928-) [Canadian
ballerina, teacher and
choreographer]
Patricia Wilde
WHITE, PAUL HAMILTON HUME
(1910-) [Australian
medical officer, broadcaster
and author]
Jungle Doctor
WHITE, PEARL (1889-1939)
[American star of silent
motion picture serials]
The Queen of the Silent
Serials
White Queen, The. See:
MARY
White, Ramy Allison. See:
STRATEMEYER,
EDWARD L.
WHITE, RICHARD GRANT
(1821-85) [American
essayist and critic]
A Yankee
White Robe. See:
ROBERTS, JOHN
White Rose of Raby, The. See:
NEVILL, CECILY
White Rose, The Knight of the.
See: TAYLOR, ROBERT LOVE
White Savage, The. See:
GIRTY, SIMON
WHITE, STANHOPE (1913-)
[English civil servant and
author]
Sabiad
White, The. See:
HUGUES (HUGH)

WHITE, THEODORE EDWIN
(1938-   ) [American
author]
Ron Archer
Ted White
WHITE, THEODORE EDWIN.
See also:
Edwards, Norman
WHITE, WILLIAM ALLEN
(1868-1944) [American
journalist, scholar and
political leader)]
The Sage of Emporia
WHITE, WILLIAM ANTHONY
PARKER (1911-68) [Amer-
ican critic and writer of
detective stories]
Anthony Boucher
H.H. Holmes
WHITE, WILLIAM HALE
(1831-1913) [English author]
Mark Rutherford
White Woman of the Genessee,
The. See:
JEMISON, MARY
White, Zita. See:
DENHOLM, THERESE
MARY ZITA WHITE
WHITEHALL, HAROLD
(1905-   ) [Anglo-
American educator and
author]
Fritz Whitehall
WHITEHEAD, DONALD
FORD (1908-   ) [American
journalist]
Don Whitehead
WHITEHEAD, WALTER
EDWARD (1908-)
[British business
executive]
Commander Whitehead
The Embodiment of
Schweppervescence
Whitehorn, Katharine. See:
LYALL, KATHARINE
ELIZABETH
Whitehorn, Washington. See:
BELLAW, AMERICUS
WELLINGTON
WHITEHOUSE, ARTHUR
GEORGE (1895-   ) [British

cartoonist and writer]
Arch Whitehouse
WHITEMAN. See also:
WHITMAN
WHITEMAN, GEORGE FREDERICK
CARL (1877-1958)
[Australian actor, dramatic
critic and theater manager]
Sydney W. Carroll
WHITEMAN, PAUL (1891-1967)
[American dance orchestra
conductor]
The Dean of American
Popular Music
King of Jazz
Pops
Whitey. See:
BERQUIST, BERNARD H.
FORD, EDWARD CHARLES
KAUFMAN, MARTIN ELLIS
MITCHELL, GORDON B.
PIETRUSZKA, ANTHONY
FRANCIS
YOUNG, LEMUEL FLOYD
WHITFIELD, JOHN HUMPHREYS
(1906 -) [British educator
and author]
Gerone Pilio
Whitfield of Nova Scotia, The.
See: ALLINE, HENRY
Whitfield of the Stage, The.
See: GARRICK, DAVID
QUIN, JAMES
WHITING, MARGARET
ELEANORE (1924-   ) [Amer-
ican singer and actress]
Madcap Maggie
Whitinger, R.D. See:
PLACE, MARIAN
TEMPLETON
Whitley, George. See:
CHANDLER, A. BERTRAM
WHITMAN. See also:
WHITEMAN
WHITMAN, JOHN LORIN
(1862-1926) [American
prison guard and penologist]
The Beloved Jailer
The Boy Guard
WHITMAN, WALTER (1819-92)
[American poet]
The Good Gray Poet

Walt Whitman
WHITNEY, ARTHUR CARTER
(1908-) [American
professional baseball
player]
Pinkey
WHITNEY, ELI (1765-1825)
[American inventor of
the cotton gin]
The Father of the Cotton
Gin
Whitney, Elliott. See:
SAYLER, HARRY
ELLIOTT
Whitney, Hallam. See:
WHITTINGTON, HARRY
Whitney, J. L. H. See:
TRIMBLE, JACQUELYN
WHITNEY
WHITNEY, JOHN HAY (1904-)
[American financier,
ambassador and publisher]
Jock Whitney
WHITNEY, JULIA A. (1922-65)
[Russian composer and
singer]
Yulia
Whitney, Lucia. See:
KELLER, ETHEL MAY
WHITNEY, MOXAM (1919-)
[American composer,
conductor and musician]
Moxie Whitney
Whitney, Peter. See:
ENGLE, PETER KING
WHITON, JAMES NELSON
(1932-) [American
writer]
Boyd Boylan
WHITON, JAMES NELSON.
See also:
Bolo, Solomon
WHITSON, JOHN HARVEY
(1854-1936) [American
minister, educator and
author of dime novels]
Luke Garland
Captain Hazelton
Colonel Hazelton
Frank Merriwell
Arthur Sewell
Lieut. A. K. Sims

Burt L. Standish
Robert Steel
Addison Steele
Maurice Stevens
Russell Williams
WHITTAKER, FREDERICK
(1838-89) [Anglo-American
author]
Launce Poyntz
WHITTEMORE, ARTHUR
(1916-) [American concert
pianist]
Buck Whittemore
WHITTIER, JOHN GREENLEAF
(1807-92) [American poet]
The Burns of America
The Poet Laureate of New
England
The Puritan Poet
The Quaker Poet
The Wood-thrush of Essex
WHITTINGTON, HARRY (1915-)
[American editor and author]
Whit Harrison
Kel Holland
Harriet Kathryn Myers
Steve Phillips
Clay Stuart
Hondo Wells
Harry White
Hallam Whitney
WHITTINGTON, RICHARD
(1358?-1423) [English
merchant, mayor of London]
Dick Whittington
Whittle, Tyler. See:
TYLER-WHITTLE,
MICHAEL SIDNEY
Whittlebot, Hernia. See:
COWARD, NOEL PEIRCE
Who Remembers, One (Hafiz).
See: SHAMS UD-DIN
MOHAMMED
Who Speaks, One (Uei Tlatoani).
See: MONTEZUMA II
WHYTE [Whyte]. See also:
WHITE
White
Whyte, Violet. See:
STANNARD, ELIZA
VAUGHAN
WHYTE, WILLIAM PINKNEY

(1824-1908) [American
lawyer and politician;
Governor of and repre-
sentative from Maryland]
The Grand Old Man from
Maryland
Wi-chash-ta-Ish-nan-nah.
  See: PHILLIPS,
  WALTER SHELLEY
WIBBERLEY, LEONARD
  PATRICK O'CONNOR
  (1915-) [Irish editor,
  correspondent and author]
  Leonard Holton
  Patrick O'Connor
Wicked Lord Lyttelton, The.
  See: LYTTELTON,
  THOMAS, 2ND LORD
  LYTTELTON
Wicked, Old. See:
  GODFREY, HOLLEN
WICKER, IREENE SEATON
  (1905-) [American
  radio script writer,
  singer and actress]
  The Singing Story Lady
WICKHAM. See:
  WYKEHAM (WICKHAM),
  WILLIAM OF
Wickham, Mary F. See:
  BOND, MARY FANNING
  WICKHAM
Wickham, Mary Fanning. See:
  BOND, MARY FANNING
  WICKHAM
WICKLIFFE, CHARLES
  ANDERSON (1788-1869)
  [American lawyer and
  politician; congressman
  from Kentucky]
  Duke
WICKLIFFE, JOHN
  (c.1324-84) [English
  religious reformer]
  Doctor Evangelicus
  The Gospel Doctor
  The Morning Star of the
  Reformation
WICKS, KATHARINE GIBSON
  (1893-) [American
  author]
  Katharine Gibson

WIDDEMER, MABEL CLELAND
  (1902-) [American librarian
  and author]
  Mabel Cleland
  Mabel Cleland Ludlum
  Widow Bedott, The. See:
  WHITCHER, FRANCES
  MIRIAM BERRY
WIEDERRECHT, MARTHA
  (1926-) [American singer]
  Martha Wright
WIELAND, CHRISTOPHER
  MARTIN (1733-1813)
  [German poet and author]
  Der Meister (The Master)
  The Voltaire of Germany
Wiener, Henri. See:
  LONGSTREET, STEPHEN
WIENER, NORBERT
  (1894-1964) [American
  mathematician and author]
  The Father of Automation
  W. Norbert
WIERSBE, WARREN WENDELL
  (1929-) [American Baptist
  pastor and author]
  Dave Warren
WIEZELL, RICHARD JOHN
  (1933-) [American
  educator, editor and
  author]
  Andrew John Field
Wife, Haydn's. See:
  BOCCHERINI, LUIGI
Wife, Josiah Allen's. See:
  HOLLEY, MARIETTA
Wife, The Baker's. See:
  MARIE ANTOINETTE
Wife, The Bonny Brown. See:
  JACKSON, RACHEL
  DONELSON
WIGGER, RALF HAROLDE
  (1899-) [American motion
  picture actor]
  Ralf Harolde
Wiggs, Johnny. See:
  HYMAN, JOHN
  WIGGINTON
WILBERFORCE, SAMUEL
  (1805-73) [Bishop of
  Winchester]
  Soapy Sam

Wilbur Fawley. See:
    FAULEY, WILBUR
    FINLEY
Wilbur Jones, Captain. See:
    EDWARDS, WILLIAM
    BENNETT
Wilby, R. Hunt. See:
    EYSTER, WILLIAM
    REYNOLDS
WILCOX, COLLIN (1924-)
    [American designer and
    author]
    Jeffrey Collins
WILCOX, JESSICA (1925-)
    [American model and
    businesswoman]
    Candy Jones
WILD [Wild]. See also:
    WILDE
    Wilde
Wild Bill. See:
    DAVIS, WILLIAM
    STRETHEN
    DAVISON, WILLIAM
    ELLIOTT, GORDON
    HICKOCK, JAMES BUTLER
Wild Bill the Pony Express
    Rider. See:
    CODY, WILLIAM
    FREDERICK
Wild Boy, The. See:
    HAUSER, KASPAR
    PETER THE WILD BOY
Wild Bull of the Pampas, The.
    See: FIRPO, LUIS
    ANGEL
WILD, HENRY (born c.1684)
    [English tailor and
    linguist]
    The Arabian Tailor
    The Learned Tailor
Wild Horse Charlie. See:
    ALEXANDER, CHARLES
    W.
Wild Humorist of the Pacific
    Slope, The. See:
    CLEMENS, SAMUEL
    LANGHORNE
WILD, JONATHAN (c.1682-1725)
    [English criminal]
    The Great
Wildcatters, The King of the.
    See: BENEDUM, MICHAEL

Wildcatters, The King of the
    Texas. See:
    CULLEN, HUGH TROY
WILDE [Wilde]. See also:
    WILD
    Wild
WILDE, CLEO (1932-)
    [American singer]
    Cathrine Wilde
WILDE, JANE FRANCISCA
    SPERANZA, LADY
    (1826-96) [Irish poet; mother
    of OSCAR WILDE]
    Speranza
WILDE, JIMMY (1892-)
    [Welsh professional prize
    fighter]
    The Welsh Wonder
Wilde, Kathey. See:
    KING, PATRICIA
WILDE, OSCAR FINGAL
    O'FLAHERTIE WILLS
    (1856-1900) [Irish poet,
    playwright and author]
    C. 3. 3.
    I. Playfair
    Sebastian Melmoth
    Oscar Wilde
Wilde, Patricia. See:
    WHITE, PATRICIA LOR-
    RAIN-ANN
WILDEN-HART, BERNARD JOHN
    (1881-) [British economist,
    author and lecturer]
    By Professor Wilden-Hart
Wilder. See:
    Wylder
Wilderness, The Apostle of the.
    See: BRECK, JAMES
    LLOYD
Wilderness, The Gamecock of
    the. See:
    MARBLE, DANFORTH
Wildest Tenor Man, The
    World's. See:
    COBB, ARNETT CLEOPHUS
Wilding, William West. See:
    PATTEN, WILLIAM GILBERT
Wildwood, Will. See:
    POND, FREDERICK EUGENE
WILES, GREENBURY F. (fl.
    1861-65) [American Civil
    War Union general officer]

1074

Old Whiskers
Wiley, Margaret L. See:
    MARSHALL, MARGARET
    WILEY
Wilfrid Lawson. See:
    WORSNOP, WILFRID
WILHELM, GEORG (1885-)
    [German motion picture
    director]
    G. W. Pabst
Wilhelmina Amelia Skeggs,
    The Honorable. See:
    THACKERAY, WILLIAM
    MAKEPEACE
WILHOITE, DONALD MACRAE,
    JR. (1909-) [American
    composer, singer and
    pianist]
    Don Raye
WILKENS, MAYBRITT (1933-)
    [Swedish motion picture
    actress]
    May Britt
WILKES-HUNTER, RICHARD
    (1906-) [Australian
    author]
    Dean Ballard
    Marc Brody
    Tod Conrad
    Alex Crane
    Shane Douglas
    James Dunn
    Peter Gordon
    Kerry Mitchell
    C. M. O'Neill
    Kent Sanders
    Alan Shulberg
Wilkie. See:
    COLLINS, WILLIAM
    WILKIE
WILKIE, FRANC BANGS (1832-
    92) [American editor and
    author]
    Poliuto
WILKIE, SIR DAVID (1775-
    1841) [Scottish genre
    painter]
    The Scottish Teniers
WILKIE, WILLIAM (1721-72)
    [Scottish poet]
    The Scottish Homer
WILKINSON, CHARLES BURN-
    HAM (1916-) [American

football coach and physical
    fitness consultant]
    Bud Wilkinson
    The Golden Man of the Gridiron
WILKINSON, JOHN DONALD
    (1929-) [British Church of
    England priest and author]
    Maximus Ironmaster
WILKINSON, LORNA HILDA
    KATHLEEN (1909-)
    [British author]
    Lorna Deane
Wilkinson, Louis. See:
    MARLOW, LOUIS
WILKINSON, MRS. MARGUERITE
    OGDEN (1883-1928)
    [American poet]
    Harley Graves
WILKINSON, NICHOLAS
    (c. 1575-1623)
    [English actor]
    Nicholas Tooley
WILKINSON, RONALD (1920-)
    [British physician and
    author]
    Ronald Scott Thorn
Will. See:
    BIRD, WILLIAM RICHARD
    CUPPY, WILLIAM JACOB
    DILLON, WILLIAM A.
    DURANT, WILLIAM JAMES
    FOWLER, WILLIAM
    RANDOLPH
    IRWIN, WILLIAM C. K.
    OURSLER, WILLIAM
    CHARLES
    ROGERS, WILLIAM PENN
    ADAIR
Will B. Good. See:
    ARBUCKLE, ROSCOE
Will, Belted. See:
    HOWARD, LORD WILLIAM
Will Benton. See:
    PAINE, LAUREN
Will Bradley. See:
    SCHWICHTENBERG,
    WILBUR
Will C. Brown. See:
    BOYLES, CLARENCE
    SCOTT, JR.
Will Carleton. See:
    BARTLETT, FREDERICK
    ORIN

1075

Will Curtis. See:
 NUNN, WILLIAM CURTIS
Will Dexter. See:
 COOMES, OLIVER
Will, Doctor. See:
 MAYO, WILLIAM JAMES
Will Ermine. See:
 DRAGO, HENRY
 SINCLAIR
Will Geerlink. See:
 HOFDROP, WILLIAM
 PIM
Will H. Houghton. See:
 HOUGHTON, WILLIAM
 HENRY
Will Laurence. See:
 SMITH, WILLARD
 LAURENCE
Will O. Grove. See:
 BRISTER, RICHARD
Will Rossiter. See:
 WILLIAMS, W.R.
Will Stewart. See:
 WILLIAMSON, JOHN
 STEWART
Will, The Ambassador of
 Good. See:
 ROGERS, WILLIAM
 PENN ADAIR
Will, The People's. See:
 PITT, WILLIAM
Will Travers. See:
 ROWLAND, DONALD
 SYDNEY
Will Watson. See:
 FLOREN, LEE
Will Wildwood. See:
 POND, FREDERICK
 EUGENE
Willadsen, Gene. See:
 LYNN, JANE
 THURSTON
Willard, Charles. See:
 ARMSTRONG, JOHN
 BYRON
WILLARD, FRANCES
 ELIZABETH (1839-98)
 [American educator and
 reformer]
 The Silver-tongued and
 Golden-Hearted
WILLARD, JOSIAH FLINT

(1869-1907) [American
 author]
 Josiah Flynt
Willard Parker. See:
 VAN EPS, WORSTER
WILLBANKS, ALEXANDER
 (fl. early 20th cent)
 [American Negro Baptist
 preacher and evangelist]
 The Black Billy Sunday
Willem de Polman. See:
 NICHOLS, DALE
 WILLIAM
Willem the Elder. See:
 VELDE, WILLEM VAN DE
Willem the Younger. See:
 VELDE, WILLEM VAN
 DE
WILLETT, BROTHER FRAN-
 CISCUS (1922-) [American
 Roman Catholic religious
 educator and author]
 Ian Bond
 Brother Jeremy Premont
 Brother Orrin Primm
WILLETT, EDWARD (1830-89)
 (American attorney,
 journalist and author]
 Carl Brent
 J. Stanley Henderson
Willey, Robert. See:
 LEY, WILLY
WILLIAM. See also:
 FREDERICK WILLIAM
 KING OF WILLIAM, JAMES
William. See:
 DIETERLE, WILHELM
 Hirsch, William Randolph
WILLIAM (1143-1214)
 [King of Scotland]
 The Lion
 The Lyon
WILLIAM (died 1226) [Natural
 son of ROSAMUND
 CLIFFORD and HENRY II
 of England]
 Long Sword
WILLIAM (1227-56) [King of
 Germany]
 William of Holland
WILLIAM I (886-918) [Count of
 Auvergne and Duke of

Aquitaine]
The Pious
WILLIAM I (1027-87)
[Duke of Normandy
and King of England]
William the Bastard
William the Conqueror
William the Norman
WILLIAM I (1120-66) [King of
Sicily]
The Bad
WILLIAM I (1533-84) [Prince
of Orange and chief
founder of the Dutch
Republic]
The High-born Demosthenes
William the Silent
WILLIAM II (1056?-1100)
[King of England]
The Red King
Rufus the Red
William Rufus
WILLIAM II (1166-89) [King of
Sicily]
The Good
WILLIAM II (1859-1941) [Emperor
of Germany and King of
Prussia]
Kaiser Bill
The Kaiser
WILLIAM III (1650-1702) [King
of England]
Dutch Billy
William of Orange
WILLIAM IV (1765-1837) [King
of England]
The Sailor King
Sailor William
Silly Billy
William Allen, Rise up. See:
ALLEN, WILLIAM
William and Robert Whistlecraft.
See: FRERE, JOHN
HOOKHAM
William Arthur. See:
NEUBAUER, WILLIAM
ARTHUR
William Atheling. See:
POUND, EZRA LOOMIS
William Augustus Conway. See:
RUGG, WILLIAM
AUGUSTUS

William B. Perry, Captain.
See: BROWN, WILLIAM
PERRY
William Bentley. See:
BLANCHARD, WILLIAM
William Bolitho. See:
RYALL, WILLIAM
BOLITHO
William Brayce. See:
ROWLAND, DONALD
SYDNEY
William Buchanan. See:
BUCK, WILLIAM RAY
William C.L. Thompson. See:
EDWARDS, WILLIAM
BENNETT
William Carleton. See:
BARTLETT, FREDERICK
ORIN
William Cooper. See:
HOFF, HARRY SUMMER-
FIELD
William Donovan. See:
BERKEBILE, FRED
DONOVAN
William Ernest. See:
BERKEBILE, FRED
DONOVAN
William F. Cody, Colonel. See:
CODY, WILLIAM
FREDERICK
William F. Lanne. See:
LEOPOLD, NATHAN F.
WILLIAM FREDERICK
(1776-1834) [Duke of
Gloucester]
Silly Billy
William Gunther. See:
SPRECHER, WILLIAM
GUNTHER
William Haggard. See:
CLAYTON, RICHARD
HENRY MICHAEL
William Henry Sedley-Smith. See:
SEDLEY, WILLIAM HENRY
William Holden. See:
BEEDLE, WILLIAM
FRANKLIN
William Hunter Kendall. See:
GRIMSTON, WILLIAM
HUNTER
William Hutchins. See:

TYNDALE (TINDALE),
WILLIAM
William Irish. See:
HOPLEY-WOOLRICH,
CORNELL GEORGE
William James Florence. See:
CONLIN, BERNARD
William Jason. See:
MACHLIN, MILTON
ROBERT
William Jennings Bryan, The
Second. See:
LEE, JOSHUA BRYAN
William K. Reilly. See:
CREASEY, JOHN
William Lancaster. See:
WARREN, JOHN BYRNE
LEICESTER
William Lee. See:
BURROUGHS, WILLIAM
SEWARD
William McClelland. See:
STRONG, CHARLES
STANLEY
William March. See:
CAMPBELL, WILLIAM
EDWARD MARCH
William Marshal, Gent. See:
WALPOLE, HORATIO
William Masters. See:
COUSINS, MARGARET
William Morrison. See:
SAMACHSON, JOSEPH
William Morton. See:
FERGUSON, WILLIAM
BLAIR
William Murry. See:
MORRIS, CHARLES SMITH
William Nadir. See:
DOUGLASS, WILLIAM
William O. Berch. See:
COYNE, JOSEPH E.
William of Malmsbury. See:
SOMERSET, WILLIAM
William of Ruysbroeck (Rubrouck).
See: RUBRUQUIS,
GUILLAUME
William Paul. See:
EICHER, ETHEL
ELIZABETH
William, Sailor. See:
WILLIAM IV

William Shepard. See:
WALSH, WILLIAM SHEPARD
William Small. See:
EVERSLEY, DAVID
EDWARD CHARLES
William Starret. See:
McCLINTOCK, MARSHALL
William Terriss. See:
LEWIN, WILLIAM
CHARLES JAMES
William, The People's. See:
PITT, WILLIAM
William Tibbetts. See:
BRANNON, WILLIAM T.
William, Warren. See:
KRECH, WARREN
William West Wilding. See:
PATTEN, WILLIAM
GILBERT
WILLIAMS, ALEX (fl. c.1826)
[American politician and
prominent citizen of
Greenville, Tennessee]
Alexander the Great
WILLIAMS, ANDREW (1930-)
[American singer]
Andy Williams
WILLIAMS, ANNA BOLLES
(1840-) [American author]
J.A.K.
Williams, Beryl. See:
EPSTEIN, BERYL
WILLIAMS
Williams, Bill. See:
KATT, WILLIAM
Williams, Bransby. See:
PHAREZ, BRANZBY WILLIAM
WILLIAMS, CHARLES MELVIN
(1908-) [American jazz
musician (trumpet, leader)]
Cootie Williams
WILLIAMS, CLYDE C. (1881-)
[American frontiersman,
lecturer and author]
Slim Williams
Williams, Cris. See:
DE CRISTOFORO, R.J.
WILLIAMS, DAVID ROGERSON
(1776-1830) [American
pioneer manufacturer,
general officer and congress-
man from South Carolina]

Thunder and Lightning
Williams
WILLIAMS, EDWARD
(1745-1826) [Welsh poet
and editor]
Iolo Morgannwg
The Welsh Shakespeare
WILLIAMS, EGBERT AUSTIN
(c.1876-1922) [American
Negro comedian, minstrel
and singer]
Bert Williams
WILLIAMS, EIRLYS OLWEN
(fl. 1959) [British author]
Eirlys Trefor
WILLIAMS, ELEAZAR (c.1789-
1858) [Canadian Indian
scout and missionary]
The Lost Dauphin
WILLIAMS, ELMA MARY
(1913-) [English author]
Jane Oxford
Williams, Francis B. See:
BROWIN, FRANCES
WILLIAMS
Williams, Frederick Benton.
See: HAMBLEN,
HERBERT ELLIOTT
WILLIAMS, G. MENNEN (1911-)
[American lawyer and
statesman]
Soapy Williams
WILLIAMS, GEORGE DALE
(1917-) [American jazz
musician (arranger)]
Fox Williams
WILLIAMS, GEORGE
VALENTINE (1883-1946)
[English writer of mystery
stories]
Douglas Valentine
Vedette
Valentine Williams
WILLIAMS, GRIFFITH E., III
(1905?-59) [American jazz
musician (piano, composer,
leader)]
Griff Williams
WILLIAMS, GUINN (1900-62)
[American motion picture
actor]
Big Boy Williams

Williams, Hawley. See:
HEYLIGER, WILLIAM
WILLIAMS, ISRAEL (1709-88)
[American politician and jurist]
The Monarch of Hampshire
WILLIAMS, JAMES (1796-1869)
[American editor and
author]
Old Line Whig
WILLIAMS, JAMES DOUGLAS
(1808-80) [American
politician; Governor of
Indiana]
Blue Jeans Williams
Williams, Joel. See:
JENNINGS, JOHN E., JR.
WILLIAMS, JOHN (1664-1729)
[American captive of Indians]
The Redeemed Captive
WILLIAMS, JOHN (1761-1818)
[British satirist, critic and
poet]
Anthony Pasquin
WILLIAMS, JOHN (1796-1839)
[English missionary]
The Martyr of Erromango
WILLIAMS, JONATHAN CHAMBER-
LAIN. See:
Chamberlain, Theodore
WILLIAMS, LEWIS (1786-1842)
[American politician;
congressman from North
Carolina]
The Father of the House
Williams, Mary Lou. See:
SCRUGGS, MARY ELFRIEDA
Williams, Michael. See:
St. JOHN, WYLLY FOLK
WILLIAMS, MYRNA (1902-)
[American motion picture
actress]
Myrna Loy
Williams, Pete. See:
FAULKNOR, CLIFFORD
VERNON
WILLIAMS, RENWICK (died
1790) [English multiple
murderer of women]
The Monster
WILLIAMS, ROGER (c.1604-83)
[English founder of Rhode
Island]
The Apostle of Toleration

The Banished Preacher
The Indian's Friend
The Rebel of Salem
Williams, Russell. See:
  WHITSON, JOHN HARVEY
WILLIAMS, SARAH (1841-68)
  [British poet]
  Saidie
WILLIAMS, THEODORE
  SAMUEL (1918-)
  [American professional
  baseball player]
  The Big Guy
  The Kid
  The Splendid Splinter
  Ted Williams
WILLIAMS, THOMAS LANIER
  (1914-) [American
  playwright, novelist
  and short story writer]
  Tennessee Williams
WILLIAMS, W.R. (1867-1954)
  [American composer and
  publisher]
  Will Rossiter
WILLIAMSON, CLAUDE
  CHARLES H. (1891-)
  [British Roman Catholic
  priest, educator and
  author]
  Felix Hope
WILLIAMSON, ELLEN DOUGLAS
  (fl. 1927-65) [American
  author]
  Ellen Douglas
WILLIAMSON, GEOFFREY
  (1897-) [British editor
  and author]
  Alan Hastings
WILLIAMSON, JOHN STEWART
  (1908-) [American
  teacher and author]
  Will Stewart
  Jack Williamson
Williamson, Sonny Boy. See:
  MILLER, RICE
WILLIAMSON, THAMES ROSS
  (1894-) [American
  novelist]
  S.S. Smith
WILLIAMSON, WILLIAM HENRY
  (1870-) [British novelist]

W. Dane Bank
W. Shaw Heath
Willibald Alexis. See:
  HÄRING, GEORG WILHELM
  HEINRICH
WILLIBRORD (c.657-738)
  [English missionary]
  The Apostle of the Friesians
Willie. See:
  COOK, JOHN
  HOPPE, WILLIAM
  FREDERICK
  MOSCONI, WILLIAM
  JOSEPH
  SHOEMAKER, WILLIAM
  LEE
  Willy
Willie Bobo. See:
  CORREA, WILLIAM
Willie Dennis. See:
  DE BERARDINIS,
  WILLIAM
Willie Dunn, Blind. See:
  MASSARO, SALVATORE
Willie Edouin. See:
  BRYER, WILLIAM
  FREDERICK
Willie, Joe. See:
  NAMATH, JOSEPH
  WILLIAM
Willie, Lumpy. See:
  CHAPELSKI, ALEX
  SAMUEL
Willie the Lion. See:
  SMITH, WILLIAM HENRY
  JOSEPH BERTHOL BONA-
  PARTE BERTHOLOFF
Willie the Wallop. See:
  MAYS, WILLIE HOWARD
Willie, Wee. See:
  KEELER, WILLIAM HENRY
Willie, Weeping. See:
  WINTER, WILLIAM
Willie, Woodbine. See:
  KENNEDY, REV. GEOFFREY
  ANKETELL STUDDERT
WILLIS, CORINNE DENNENY
  (fl. 1944-61) [American
  teacher, librarian and author]
  Patricia Denning
WILLIS, GEORGE ANTHONY
  ARMSTRONG (1897-)

[Canadian humorous
writer]
Anthony Armstrong
Willis, Hal. See:
    FORRESTER, CHARLES
    ROBERT
Willis, Lowell E. See:
    DAVIS, HORACE
    BANCROFT
WILLIS, NATHANIEL PARKER
    (1806-67) [American
    poet, author and editor]
Philip Slingsby
N. P. Willis
Willis T. Ballard. See:
    BALLARD, WILLIS
    TODHUNTER
Willoughby Hodgson, Mrs. See:
    HODGSON, AGNES
WILLS [Wills]. See also:
    WELLES
    WELLS
    Wells
WILLS, HELEN NEWINGTON
    (1906-) [American
    tennis player and author]
Little Miss Poker Face
WILLS, MAURICE MORNING
    (1932-) [American
    professional baseball
    player]
Maury Wills
Wills, Thomas. See:
    ARD, WILLIAM THOMAS
Willy, joint pseud. of
    SIDONIE GABRIELLE
    COLETTE (1873-1954) and
    her husband HENRI
    GAUTHIER-VILLARS (1859-
    1931) [French novelists]
Willy. See also:
    COLETTE, SIDONIE
    GABRIELLE
    GAUTHIER-VILLARS,
    HENRI
    POGANY, WILLIAM
    ANDREW
    SUTTON, WILLIAM
    Willie
Willy Brandt. See:
    FRAHM, HERBERT
    ERNEST KARL

Willy, Kinmont. See:
    ARMSTRONG, WILLIAM
Wilma Dykeman. See:
    STOKELY, WILMA
    DYKEMAN
Wilma George. See:
    CROWTHER, WILMA
    BERYL
Wilmer, Dale. See:
    Masterson, Whit
WILMOT, FRANK LESLIE
    THOMSON (1881-)
    [Australian author]
Maurice Furnley
WILMOT, JOHN (1647-80)
    [Earl of Rochester;
    English nobleman]
Virgin Modesty
Wilmot, Major Walt. See:
    HARBAUGH, THOMAS
    CHALMERS
Wilmouth Houdini. See:
    HENDRICKS, FREDERICK
    WILMOTH
Wilmshurst, Zavarr. See:
    BENNETT, WILLIAM
WILNA, ELIJAH (ELIAS) (1720-
    97) [Lithuanian cabalist
    and Hebrew scholar]
Elijah (Elias) Ben Solomon
Gaon Elijah of Wilna
Wilson. See:
    BARRETT, WILLIAM HENRY
WILSON, ALBERT WILLIAM
    (1909-) [English author]
Yates Wilson
WILSON, AUGUSTA JANE
    EVANS (1835-1909)
    [American novelist]
Augusta Jane Evans
WILSON, CHARLES McMORAN
    (1882-) [British physician
    and author]
Lord Moran
WILSON, CHARLES MOSEMAN
    (1858-1917) [American
    attorney and estate
    administrator]
The One-man Trust Company
Wilson, Charlotte. See:
    BAKER, MRS. KARLE
WILSON, CHRISTOPHER NORTH

(1785-1854) [Scottish
 journalist]
John
WILSON, CLEROW (1935-)
 [American Negro comedian
 and entertainer]
Flip Wilson
Wilson, Dave. See:
 FLOREN, LEE
WILSON, EDITH BOLLING
 GALT (1872-1961) [Wife
 of President THOMAS
 WOODROW WILSON]
The First Lady of the Land
The First Lady of the World
WILSON, FLORENCE (1894-1968)
 [Australian concert
 and opera singer]
Florence Austral
WILSON, FLORENCE ROMA
 MUIR (1891-1930)
 [English novelist]
Romer Wilson
Wilson Gage. See:
 STEELE, MARY
 QUINTARD GOVAN
Wilson, George. See:
 BLAND, GEORGE
WILSON, HENRY (1812-75)
 [American politician; Vice
 President of the United
 States]
The Cobbler
The Natick Cobbler
Wilson, Henry. See:
 COLBATH, JEREMIAH
 JONES
WILSON, IDA LEWIS
 (1841-) [American
 lighthouse keeper]
The Grace Darling of
 America
Wilson, J. Arbuthnot. See:
 ALLEN, CHARLES
 GRANT BLAIRFINDIE
Wilson, Jack. See:
 WOVOKA
WILSON, JAMES (1835-1920)
 [Scottish-American poli-
 tician; Secretary of
 Agriculture]
Tama Jim

WILSON, JAMES (1900-47)
 [American professional
 baseball player]
Ace Wilson
WILSON, JAMES FALCONER
 (1828-95) [American
 politician, congressman
 from Iowa]
Jefferson Jim
WILSON, JAMES GRANT
 (1832-1914) [American
 editor, biographer and
 soldier]
Allen Grant
WILSON, JEREMIAH JONES
 COLBATH (1812-75)
 [American political leader;
 18th Vice-President of
 United States]
Henry Wilson
WILSON, JOHN (fl. early 19th
 cent.) [American pioneer
 in Missouri]
Cave Wilson
WILSON, JOHN (1785-1854)
 [Scottish essayist, poet
 and novelist]
Christopher North
WILSON, JOHN ALFRED
 BAYNUM (1848-)
 [American clergyman]
The Phenomenal Presiding
 Elder
Wilson, John Burgess. See:
 BURGESS, ANTHONY
WILSON, LEWIS ROBERT
 (1900-) [American pro-
 fessional baseball player]
Hack Wilson
WILSON, MARGARET
 (1882-) [American author]
An Elderly Spinster
Elizabeth West
Wilson, Marie. See:
 WHITE, KATHLEEN
 ELIZABETH
WILSON, NORMAN SCARLYN
 (1901-) [British educator
 and author]
Anthony Webb
Wilson, R.A. See:
 KING, ROBERT

WILSON, RICHARD HENRY
(1870-) [American
educator and author]
Richard Fisguill
WILSON, ROBERT FORREST
(1883-1942) [American
author and
journalist]
Forrest Wilson
WILSON, ROGER C. (1912-)
[American composer,
conductor and arranger]
Thomas Ahrens
Stewart London
Benton Price
Walter Price
Lee Rogers
Harold West
WILSON, ROGER HARRIS
LEBUS (1920-) [American
writer and professor of
medicine]
Roger Harris
Wilson, Romer. See:
O'BRIEN, FLORENCE
ROMA MUIR
WILSON, ROSSIERE (1919-)
[American jazz
musician (drums)]
Shadow
WILSON, SAMUEL (fl. early
19th cent.) [American
meat packer]
Uncle Sam
WILSON, STANLEY KIDDER
(1879-) [American
author]
Pliny the Youngest
Wilson, Steve. See:
GOLDENBERG, EMANUEL
WILSON, T.P. CAMERON
(1889-1918) [English poet
and novelist]
Tipuca
WILSON, THEODORE (1912-)
[American jazz
musician (piano, composer,
leader)]
Teddy Wilson
WILSON, THOMAS WOODROW
(1856-1924) [28th President
of the United States]

Coiner of Weasel Words
Phrasemaker
Professor
The Schoolmaster in Politics
Woodrow Wilson
WILSON, THOMAS WOODROW.
See also:
Big Three, The
Duumvirs, The (The
Duumvirate)
WILSON, WILLIAM ABNER
(1864-1928) [American
civic leader in Houston,
Texas]
The Builder of the City of
Houston
Wilt. See:
CHAMBERLAIN, WILTON
NORMAN
WILT, FREDERICK LOREN
(1920-) [American athlete
and government employee]
Fred Wilt
Wilt the Stilt. See:
CHAMBERLAIN, WILTON
NORMAN
Wilton, Captain Mark. See:
MANNING, WILLIAM
HENRY
Wily, The. See:
FERDINAND V
Wimbledon, The Philosopher of.
See: HORNE, JOHN
WIMP, KATHRYN ELIZABETH
(1920-) [American jazz
musician (singer)]
Kay Davis
Winch, John. See:
LONG, MRS. GABRIELLE
MARGARET VERE
CAMPBELL
WINCHCOMB, JOHN (fl. 16th
cent.) [English clothier]
Jack of Newbury
WINCHEL, WALTER (1897-1972)
[American gossip columnist
and radio personality]
America's One-man Newspaper
Walter Winchell
WINCHESTER. See:
ETHELWOLD OF
WINCHESTER

WINCHEVSKY, MORRIS
(1856-1932) [Lithuanian
poet]
The Ghetto Poet
WINCHILSEA, ANNE FINCH,
COUNTESS OF (1661-1720)
[English poet]
A Lady
Wind, The. See:
WAYNE, ANTHONY
Wind, The Dry. See:
GUYER, ULYSSES SAMUEL
WINDER, MAVIS ARETA
(1907-) [New Zealand
author]
Mavis Areta
Mavis Areta Wynder
Windermere. See:
HURD, PERCY ANGIER
Windsor, Anne. See:
DEWEY, ANNETTE
BARRETT
Windsor, Duke of. See:
EDWARD VIII
Windsor, Edward of. See:
EDWARD III
WINDSOR-GARNETT, JOHN
RAYNHAM (fl. 1931)
[British clerk in holy
orders and author]
Othere
Windsor, Marie. See:
BERTELSON, EMILY
MARIE
Windsor, Rex. See:
ARMSTRONG, DOUGLAS
ALBERT
Windy Wales. See:
KNOTTS, DON
WINE-GAR, FRANK (1901-)
[American composer and
conductor]
Fran Wine-Gar
Winfield, Arthur M. See:
STRATEMEYER,
EDWARD L.
Winfield, Edna. See:
STRATEMEYER,
EDWARD L.
Winfield, Leigh. See:
YOUNGBERG, NORMA
IONE RHOADS

WINFRID (WYNFRITH) (c. 680-
c. 755) [English archbishop
and missionary]
The Apostle of Germany
St. Boniface
WING, FRANCES SCOTT
(1907-) [American editor,
journalist and author]
Frances V. Scott
WING, JOSEPH ELWYN
(1861-1915) [American
farmer, lecturer and
agricultural journalist]
Alfalfa Joe
Wing, Old One. See:
MARTIN, JAMES GREEN
WINGENBACH, CHARLES
EDWARD (1938-) [American
journalist, editor and
author]
Raoul de Liancourt
Wingy. See:
MANONE, JOSEPH
MATHEWS
Winifred Graham. See:
CORY, WINIFRED MURIEL
Winifred Woodley. See:
HEDDEN, WORTH TUTTLE
Winn. See also:
WINNE
Wynn
WYNNE
Wynne
Winn, Mary Elfrieda. See:
SCRUGGS, MARY ELFRIEDA
Winn, Mary Lou. See:
SCRUGGS, MARY
ELFRIEDA
WINNE. See also:
Winn
Wynn
WYNNE
Wynne
WINNE, ROBERT BRUCE
(1920-) [American motion
picture actor]
Robert Hutton
WINNEBRENNER, LE ROY
(1932-) [American child
motion picture actor]
Baby Le Roy
WINNER, SEPTIMUS (1827-1902)

[American song
writer]
Alice Hawthorne
Winnie. See:
CHURCHILL, SIR
WINSTON LEONARD
SPENCER
Winnie Davis, The Daughter
of the Confederacy. See:
DAVIS, VARINA ANNE
JEFFERSON
Winnie Lightner. See:
HANSON, WINIFRED
WINNIFRITH, JOANNA (1914-)
[British motion picture
actress]
Anna Lee
Winslow, Amos, Jr. See:
COBB, SYLVANUS, JR.
Winslow, Donald. See:
ZOLL, DONALD ATWELL
Winslow, George. See:
WENZLAFF, GEORGE
Winslow Rhode. See:
ROE, FREDERIC GORDON
WINSLOW, ROSE GUGGENHEIM
(1881-) [American poet
and author]
Jane Burr
WINSTON, JOHN ANTHONY
(1812-71) [American
politician; Governor of
Alabama]
The Veto Governor
Winston P. Sanders. See:
ANDERSON, POUL
WILLIAM
WINTER, BEVIS (1918-)
[British editor and
author]
Al Bocca
Peter Cagney
Gordon Shayne
WINTER, ELIZABETH CAMP-
BELL (1841-1922)
[Scottish novelist]
Isabella Castelar
Winter, Herbert. See:
ELLINGFORD, ROBERT
FREDERICK
Winter, John Strange. See:
STANNARD, HENRIETTA

ELIZA VAUGHAN
Winter King, The. See:
FREDERICK V
Winter Queen, The. See:
STUART, ELIZABETH
Winter, R.R. See:
WINTERBOTHAM, RUSSELL
ROBERT
WINTER, WILLIAM (1836-1917)
[American author and
biographer]
Weeping Willie
WINTERBOTHAM, RUSSELL
ROBERT (1904-)
[American author]
Ted Addy
J. Harvey Bond
Franklin Hadley
R.R. Winter
Winterfield, Charles. See:
WEBBER, CHARLES
WILKINS
Winters, Jack. See:
TALENT, LEO
WINTERS, JANET LEWIS
(1899-) [American
novelist and poet]
Janet Lewis
WINTERS, JONATHAN HARSH-
MAN (1925-) [American
comedian]
Johnny Winters
Winters, Shelley. See:
SCHRIFT, SHIRLEY
Winterton, Gale. See:
ADAMS, WILLIAM TAYLOR
WINTERTON, PAUL (1908-)
[British journalist,
correspondent and author]
Roger Bax
Andrew Garve
Paul Somers
WINTHROP, JOHN (1588-1649)
[Anglo-American colonist;
governor of Massachusetts
Bay Colony]
The American Nehemiah
The Father of Massachusetts
WINTHROP, JOHN (1639-1707)
[American soldier and
colonist]
Fitz-John

WINTHROP, LAURA
(1825-89) [American
author and poet]
Emily Hare
WINTHROP, ROBERT (1896-)
[British comedian and
entertainer]
Bud Flanagan
Winton, Captain Walt. See:
HARBAUGH, THOMAS
CHALMERS
Winton, F. S. See:
HARBAUGH, THOMAS
CHALMERS
Winton, Harry. See:
HARBAUGH, THOMAS
CHALMERS
Winton, John. See:
PRATT, JOHN
Winwar, Frances. See:
GREBANIER, FRANCESCA
VINCIGUERRA
Winwood, Estelle. See:
GOODWIN, ESTELLE
Winwood, Rett. See:
COREY, FRANCIS
ADELBERT
Wire King of America, The.
See: GATES, JOHN
WARNE
Wires, The Wizard of the. See:
EDISON, THOMAS ALVA
WIRZ, CAPTAIN HENRY
(1822-65) [Swiss-born
Confederate officer;
superintendent of
military prison at Ander-
sonville, Georgia]
Death on a Pale Horse
Wisdom, The Prince of Wit
and. See:
ROGERS, WILLIAM PENN
ADAIR
Wise. See:
DJANG, YUAN SHAN
WISE, ARTHUR (1923-)
[British educator and
author]
John McArthur
Wise Charley. See:
McNARY, CHARLES LINZA
WISE, DANIEL (1813-98)

[American Methodist
clergyman, editor and
author]
Francis Forester
Lawrence Lancewood
Wise Doctor, The. See:
WESSEL, JOHANN
Wise, Gildas the. See:
SAPIENS (BADONICUS),
GILDAS
WISE, HENRY ALEXANDER
(1806-76) [American Con-
federate army officer and
politician; congressman
from Virginia]
The Harry Percy of the House
Old Chinook
WISE, HENRY AUGUSTUS
(1819-69) [American naval
officer and author]
Harry Gringo
WISE, ISAAC MAYER
(1819-1900) [Bohemian-
American Jewish rabbi]
The Moses of America
WISE, JOHN (1652-1725)
[American Congregational
clergyman and author]
Amicus Patriae
The First Great American
Democrat
Wise Men. See:
Three Wise Men
Wise Men of Greece, The Seven.
See: Seven Sages of
Greece, The
WISE, ROBERT RAYMOND
(1928-) [American jazz
musician (tenor saxophone)]
Buddy Wise
Wise, The. See:
CHARLES V
LEO VI
Wise, The (El Sabio). See:
ALFONSO X
Wisecracker, The. See:
WALKER, JAMES JOHN
WISEMAN, RICHARD (1622?-76)
[English surgeon]
The Father of English
Surgery
Wisest Fool in Christendom, The.

See: JAMES I
Wisest Man of Greece, The.
See: SOCRATES
Wishart, Henry. See:
SHEPHERD, ROBERT
HENRY WISHART
Wiskers. See:
TINKHAM, GEORGE
HOLDEN
Whiskers
WISNER, EDWARD (1860-1915)
[American pioneer in
land reclamation]
The Father of Reclamation
WISWELL, THOMAS GEORGE
(1915-) [American
checker and chess
champion; writer on both
games]
Tom Wiswell
Wit and Wisdom, The Prince
of. See:
ROGERS, WILLIAM PENN
ADAIR
Witch Finder Generall, The.
See: HOPKINS, MATTHEW
Witch Hazel. See:
SMITH, FRANCIS
SHUBAEL
Witch of Balwery, The Great.
See: AIKEN,
MARGARET
Witch of Wall Street, The.
See: GREEN,
HENRIETTA HOWLAND
Withers, E. L. See:
POTTER, GEORGE
WILLIAM, JR.
Witherspoon, Halliday. See:
NUTTER, WILLIAM H.
Without a Rival, The Poetic
Actress. See:
MURRAY, ALMA
Without a Skin, The Man. See:
CUMBERLAND, RICHARD
Without Fear and Without
Reproach, The Knight.
See: BAYARD, PIERRE
DU TERRAIL,
CHEVALIER DE
Without Reproach, The Knight.
See: BARBAZAN, AR-

ARNAULD GUILHELM DE
Without Reproach, The Knight
Without Fear and. See:
BAYARD, PIERRE DU
TERRAIL, CHEVALIER
DE
Witling of Terror, The. See:
VIEUZAC, BERTRAND
BARÈRE DE
Witness, Eye. See:
BENNETT, JAMES
O'DONNELL
FOE, DANIEL
Witness, The Ideal Scientific.
See: SPILSBURY, SIR
BERNARD HENRY
Wits. See:
Hartford Wits, The
Witz
WITTE, GLENNA FINLEY
(1925-) [American
broadcasting producer,
librarian and author]
Glenna Finley
Witty Nellie, Pretty. See:
GWYN (GWYNNE),
ELEANOR
Witz. See:
DINGELL, JOHN DAVID
Wits
Wizard, Earl, The. See:
PERCY, SIR HENRY
Wizard, Mr. See:
HERBERT, DONALD
JEFFRY
Wizard of American Drama,
The. See:
BELASCO, DAVID
Wizard of Kinderhook, The. See:
VAN BUREN, MARTIN
Wizard of Menlo Park, The.
See: EDISON, THOMAS
ALVA
Wizard of the Albany Regency,
The. See:
VAN BUREN, MARTIN
Wizard of the North, The. See:
SCOTT, SIR WALTER
Wizard of the North, The Great.
See: ANDERSON, JOHN
HENRY
Wizard of the Saddle, The. See:

FORREST, NATHAN
BEDFORD
Wizard of the Wires, The. See:
EDISON, THOMAS
ALVA
Wizard of Tomassee, The. See:
PICKENS, ANDREW
Wizard of Word Music, The.
See: POE, EDGAR ALLAN
Wizard, The. See:
SCOTT, SIR WALTER
Wizard, The Automobile. See:
FORD, HENRY
Wizard, The Electrical. See:
STEINMETZ, KARL
AUGUST RUDOLF
Wizard, The Plant. See:
BURBANK, LUTHER
Wizard, The Wondrous. See:
SCOTT, MICHAEL
WODEHOUSE. See also:
WOODHOUSE
WODEHOUSE, PELHAM GREN-
VILLE (1881-) [Anglo-
American author, humor-
ist and playwright]
Plum
P.G. Wodehouse
Woden. See also:
Wooden
Woden, George. See:
SLANEY, GEORGE WILSON
Wodge, Dreary. See:
GOREY, EDWARD ST.
JOHN
WOFFINGTON, MARGARET
(1714?-60) [Irish actress]
Peg Woffington
WOHLBRUCK, ADOLF (1900-)
[German motion picture
actor]
Anton Walbrook
WOJCIECHOWSKA, MAIA
(1927-) [Polish-American
author]
Maia Rodman
WOLCHOK, SAMUEL (1896-)
[Russian-American
labor union official]
Sam Wolchok
WOLCOT. See also:
Walcott

WOLCOTT
WOOLLCOTT
WOLCOT, JOHN (1738-1819)
[British satirist and poet]
Peter Pindar
WOLCOTT. See also:
Walcott
WOLCOT
WOOLLCOTT
WOLCOTT, ONA (1906-55)
[American dancer and
motion picture actress]
Ona Munson
Wolf. See:
PUTNAM, ISRAEL
THOMPSON, ERNEST
SETON
WOLFE
Wolfe
WOLFF
WOLFFE
WOOLF
Wolf, Frederick. See:
DEMPEWOLFF,
RICHARD FREDERIC
WOLF, GEORGE (1777-1840)
[American educator]
The Father of the Public
School System of Penn-
sylvania
WOLF, MIRIAM BREDOW
(1895-) [American medical
secretary and writer]
Miriam Bredow
Wolf of Badenoch, The. See:
STEWART, SIR
ALEXANDER
Wolf of France, The She. See:
ISABELLA OF FRANCE
Wolf of the Underworld, The
Lone. See:
MILLMAN, HARRY
Wolf, The Great. See:
TRYON, WILLIAM
Wolf, The She. See:
LINCOLN, MARY TODD
WOLF, THOMAS J., JR. (1925-)
[American composer, ar-
ranger and pianist]
Tommy Wolf
WOLFE [Wolfe]. See also:
WOLF

1088

Wolf
WOLFF
WOLFFE
WOOLF
Wolfe, Billy de. See:
JONES, WILLIAM
ANDREW
WOLFE, THOMAS KENNERLY,
JR. (1931-) [American
journalist, essayist and
author]
Tom Wolfe
WOLFF. See also:
WOLF
Wolf
WOLFE
Wolfe
WOLFFE
WOOLF
WOLFF-BEKKER, ELISABETH
(BETJE) (1738-1804)
[Dutch novelist,
essayist, poet and
translator]
Silviana
WOLFFE. See also:
WOLF
Wolf
WOLFE
Wolfe
WOLFF
WOOLF
WOLFFE, YOLANDE MARI
(1940-) [English jazz
musician (singer)]
Yolande Bavan
WOLLHEIM, DONALD ALLEN
(1914-) [American
author]
David Grinnell
WOLSEY. See also:
WOOLSEY
WOLSEY, THOMAS (1475?-1530)
[English statesman and
cardinal]
Cardinal Wolsey
WOLSEY, WILLIAM FRANKLYN
(1904-) [Canadian quack
educator and diploma mill
operator]
The Archbishop John I of
Vancouver

Uncle Bill
Woman, A Greedy. See:
PENNELL, ELIZABETH
Woman, America's Premier Air.
See: PUTNAM, AMELIA
EARHART
Woman Authors of America, The
Dean of. See:
TARBELL, IDA MINERVA
Woman, Hollywood's Busiest and
Most Versatile. See:
HOPPER, ELDA FURRY
Woman in Black, The. See:
GILBERT, MARIE DOLORES
ELIZA ROSANNA
Woman of Rev. XII, The. See:
SOUTHCOTT, JOANNA
Woman of the Genessee, The
White. See:
JEMISON, MARY
Woman of Tutbury, The Fasting.
See: MOORE, ANNE PEGG
Woman, The Bird. See:
SACAJAWEA (SACAGAWEA)
Woman, The Chief Old. See:
STEVENS, THADDEUS
Woman, The First American
Newspaper. See:
CROLY, JANE CUNNING-
HAM
Woman, The Preaching. See:
SPRAGUE, ACHSA W.
Woman, The Traipsin'. See:
THOMAS, JEANETTE BELL
Woman, The World's Funniest.
See: DAVIS, JOAN
Woman, The World's Most
Admired. See:
ROOSEVELT, ANNA
ELEANOR
Woman Who Always Prays, The.
See: DUCHESNE, ROSE
PHILIPPINE
Woman Who Always Speaks Her
Mind, The. See:
COX-OLIVER, EDNA MAY
Woman's Congresswoman, The
Farm. See:
KNUTSON, CORNELIA
GJESDAL
Won a Fight, The Dead Man Who.
See: DOUGLAS, JAMES

Wonder Boy. See:
    KRAMER, STANLEY E.
Wonder Boy, The Barnum. See:
    BARNHUM, H. B.
Wonder Magician, The Child.
    See: DUNNINGER, JOSEPH
Wonder of the World, The.
    See: FREDERICK II
    OTTO III
Wonder, The Boy. See:
    HARRIS, STANLEY
    RAYMOND
    HOPPE, WILLIAM
    FREDERICK
    LEE, JOSHUA BRYAN
Wonder, The Cornish. See:
    OPIE, JOHN
Wonder, The Little. See:
    GRAVELET, JEAN
    FRANÇOIS
Wonder, The Welsh. See:
    WILDE, JIMMY
Wonder, The World's. See:
    ELIZABETH I
Wonderful Doctor, The (Doctor
    Mirabilis). See:
    BACON, ROGER
Wonderworker. See:
    GREGORY THAUMATURGUS
Wondrous Maid, The. See:
    JOAN OF ARC (JEANNE
    D'ARC)
Wondrous Three, The, joint
    nickname of EDMUND
    BURKE (1729-97),
    CHARLES JAMES FOX
    (1749-1806) and WILLIAM
    PITT (1759-1806) [English
    statesmen]
Wondrous Three, The. See also:
    BURKE, EDMUND
    FOX, CHARLES JAMES
    PITT, WILLIAM
Wondrous Wizard, The. See:
    SCOTT, MICHAEL
WONG LIU TSONG (1902-60)
    [Chinese-American motion
    picture actress]
    Anna May Wong
WONG TUNG JIM (1899-)
    [Chinese cinematographer]
    James Wong Howe

WOOD, ANTHONY (1632-95)
    [English antiquary]
    Anthony à Wood
WOOD, CHARLOTTE DUNNING
    (1858-) [American author]
    Charlotte Dunning
WOOD, ELLEN PRICE
    (1814-87) [English novelist]
    Mrs. Henry Wood
WOOD, GLORIA (1919-)
    [American motion picture
    actress]
    K. T. Stevens
WOOD, JAMES PLAYSTED
    (1905-) [American
    educator and author]
    James St. Briavels
    Henry Soudley
Wood, Kirk. See:
    STAHL, LEROY
Wood, Natalie. See:
    GURDIN, NATASHA
Wood-pulp. See:
    MILLER, WARNER
WOOD, SAMUEL GROSVENOR
    (1884-) [American
    motion picture director and
    producer]
    Sam Wood
Wood, Serry. See:
    FREEMAN, GRAYDON LA
    VERNE
WOOD, SIR HENRY JOSEPH
    (1869-1944) [English
    conductor]
    Paul Klenovsky
Wood, Sue. See:
    TAYLOR, MARY VIRGINIA
Wood-thrush of Essex, The. See:
    WHITTIER, JOHN GREEN-
    LEAF
WOOD, VIOLET (1898-) [English
    author]
    Quality Wood
Woodbine Willie. See:
    KENNEDY, REV. GEOFFREY
    ANKETELL STUDDERT
WOODBRIDGE, TIMOTHY
    (1784-1862) [American blind
    Presbyterian clergyman]
    The Blind Minister
Woodchuck Lodge, The Laird of.

See: BURROUGHS, JOHN
Woodcott, Keith. See:
    BRUNNER, JOHN KILIAN
    HOUSTON
Wooden. See also:
    Woden
Wooden Joe. See:
    NICHOLAS, JOE
Wooden Leg. See:
    STUYVESANT, PETER
Wooden-shoe Statesman, The.
    See: WATSON, JAMES
    ELI
WOODERIDGE, KATHLEEN
    MABEL (1914-) [English
    author]
    Kathleen Partridge
Woodford, Jack. See:
    WOOLFOLK, JOSIAH PITTS
WOODHOUSE. See also:
    WODEHOUSE
WOODHOUSE, MARTIN (1932-)
    [British author]
    John Charlton
WOODHULL, VICTORIA
    CLAFLIN (1838-1927)
    [American lecturer, author
    and editor]
    The Terrible Siren
Woodley, Winifred. See:
    HEDDEN, WORTH TUTTLE
WOODMAN, JAMES MONROE
    (1931-) [American author]
    Jim Woodman
Woodman, The American. See:
    AUDUBON, JOHN JAMES
    FOUGÈRE
Woodrook, R.A. See:
    COWLISHAW, RANSON
Woodrow. See:
    WILSON, THOMAS
    WOODROW
WOODRUFF, EDWINA (1909-)
    [American motion picture
    actress]
    Edwina Booth
WOODRUFF, JULIA LOUISA
    MATILDA (1833-1909)
    [American author]
    W.M.L. Jay
Woodruff, Philip. See:
    MASON, PHILIP

WOODRUM, CLIFTON
    ALEXANDER (1887-)
    [American politician,
    congressman from Virginia]
    The Choirmaster of the House
WOODS, FREDERICK (1932-)
    [British editor and author]
    Lawrence Ives
Woods, Nat. See:
    STRATEMEYER,
    EDWARD L.
Woods, The Bull of the. See:
    SUMNER, CHARLES
WOODWARD, A. AUBERTINE
    (1841-) [American trans-
    lator and author]
    Auber Forestier
WOODWARD, GRACE STEELE
    (1899-) [American
    author]
    Marion S. Doane
Woodward, Lilian. See:
    MARSH, JOHN
WOODWARD, PATTI (1880-1967)
    [American motion picture
    actress]
    Jane Darwell
WOODWARD, THOMAS JONES
    (1940-) [English singer
    of popular songs]
    Tom Jones
    Tommy Scott
WOODWORTH, SAMUEL
    (1784-1842) [American
    editor, poet and playwright]
    Selim
Woody. See:
    ALLEN, HEYWOOD
    GUTHRIE, WOODROW
    WILSON
    HERMAN, WOODROW
    CHARLES
    JENSEN, FORREST
    STRODE, WOODROW
Wool-carder President, The.
    See: FILLMORE, MILLARD
WOOLEY. See also:
    WOOLLEY
    Wooly
WOOLEY, EDWARD MOTT
    (1867-) [American author]
    Richard Bracefield

Robert Bracefield
WOOLLEY. See also:
    WOOLEY
    Woolly
WOOLLEY, CATHERINE
    (1904-) [Writer of
    literature for
    juveniles]
    Jane Thayer
WOOLLEY, EDGAR MONTILLION
    (1888-1962) [American
    professor, stage and
    motion picture actor]
    Monty Woolley
WOOLLEY, SHEB (1921-)
    [American composer,
    guitarist and singer]
    Ben Colder
WOOLF. See also:
    WOLF
    Wolf
    WOLFE
    Wolfe
    WOLFF
    WOLFFE
WOOLF, ADELINE VIRGINIA
    (1882-1941) [British
    novelist, short story
    writer and literary critic]
    Virginia Woolf
WOOLFOLK, JOSIAH PITTS
    (1894-1971) [American
    author]
    Jack Woodford
WOOLLCOTT. See also:
    Walcott
    WOLCOT
    WOLCOTT
WOOLLCOTT, ALEXANDER
    HUMPHREYS (1887-1943)
    [American dramatic critic,
    actor and writer]
    The Town Crier
    Louisa May Woollcott
Woolrich, Cornell. See:
    HOPLEY-WOOLRICH,
        CORNELL GEORGE
WOOLSEY. See also:
    WOLSEY
WOOLSEY, MARYHALE (1899-)
    [American musician, club-
    woman and author]

Eugenia Hale
Mary Hale
Terry Snow
WOOLSEY, SARAH CHAUNCEY
    (1835-1905) [American
    author of children's stories]
    Susan Coolidge
WOOLSON, CONSTANCE
    FENIMORE (1840-94)
    [American novelist]
    Anne March
Woolly. See also:
    WOOLY
    WOOLLEY
Woolly-head. See:
    JULIAN, GEORGE
        WASHINGTON
Woolly Bob. See:
    RICH, ROBERT FLEMING
WORBOYS, ANNETTE ISOBEL
    (fl. mid-20th cent.) [New
    Zealand educator and
    author]
    Annette Eyre
    Anne Eyre Worboys
Worcester County, The Marrying
    Justice of. See:
    DAVIS, WALTER ALONZO
Worcester, The Moon-faced
    Senator from. See:
    HOAR, GEORGE FRISBIE
Word, Ann of the. See:
    LEE (LEES), ANN
Word Master (Lavengro). See:
    BORROW, GEORGE HENRY
Word Music, The Wizard of. See:
    POE, EDGAR ALLAN
Worde, Wynkyn de. See:
    VAN WYNKYN, JAN
Words, Coiner of Weasel. See:
    WILSON, THOMAS
        WOODROW
Wordsworth, Dora. See:
    QUILLINAN, DOROTHY
        WORDSWORTH
Wordsworth, The American. See:
    BRYANT, WILLIAM CULLEN
WORDSWORTH, WILLIAM
    (1770-1850) [English poet]
    The Bard of Rydal Mount
    The Cumberland Poet
    The Poet of the Excursion

Work at Fisk University, The
Father of Organized
Alumni. See:
PROCTOR, HENRY HUGH
Work in Christian America, The
Father of Foreign
Mission. See:
MILLS, SAMUEL JOHN
WORKMAN, WILLIAM HENRY
(1839-1918) [Pioneer and
civic leader in Los
Angeles, California]
Uncle Billy
Works, The Father of Good.
See: MOHAMMED II
World, Bar None, The Greatest
Pilot in the. See:
BALCHEN, BERNT
World, Censor of the Proud.
See: ARETINO, PIETRO
World Citizen No. 1. See:
DAVIS, GARRY
World, Conqueror of the
(Alamgir). See:
MOHAMMED
World, Mr. See:
REEVES, STEPHEN
World, One of the Supreme
Colorists of the. See:
TURNER, JOSEPH MAL-
LORD WILLIAM
World, The Biggest Hotel Man
in the. See:
HILTON, CONRAD
NICHOLSON
World, The Conqueror of the.
See:
ALEXANDER III
JAHINGIR
World, The First Lady of the.
See: WILSON, EDITH
BOLLING GALT
World, The Funniest Clown in
the. See:
CLARK, ROBERT EDWIN
World, The Greatest Botanist
in the. See:
BARTRAM, JOHN
World, The Joan of Arc of the
Modern Religious. See:
UTLEY, ULDINE
World, The Liberator of the New.

See: FRANKLIN, BENJAMIN
World, The Light of the. See:
SIGISMUND
World, The Terror of the. See:
ATTILA (ETZEL) (ETHELE)
World, The Wonder of the.
See: FREDERICK II
OTTO III
World War Croesus, The. See:
McADOO, WILLIAM GIBBS
World's Funniest Woman, The.
See: DAVIS, JOAN
World's Greatest Alto Saxophone
Player, The. See:
DORSEY, JAMES
World's Most Admired Woman,
The. See:
ROOSEVELT, ANNA
ELEANOR
World's Most Prolific and
Popular Writer of Thrill-
ers, The. See:
OPPENHEIM, EDWARD
PHILLIPS
World's Most Pulchritudinous
Evangelist, The. See:
McPHERSON, AIMEE
SEMPLE
World's No. 1 Industrial
Architect, The. See:
KAHN, ALBERT
World's Sweetheart, The. See:
SMITH, GLADYS MARY
World's Top Boots-and-Saddle
Star, The. See:
SLYE, LEONARD
World's Wildest Tenor Man, The.
See: COBB, ARNETT
CLEOPHUS
World's Wonder, The. See:
ELIZABETH I
WORLOOU, LAMBROS (1915-)
[Greek-Egyptian singer]
Georges Guetary
Worne, John. See:
WYLIE, JAMES
WORSHAM, LEWIS ELMER, JR.
(1917-) [American golfer]
Lew Worsham
WORSNOP, WILFRID (1900-66)
[British stage and motion
picture actor]

Wilfrid Lawson
WORTH, ADAM (1844-1902)
[American master
criminal and international
thief]
Edouard Grau
The Napoleon of Crime
WORTS, GEORGE FRANK
(1892-) [American author]
Loring Brent
Would-be Cromwell of America.
See: ADAMS, SAMUEL
WOUSAMEQUIN. See:
OUSAMEQUIN (WOUSAME-
QUIN)
WOVOKA (1856?-1932) [Piute
Indian mystic and
prophet]
Jack Wilson
WOXHOLT, GRETA (1916-)
[Norwegian motion
picture actress]
Greta Gynt
WRAY. See:
RAY (WRAY), JOHN
Wrestler, The Grand. See:
LINCOLN, ABRAHAM
Wrestler, The Great. See:
LINCOLN, ABRAHAM
Wright, Amos. See:
MAGOUN, FREDERICK
ALEXANDER
WRIGHT, ARCHIBALD LEE
(1916?-) [American
Negro professional
boxer and actor]
Archie Moore
WRIGHT, BENJAMIN (1770-
1842) [American senior
engineer of the Erie
Canal]
The Father of American
Engineering
WRIGHT, CHARLES (1927-)
[American jazz musician
(drums)]
Specs Wright
WRIGHT, CHARLES BARSTOW
(1822-98) [American
railroad president and
financier]
The Father of Tacoma

WRIGHT, ELINOR BRUCE
(1921-) [English author]
Elinor Lyon
WRIGHT, ENID MEADOWCROFT
LaMONTE (1898-)
[American teacher, editor
and author]
Enid LaMonte Meadowcroft
WRIGHT, FORREST GLENN
(1902-) [American pro-
fessional baseball player]
Buckshot Wright
WRIGHT, FRANCES (1795-1852)
[Anglo-American social
reformer]
Fanny Wright
WRIGHT, JOSEPH (1734-97)
[English genre and portrait
painter]
Wright of Derby
WRIGHT, MABEL OSGOOD
(1859-1934) [American
author]
Barbara
Wright, Martha. See:
WIEDERRECHT, MARTHA
WRIGHT, MARY KATHRYN
(1935-) [American profes-
sional golfer]
Mickey Wright
WRIGHT, MARY PAMELA
GODWIN (1917-)
[British teacher and author]
Mary Bawn
WRIGHT, PAULA RAMONA
(c.1928-) [American
model and motion picture
actress]
Paula Raymond
Wright, Robert B. See:
BRUCE, ROBERT
Wright, Rowland. See:
WELLS, CAROLYN
WRIGHT, SILAS (1795-1847)
[American politician;
congressman from New
York]
The Cato of the Senate
WRIGHT, WILLARD HUNTINGTON
(1888-1939) [American
author and fine arts critic]
S.S. Van Dine

WRIGHT, WILLIAM (1829-98)
[American journalist and
author]
Dan De Quille
Writer of the Restoration
Period, The Greatest.
See: DRYDEN, JOHN
Writer of Thrillers, The
World's Most Prolific and
Popular. See:
OPPENHEIM, EDWARD
PHILLIPS
Writers for Boys, The Dean of
Sports. See:
BARBOUR, RALPH HENRY
Writers, The Spenser of
English Prose. See:
TAYLOR, JEREMY
WROBLEWSKI, PTASZYN (1936-)
[Polish jazz musician
(tenor saxophone, com-
poser)]
Jan
Wrong-way. See:
CORRIGAN, DOUGLAS
GEORGE
Wry-mouthed. See:
BOLESLAV III
WU, LADY (died 704)
[Empress of China]
The Divine Empress
The Poisoner
WU, NELSON IKON (1919-)
[Chinese educator and
author]
Lu-ch'iao
Wuckie, Ducky. See:
MEDWICK, JOSEPH M.
Wunnakyawhtin U Ohn Ghine.
See: MAURICE, DAVID
JOHN KERR
WUPPERMAN, FRANCIS
(1890-1949) [American
motion picture actor]
Frank Morgan
WUPPERMAN, RALPH
(1882-1956) [American
lawyer, stage and motion
picture actor]
Ralph Morgan
Wyandotte, Steve. See:
THOMAS, STANLEY

WYCLIFFE. See:
WICLIFFE
Wycliffe, John. See:
BEDFORD-JONES, HENRY
JAMES O'BRIEN
WYCOFF, LEON (1903-)
[American stage and
motion picture actor]
Leon Ames
WYKEHAM (WICKHAM),
WILLIAM OF (1324-1404)
[English prelate and
statesman]
The Father of the English
Public School System
Wylcotes, John. See:
RANSFORD, OLIVER
Wylder, Lennox. See:
TURNER, DR. WILLIAM
MASON
WYLIE, JAMES (1875-)
[British barrister and
author]
John Worne
Wylie Watson. See:
ROBERTSON, JOHN WYLIE
Wyman, Jane. See:
FULKS, SARAH JANE
Wymar Port. See:
JUDY, WILL
WYND, OSWALD MORRIS
(1913-) [Scottish author]
Gavin Black
Wynder, Mavis Areta. See:
WINDER, MAVIS
ARETA
Wyndham. See:
LEWIS, PERCY WYNDHAM
WYNDHAM, LEE (1912-)
[Russian-American editor,
critic and author]
Jane Lee Hyndman
WYNFRITH. See:
WINIFRID (WYNFRITH)
Wynkyn de Worde. See:
VAN WYNKYN, JAN
Wynn. See also:
Winn
WINNE
WYNNE
Wynne
Wynn, Alfred. See:

BREWER, FRED ALDWYN
Wynn, Charles. See:
    WEINBERG, CHARLES
Wynn, Ed. See:
    LEOPOLD, ISAIAH EDWIN
WYNNE [Wynne]. See also:
    Winn
    WINNE
    Wynn
Wynne, Brian. See: GARFIELD
    BRIAN WYNNE
Wynne, Frank. See:
    GARFIELD, BRIAN WYNNE
Wynne, May. See:
    KNOWLES, MABEL
    WINIFRED
Wynne, Pamela. See:
    SCOTT, WINIFRED MARY
WYNNE-TYSON, ESME (1898-)
    [British actress, play-
    wright and novelist]
    Amanda
    Peter de Morny
    Diotima
WYNNE-TYSON, TIMOTHY JON
    LYADEN (1924-)
    [British publisher and
    author]
    Michel Fourest
    Jeremy Pitt
WYNTER, DAGMAR (c.1930-)
    [British motion picture
    actress]
    Dana Wynter
Wynyard, Diana. See:
    COX, DOROTHY ISOBEL
Wyoming Bill. See:
    PATTEN, WILLIAM
    GILBERT
WYSS, JOHANN RUDOLF
    (1781-1830) [Swiss
    philosopher and librarian]
    David Wyss

X

X, Flying Officer. See:
    BATES, HERBERT
    ERNEST
X.J. See:
    KENNEDY, JOSEPH

X, Malcolm. See:
    LITTLE, MALCOLM
X, Monsieur. See:
    PARODI, ALEXANDRE
X.X. See:
    STREET, CECIL JOHN
    CHARLES
Xariffa. See:
    TOWNSEND, MARY ASHLEY
    VAN VOORHIS
XAVIER, ST. FRANCIS
    (1506-52) [Spanish Jesuit
    missionary]
    The Apostle of the Indies
XENOPHON (c.430-after 357 B.C.)
    [Greek historian]
    The Attic Muse
    The Muse of Greece
Xensi, Duke of. See:
    HOLM, H.H. FRITS
    VILHELM
Ximines, Cardinal. See:
    CISNEROS, FRANCISCO
    XIMINES DE
Xocoyotzin (Furious One). See:
    MONTEZUMA II
Xystus. See:
    SIXTUS

Y

Y.A. See:
    TITTLE, YELBERTON
    ABRAHAM
Y.L.G. See:
    GORDON, JUDAH LOEB
Y.R. Chao. See:
    JAW-YUARENN
Y.Y. See:
    LYND, ROBERT
    TSU, ANDREW YU-YUE
Yakumo Koizumi. See:
    HEARN, PATRICIO LAF-
    CADIO TESSIMA CARLOS
Yalag. See:
    GORDON, JUDAH LOEB
Yale, Frankie. See:
    UALE, FRANCESCO
Yale Rowing, The Grandfather of.
    See: SHEFFIELD, GEORGE
    ST. JOHN

YAMASHITA, TOMOYUKI
(1885-1946) [Japanese
general officer, executed
as war criminal]
The Tiger of Malaya
YANCEY, WILLIAM LOWNDES
(1814-63) [American
orator; advocate of seces-
sion]
The Orator of Secession
YAÑEZ, AGUSTÍN (1904-)
[Mexican author]
Monico Delgadillo
Yank Lawson. See:
LAUSEN, JOHN R.
Yankee. See:
HILL, GEORGE HANDEL
ROBINSON, FAYETTE
LODAWICK
Yankee, A. See:
WHITE, RICHARD
GRANT
Yankee Clipper of the Accordion,
The. See:
CONTINO, RICHARD
Yankee Clipper, The. See:
DIMAGGIO, JOSEPH PAUL,
JR.
Yankee King, The. See:
SICKLES, DANIEL EDGAR
Yankee Sullivan. See:
AMBROSE, JAMES
Yankees, The Father of all the.
See: FRANKLIN,
BENJAMIN
YANKS, BYRON (1928-)
[American concert pianist]
Byron Janis
Yardbird. See:
PARKER, CHARLES
YARMOLINSKY, MRS. AVRAHM
(1895-) [American poet]
Babette Deutsch
YASIN, KHALID (1940-)
[American jazz musician
(piano, composer)]
Larry Young
Yates. See:
WILSON, ALBERT
WILLIAM
YATES, ALAN GEOFFREY
(1923-) [British author]

Carter Brown
A.O. Yates
Yates, Dornford. See:
MERCER, CECIL WILLIAM
YAUKEY, GRACE SYDEN-
STRICKER (1899-)
[American author]
Cornelia Spencer
Yea and Nay, Richard. See:
RICHARD I
YEAKLEY, MARJORY HALL
(1908-) [American editor
and author]
Lucile Blair
Marjory Hall
Carol Morse
Yeates, Mabel. See:
PEREIRA, HAROLD
BERTRAM
YEATMAN, JAMES (1818-)
[American sanitation
advocate; active in estab-
lishing the Western Sanitary
Commission]
Old Sanitary
Yechton, Barbara. See:
KRAUSÉ, LYDA FARRINGTON
Yehoash. See:
BLOOMGARDEN, SOLOMON
Yehudah Lieb. See:
GORDON, JUDAH LOEB
Yehudah Lion. See:
GORDON, JUDAH LOEB
Yellow Bird (Chees-quat-a-law-
ny). See:
RIDGE, JOHN ROLLIN
Yellowplush, Charles, Esq. See:
THACKERAY, WILLIAM
MAKEPEACE
Yellowstone. See:
KELLY, LUTHER SAGE
Yendys, Sydney. See:
DOBELL, SYDNEY
THOMPSON
Yerrit, Miss. See:
TERRY, SARAH BALLARD
Yetta Bronstein. See:
ABEL, JEANNE
Yip. See:
HARBURG, E.Y.
Ylla. See:
KOFFLER, CAMILLA

Yma Sumac. See:
    CHAVARRI, EMPERATRIZ
Yodeling Cowboy, Oklahoma's.
    See: AUTRY, GENE ORVAN
YOELSON, ASA (1886-1950)
    [Russian-born American
    actor and singer]
    Jolie
    Al Jolson
Yogi. See:
    BERRA, LAWRENCE
    PETER
Yolande Bavan. See:
    WOLFFE, YOLANDE
    MARI
Yorick. See:
    WARD, JAMES WARNER
Yorick, A.P. See:
    TINDALL, WILLIAM YORK
Yorick, Mr. See:
    STERNE, LAURENCE
YORK, ALVIN CULLUM
    (1887-1964) [American
    soldier, World War I
    hero and winner of Con-
    gressional Medal of Honor]
    Sergeant York
YORK, HENRY BENEDICT
    MARIA CLEMENT STUART
    (1725-1807) [Churchman;
    last male descendant of
    the Stuart dynasty of Great
    Britain]
    Cardinal York
York, Jeremy. See:
    CREASEY, JOHN
York, Stephen. See:
    LINSKILL, MARY
York, The Pearl of. See:
    CLITHEROW, MARGARET
    MIDDLETON
YORKE, HENRY VINCENT
    (1905-) [English novelist]
    Henry Green
Yorke, Margaret. See:
    NICHOLSON, MARGARET
    BEDA LARMINIE
Yorke, Suzy. See:
    BURTON, JOAN EILEEN
    VERONICA
YORKIN, ALAN (1926-)
    [American television
    and motion picture

director]
    Bud Yorkin
York's Tall Son. See:
    PORTER, WILLIAM TROTTER
YORTY, SAMUEL WILLIAM
    (1909-) [American poli-
    tician; Mayor of Los
    Angeles]
    Sam Yorty
YOSHKIN, NICOLAI (1907-)
    [Russian stage and motion
    picture actor]
    Martin Kosleck
Yosimura, Huyukiko. See:
    TERADA, TORAHIKO
YOST, FIELDING HARRIS
    (1871-1946) [American
    football coach]
    Hurry Up Yost
YOU, DOMINIQUE (1775-1830)
    [French pirate on American
    Gulf Coast; associate of
    JEAN LAFITTE]
    Captain Dominique
Young. See:
    CROME, JOHN BERNAY
Young Adventurer, The. See:
    STUART, CHARLES
    EDWARD LOUIS PHILIP
    CASIMIR
YOUNG, ANGUS (1919-) [British-
    Canadian motion picture
    actor]
    Alan Young
Young, Annie. See:
    DUPUY, ELIZA ANN
YOUNG, ARTHUR (1741-1820)
    [English agriculturist]
    The Father of Modern
    Agriculture
YOUNG, ARTHUR HENRY
    (1866-1943) [American
    cartoonist and author]
    Art Young
Young, Billy. See:
    D'ARCY, COLIN
Young Chevalier, The. See:
    STUART, CHARLES ED-
    WARD LOUIS PHILIP
    CASIMIR
Young, Clarence. See:
    STRATEMEYER,
    EDWARD L.

Young Composer in America,
The Most Talented. See:
GOULD, MORTON
Young Cub, The. See:
FOX, CHARLES JAMES
YOUNG, DENTON TRUE
(1867-1955) [American
professional baseball
player]
Cy Young
Young Detective, The. See:
ROLFE, MARO O.
YOUNG, DOROTHEA BENNETT
(1924-) [British author]
Dorothea Bennett
Young, Edward. See:
REINFELD, FRED
YOUNG, EMILY HILDA (1880-
1949) [English novelist]
The Apostle of Quiet People
YOUNG, EUGENE (1919-)
[American jazz musician
(trumpet, composer)]
Snooky Young
Young, Gig. See:
BARR, BYRON
YOUNG, GRETCHEN (1913-)
[American motion
picture and television
actress]
Loretta Young
Young Hickory. See:
HILL, DAVID BENNETT
POLK, JAMES KNOX
TYLER, JOHN
Young Hotspur. See:
INGERSOLL, RALPH
ISAACS
YOUNG, JAMES OSBORNE
(1912-) [American jazz
musician (trombone,
singer)]
Trummy Young
YOUNG, JANET RANDALL
(1919-) [American
author]
Janet Randall
Jan Young
Young Juvenal, The. See:
LODGE, THOMAS
Young, Larry. See:
YASIN, KHALID
YOUNG, LEMUEL FLOYD

(1907-) [American pro-
fessional baseball player]
Pep
Whitey
YOUNG, LESTER WILLIS
(1909-) [American jazz
musician (tenor saxophone)]
Pres Young
Young Marshal, The. See:
CHANG-HSUEH-LIANG
Young Mose, The Same. See:
WEINBERGER, MOSES
Young, Nacella. See:
TATE, VELMA
Young Napoleon, Little Mac the.
See: McCLELLAN, GEORGE
BRINTON
Young Palma (Palma Giovane).
See: PALMA, JACOPO
YOUNG, PERCY MARSHALL
(1912-) [British educator,
musician and author]
Percy Marshall
Young Pretender, The. See:
STUART, CHARLES EDWARD
LOUIS PHILIP CASIMIR
YOUNG, ROBERT WILLIAM
(1916-) [American
editor, publisher and
author]
Bob Young
Young Roscius, The. See:
BETTY, WILLIAM HENRY
WEST
Young, Rose. See:
HARRIS, MARION ROSE
YOUNG
Young Sir Henry. See:
VANE, SIR HENRY
Young, The (Le Jeune). See:
LOUIS VII
YOUNG, THOMAS (1587-1655)
[English churchman and
pamphleteer]
Thomas Junius
YOUNG, THOMAS (1731/2-77)
[American patriot and
physician]
Philodicaius
YOUNG, THOMAS. See also:
Smectymnuus
Young Thunderbolt. See:
LEA, LUKE

Young Torquemada. See:
    MITCHEL, JOHN PURROY
Young 'un. See:
    Old 'un
YOUNG, WILLIAM HAMILTON
    (1836-1908) [American
    telegraph operator and
    executive with
    Western Union Telegraph
    Co.]
    Ham Young
YOUNG, WILLIS LESTER
    (1909-) [American jazz
    musician (tenor saxophone)]
    Lester Young
YOUNGBERG, NORMA IONE
    RHOADS (1896-)
    [American teacher and
    author]
    Leigh Winfield
Younger Columbia, The. See:
    COLUMBAN
    (COLUMBANUS), ST.
Younger, J.H. Rosney the. See:
    BOËX, SERAPHIN JUSTIN
    FRANÇOIS
Younger, Jan the. See:
    BRUEGHEL (BREUGHEL),
    JAN
Younger, Lorenzo the. See:
    MEDICI, LORENZO DE'
Younger, Pieter the. See:
    BRUEGHEL (BREUGHEL),
    PIETER
    BURMAN (BURMANN),
    PIETER
Younger, The. See:
    APOLLINARIS
    ARNOBIUS
    BRUEGHEL (BREUGHEL),
    PIETER
    BURMAN (BURMANN),
    PIETER
    CATO, MARCUS PORTIUS
    CEPHISODOTUS
    CHANNING, WILLIAM
    ELLERY
    COLMAN, GEORGE
    COOPER, RICHARD
    CRANACH, LUCAS
    CYRUS
    DONNE, JOHN

    EDWARDS, JONATHAN
    EGAN, PIERCE
    FLETCHER, GILES
    GAMALIEL OF JABNETH
    HALS, FRANZ
    HOLBEIN, HANS
    HOMER
    KILLIGREW, THOMAS
    MEER, JAN VAN DER
    PITT, WILLIAM
    POMPEY, SEXTUS
    POMPEIUS MAGNUS
    SECUNDUS, GAIUS PLINIUS
    CAECILIUS
    SENECA, LUCIUS ANNAEUS
    STRAUSS, JOHANN
    STROZZI, FILIPPO
    STURE, STEN
    TAYLOR, ISAAC
    TENIERS, DAVID
    VAN DE VELDE, WILLEM
    VISCHER, HERMANN
    VISCHER, PETER
    WARTON, THOMAS
Younger, The (El Mozo). See:
    HERRERA, FRANCISCO
Younger, The (Il Giovane). See:
    PALMA, JACOPO
Younger, Thomas Brown the. See:
    MOORE, THOMAS
YOUNGER, THOMAS COLEMAN
    (1844-1916) [American
    desperado; member of gang
    headed by JESSE WOODSON
    JAMES]
    Cole Younger
Younger, Willem the. See:
    VELDE, WILLEM VAN DE
Youngest Headliner, Vaudeville's.
    See: WEST, MAE
Youngest, Pliny the. See:
    WILSON, STANLEY
    KIDDER
Your Obedient Servant. See:
    WELLES, GEORGE ORSON
Your Uncle Feininger. See:
    FEININGER, LYONEL
Youth, The. See:
    ALMAGRO, DIEGO DE
YOXALL, HARRY WALDO (1896-)
    [British publishing
    executive and author]

F.H. Partington
Yu-ho, Tseng. See:
   ECKE, BETTY TSENG
   YU-HO
Yu, James T.C. See:
   TSUNE-CHI, YU
Yu, K'uan Yu. See:
   LUK, CHARLES
Yuan, Lei Chen. See:
   JAEGHER, RAYMOND-
   JOSEPH DE
Yul Brynner. See:
   KHAN, TAIDJE
YULE, JOE, JR. (1920-)
   [American motion picture
   actor and entertainer]
   Mickey McGuire
   Mickey Rooney
Yulia. See:
   WHITNEY, JULIA A.
Yun, Tan. See:
   LIN, ADET JUSU
Yves Duplessis. See:
   JAURAND, YVONNE
Yves Montand. See:
   LIVI, YVES (YVO) (IVO)
Yvonne de Carlo. See:
   MIDDLETON, PEGGY
   YVONNE

Z

Z.Y.Z. See:
   SYKES, ARTHUR ALKIN
Z.Z. See:
   ZANGWILL, LOUIS
Z.Z. Smith. See:
   WESTHEIMER, DAVID
Zach. See:
   TAYLOR, ZACHARY
   Zack
Zach, Old. See:
   TAYLOR, ZACHARY
ZACHARIAS, BASILEIOS (1850-
   1936) [Anglo-Greek
   armaments magnate and
   financier]
   Sir Basil Zaharoff
   The Mystery Man of Europe
ZACHARY (died 752) [Supreme
   Pontiff of Roman Catholic

Church]
   Pope Zachary
   St. Zachary
Zachary Ball. See:
   MASTERS, KELLY R.
ZACHARY, RUBIN (1915-)
   [American jazz musician
   (trumpet)]
   Zeke Zachary
ZACHOS, JOHN CELIVERGOS
   (1820-98) [American
   educator and clergyman]
   Cadmus
Zack. See:
   TAYLOR, JAMES WREN
   Zach
Zadkiel. See:
   LILLY, WILLIAM
   MORRISON, RICHARD
   JAMES
ZAHARIAS, MILDRED
   DIDRIKSON (1914-56)
   [American athlete]
   Babe Didrikson
Zaharoff, Sir Basil. See:
   ZACHARIAS, BASILEIOS
ZAJDLER, ZOË GIRLING
   (c.1907-) [Irish writer and
   journalist]
   Martin Hare
Zakhmi Dil. See:
   HILTON, RICHARD
Zale, Tony. See:
   ZALESKI, ANTHONY
   FLORIAN
ZALESKI, ANTHONY FLORIAN
   (1913-) [American profes-
   sional boxer; world's middle-
   weight champion]
   Tony Zale
ZAMPIERI, DOMENICO (1581-
   1641) [Italian painter]
   Il Domenichino
Zan Ganassa. See:
   NASELI, ALBERTO
ZANARDI-LANDI, ELIZABETH
   MARIE (1905-)
   [Italian actress, lecturer
   and novelist]
   Elissa Landi
ZANGWILL, LOUIS (1869-)
   [British author]

Z. Z.
ZANVILLE, BERNARD
(1913-) [American
motion picture actor]
Dane Clark
Zany of Debate, The. See:
CANNING, GEORGE
Zápolya, Sigismund
(Szapolyai). See:
JOHN II
Zápolya (Szapolyai). See:
JOHN I
Zara, Louis. See:
ROSENFIELD, LOUIS
ZARA
ZARCHY, HARRY (1912-)
[American commercial
artist and author]
Roger Lewis
Zaturenska, Maria. See:
GREGORY, MRS. HORACE
MARYA
ZAUNER, FRANZ PAUL
(1876-) [German author]
Dr. F. Pezet
Zavarr Wilmshurst. See:
BENNETT, WILLIAM
ZAWADSKY, PATIENCE
(1927-) [American
television writer, pro-
ducer, actor and
researcher]
Patience Hartman
Becky Lynne
Zeb. See:
JULIAN, SEBASTIAN
Zeb, Old. See:
WEAVER, ZEBULON
Zedekiah. See:
MATTANIAH
Zeffirelli, Franco. See:
CORSI, FRANCO
ZEFFIRELLI
Zeffros Vradinos. See:
HATZIDAKIS, NICHOLAS
Zehrzy-Wehrzy. See:
SHARP, MARJORIE
BARNHILL ZEHR
ZEIDLER, LEATRICE JOY
(1899-) [American
motion picture actress]
Leatrice Joy

ZEIGER, HENRY ANTHONY
(1930-) [American editor
and author]
James Peterson
ZEIGERMAN, GERALD (1939-)
[American author]
Ziggy Gerald
Zeke. See:
ZACHARY, RUBIN
Zeke Manners. See:
MANNES, LEO
ZELAZNY, ROGER (1937-)
[American social insurance
specialist and author]
Harrison Denmark
ZELLE, MAGARETE GERTRUDE
(1876-1917) [Dutch dancer
and spy]
Mata Hari
Zena Collier. See:
SHUMSKY, ZENA FELDMAN
ZENO (ZENON) (died 491)
[Byzantine emperor]
The Isaurian
Zenobia, Alexandria. See:
BRONTË, ANNE
Zenobia Bird. See:
LEFEVRE, LAURA
ZENOBIA
ZENON. See:
ZENO (ZENON)
ZEPHYRINUS (died 217) [Supreme
Pontiff of Roman Catholic
Church]
Pope Zephyrinus
St. Zephyrinus
Zeppo Marx. See:
Four Marx Brothers, The
Zero. See:
MOSTEL, SAMUEL JOE
Zeta. See:
COPE, VINCENT ZACHARY
FROUDE, JAMES ANTHONY
Zita
ZITO
Zette, Poum et. See:
SIMENON, GEORGES
Zeus. See:
SANDERS, DANIEL
JACKSON
Zez. See:
CONFREY, EDWARD E.

1102

ZIEGFELD, FLORENZ, JR.
(1869-1932)
[American theatrical
producer]
Flo Ziegfeld
Ziggy Elman. See:
FINKELMAN, HARRY
Ziggy Gerald. See:
ZEIGERMAN, GERALD
Zigzag. See:
SYKES, ARTHUR ALKIN
ZILVERITCH, FANNY (1909-)
[Hungarian motion
picture actress]
Franceska Gaal
ZIM, SONIA BLEEKER
(1909-) [Russian-
American anthropologist
and author]
Sonia Bleeker
Zimisces. See:
JOHN I
ZIMMERMAN, ETHEL AGNES
(1909-) [American
musical comedy and
motion picture singer and
actress]
Ethel Merman
ZIMMERMAN, ROBERT
(1941-) [American poet,
composer and folk
singer]
Bob Dylan
Zimri. See:
BUCKINGHAM, GEORGE
VILLIERS, 2ND DUKE
OF
Zingaro, Lo. See:
SOLARIO, ANTONIO
Zinken. See:
HOPP, SIGNE MARIE
ZIONCHECK, MARION A.
(1900-36) [Polish-
American playboy and
politician; congressman
from Washington State]
The Congressional Playboy
Seattle's Sensational Son
Zita. See also:
Zeta
ZITO
Zita White. See:

DENHOLM, THERESE
MARY ZITA WHITE
ZITO. See also:
Zita
Zeta
ZITO, SALVATORE (1933-)
[American composer and
arranger]
Torrie Zito
Zog I. See:
ZOGU, AHMED BEY
ZOGBAUM, BAIRD LEONARD
(c.1889-1941) [American
critic and poet]
Baird Leonard
ZOGU, AHMED BEY (1893-)
[King of Albania]
Zog I
ZOILUS (fl. 4th cent. B.C.)
[Greek rhetorician]
The Scourge of Homer
(Homeromastix)
ZOINO, VINCENT EDWARD
(1928-) [American actor]
Vincent Edwards
Zola, The German. See:
KRETZER, MARY
ZOLL, DONALD ATWELL
(1927-) [American educator
and author]
Donald Winslow
ZONIK, ELEANOR DOROTHY
(1918-) [British educator,
actor, director and author]
Eleanor Dorothy Glaser
Zoölogy, The Father of American.
See: SAY, THOMAS
Zoot. See:
SIMS, JOHN HALEY
Zorina, Vera. See:
HARTWIG, EVA BRIGITTA
ZOROASTER (630/618 B.C.-553/541
B.C.) [Founder of
Zoroasterism and author
of the Gathas]
The Bactrian Sage
Zorro, El. See:
VIGARA, RAFAEL MARTÍN
ZOSIMUS (died 418) [Supreme
Pontiff of Roman Catholic
Church]
Pope Zosimus

St. Zosimus
Zoyara, Ella. See:
    KINGSLEY, OMAR
Zsa Zsa, See:
    GABOR, SARI
ZUCCA, RITA LOUISE (1912-)
    [American-born radio
    propagandist for Nazi
    government]
    Axis Sally
ZUCKER, DOLORES MAE
    BOLTON (fl. 1964) [Amer-
    ican editor and author]
    Dee Hill
    Devera Myles
ZUDEKOFF, MOE (1919-)
    [American jazz musician
    (trombone, leader)]
    Buddy Morrow
    Muni Morrow
ZUKOR. See also:
    CZUKOR
ZUKOR, ADOLPH (1873-)
    [Hungarian-American
    film producer]
    Pop
ZÚÑIGA, JOSÉ (1932-)
    [Colombian bullfighter]
    Joselillo de Colombia
Zup. See:
    ZUPPKE, ROBERT
        CARL
ZUPPKE, ROBERT CARL
    (1879-) [American
    football coach]
    Zup
Zurito. See:
    HABLA, MANUEL DE LA
ZURKE, ROBERT (1910-44)
    [American jazz musician
    (piano)]
    Bob Zurke
    The Old Tomcat of the Keys
Zutty. See:
    SINGLETON, ARTHUR
        JAMES